Korea's Place in the Sun

A MODERN HISTORY

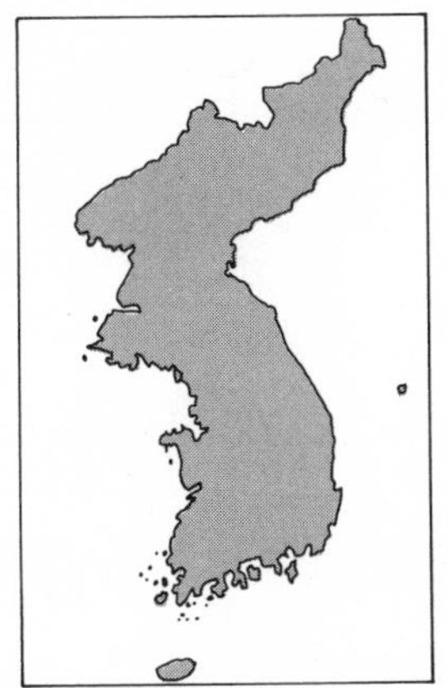

ALSO BY BRUCE CUMINGS

The Origins of the Korean War

Volume 1: Liberation and the Emergence of Separate Regimes, 1945–1947

Volume 2: The Roaring of the Cataract, 1947–1950

War and Television

Korea's Place in the Sun

A MODERN HISTORY

UPDATED EDITION

Bruce Cumings

W. W. NORTON & COMPANY
New York London

For Ian and Benjamin

Printed in the United States of America
First published as a Norton paperback 1998;
Updated edition published in 2005

Manufacturing by The Maple-Vail Book Manufacturing Group
Book design by Charlotte Staub

Library of Congress Cataloging in Publication Data

Cumings, Bruce, 1943–
Korea's place in the sun : a modern history / Bruce Cumings.
p. cm.
Includes bibliographical references and index.
ISBN 0-393-04011-9
1. Korea—History—20th century. 2. Korea (South)—History.
3. Korea—History—1864–1910. I. Title.
DS917.C86 1997
951.9'03—dc 20 96-15398
CIP

ISBN 0-393-31681-5 pbk.

W. W. Norton & Company, Inc.
500 Fifth Avenue, New York, N.Y. 10110
www.wwnorton.com

W. W. Norton & Company Ltd.
Castle House, 75/76 Wells Street, London W1T 3QT

2 3 4 5 6 7 8 9 0

Contents

Preface to the Updated Edition

With this updated edition of *Korea's Place in the Sun*, I have sought to bring the book current, which proved fairly easy for two reasons. First, in the past decade South Korea has developed politically much along the lines that my narrative suggested, with its strong civil society and democratizing politics yielding the successive elections of two former dissidents—first Kim Dae Jung and then Roh Moo Hyun. Second, North Korea is stuck in the aspic of its own failure to find a new path that would enable it to meet the challenges of the twenty-first century, and after George W. Bush took office in 2001, U.S.–North Korean relations returned to the pattern of confrontation and stalemate that marked the Cold War years, enabling the North to dust off its well-practiced strategies of obstinacy and recalcitrance. Thus it is difficult to say that much changed during President Bush's first administration, and the likelihood for the second is more of the same—stalemate.

Only two episodes in the past decade merit extended discussion: the first is the financial crisis in 1997–98, which bankrupted the South Korean economy and rang the curtain down on the decades-long discourse about "the Korean miracle." That high American officials were instrumental in trying to refashion the Korean model of development that they had for so long—and so loudly—supported caused a spate of "anti-Americanism" at the time, something that was only deepened with the arrival of the Bush administration, amid a growing estrangement between Seoul and Washington over how to deal with the North. The second episode was a sincere attempt by the administration of President Bill Clinton to engage North Korea in the late 1990s, one that nearly achieved major success in 2000. Readers will find much food for thought in these two experiences, both of which departed dramatically from the general pattern of Korean history in the past six decades.

So, this version is a modest effort to bring the book up to date rather than a full revision, which can happen only after the shape and trajectory of Korea in the twenty-first century become clear. I would like to thank Steve Forman and Sarah England of W. W. Norton for suggesting that an updating would be appropriate, and for seeing this version through to publication. Professor Elaine Kim of the University of California at Berkeley was also kind enough to dun the publisher about bringing the book current. Writing now in this new century, I remain amazed and humble before the turbulence and complexities of Korea's modern history.

that an updating would be appropriate, and for seeing this version through to publication. Professor Elaine Kim of the University of California at Berkeley was also kind enough to dun the publisher about bringing the book current. Writing now in this new century, I remain amazed and humble before the turbulence and complexities of Korea's modern history.

Preface and Acknowledgments

The idea for this book germinated when John W. Boyer, dean of the college at the University of Chicago, provided me with some summer money to prepare a reader on Korea for the college's justly respected civilization program. Some years later when I told him—a historian of Germany and Austria—my book title, he could not suppress a laugh: it seemed a bit Bismarckian. The Greek word *asu* and the Latin word *oriens* connoted "rising sun" or "the east," and for centuries everything east of Istanbul signified "lands of the rising sun," just as *occidens* conjured the territory of the setting sun; Martin Luther identified Europe with the *Abend* (or evening) land, the Orient with the *Morgen* (morning) land.[1] Now only Japan claims to be a land of the rising sun, and only anxious Americans identify their country with the setting sun. The world that has given us rises and falls and periodic eclipses is not that of Greece and Rome, however, but the industrial epoch, with its relative handful of advanced industrial states and their incessant competition. It is that solar system that Korea has now joined (and that is all I mean by the title).

To the left is the *kangnido,* a map of the known world drawn by Korean cartographers in 1402, nearly a century before the Western voyages to the Americas. Korea, the "Eastern country," hangs like a large grapefruit next to China, into which is collapsed India and South Asia. The Japanese islands are insignificant, placed down near the Philippines. This map may be old, but it tells us what Koreans think about their country and always have: an important, advanced, signifi-

1. I knew the etymology of "Orient," but I am grateful to the historian Anders Stephanson for telling me about Herodotus' usage of *asu* and Luther's analogous division of West and East.

cant country, which may have been "a shrimp among whales" during the imperial era, a small country jammed cheek-by-jowl against great powers during the Cold War, a poor and divided country after the Korean War, but now is a nation reoccupying its appropriate position in the world.

Korea is roughly the size of England, with a population in both Koreas approximating that of unified Germany. If it were not a peninsular promontory of China, we would not think of it as a small country (no one thinks of Japan or England as a small country). Many Americans also believe Korea is "remote" or "far-off"; for different reasons the Japanese enjoy referring to North Korea as "the remotest country." Northeast Asia is remote only from the Eurocentric and civilizational standpoint of "the West"—something much prized these days because it is much threatened. Many Westerners still believe that European civilization "has had some unique historical advantage, some special quality of race or culture or environment or mind or spirit, which gives this human community a permanent superiority over all other communities, at all times in history and down to the present."[2] We will find that Koreans think about the same thing, except they replace Europe with their own country—or, historically, China. Beijing sits in the middle of the *kangnido* because it was the seat of known civilization.

What is meant by modern Korea? When other countries start acting a bit like Western ones, we often say they "modernize." Today we have many such countries, but according to some recent accounts none—including the economic giant Japan—know true freedom as do the nations of Europe. Somehow this prize at the end of the modernizing rainbow remains elusive. The twentieth century was so full of stunning events, however, running the full spectrum from the great and wonderful to the horrible and unimaginable, that we can no longer use the term "modern" as a sign of tribute, or progress as a sign of approbation. Modern has meant that people work in industrial settings, use advanced technology as a tool, live in cities or suburbs, enjoy or suffer the attentions of the most industrially advanced nations, and experience a democratic or an authoritarian politics rather different from previous political forms. The twentieth century was one of industrialization and technological change, the world-ranging power of those nations having both and putting both to good military use, and the full emergence of masses of the population as political participants. The modern is not a sign of superiority but a mark, a point, on a rising and falling scale. Korea began the twentieth century near the bottom of that scale and begins the twenty-first near the top. Along the way there have been many gains and many losses, and a remarkable

2. Blaut (1993), pp. 1–3.

story of human triumph over adversity. But we now have a modern Korea.

Korea presents the Westerner not with a smooth narrative of progress toward industrial mastery, however, but with a fractured, shattered twentieth-century history. In 1910 it lost its centuries-old independence and remained an exploited colony until 1945. Then came national division, political turmoil, a devastating war, and the death and dislocation of millions—which only left Korea still divided and in desperate poverty. A decade later South Korea began to industrialize, and today it has a mostly democratic politics, but only after two military coups and several popular rebellions. North Korea developed more quickly after the war, but soon reaped the diminishing returns of a political and economic system designed to remedy the problems of the 1930s, not those of the 1960s or 1990s. For several years many analysts have said that North Korea is on the verge of collapse, but the peninsula remains divided and subject to all the conflicts and passions that the rest of the world knew during the long years of the Cold War. How Koreans will reconcile their two different systems and finally unify the country remains a mystery for the future.

So, this is another theme: modern, yes; whole, no. A related theme is the marginal beginnings of Korea's modern effort. No Westerner imagined a modern Korea in 1900, none predicted it in 1945, and experts still did not envision it just a generation ago. Instead, Korea seemed lacking in everything that counted in the West: bustling commerce, empirical science, a stable middle class, a spirit of enterprise, innovative technology. How, then, did the Koreans do it? Something must have been missed, something overlooked, in observations of old Korea. It might have been history that was overlooked. Korea's long past of continuous existence on one territory may light our path to an understanding of one of the twentieth century's most remarkable achievements. It is with this history that we will begin, seeking to comprehend its legacies for our own time.

There are also other problems we will want to examine: race, for example. Elaine H. Kim has written that most Americans see Koreans "primarily through the lens of race; they see us as all alike and caring only about ourselves."[3] Too many Koreans look through that same lens, thinking they have some essential quality making them and only them real Koreans, tracing a unique, homogeneous bloodline back some five thousand years. All too many non-Koreans think they and only they really *know* what makes Koreans tick. When I say, "Koreans do this, Koreans do that," I use a shorthand. In reality there is no homogeneous

3. Elaine H. Kim in Aguilar-San Juan (1994), p. 73.

category called Korean—no racial essence, no homogeneous ethnicity, no unique genetic stamp. Koreans come in all shapes and sizes, and the full human range of personality types.

The twentieth-century Korean is a complex mixture of ancient peoples who traversed the Korean peninsula, certainly including Japanese, Chinese, Manchu, and many other East and Central Asian ethnicities, but perhaps also including peoples known historically as Caucasians. (I once read a book entitled *Koreans Are White.*) Archaeological science has recently shown that the Korean genetic pool of DNA, like the Chinese pool, has many affinities with European DNA, and fewer with African or Middle Eastern DNA—that is, an infinitesimally smaller range of DNA than is found in Africans, who have the largest pool of DNA, a range that makes no difference whatsoever in human behavior. Science has proved race to be a stupidity, however much weight it may exercise in our social and political life.

If race is a stupidity, hierarchy and inequality are difficult concepts for Americans, especially younger ones, to grasp. Yet hierarchy and inequality were deeply ingrained in Korean society until just the past few decades, and for many Koreans these remain not just "facts of life" but *ideals* of how to organize a proper society. Since we seek in this book an understanding, an act of empathy for Korea, we should try—temporarily—to disabuse ourselves of American assumptions that get in the way of knowing, of seeing, a truly different society: a brief encounter not with the aberrant but with the different.

A suspension of judgment to achieve an understanding is precisely what made Alexis de Tocqueville such a brilliant student of American society. He wasn't so sure that 1840s America really promoted the individual nonconformity and egalitarianism prized in its values (and it didn't do so at all in the slaveholding South), but it did well enough to make a stark contrast with aristocratic France:

> *Individualism* is a novel expression, to which a novel idea has given birth. Our fathers were only acquainted with *égoisme* (selfishness). . . . Individualism is a mature and calm feeling, which disposes each member of the community to sever himself from the mass of his fellows and to draw apart with his family and friends, so that after he has thus formed a little circle of his own, he willingly leaves society at large to itself.[4]

When we think about the hierarchy and inequality that marked Korean society, it is crude and unhelpful to begin with the dictatorship

4. Tocqueville (1945), p. 104.

in North Korea or the patriarchy of the South. We should "think rather of the child" (in Louis Dumont's words about a different society)

> slowly brought to humanity by his upbringing in the family, by the apprenticeship of language and moral judgment, by the education which makes him share in the common patrimony. . . . Where would be the humanity of this man, where his understanding, without this training or taming, properly speaking a creation, which every society imparts to its members, by whatever actual agency?[5]

Korean mothers, it seems to me, often look upon their child in just this way: not merely a biological outcome but a being to be shaped and reared as a human creation, like a work of art. The premise of the maternal sculptor, however, must be her "knowing what's best for the child," her unquestioned authority.

It is a small step to the idea that family rearing principles can be extended to politics, to the state, and to the family-state of ancient kings or of Kim Il Sung (at least in the imaginings of his ideologues). The individual is not an atom, detached from society, but the building block of the whole, the basis of a society conceived organically. The problem for our understanding is that *all* societies evolved through an organic conception (see Tillyard's marvelous reconstruction of Elizabethan England, for example),[6] but in America we have left that idea so far behind that we really have few ways to fathom a society still captured between ancient organic conceptions and "modern" individualistic ones.

Hierarchy conjures in our minds notions of illegitimate privilege, arbitrary command, and unfree subordination. Dumont said of India that hierarchy instead conferred "degrees of dignity," religiously originated and then, later, socially defined.[7] This means several things: an apportioning of dignity, some greater, some lesser; degrees of personal rank in relation to the whole; but also an attribution of dignity to all who are part of the society. "Knowing one's place," an idea that we abhor, nonetheless was something honorable, dignified, a locus where human beings could realize themselves. Hierarchy without shame, hierarchy that is self-conscious but without conscious abuse, without necessarily infringing on what it means to be human: think about it.

The United States, founded on ideas of liberty and equality, often experiences "unfreedom" only as an aberration. Yet our former colonizer, England, is still a country of wide liberty and little equality. Fur-

5. Dumont (1980), p. 5.
6. Tillyard (1942).
7. Dumont (1980), pp. 65–66.

thermore, our egalitarian and democratic disgust with hierarchy, which makes of America such a rich and diverse society, may have the unexpected consequence of leaving us bereft of ways to understand manifest inequality, or even to organize in our minds the society that we experience: and thus we have easy recourse to racism, which offers the most obvious way to distinguish and separate people amid the general equality.[8] There is, however, no question in my mind that the American organization of society in our time, speeded by a globe-ranging media, carries every alternative social form before it. It is deeply popular because it convinces people everywhere that they can live a life of carefree individuality, and thus it transforms and dissolves the alternatives one after another, including old Korea. We can now begin an appreciation of that venerable but rapidly disappearing thing: old Korea.

In this book meant for the general reader I have tried to keep footnotes to a minimum, with most making quick reference to a book in the bibliography that offers further reading on the subject at hand; for the same reason, to the extent possible I have stayed away from Korean words in the text, large numbers of Korean names, and Korean-language sources. Still, there will be all too many Kims: about one-third of Koreans have that last name (some three hundred Korean family names circulate, but only a handful are in wide use). At one point the North Korean leadership consisted of Kim Il Sung, Kim Il, and Kim Jong Il, in that order; only the first and the last were related. Unless I say so, the reader may assume that none of the Kims, Paks, Yis, or Chŏngs are relatives. With the exception of Syngman Rhee and one or two other people, the family name always comes first; for well-known people like Rhee, Park Chung Hee, Kim Dae Jung, and Kim Il Sung, I have rendered the name as they do in English. Otherwise I have used the McCune-Reischauer system of transliteration for Korean and the Wade-Giles system for Chinese.

I have written other books dealing with modern Korean history. Everything in this book, however, has met a fresh assessment and as much familiarity as I can muster with recent work by my colleagues. I reserve the right to retain interpretations that still seem correct to me and to revise views that may have been found in my work before, on the principle that to change one's mind is a sign of growth. Readers familiar with my work will be able to trace both, but I see no need to do that for the reader coming to it for the first time. My involvement with Korea now runs to three decades, and from time to time I will also revisit that personal experience with the reader.

Many people have helped me with this book, especially my graduate

8. Dumont (1980), pp. 15–17.

and undergraduate students in modern Korean history, who have been far too numerous to list here without slighting someone dear to me; still, I want to give special mention to Charles Armstrong, Suk-jun Han, Ken Kawashima, Dongno Kim, Nyung Kim, Henry Em, Paul Nam, Joyce Park, Kie-Duck Park, Michael Shin, and Yul Sohn. Vivian Lee helped me compile an extensive bibliography of modern Korea, only a small part of which is cited in this book.

I would like to thank my agent, Elaine Markson, for encouraging this project and for placing the book so well, and Henning Gutman and Steven Forman of W. W. Norton for their excellent advice, editorial and otherwise. Otto Sonntag's painstaking copyediting is unsurpassed in my experience. Charlotte Staub also deserves credit for her fine book design. John Boyer and Sheila Biddle of the Ford Foundation deserve thanks for the summer grant that enabled me to begin the book. Regina Rogers Doi was so generous as to let me use the peace and quiet of her lovely home to write the first draft of the manuscript. The friendship and scholarship of James Palais are always an inspiration to me, even if his prepublication critique of this text caused my hair to gray even more; Donald Clark's energetic and supportive reading also aided me greatly, and both scholars saved me from many mistakes. I composed this volume while beginning to edit the modern volume of the *Cambridge History of Korea*, and I thank the contributors to that book. Of course, I bear all responsibility for interpretations, errors, and idiocies in my text.

Meredith Woo-Cumings (Jung-en Woo) always seeks to instruct me about the mysteries of life, but through direction and indirection she has also taught me much about the country she hails from. My father-in-law, Y. H. Woo, is a fount of knowledge about modern Korea. Ian Woo Cumings was born before this book was conceived and Benjamin Woo Cumings was born in the middle of its development; both sustained me with their wit and diversions. When I could not be with them, my mother Eleanor S. Cumings was always eager to baby-sit.

The organization of this book is neither chronological nor analytical, but some chronology is necessary for order, and some analysis for setting off what is distinct and separate, or familiar with a difference, in Korea's experience. The first chapter is a long introduction to the background of modern Korea, but not nearly long enough: covering year one to the 1860s, it seeks to retrieve elements in the Korean past salient for our contemporary understanding. This is not my field, nor is it my main subject, and I have relied on excellent recent work by my colleagues to guide me. Chapter 2 is the first in this modern history, the modern being marked by the arrival of the big powers in Korea. There follows an account of Korea's capture by a Japan that adapted itself more quickly to the industrial era than did Korea, giving it a temporary leg up on its near neighbor. Middle chapters examine Korea's determining crisis at mid-century, which began in the ashes of Japan's defeat and ended with two thoroughly divided nations inhabiting the same peninsula. Chapters 6 and 7 look at South Korea's rise to industrial strength under incessant prodding from an authoritarian and interventionist state, and the popular resistance to that which ultimately produced a relatively industrialized, relatively democratic country—in other words, a modern Korea. Chapter 8 examines the North Korea of Kim Il Sung, just as chapter 10 begins with the accession of his son to power, the 1990s crisis in U.S.-Korean relations, and the prospects for reunifying Korea. In between is a chapter about the Korean experience in this country: a requirement in a book written by an American, for Americans, and for Koreans who are now of America.

This American perspective may strike Koreans as a liability, but I work in the United States and consider myself as American as apple pie, so it can't be helped. It might also be a blessing: there is no such thing as "a thing in itself"; we can know our world only through comparison and analogy and metaphor, through a perspectival stance that reconnoiters the object of our desire as it illumines ourselves. In his last book, *L'Identité de la France,* Fernand Braudel wrote,

> The historian can really be on an equal footing only with the history of his own country; he understands almost instinctively its twists and turns, its originalities, and its weaknesses. Never can he enjoy the same advantages, however great his learning, when he pitches camp elsewhere. So I have saved my white bread until last; there is some left for my old age.

Because of a similar intuition my tent has been pitched at the intersection of East Asia and America, just as I have lived my life at that crossing since I was twenty-two. I am also putting away some white bread, just in case I need it in my old age.

Korea's Place in the Sun

A MODERN HISTORY

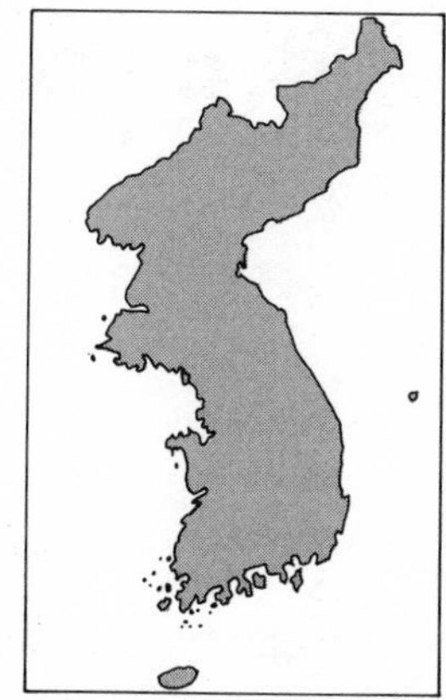

0 50 100 150 200 250 300 km
0 50 100 150 200 miles
RUSSIA
Vladivostok
CHINA
Tumen R.
Najin
Ch'ŏngjin
Yalu R.
Hyesanjin
Manp'ojin
Kanggye
Kilchu
Suiho (Sup'ung) Reservoir
Chosan
Changjin (Chosin) Reservoir
Mup'yŏng-ni
Pujon Reservoir
Sŏngjin
Antung (Dandong)
Yudam-ni
Hagaru
Kot'o-ri
Sudong
Iwŏn
Onjŏng
Huich'ŏn
Unsan
Sinŭiju
Ch'ŏngch'ŏn R.
Ipsŏk
Taedong R.
Hamhŭng
Hŭngnam
Chŏngju
Anju
Kunu-ri
Yŏngwŏn
Tŏkch'ŏn
Sinanju
Chinhŭng-ni
EAST SEA
(Sea of Japan)
P'YŎNGYANG
Wŏnsan
Ceasefire line
Chinnamp'o
Imjin R.
Hwach'ŏn Reservoir
Sariwŏn
Yesŏng R.
P'yŏnggang
Kŭmsŏng
Kansŏng
Hwangp'o-ri
Taep'o-ri
P'anmunjŏm
Kŭmhwa
Kaesŏng
Inje
38°
38°
Ch'unch'ŏn
Sabangu
Ŭijŏngbu
Kangnŭng
Hongch'ŏn
Ongjin Peninsula
Kimp'o Peninsula
Yangp'yŏng
Hoengsŏng
Chip'yŏng-ni
Ullŭng-do
Inch'ŏn
SEOUL
T'AEBAEK MOUNTAINS
Suwŏn
Wŏnju
Yŏju
Chech'ŏn
Osan
Han R.
Ch'ŏnan
Ch'ŏnŭi
Choch'iwŏn
Kŭm R.
MOUNTAINS
YELLOW SEA
Taejŏn
P'ohang
Kunsan
SOBAEK
Taegu
Kyŏngju
Naktong R.
Nam R.
Masan
Kwangju
Chinju
Pusan
KOREA STRAIT
Mokp'o
Kŏje-do
JAPAN
Yŏsu
Tsushima
HONSHU
Shomonoseki
Fukuoka
Cheju-do
KYUSHU
CHAZAUD

Korea

CHAPTER ONE

The Virtues

One might trace the history of the limits, *of those obscure actions, necessarily forgotten as soon as they are performed, whereby a civilization casts aside something it regards as alien. Throughout its history, this moat which it digs around itself, this no man's land by which it preserves its isolation, is just as characteristic as its positive values.*
—*Michel Foucault*

Like most other people on this earth, contemporary Koreans in North and South think they have escaped history and tradition in the dizzying pace of an energetic twentieth century. Meanwhile, they move in ways that would be inexplicable without investigations of a much longer period—the poorly recorded millennium before 1400, and especially the well-recorded half-millennium of the Chosŏn dynasty (1392–1910). To grasp "modern" Korea we will first need a tour through previous centuries, to make the point that you may forget about history, but history will not forget about you.

Consider this statement on Korean history around the time of Christ: "The significance of sinicised Choson, and later settlements in Korea sponsored by the Han emperors, lay in their long-term cultural influence on Japan. In time the Korean peninsula became the main conduit through which Chinese culture flowed to the Japanese islands." This was written in 1993, in a good book.[1] It could have been written at any time since Japan rose up more quickly in the Western imagination than did Korea—namely, after 1868—but not before. What's wrong with the quoted statement? First, Korea was never "Sinicized," although it came close in the period 1392–1910. Certainly it was not Sinicized at a time when walled mini-states contested for power on the peninsula. Second, is there no other significance to Korea than its "long-term" effects in

1. Cotterell (1993), pp. 46–47.

conducting Chinese influence by remote control to Japan? Was that influence unchanged by its passage through Korean hands? Did China exercise no "cultural influence" on Korea, but only on Japan? If not, why not? If so, why emphasize and dwell upon Japan, and not Korea?

I could go on, but we may say that from the inroads of the Western imperial powers in East Asia right down to the moment at which I am writing, non-Koreans have had trouble taking Koreans seriously, in understanding Koreans as actors in history. Imagine a European version of this: Greek and Roman culture passed through country X along about 200 B.C. to A.D. 1400 (the above author's time frame) and had a definitive effect on . . . England. We need not name country X to see the deficiencies of such a statement. Great Britain, like many other European countries, lived and evolved in the instructive shadow of Greek and Roman civilization. In Edinburgh perched on a hilltop overlooking the sea, we happen upon a partial reconstruction of the Parthenon, a thousand miles from the real thing. Does that make of Scotland a mere reflection of Greek glory, a vessel, a conduit? Of course not.

It is the history of the past century, in which Korea fell victim to imperialism and could not establish its own constructions of the past, which makes us think that if Koreans are Confucians, or Buddhists, or establish a civil service exam system, they must therefore have become "Sinicized." The world is more complex than that, and Korean history is stronger than that. Koreans made Confucius their own just as Renaissance thinkers made Plato and Aristotle their own; that Confucius' grave was in Shantung, just across the Yellow Sea from Korea, made the adaptation all the easier. The real story is indigenous Korea and the unstinting Koreanization of foreign influence, not vice versa.

In his masterful book *After Virtue,* Alasdair MacIntyre persuades readers in the twentieth century to understand that the ideas inhabiting their minds are fragments of a lost totality, whether they fancy themselves Lockean liberals, Augustinian Catholics, or Aristotelian rationalists. There is simply no possibility of recapturing the disappeared whole, a world where such systems of thought were the *only* ideas, structuring the totality of human interaction and inhaled like the air we breathe. It is the same with Korea, where a world view suffused with Confucian, Buddhist, and nativist ideas defined what it meant to be Korean for millennia, only to be lost with a poof in our time. Still, there are the remnant fragments of this world in Korean minds, which help to explain why many Koreans do the things they do, and how they have adapted themselves to modern life.

Old Korea was a universe all of its own, a fully realized human history like no other. It was a world defined by virtue, and if the virtues may be in retreat in contemporary Korea, as they are everywhere else, they still animate Korean minds: minds that are "front-end loaded" whether they know it or not, with thousands of years of history, and deeply felt morality. Today we connote those virtues with the catchall term "Confucianism." This is often said to be a conservative philosophy, stressing tradition, veneration of a past golden age, careful attention to the performance of ritual, disdain for material things, commerce, and the remaking of nature, obedience to superiors, and a preference for relatively frozen social hierarchies. If Confucianism had those tendencies, it also had others—a salutary loyalty to one's family, for example, which might translate into competition with other families over material wealth; an emphasis on moral remonstrance, for another, which gives to students and scholars an ethical stance from which to speak truth to power. Much commentary on contemporary Korea focuses on the alleged static, authoritarian, antidemocratic character of this Confucian legacy. Yet one-sided emphasis on these aspects would never explain the extraordinary commercial bustle of South Korea, the materialism and conspicuous consumption of new elites, or the determined struggles for democratization put up by Korean workers and students. At the same time, the assumption that North Korean communism broke completely with the past would blind one to continuing Confucian legacies there: its family-based politics, the succession to rule of the leader's son, and the extraordinary veneration of the state's founder, Kim Il Sung.

Running silently alongside this Confucian stream is a mighty river of inarticulate axiom and belief, a native strain of thought that inhabits the minds of the uneducated, the unlettered, the cloistered, hidden-and-forbidden woman, the bent peasant in the rice field, the old man hustling through the streets of Seoul with a hundred pounds of baggage on his wooden A-frame, the industrial worker howling to the moon under the dull influence of *makkŏlli,* the inquisitive young child, the young couple enthralled in the mutual discovery of their own sexuality, the invisible outcaste. That mind sits under the breastbone and not between the ears: as Richard Rutt put it, "Koreans, like the Chinese and the Hebrews, think of the heart, not the head, as the seat of thought."[2] When they say, "I think," they point to their chest. Mind is mind-and-heart or *sim,* a visceral knowledge that joins thought with emotion and that has an honored position in Western civilization in the thought of Plato.

The Korean mind-heart is attuned to the spirits that inhabit the nature of all things (bears, crickets, trees, flowers, homes, rivers, mountains), the ghosts and goblins that walk the night, the shamans who cast spells, the heterodox women who unite mind and body in the writhing incantations of the *mudang* sorcerer. This is the human mind connected to the

2. Rutt in Gale (1972), p. 87.

viscera and the body in touch with its natural environment, and out of it comes superstition, intuition, revelation, insight, madness, wisdom, and, above all, freedom. It is the purest Korean tradition, infusing songs, poems, dances, dreams, and emotions; it resists all attempts to excise the senses and bank the fires of passion. It is the Korea that I, a Western rationalist, know least about: ghosts and demons I can't see, wailing and screaming I can't hear, forces for good or evil I can't feel, foot-stomping, throat-shrieking, hand-waving experience that goes on without me. An observant American visitor to Korea a century ago, a scientist and traveler named Percival Lowell, had this to add: "The Koreans are passionately fond of scenery. The possessions of each province in this respect are not only thoroughly known, but they are systematically classified and catalogued. A grove of trees is celebrated here, the precipices of a mountain there, the moonlight falling on a pool of water in a third spot. . . ."[3] Somehow I think this is the most authentic, fully human Korea—perhaps because it is the Korea we are always warned against. From this native source, I think, comes the earthy, expansive, bouncy, kinetic energy the foreign traveler senses in Koreans, so attractive and compelling, and finds lacking in Korea's neighbor to the East. To all those anonymous invigorating people, I raise a cup of *soju*.

ORIGINS OF THE KOREAN NATION

Koreans emerged as a people on a mountainous peninsula surrounded on three sides by water. Someone once said that if the Korean peninsula were flattened with an iron, it would be as big as China. Koreans associate the origin of their history with the great crater-lake mountain on their northern border, Paektusan, or White Head Mountain: they remain today a "mountain people," who identify with hometowns and home regions that, so they argue, differ greatly from other places in Korea. To the foreigner this regionalism often seems exaggerated, but it exercises very real influence—for example, on recent voting patterns in South Korea. No doubt it exercised much greater influence when few Koreans lived in cities, inhabiting a universe called their own village, and walking for hours just to reach a town on the other side of a foothill.

The peninsula was also surrounded on three sides by other people: Chinese to the west, Japanese to the east, and an assortment of influences to the north: "barbarian" tribes, aggressive invaders, and, in the past century, an expanding and deepening Russian presence. Although

3. Lowell (1888-A), p. 59.

Japan exercised strong influence in the late 1500s and again in the past century, in ancient times the peoples and civilizations on the contiguous Asian continent were far more important to Korean history. The northern border between Korea and China formed by the Yalu and Tumen rivers has been recognized by the world for centuries, much longer than comparable borders in Europe, and so one might think these rivers always constituted Korea's northern limits. In fact, Koreans ranged far beyond these rivers, well into northeastern China and Siberia, and neither Koreans nor the ancient tribes that occupied the plains of Manchuria considered these riparian borders to be sacrosanct. The harsh winter climate also created frozen pathways for many months, facilitating the back-and-forth migration out of which the Korean people were formed.

The imagined beginning of the Korean nation, for the contemporary North and South, was the third millennium B.C. when a king named Tan'gun founded Old Chosŏn (sometimes translated as "morning calm," Chosŏn remains the name of the country in North Korea, whereas South Koreans use the term Han'guk, a usage dating from the 1890s; the Western name Korea comes from the Koryŏ dynasty, 918–1392). According to a surviving text from the Koryŏ period,[4] Chinese historians wrote that Tan'gun built his royal palace near modern-day P'yŏngyang and established a state called Chosŏn, in the same era as a legendary founder of China, Emperor Yao. James Gale was much closer to the truth when he wrote that Korea "takes its beginnings in the misty ages of the past that elude all attempts at close investigation, ages that lie somewhere between that of man and those of angels and spirit beings, joining heaven on the one hand and earth on the other."[5]

The Koryŏ text gave this version of Tan'gun's birth (there are several others):

> In those days there lived a she-bear and a tigress in the same cave. They prayed to Hwanung [the king who had descended from heaven] to be blessed with incarnation as human beings. The king took pity on them and gave each a bunch of mugwort and twenty pieces of garlic, saying, "If you eat this holy food and do not see the sunlight for one hundred days, you will become human beings."
>
> The she-bear and the tigress took the food and ate it, and retired into the cave. In twenty-one days the bear, who had faithfully observed the king's instructions, became a woman. But the tigress, who had disobeyed, remained in her original form.

4. Illyŏn, *Samguk yusa,* pp. 32–33. This is a thirteenth-century text, which relied on sources no longer extant.
5. Gale (1972), p. 93.

> The bear-woman could find no husband, so she prayed under the sandalwood tree to be blessed with a child. Hwanung heard her prayers and married her. She conceived and bore a son who was called Tan'gun Wanggŏm, the King of Sandalwood.[6]

Of obscure origin, Tan'gun has nonetheless exercised his influence on Koreans in every century since Christ, and no doubt many before; the legend above was not manufactured in the Koryŏ period, as Japanese historians have claimed, but can be found illustrated on some stone slabs from a family shrine in Shantung, across the Yellow Sea from Korea, that dates to A.D. 147.[7] A temple erected in Tan'gun's honor in 1429 stood in P'yŏngyang right up until the Korean War blew it to smithereens in the 1950s.

Nationalist historians assert a linear, homogeneous evolution of the Korean people from the distant point of Tan'gun's appearance to the Korean of today. Moreover, the king was not just a person: he was also a continuous presence from the time of Tan'gun down to the present, a vessel filled by different people at different times, who drew their legitimacy from this eternal lineage. Under its first president, for example, South Korea used a calendar in which Tan'gun's birth constituted year one—setting the date at 2333 B.C. And in September 1993 North Korea interrupted the ongoing nuclear crisis involving the United States to announce with great fanfare the discovery of Tan'gun's tomb and a few remains of his skeleton, at a site close to P'yŏngyang:

> The founding of KoJoson [Old Chosŏn] by Tangun 5,000 years ago marked an epochal occasion in the formation of the Korean nation. With the founding of the state of KoJoson an integrated political unit was established, the blood ties and cultural commonness of the population were strengthened and their political and economic ties became closer, which gave momentum to the formation of the nation. . . . The Koreans are a homogeneous nation who inherited the same blood and culture consistently down through history.[8]

Kim Il Sung toured the site later that month, and a year after that his son, Kim Jong Il, dedicated a museum in the same place. All the scribes came forward to proclaim Koreans the oldest (and therefore finest) people in the world, with one continuous line of history from the thirtieth century B.C. down to the present.

6. Illyŏn, *Samguk yusa,* pp. 32–33; see a slightly different translation by Peter Lee in Lee (1993), p. 6.
7. Lee (1993), p. 5.
8. Korean Central News Agency (P'yŏngyang—hereafter KCNA), Nov. 26, 1993.

Whatever one makes of this latest discovery or the she-bear myth, this is clearly a Korean story: few other peoples (the Japanese and the Israelis come to mind) assert such distant origins, with a continuously distinct ethnicity and language down to our time. Few place such inordinate attention on the female issue of a prodigal son, or the son's prodigious talents (the North Koreans claimed that Tan'gun's unearthed pubic bone was unusually large; ancient texts sometimes gave the length of the king's phallus, but only if it was something to write home about.)[9] Few peoples eat as much garlic. Above all, few of the world's peoples live in a nation with no significant ethnic, racial, or linguistic difference: Korea is indeed one of the most homogeneous nations on earth, where ethnicity and nationality coincide. It is pleasant for Koreans to think they were always that way; it is a dire mistake to think that this relative homogeneity signifies a common "bloodline" or imbues all Koreans with similar characteristics.

Unfortunately there is no written history of Korea until the centuries just before the birth of Christ, and that history was chronicled by Chinese scribes. Excavations at Paleolithic sites, however, have determined that human beings inhabited this peninsula half a million years ago, and people were also there seven or eight thousand years ago, in the Neolithic period—as revealed by the ground and polished stone tools and pottery they left to posterity. Around 2000 B.C. a new pottery culture spread into Korea from China, bearing prominent painted and chiseled designs. These Neolithic people practiced agriculture in a settled communal life and are widely supposed to have had consanguineous clans as their basic social grouping. Korean historians of today sometimes assume that clan leadership systems characterized by councils of nobles called *hwabaek,* institutions that emerged in the subsequent Silla period, go back to these Neolithic peoples, as would the Tan'gun myth. But there is no hard evidence to support such imagined beginnings for the Korean people, unless one credits the recent discovery in North Korea, which few outside historians are yet willing to do.

By the fourth century B.C., however, a number of small states on the peninsula had survived long enough to come to the attention of China, and the most illustrious was Old Chosŏn, which some historians locate along the banks of the Liao River in southern Manchuria, and others along the Taedong River, which runs through P'yŏngyang and northwestern Korea.[10] Chosŏn prospered into a civilization based on bronze

9. "King Kyŏngdŏk's male organ was eight inches long," *Samguk yusa,* p. 113.
10. These two sites are of course far apart; archaeological evidence either does not exist or is mixed on exactly where Old Chosŏn was located. Some historians think that any conclusions about Old Chosŏn must be purely speculative, given the state of our knowledge.

culture and a political federation of many walled towns, which (judging from Chinese accounts) was formidable to the point of arrogance. Composed of a horse-riding people who deployed bronze weapons, Chosŏn extended its influence to the north, taking most of the Liaot'ung basin. But the rising power of the North China state of Yen (1122–255 B.C.) checked Chosŏn's growth and eventually pushed it back to territory south of the Ch'ŏngch'ŏn River (located midway between the Yalu and the Taedong rivers).

As the Yen gave way in China to the Ch'in Empire and the Han dynasty (206 B.C.–A.D. 200), Chosŏn declined and refugee populations migrated eastward. Out of this milieu emerged a man named Wiman, who assumed the kingship of Chosŏn sometime between 194 and 180 B.C. Wiman's Chosŏn was a meld of Chinese influence and the old Chosŏn federated structure; apparently reinvigorated under Wiman, this state again expanded across hundreds of miles of territory. Its ambitions ran up against a Han invasion, however, and Wiman Chosŏn fell in 108 B.C. These developments coincided with the emergence of iron culture, making possible a sophisticated agriculture based on implements such as hoes, plowshares, and sickles. Cultivation of rice and other grains increased markedly, thus enabling the population to expand. From this point onward there is an unquestioned continuity in agrarian society down to the emergence of a unified Korean state many centuries later, even if we are not yet willing to call the peoples of the peninsula "Korean."

Han Chinese built four commanderies to rule the peninsula as far south as the Han River (which flows through Seoul), with a core area at Lolang (Nangnang, in Korean; the location is near modern-day P'yŏngyang). It is illustrative of the relentlessly different historiography practiced in North and South Korea today—as well as of the dubious projection backward of Korean nationalism that both sides engage in—that DPRK historians deny that the Lolang District was centered in Korea and place it northwest of the peninsula, possibly near Beijing. Perhaps this is because Lolang was clearly a Chinese city, the site of many burial objects showing the affluence of the Chinese overlords and merchants who lived in it, with many of the artifacts unearthed by a Japanese archaeologist named Sekino Tadashi under the direction of the colonial governor-general, in 1913. (Perhaps the North Koreans have a point, after all.)

THE PERIOD OF THE THREE KINGDOMS

For about four centuries Lolang was a great center of Sino-Korean statecraft, art, industry (including the mining of iron ore), and commerce. Its influence carried far and wide, attracting immigrants from China and exacting tribute from several states south of the Han River. In the first three centuries A.D. a large number of so-called walled states in southern Korea grouped themselves into three federations, known as Chinhan, Mahan, and Pyŏnhan; rice agriculture had developed in the rich alluvial valleys and plains to the point where reservoirs for irrigation could be established. Chinhan was situated in the middle part of the southern peninsula, Mahan in the southwest, and Pyŏnhan in the southeast. The state of Paekche, which soon came to exercise great influence on Korean history, emerged first in the Mahan area; no one is certain when this happened, but the state certainly existed by 246, since Lolang mounted a large attack on it in that year. That Paekche was a centralized, aristocratic state blending Chinese and indigenous influence is not doubted, however, nor is its growing power: within a hundred years Paekche had demolished Mahan and occupied what today is the core area of Korea, around Seoul. It is said that the common Korean custom of father-to-son royal succession began with King Kŭn Ch'ogo of Paekche, and his grandson inaugurated another long tradition by adopting Buddhism as the state religion (in 384).

Meanwhile, two powerful states had emerged north of the peninsula around the time of Christ—Puyŏ in the Sungari River basin in Manchuria and Koguryŏ, Puyŏ's frequent enemy, to its south near the Yalu River. Koguryŏ, which would also exercise a lasting influence on Korean history, developed in confrontation with the Chinese. Puyŏ was weaker and sought alliances with China to counter Koguryŏ, but eventually succumbed to it around A.D. 312. Koguryŏ was now expanding in all directions, in particular toward the Liao River in the west and toward the Taedong River in the south. In 313 it occupied the territory of the Lolang Commandery and came into conflict with Paekche.

Peninsular geography shaped the political space of Paekche and Koguryŏ, and a third kingdom called Silla that fills out the trilogy. In the central part of Korea the main mountain range, the T'aebaek, runs north to south along the edge of the Sea of Japan. Approximately three-fourths of the way down the peninsula, however, roughly at the thirty-seventh parallel, the mountain range veers to the southwest, dividing the peninsula almost in the middle. This southwest extension, the Sŏbaek Range, shielded peoples to the east of it from the Chinese-occupied portion of the peninsula, but placed no serious barrier in the way of expansion into or out from the southwestern portion of the peninsula. This was Paekche's historic territory.

Koguryŏ, however, ranged over a wild region of northeastern Korea and eastern Manchuria subjected to extremes of temperature and structured by towering mountain ranges, broad plains, and life-giving rivers;

the highest peak, Paektusan, occupies the contemporary Sino-Korean border and has a beautiful, crystal-pure volcanic lake at its summit, called Ch'ŏnji, or Pond of Heaven. It is 500 meters from the summit, with surrounding peaks at nearly 3,000 meters above sea level. A famous Korean monk named Tosŏn, who combined Buddhist and Taoist practices of geomancy, saw the Korean peninsula as "a branching tree with its roots at Mt. Paektu."[11] Meanwhile, in 1942 a German geographer assayed the traveler's breathtaking vista—"a view of monumental grandeur"—from the rim of the crater, with a vast expanse of virgin forests below:

> Gazing outwards, he scans over the slopes with their white patches and downward to the sheer unending plateau with its immense forests. Gazing inward his eye looks down 500 m[eters] over steep precipices to the broad surface of the lake, which appears to be motionless, even when storms are raging overhead. In good weather it is a radiant dark blue, and the forms and colors of the caldera walls are reflected in perfect clarity. The reds of the lower lavas, the gray and black of the higher ones, the gleaming yellowish white of the pumiceous sand appear double their actual size in the reflection and are all the more impressive. All observers agree that the contrasts that this twofold view unite make the scene . . . one of the most enthralling sights on earth.[12]

Koguryŏ branched far and wide from this mountain, from contemporary Vladivostok to Port Arthur, from the thirty-eighth parallel to Changch'ün in Manchuria. Like Koguryŏ, North Korea utilized this mountain as part of its founding myth, and now Kim Jong Il is said to have been born on the slopes of Paektusan, in the desperate year of 1942 (he was actually born along the Russo-Chinese border south of Khabarovsk, and accounts conflict as to whether he was in China or in Russia). Unsurprisingly, it is also the Koguryŏ legacy that the Democratic People's Republic of Korea (DPRK) claims as the mainstream of Korean history.

Certainly Koguryŏ bowed to no one in championing its own kings: the founder, Chumong, was not merely the son of heaven, a great archer and horseman, and strong as a mature man at the age of seven; he could also walk on water. Once when enemy warriors were hot on his heels, legend has it, Chumong drew up short in front of a wide river. When he was about to be captured, "immediately a host of fish and turtles gathered together on the surface to form a bridge so that Chumong and his party could cross. Then they dispersed and sank back into the depths, leaving

11. Lee (1984), p. 107.
12. Lautensach (1945), p. 243.

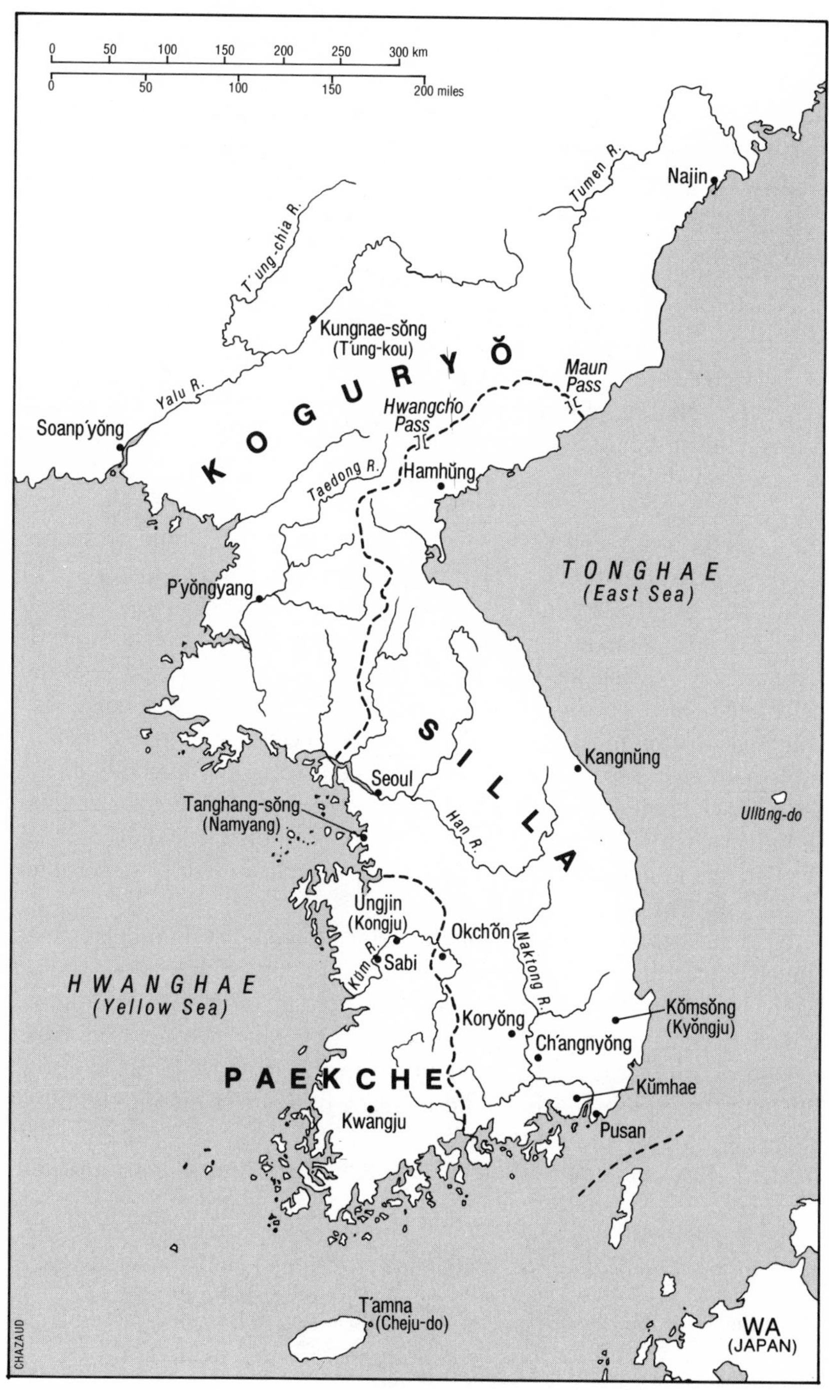

The Three Kingdoms

the pursuers on horseback with no way to cross." Chumong "gave the name Koguryŏ to his land from his family name Ko, meaning high, because he was begotten by the sun on high."[13] North Korea's Kim Il Sung, also a sun-king, called himself by an old Koguryŏ term meaning maximum leader *(suryŏng)*[14] and privileged a direct line from that ancient kingdom through the Koryŏ dynasty and down to the present.

It is the glories of a third kingdom, however, that first constituted the main current of Korean lineage according to South Korean historiography. The Silla state to the southeast eventually became the repository of a rich and cultured ruling elite, with its capital at Kyŏngju, north of the port of Pusan. The presidents who ruled South Korea either as dictators or as elected leaders from 1961 through 1996 all came from this region, and most Republic of Korea (ROK) historians privilege Silla's historical lineage; the author of Syngman Rhee's ideology, the first minister of education, named An Ho-sang, produced his own "Juche"[15] philosophy and located its origin with Silla. It is the southwestern Paekche legacy that is the casualty of divided Korea, with the people of the Chŏlla provinces suffering discrimination by Koreans of other regions and by historians in North and South; fortunately the discovery of King Muryŏng's tomb (501–23), near Kongju, revealed to twentieth-century scholars the brilliant artistry of Paekche, with finely filigreed gold crowns that rival the celebrated crowns of Silla. One painter of Paekche ancestry in Japan was said to be the foremost court artist of the ninth century, "the first memorable painter in Japan, the first to bring landscape, for example, to the level of a dignified art."[16] Taken together, the three kingdoms continue to influence the history and political culture of Korea; it is not unusual for Koreans to assume that regional traits that they favor or despise go back to the Three Kingdoms period.

Were these three kingdoms inhabited by "Koreans"? Certainly some of the characteristics of each kingdom had survivals in unified Korea, as we will see. But there was way too much warfare, migration, and intermingling to make for a homogeneous race of people, distinct from their neighbors, and far too little verifiable historical material for us to know the boundaries, ethnic stock, and lingustic differences among the three states, or among these three and the states in western Japan, for that matter.[17] Koguryŏ unquestionably merged with Chinese and northern

13. Both from Illyŏn, *Samguk yusa*, p. 46.
14. For *suryŏng* as a Koguryŏ term for the king, see Lee (1984), p. 89.
15. "Juche" is the North Korean spelling of *chuch'e*, a term we will have much to say about below.
16. Alexander Soper, quoted in McCune (1962), p. 99.
17. Farris (1994), pp. 2–4.

ethnic stocks, and the two southern kingdoms had much intercourse with peoples inhabiting the Japanese islands, especially western Kyushu. Recent evidence suggests that as many as one-third of the residents of Japan's Tomb period (A.D. 300–700) could trace their recent ancestry back to Korean roots.[18] It is best, I think, to hypothesize that the gene pools of contemporary Koreans and Japanese must inevitably have had an ancient, common root, just as northern Chinese and Mongol peoples cross-fertilized with inhabitants of the peninsula. So we have no unique, homogeneous races in Korea and Japan, however much both peoples want to believe in such things, but a common human stock that branched off culturally and linguistically at some unknown point, thereafter to have a relatively independent historical development, but with only the slightest DNA trace of racial difference.

Silla evolved from a walled town called Saro, and although Silla historians are said to have traced its origins back to 57 B.C., contemporary historians regard King Naemul (356–402) as the ruler who first consolidated a large confederated kingdom and who established a hereditary kingship. His domain was east of the Naktong River in today's North Kyŏngsang Province. A small number of states located along the south central tip of the peninsula facing the Korea Strait did not join either Silla or Paekche, but instead formed a Kaya league that maintained close ties with states in what is now Japan. Kaya was eventually absorbed by its neighbors in spite of an attack by Wae forces from Kyushu[19] against Silla on their behalf in A.D. 399, an attack Silla repelled with help from Koguryŏ. For the next two decades the Koguryŏ army was stationed in Silla.

Centralized government probably emerged in Silla in the last half of the fifth century, as the capital became both an administrative and a marketing center. In the early sixth century its leaders introduced plowing by oxen and built extensive irrigation facilities. Increased agricultural output was the result, permitting further political and cultural development, including the formulation of an administrative code in 520, the creation of a hereditary "bone-rank" system for designating elite status, and the adoption of Buddhism as the state religion around 535 (Paekche and Koguryŏ adopted Buddhism earlier).

18. Ibid., p. 29.

19. Wae is the Korean pronunciation of the more common Wa. It is wrong to call these forces simply "Japanese," as some historians like to do. These were most likely people from Kyushu Island, but some experts think *Wae* refers to people from the Korean peninsula; basically the evidence isn't good enough for us to know one way or the other. It is likewise wrong for Japanese historians to claim some sort of early influence or tributary relationship with Korea; during these centuries Korea's influence on Japan was far greater than Japan's influence on Korea.

Silla was weaker than Koguryŏ militarily; indeed, by the beginning of the fifth century Koguryŏ had achieved undisputed control of all of Manchuria east of the Liao River as well as of the northern and central regions of the Korean peninsula. At this time it had a famous leader with an appropriate name: King Kwanggaet'o, whose name translates roughly as "the king who widely expanded the territory." Reigning for twenty-one years (391–412), from the age of eighteen, he conquered sixty-five walled towns and 1,400 villages, in addition to assisting Silla in fights with Wae forces from Japan. Kwanggaet'o was the master of northern Korea and much of Manchuria; in 427 he settled the Koguryŏ capital at P'yŏngyang, a junction of alluvial plains and rivers, which became the center of this large nation. But as Koguryŏ's wide domain increased, it confronted China's Sui dynasty (581–618) in the west and Silla and Paekche to the south.

Silla attacked Koguryŏ in 551 in concert with King Sŏng of Paekche. After it conquered the upper reaches of the Han River, Silla turned on Paekche forces and drove them out of the lower Han area. While a tattered Paekche kingdom nursed its wounds in the southwest, Silla allied with Chinese forces of the Sui and the successor T'ang dynasty (618–907) in combined attacks against Koguryŏ. These were immense clashes between hundreds of thousands of soldiers on each side, and they reshaped the face of Northeast Asia. First Koguryŏ armies drove across the Liao River in 598 and beat back several Sui attempts to dislodge them. Neither could the Sui emperor Yang Ti defeat the Koguryŏ armies at their Liaotung fortress, so he boldly launched an enormous invasion of Koguryŏ in 612, marshaling more than one million soldiers and sending one-third of this force against the capital at P'yŏngyang. The Koguryŏ commander, a scholar and soldier named Ŭlchi Mundŏk, arranged successive defeats, feints, and retreats, in order to lure the Sui forces into a trap along the Ch'ŏngch'ŏn River, thirty miles north of P'yŏngyang, where—finally—he awaited the Chinese. There he prepared for the occasion a poem, which he sent to the opposing commander:

> Your divine plans have plumbed the heavens;
> Your subtle reckoning has spanned the earth.
> You win every battle, your military merit is great.
> Why then not be content and stop the war?

The Chinese were unimpressed. So the Koguryŏ forces attacked the enemy from all sides, cutting the Sui forces to pieces; nine armies fled in disarray toward the Yalu River. Perhaps as few as three thousand Sui soldiers survived to retreat into China; their defeat contributed to the fall of the dynasty in 618.[20] The newly risen T'ang emperor T'ai Tsung launched another huge invasion in 645, but Koguryŏ forces won a striking victory in the siege of the An Si fortress, forcing T'ai Tsung to withdraw.

Koreans ever since have seen these victories as sterling examples of resistance to foreign aggression. There is much merit to the argument; had Koguryŏ not beaten them back, all the states of the peninsula might have fallen under long-term Chinese domination and ultimate absorption. Thus commanders like Ŭlchi Mundŏk became models for emulation thereafter, especially during the Korean War (1950–53).

Paekche could not hold out under combined Silla and T'ang attack (the latter landed an enormous invasion fleet on the southwest coast in 660), however, and it quickly fell under their assaults. T'ang pressure had also weakened Koguryŏ, and after eight successive years of battle it gave way from both external attack and internal strife accompanied by several famines. It retreated to the north, enabling Silla forces to advance and consolidate their control up to the Taedong River, which flows through P'yŏngyang. Silla thus emerged on top in 668, and it is from this famous date that many historians speak of a unified Korea. The period of the Three Kingdoms thus ended, but not before all three states had come under the long-term sway of Chinese civilization by introducing Chinese statecraft, Confucian philosophy, Confucian practices of educating the young, and the Chinese written language (Koreans adapted the characters to their own language through a system known as *idu*). The Three Kingdoms also introduced Buddhism, the various rulers seeing a valuable political device in the doctrine of a unified body of believers devoted to Buddha but serving one king. In addition, artists from Koguryŏ and Paekche perfected a mural art found on the walls of tombs, and took it to Japan, where it deeply influenced Japan's temple and burial art. Some Korean scholars maintain that Paekche "conquered" Japan,[21] which raises any number of questions (for example, What was "Japan"?), but many Korean and Western historians now believe that the wall murals in royal tombs in Japan suggest that the imperial house lineage may have had a Korean origin; perhaps that is why Japanese archaeologists are slow to open more imperial tombs (most of the great ones are still off-limits to archaeological research).

That Koreans profoundly influenced Japanese development, there is no doubt: as one Japanese historian put it, Paekche art "became the

20. Compiled from several histories; the poem, translated by Peter Lee, along with a similar account, can be found in Lee (1993), p. 38.
21. For example, Hong (1988), p. 5.

basis for the art of the Asuka period (about 552–644),"[22] and the tomb murals clearly do show a strong Koguryŏ influence. Nationalistic scholars in Japan try to deny all this, just as their counterparts in both North and South see Korea as the onetime ruler of Japan and "the fount of all ancient Japanese civilization."[23] Recent evidence, weighed dispassionately, shows that Japan got from old Korea advanced iron products, armaments, horse trappings, gold and silver jewelry, pottery, and new methods of statecraft, some of it copied from China and some originated by inhabitants of Korea. In particular, "nearly all the iron to make the first Japanese weapons and tools" came from Korea, and the Japanese learned that the Koguryŏ method of armoring both horse and rider was "the most deadly military technology in the world before the advent of gunpowder." An American scholar puts the point discreetly: "one may be inclined to agree with those experts, Korean and Japanese, who see Korea as the wellspring of Japanese culture before 700."[24]

KOREA UNDER SILLA

Silla and Paekche had sought to use Chinese power to best the Koguryŏ kingdom, inaugurating another tradition of involving foreign power in Korean internal disputes. Silla's reliance on T'ang forces to consolidate its control had a price, however, since Silla then had to resist encroaching T'ang forces, which limited its sway to the area south of the Taedong River. But its military force, said by Korean historians to have been bolstered by an ideal of the aristocratic, youthful warrior *(hwarang)*, was formidable and had seized Paekche territories by 671; aided by a Koguryŏ general named An Sŭng, it then pushed the T'ang commanderies off the peninsula by 676. Silla thereby guaranteed that the development of the Korean people would take an independent form.

The warrior oath of the *hwarang* symbolized the mix of Buddhism and Confucianism that had come to characterize Korean thought by this time. In the early 600s a famous monk named Wŏn'gwang required the *hwarang* braves to honor five injunctions: loyalty to the king, filial love toward one's parents, fidelity in friendship, bravery in battle, and chivalry in warfare (no wanton killing).[25] It would not have occurred to Western visitors in late-nineteenth-century Korea that it had a military

22. Hatada (1969), p. 20.

23. Farris (1994), pp. 24–25.

24. Ibid., pp. 3–4, 7–15, 27.

25. The *hwarang* ideal is a common theme in the way Koreans think about Silla, but Richard Rutt could find little evidence of it in the extant sources. See Rutt, "The Flower Boys of Silla," *Transactions of the Korea Branch of the Royal Asiatic Society,* no. 38, pp. 1–66.

tradition like Japan's, but for centuries it clearly did—manifest in the sterling Koguryŏ and Silla battlefield successes against China.[26] Koguryŏ's military prowess existed alongside Confucian education: in 372 it established a national Confucian academy, and in the local towns young men came of age reading the five great classics of Confucian learning.

In spite of Silla's military triumphs in the seventh century, broad territories of Koguryŏ were not conquered, and a section of the Koguryŏ elite under a general named Tae Cho-yŏng established a successor state known as Parhae above and below the Yalu and Tumen boundaries. Parhae saw itself as the embodiment of old Koguryŏ, and its strength forced Silla to build a northern wall in 721 and kept Silla forces permanently below a line running from present-day P'yŏngyang in the east to Wŏnsan in the west. As one prominent historian has written, "Silla and Parhae confronted each other hostilely much like southern and northern halves of a partitioned nation,"[27] and North Korea today looks back to Parhae for lessons in post–Cold War survival. (It is by no means clear that such things would be written had Korea not been divided in 1945, however.) By the eighth century Parhae controlled the northern part of Korea, all of northeastern Manchuria, and the Liaot'ung peninsula. Like Silla, Parhae continued to be influenced deeply by the Chinese civilization of the T'ang, sending students to the capital at Ch'angan (many of whom passed the civil service exams there) and modeling its own capital city on Ch'angan—just like the ancient city of Kyoto in Japan.

According to some sources, Parhae people settled Paektusan mountains and valleys more densely than was the case in the twentieth century.[28] Unlike the Japanese, Parhae people were by this time sleeping on *ondol* floors, heated by a system that involves sending flues from a central hearth through the floors of each room—and that is still in wide use in contemporary Korea, with the stone flues covered by waxed and polished rice paper. Ice may form in a water jug on the table, while a person sleeps comfortably on a toasty warm *ondol,* so it is not unlikely that the good citizens of Parhae passed their Manchurian winters likewise. A master poet of the twelfth century, Yi Kyu-bo, had it this way:

> Beneath the winter's moon the biting cold
> Sharp-toothed sets fingers on my quivering skin.
> At last—good luck—a fire blows 'neath the floor
> With heat awakening from its faggot brand.

26. One of the best sources on early Korean military history is John C. Jamieson, "The *Samguk Sagi* and the Unification Wars" (Ph.D. diss., University of California at Berkeley, 1969).

27. Lee (1984), p. 71.

28. Lautensach (1945), p. 239.

The welcome warmth is like the breath of spring,
And friendly grows the blanket at its spell.[29]

A seventeenth-century shipwrecked Dutchman, Hendrik Hamel, found a two-class system for Korean homes, which he did not like, but also warm floors, which he did. There were tile roofs for the rich and mandated straw thatch huts for the poor: "No Man can cover his House with Tiles, unless he have leave, so to do." Hamel went on,

> The Floors are all vaulted, and in Winter they make a Fire underneath, so that they are always as warm as a stove. The Floor is cover'd with Oil'd Paper. Their houses are small, but one Story high. . . . The Nobility have always an Apartment forward, where they receive their Friends. . . . [B]efore their Houses [is] a large Square, or Bass Court, with a Fountain, a Fish-pond, and a Garden with covered Walks. The Womens Apartment is in the most retir'd part of the House, that no body may see them.[30]

Contacts between Silla and T'ang were also many and varied, as large numbers of students, officials, and monks traveled to China for study and observation. In A.D. 682 Silla set up a national Confucian academy to train high officials, and later instituted a civil service exam system somewhat like that of the T'ang, but with typically Korean hereditary restrictions on who could sit for the exams. If anything, Parhae borrowed its central government more directly from T'ang systems than did Silla; its culture melded indigenous and T'ang influences, but its level of civilization was still high enough to bestir the Chinese to call it a "flourishing land in the East."[31]

Silla also developed a thriving indigenous civilization, one of the most advanced in the world. Its capital at Kyŏngju had upwards of one million residents[32] and was renowned as the "city of gold," where the aristocracy pursued a high culture and extravagant pleasures. T'ang dynasty historians wrote that elite officials possessed thousands of slaves, and like numbers of horses, cattle, and pigs. Their wives wore pure-gold tiaras and earrings of delicate and intricate filigree. Scholars studied the Confucian and Buddhist classics and perfected state administration, while developing advanced methods for astronomy and calendrical science. The famous seventh-century Ch'ŏmsŏngdae observatory, where the queen sat and pondered the heavens, still stands today. Advanced math-

29. Yi Kyu-bo, trans. James Gale, in Gale (1972), p. 180.
30. Hamel, in Ledyard (1971), p. 216.
31. Lee (1984), pp. 88–91; Parhae is Pohai in Chinese.
32. Illyŏn counted nearly 179,000 households in Kyŏngju at the height of the Silla period. See *Samguk yusa*, p. 48.

ematics informed the surrounding Buddhist architecture, and refined woodblock printing made possible the production of many Buddhist sutras and classic Confucian texts. Arab travelers also discovered and wrote about the wonders of Silla, coming to Korea overland from China and by ship *(dhow);* many settled down to live out their lives in this bountiful state. The Arab historian Masuid wrote about Silla in his *Meadows of Gold and Mines of Precious Stone* (947), "Seldom has a stranger who has come there from Iraq or another country left it afterwards. So healthy is the air there, so pure the water, so fertile the soil and so plentiful all good things."[33] Presumably these Arab sojourners also married, putting a bit of Semitic seed into the hallowed Korean bloodlines.

Buddhists came on pilgrimages to Kyŏngju from as far away as India. The Dharani sutra, written by Silla scholars and found recently at the foot of the "Pagoda That Casts No Shadow," dates to 751 and is the oldest remaining example of woodblock printing in the world. Meanwhile, "Pure Land" Buddhism united the mass of common people, who could become adherents merely by repeating simple chants—maybe a bit like Hare Krishna enthusiasts of today. The crowning glories of the "city of gold" were the Pulguk-sa temple in Kyŏngju and, over winding paths through nearby hills upon a cliff with a majestic view of the ocean, the Sŏkkuram grotto. Both were built around 750, and both are home to some of the finest Buddhist sculpture in the world:

> The Sŏkkuram was modeled after the stone cave temples of China, but in China these were cut into the face of natural rock cliffs, whereas the Sŏkkuram is a man-made stone grotto . . . [with] a rectangular antechamber and a circular interior chamber with a domed ceiling formed by carefully cut blocks of stone. This domed ceiling evidences not only great technical skill but also a solidity reflecting sophisticated knowledge of the mechanics of stress.[34]

No mortar was used in the construction of this solitary chapel. Four Deva kings stand guard along the passageway to the interior chamber where sits a giant statue of the Sakyamuni Buddha cut from solid granite, a serene and impassive expression on his great round face, his left hand with palm open connoting meditation, the right hand down to "call the earth to witness"—suggesting to Koreans a militant posture, a determination to protect Korea from invasion across the sea.

Carved into the circular walls of this chamber are the likenesses of Buddha's disciples, arrayed behind the Buddha as it receives the rising sun from the horizon of the East Sea. An eleven-headed *kwansŭm*

33. Quoted in Lautensach (1945), p. 40.
34. Lee (1984), p. 87. See also the fine description in McCune (1962), pp. 92–96.

behind the Buddha symbolizes its all-seeing power and is among the most beautiful of all Korean sculptures. The effect on the pilgrim who climbs up to the grotto to await the dawn is overwhelming; perhaps an American can experience a similar effect by sitting in the rotunda of the magnificent Jefferson Memorial in Washington, watching the first rays of sun strike the tidal basin.

The symbolism is all the more striking, for beyond the horizon sits the rising sun of Japan. I thought of this once when a prominent Japanese scholar waxed enthusiastic about the heaven-sent geographic isolation of his home islands, separated by broad seas from the turmoil of the Asian mainland. He thought it was the main reason why Japan had a different (and of course superior) development. Called upon to comment on his paper, I remarked that the Sŏkkuram Buddha and many Koreans probably hoped to wake one morning and find that the islands were no longer there. The professor stomped out of the room, refusing to respond to me.

Maybe I deserved it, maybe not; in any case, let me say something even more offensive to Japanese sensibilities: where did *Nippon* come from? It is from the perspective of the Sŏkkuram Buddha gazing out over the sea that the characters "rising sun" or "root of the sun" seem pertinent; it would not occur to the people of those islands themselves. Thus an early translator of the *Nihongi* (or *Chronicles of Japan*), William Aston, surmised, "I have little doubt that Nippon, as a name for Japan, was first used by Corean scholars who came over in numbers during the early part of the seventh century. . . . In 670 it was formally notified to one of the Corean Kingdoms that this would be the name of the country in the future. . . ."[35]

Silla's high civilization was exemplified in this incomparable sculpture, and its longevity may be felt among the many high, round burial tumuli that still sculpt the physiognomy of Kyŏngju. That many of the homes of the true silent majority are still unopened is evidence of the respect Koreans believe to be due them. Most of these were tombs of the aristocracy, the hereditary "true bone" elite, built according to geomantic desiderata promulgated by the great monk Tosŏn. According to him, "in the lie of the land there is decay or prosperity, . . . and by selecting a flourishing or propitious site . . . for constructing a tomb," the family would enjoy good fortune.[36] The linkage of bones *(kol)* with hereditary bloodline *(ch'ŏng)* has exercised a strong influence on Koreans well into this century.

35. William George Aston, trans., *Nihongi* (Chronicles of Japan) (Tokyo: Tuttle, 1972), quoted in Hong (1988), p. 219.
36. Ki-baik Lee's paraphrase of Tosŏn, in Lee (1984), p. 107.

Silla's power began to dissipate in the ninth century when influential regional leaders splintered central power and rebellions shook the state's foundations (some rebels were called "the Red Trousers"). The northern state of Parhae, straddling both sides of the Yalu River, still existed although it was under severe pressure from Khitan warriors and was riven within by ethnic splits between remnant Koguryŏ and Malgal peoples, who were also part of the Parhae state.[37] Silla's decline encouraged "restorationists" of both the defeated Paekche and the still-extant Koguryŏ (through the vehicle of Parhae) to try and bring this great dynasty to an end. A warrior named Kyŏnhwŏn founded "Later Paekche" at Chŏnju in 892, and one named Kungye founded "Later Koguryŏ" at Kaesŏng, in central Korea; Kyŏnhwŏn sought to have his fourth son succeed him, which enraged his first son: so he confined his father in a temple and claimed the throne for himself. The father did not take kindly to this affront, escaping to join forces with Wang Kŏn, the son of Kungye, who succeeded to the throne in 918. This turned out to be a good move, since Wang Kŏn won out. Viewing himself as the legitimate successor to Koguryŏ, he shortened the name to Koryŏ ("high mountains and sparkling waters") and became the founder of a new dynasty by that name (918–1392)—whence comes the modern term "Korea."

UNIFICATION BY WANG KŎN IN THE NAME OF KOREA

Wang Kŏn's army fought ceaselessly with Later Paekche for the next decade, with Silla utterly in retreat. After a crushing victory over Paekche forces at present-day Andong in 930, Koryŏ got a formal surrender from Silla and proceeded to conquer Later Paekche by 935—amazingly, with troops led by the former Paekche king Kyŏnhwŏn, whose son had treacherously cast him aside. After this accomplishment Wang Kŏn became not just a unifier but a magnanimous one. Regarding himself as the proper lineal king of Koguryŏ, he embraced survivors of the Koguryŏ line who were fleeing the dying Parhae state, which had been conquered by Khitan warriors in 926. (This marked the last time that a Korean state dominated large areas of Manchuria, but the experience still encourages many Korean nationalists to lay sovereign claim to large swatches of what is now northeastern China.) Wang Kŏn then took a Silla princess as his wife and treated the Silla aristocracy with unexampled generosity. He established a regime embodying the remnants of the Later Three King-

37. The presence of many Malgals leads some historians to say that Parhae should not be treated as a successor state to Koguryŏ. Chinese and North Korean historians differ with each other profoundly on that point; the North Koreans are supported by some southern historians, and contemporary nationalism muddies attempts to sort out the truth.

doms and thereby accomplished a true unification of the peninsula.[38] The Koryŏ dynasty ruled for just short of half a millennium, and in its heyday ranked among the most advanced civilizations in the world.

With its capital at Kaesŏng, a town north of Seoul bisected by the thirty-eighth parallel, the Koryŏ dynasty's composite elite also forged a tradition of aristocratic continuity that lasted down to the modern era. The elite fused aristocratic privilege and political power through marriage alliances and control of land and central political office, and fortified this class position to the point of impregnability by making it hereditary. Koryŏ established a social pattern in which a landed gentry mixed its control of property with a Confucian- or Buddhist-educated stratum of scholar-officials, usually residing in the capital; often a scholar and a landlord was one and the same person, but in any case landed wealth and bureaucratic position were powerfully fused. At the center a bureaucracy influenced by Confucian statecraft emerged; it thereafter sought to influence local power and thus militated against the Japanese or European feudal pattern of castle towns, landed domains, and parcelized sovereignty all backed by a strong military class (although Korea came close to the feudal pattern in the ninth and tenth centuries, when strong walled-town lords and military commanders challenged central power).

By the thirteenth century there were two government groupings in Koryŏ, those of the civil officials and the military officials; at that time the military people were stronger, but thereafter both were known as yangban (the two orders). Below the hereditary aristocracy were common people like peasants, clerks, and merchants; below these were outcaste groups of butchers, tanners, and entertainers who were called *ch'ŏnmin* and who led a caste-like existence, often in separated and ostracized villages, and whose status fell upon their children as well. Likewise slavery was hereditary (matrilineally), and slaves may have constituted as much as 30 percent of Koryŏ society.[39]

We will call this sociopolitical pattern "agrarian bureaucracy," to distinguish it from feudalism, and will return to it when it reached its fully developed form, in the subsequent Chosŏn period. Although this social system evolved over centuries, its chief characteristic was a strong and enduring tension between central bureaucratic power and provincial landed wealth; it is close to the Chinese system in its statecraft and philosophy, but with more entrenched local power than China's, often resembling the Japanese feudal pattern of a fusion between landownership and aristocratic status in the localities, with outcaste groups like the

38. Lee (1984), p. 103.
39. The best study is Palais (1996), chap. 6.

eta or *burakumin* who are (with minor exceptions) essentially unknown in China.[40] We can compare the social system to that of areas in China where agrarian wealth based in wet-paddy rice farming predominated, such as the Canton delta, but it featured less social mobility, since the Chinese mostly gave up hereditary status after the Song period.

After the founding of Koryŏ, favored officials received land grants (or prebends) as rewards for supporting the dynastic unification, giving them tax collection rights. Meanwhile, large landed families held their land in perpetuity and could bequeath it to their survivors; its produce was at the service of the owner, after taxes were paid. It thus constituted private property, in spite of stipulations to the effect that all the land in the country belonged to the king. This system, in which land was worked mostly by tenants who paid rent in kind, often produced vast estates of great wealth worked by hundreds of tenants or slaves, and in its essential form persisted through the subsequent Chosŏn period and the Japanese colonial period. Family landholding became more important than office holding in perpetuating aristocratic dominance over time, although having an officeholder in the family was a good form of insurance. The wealthy, aristocratic landlord, often residing in the capital cities of Kaesŏng or Seoul, became a benefaction or a plague (depending on your point of view) from early Koryŏ down to modern times, and an egalitarian redistribution of the land became a focal point of Confucian reformers, capitalist modernizers, and communist agitators alike. As for the peasants who worked this land, their only escape was often flight into the mountains; one Koryŏ "long poem" *(changga)* put it his way:

> Let us live, let us live,
> Let us live in a green mountain,
> Eating wild grapes and vine berries,
> Let us live in a green mountain.

Other peasants rose up in rebellion, like the insurrections in the last decade of the twelfth century that shook the dynasty. A rebel named Manjŏk sought to inflame the slaves in Kaesŏng in 1198 with this stirring speech, given to a multitude gathered at Kaesŏng's North Mountain:

> Are generals and ministers born to . . . glories? No! For when the time is right anyone at all can hold these offices. Why then should we only work ourselves to the bone and suffer under the whip? . . . If each one

40. This pattern was reinforced by the central state's expectation that the villages would govern themselves; the county magistrate worked with prominent yangban families much as the king solicited advice from the great families of the capital. See Fujiya Kawashima's chapter in the forthcoming *Cambridge History of Korea*, vol. 3.

kills his master and burns the record of his slave status, thus bringing slavery to an end in our country, then each of us will be able to become a minister or general.[41]

The Koryŏ aristocracy was by no means a class without merit, however. It admired and interacted with the splendid Chinese civilization that emerged during the contemporaneous Song dynasty (960–1279). Official delegations and ordinary merchants brought Koryŏ gold, silver, and ginseng to China in exchange for Song silks, porcelains, and woodblock books. Finely crafted Song porcelains stimulated Koryŏ artisans to produce an even finer type of inlaid celadon pottery; unmatched in the world before or since for the pristine clarity of its blue-green glaze and the delicate art of its inlaid portraits (usually of flowers or animals), twelfth-century Koryŏ celadon displayed the refined taste of aristocrats and later had great influence on Japanese potters. But it also was a relatively unadorned, guileless pottery. As William B. Honey put it,

> The best Corean wares were not only original, they are the most gracious and unaffected pottery ever made. They have every virtue that pottery can have. . . . It seems to speak at first of a serenely happy people, and only later in a time of extreme poverty does its graciousness give way to a wild austerity which is admirable in a different way. This Corean pottery, in fact, reaches heights hardly attained even by the Chinese.[42]

Like China, Korea also sent out trading ships: Yesŏng harbor, near the capital, was an international commercial port, where Arab ships brought spices and medicines in return for Koryŏ's leathers and furs. There was also much trade with Japan, a fact that allows us to imagine in this period an East Asian international system of great fluidity and a confident, worldly Korea that was the antithesis of the subsequent "Hermit Kingdom." But we have to imagine it, because so few sources still exist that would allow us truly to write its history.

Scholars have long pondered the rapid commercial and industrial development of the Song period, and the wide trading network that culminated in Admiral Cheng Ho's seven seafaring expeditions to the Persian Gulf and the African coast in the period of Yi Sŏng-gye and Sejong, that is, 1405–33. The question is, Why did this fruitful period come to an end? We might ask the same of Koryŏ. Why did Sung and Koryŏ inventions have to be reinvented in the West, why no steady march from there toward science, toward capitalism, toward modernity? Even the

41. Quoted in Lee (1984), pp. 144, 168.

42. Honey, *The Ceramic Art of China and Other Countries of the Far East,* p. 167, quoted in McCune (1962), p. 174.

best historians cannot resist indulging themselves in this progressive (and therefore anachronistic) logic: we find Fernand Braudel at the end of his illustrious career, for example, bewildered by "the immobility of the Far East, its extraordinary fidelity to its own ways," fretting about whether it dropped back or "remained where it was," wondering why it was ahead of the West for so long and then got "outdistanced." His tentative answer is that East Asian civilization "very early achieved remarkable maturity, but in a setting that made some of their essential structures almost impervious to change."[43]

A few questions for this eminent historian of the *longue durée* from the perspectival optic of today: What if the East Asian civilizations have not yet reached maturity? If "fidelity to its own ways" is so central, why is East Asian capitalism so formidable today? If Korea, Japan, and China were so impervious to change, why have they changed so dramatically in such a brief period of human history? Perhaps history was not so unchanging in East Asia after all; perhaps we simply do not know enough to chart its changes. Braudel may have been the greatest historian of our time: it just goes to show that you can't fully trust any of them to get things right.

What should we learn from this exercise—not to believe our good historians? Not at all: we should learn the old baseball adage that every human being puts on his pants one leg at a time. The Korean of Koryŏ ate his food in the morning, went to bed at night, honored his parents, made love to his wife, fretted about his children, weighed his life chances, prepared to meet his maker, much as we do and in full possession of all our creative faculties. Furthermore, the way of Koryŏ might one day, centuries hence, come to be considered better than the way of change, progress, tumult—history on the upward curve toward Valhalla—that even Braudel cannot shake out of his head. Once when asked to comment on the meaning of the French Revolution, Mao Tse-tung said, "It's too early to tell." A little Eastern wisdom for our French progressives. . . .

Buddhism coexisted with Confucianism throughout the Koryŏ period, richly influencing the daily life of society and perhaps bequeathing to modern Korea its characteristic eclecticism of religious belief: Koreans are often Confucianists, Buddhists, and Christians at the same time. Koryŏ Buddhist priests systematized religious practice by rendering the Korean version of the Buddhist canon into mammoth woodblock print editions, known as the Tripitaka. The first was completed in 1087 after a lifetime of work, but was lost; another, completed in 1251, can still be viewed today at the Haein-sa temple. Its accuracy and its exquisite calli-

43. Braudel (1994), p. 168.

graphic carvings make it the finest example of some twenty Tripitaka created in East Asia. By 1234, if not earlier, Koryŏ had also invented movable metal type, two centuries before its inception in Europe.

Meanwhile, Confucian worthies like Ch'oe Ch'ung established many private academies for studying the classics, and the two great philosophical doctrines lived easily with each other, side-by-side as it were. Nor was Koryŏ Buddhism just of the otherworldly variety: many monks got rich from commerce, agriculture, animal husbandry, wine making, and loans at high interest; furthermore, it was a state religion, merging philosophy with political power. And finally, during the Koryŏ and later periods these were fighting monks: the Koryŏ "subdue demons corps" held off Jurchen invaders, just as monkish guerrillas later helped turn back Japanese invasions.

This high point of Koryŏ culture coincided with internal disorder and the rise of the Mongols, whose power swept over most of the known world during the thirteenth century. Koryŏ was no exception, as Mongol forces invaded and demolished Koryŏ's army in 1231, forcing the Koryŏ government to retreat to Kanghwa Island (north of modern-day Inch'ŏn), a ploy that exploited the Mongol horsemen's fear of water. But after a more devastating invasion in 1254, in which countless people died and some 200,000 were captured, Koryŏ succumbed to Mongol domination and its kings came to intermarry with Mongol princesses (more exotic seed for the bloodlines). The Mongols then enlisted thousands of Koreans in ill-fated invasions of Japan in 1274 and 1281, using crafts made by Korea's great shipwrights. The Kamakura shogunate turned back both invasions with help, as legend has it, from opportune typhoons known as the "divine wind," or *kamikaze.* The last period of Mongol influence was marked by the appearance of a strong bureaucratic stratum of scholar-officials (literati; called *sadaebu* in Korean). Many of them lived in exile outside the capital and used their superior knowledge of the Confucian classics to condemn the excesses of the ruling families, who were backed by Mongol power.

The overthrow of the Mongols by the Ming dynasty in China (1316–1644) gave a rising group of military men, steeled in many battles against coastal pirates from Japan, an opportunity to contest for power. When the Ming claimed suzerainty over former Mongol domains in Korea, the Koryŏ court was divided into pro-Mongol and pro-Ming forces. Two generals marshaled their forces for an assault on Ming armies in the Liao-t'ung peninsula; one of them, Yi Sŏng-gye, had an abrupt change of mind: he reached the Yalu River only to turn back and charge toward the Koryŏ capital, which he subdued quickly. He thus became the founder of Korea's longest-ruling dynasty, the Chosŏn (1392–1910), which lasted down to this century. The new state was named Chosŏn, harking back to the Old Chosŏn kingdom fifteen centuries earlier, and its capital was built at Seoul.

THE CHOSŎN PERIOD: FLORESCENCE

General Yi announced the new dynasty by mobilizing 200,000 laborers to surround the new capital with a great wall; it was completed in six months in 1394, and scattered remnants of it still stand today. Like Wang Kŏn, he was generous to his defeated Koryŏ antagonists. The last Koryŏ king, Kongyang, he sent off to comfortable exile in Samch'ŏk, a town on the remote middle part of the east coast; another prominent Koryŏ clan, the U family, went the same way and can still be found in Samch'ŏk today—my in-laws, as it happens.[44] Such magnanimity encouraged one writer to wax poetic about Yi Sŏng-gye's virtues—a typical example of how Koreans sing the manifold praises of their leaders, especially dynastic founders:

> His presence is the mighty warrior, firm
> He stands, an eagle on a mountain top;
> In wisdom and resource none can compare,
> The dragon of Namyang is he.
> In judgment on the civil bench,
> Or counsel from the warrior's tent, he rules;
> He halts the waves that roll in from the sea,
> And holds the sun back from its heavenly course.[45]

According to another legend, Yi's father, Yi Cha-ch'un—a military officer from Hamhŭng—had this experience:

> One day in bright spring Chach'un dreamed at high noon a wonderful dream—an old man with a long white beard, wearing a high hat and a flowing robe, stood before him with both hands to his brow and said, I am the guardian deity of Paektusan and I have come to foretell a good fortune that is visiting your family. If you offer prayers with devotion to the famous mountains and rivers you will get a noble son.[46]

The new king's sons, however, were less than magnanimous and all too numerous. As every Korean knows, Yi Sŏng-gye's reign began with a remarkable power struggle within the royal family; like many other such affairs, this one bequeathed a model text for the unceasing gossip

44. King U (1374–88) devoted his last years on the throne to hunting, drinking, and womanizing—or so the annals say. (I am indebted to John Duncan for this reference.)
45. Translated by James Gale, in Gale (1972), p. 222.
46. "In the Reign of King T'aejo," in Ha Tae-hung, *Behind the Scenes of Royal Palaces in Korea* (Seoul: Yonsei University Press, 1983), p. 3.

about the presumed tensions within every governing household, including those in Seoul and P'yŏngyang today. A dynasty as long-lived as this one should have such stories at its inception.

General Yi was a prodigious head of his own household, fathering eight sons and five daughters by two wives. The fifth son by the first wife, Yi Pang-wŏn, was the strongest and introduced many of the reforms that subsequently reshaped Korean society. It was Pang-wŏn who arranged for the Ming emperor Hung Wu to invest his father on the throne (a tribute of 9,800 horses helped); the Hung Wu emperor also chose Korea's new name, that is, the old name of Chosŏn.[47] The first wife died in 1392, an unlamented event since the king favored the second wife, Queen Kang. Hearkening to his beloved, in 1393 the king chose her second son, Pang-sŏk, as his successor. Four years later Queen Kang also died, however, just as the king passed his *hwan'gap* (sixty-year cycle), thus entering his "second life." Terrible events worthy of a Shakespeare tragedy were thus set in motion.

In 1398 Yi Pang-wŏn mobilized troops in Seoul and struck at the two sons by the second marriage. Battles raged across the city. Both of Queen Kang's sons were killed, and a famous Confucian reformer and adviser to the king, Chŏng To-jŏn, was beaten to death. "On this the old king, enraged beyond words, cut off his daughter's glossy hair, shook the dust of the accursed city from his feet and made his way back to Hamhŭng. For ten long years he remained in exile, a grinning spectre. . . ." Yi Pang-wŏn had the eldest son by the first marriage installed as a figurehead king, while sending messengers to his father to beg forgiveness. One of them, Pak Sun, thought he had achieved peace and turned back toward Seoul, only to be struck in his spine with an arrow. Finally Pang-wŏn came to his father begging for mercy, and just missed the same fate when an arrow meant for him hit a tree—behind which Pang-wŏn was hiding: "On this the old man threw him the state seal and said, 'Take it, you rascal, since that's what you want.' "[48] Pang-wŏn did so, taking the throne for himself in 1400 and reigning for nearly twenty more years.

THE TRANSFORMATION OF KORYŎ SOCIETY

Yi Sŏng-gye surrounded himself with the best intellects at the end of the fourteenth century, including a famous Buddhist monk who called himself Muhak, that is, "no knowledge." (Muhak had the same idea as Jean-Paul Sartre, who once wrote that all his work was conditioned by his own ignorance.) It was this monk who shepherded the king to exile

47. Rutt in Gale (1972), p. 342.
48. Gale (1972), pp. 223–24.

in Hamhŭng and who uttered the phrase I like best from the Korean philosophers: "Among all the actions of life, those of a tiny baby are best." A Confucian scholar once described Muhak in this way:

He was a peerless son of meditation,
A teacher of the Fathers. . . .
As one born to highest honour
He cared not for sounding praises.
His prophet-vision was unlimited;
God gave him lengthened life,
Seventy and nine long years.
Whence came he at his birth?
The sun's rays shot him forth.
Whither now depart his steps
Up beyond the lotus flower?[49]

Yi was also advised, however, by the same Chŏng To-jŏn whom his son killed, and Chŏng was the man behind changes that mark a watershed in Korean history—ones that transformed the Buddhist-shaped society that Muhak represented—just as Yi's grandson Sejong presided over so many new achievements. Yi Sŏng-gye began to reform the land system, destroying the prebendal privileges of the Koryŏ elite. Except for land doled out to loyalists called "merit subjects" (on the pattern followed by early Koryŏ leaders), Yi Sŏng-gye declared everything to be owned by the state, thus undercutting Buddhist temples (which held a lot of farm land) and locally powerful clans—both of which had exacted high rents from peasants, leading to social distress in the late Koryŏ period. These reforms also, of course, enhanced the taxing power of the central government.

Buddhist influence and complicity in the old system made it easier for the literati to urge the extirpation of Buddhist economic and political influence, and exile in the mountains for monks and their disciples. Indeed, the literati accomplished a deep Confucianization of Chosŏn society, which particularly affected the position of women. Although many women were prominent in Koryŏ society, they were now relegated to domestic chores of child rearing and housekeeping, as so-called inside people. Up until the recent period the woman's role in Korean society seemed to be as old as the bones in ancestral graves, just as central and just as hidden, and just as unchangeable. Some recent scholarly spadework, however, has shown us what we should have known—that the social position of women is at its origin a political question.

Koryŏ society had been influenced by Confucianism, but more so by

49. Gale's translation of a poem by Pyŏn Kye-ryang, in Gale (1972), p. 227.

Buddhism, the state religion of the time. Koryŏ practice was different from the Chinese, emphasizing a more matrilineal system. It was by no means a matriarchy, but it wasn't nearly the patriarchy prevalent in later centuries. The husband was welcomed into the wife's house, where the children and even grandchildren would live. Husbands were happy to take this route because woman shared rights of inheritance with their male siblings (women were endowed with more than their beauty). Women were so valuable that men wanted several; a Chinese envoy in 1123 found a wealthy man in Kaesŏng with four. But plural wives were not dependent on one man; often living apart, they had their own economic underpinnings. Detailed ritual did not surround the act of marriage, nor the relations between sexes: "the general free and easy contact between the sexes amazed . . . Chinese observers." Women took serial husbands if not several at the same time, there being no restrictions on widows' remarrying.[50]

The new elite that seized power in 1392 was more or less the old elite, in that property relations were not deeply disordered, many scholar-officials remained at their posts, and new social forces did not push up from below. It was more a renovation than a revolution.[51] The new leaders did think, however, that Koryŏ had fallen because of the error of its ways, especially its Buddhist ways, and so they soon embarked on major reforms. The leader was Chŏng To-jŏn, whom we met before. A revered scholar who had been exiled to Naju, in Chŏlla Province, from 1375 to 1383, he had tasted the degree of raw hatred for the ruling elite that prevailed among dirt-poor and heavily taxed peasants. To them, the Confucian literati "seemed a breed apart and not to be trusted."[52] With the king's help, he was positioned to change all this with a thorough rectification of the Korean social order. Although the changes did not come at once but evolved over the next two centuries, in retrospect Chŏng was one of the originators of a profound reformation.

All the reforming came in the name of Neo-Confucianism and Chu Hsi, the great progenitor of this doctrine. Much of what we now reckon as "Korean culture" or "Korean tradition" was the result of this major social reorganization accomplished by self-conscious ideologues, who got going in the fifteenth century. What started as a military putsch by General Yi ended up centuries later in the apparent solidity of a hierarchical Confucian society, much like the one Westerners first encoun-

50. Deuchler (1992), pp. 66–72, 277.

51. John Duncan has done the major work on the transition from Koryŏ to Yi. See Duncan, "The Social Background of the Founding of the Chosŏn Dynasty: Change or Continuity?" *Journal of Korean Studies* 6 (1988–89): 39–79, and his forthcoming book.

52. Chai-sik Chung, "Chŏng Tojŏn: 'Architect' of Yi Dynasty Government and Ideology," in de Bary and Haboush (1985), p. 62.

tered. The Chosŏn dynasty founders believed that they had instituted a system that paid more fealty to Confucianism than did China itself; their fealty was to Chu Hsi's Neo-Confucian orthodoxy, and they saw the Wang Yang-ming school in the sixteenth century as "a grave deviation from the truth." Subsequent scholars have agreed: Michael C. Kalton argues that Korea became "the most Neo-Confucian of all East Asian societies."[53]

To restore Korean society to its proper path meant to use the virtues to discipline the passions and the interests. Kwŏn Kun, another leading thinker of the early period, drew a famous organic diagram to illustrate the unity of man with heaven, and mind with nature. The human intellect, through long cultivation of the virtues, would control and discipline the emotions and the will and root out the evil of passion and desire. After long study, according to Kwŏn's diagram, the superior man might become a sage whose perfect integrity approximated the greatness of heaven. Another early reformer, Cho Chun, used an organic analogy to argue that the principles of society ought to be like blood vessels in the body—effective transmission belts through which the state's edicts moved. The state would give body to society in the same way that doctrine gave correct bearing to the man, and thus doctrine and edict should brook no deviation.[54] These ideas evolved into the master organizing principles of Korean society for centuries.

The unquestionable effect of the new laws, if not their clear intent, was a slow-moving but ultimately radical change in women's social position and an expropriation of their property (it was probably complete by the late fifteenth century). The latticework of Korean society in the Chosŏn period consisted of "highly structured patrilinear descent groups"—families in the great chain linking past and present, but newly founded in primogeniture and strict lineage exogamy. The nails in the latticework, the proof of its importance and existence over time, were the written genealogies *(chokpo)* that positioned families in the hierarchy of property and prestige. Property could be land or titles or eligible sons and daughters, but usually it was all three.[55] The daughter did not merit a name before she was betrothed, yet she was a key link in solidifying family alliances. To send a daughter off to another house (which is the term Koreans use when she marries) was to make a strategic choice for one's own family fortunes. To send a daughter who could bring forth

53. Haboush (1988), pp. 23–24; see also Kalton's chapter in the forthcoming *Cambridge History of Korea,* vol. 3.

54. "Diagram of Heaven, Man, Mind and Nature, Conjoined as One," in Kalton's chapter in *The Cambridge History of Korea,* vol. 3; Cho Chun is quoted in Deuchler (1992), p. 108.

55. The best account of these reforms is Deuchler (1992).

sons was even better, for with the birth of the son a woman achieved her designated place in the new family, and got an honored name: so-and-so's mother. An exuberant if anonymous observation from the 1920s makes the point:

> If there is any matter in which a Korean's spirit comes to a state of white heat, it is marriage. [S]he is a born match-maker, a born marrier. [S]he will have who married to whom, finished and done, before the sun goes down.
>
> What money is to the son of the west, marriage is to the Korean: every man is after it. . . . Theoretically he says, "Let me be married in the spring when the plum blossoms greet me, and when the peach flowers and apricots tint the hill-side;" but he never thinks of his bride as his peach- or plum-blossom. Spring is the mating season and he would mate. He wants to be married, not for selfish pleasure, nor because a little sugar-coated heart longs to rest in his love and be looked after. Not a bit of it: he wants a son, a son of his very own. He wants him wildly, unreasonably; anything for a son.[56]

All this is not to say that the choice was easy; family alliances combined material wealth, social standing, and perpetuation of both over time. Nothing was left to chance, including chance itself: the same author continues,

> In the choice of bride, the old elements are still consulted; metal, wood, water, fire, earth. Everybody has his fixed element, according to the day, month, hour and year in which he was born. A girl marked "metal" is crossed off when a "wood" boy is in question. A "fire" girl and a "water" boy mated would mean fuss and steam and sizzle, while a "wood" girl and a "water" boy would fall within the encompassing sphere of good luck.

Now, let me just add from discreet personal experience and observation that the formula has not changed today, either; it still involves all the old elements, even as young people try desperately to avoid them (and often succeed). The gravest and most admirable element of all is respect for one's parents, honor to the aged, and offerings to the ancestral dead.

Koreans quite naturally think that their system is unique, or perhaps shared with China, but better. That it was not is evident in Tocqueville's analysis of aristocratic nations, upon which it would be hard to improve:

> As families remain for centuries in the same condition, often on the same spot, all generations become, as it were, contemporaneous. A

56. Quoted in Gale (1972), pp. 109–10.

> man almost always knows his forefathers and respects them; he thinks he already sees his remote descendants and he loves them. He willingly imposes duties on himself towards the former and the latter, and he will frequently sacrifice his personal gratifications to those who went before and to those who will come after him. . . . As the classes of an aristocratic people are strongly marked and permanent, each of them is regarded by its own members *as a sort of lesser country,* more tangible and more cherished than the country at large. As in aristocratic communities all the citizens occupy fixed positions, one above another, the result is that each of them always sees a man above himself whose patronage is necessary to him, and below himself another man whose co-operation he may claim. Men living in aristocratic ages are therefore almost always closely attached to something placed out of their own sphere, and they are often disposed to forget themselves. . . . Among democratic nations new families are constantly springing up, others are constantly falling away, and all that remain change their condition; *the woof of time is every instant broken, and the track of generations effaced.* Those who went before are soon forgotten; of those who will come after, no one has any idea. . . . Aristocracy has made a *chain* of all the members of the community, from the peasant to the king; democracy breaks that chain and severs every link of it.[57]

These observations are richly revelatory of what Koreans have thought (at least since the fourteenth century) and of the future that democracy holds for them. But they also tell us that Koreans are by no means alone in nourishing such practices.

The lineage group organized society at the top, in such a way that most of the Chosŏn elite came from a relative handful of eminent families, tracing their line back to a prominent male (thus spawning an entire field of inquiry—*pohak,* or the discipline of family lineages). And it organized society at the bottom, with many Korean villages having but one clan. (Some 15,000 "single-lineage villages" remained in 1930s Korea.)[58] At the top were the yangban, literally meaning the two ranks (military and civilian) that staffed the Chosŏn dynasty, but designating a potent aristocratic fusion of landed wealth and political power.

Historians still debate the precise definition of the yangban, but it clearly was an elite different from that in China or Japan. Elite status in Korea, unlike that in China, was hereditary: you had to demonstrate that at least one ancestor in the previous four generations had been a yangban. To be a "distinguished ancestor" against which your progeny could make their subsequent claims, it was good to be a landowner, an official,

57. Tocqueville (1945), p. 105 (emphasis added).
58. Deuchler (1992), p. 9.

and, above all, a scholar: in short, a literatus or Mandarin or "scholar-official." Best of all was to combine all three in one person or family. Running close behind was the virtue of marrying well, that is, finding a daughter from another prominent family. Silla society, as we have seen, had a hereditary caste system known as the bone-rank system, and since one's status in the society was so much influenced by birth and lineage, from that early point onward each family and clan sought to maintain genealogical records with meticulous care. Since only male offspring could prolong the family and clan lines and were the only ones whose names registered in the genealogical tables, the birth of a son was greeted with great fanfare. Such historical influences remain strong in both Koreas today, where first sons and their families often live with the male's parents and where all the stops are pulled out to the end of fathering a boy.

The first son, Korean ritual had it, was the only offspring with *chŏngch'e,*[59] the right stuff making him the exclusive heir of his father's full panoply of privilege and obligation. *Chŏngch'e* literally means something like correct basis or substance or constitution, and from it comes every Korean father's attempt to put his first son in his place—the last and best-known attempt being Kim Il Sung's. He took the *ch'e* character into his Juche doctrine, and the *chŏng* character into his eldest son's name (Jong Il), thus to provide a succession for the ages: the correct idea, carried forth by the correct man. Tseng Tzu, Confucius' disciple, put it this way: "When proper respect towards the dead is shown at the End and continued after they are far away, the moral force of a people has reached its highest point."[60]

Those at the top thus wove a web of property, status, and lineage that was well nigh impenetrable from below through much of the dynasty. In Korea as in China, of course, the majority of peasant families could not spare a son from the fields to study for the exams anyway, so upward social mobility was sharply limited in both societies. In Korea the limit was specifically hereditary as well, leading to less mobility than in China and attitudes toward class distinctions that often made them indistinguishable from castes.

Records showing how many people qualified as yangban are scattered, and there is a lot of debate among scholars about how to identify them; research into a few collections of household registers from the late seventeenth century yielded a figure of somewhere between 9 and 16 percent of the population who counted themselves as yangban. By the nine-

59. Deuchler (1992), p. 178. *Ch'e,* as we will see later, means "body," and many other meanings derive from that root.
60. Quoted in Deuchler (1992), p. 179.

teenth century the category had been diluted, and often a much larger number claimed aristocratic status. A major study of all who passed civil service exams at the high *munkwa* level in the Chosŏn dynasty (some 14,600 over five centuries), however, showed remarkable persistence in those elite families producing students to sit for the exams; twenty-one of the leading clans produced 40 percent of *munkwa* degree holders, and thirty-six clans produced 53 percent.[61] Other studies have documented the persistence of tightly held elite privilege into the early twentieth century. Even in 1945, one can say, this aristocracy was substantially intact—although its effective demise came very soon thereafter.

Korea's traditional class system also included the majority who were peasants; minorities of petty clerks and merchants; and so-called base classes, caste-like hereditary groups *(paekchŏng)* such as butchers, leather tanners, and beggars. Although merchants ranked higher than persons in lowborn classes, Confucian elites frowned on commercial activity and squelched it as much as possible right down to the twentieth century. Peasants ranked higher than merchants because they worked the life-giving land, but the life of the peasantry was almost always difficult during the dynasty, especially in the later centuries; most peasants were tenants, required to give up at least half of their crop to landlords as tax, and subject to various additional exactions. Many reformist scholars called for an egalitarian redistribution of the land, but to no avail. The lowborn classes were probably worse off, however, given very high rates of slavery for much of the Chosŏn period. One source reports more than 200,000 government slaves in Seoul alone in 1462, and a 1663 register suggests that as much as 75 percent of Seoul's population may have been slaves. The Bureau of Slave Administration maintained files on all slaves and on litigation regarding ownership. Probably about 30 percent of the entire population consisted of slaves.[62] Of slaves there were two types—those owned by the state or owing service to the state and those bought and sold privately, mostly for work in the home or on the land. Prices for slaves, like almost all other prices, were set by the government (this will not surprise foreign businessmen who have worked in contemporary Korea). Many slaves had their own households, with living conditions not unlike those of poor tenant farmers—except that slave status was strictly hereditary (although determined by the mother's status, in

61. Edward Wagner, "The Ladder of Success in Yi Dynasty Korea," *Occasional Papers on Korea*, no. 1 (1973): 1–8.

62. See Fujiya Kawashima's chapter in the forthcoming *Cambridge History of Korea*, vol. 3; also Palais (1996), which is the major account of Korean society in the period, with much new information on slavery and a theorization of Chosŏn as a "slave society" (pp. 208–70).

this case) and also organic: slaves were the "hands and feet" of the yangban, just as one could barely be considered a yangban without a complement of slaves to do the dirty work.

In spite of hereditary status, however, rates of escape from slavery and manumission were also unusually high. Why this should have been so is hard to determine, but it suggests a less onerous type of slavery than, say, what faced blacks in the American South. Still, as late as the 1920s it was not uncommon for a person to be known simply as "so-and-so, slave," with no surname. It may be that *paekchŏng* outcastes were even worse off than slaves, since they often lived in isolated villages in the middle of old riverbeds and the like, and had more trouble escaping their status—perhaps because working with animals and the dead was all they knew.

What are the *paekchŏng* and *ch'ŏnmin?* Korea and Japan have stigmatized these "base classes," just as India did with its "untouchables." In all three countries butchers are included in the category, leading Dumont to ask if the stigma might owe to "the nauseating smell" of animal skins being treated or cooked. But it is more than that, he writes; it is "the attribution of a massive and permanent impurity to certain categories of people." The son inherits the butcher's station even if he does no fetid slaughtering. Really it is an "extreme portioning out," Dumont argues, of the central category of hierarchy.[63]

Korea was not a caste society but rather one with certain castes; but Dumont's point still holds, particularly regarding the extremely fine distinctions drawn between rank, status, and grade. The Korean hierarchy was so successful that the highborn were the high livers; more than that, they got to enter at the top of the hierarchy of the afterlife as well, together with their servants. Class and status hierarchies also were built into the Korean language, so that today one still addresses superiors and inferiors quite differently and should speak to elders only with elaborate honorifics. Verb endings and conjugations will differ according to station. Because the path backward to this extraordinary hierarchy has been so short, given Korea's recent industrialization, egalitarianism has often been an ideal falling on deaf ears in both halves of Korea.

Confucian doctrines of hierarchy in the Chosŏn dynasty did not stop at the water's edge but also informed a foreign policy known as "serving the great" *(sadae),* that great thing being China—and not just China, but China of the Ming. If a country wanted to associate itself with something great, the Ming, China's greatest dynasty, was not a bad choice. In any case, it was the choice that Yi Sŏng-gye made at the beginning of the

63. Dumont (1980), p. 47.

dynasty because it helped him triumph over the Koryŏ aristocracy, and successive rulers were happy to bask in Ming glories. Chosŏn lived within the Chinese world order, radiating outward from the "Middle Kingdom" to associated states, of which Korea was the most important. It was China's little brother, a model tributary state, and in many ways its chief ally.

The central government's ultimate weakness, particularly in the latter stages of the Chosŏn dynasty, was its inability to extract resources effectively—primarily because of the aristocracy's power. The state's taxing power was strong on paper, but competent taxation required frequent surveys of the extent and value of property, just as it does in any American city. The rural aristocracy succeeded in blocking cadastral or land surveys for decades at a time; there were virtually none in the first half of the nineteenth century (the state undertook major surveys in 1663–69, 1718–20, and 1820, the latter being very incomplete). The cause was "the fusion of aristocratic status with private landownership, an amalgam that was almost as resistant to the fiscal encroachments of the central government as a bona fide feudal nobility."[64] The administrative setup was strong from the center down to the county level, as in China, with local magistrates appointed by the center and subject to frequent rotation, lest they get too involved with the localities. Below the counties, however, local influentials (meaning strong clans and elders) controlled everything. They pressured (and often bribed) local clerks to keep their lands off the tax rolls.

In truth, the yangban were exempt not just from an effective land tax but from nearly all the exactions placed upon commoners—most other taxes, corvée labor, military conscription. Good Confucians who disdained working with their hands, they literally believed the world owed them a living. For the most part they got it, and when they didn't they would still avoid manual labor even to the point of starvation, because soiling their hands would irremediably diminish their social status. Yi Kyu-gyŏng, a reformer writing in the ill-fated 1830s, had this to say:

> In the past, the number of [yangban] were no more than one quarter of the population, but at present they take up almost half the population. Do they engage in agriculture or commerce? Can they be recruited into the royal guards or the army? . . . Can you make them pay silk, cloth, or ramie for the land, labor or tribute taxes? Can you limit their landholdings? . . .
>
> Because the orders of the court are not applied to the yangban, the household, miscellaneous labor service, and the personal service taxes

64. Palais (1975), p. 58.

> are not applied to the yangban. In a system of land taxation, nothing is more important than equalizing distribution of taxes among people, but the evil of unequal distribution exists because of them.[65]

To be a yangban male thus was to be everything and give nothing: not military service, not labor, not even taxes. To work with one's hands was beneath him; to possess a lot of slaves, a mark of his station in life. To progressive Westerners in the nineteenth century, Korean yangban lacked every modern virtue: they seemed idle, lazy, profligate, totally lacking in the enterprising spirit and work ethic that (they thought) built the West. But to Koreans they were the virtuous, the men of reason and contemplation, the exemplars of ethical behavior and good governance, people to look up to.

The purified social order was one in which yangban were pure and everyone else was not. The pure were at the top, having perfected the social order, and all others ought to know their place, and the difference between noble and base. Everything distinguished the yangban from the commoner, including the size of one's home, the educational opportunity of one's children, dress and the manner of address, even body language, one's carriage; above all, commoners did not record their family lines in genealogies, and slaves had no surnames to record, so there was no record of past merit and thus no prospect of current or future reward.

But there was a redeeming virtue: the ideology itself, the Neo-Confucian world view, claimed that human nature had no essential quality at the start, therefore was mutable and subject to external ministrations that would yield internal perfection. The human soul was indifferent at the beginning, neither good nor bad, but existed to be constructed through the right means. This echo of Plato (engineer of the soul) and Locke (the mind as tabula rasa) combined to leaven the Confucian view of people: human-all-too-human, the human being was nevertheless capable of perfection. It was by no means self-evident to Confucians that humans were "born equal"—quite the contrary. But through the discipline of the mind, people could become not just equal but superior beings: true gentlemen. It was an entirely secular stance, because it sought ennoblement in this life and eternal verification of that nobility in the afterlife, through the worship of one's grateful progeny. Ancestor worship, as it is usually called, is Korea's most important and venerable tradition, surrounded by and imbricated with elaborate ritual (even if it had less than a venerable beginning, having been instituted with a new law in 1390). But why wouldn't we want to offer obeisance to an ancestor who had guaranteed social position or married well or bequeathed

65. Quoted in Palais (1975), pp. 98–99.

land to several generations? Was this not the way to success in the here and now?

THE FAMILY, MOBILITY, EDUCATION

The classic text for inculcating proper ideas, read over and over by commoner and king alike, was the *Ta-Hsüeh,* or *Great Learning.* According to it (in Legge's translation), the ancient sages did this:

> Wishing to order well their States, they first regulated their families. Wishing to regulate their families, they first cultivated their persons. Wishing to cultivate their persons, they first rectified their hearts *(sim).* Wishing to rectify their hearts, they first sought to be sincere in their thoughts. Wishing to be sincere in their thoughts, they first extended to the utmost their knowledge.[66]

A simple text, it has resonated down through the Korean ages with its ringing call first to rectify oneself, then one's family, and finally the state. From the individual to the society and polity, all were to be put in harmonious order, through the three "do thises" and the four "do thats" that characterized later Chinese and Korean thought. King Sŏngjong of Koryŏ said this: "in governing the country . . . nothing surpasses filial piety *[hyo]*"; it constitutes "the core of all virtues."[67] The proper relationship between father and son was the most important of the filial relations, the basic paradigm "for all hierarchical relationships in a moral society."[68] What is most interesting about these two statements, perhaps, is that one comes from the Koryŏ period and the other from South Korea in the 1970s.

The principle of filial piety was hierarchy within a web of duties and obligations: the son obeyed the father, the father provided for and educated the son. Daughters obeyed mothers (and mothers-in-law), younger siblings followed older siblings, wives were subordinate to husbands. The superior prestige and privileges of older adults made longevity a prime virtue. In politics, the principle held, a village followed the leadership of venerated elders and citizens revered a king or emperor, who was deemed the father of the state. In international affairs, the Chinese emperor was the big brother of the Korean king. Transgressors of these elaborate rules were regarded as uncultured beings unfit to be members of society.

66. James Legge, *Confucius: Confucian Analects, the Great Learning, and the Doctrine of the Mean,* trans. and annotated by Legge (1893; reprint, New York: Dover, 1971), pp. 357–58.
67. "Rescript on Filial Piety," from the *Koryŏ-sa,* trans. Hugh Kang, in Lee (1993), p. 319.
68. Janelli and Janelli (1982), p. 50.

The story of Sim Ch'ŏng features Korea's most famous filial child.[69] She sold herself to seamen wanting a fifteen-year old virgin of great beauty to offer as a sacrifice to the sea, so that her blind father could have the money to buy rice to donate to a temple, an act that would restore his sight. The tale was often told in *p'ansori,* an art form widely popular in nineteenth-century Korea; the *p'ansori* songs emphasized the Confucian virtues and had one singer and one drummer, the singer narrating both male and female parts.

Korean child-rearing practices that emerged from this philosophy generate an enormous debt of love and gratitude. When I lived with a Korean family having two small children, I was not so surprised at the obvious love the parents manifested for them, but was flabbergasted by their indulgence. Both kids were happy, free birds who roamed the house at will, had no routine, played to their heart's content, ate and evacuated on demand, and frolicked freely, hearing no raised voices and suffering virtually nonexistent punishment. At length they would collapse in their parents' arms and sleep with them all night.[70] To an American of Calvinist lineage, in whose view the sins of the parents were soon visited upon the children with due moral opprobrium and guilt, this looked like a recipe for making adults with no superegos, loose cannons who would soon bedevil civil society. But there was nothing of the sort; soon the schools provided all the discipline necessary to young people who were as healthy mentally as any parent could hope. Much earlier, Hamel made similar observations: "Parents are very indulgent to their Children," he wrote, "and in return are much respected by them. They depend upon one anothers good Behaviour," providing an ultimate corrective to childhood abandon.[71]

Such practices may not produce strongly independent individuals, sure of their personal identity; Koreans "view themselves primarily as extensions of their parents"—at least that is what Percival Lowell thought in 1888 and what many anthropologists still think[72]—but it by no means inhibits personal mastery and rock-like psychological security, even amid considerable poverty; furthermore, the wayward winds of individualism grow cold and uncomforting in the later years. The Korean way may or may not be a "better" way to raise children, but it certainly is a venerable and dignified way to create strong human beings, solid in their attachments.

69. An award-winning translation of "The Song of Shim Ch'ŏng" by the late Marshall R. Pihl was reprinted in *Korea Journal* 35, no. 3 (Autumn 1995): 85–98.

70. For scholarly confirmation of these practices by two observant anthropologists, see Janelli and Janelli (1982), pp. 31–32.

71. Hamel, quoted in Ledyard (1971), p. 219.

72. See Janelli and Janelli (1982), p. 36, for various citations.

The attachments and the filial gratitude are so strong that Korean children feel acute guilt when parents pass away, and from this come extended and emotional mourning practices—lasting three years in the old days, for a son who lost his father. Hamel again, from the seventeenth century:

> As soon as one dies, his Kindred run about the Streets shrieking, and tearing their Hair. Then they take special care to bury him honourably in some part of a Mountain, shown them by a Fortune-teller. . . . In the Morning at break of day, they set out with the Body, after a good Repast, and making merry all the the Night. . . . Every Full Moon they cut down the Grass that grows on the Grave, and offer new Rice there. That is the greatest Festival next to the new Year.

There then followed a three-year period of mourning, the breaved dressed in hemp and "a sort of Sack-Cloth," with a large, umbrella-like hat made of green woven reeds—shaped to prevent the wearer from looking up to heaven, because he was guilty of the death of his parent. Mourners carried a cane, connoting the departed father, and never bathed during this long period of bereavement. At length, "when the Children have fully perform'd the Duty they owe to Father and Mother by means of this tedious Ceremony . . . the eldest Son takes possession of the house that belongs to him, with all the Lands depending on it."[73]

In addition to filial virtues, the practical glue holding the system together was education, the paradigmatic figure being the "true gentleman," the virtuous and learned scholar-official who was equally adept at poetry and at statecraft. The primary route to bettering a family's station in life was through education, a kind of socio-academic upward mobility; study therefore went on ceaselessly, morning, noon, and night: just as it does for Korean schoolchildren today, who may sleep as few as four hours a day. The eye of the needle through which every family hoped their children would pass was the civil service examination system.

Throughout the Chosŏn dynasty all official records, all formal education, and most written discourse was in classical Chinese, as were the examinations that constituted the core of Korean civilization and upon the outcome of which "hung preferment to office, a place in the sun and a name never to be forgotten."[74] For children whose families could spare them from the fields, a regimen of study began when a child first

73. Hamel, quoted in Ledyard (1971), pp. 219–21; also Rutt, in Gale (1972), p. 38. More on mourning rituals can be found in Deuchler (1992), pp. 192–93.

74. Gale (1972), p. 181. The records include the *Chosŏn wangjo sillok*, or dynastic annals, and the *Sŭngjŏngwŏnilgi*, the daily record of the royal secretary's office, more than three thousand volumes of which are still extant.

acquired speech and did not end until he had reached the highest station his talents could afford him. Education meant socialization into Confucian norms and virtues that began in early childhood with the reading of the Confucian classics, for king and commoner alike. Korean students had to master the extraordinarily difficult classical Chinese language, thus to master tens of thousands of written characters and their many meanings; rote memorization was the typical method. James Gale remembered that his "first recollection of Korea began with hearing the little children in the thatch-roofed school shouting in unison: *'Hanŭl ch'ŏn, tta chi, kamŭl hyŏn, nuru hwang'*. . . . They were all reciting the Thousand-character Classic. . . ."[75]

The figure of the disciplinarian Korean mother, hovering about her child and attending to his needs so long as he keeps his nose in the books, is a character as familiar to Korean society today as it was then. To say that Korean mothers take education seriously is only to begin to understand them; one woman, a writer well known in Korea, emigrated to Long Island so that her two sons could go to Harvard. By the seventh grade both sons had outscored most high school seniors on the College Board exams and thereafter never earned less than straight A's. Soon, however, the mother learned that Harvard might have regional quotas for admission: so she moved the family to Texas, thinking there would be fewer applicants from the Lone Star State than from Long Island.

How *long* have Koreans taken education seriously? Well, when Hamel, the Dutch sailor who found himself beached quite unexpectedly on Cheju Island in 1653, got his feet on the ground, he found Koreans indulging in a "national devotion to education." Indeed, aristocrats and "Free-men" alike "take great care of the Education of their Children, and put them very young to learn to read and write, to which the Nation is much addicted." The elders give to the young scholar "an Idea of Learning, and of the Worth of their Ancestors, and telling them how honourable those are who by this means have rais'd themselves to great Fortunes, which breeds Emulation, and makes them students. It is wonderful to see how they improve by these means, and how they expound the Writings . . . wherein all their Learning consists." Venerated teachers, Hamel thought, were "the greatest Men in the Kingdom," and aspiring to similar honors was "often the ruin of the Candidates."[76]

The examination system required of every candidate that he begin with his family pedigree, the name and rank of the last three generations of his father's line, and the clan home of his mother's line. The substance of the exam was mastery of Confucian classical texts, along with disqui-

75. Gale (1972), p. 149.
76. Ledyard (1971), pp. 123, 218–19.

Swaddled Korean women on the streets of Seoul, circa 1900. *Courtesy of Carlo Rosetti,* Corea e Coreani *(Korea and Koreans) (Bergamo: Instituto Italiano d'Arti Grafiche, 1904).*

sitions on statecraft, bureaucracy, and ritual. Some scholars say that commoners sat for exams in the early Chosŏn dynasty, but if they did at one point or another, they were exceptions proving the rule of aristocratic dominance. Later the dynasty instituted a system of private academies, or *sŏwŏn;* by 1700 there were over six hundred of them, or more than the total number in China.[77] Westerners traveling to villages in the late nineteenth century often commented on the picturesque sight of a venerable elder surrounded by a small group of young students, reciting the classics.

If society was structured by three relationships (ruler and subject, father and son, husband and wife), behavior obeyed five injunctions: honor thy ruler, thy father, and thy elder brother; place man and wife in different realms of duty and obligation; and let faithfulness unite friends.[78] Marriage was not about love between man and wife, but "a bond of love between two surnames," in the antiseptic language of the *Li Chi,* or Book of Rites. The Chosŏn wife soon found herself in an impenetrable inner sanctum, bereft of property, and in someone else's house. She was the nameless person given to the husband's family; she was the inside person whose best (and usually realized) hope was to rule the inner sanctum; she was denied rights of inheritance that passed on about the only real wealth Korea had: land and its products and

77. Haboush (1988), p. 17.
78. Deuchler (1992), p. 110.

dwellings. And this was the yangban wife: imagine what life was like for the 30 percent of all women who were simply slaves.

A self-conscious doctrine at the beginning of the dynasty, this became over time the ethos that soaked Korean society, governed by a thousand ritual observances. By the sixteenth century a yangban woman had to be married for years before daring to move in the outer world of society, and then only in a cocoon of clothing inside a cloistered sedan chair, carried by her slaves. In the late nineteenth century foreigners witnessed these same cloistered upper-class women, clothed and swaddled from head to toe, wearing a green mantle over their heads and bringing the folds across their faces, leaving only the eyes exposed. Like the blind men of Seoul, they would come out after the nightly curfew, after the bells rang and the city gates were closed against tigers, and find a bit of freedom in the darkness. As Angus Hamilton reported, "The spectacle of these white spectres of the night, flitting from point to point, their footsteps lighted by the rays of the lantern which their girl-slaves carry before them, is as remarkable as the appearance of Seoul by daylight, with its moving masses all garmented in white."[79] These days many Korean women marry men by choice, just as many still let their mothers select husbands; many women dress as they please, but many more maintain a chaste public appearance. (In the summer of 1994 a widely reported incident occurred in Seoul in which an old man slapped a young woman for going around with a bare midriff; the woman was arrested.) In prominent families women are still remembered to posterity by their entries on the husband's genealogy; if they are later divorced, which happens with increasing frequency, their names are erased.

The position of women is a critical window to any civilization, a core element that appears immutable. Because it is so close to home, because we all come of woman into our own societies and spend a great part of our lives trying to understand that fact, self-conscious reflection on what woman means to our own history is almost impossible. Far simpler is the outsider's window on a different society, where we instantly mark the distance between our ways and theirs. Hardly any foreigner, myself included, has applauded the condition of Korean women. The first impression, at least until recently, was perhaps the worst. My good friend and co-teacher in the late 1960s, Mr. Kang, did not bother to introduce me to his wife for several months, even though he had met mine many times. When we finally did meet, she walked about five paces behind us in virtual self-effacement. She was, in other words, a proper wife of the old school.

Should a woman in old Korea have taken it upon herself, for whatever

79. Hamilton (1904), p. 39.

reason, to dispatch her husband, here was one likely result in the seventeenth century, according to the errant Dutchman Hamel: "she is bury'd alive up to her shoulders, in a High-way that is much frequented, and by her is laid an Axe, with which all that pass by, and are not noble, are oblig'd to give her a Stroke on the Head till she is dead." Should a woman commit adultery and her husband kill her, Koreans responded like Texans: he was "in no danger for doing so." Men, however, were in no danger from anyone for taking concubines: "A Man may keep as many Women as he can maintain, and repair to them at all times without scandal." But it was not all one-way, not all a double standard: "If a marry'd Man be taken lying with another Man's Wife, he is to suffer Death," and, in a nice Korean touch, "the Criminal's Father . . . must be the Executioner."[80]

A sharp stricture of the new Chosŏn dynasty legislation added injury to the grief of widowed women. They were never supposed to marry again, and most did not (in the Koryŏ period they had frequently done so), making of the widow in the village a stock character in vernacular novels. The reasoning was that marriage was "an affair between 'two surnames,' "[81] and the widow's loyalty to the adopted family was a form of property. Occasionally widows still did remarry, of course, and there was a certain human tolerance of second marriages, especially among poor women. A third marriage, however, got a woman classified as purely promiscuous. Men controlled the body politic, and the bodies of women. As the national code of 1469 put it, "thrice-married women are listed together with licentious women, and their sons and grandsons are barred from the examinations. . . . For a woman of a poor and lowly house . . . if her parents and relatives decide that she should marry for a second time, this does not harm propriety." For yangban women, however, "a marriage once concluded cannot be changed within a lifetime. . . . [T]he sons and daughters of twice-married women will no longer be listed as members of the upper class."[82]

Concubinage has been another bane of women in Korea, right down to the present: "the differentiation between main wives and concubines *(ch'och'ŏp)* became one of the sharpest as well as most tragic social dividing lines in Korean society."[83] It would be wrong, however, to think of a second or third wife as having no standing. The patriarch of my father-in-law's family ran a *makkŏlli* brewery in Samch'ŏk. His daily routine included drinking in the afternoon and continuing into the night,

80. Hamel, quoted in Ledyard (1971), pp. 211–12, 217.
81. Deuchler, in Lee (1993), p. 563.
82. Translation by Martina Deuchler, in Lee (1993), pp. 564–65.
83. Deuchler, in Lee (1993), p. 559.

sometimes jumping into the wine vats to frolic; he chain-smoked unfiltered cigarettes and had four wives. He died at the age of ninety-four, when he was hit by a truck. In his will he left the yearly proceeds of the brewery to his second wife, with the property to revert to the main lineage when she passes away. I know this woman; she is a person of much dignity and towering strength, not to mention ability to drink me under the table; the family treats her with honor, and she evinces no sign of second-class citizenship (even though everyone knows her situation).

KOREA IN THE SUN

The fifteenth century marked Korea's premodern apogee, in addition to being a time when Neo-Confucian reformers reigned almost alone. As a nation and a culture Korea was far ahead of a Europe that had not yet discovered the New World. Europe was stagnant economically and technically, whereas Korea had movable type long before Gutenberg's celebrated Bible. Its scientists invented a gauge to measure rainfall in 1442, two hundred years before a similar instrument was devised in Europe, and made important progress in agronomy. Korea's mathematicians were advanced, using concepts like negative numbers and polynomial equations centuries before Europeans did.[84] A wizard named Chang Yŏng-sil specialized in sundials and astronomical clocks (he even made a cuckoo clock that struck on the hour), while others refined Chinese and Arabic calendrical science. Military technicians produced new forms of cannon and artillery, and scientists codified Korean medical science in encyclopedias.[85] Of course, European science and technology advanced rapidly after the discovery of the New World in 1492, just as Korean skills have progressed quickly in the century since it began to interact with the world system.

In its pinnacle century the Chosŏn dynasty also enjoyed its greatest king. To revisit the fifth son of the first wife of Yi Sŏng-gye, that is, the militant Yi Pang-wŏn, he was not lacking in other talents as well. He was even more fecund than his father, siring twelve sons and seventeen daughters. The third son was magical—a talented student and a person of great heart. Pang-wŏn was happy to yield the throne to him at the age of twenty-two: given the reign name Sejong, he became Korea's sage king (1418–50). His father retired to a palace that sat on the grounds of what is now Yŏnsei University in Seoul, with no ill will and no flying arrows.

84. See Don Baker's contribution to the forthcoming *Cambridge History of Korea.*
85. Lee (1984), pp. 192–97. On Korean science more generally see Jeon (1974).

Koreans had invented movable metal type printing around 1234, as we saw above, and perfected the method in 1403; Sejong quickly put technicians to work mechanizing the process. In 1420 he asked a secretary, Yi Ch'ŏn, to have new castings made in the foundry: "In seven months the work was done, a great improvement over former efforts. The printers were highly pleased and were able to set up more than twenty pages a day. . . . We are prepared now to print any book there is and all men will have the means of study."[86] The technology of the new process was described by Sŏng Hyŏn:

> First, logographs are engraved on *hwangyang* wood; then flat print plates are prepared with soft clay collected from the seashore where seaweed grows. And then the wooden graphs are pressed against the clay to produce impressions of the graphs. Both print plates are placed together and molten copper is poured through a hole to flow downward, filling the indentations until each graph is formed. The graphs are then removed and refined. . . . The typekeeper lines up the needed graphs on the manuscript papers and then places them on a plate called the upper plate. The graph leveling artisan fills in all the empty spaces between type on the upper plate with bamboo and torn cloth, and tightens it so that the type cannot be moved. The plate is then handed over to the printing artisan to print.[87]

Sejong was known to direct this work personally, appearing at the new foundries with wine and food for the workers. His greatest achievement was the excellent, scientific Korean written alphabet *(han'gŭl)* that was systematized under his reign. The official explanation for Sejong's radical change was this:

> The sounds of our language differ from those of China and are not easily conveyed in Chinese writing. In consequence, though one among our ignorant subjects may wish to express his mind, in many cases he after all is unable to do so. Thinking of these, my people, with compassion, We have newly devised a script of twenty-eight letters, only that it become possible for anyone to readily learn it and use it to advantage in his everyday life.[88]

It is one of the world's premier alphabets for accurately representing the sounds of words, and has attracted the interest of many linguists. Some linguists argue that Korean is part of the Uralic-Altaic group of

86. Quoted in Gale (1972), p. 233. For a good description of the casting process in 1403, see Rutt, in Gale (1972), pp. 52–53, and Gale, pp. 224–25.

87. "On Printing," trans. Yong-ho Ch'oe, in Lee (1993), p. 537.

88. Quoted in Lee (1984), p. 192. (There are now twenty-four letters in the Korean alphabet.)

languages, including Turkish, Hungarian, Finnish, and Japanese, and in spite of long influence from written Chinese, Korean remains very different in lexicon, phonology, and grammar; indeed, its grammar is very similar to Japanese—suggesting a close association at some point in the lost past. Since *han'gŭl* also had a standard pronunciation for every Chinese character, and given all the mutually incomprehensible dialects in China pronouncing the same written language but without an alphabet, some American missionaries from Korea recommended the use of *han'gŭl* in China as well (obviously without much luck).

Predictably the yangban officials did not like either of these innovations, since both threatened their monopoly of the word, and therefore of everything else. One wrote, "Only such peoples as the Mongols, Tanguts, Jürchens, Japanese and Tibetans have their own writings. But this is a matter that involves the barbarians. . . . [B]arbarians are transformed only by means of adopting the Chinese ways; we have never heard of the Chinese ways being transformed by the barbarians."[89] *Han'gŭl* nonetheless became popular among peasants and military men, who took instructions on how to do their work from popular vernacular guides, and among women, who used the new alphabet to communicate with each other through letters or with themselves through diaries. The rapid movable type expanded book publications of all sorts, yielding a vibrant historiography. By the end of the century, the Chinese classics were beginning to be translated into the new alphabet. The alphabet did not come into general use until the twentieth century, however, since the literati succeeded in associating any consequential knowledge with Chinese writing; since 1948 the North Koreans have used the Korean alphabet exclusively, while the South Koreans retain usage of a mixed Sino-Korean script.

Sejong was renowned as a kind-hearted king, of gentle, scholarly soul. Lee Kwan Yew of Singapore could learn from him in our time, since Sejong outlawed flogging on the back and buttocks: "It endangers a man's life to beat him after this fashion; we shall have no more of it." He took pity on Korea's many outcaste groups, trying to find ways to merge them with the commoner population. It was a noble goal, but for once he failed. He urged the people to turn away from superstitions, like *p'ungsu* or geomancy: "The prosperity of the state depends on the character of the government and not on the vagaries of wind and weather."[90] Here, too, he failed.

King Sejong got the plaudits with which Korean scribes wrote his epitaph the hard way—he earned them: *yŏngmun, yemu, insŏng, myŏng-*

89. Translation by Yong-ho Ch'oe, in Lee (1993), p. 519.
90. Gale (1972), p. 234; Lee (1984), p. 188.

hyo—"florescent scholar, sagacious warrior, benevolent sage, resplendently filial son."[91] Koreans as much as or more than any other people believe in spirits, and for centuries after his death there were said to be many sightings of Sejong. We rationalists dismiss such claims as nonsense, but familiarity with Korea breeds humility. James Gale was a good Christian, but Korea shook his certainty that only Jesus Christ could come again: he wrote that "in the mind of Korea . . . appearances of the dead are possible," and cited the London Society for Psychical Research as potential confirmation.[92] I never met my mother-in-law, a powerful woman who reared seven children, attended to a husband of weighty responsibility, and ran a taxicab company in Seoul—because she died before my marriage. That is, she died, appeared to me in a dream at the crack of dawn, told me always to look after her daughter, and two hours later the phone rang . . . announcing her death of a sudden heart attack at a distance of ten thousand miles.

YŎNGJO AND SADO

Fathers may have been kings of the Korean household, but a kingly household was different still. The king's first son was groomed for rule from his earliest days, and if he did not pan out, there was no meritocracy to restrain excess. If the first son could not cut the mustard, perhaps a second son could; but if none of them could, the succession to the throne still remained a matter for the royal inner sanctum to resolve. We saw the violence that attended such conflicts at the beginning of the dynasty. But after the period of radical reform, Neo-Confucian doctrine and new family patterns slowly became customary, yielding new patterns of normalcy—and pathology—from the level of the court on down.

Readers who have followed events in North Korea in recent years will instantly draw parallels with "Great Leader" Kim Il Sung giving way to "Dear Leader" Kim Jong Il, his first son, just as those who know South Korea will see this family principle repeated throughout the realm of the truly powerful there as well, namely, the giant conglomerates that dominate the economy. But Korean history yields a stunning example of the Oedipal and Shakespearean ways in which primogeniture affects high politics and vice versa, in the epic of Yŏngjo and his first son, Sado.[93]

91. Rutt's translation, in Gale (1972), p. 333.

92. Gale (1972), p. 231.

93. JaHyun Kim Haboush is the standard reference here, both in her excellent account of Yŏngjo's long and distinguished reign (Haboush 1988) and through her analysis and translation of Lady Hong's memoir (Haboush 1996). In the following I rely on her accounts, and on the extant translation of Lady Hong's memoir (Lady Hong 1985).

Yŏngjo was not the greatest of Chosŏn dynasty kings (he came close, but Sejong was more important), but he was the longest reigning (all the way from somnolent 1724 to providential 1776) and the one who did precisely what the Confucian busybodies wanted him to do, by way of preparing himself for his august responsibilities. He did everything asked of him, which usually meant reading everything he was asked to read—primarily the classic texts of Confucian virtue and statecraft—over and over. In 1725 he spent four months on *The Analects,* and forty years later, four more months on them. He studied Mencius for twenty-one months, in 1725–27, and came back to it for a full year in 1763–64. He read *The Great Learning* and *The Doctrine of the Mean (Chung-yung)* as many as eight times. If that doesn't sound like much, each "time" involved from one to twenty-two months of study over the period 1727–62, because "reading" meant not quiet time with a good book in the evening but an absorption so compelling that it created a state of mind, one so informed by the thoughts of the masters that doing right (by their lights) would be axiomatic and become automatic. As the eminent scholar Yulgok wrote, the point of "reading books" was to study "scrupulously by turns, continuously striving for understanding, thus making their meanings and their principles clearer daily."[94]

Yŏngjo, in other words, was the ideal Confucian prince, and he turned into a formidable political leader whose daily problems and strategies would be familiar to any chief executive. His agony was that his son Sado was the worst prince in Korean history: indeed, he had no idea what it meant to be a prince, or, if he did, he did not like it. And so his regency ended in high tragedy, inside a sealed rice chest set out in the royal garden by his very own father, in the year 1766. It was, ironically, a gross transgression of kingly virtue done in the interest of effective kingly succession.[95] Lady Hong was Sado's wife, betrothed at age ten, and mother of King Chŏngjo; all records were purged following this affair, known to Koreans as the Imo incident, after the year it happened (1762). Lady Hong, however, kept a detailed memoir of her husband's behavior.

Sado exemplified all the weaknesses of the Korean royal system, and hardly any of its strengths. Afforded every privilege, doted on by a hundred ladies-in-waiting, indulged by his father, and worshiped by his people, he advanced not from playful childhood to Confucian adulthood but

94. Quoted in Haboush, "The Education of the Yi Crown Prince: A Study in Confucian Pedagogy," in de Bary and Haboush (1985), p. 193.

95. See Nietzsche's discussion of Oedipus the King's analogous dilemma in *The Birth of Tragedy and The Case of Wagner,* trans. Walter Kaufmann (New York: Random House, 1967), pp. 67–70.

from prolonged adolescence to palpable neurosis to a very well-documented schizophrenia. If he is an unquestioned special case, his life's trajectory makes a more general point: Korean children are children well into their teens, and adolescents *(chŏngnyŏn,* youths) preparing for adulthood well into their thirties or even forties, and "adults" only when the father gives over the family responsibilities to the son and his wife, whereupon the father enters the hallowed (*hwan'gap,* sixtieth birthday) realm of revered elder and relative freedom.

Amid intense anxiety in Seoul that Yŏngjo had as yet produced no heir, Sado was born in 1735. His father sometimes wondered if this brilliant and industrious child was overdoing it (in 1735, for example, Yŏngjo worried that he might be "too earnest and unbending").[96] Meanwhile, various ladies-in-waiting indulged the son with war games and toy weapons. By his thirteenth year, however, Sado was being scolded by the king about his sloth and lack of virtue, and he became halting and queasy in audiences with his father; he would delay getting dressed in the morning to avoid such encounters, putting on one robe after another and then throwing each to the ground in a rage. Part of this, no doubt, was the ritual of the time, which required Sado to prostrate himself before his father, but much more of it was a father enraged by his son's failure to turn out as expected. The king rebuked Sado all the time, once so terribly that Sado threw himself into a well.

This was but one of many signs of developing neurosis, and more soon followed. By his twenty-third year Sado had graduated from adolescence to madness. The thought of getting dressed terrified him, so he destroyed one suit after another before finding the one he could bring himself to wear. He took a mistress from among the ladies-in-waiting, something strictly proscribed by custom. He began to murder the court eunuchs, first by beating and then by decapitation (he once entered his wife's chamber carrying the bloody head of one such victim). And he tried more than once to kill himself. In one vain attempt at reconciliation between father and son, after Yŏngjo asked him why he killed people and animals, Sado grabbed his father's robes and blurted this out:

> "Because I am hurt," answered the prince.
> "Why are you hurt?" the king asked.
> "I am hurt because you do not love me and also, alas, I am terrified of you because you constantly rebuke me."[97]

96. Haboush (1988), p. 173.
97. Lady Hong (1985), p. 70. Haboush has a slightly different translation: "I am sad that you don't love me, and terrified when you criticize me. All this turns to anger." Haboush (1988), p. 199.

Then he detailed for Yŏngjo more about his grisly murders. A sign of the autonomy of the court was that no one suggested doing anything about these murders.

Soon Sado was back to his marauding and womanizing, not stopping even before the virtue of Buddhist nuns. He murdered servants, court physicians, shamans, and bearers of bad tidings. He had orgies in his palace with *kisaeng* girls and servants. In 1760 he began going into town in disguise, killing people at random. Finally, in 1762 his mother, even though she did not think her son wholly at fault, asked the king to put him to death; the king, however, unable to see his son's illness, still thought all his faults were owing to a lack of filial piety. Overcome with grief and guilt, Sado's mother was in agony—thinking she should never have uttered the thought: "even the grass will not grow on my grave." Soon she developed "a malignant tumor on her back" and shortly afterward died.[98]

Sado slept in a box resembling a coffin and then moved to a hole in the floor covered with planks and dirt. Yet at times he would return to sanity, act the good prince, recite the classics, pledge to do better, all as if nothing had happened. These hallucinations astonished his wife; she wrote that Sado seemed to be "not one person, but two"—a startlingly "modern" observation, since Sado was clearly schizophrenic. Sado's crypt-like sleeping habits prefigured the denouement of this story. When he arose, rumor had it, he plotted parricide. And while Sado slept, his father pondered filicide.

The minimax solution to this dilemma was for Sado to kill himself, as his mother had suggested to her regret, and as his father now urged him time and again to do (while Sado lay prostrate at his feet), as the only way out and his duty to the familial line. After enough repetition, Sado tried to strangle himself, to no avail. So one fine morning Yŏngjo called his son out to a nearby shrine, with a military guard and most of the high officials in attendance. Yŏngjo then led the procession to a pavilion used for gazing at the moon (the moon being a symbol of the king's son) and said this: "If I die, our three-hundred-year dynastic line would end. If you die, the dynasty can be preserved. It would be better if you died." This had a perfect royal logic. Yŏngjo waved his sword over Sado's head, yelling, "Kill yourself, kill yourself fast." Sado tried again to strangle himself, only to fail (in his father's eyes) even at this final act. By early evening the king was tired of pleading: "Aren't you ever going to kill yourself?" he asked.

Then attendants brought a large rice chest into the courtyard, and Yŏngjo demanded that his son get in—"fast." Sado cried on his father's

98. Lady Hong (1985), pp. 89–92, 101, 106–7.

The wall near Suwŏn built in 1780 by Prince Sado's son, King Chŏngjo, for his remove from Seoul—one that never came. *Courtesy of Joo Myong-dok,* Korean Traditions: As Seen through Paper Windows *(Seoul: Seoul International Publishing House, 1981).*

robes, begging to be spared, but to no avail. Thirteen hot July days later, Sado expired in this same chest. It was the logical outcome to the catch-22 the king found himself in, since to execute the son for his crimes would tarnish the royal family and simply to kill him would be a crime. So the mad son was left to rot in the broiling sun, and many Koreans and their admirers have since justified the act. As Gale put it, "for a son to rise against his father is the blackest crime imaginable."[99] But only his wife and his late mother knew the truth: "all [this] is caused by disease; he is not a criminal."

The king died in 1776, when George Washington was forty-four years old; Yŏngjo's reign was almost as long as George III's of fifty-nine years, as James Gale noted, and longer than that of any other Korean king. A new democracy was being born on one side of the earth, and an old monarchy was at peace on the other. Gale had this unusual opinion of these events:

> We think of the oriental as under the iron heel of despotism, whereas the truth is he was usually very content and in most cases left happily alone. Our ideal of government is a noisy democracy; his, a wise and good ruler. If one but take the trouble to read and compare history carefully, the conclusion will undoubtedly be that on the whole his is much the better choice. Tyrants sometimes he has had, but single ones;

99. Gale (1972), p. 287; Haboush also justifies Yŏngjo's actions.

> we have had tyrants, swarms of them. Aristotle knew well what he was talking about when he said, "democracy is the acme of tyranny."[100]

Chŏngjo, Sado's son, succeeded to Yŏngjo's throne and forever resented his father's death. He built a wall around Suwŏn, south of Seoul, thinking to move the capital there. But he never did.

For more than a century after its founding, Chosŏn flourished as an exemplary agrarian bureaucracy deeply influenced by a cadre of learned scholar-officials, steeped in the doctrines of Neo-Confucianism. Koreans today describe this traditional system and its contemporary legacies as "feudal," but we cannot call the Chosŏn dynasty feudal. Like Koryŏ, it lacked classic features of feudal society. It was instead a classic agrarian bureaucracy. We can see the kernel of the system in Hendrik Hamel's observation in 1653:

> *Corea* is subject to a King whose Power is absolute (tho' he pays an Acknowledgement to the *Tartar,*) and he disposes of all things as he pleases, without asking any bodies Advice. There are no Lords of peculiar places . . . [but] all the Great Mens Revenues arise out of those Estates they hold during pleasure, and from the great number of their Slaves. . . .[101]

It was bureaucratic because it possessed an elaborate procedure for entry to the civil service, a highly organized civil service itself, and a practice of administering the country from the center and from the top down. Thus, unlike a feudal system, Korea had strong central administration and many officials who ruled through a civilian bureaucracy, not through provincial lords who fused civil and military functions. The system rested upon an agrarian base, making it different from modern bureaucratic systems; the character of Korea's agrarian-bureaucratic interaction also provided one of its departures from the typical Chinese experience, to which it is the most comparable. Conflict between bureaucrats seeking revenues for government coffers and landowners hoping to control tenants and harvests was a constant source of tension during the Chosŏn dynasty, and in this conflict over resources the landowners often won out. Theoretically owned by the state, private landed power was stronger and more persistent in Korea than in China. Korea had a centralized administration, to be sure, but the ostensibly strong center was more often a façade concealing the reality of aristocratic power: "In fact, the social elite controlled the bureaucratic structure, kept it rela-

100. Gale (1972), p. 294.
101. Ledyard (1971), p. 207.

tively weak, and used it to check royal authority."[102] At the local levels the elite captured officials called *ajŏn,* often common clerks, who worked with important families below the county level.

Thus Korea's agrarian bureaucracy was superficially strong but actually rather weak at the center. The state ostensibly dominated the society, but in practice landed aristocratic families could keep the state at bay and perpetuate their local power for centuries. This pattern persisted until the late 1940s, when landed dominance was obliterated in a northern revolution and attenuated in southern land reform; since that time the balance has shifted toward strong central power and top-down administration of the whole country in both North and South Korea. Precisely because of the tension between central power and landed wealth, however, Korea's leaders could achieve stability over time by playing one force off against the other, since each end of this connection needed the other. This was a supple and adaptable system for governing Korea; otherwise how could it have lasted for five hundred years? But it was not a system that could be mobilized to keep the imperial powers at bay in the late nineteenth century; instead it fell before them: "The balance of power between monarchy and aristocracy was an asset for the maintenance of stability," Palais has written, "but it was a liability when Korea was faced with the need to expand central power to mobilize resources for defense and development."

The politics of the center reflected a system of checks and balances that kept most kings from accumulating despotic power. Consort clans, royal censors, a recalcitrant bureaucracy, and an ethic of scholarly remonstrance held the king's power within delimited boundaries. In many ways the kingship was analogous to the office of the American presidency: the powers are there for one who knows how to use them, but their effective exercise depends very much on executive style and personality. Nor was the Korean king surrounded by moats of mystery and symbolism, like the powerless figurehead of the Japanese emperor. The Korean monarch could punish officials, send secret inspectors around the country to check on bureaucrats' performance, invoke moral virtues stressing loyalty to the father figure, or put armies in motion. Above all, however strong the king's force of will and political skills, he could not directly threaten the interests of the landed aristocracy, just as aristocrats needed him for legitimacy and the perpetuation of their privileges.

This was the Korean king, indeed, but not the one that Westerners imagined when they first laid eyes on the Korean court. The wife of

102. Palais (1975), p. 5. This is the best source on Korea's agrarian bureaucracy.

The Taewŏn'gun, father of King Kojong.

Kojong's American physician, Hattie Heron, described the king, his retinue, and his young prince this way in 1890:

> The king in his red satin robe, all embroidered in gold . . . the pleasant voice of the little queen as she talked to the prince through the bamboo screen which hid her from sight. . . .
>
> The little prince was actually seen bundling himself over a back balcony all undignified, and scampering through the long verandah until he came to the door of the king's audience chamber, where he solemnly took his place beside his majesty and looked as much as ever like a very pretty, proper wax figure, while all the old grey-headed officials and time-worn eunuchs bowed before him, bumping their heads on the stone floor again and again.
>
> The little herons could also see the army of attendants and maids in long blue silk skirts and yellow jackets hovering about his little kingship all day long, powdering his face, painting his lips and fingertips, shaving the top of his head, pulling out his eyebrows, cutting his food into the daintiest of morsels, fanning him with monstrous long-handled fans, never leaving him alone a moment, even at night guarding and watching by his bedside, singing him to sleep with a queer little lullaby that has been sung to baby kings in the Land of the Morning Calm for the past three hundred years.[103]

As Mel Brooks put it in one of his films, "It's fun to be king."

Self-conscious Neo-Confucian ideologues may have attempted to sweep out Buddhism and install a new orthodoxy, but throughout the Chosŏn period common people retained attachments to Buddhist practices and to folk religions, shamanism, geomancy, and fortune-telling, influences condemned both by Confucians and by the modern world. Nonetheless, they remain strong today in Korea and in some ways constitute a "second tradition," in conflict with the elite culture. This Korean mass culture created remarkably lively and diverse art forms: uniquely colorful and unpretentiously naturalistic folk paintings of animals, popular novels in Korean vernacular, and characters like the *mudang,* female shamans who summon spirits and perform exorcisms in *kŭt* rituals. In this second tradition, women frequently found freedom to express their artistic creativity, outside the confines of the reigning virtues. Novels also attacked the inequities of the class system, the most scathing being Hŏ Kyun's *Hong Kil-tong,* written in the early 1600s. The most famous, however, is *The Tale of Ch'unhyang,* which championed the humanity of commoners and outcastes. It is Korea's favorite story, still read and performed widely in South and North Korea. An older poetic form, made

103. Quoted in Gale (1972), pp. 17–18.

up of short stanzas and called *sijo*, became another vehicle for free expression of distaste for the caste-like inequities of Korean society.

THE CHOSŎN PERIOD: DECLINE

A combination of literati purges in the early sixteenth century, Japanese invasions at the end of it, and Manchu invasions in the middle of the next century severely debilitated the Chosŏn state, and it never again reached the heights of the fifteenth century. This period also saw the Manchus sweep away the Ming dynasty in China, ending a remarkable period when Korean society seemed to develop apace with China, while making many independent innovations. Yŏngjo's period is thought by Koreans to be one of renaissance after the Japanese and Manchu invasions, and to some extent it was (his policies diminished factional rivalry among the officials), but even then times were tough and epidemics killed hundreds of thousands of people (in 1749, for example), and "the spectacle of starving people eating corpses was common."[104]

First of all, Korea suffered devastating foreign invasions. The worst came shortly after the warlord Hideyoshi Toyotomi ended Japan's internal disorder and unified the territory; he launched an invasion that landed 158,700 Japanese soldiers at Pusan in May 1592, but the eventual goal was to put China under his wing. At this the Chosŏn court took flight not to Kanghwa Island, its usual refuge, but to the Yalu River, infuriating ordinary Koreans and leading slaves to revolt and burn the registries. Japanese forces now marched through the peninsula at will. Just in the nick of time, however, a remarkable admiral named Yi Sun-shin appeared on the scene and devastated Japanese shipping in the coastal waters off Korea.

Admiral Yi had at his disposal the world's first armor-clad warships, the famed "Turtle Ship"—with iron plates on its top, a large sail reminiscent of Chinese "junks," a dozen sailors pulling long oars from within, cannon at every point to blow the Japanese out of the water, and a dragon at the head to scare the hell out of everyone. The first ship was built by an engineer named Na Tae-yong, according to Yi's model; it was nearly sixty-five feet long, fifteen feet amidships, with sides nearly eight feet high, covered by thick wooden boards. The hull was covered with protective iron plates, with long iron spikes on its shell back. The fearsome dragon's head on the prow had four guns inside, shooting flying thunder bombs made of gunpowder and iron splinters, and also laying

104. Hatada (1969), p. 87.

down a protective smoke screen.[105] All in all, it was an important invention in the annals of warfare and testimony to Korean shipbuilding prowess in the long centuries before a seclusion policy closed the country off.

Admiral Yi's forces cut Japan's supply routes and, combined with the dispatch of Ming forces and 22,000 soldiers in "righteous armies" that rose up to wage guerrilla warfare (even Buddhist monks participated), caused the Japanese to retreat to a narrow redoubt near Pusan—let's call it an early Pusan perimeter. After desultory negotiations and delay, Hideyoshi launched a second invasion in 1597. The Korean and Ming armies were ready this time: Yi Sun-shin returned with a mere dozen warships and dealt a crushing defeat to the Japanese in the narrow straits off Mokp'o, between Chindo and a promontory pushing out around the port. Yi waited patiently with his fleet for the enemy to come through this channel and then wrecked over three hundred Japanese ships. In the midst of battle, however, he learned that his beloved mother had died: "How could the sun in heaven be so dark," he wrote in his war diary.[106] Soon the great conquerer Hideyoshi also died, of heartbreak, as the story goes, and another sun went down. Japanese forces withdrew to their home islands, where they nursed a policy of isolation for the next 250 years—taking with them the ears of tens of thousands of Korean and Chinese soldiers, where they remained buried in Kyoto down to the present (they were finally unearthed and returned to Korea in 1994).

This Korean victory came at almost the same time that England subdued Ireland,[107] leading to a long-term dependency and endless trouble. Unlike Ireland, Korea won, but paid a terrible price for turning back invasions that would otherwise have substantially recast East Asian history. Yi Sun-shin did not live to hear of his own glory, since an errant cannon shot killed him as the war concluded (a grandiose statue of this conqueror now stands in the center of Seoul, however). The peninsula was devastated by the intense fighting. Refugees flowed up and down its length, famine and disease ran rampant, and basic class relationships were overturned by widespread destruction of land registers. To some extent this early-modern war may have propelled the Chosŏn dynasty toward a more rapid decline; Japan suffered far less and profited from kidnapping many Korean artisans who, in the words of a Korean historian, "then became the instruments of great advance in the ceramic art"

105. Yi Sun-shin (1977), p. xxv; Palais (1996), pp. 78–84, has an excellent account of the invasions.

106. Yi Sun-shin (1977), pp. 260–61; Palais (1996), p. 83.

107. See Michael Hechter, *Internal Colonialism: The Celtic Fringe in British National Development, 1536–1966* (Berkeley: University of California Press, 1975), pp. 67, 97–103.

of Japan.[108] Certainly this war bred a lasting antipathy toward the Japanese, now commonly referred to as island "dwarfs" *(wae).*

Korea had barely recovered when the Manchus invaded from the north, fighting on all fronts to oust the Ming dynasty. Invasions in 1627 and 1637 achieved the goal of establishing tributary relations between Korea and the Manchu or Ch'ing dynasty (1644–1911), but they were less deleterious than the Japanese invasions, except in the northwest, where Manchu forces wreaked havoc. More important was the perception that when the Ming fell it was a disaster for Koreans: rule of China by northern barbarians was "tantamount to the disintegration of civilization." Soon came the idea that Korea was the last bastion of Confucian orthodoxy and the true civilization.[109] Koreans built a secret shrine to the Ming in 1704 (the Altar of Great Retribution, or Taebodan) and built another one in 1717. "Revere the Ming and resist the Ch'ing" became a fond couplet for the literati.

Thereafter the dynasty enjoyed a period of revival which, had it continued, might have left Korea much better prepared for the encounter with the West. The Confucian literati were particularly reinvigorated by an intellectual movement advocating that philosophy be geared to solving real problems of the society. Known as *silhak* (practical learning), it included people like Yu Hyŏng-wŏn (1622–73), who exiled himself to a small farming village and pored over the classics in search of reform solutions to the social problems he observed. He developed a thorough, detailed critique of nearly all the institutional aspects of Chosŏn politics and society, and a set of concrete reforms to invigorate it.[110]

Why did learning need to be "practical"? In part because the heights scaled by Korean Neo-Confucians in previous centuries were as arid as they were sublime. Korean metaphysics was virtually unmatched elsewhere in East Asia in the writings of T'oegye (also known as Yi Hwang [1501–70], known to posterity as "Korea's Chu Hsi," after the Chinese founder of the Neo-Confucian school, also has a street named for him in downtown Seoul). Korean Neo-Confucians were the peers of any Chinese scholar, but they competed in speculative metaphysical exercises about whether the formative constituency of the universe was material *(ki)* or spiritual *(i)* or perhaps both, with no way to choose between competing doctrines except by the erudition of each protagonist—which tended to be judged according to which school you belonged to (T'oegye favored *i,* but an equally famous contemporary, Yulgok, favored *ki*). By the time these talented ideologues were done with their expositions, they

108. Lee (1984), p. 215.

109. Haboush (1988), pp. 23–24.

110. Palais (1996) discusses Yu's critique of Chosŏn society.

could have you believing they had created the universe all by themselves. *Silhak* was thus an antidote, a recourse to reality, the analogue of Deng Xiaoping's late 1970s cry to "seek truth from facts" after decades of scholastic nonsense by Maoist ideologues.

The doctrinaire version of Confucianism dominant during the Chosŏn dynasty made squabbles between elites particularly nasty. The reigning doctrines rewarded scholar-officials for arid scholasticism and obstinate orthodoxy. First you had to commit your mind to one or another side of abstruse philosophical debate; only then could the practical affairs of state be put in order. Such mind-sets exacerbated a series of political upheavals beginning in the mid-fifteenth century (known as the "literati purges") and lasting more than a hundred years, to be followed by hereditary factional feuding down to the end of the dynasty. The losers often found their persons, their property, their families, and even their graves at risk from victors determined to extirpate their influence—always in the name of a higher morality, even if the conflicts were usually about political power. Later in the dynasty the concern with ideological correctness also influenced more mundane factional conflicts that debilitated central power.

With that off the chest, we can also say that few civilizations have ever produced people of higher learning, better moral bearing, or more finely honed integrity than the old fogies of the Chosŏn period. As Gale put it, "The more I study them the more I honour the sincerity, the self-denial, the humility, the wisdom, the devotion that was back of the first founders, great priests of the soul."[111] They embodied the venerable principle of superior moral example, and they cast a humbling shadow that carries down to our time.

Neo-Confucian thought exemplified the pronounced Korean concern with the power of ideas, still visible in North Korea's *chuch'e* doctrine, which assumes that rectification of the mind must precede correct action, even to the point of committing the Marxist heresy that ideas determine human reality. By the end of the sixteenth century the ruling elite had so homogenized its ideology that few heterodox miscreants were left: all were presumably united in one idea. The "one idea" was a world conceived as a single unity, with the Chinese emperor and the Korean king in communion with heaven, and an a priori harmony between humans, animals, and nature on earth. Neo-Confucians "viewed the universe as a single organic whole, a living physical continuum including humans and all other creatures in a harmonious unity." What distinguished people from animals was their capacity for self-development, for self-perfection. Yulgok referred to humans as "inte-

111. Gale (1972), p. 79.

gral," unlike animals, and sages as perfectly integral, after long self-cultivation. The proper human organism was a merging of mind and body; the deepest form of knowledge was that which united rationality and the emotions, which is why Koreans use the word *sim* (literally, "heart," but in this context usually translated as "mind-and-heart") and point to their chests when they talk about "thinking."[112]

Silhak scholars were not very far out of this metaphysical loop, but they were concerned with real-world problems and human suffering. They were people who had been thrown out of office or eclipsed or who belonged to socially restricted groups, like the *chungin* (a group of clerks and government workers, known by the area they occupied in downtown Seoul). Chŏng Yag-yong (1762–1838), or Tasan, is thought to have been the greatest intellectual of his time, producing several books that offered his views on administration, justice, and the structure of politics. He developed original and radical ideas on land reform. Still others, like Yi Su-gwang (1563–1628), traveled to China and returned with the new Western learning then spreading in Beijing, while Yi Ik (1681–1763) wrote a reformist treatise entitled *Record of Concern for the Underprivileged.*

COMMERCIAL FERMENT?

No traveler ever thought that Korea was a commercial country before the 1860s, if not the 1960s. No ruling elite seemed so intent on squashing incentives to get rich via Adam Smith's presumably universal propensity to truck and barter. The Confucian hierarchy of scholar/farmer/artisan/merchant, Gale wrote, "not only killed manufactures of all kinds, but has put the merchant in a class little better than a pariah. Though rolling in wealth, he may not lift up his eyes to the lettered sage, who, deeply steeped in the classic lore, knows not where tomorrow's meal will come from."[113] Many scholars have discredited the Weberian idea that China had little or no commerce, owing to the baneful influence of Confucianism, and no doubt much Korean commerce has missed the traveler's or the historian's eye. But the smaller scale of the country may also have made the Confucian ideal more perfectable.

In the late nineteenth century Korea had no large commercial cities and no commercial class worthy of the name (which is not to say there were no merchants). Officials' first instinct in dealing with foreign trade in the later Chosŏn was to cut it off or to grant a monopoly on it to

112. Kalton (1994), pp. xxxiv, 127. Thus Ugye's letter to Yulgok referred to "the whole body and the mind-and-heart *[sim],*" each interdependent (p. 141).
113. Gale (1972), p. 108.

a favored friend. Some scholars have been able to find indications of commercial development in the eighteenth century, but their findings are disputed by other historians; Kaesŏng may have remained the domicile of merchants in the Chosŏn period, as it was in the Koryŏ, but their purview had to be limited: for example, they had an insignificant portion of the trade with Japan.[114] Korea was the least commercial of the East Asian nations.

I had heard this before going to Korea for the first time, in 1967, and had trouble squaring such accounts with the extraordinary hubbub of Seoul's bustling street markets, especially the vast, labyrinthine South Gate market, where almost anything could be bought for the right price—including American consumer goods, which funneled through the U.S. Army post exchange to the *ttokkebbi sijang*, or "phantom market," with lightning speed. A buyer who didn't haggle over the posted price was thought to be a fool; a seller who didn't work eighteen hours a day was thought to be a lout. This was small, family-based commerce, and it flourished in the freest of all markets, namely, the "black market" in valued goods that one could find on any street corner. Wherever the state stepped in, however, the market function was in jeopardy—and it stepped in most of the time.

There were always markets in Seoul, little shops stretched along the main street called Chongno, but these were licensed by the state and leased to the merchants who occupied them. For staple consumer items like silk, cotton, tobacco, salt, and paper, the state gave monopoly rights to certain merchants in return for reliable tax revenue. Itinerant peddlers *(pobusang)* carried other items from town to town on their backs or in pushcarts, hawkers who can still be seen in some parts of South Korea and known by their characteristic sounds—songs, chants, yells, howls, or the rhythmic clicking of large iron scissors. If peddlers made any real money (which they rarely did), they faced an obstacle, because for much of the dynasty the coinage was so heavy that they needed a donkey or several servants to haul it around on a rope (if the coins were light, officialdom thought, greedy people would hoard them).

It seems that the Koryŏ period was different, for it saw a flourishing international trade along the coasts and many rich merchants in the capital at Kaesŏng. The flinty scholar-officials who ran the Chosŏn state, however, wanted to nip commerce in the bud everywhere (even though they failed now and then). Broad commerce would mean less control, the rise of upstarts, alternatives for the peasantry, freedom for the slave. Somewhat as in their imposition of order and ritual on the family unit,

114. Deuchler (1977), p. 75.

these ideologues wanted to make sure that their caste-like social order would find no exit through the marketplace. Trade with China was something of an exception, carried on as part of tribute missions; with Japan, however, the instinct was to constrict trade to a bare minimum. Traders on Tsushima Island, the only venue, frequently importuned the Koreans to boost existing limits on trade (fifty ships a year, so much rice per year, etc.), usually to no avail. One of the key reasons why late-twentieth-century Korean commerce developed so strongly is thus the demise of the yangban aristocracy, as the interests displaced the virtues.

Still, it would be a mistake to think that Chosŏn society was unchanging, that nobody but a handful of officials got rich. As historians like Kang Man-gil and Kim Yŏng-sŏp have shown, agricultural output grew remarkably in the early seventeenth century because of new techniques for transplanting rice and double cropping, with corresponding developments in irrigation methods. The transplanting of seedlings dramatically reduced the labor required to cultivate rice and yielded larger fields; the gains in labor time enabled some farmers to move into production of commercial crops like ginseng, tobacco, and cotton for the domestic and Chinese markets. The use of coins for commerce and for paying wages increased, and handicraft production began to emerge from government control. The old Koryŏ capital at Kaesŏng became a strong center of merchant commerce and conspicuous wealth.

Some scholars see in this activity the emergence from below of a class of rich peasants and commoner landlords, and the beginnings of wholesale commerce by middlemen who purchased grain, ginseng, rice wine, and salt for resale at home and in China.[115] Many wealthy merchants lived in Kaesŏng, and by the end of the eighteenth century Seoul had developed big private markets located at East Gate, at South Gate, and along the Chongno thoroughfare. A group of people known as *kaekchu,* who were wholesale merchants and innkeepers, providing storage, lodging, and banking services for merchants, were important in Korean commerce. Still, they were not comparable to the great banking houses of Kyoto, which grew through loans to samurai and the periodic commerce and exchange generated by the requirement that feudal lords live for a period of time in the capital (the *sankin kotai* system). The *kaekchu* were well positioned to take advantage of rapidly developing trade after 1876, however, and did so.

Korean scholars also had an inkling of Western progress in the late Chosŏn period, through information trickling in from Beijing. In 1631 Chŏng Tu-wŏn returned from China with world maps, books on Western

115. Lee (1984), pp. 226–28. See Palais (1996) for the most complete account of pre-nineteenth-century Korean commerce and the issues raised in the literature about it.

science, a working musket, a new telescope, and even an alarm clock. Around this time a Dutchman named Weltevree washed up on Korean shores from a shipwreck, soon to be followed by an entire Dutch crew that abandoned ship on Cheju Island. Weltevree stayed in Korea until his death under the name Pak Yŏn, and Hendrik Hamel stayed long enough to write a fascinating account of seventeenth-century Korea, as we have seen.[116] Pak Chi-wŏn journeyed to Beijing in 1780 and wrote *Jehol Diary,* which compared social conditions in Korea unfavorably with those he observed in China. Unfortunately there was no substantial Korean equivalent to the "Dutch learning" by which Japanese scholars opened an early window on the West, through Dutch residents and Catholics in the port city of Nagasaki. In the seventeenth century more Western learning filtered into Korea, usually under the auspices of a spreading Catholic movement (which attracted commoners above all by its creed of equality before the Lord), but this did not stimulate a ferment such as that which led to new technologies in Japan and helped it get off the mark quickly in 1868.

To the extent that all this activity augured an independent path toward economic growth for Korea, it is unfortunate that a big retrogression occurred in the early nineteenth century, leaving little evidence of such commercial bustle by the time Westerners began to arrive on Korean shores. The general observation was that Korea's merchants were "an undistinguished lot, despised socially by the upper class, perennially worrying about the preservation of their monopoly rights, and distrusted by the general population."[117]

A series of bad harvests in the early 1800s pushed many peasants into vagabondage or slash-and-burn farming *(hwajŏn)* in the mountains, and others into open rebellion. Greedy tax collectors were often the stimulus for revolt; they stretched their hands even into the mountains, seeking to collect from *hwajŏn* farmers (who were often quite numerous). The biggest eruption was the Hong Kyŏng-nae Rebellion (1811); in typical fashion Hong had failed the civil service exams and had no chance for an official career; after working as a professional geomancer, he took to organizing peasants against the government. Severe famines in P'yŏngan Province produced the raw material for an explosion that soon engulfed a large area north of the Ch'ŏngch'ŏn River. Although this uprising was suppressed, sporadic rebellions broke out right down to the 1890s, when the Tonghak rebels vastly enlarged the domain of conflict.

In the end, why so little evidence of commerce in nineteenth-century

116. Ledyard (1971).

117. Daniel Juhn, "Nationalism and Korean Businessmen under Japanese Colonial Rule," *Korea Journal* 17, no. 1 (Jan. 1977): 4.

Korea? Braudel had this observation: "Despite what many Sinophile specialists and historians maintain, [East Asia's] economic achievements were modest and, to be frank, backward compared with those of the West. . . . Her inferiority lay in her economic structure, her market outlets and her merchant middle class, less well developed than that of Islam or the West." He went on to cite the absence of free cities, "entrepreneurs eager to make profits" (which were "a spur to progress" in the West), nonexistent or inadequate credit systems, and an ethic determining that money, once made, ought to be used "to lead a comfortable life . . . and above all to discharge their obligations to their parents and their whole family."[118]

I think Braudel's judgment is just about right, minus the theoretical aside that entrepreneurial profit was essential to progress in the West (maybe it was, maybe not; but this is not our question). The question we posed, however, is a Western and a timebound one: Why didn't Koreans do what we did? It assumes an answer about how the West "did it," and asks a question about the East that is quickly becoming obsolescent. It is plausible that in a few decades from now the central question of historians may be, How did East Asia "do it," and what happened to "the West"?

CONCLUSION

In the 1860s Koreans, like their neighbors in China and Japan, looked back on a well-understood history that was about to be no more: their own. The irruption of a technically superior West in the East meant inevitable change, which washed away the old order in East Asia. Attuned to looking to the past for answers to current problems, their sages were not silent about remedies against the impending deluge; it's just that none of them worked. Nothing could be done about it, and nothing was done about it, save for jumping in this tide and rolling forward with it. That will be the rest of this story. Here we can close this chapter on old Korea and commemorate it in the words of Hong Yang-ho (1724–1802), who sought to tell Koreans of their real place in the world, through the meanderings of that symbol of fertility and procreation given to newlyweds—the goose:

> In the late autumn of the year *chŏngyu* (1777), a farmer from the Tumen River caught two wild geese, cut their wings and brought them to me. . . . One day he came to me and said, "These birds, sir, are better-flavoured than pheasant. I advise your Excellency to kill and eat them." "God forbid," said I. "Wonderful birds such as these were never

118. Braudel (1994), pp. 194–95.

intended for slaughter. Have not you noticed that when they fly they observe the strictest order *(ye);* when they mate, they are true to another, righteous *(ŭi);* in their migrations they follow the warmth of the sun, wise *(chi);* and though they go far afield you can always depend upon their sure return, trustworthy *(sin);* they never make war on other creatures with bill or claw, they love *(in)*. Only mere birds with feathers, and yet they possess all the Five Virtues—*in, ŭi, ye, chi, sin. . . .*"

I therefore fed them every day . . . till their wings were grown. Then I took them to the peak near by and let them fly off with this message:

> Now don't go North
> Where larchwoods moan, and hairy beasts go by,
> Where roaring speeds the Amur on its way. . . .
>
> Nor yet go South,
> Where fiery dust breaks on the smothery air,
> with boiling waters seething everywhere. . . .
>
> Nor go you East. Cross not the sea;
> For wild waves mount and echoing roar their will. . . .
> Black, too, the women's teeth, tattoed the men,
> Equipped with cunning and a practiced hand. . . .
>
> Avoid the West—the treacherous Yalu's stream,
> For there the great unwashed barbarian hides,
> With wild disordered speech and half-hung hair. . . .
>
> But here's the place for you, in this green land
> Of ours where first the sun alights, safeguarded
> By the stars and sheltered by the sky. . . .
> Go nowhere; find your place within this land. . . .[119]

119. Hong was a poet, a statesman (a *taejehak,* or secretary of state), and an envoy to China. This excerpt is from his *Letting Go the Wild Geese,* as translated in Gale (1972), pp. 290–92.

CHAPTER TWO

The Interests, 1860–1904

The pacific is the ocean bride of America—China & Japan & Corea—with their innumerable islands, hanging like necklaces about them, are the bridesmaids, California is the nuptial couch, the bridal chamber, where all the wealth of the Orient will be brought to celebrate the wedding. Let us as Americans—see to it that the "bridegroom cometh." . . .

—Commodore Robert W. Shufeldt

East Asia was "opened" by Western imperialism in the middle part of the last century, in about three decades. China was the first to succumb, during the Opium Wars of 1839–42; Japan came next when Commodore Matthew Perry's "black ships" appeared in Tokyo Bay in 1853; Korea came last, not because it was stronger, but perhaps because it was more recalcitrant. It did not sign its first international treaty until 1876—with Japan, instead of a Western power. Korea's descent into the maelstrom of imperial rivalry was quick after that, however, as Japan imposed a Western-style unequal treaty, giving its nationals extraterritorial legal rights and opening several Korean ports to international commerce.

Here is the beginning of modern Korea: its leaders no longer could shape events as they wished. For the first time in its history, the country was shaped from without more strongly than from within. Still, there was a dramatic effort at reform from within, and not just in Korea: throughout East Asia arrived the Indian summer of the Confucian system. In Korea, China, and Japan the decade of the 1860s was a time of reform on the old model—a "restoration" in China, "conservative reconstruction" in Japan.[1] In all three countries the reformers moved vigor-

1. See Wright (1966), the best account of the Chinese reforms; also Totman (1980), p. xxiii.

ously and with considerable success by past standards, because they were all reading the same classical texts and were all deeply threatened from without. The Taewŏn'gun (Yi Ha-ŭng, 1821–98) led Korea's reform effort from 1864 to 1873, illustrating the resilience of the old system when it had no choice but to put its domestic house in order. All three programs failed, however, to do anything about the challenge facing East Asia from imperialism. Only a different kind of reform worked, the radical post-1868 Meiji movement toward state building and industrialization in the name of "restoration."

A curious surge of activity in the old East Asian system saw Japan and China competing for influence in Korea, just as a new system brought in Western interests. As part of its own reform effort, led by an outstanding reformer named Li Hung-chang, China sought to reassert its traditional position in Korea by playing the imperial powers off against each other, and arranging more unequal treaties between Korea and the United States, Britain, and Germany (all in 1882). This split the Korean elite into groups that followed one or another power and its ideas (although one could be Korean and "pro-Chinese" or "pro-Russian" at the same time) and groups that sought to benefit from the weight of each power in Korea; they influenced policy down to the final annexation of Korea by Japan in 1910.

Amid the Taewŏn'gun's activities there were fits and starts in different and newer directions, but it was not until 1894 that Korea began its "modernization" in earnest—a mere century ago. A major rebellion at home, Japan's defeat of China, and a stalemate in the power balance gave Korea a brief decade in which it sought to industrialize its economy, enlighten its citizens, and begin a brief experiment with a kind of democracy. It wasn't enough time, of course, and thereafter the Japanese closed off independent Korean initiative. Meanwhile, many Westerners came to Korea for the first time, and they had lots to say about a country they found most curious. First, however, we will look at Korea's old pattern of foreign relations and the abrupt change that came with the imposition of a Western system.

THE HERMIT KINGDOM

Korea was known long before the nineteenth century as a country where foreigners were met with mistrust and dispatched as quickly as possible back to their homes: to those who knocked at its gates, Korea said in effect, "We have nothing and we need nothing. Please go away." Shipwrecked Japanese and Chinese sailors received good treatment before they were sent packing, but Occidentals—especially Dutch sailors like Hendrik Hamel, who became the first Westerners to live in Korea—had a different experience. They had two choices: stay and assimilate, or escape if they could.[2]

Basil Hall, captain of a British man-of-war that dropped anchor in 1816 among some Korean islands on the west coast, reported that the islanders "expressed some surprise on examining our clothes," but after that "took very little interest in anything belonging to us. Their chief anxiety was to get rid of us as soon as possible." Charles Gutzlaff, another early-nineteenth-century traveler to Korea, at first concluded that he had found "the most misanthropical people in the world," importuning every intruder with the stock question "What time do you think to depart?" But later he blamed the government for the relentless exclusionary impulse, and for the general poverty of the country. The people he met—mainly fishermen—were "good-humoured and obliging," he thought, and often sound in their judgment, except when confronted with the epic of Jesus Christ, which did not arouse their interest, leading Gutzlaff to conclude that "such callousness of heart bespeaks a great degree of mental apathy."[3]

In 1832 the British East India Company sent the *Lord Amherst* to Korea, but the ship was turned away on grounds that it contravened Korean law to engage in foreign commerce. After another try, in 1845, the Chinese imperial commissioner in Hong Kong explained to the British that Korea "could not be opened to trade by China, for it was not a part of China"; nor could Korea open itself to trade, since "it was not independent."[4]

Even comparatively well-traveled Koreans who were part of embassies to China impressed Europeans as far more xenophobic than the Chinese. Jesuit missionaries to Beijing in the sixteenth century thought the Koreans they encountered in the capital were surly, standoffish, and all too self-contained—just as Europeans in the same city three centuries later spoke of "these strangely-coated people, so proud, so thoroughly uninterested in strangers, so exclusive, so content to go their own way."[5] Korea's seclusion policy was partly a reaction to foreign predations, but also expressed its national self-sufficiency, its achievement of virtual economic autarky, and its valued place within the Chinese world order.

When I first traveled to North Korea, in 1981, I materialized at the airline ticket office in Beijing and asked where I might buy a ticket to

2. Ledyard (1971), p. 101. The Dutch sailors are often blamed for the strands of brown and red hair among Koreans today—or so Koreans say.

3. Gutzlaff (n.d.), p. 232.

4. K. H. Kim (1980), p. 40.

5. Gale (1972), pp. 299, 303. Of course, the Chinese exacerbated Korean xenophobia by putting sharp restrictions on what Koreans could do in the capital.

P'yŏngyang. The already narrow eyes of my Chinese interlocutor narrowed a bit more, and momentarily a tall Korean emerged from behind a door. As we scrutinized each other, it occurred to me that he had both the look and the greased pompadour of the rock-and-roll pioneer Little Richard. No doubt his impressions of me were equally peculiar. He asked me in Chinese where I came from, and my answer (Yankee) put a special edge on the second question, which was why would I want to visit his country. His third question was whether I had done penance for American crimes in Korea. By the time he thought up his fourth question, however, he was warming to me in the imperceptible manner of a glacier catching the first rays of the spring sun; it helped that we had switched to Korean.

The historian Key-Hiuk Kim uses the term "exclusionism" to distinguish Korean isolationism from the other varieties, suggesting a positive holding at arm's length, and also implying something of an understatement. Exclusionism was especially strong in the nineteenth century, since Koreans were not unaware of the increasing Western presence in East Asia, but it was a relatively recent phenomenon in Korea's long history. Worries about foreign pressure probably dated from the Mongol invasions of the thirteenth century and were sharply imbedded in the popular consciousness by Hideyoshi's depredations. In earlier periods Korea was thought very worldly and very wealthy, as we learned from the Arab travelers who fell in love with Silla. A deeply textured pattern of interaction with China, Japan, and Southeast Asia, especially during the heydays of coastal trade in the Koryŏ period when Koreans looked upon the outside world with relative security and tranquillity, no doubt made Korea a very different place.

Korea after the Mongol invasions, however, can be compared to an island rather than a peninsula. Like the Sŏkkuram Buddha, it was still open to the east and did not fear the island people in Japan, save for some pirates who squatted on Japanese territory and marauded along the Korean coast. It was no longer open to the north, however: it built a wall from the western end of the Yalu River to the sea, thus to define self and other, hygiene and plague, civilization and scourge. This border was not like the Khyber Pass, protecting India against the nomads, but neither was it like China's Great Wall, ranging over thousands of miles. White Head Mountain and the range running up to it posed a formidable barrier, as did the climate; the mere addition of a wall might do the trick and achieve closure. Hideyoshi's sixteenth-century invasions changed the calculus of the pacific East, however, and only after that can we speak of a Hermit Kingdom. If Japan saw itself as an island nation protected by divine winds, Korea became a peninsular island protected by a divine mountain and a severe anti-Japanese allergy.

Korea was relatively content in its relations with one country—China—and anxious to keep everyone else at bay. The Chinese hardly received a big welcome on the peninsula, however, at least after the Ming dynasty fell to the Manchus. Korea was indeed a tributary state to China, but it had not always been so: the leaders of the Chosŏn dynasty pushed for a close association with the Ming, as we have seen, for the same reasons that Renaissance figures wanted a close association with the Greeks: here was the pinnacle of world culture, toward which Korea wished to elevate itself.

Three official embassies traveled to China every year, at the New Year, the birthday of the emperor, and the birthday of the crown prince; later they were supplemented with another mission, at the winter solstice. A new king in Korea or the death of an emperor in China occasioned special missions, since the Korean kings sought investiture by the Chinese Son of Heaven. From 1637 until the end of the practice, in 1881, Korea sent a total of 435 special embassies and missions to China. Under the rubric of these embassies much cultural and commercial exchange took place, with a lively trade in furs, ginseng, horses, silk, and porcelain. Although some scholars make much of this limited trade, the relationship was founded less on self-interest than on the virtues of the Confucian order, in which China was big brother to Korea and each bore obligations to the other.[6]

Chinese and Korean diplomats rarely discussed internal affairs in either country, or even their respective external affairs. If the Korean king got his investiture from China, this was a mere ritual in which the Koreans made the political choices, not the Chinese. The few Chinese officials who traveled to Korea followed strict guidelines and protocol, journeying down one route to the capital from the border and never venturing into the interior. After the Ming fell, Chinese visitors were cloistered in one palace in Seoul and allowed no outside fraternization. As William Elliot Griffis wrote, "While the entire body of Coreans, dignitaries, servants, merchants, and cartmen enter Peking, and all circulate freely in the streets among the people, the Chinese envoy to Seoul, must leave his suite at the frontier, and proceed to the capital with but a few servants, and there dwell in seclusion."[7] (I was reminded of this when I met a Soviet diplomat in P'yŏngyang in 1981 and asked him about his life: "It is like living in a submarine. We don't go out. We have to get a permit to go to the countryside. We play soccer on Sundays with the diplomatic community—all except for the Albanians.")

"In external as well as internal affairs," Key-Hiuk Kim has written,

6. K. H. Kim (1980), pp. 6–9.
7. Griffis (1888), p. 220.

"Korea was fully autonomous, free to maintain relations with any country so long as such relations did not conflict with its tributary obligations to China."[8] Koreans revered things Chinese, and China responded by being for the most part a good neighbor, giving more than it took away. Absolutely convinced of its own superiority, exercising a light-handed suzerainty, China assumed that enlightened Koreans would follow it without being forced; it indulged in a policy that might be called benign neglect of things Korean, thereby allowing Korea substantive autonomy as a nation.

With Japan relations were always different. Korea's interactions with Japan were intense and frequent through long stretches of history, and, as we have seen, archaeological evidence suggests a much closer ethnic and cultural affinity than contemporaries prefer to admit. Here, too, Chosŏn Korea formalized older patterns by adopting a correct Confucian policy of "neighborly relations" *(kyorin)* with Japan. A year after King T'aejong's investiture by the Ming (1404), the third Ashikaga shogun, Yoshimitsu, also received Ming blessings as "King of Japan," putting Korea and Japan on an equal footing and thereby inaugurating the *kyorin* system.[9] Korean embassies visited Edo from time to time, but merely to exchange messages and gifts; it was a relationship of equality, but not a very important one to Koreans. Neither was it one to be feared. Koreans, after all, not only thought themselves to be but in fact were closer to the fount of Chinese civilization. Like American advocates of the virtues of "the West" these days, they used this proximity to look down on Japanese civilization.

The island of Tsushima was the medium of contact between Korea and Japan for centuries, and many scholars consider this island to have been a semitributary of Korea. Traders went back and forth from Ch'oryang, near Pusan, where sat Japan House: a large walled "factory" of homes, shops, and warehouses, it was the only place at which a Japanese could land on Korean soil. Covering about fifty acres and facing the sea, a high wall punctuated with watchtowers sequestered the compound from the rest of terra firma—Korea—as if someone might catch a disease by scaling it. To complete the circle, Japanese ships could drop anchor only in a lagoon surrounded by breakwaters.

Two miles down a narrow dirt path was the walled town of Pusanjin, a community of Korean merchants. In between were a couple of houses harboring interpreters and some motley assistants.[10] Here was the prophylactic bottleneck through which "trade" was conducted, an exquisite

8. K. H. Kim (1980), p. 9.
9. H. K. Kim (1980), pp. 15–16.
10. Deuchler (1977), p. 69.

illustration of the old Confucian maxim that trade was the only human activity in which the winner was disgraced. Japan House was the nodal point at which two bureaucratic empires touched and then recoiled—a perfect example of the premodern international system, the perfect antithesis of the nineteenth-century empire of free trade and "open doors."

After Hideyoshi's depredations both Japan and Korea formally adopted seclusion policies, and even if one can exaggerate their mutual isolation—there was still considerable contact[11]—they did hold each other at a distinct arm's length. The invasions cut off all trade, of course, but it was restored in 1609 and that trade agreement governed the relationship right down to the 1870s. Twenty-one ships made up the annual quota of trade in the seventeenth century, but it had been as high as fifty ships per annum in earlier periods. (Koreans had supported this early trade as a way of putting an end to the plundering by pirates based in Japan, or to turn the pirates into traders.)[12] An elaborate protocol governed every interaction, since it was unthinkable to Japanese and Koreans alike that their ruler could deal with the other on equal terms (even though that was the premise of the *kyorin* system). The shogun and the king had no formal correspondence, as both thought it beneath their station. Tsushima was the active party pushing for more and more contact. The lords of the island were more interested in sending trade Korea's way than the Koreans were in receiving it; Koreans reluctantly continued a practice that had few virtues in their eyes, except that it stifled smuggling.[13] This was the isolated Korea that Westerners "discovered" at the beginning of the nineteenth century; it was also a Korea in decline and rent by political squabbling.

Foreigners found the dynasty near its lowest point in four centuries. Through much of the nineteenth century Korea had no strong king, only a succession of child kings and weaklings. Queen dowagers and their clans (especially the Andong Kims) controlled the government and dominated the court behind the scenes. Sunjo was but ten years old when he became king in 1800; Hŏnjong, who came to the throne in 1834, at the age of eight, died suddenly fifteen years later, and Dowager Queen Kim, fifty-nine years old, picked the third son of Prince Chŏn'gye to be the king. He was nineteen years old and had no accomplishments of note; royal messengers dragged him back to Seoul from where they found him, behind a cow and a plow on Kanghwa Island, and made him the twenty-

11. See Toby (1984).
12. Deuchler (1977), p. 3.
13. Ledyard (1971), pp. 84–86; see also Toby (1984).

fifth Chosŏn dynasty king, Ch'ŏlchong. As Gale commented, he was someone with whom Dowager Queen Kim "might play as a college girl does with her tennis ball." Thus were born "contests between queens, clan fights, palace intrigues, all of which lent themselves to Korea's speedy downfall."[14]

Ch'ŏlchong died at the age of thirty-two in January 1864, a victim of the excesses and extravagances of the court. Three dowagers now dueled in the palace: Queen Cho, mother of King Hŏnjong; Queen Hong, Hŏnjong's wife; and Queen Kim, wife of the just-deceased king. The ball they batted around now was the absence of a direct heir to the royal line; the new king would have to be an adoptee from one of the consort clans. Queen Kim of the Andong coterie summoned a retired minister nearing eighty and told him to go find the eleven-year-old son of Prince Hŭngsŏn, who turned out to be flying a kite in a nearby garden. Runners perched him on a royal sedan chair and carried him off to the palace. Before anyone else (including Queen Kim) could act, Dowager Cho rushed forward exclaiming "My son!" and grabbed his hand and took him behind the queenly curtain. Presently she announced through the veil, "I have made the new king the son of Ikchong. . . . I have hung up the screen and now take command of the government." The assembled ministers had no choice but to bow and accept the nation's fate. Why?

If we think about this thing called "the state," it can be a set of representative institutions, a bureaucracy, or the exercise of sovereign power by a dowager. As Marx once wrote of the German monarchy, state sovereignty can be "sprinkled" by the king, as if he were wielding a salt shaker. Dowager Cho cast her salt and thus was produced King Kojong, adopted son of Ikchong (who had died twenty-two years before Kojong's birth), last monarch of Korea, and fateful historical symbol.[15]

Kojong's father was Yi Ha-ŭng, alias Prince Hŭngsŏn, alias the Taewŏn'gun, great-grandson of Prince Sado on the Min side; many historians believe he conspired with Dowager Cho to select his son, since her clan, the P'ungyang Chos, was much weaker than the Andong Kims. Gale had this to say:

> What to do with Prince Hŭngsŏn, father of the [new] king[?] What forms of ceremony . . . ? What dress? What place in the government? He could not bow as other officials did because that would mean bowing to his son. . . . Through the influence of Queen Cho . . . he became

14. Gale (1972), p. 305; Palais (1975), pp. 24–26.

15. Gale (1972), pp. 306–7. This story makes good reading; the account in Palais (1975), pp. 26–27, is less apocryphal, but no one quite seems to know why the Andong Kims let Dowager Cho get away with this.

regent and ruler absolute with the title *Taewŏn'gun,* "Prince of the Great House." For nine years his heavy hand was felt.[16]

There remained the question of Kojong's marriage. The Taewŏn'-gun's wife—Kojong's mother—fixed her eyes upon a daughter of the powerful Min clan. For complicated genealogical reasons, this meant in effect that Kojong would be marrying his aunt, at the pubescent age of thirteen. Undaunted, his mother went ahead with it anyway (the ceremony was held in 1866). The Taewŏn'gun, upon seeing the bride, "remarked that she was a woman of great determination and much poise of manner. He was somewhat disturbed at this. Later . . . he said, 'She evidently aspires to be a doctor of letters; look out for her.' "[17] Indeed, yon Queen Min had a lean look, and the Taewŏn'gun should have acted on his first impression. Instead, he inadvertently produced "the ablest female politician in the history of the dynasty."[18]

Meanwhile, the Taewŏn'gun ruled Korea with an iron fist from 1866 to 1873, and was an axis of politics for two decades thereafter. These two strong personalities—the Taewŏn'gun and the king's queen—swayed the young Kojong and shaped Korean politics for the rest of the century. Moreover, they didn't like each other: five years after her marriage Queen Min bore a son who died within three days; it was rumored "that the boy died after the Taewŏn'gun administered some kind of ginseng palliative." From that day onward she abominated the now dominant regent and waited for a ripe time to oust him from power.[19] By then it was 1871, however, and Korea was no longer sequestered in its own universe.

OPENINGS ABORTIVE AND OTHERWISE

What did it mean in the nineteenth century to "open" a country? Sometimes opening means discovery: as in, Perry discovered Japan. But Japan had been there all along; the Japanese did not know they were about to be discovered. Sometimes opening means enlightenment, as in the open-minded person, or the European Enlightenment. Sometimes opening means free trade and commerce. Sometimes opening connotes an ideological position. Sometimes opening means subjugation. In the Korean case it had all these meanings for the West and Japan, as we will see. What did it mean to Koreans? Koreans thought their country was as

16. Gale (1972), pp. 306–7.
17. Gale (1972), p. 308–9.
18. Palais (1975), p. 45.
19. Palais (1975), p. 45.

open as they wanted it to be—which, from the Western standpoint, was not very open. Many North Koreans think the same thing today. Meanwhile, recent American administrations have set as their task the "opening" of a Korean country, namely, the Democratic People's Republic of Korea. How can we account for the persistence over time of a demand for "opening," and for continued Korean recalcitrance?

In the modern era "opening" has been the implicit or explicit goal of every Japanese and American leader when thinking about Korea. But "opening" was the beginning of the end for old Korea, for the Sinic universe it inhabited, for a way of thinking about the relations between nations, for a way of thought. And from this we can deduce that the ulterior intent of opening was to destroy that old Korean universe in the name of progress: as in the breaking of the organic integrity of an eggshell, Korea (like Humpty Dumpty) would become an omelet. We don't think of "opening" this way, because we saturate the concept with all that is good and progressive. That this was inevitable, unavoidable, rational, advanced, demanded by the times, modern—all the high-flown characterizations that come to mind—is not the point. The point is that the very normalcy of this demand, its very reasonableness, made Korean recalcitrance all the harder, and all the more interesting. Koreans recognized the "modern" Rumpelstiltskin for what it really was: the virus that would destroy a unique Korean way in the world and pose for contemporary Koreans a question that absolutely never would have occurred to them before 1876: what does it mean to be Korean?

That this virus came first in the form of a newly rising Japan made Korean choices all the harder. Here was a nation never more than Korea's equal, knocking at its door in the name of a doctrine utterly alien to both, calling itself modern and reversing black and white by proposing that Valhalla was to be found in an endless pursuit of future happiness, not through a careful culling of lessons from a golden age in the past. The knocking was loud, insistent, and soon at the point of a gun.

The Sino-Korean tributary system was one of inconsequential hierarchy and real independence, if not equality. The Western system that Korea encountered, however, was one of fictive equality and real subordination. It was the British who did the most to propel the doctrine of sovereign equality around the world, confounding and undermining their imperial practice with an abstract, idealist theory that transferred notions about the free market to international politics: if every entrepreneur ought to be the equal of any other entering the marketplace, so every nation was equal and sovereign before the bar of international law. Or as Karl Polanyi put it, "in the liberal theory, Great Britain was merely another atom in the universe . . . and ranked precisely on the same footing as Denmark and Guatemala."[20] It was under this system that Korea "opened," and lost its independence for the first time since the Mongol conquests and far more completely than in that thirteenth-century interlude.

The first requests for opening came from Catholic priests and missionaries, and the Korean response was predictable: for a people who prized ideas and thought that ideas had consequences, the Bible was just another book, and Catholics looked like people with an allegiance to a place called Rome, come to do Korea no good—like other foreign predators. In 1784 a Korean named Yi Sŭng-hun tagged along with his father on a tributary pilgrimage to Beijing, and returned as a baptized Catholic convert. A Catholic priest smuggled himself into Korea in 1795, and by 1801 massacres of Korean converts had begun—only to increase in the 1830s when French priests made special efforts to penetrate the country. Seventy-eight Catholics, including three French priests, were murdered in 1839.[21] It was pretty terrible, but in some ways Korean leaders understood what was at stake. After all, one Korean Catholic named Hwang Sa-yŏng had been nabbed in 1801 carrying an infamous "silk letter" to the French bishop in Peking, asking that one hundred Western ships with tens of thousands of men be dispatched to help with the Vatican's work in Korea.[22] When Koreans launched more bloody pogroms against native Catholics in the 1860s, in which thousands died (reportedly, eight thousand Korean converts were massacred), the link between missionaries and gunboats was just as clear: the French threatened to mount a punitive expedition.

Koreans found this incomprehensible: they told the French that they would understand perfectly the execution of their own nationals in France, should they try to disseminate Korean views there. French troops landed on Kanghwa Island, north of Inch'ŏn, in 1866, but Seoul mobilized twenty thousand men and easily pushed the French forces back to the sea. This convinced Koreans that their forcible defense policies were correct, and propelled the French southward, toward their eventual colonization of Indochina.[23]

The United States also tried its hand at opening up Korea in 1866, when the merchant schooner *General Sherman* sailed up the Taedong River toward P'yŏngyang. A heavily armed ship with a mixed crew of Americans, British, and Chinese, it received the message that it was not just Christianity that contravened Korean law but also foreign commerce.

20. Polanyi (1944), p. 207.
21. Kwang-Ching Liu, foreword to K. H. Kim (1980), p. xi; also K. H. Kim (1980), p. 36.
22. K. H . Kim (1980), p. 35; Palais (1975), p. 178.
23. K. H. Kim (1980), p. 48–50.

Undaunted, the *Sherman* forged ahead. Shortly a hostile crowd gathered on the shore, into which the frightened sailors unloaded their muskets. After that volley the provincial governor, a much respected and temperate official named Pak Kyu-su (who later negotiated the first treaty with Japan), ordered the *General Sherman* destroyed. The tide obligingly receded, grounding the vessel. The Koreans killed all its crew in battle and burned the ship—unwittingly taking revenge for an Atlanta that could not.[24]

It was a dastardly act, the authorities in Washington declared; what an outrageous affront to a peaceable bunch of people who just happened to be sailing a man-of-war up the river to P'yŏngyang! None other than Secretary of State William Seward, architect of westward expansion, proposed a joint expedition with the French to punish the Koreans, and Commodore Robert W. Shufeldt (who fancied himself Korea's Commodore Perry) determined to "go up the 'Ping yang' river at the proper season and inflict proportionate punishment."[25] But it did not happen until 1871. By then the U.S. government had decided to open Korea's ports by force, and put Fredrick Low in command of the American expedition.

In this famed "Little War with the Heathen," as the *New York Herald* called it, the American Asiatic Squadron included the warships *Monocacy* and *Palos,* plus "four steam launches, and twenty boats, conveying a landing force of six hundred and fifty-one men, of whom one hundred and five were marines." When the formation got near Kanghwa, twelve native Christians approached, trying to communicate with the Americans. The flotilla steamed through the straits near the island, where it took sharp fire from newly cast Korean cannons. Marines hit the beaches of Kanghwa and sought to capture several Korean forts. These were filled with Korean tiger fighters renowned for their courage, who battled ferociously; when their weapons were empty, they threw sand in the Americans' eyes and fought to the last man in hand-to-hand combat.

In the end about 650 Koreans died, according to William Griffis:

> Two hundred and forty-three corpses in their white garments lay in and around the citadel. Many of them were clothed in a thick cotton armor, wadded to nine thicknesses, which now smouldered away. A sickening stench of roasted flesh filled the air. . . . Some of the wounded, fearing their captors worse than their torture, slowly burned to death. . . .

24. There are several accounts of this incident, but the most interesting is the one taken down firsthand by Gale (1972), pp. 310–11, from an old hermit of P'yŏngyang named Chŏng Hŭi-jo.

25. Quoted in Drake (1984), p. 107.

Commander Low thought the Koreans fought back with a courage "rarely equalled and never excelled by any people."[26] After some desultory and fruitless negotiations, the Americans withdrew. Once again Korean leaders were convinced that their anti-foreign policy worked.

The "Little War with the Heathen" was little noted nor long remembered in the United States, but more than a century later my North Korean hosts were pleased to show me the stone monument that still marks the spot where the *General Sherman* burned. It is not far from Kim Il Sung's birthplace, and my hosts assured me that his great-grandfather had led the charge. Much like North Koreans today, Koreans of that era thought that their staunch moral virtue had sent the foreigners packing, even if their weapons were technologically backward.

Meanwhile, various freebooters took diplomacy into their own hands with personal invasions of Korea's territory. The most famous and grotesque of these episodes was carried out by one Ernst Oppert, a German trader and adventurer. Oppert held many odd views, among them that some Koreans (the upper class) were "caucasian" while others (the lower classes) were "mongolian." Mainly, though, Oppert was beside himself with the arrogant insularity of Korea, "too deeply convinced of its own invincibility to fear any assault from foreigners." Korea was still in 1880 "a 'forbidden land,' a land which no foreigner dares to enter without running the risk of paying for his hardihood with his life." Explorers might trek to the North Pole, or into darkest Africa, and yet here, "within a day's steam from the nearest Chinese coast . . . we do not venture to demand admission because a semi-barbarous Government, against the wishes of its own people, chooses to write 'no entrance' over its doors, and bids defiance to the whole civilized world." He hoped the time would soon come, however, when "it will be taught the contrary" and then be forced to admit "the absurdity of its belief in its own superior bravery and power."

Kim Ronyoung in her novel *Clay Walls* used the metaphor to symbolize old Korea, the position of women, and the walls between her and Anglo-Saxon Americans in Los Angeles (see chapter 9). To Oppert, however, Korean walls symbolized an insolent unwillingness to trade. But then they looked weak to him, so he was optimistic: "The Corean walls are . . . miserably constructed of irregular and uneven stone blocks, and every one of them would tumble down at the first shock from the balls of any moderately-sized guns."[27] After being rebuffed in his first attempt to truck and barter in 1866, he got the bright idea to raid the tomb of the

26. K. H. Kim (1980), pp. 56–61; Griffis (1889), pp. 412–18.
27. Oppert (1880), pp. 1, 5–7, 21, 104.

Taewŏn'gun's father, grab his bones, and hold them for ransom. Surely this would get the Koreans to see the virtues of free trade, or so he thought. Oppert and his fellow pirates landed on the coast from several ships in 1868 and moved stealthily inland toward the grave; soon Korean troops confronted them, and their "moderately-sized" balls ended Oppert's vandalism, sending his men scampering back to their ships.[28]

The United States became the first Western nation to open Korea, concluding a treaty in 1882. But there was no American Commodore Perry: instead, a Chinese official managed the whole business of hooking Korea into the Western system, as we will see. Meanwhile, Japan had already made its own treaty. When Japan itself opened up and began an active diplomacy in the 1860s, it initially sought to deal with Korea through a fictive "tributary" relationship that only the Japanese recognized, with dubious and antique historical arguments that things between the two nations had surely been thus-and-so, long before any written records existed. The Koreans responded with a predictable loathing and contempt for this idea, leading the Japanese to join Oppert in exclamations about Korean "insolence." Soon it got worse.

In 1869 a Korean official in Pusan, An Tong-jun, told an envoy from Tsushima that Korea could not tolerate his use of the term "emperor" for the new Japanese leader. "Meiji emperor" was a misnomer because there was but one emperor, and he was in China; Japan's monarch was a king of the same rank and honor as the Korean king and nothing more. Mr. An thus demanded that the envoy return home forthwith—which he did, but his superiors were not happy. Now Japan toyed with simply calling it a walk by invading Korea. This would put a quick stop to Korean insolence, show the Western powers what kind of stuff the new Japan was made of, and stimulate unity in a country theretofore divided along feudal lines. After some spirited debate and formidable support for an invasion, the proposal was shelved.

Japanese envoys again knocked on the Korean door in 1873, now gussied up as proxies of a "modern" nation. The Tongnae prefect, Chŏng Hyŏn-dŏk, noticed that with Japan's new legal dressing came a change in attire—namely, Western suits—and decided that people dressed this way could no longer be considered Japanese and would not be permitted to trade at Pusan. Just to make the point stick, he addressed the envoys with a low and blunt language that accorded with his judgments about their sartorial dementia. Chŏng acted just as any Korean official would have in previous decades and centuries, since they had always thought the Japanese backward in their halting efforts at following the Chinese

28. Palais (1975), p. 21.

and Korean way, and their rapid Westernization after 1868 merely proved yet again their wayward nature. Back in Tokyo, however, Japanese leaders were less than impressed with Mr. Chŏng.

Baron Saigō, the most powerful figure in the new government, determined upon gunboat diplomacy to teach such people a lesson, pushing hard for a campaign against Korea. But other important leaders counseled restraint, lest the new reforms be endangered by a provocative and premature expansionism. The arguments on both sides of the issue were fierce, but at length the Meiji leadership chose to stay its hand. "Korea was spared the horror of war with Japan by a hair's breadth. . . ."[29] Saigō and his allies lost the argument and left the government, and in this way modern Japan's founding political crisis over what to do about recalcitrant Korea ended, concluding for the time being a key debate in Japan's definition of itself as a modern country. Koreans, of course, could not be expected to applaud this outcome, but wondered why the idea had come up in the first place—and later connected it to Japan's colonization of Korea by asserting an unbroken chain of imperial agression toward its near neighbor. But the chain was broken in 1873, not to be linked again until the Russo-Japanese War. What broke it was a frontal demand for war in Korea, followed by a critical decision that Japan should first put its own house in order through the new reform program, before getting embroiled in foreign adventures.

Thereafter Japan busied itself not in occupying Korea but in establishing equality with China, which in some ways it had done in a treaty signed in 1871. This agreement then provided a basis for challenging China's position in Korea, widely called a "suzerainty" but, as we have seen, not one that amounted to much. As a means to this end Japan sought the same privileges in Korea that the Western imperial powers already had in China and Japan; it was a simple matter of giving literal interpretation to the Western buzzwords about the sovereign equality of all nations, and then pushing for the same superior rights and privileges that the Western imperialists had gotten by using this same lingo as a cover.

The Taewŏn'gun had a simple foreign policy: no treaties, no trade, no Catholics, no West, and no Japan. He viewed Japan's progressive reforms as yet more evidence of how far it had fallen from the way, how little the island people really understood the virtues of a Sinic world order. Pak Kyu-su also remonstrated with the court about Japan's aggressive designs: "rich country, strong army" might be Japan's new slogan,

29. Palais (1975), p. 22; K. H. Kim (1980), pp. 94–99, 115–18, 124–35, 177–84; more generally see Conroy (1960).

he said, but the wealth and power of a nation came from moral rectitude, not shows of force. (Pak was the official who, a decade earlier, had inquired what the schooner *Sherman* might be doing in the middle of the Taedong River.) In this he was joined by the caustic Confucian Ch'oe Ik-hyŏn, who expressed Korean fear and loathing of Japan's new ways in pungent language: "The Japanese who come today are wearing Western clothes, are using Western cannons, and are sailing upon Western ships; this indeed is clear proof that the Japanese and the Westerners are one and the same." Coming on the heels of a rapprochement with Japan, Ch'oe thought, would be an unstoppable string of calamities: the exchange of Korean daily necessities for Japanese trinkets, more Japanese running hither and yon through the countryside, more Christian converts, and the defiling of Korean woman. Best to keep the Japanese out; they were "wild animals that only crave material goods and are totally ignorant of human morality." Ch'oe took the extreme measure of gathering together fifty scholars and marching to the palace to beseech King Kojong with this memorial. Wielding axes in their hands, they offered their necks to the king should he wish to exchange them for the scholars' convictions.[30]

Having gotten the crusty Taewŏn'gun out of the way in 1873, however, Kojong decided he would seek to embrace the new Japan—thus to contain it. It wasn't a very good idea, either. His 1874 policy of "reconciliation" yielded within two years Japan's first success at the unequal-treaty business, imposing upon Korea the Kanghwa Treaty, by which we date Korea's "opening" (even if the actual opening came a bit later). Meanwhile, Ch'oe Ik-hyŏn found himself in the docket for his reiteration of primordial Korean verities.

Like the Western powers, including the United States, the Japanese chose gunboats and the by now perennial target Kanghwa Island to make their point. In 1875 they first provoked island guns by entering an area known to be off-limits to foreign ships, and then silenced shore-bound Korean cannons with a fusillade from the warship *Unyō*. For good measure the *Unyō* also destroyed a Korean fort near Inch'ŏn, killing many of its defenders. A few months later, after Chinese-mediated attempts failed to resolve difficulties growing out of this affair, Japan landed some four hundred troops on Kanghwa as an earnest of its intent to force treaty negotiations upon Korea; a Japanese squadron with as many as four thousand men reconnoitered offshore.

Some Koreans wanted to take the Japanese on headfirst. Yi Hang-no, formerly a court censor, urged Kojong to mobilize the army:

30. Palais (1975), pp. 264–65; Deuchler (1977), p. 43.

> The bandit troops are no more than pirate plunderers. We should attack them in one fell swoop. . . . If they are allowed to grow big like a dragon in his lair, then it will be difficult to suddenly attack and destroy them. I humbly beg the king to immediately order troops to be sent to attack the evil and dirty [scum], so they will not dare to squat all over our borders.[31]

The Japanese show of force turned Kojong's mind in the opposite direction, however, and on February 27, 1876, the two countries signed the treaty. It was diplomacy with a gun to the temple, an offer Korea couldn't refuse. Article 1 recognized Korea as an "autonomous" *(chaju)* state with sovereign rights the same as Japan's, a good example of ersatz legal boilerplate that would not get Koreans a bowl of rice in Tokyo unless they had fifteen sen. The article really meant that Japan no longer found any Chinese position in Korea worthy of its respect. Other articles gave Japan rights to search for new ports in five Korean provinces, survey Korean waters, conduct business and trade without interference, and protect its merchants in Korean ports under extraterritorial privileges. As for Korean privileges in Japan, there were none. Korea got a few minor concessions that saved a bit of face, but it inked the treaty mainly because it could not hope to win the war that Japanese troops and gunboats clearly threatened.[32]

In one book after another, we find this phrase: it was Korea's first modern treaty.[33] Surely it was, but what might "modern" mean in this context? Fair? Equal? In accord with international law? Concluded by sovereign nations? A lawyer in a courtroom could get an affirmative verdict on all these points; the treaty was integral to the "common law" of the Western imperial system. Concluded in the name of sovereign equality and against the putative hierarchy of the Chinese world order, the real effect of the treaty was to erase the centuries of essential equality between Japan and Korea. The consequences of this transformation were not long in coming, and live with us to this day.

This was not, however, an opening with much of an immediate punch in 1876. Japan was too preoccupied at home with the Satsuma Rebellion of 1877 and other pressing matters, and so it did not push its advantage. Temporarily the Korean field was left to the Chinese, who began to assert themselves for the first time in more than two centuries—also in the name of the new diplomacy and the Western state system. The vehicle for this reassertion was China's great leader of the late nineteenth century, a man who operated effectively on the new domestic terrain of

31. Quoted in Palais (1975), p. 264.
32. Palais (1975), p. 259; Deuchler (1977), p. 47.
33. For example, Deuchler (1977), p. 48.

"self-strengthening" and the new international terrain of diplomatic rivalry: Li Hung-chang.

The question was how to "reassert" a position in Korea that had never meant much, where the king "pays an Acknowledgement to the *Tartar,* . . . [and] disposes of all things as he please," in the words of Hendrik Hamel. In 1875 one Chinese official, Shen Pao-chen, explained to the Japanese that Korea "was a dependent of China and subject to the control of the Board of Rites," that is, not the office responsible for foreign affairs (the Tsungli Yamen). Called upon then to define "dependent country" *(shuguo* or *shupang),* "Shen stated that Korea was left to her own devices in internal matters . . . and that she also possessed complete power of decision in the field of foreign affairs."[34] Exactly so; Shen spoke as if he were answering an exam question. But it was not the answer an assertive China was looking for, nor was it inclined to impress a Japan eager to make Korea independent of Chinese "suzerainty," in order to get busy subordinating both.

In August 1879 Li sent a letter to Yi Yu-wŏn, a former chief state councillor with much experience with China.[35] Taking up the traditional role as Korea's guardian against foreign predation, Li urged upon him an old Chinese idea that might have merit in the new era: let the barbarians control the barbarians. Korea, he wrote, was a nation of literary merit and elevated statecraft, but these very virtues would leave it prey to a much rougher power politics. The imperial tide was irreversible, but it could be checked and perhaps controlled through the interplay of realpolitik and treaty obligations. Li recommended that Korea sign treaties with three Western powers that so far had not displayed much interest in Korea—namely, Great Britain, Germany, and the United States—as a means of holding back Japanese and Russian ambitions. Korea, in short, should lodge itself in the web of the new diplomacy by allying with the less attentive spiders.

Yi Yu-wŏn responded that Korea did not desire intercourse with other nations. It preferred its long-standing policy of seclusion, buttressed by China's historical support: "Neither Japan nor the West dare behave with license before your excellency's imposing power. . . . [O]ur inferior country places eternal reliance upon your great virtue."[36] It was not a time for the old virtues, however, and ultimately King Kojong relented and signed another unequal treaty: this time with the United States of America.

In 1880 a councillor in China's mission in Tokyo, Huang Tsun-hsien,

34. Deuchler (1977), p. 27.
35. K. H. Kim (1980), pp. 241, 284–89.
36. Quoted in H. K. Kim (1980), p. 289.

wrote something called "Korean Strategy" *(Chaohsien t'se-lüeh).* The time for seclusion was over, he argued, and the time for internal self-strengthening had arrived in East Asia. Korea needed to buy time for that, and new alliances were the answer. The United States, Huang thought, had always "upheld justice" and had never allowed the European powers "to freely perpetrate their evil deeds." If that might not turn out to be true, at least the United States was well across the Pacific and more or less minding its own business—as was Japan for the time being, preoccupied with reform at home. Russia, on the contrary, threatened Korea. In good Chinese fashion, Huang summed up the new policy in a pithy phrase: *ch'in Chung, chieh Jih, lien Mei*—stay close to China, associate with Japan, ally with America.[37]

A Korean envoy in Japan, Kim Hong-jip, took Huang's booklet home to Kojong, who was impressed and recommended it to the ministers of state. Soon he set up a rudimentary foreign office: predictably he used the Chinese model of the Tsungli Yamen. It wasn't doing the Chinese a whole lot of good in this new era, but never mind: Korea now had the T'ongnigimu Amun, with somewhat broader functions than the Chinese version, combining foreign affairs and defense functions. (It never amounted to much.) Kojong also dispatched a secret mission to Japan to survey its recent changes, in "sightseeing group" masquerade. A Korean in Pusan tipped the Japanese off, however, and a top Meiji leader, Inoue Kaoru, took the delegation by the hand through new factories, shipyards, arsenals, and schools. They returned after four months and told Kojong that they were less than impressed: the Japanese were still a fickle lot, and their recent progress was much overrated.[38]

Meanwhile, the word spread about all this foreign activity, and once again Korea's Confucian sentinels were outraged. A joint memorial to the throne soon arrived, signed by scholars from every province. Kojong's actions signaled not reform, they wrote, but the impending deluge that would sweep Korea away. One denounced Huang as a Christian heretic, and another called Kim Hong-jip a traitor for showing Huang's "Korean Strategy" to the king; these were the useless "opinions of a foreigner." Yi Man-sŏn scoffed at the idea that America was a species of barbarian different from the rest. Others demanded simply that all foreign books in Korea be burned. The memorials recommended that everything else be "corrected": relations among the people, educational practice, military training, any and all heterodox ideas. Things finally came to a head, so to speak, when Kojong had one of the Confucian

37. Lee (1988), p. 25. Lee notes the naïveté of this analysis of the United States, which soon acquired colonies itself.

38. Han (1974), pp. 376–78; Deuchler (1977), pp. 92–102.

miscreants decapitated in a show trial outside Seoul's gates on September 13, 1881, and then banished the rest.

The man who lost his head for his ideas was the Confucian scholar Hong Chae-hak (the characters mean Hong-in-the-midst-of-cranes), of Kangwŏn Province. We should pause to give the man his due. He had argued, like Ch'oe Ik-hyŏn, Pak Kyu-su, and many others before him, that Japan and the West were peas in a pod, that they all meant affliction and ruin to Korea; better to hoist up the gates and set the Five Armies in motion. What can we call people like Mr. Hong? Illogical, irrational, obscurantist, traditionalist, anachronistic, myopic, arrogant, obtuse, stubborn, backward, posterior, positively dorsal. That is in fact what they have been called by most of the modern scholarship, which, as it happens, echoes the views of the man who thought destiny had called him to crank open old Korea, Commodore Shufeldt (he was outraged by Korea's "contemptuous exclusiveness").[39] We might, however, want to call them patriots. Or conscientious scholars, men of principle, virtue, strength, vigor; they let out learned wails for the fate of old Korea, and correctly predicted the shot that came a few short years later.

Were they conservatives? In America a conservative is usually someone nostalgic for a social order that seems to have died out four decades earlier, in one's youth.[40] A liberal lives happily in the present, looking toward the yet more progressive future. We cannot understand a person steeped in the lore, life, and wisdom of three millennia, watching his world crumble before his eyes. We will meet more people like Hong Chae-hak, right up to the point where Korea itself was snuffed out in 1910, people willing to give their lives for a disappearing universe. One cannot read their ideas in their fullness without mist forming on the eye. So we should honor these people with a name: "hermits" might do, but they were much more than that. "Conservatives" would not begin to capture their age-old wisdom. From now on let's call this the Hongian legacy, in honor of scholar Hong-amid-cranes, who had his head handed to him for his virtue and courage.

39. Drake (1984), p. 105. I will spare the scholars, but cull from the scholarly literature some illustrations of my point for the reader: "traditional seclusion," "arrogance of seclusion," "obscurantist sophistry," "obtuse arrogance," "backward mentality," "anachronistic and myopic," "innovation was the enemy," so on and so forth.

40. Not always, of course. Senator Robert Byrd (Democrat of West Virginia) spoke words in 1995 that sound Confucian—were they not so Roman: "Instilled in the Roman was the discipline and the respect for authority that were taught in the home. The Roman family was the cornerstone of the Roman society and the Roman body politic." Rome fell, Senator Byrd thought, when "the Romans, like Americans in recent decades, lost their reverence for their gods, [and] their veneration of their ancestors." *Los Angeles Times*, Jan. 29, 1995, p. M3.

The motive force in Korean diplomacy was still China, and not King Kojong and his advisers. Li Hung-chang did all he could to realize Huang's balance-of-power policy, including everything but dot the i's and cross the t's of the 1882 treaty with the United States (maybe he did that too). Li and Commodore Shufeldt secretly negotiated the deal in China, even to the point of choosing Korea's new national flag (and still the flag of South Korea), and then presented the finished document to the Koreans. As Frederick Drake has aptly put it, Shufeldt "was discussing the treaty with the viceroy of Chihli . . . , writing it in Tientsin in the Chinese language, and arranging it through the agency of China's diplomats for a Korean official he had never formally met and had seldom seen!"[41] (From time to time Li consulted with the Korean representative in Tientsin, Kim Yun-sik, but Kim was not part of the treaty negotiations with Shufeldt.)

A Chinese official took Shufeldt to Inch'ŏn to sign the treaty, weighing anchor in heavy fog on the ship *Swatara* on May 8 and arriving off Korea the next day. On May 20 Shufeldt presented his credentials to Korean officials, with this prefatory flourish: "Great America. Imperial Decree of Commodore Shufeldt U.S.N. Special Envoy with full power." He came ashore two days later to sign the treaty. Little noticed back home, the achievement nonetheless duly impressed the commodore: he had accomplished, he later wrote, "the feat of bringing the last of the exclusive countries within the pale of Western Civilization."[42]

Li Hung-chang made sure that another naval officer arrived to sign the British treaty five days later, with a German envoy hot on his heels by June. The three treaties were identical in substance, and they signaled Li's success at taking over Korea's foreign policy. All he had really wanted to do was find a way to protect China's eastern flank.[43] As for Shufeldt, he was proud to the point of prurience with his climactic feat: he now hoped that Korea and China would come to look beyond Japan for the source of the rising sun, and then (mixing metaphors) come together on the bridal couch with a new American empire of the Pacific:

> As everything that is bright comes from the East—even as the sun rises in the East & as still the Star of Empire westward takes its way—so China must look to the shores of America for a new Civilization & a more vigorous regeneration. This is the natural course of events, the true march of human progress, the irresistible flow of the human tide. . . .
>
> The pacific is the ocean bride of America—China & Japan & Corea—

41. Drake (1984), p. 292.
42. Drake (1984), pp. 296–98.
43. Kwang-Ching Liu, foreword to K. H. Kim (1980), pp. xvi–xvii.

> with their innumerable islands, hanging like necklaces about them, are the bridesmaids, California is the nuptial couch, the bridal chamber, where all the wealth of the Orient will be brought to celebrate the wedding. Let us as Americans—see to it that the "bridegroom cometh" . . . let us determine while yet in our power, that no commercial rival or hostile flag can float with impunity over the long swell of the Pacific sea. . . . It is on this ocean that the East & the West have thus come together, reaching the point where search for Empire ceases & human power attains its climax.[44]

The three Western nations got extraterritorial rights in Korea for their citizens, consular representation, fixed tariffs, port concessions, and other benefits; Korea got a commonplace "use of good offices" clause that, ever since, has been misinterpreted by Koreans who think it meant that the United States would or should protect them from Japan. The agreements also called for the dispatch of Korean students to the West, who quickly took advantage of this provision. The main point is made by a fine historian: the treaties "violated Korean sovereignty,"[45] whether under the old rules or the new. Korea was now fully hooked into the system of unequal treaties, a process begun by Japan and finished by China—both of which were then subject to the same system.

It wasn't long before Americans besides Shufeldt began arriving in Korea. The first representative, Lucius Foote, traveling with a small group on the now peaceable USS *Monocacy,* reached Inch'ŏn in May 1883. The naval attaché George Foulk followed a year later. Neither made much of an impression, although lots of Koreans turned out to gape at them. Far more important was Horace Allen, who arrived in 1884, just in time to save Min Yŏng-ik's life at a fateful dinner on December 4. Of Allen, we will soon hear much more.

RESTORATION, REFORM, REVOLUTION

As we saw, the early nineteenth century witnessed a period of sharp decline in Korea's fortunes. Agricultural production suffered, with many peasants escaping into slash-and-burn agriculture in the mountains. Popular uprisings began in 1811 and came and went through the rest of the century, culminating in the Tonghak (Eastern Learning) movement of the 1860s, which eventually spawned a major peasant rebellion in the 1890s. Korean leaders were aware that China's position had been transformed by the arrival of powerful Western gunboats and traders, but reacted to the Opium Wars by shutting Korea's doors even tighter.

44. Quoted in Drake (1984), pp. 115–16.
45. Han (1974), p. 387.

Furthermore, through its successful rebuff of French and American gunboat diplomacy, the regime was encouraged to think it could hold out indefinitely against external pressure.

The Taewŏn'gun took power in 1864 and was a determined reformer, on the classical pattern of rectifying state and society. He led an energetic program to discipline the royal clans, bring in new blood, straighten bureaucratic practice, strengthen central control, and, above all, attack the vested interests of the yangban elite—especially their tax privileges. As the historian of this episode wrote,

> The basic goals of the Taewongun were to preserve the country and the dynasty by removing the superficial causes of peasant discontent (bureaucratic corruption, illicit taxation, official usury), restoring the power and prestige of the throne to earlier levels, increasing the central government's control over financial resources, eliminating subversive and heterodox doctrines, and building up military strength by traditional means. His approach was primarily pragmatic . . . and he did not hesitate to step on the toes of the social elite, the older bureaucratic factions, or the Confucian dogmatists.[46]

Horror of all horrors, he slapped taxes on the aristocracy.

Nevertheless, the Taewŏn'gun's restoration *(chunghŭng)* had nothing in common with the restoration of the imperial house that marked Japan's break with the past. There was no new ideology, no new connection with the people, no new pattern of state politics, no plan for using Western technology to build a new country: the Taewŏn'gun was in fact trying to recapture the halcyon days of Sejong in the fifteenth century.[47] In other words, it was a real restoration, like the T'ung-chih period in China, and not a revolution trying to camouflage itself in old clothes. To use a different metaphor, the Meiji leaders were pouring new wine into old bottles; the Koreans were pouring old wine into old bottles. The question was, Which wine?

The Taewŏn'gun was a strong political leader and a man of action, and many of his reforms were effective; he had taken on the aristocracy, however, and thereby upset the true power balance in Korea's agrarian bureaucracy. That was the main rock on which he foundered, for he was a conservative and not a radical: he had no intention of smashing the yangban. Korea faced a crisis in the 1860s both at home and abroad, and there were others besides the Taewŏn'gun, just as sincere, who thought that people and not institutions should be rectified. One was a venerable scholar named Yi Hang-no, who "had spurned opportunities for office

46. Palais (1975), p. 3.
47. Palais (1975), p. 42.

A foreign diplomat gets ready to leave his compound in a sedan chair, circa 1900. *Courtesy of Carlo Rosetti.*

in preference for a life of study and moral self-cultivation." In 1866, as the battle with French forces ensued on Kanghwa Island, Yi lauded the Taewŏn'gun for his strong, exclusionist foreign stance but chided him for his domestic policies. The essence of the latter should be moral rectification. Sounding like Benjamin Franklin but actually harking back to Sejong's well-known habits, he wrote,

> If from now on the King starts by rising early and going to bed late, and if the ministers take oaths among themselves to cut out the evils of parties and merriment, be diligent in cultivating frugality and virtue, do not allow private considerations from taking root in their minds, and do not use artifice as a method of operation in government affairs, then the officials and common people will all cleanse and purify their minds. . . .
>
> Put a stop to construction projects; put an end to government which exacts taxes from the people; abandon the habits of luxury and extravagance; make the palace humble and partake simply and sparingly of food and drink; shun fancy clothes and devote all efforts to the people's affairs. . . . Then the strength of the people will be greatly extended and public opinion will be in harmony, and the people will look up to you

> as a father and mother. . . . Only after things are done like this can the Western barbarians be driven off and the state preserved.

Ch'oe Ik-hyŏn (another Hongian whom we met before) was taken by his father to study at Yi Hang-no's knee in 1846, at the age of thirteen. Ch'oe was just as active on the domestic front as in regard to foreign policy; like his mentor, he urged a return to the virtues. With the end of the Taewŏn'gun's regency drawing near in 1873, he wrote this:

> If [the king's] mind is as clear as pure water, his desires will be purified and disappear, and Heaven's principles will flow [everywhere]. When it comes to government orders and carrying them out, what should be done will be done with the ferocious force of lightning and wind. . . . [T]he Way will be established without doubt.[48]

Yi Hang-no and his disciple had no better remedy for Korea's plight than did the Taewŏn'gun; they just had unshakable will and convictions and lived their lives according to the dictates of ethics and morality. They were immovable objects meeting an irresistible force, and thus their remonstrance led to the collapse of the consensus underpinning the Taewŏn'gun's reform program. As for King Kojong, such people were simultaneously his critics and his teachers, and their judgments moved him. Whatever one may say about the reasons for Korea's collapse, such individuals were sublime and exercised a haunting influence on both the king and the progressive younger generation, neither of whom could ever quite be sure that the Hongians were not right. To paraphrase Yeats, the best had all conviction and passionate intensity while the ceremony of progressive innocence drowned the young, and so the Confucian middle held.

With resolute Hongians the only thing to do was get them out of the way. Some officials thought Ch'oe Ik-hyŏn had slandered the king and ought to be executed like Hong Chae-hak for lèse-majesté, but Kojong instead banished him to Cheju Island. Then he took over the reins of government, retiring the redoubtable Taewŏn'gun.[49] Kojong came back to direct power, and thereafter Korea's reform possibilities were stalemated by the Taewŏn'gun and various Hongians on one side or by progressive reformists like Kim Ok-kyun on the other, and by the political ambitions of Queen Min's group (deploying their important ties to the Chinese) who prefered the status quo "middle." Ultimately, the king's new leadership carried Korea from the mid-1870s through to the Sino-

48. Palais (1975), pp. 180–81, 191.
49. This is a very involved business, drastically summarized here; for the details, see Palais (1975), pp. 182–201, 284–86.

Japanese War in 1894, by which time the old government was a puck on a shuffleboard controlled by the big powers.

Meanwhile, various Korean reform movements sought to get off the mark in the 1880s, influenced by either Japanese or American progressives. In the 1880s we can see paths not taken, or roads embarked upon which later worked for Korea, but in searching out the origins of Korean modernity we must remember that people in the 1880s did not know which path would succeed (as we do). A handful of yangban went to China to examine its new arsenals, the fruit of Li Hung-chang's "self-strengthening" movement, and returned with new ideas for improving the Korean military. Some young progressives looked to America with hope, encouraged by the many missionaries who sponsored schools of all sorts, but especially the Paejae School for Boys and the Ewha School for Girls, both inaugurated in 1886; meanwhile, in the Royal English School, American missionaries gave yangban students their English lessons. Such schools quickly became alternative avenues of upward mobility in Korea's rigid social system.

Others looked to Japan—young men who later became famous like Kim Ok-kyun, Pak Yŏng-hyo, Sŏ Chae-p'il, Sŏ Kwang-bŏm, Yun Ch'i-ho, and Yu Kil-chun. Several were yangban who had their careers blocked by the Min faction. Yun went on to become an influential modernizer in the twentieth century, Yu became the first Korean to study in the United States (at the Governor Drummer Academy, in Massachusetts), and Sŏ ended up living in America. Regardless of what Korean nationalists may think of them now, Japan's model was a good choice, one made by countless young people throughout Asia who looked to Japan as a shining star of progress, proof positive that not only the "white" races could swim in the new global tides. Sun Yat-sen, Tagore, Ho Chi Minh, and any number of Koreans of all stripes who later distinguished themselves made this choice.

What is unlikely, however, is that they constituted an "enlightenment party," as some scholars have called them, or an "independence party," as others say, or that the 1880s marked a historical period of Korean enlightenment. One or two Western historians have praised "the vitality of Korea's modernization efforts,"[50] but this phase of fitful Westernization cannot remotely be compared to the Meiji Restoration (let alone the Enlightenment in Europe) and was constantly thwarted by reactionary

50. Deuchler (1977), p. 149. One source calls the unequal treaty with the United States in 1882 "one of the most significant enlightenment measures undertaken by the Chosŏn government." (It was, of course, an undertaking of Li and Shufeldt.) See Eckert (1990), p. 203.

scholars and officials. At best it was a pale reflection of China's "self-strengthening movement," both being premised on the idea that Eastern learning would still constitute the philosophical and political "base" (*t'i* in Chinese, *ch'e* in Korean), with Western science and technology for "use" *(yong)*.

The new leaders were young and ambitious, but also were "neither profound philosophers nor great theoreticians; rather, they were idealistic, reform-minded, pro-Japanese and pro-Western, and yet strongly nationalistic politicians. The main source of their inspiration was Japanese liberalism. . . ."[51] Fukuzawa Yukichi, the Japanese reformer most impressed with American modernity, was mentor to several young Koreans who were deeply impressed by Japan's new strides since 1868. Their enthusiasm knew no bounds, but it often ran ahead of thoughtfulness. Hardly French philosophes, they left little writing for posterity, and what there is usually follows in the wake of Japanese popularizers of Western thought, like Fukuzawa, or works by Western progressives of the time. Anyway, there weren't many of them—often no more than a handful. The 1880s were years of enormous technological progress, but the Western liberals of the time were often not much to write home about. Many supported the "civilizing" role of the colonial powers, just as Fukuzawa backed Japanese imperialism in Korea. The young Koreans had no workable program of reform for Korea, but even if they had had one, either their Korean opponents or the big powers would have blocked it.

Pak Yŏng-hyo's well-known "Memorial on Enlightenment" written from exile in Japan in 1888, was a laundry list of what he saw emerging in Japan, or in books about the West: promotion of industry and commerce, new military weaponry and technique, social hygiene, civil liberties, the rule of law, and so on. They were good ideas, of course; they just weren't Korean ideas and never had been—they were of and by the West. If reform means knowing what your starting point is and where you would like to go, this group was in truth alien to everyone in Seoul except the diplomatic community and the missionaries. Its members were not so much enlightened as quite properly dazzled by the progress they saw rushing toward them in the 1880s: steamships, railroads, electricity, the telegraph; all the world was stunned by this explosion of "high technology," this unrestrained progress, and the Korean reformers ran toward it.

Pak Yŏng-hyo's later career perhaps underlines these points. He returned to Korea in 1894, where he held a position in the reform cabinet tutored by Japanese advisers, and was part of Yi Wan-yong's infamous cabinet in 1910—yielding Pak an eventual appointment to the Japanese

51. Lee (1988), p. 67.

House of Lords. Later on he served on the boards of Kim Sŏng-su's large textile firm and the Korean Industrial Bank.[52]

When the reformers actually did something in 1884, their action program was all too "traditional": seize power at the top and then impose their ideas. But they added a new wrinkle: they would do it in league with the local Japanese, whom they had contacted secretly and asked to put troops at the ready. The minister to Seoul, Takezoe Shinichirō, and several resident Japanese officials plotted this action with the "enlightenment party." (Many other Japanese were also in Korea at the time—technicians who were laying a telegraph cable between the two countries, disciples of Fukuzawa who arrived as advisers on various matters; all were chaperoned by Japanese guards or soldiers.) The scene was a dinner party with foreign diplomats and Korean officials to inaugurate the new post office, on December 4, 1884; the goal was a new government; the method was a night of the long knives in which at least seven Korean officials were murdered. In the middle of it Japanese legation guards materialized to protect the king and queen, and more or less hold them hostage.

The argument of the reformers was that working within the existing Korean political system was impossible. Trying to topple it proved just as impossible; on their "first day in office," as one approving scholar called it, the conspirators issued a fourteen-point reform program. Alas, that proved to be their only day in office, as Yüan Shih-kai moved fifteen hundred Chinese soldiers into the palace where the conspirators held forth, chasing them and the Japanese soldiers over to the Japanese legation and inflicting heavy casualties. Then Yüan (who had arrived in Korea in 1882 and would soon play a dominant role in Korean affairs) grabbed the king and deposited him at his own headquarters.

By then Seoul's populace had learned of this uproarious affair. Outraged Koreans ransacked Japanese homes and marched on the legation, sending Takezoe packing quickly off to Inch'ŏn, from which he dispatched panicky cables to Tokyo. A few days later Yüan let the king go, all the high ministers came back, and they rescinded every decree and reform—they even shut down the new post office. Then came Korean negotiations with Japan: Korea protested its interference in internal Korean affairs and demanded the return of the conspirators. Japan, however, wanted an apology and an indemnity for property loss, and it made a bunch of other demands, all in spite of the blatant involvement of its representatives and nationals in this coup d'état. All that it wanted Japan got, after landing two battalions of troops and marching them into Seoul.

As for the reformers, their bid for power was as puerile and rash as it

52. Eckert (1991), p. 99.

was disastrous. As Shin Ch'ae-ho later wrote, the coup "was nothing more than a dramatic struggle between special forces in the palace" with no support among the Korean people,[53] and it either finished the reformers off or stymied them for years. Those who survived mostly took asylum in Japan (after being stuffed into boxes and smuggled aboard a Japanese freighter), and a couple of others went to the West to study. Kim Ok-kyun was murdered a decade later by another Korean in Shanghai. (The Chinese allowed the assassin to take Kim's remains home to Korea, where they were chopped up and posted for public viewing.)[54]

A brief parenthesis of potential Korean independence opened in April 1885 after Li Hung-chang and Itō Hirobumi signed the Convention of Tientsin, leading to a mutual withdrawal of their troops from Korea. Kojong's policy of using power to check power seemed momentarily to work. Just then, however, four British warships took up residence at "Port Hamilton" on Kŏmun Island, off the southeastern coast. The "great game" between Britain and Russia had arrived in Korea: both imperial powers worried that the temporary stalemate between Japan and China might open a vacuum for the other in Korea. Soon the wily Russian diplomat Alexis de Speyer moved his residence from Tokyo to Seoul; he claimed to have instructions to annex ten Korean acres for every one the British claimed, should they not vacate Kŏmun Island. Kojong importuned the "good offices" of the United States, as per the 1882 treaty; the United States paid no notice. But Speyer was just bluffing, and soon he was gone.

Thus ended "Korea's first decade of modernization," as one Western scholar put it; "Korea's response to modernization" had been inhibited by the big powers, to be sure, but "Korean conservatism" had also been a "retarding factor." Another said that the 1884 coup should have led to a revolution like the one the Meiji leaders accomplished in Japan. An omniscient genius sitting on the Korean throne could barely have done a thing about Korean "modernization" amid such a scramble for its real estate, nor was the Meiji Restoration something that came in one night: it had been prepared by decades of agrarian and urban commercialization. In fact the ten years after the Kanghwa Treaty produced a Korea that was increasingly a plaything of the great powers; even the king moved from one legation to another, and not for the last time. With the failure of a coherent and sincere restoration, and the failure of a sincere

53. Quoted in Kang Man'gil, "Contemporary Nationalist Movements and the Minjung," in Wells (1995), p. 33.

54. Han (1972), pp. 390–95; Deuchler (1972), pp. 205–11; Gale (1972), p. 315. Gale noted that however gruesome this act might be, it was no different from "Cromwell's grinning head set on a pike-point on Westminster Hall for twenty-three years."

but incoherent progressive reformism, the opportunity for state-led reform to save Korea had passed.

THE TONGHAK MOVEMENT: REFORM BY ANOTHER NAME

So far we have not had much to say about Korea's most numerous class, the millions of peasants who tilled the fields day in and day out so that the aristocracy could be free to conduct its pursuits, high-minded and otherwise. If modern Korea can be defined by the coming of the industrial powers, so it is also defined by the participation in politics of ordinary peasants: and both came at the same time. After years and decades of agricultural distress, a movement arose in the 1860s, under the name Eastern Learning, or Tonghak. It adopted a pithy slogan: "Drive out the Japanese dwarfs and the Western barbarians, and praise righteousness."[55]

At this time Korea's taxation system was an orrery of infuriating exactions, most of them attached in one way or another to agrarian production. Because it was fundamentally weak in relation to the aristocracy, the state tried to raise money every which way and grabbed everything it could put its hands on, giving next to nothing in the way of service. There were government taxes, land taxes (not one but a variety, plus surcharges and handling fees), taxes on fallow fields, military taxes (one bolt of cloth from every able-bodied male, often more ruinous than the land taxes), taxes to the local officials, taxes to the local estates, all this not counting taxes on salt, fish, boats, and many other commodities. Every living thing that could be taxed was taxed, including tiny babies and the elderly, relatives and neighbors of people who had fled the tax collector, not to mention dead people. When the tax man got you, you could pay him off by getting a loan at usurious interest—from state officials through the infamous grain loan system, or from local moneylenders, who had been a thorn in everyone's flesh from time immemorial.[56] The rational thing to do was to escape taxes, by jumping on the student roll, or the official roll, or the privileged clan roll, above all the tax- and draft-exempt yangban roll, or bribe a petty clerk to tax someone else, or just abscond to the mountains and raise your crops there. Only the sedentary subsistence peasant families, tied to the land, were always around to be fleeced.

During the 1850s a man named Ch'oe Che-u (1824–64) began propagating among peasants a doctrine called Tonghak. Like Hung Hsiu-

55. Hatada (1969), p. 100.
56. Palais (1975), pp. 100–102, and passim.

ch'üan, the leader of the massive Taip'ing Rebellion in mid-nineteenth-century China, Ch'oe had failed the civil service exams. After a period of wandering he originated a millenarian, syncretic doctrine combining what he thought were the best ideas of Confucianism, Buddhism, and Taoism into a potent mix that would protect Korea against the influx of Western learning *(sŏhak)*. Ch'oe was also influenced by Catholicism in spite of himself, but above all by native Korean beliefs in spirits and mountain deities. His main idea was the unity of heaven and mankind and thus the universal equality of all people, which he mingled with magical chants and the usual village hocus-pocus, accumulating disgruntled and tax-avoiding peasants as he went along. The hocus-pocus ranged from emptying rice bags on a mountain pass to propitiate a disgruntled spirit, to highly popular oral songs and performances called *p'ansori,* to colorful, satirical mask dances that thrilled peasants with passages like these:

> I'll eat them raw at low tide, cram my maw at high tide,
> Devour my *yangban* masters nine and ninety.
> Then I'll eat one more and lo!
> A dragon now become, mount the throne of Heaven.[57]

Peasant rebellions broke out in 1862, whereupon it was found that the military was way under strength: "the number of soldiers . . . was only a fraction of those listed on the [tax-exempt] military registers,"[58] serving the officials right for bleeding all who could be bled. But they nabbed Ch'oe in 1863 and executed him the next year, driving his followers underground for three decades.

The opening of the country in the 1870s only deepened the plight of the peasantry. Rice was now going to Japan in ever greater quantities, causing rapid rises in price (the profits of which went to middlemen) and inflation in the cost of daily necessities. Coastal fishing families lost out to Japanese fishery companies, now plying Korean waters in ever larger numbers. Droughts came in 1876–77 and again in 1888–89, especially in the rice-rich southwestern Chŏlla provinces. Tax revenues accordingly dropped, necessitating more exactions from the peasants. Korea had always had a pattern of peasant rebellions similar to China's, and once again in the 1880s the classic signs abounded: "Well-armed and organized robber bands began to appear, with bases deep in the mountains, attacking shipments of tax grain and convoys of imported goods on their way to Seoul . . . [along with] a wave of local uprisings

57. Lee (1984), p. 260.
58. Palais (1975), p. 101.

of various kinds, usually against corrupt officials."[59] The flickering flame of Ch'oe Che-u's movement now flared up again, and again in the name of anti-foreignism and reform. But unlike the Taewŏn'gun, the Tonghaks would not shrink from smashing the aristocracy.

By 1892 Tonghak demonstrations were common in the southwestern region, but the government was slow to respond; the governor of Ch'ungch'ŏng Province blithely seized rebel properties as he moved to suppress the movement. Fire signals in the mountains in early 1893 linked rebel groups together to mount wider actions, including demands that Ch'oe be rehabilitated. At least twenty thousand converged on the town of Poŭn in April, nearly taking it over before the authorities succeeded in scattering them. Soon four Tonghak leaders showed up in Seoul with a petition, kneeling for three days at the palace gates. In his response Kojong offered this:

> 500 years have passed and the world has fallen into exceeding great evils, so that every man does what is right in his own eyes—very bad! . . . What you call *hak* or "learning," said to be the honour of God, is in reality an attempt to deceive God. For what purpose do you act thus? Your building of walls, your flying of flags, your scattering of leaflets merely stir up the people. Such practices will bring a sea of troubles on Korea and end in war.[60]

Now compare the rhetoric of Tonghak leaflets:

> The people are the root of the nation. If the root withers, the nation will be enfeebled. Heedless of their responsibility for sustaining the state and providing for its people, the officials build lavish residences in the countryside. . . . We are wretched village people far from the capital, yet we feed and clothe ourselves with the bounty from the sovereign's land. We cannot sit by and watch our nation perish. The whole nation is as one, its multitudes united in their determination to raise the righteous standard of revolt. . . . [W]hen all the people can enjoy the blessings of benevolent kingly rule, how immeasurably joyful will we be![61]

The four men returned home, as the king had bid them. Suddenly wall writings appeared all over Seoul, calling for the expulsion of foreigners and the extirpation of Catholicism. Diplomats bolted their doors as the capital's grapevine claimed that tens of thousands of Tonghaks would

59. Han (1974), p. 404.
60. Gale's translation, in Gale (1972), p. 316. Gale substitutes "God" for something else, probably "heaven."
61. Lee (1984), p. 284.

soon scale Seoul's ramparts. But nothing happened for the time being.

Things came to a head about a year later after an instructive example of the ineffable arrogance and corruption of the old ruling class came to Chŏlla in the form of Cho Pyŏng-gap. Arriving as district magistrate in Kobu, he offered the peasants tax exemption if they would bring fallow land under cultivation, whereupon he proceeded to tax the now not fallow land. He put corvée laborers to work on irrigation projects and pocketed their pay for himself. Meanwhile, he accused local wealthy people of crimes, thus to blackmail them.

The Tonghak leader in the area was Chŏn Pong-jun, a village teacher *(sŏnsaeng)* so typical of local influentials in Korea and China. He gathered a thousand peasants, occupied the country office, seized weapons from an armory, demolished the irrigation reservoir Cho had forced them to build, and distributed grain stocks to the starving peasants. Seoul's response was to send down people to arrest the protesters, which touched off a general conflagration. Tonghaks rose all over the southwest, distinguished by their brightly colored headbands and waistbands; when they couldn't find guns, they sharpened bamboo sticks and honed farm tools. The provincial governor in Chŏnju sent troops to attack them, but by now many rebels had weapons and they easily overcame the government soldiers, many of whom deserted to the Tonghak. Soon one town after another in Chŏlla was in the hands of the rebels.

By now the government in Seoul was thoroughly alarmed, and the king promised to dismiss all the corrupt officials in the region. The Tonghaks said they wanted two things beyond that: fair taxation and a halt to rice exports to Japan. The authorities agreed, which only emboldened the movement. Now the whole social system came under attack: the Tonghaks tabled twelve sharp demands, including the removal of yangban oppression, the burning of slave registers, an end to the strict social hierarchy, and a general redistribution of the land. Number six demanded that *paekchŏng* outcastes no longer be required to wear "their distinctive 'P'yŏngyang hat' " (Korea's class structure, like our own at the time, showed itself in what people wore on their heads).[62] A classic peasant rebellion had turned into a modern demand for agrarian revolution—all in the name of restoring a proper moral and political order. The rebels had fought Japanese soldiers in the name of "our nation" *(uri nara),* a kind of proto-nationalism. Korea was getting more and more "modern" all the time.

Kojong detached eight hundred men from the elite capital garrison to put down the rebellion. Half of them deserted, and the other half proved

62. The twelve demands are in Lee (1984), p. 287. See also Han (1974), pp. 407–13.

no match for the Tonghaks, in spite of far superior weaponry. At the end of May the rebels took over the capital of Chŏnju. Now Kojong panicked and sought the aid of Li Hung-chang, who dispatched a flotilla to Inch'ŏn—but not before informing Tokyo, as called for under their existing "convention." Needless to say, Japan had its warships under steam forthwith. By June 10, 1894, both countries had begun to pour troops into Korea, even though the rebellion had by then been quelled. Kojong asked that the foreign troops be removed, and China proposed a mutual withdrawal. It was too late: the Japanese meant business, they held the strong hand, and they proceeded to play it. On July 23 their soldiers occupied the royal palace and took control of the king, forcing Kojong to bring the Taewŏn'gun back to power—now sponsored by Japan, in a strange twist. But then Queen Min had been pro-Chinese and an enemy of the Taewŏn'gun; the old man was happy to watch the Japanese expel her and her presumed friend Yüan Shih-kai (who fled Seoul in disguise). Two days later a Japanese man-of-war blasted Chinese ships off the Korean coast near Asan, and the Sino-Japanese War began.

One victory followed upon another, humiliating China, demonstrating Japan's newly risen power to the world, and putting the Korean state under the Japanese wing. The big losers appeared to be the rebellious peasants of Chŏlla, as the Japanese demanded and got the opening of all ports on the southwest coast—thus to export even more rice. Chŏn Pong-jun waited until October 1894, after the harvest, and then stimulated an immense peasant uprising in Chŏlla and Ch'ungch'ŏng. At least one hundred thousand people participated in these protests, with the largest crowd surging into Nonsan. Japanese forces were still fighting the Chinese, but when Tonghaks attacked their supply bases, they broke off some crack units that caught up with the main body of peasants near Kongju. After a week of fierce battle the Japanese forces routed the rebels, with great loss of life. They chased after stragglers and those who sought to escape, killing them mercilessly; they were still hunting Tonghaks down in January 1895. Meanwhile, the authorities in Seoul captured and executed Chŏn Pong-jun and several other Tonghak leaders.

The rebellion was over, and soon, so was the Sino-Japanese War. Japan was completely victorious, China's age-old relationship with Korea was severed for the next fifty years, Japan now occupied Taiwan and made the island its first colony, and China ceded rights to Port Arthur and the strategic Liaot'ung peninsula, in Manchuria. This was too big a bite by pilot fish Japan in the eyes of the other imperialist sharks, so the Tripartite Intervention (Russia, France, Germany) forced it to give up Liaot'ung. The Tonghak lived on in the *Ch'ŏndogyo* (Heavenly Way) religious movement, which influenced Korean peasants for decades thereafter and was an early stimulant of Korean nationalism. This massive rebellion also cleared the way for Korea's first truly modern reforms, as commercial and industrial efforts began and semifeudal restrictions on Korea's multitude were lifted. Although the reforms came under Japanese auspices, it is from 1894 on that we can speak of Korea's modern period. It came a couple of decades after Japan got off the mark, however, a dangerous and ultimately fatal lead time.

THE BIRTH OF MODERN KOREA

A powerless Taewŏn'gun and a new premiership under Kim Hong-jip provided the fig leaf for Otori Keisuke, the Japanese minister, and a host of Japanese and Korean aides to send reform after reform through for the signature of Kojong (who duly signed every one, and no doubt any autumn leaves that wafted across his desk). Known as the *kabo* reforms,[63] 208 separate laws were from the end of July 1894 endorsed by the king: class distinctions, slavery, the exam system, even the clothes Koreans wore, even the long pipes that symbolized yangban status, were abolished; a new State Council, with eight ministries on the Japanese model (Home Affairs, Finance, etc.), was established and new and stable coinage circulated; new tax laws unified the extraction system, with rational taxes now to be paid in cash; the practice of punishing whole families for the transgressions of criminals came to an end. No more would the high officials ride in sedan chairs, hustled along by several groaning wretches.

Now the man who had shepherded the first Korean mission to new Japan, Inoue Kaoru, arrived in Seoul to replace Otori. He quickly sent the Taewŏn'gun into his last retirement. The old man hated the new reforms almost as much as he did the Japanese; he had come back to government only because he loathed Queen Min even more. (Many assumed that he had also encouraged the Tonghak revolts.) So ended the career of a remarkable Korean leader who showed to a modern world the vigor of Confucian reform, almost as if history enjoyed exhaling the last hearty gasp of a dying order.

Under Inoue still more new laws spewed forth, calling for Japanese advisers in every ministry and reorganizing the justice system. Korea now had a legal-rational court system and a countrywide national police. All of these reforms were capped in a new constitution, promulgated in January 1895. Inoue also brought from Japan two of the 1884 conspirators, Pak Yŏng-hyo and Sŏ Kwang-bŏm, placing them in high posts. Korean nationalists naturally see in these reforms and these people only

63. The best source is Lew (1972).

the furtherance of Japan's economic and political interests in Korea,[64] and it is true that however indispensable the measures might have been, change under foreign auspices cannot substitute for autonomously activated reform. No one else saw Japan's actions in this light, however. For most Westerners, Japan in this period was a shining beacon of enlightenment; for other Asians, it was a mecca of progress; and for Koreans who had groaned under the yoke of an aristocracy that, as it neared total collapse, seemed only to exact more privilege for itself, the reforms were a welcome antidote.

What would a slave or a butcher care for the pride of the yangban, now shamed by Japan? Think of what Japan had done: in the space of two decades it had transformed its small country into a power that could humiliate China. For the first time in recorded history, civilization no longer spread outward from the Middle Kingdom; industrial might had reversed the East Asian hierarchy, with Japan now on top, Korea sticking in the middle because of these millennial reforms, and China on the bottom—"sick man of Asia." (And in the next few years the imperial powers carved China up like a Christmas turkey.) A hundred years later, that new 1890s East Asian hierarchy has still not been overturned.

Korean leaders, however, again mistook a temporary balance of power (this time between Japan and Russia) for a vacuum they could fill. They began firing pro-Japanese officials and reversing some of the 1894 reforms. A new Japanese minister, Miura Goro, had a different idea: he thought that the Taewŏn'gun, once again, could be counted on to hate the queen enough to be coaxed back into the government. In October 1895 a Japanese guard unit went to meet the Taewŏn'gun outside the West Gate of Seoul, to escort him back to Kyŏngbok Palace. A Korean "training unit" accompanied this retinue, and when it reached the palace the Japanese and Korean soldiers fought their way into the palace, grabbed Queen Min before she could run away, and stabbed her in the chest. They then dragged her out to the garden, doused her with kerosene and lit a match, hoping to destroy the evidence of their foul deed.

Japan denied any involvement, but American and Russian advisers had been in the palace and witnessed the murder. Much later, documents came to light showing that Miura had plotted every aspect of the murder with Japanese thugs, who had quietly joined the procession as it entered the palace grounds. After wide international protest, Tokyo punished some of the miscreants and got on with the reform program. Seoul now got a primary education system, open to all. The reformers overplayed their hand, however, by decreeing that all Korean men

64. See Han (1974), pp. 418–27, for example, which also has a good account of the reforms.

should have short, Western-style hair, meaning that the venerable topknot was now against the law. The most recalcitrant Korean males—Hongians all—were ordered to get a haircut. Here is how Gale once described this Korean fashion, which is thought by some historians to date back to Old Chosŏn in the third century B.C.: "On the gentleman's head was a headband, tied after long practice, tight enough to squeeze tears from the eyes. Above the band was a little cap, beautifully woven of horsehair. Above this sat the gauze hat, a cage for the topknot that you dimly glimpsed through the meshes."[65]

This affront, akin to Delilah's asking Samson to cut his tresses and coming on the heels of the queen's assassination, spawned armed uprisings all over the country. Insurgents cried out, "If you want to cut off my topknot, you'll have to cut off my head first." In the middle of this uproar, on February 11, 1896, some 120 sailors from a Russian ship docked at Inch'ŏn, accompanied by some willing Korean officials. They waltzed into the palace and—with much help from Kojong—stole the king from under the Japanese nose.

The king and the crown prince had the bright idea to disguise themselves as court ladies and use the royal women's cloistered sedan chairs to abscond to the Russian legation, thus to escape Japanese ministrations. This they did, "crouched pale and trembling" as they left the palace gates early in the morning of February 11;[66] Kojong remained in the legation for almost exactly one year. From a puck on a shuffleboard gallery he had become a shuttlecock, batted around by the powers. But nothing could move without his royal seal affixed, he was not unhappy, and so with this simple act Russia now dominated the Korean government. The Japanese had to take all this sitting down, or go to war: but antiquated China was one thing, Count Witte's new Russia another, and they were not yet ready.

Kojong fired his pro-Japanese cabinet, and yet did not really become a creature of the Russians. He continued to work with Horace Allen and other foreign diplomats and was "more Japanophobe than Russophile," in George Lensen's apt words. Although the Russians were like every other foreign mission in believing the Koreans to be hapless and unable to govern themselves without a strong foreign hand behind the king, they interfered little in domestic affairs during the period that Kojong was in the legation; indeed, it was the king who feared returning to his own palace. Thus he was no prisoner of the Czars.[67]

65. Gale (1972), p. 58.

66. Lensen (1982), pp. 583–84.

67. Lensen (1982), p. 591. Arguments to the contrary are many, but they are usually shaped not by the facts but either by the interests of British and Japanese diplomacy at the

During Kojong's sojourn in the Russian legation, however, Tokyo and Moscow began conjuring with the idea of dividing Korea into spheres of influence. Negotiations in May 1896 in Moscow nearly yielded a partition of Korea along a mid-peninsula boundary line, although apparently not at the thirty-eighth or thirty-ninth parallel as many historians have claimed. Their agreement did, however, yield a different kind of historically resonant space: one free of troops lying between the two armies at a geographic point never quite specified, that is, a demilitarized zone.[68]

In February 1897 Kojong returned to his palace and proceeded to have himself named emperor, since *wang*, or king, did not sufficiently connote the independent status he now claimed for Korea and since it furthermore allowed both Japan and China to "talk down" to him. Following an old ritual, his ministers offered this idea nine times and Kojong refused it eight times; but the ninth head knock did the magic trick. Court astrologers picked the most auspicious time for this grand event, which unfortunately turned out to be three in the morning on October 12. Undaunted, the imperial procession sallied forth. Korea became the Great Han Empire (Taehan Cheguk), whence comes the name Taehan Min'guk of the postwar Republic of Korea, and Kojong became the Emperor of Great Han, or *Taehan hwangjae*—all before dawn.

Not only his ministers but many foreign diplomats kowtowed before him, as many as nine times, depending on their rank. If the diplomats were less than overwhelmed by this new Korean empire, they were thoroughly appalled a few weeks later when Kojong spent a fortune to have the remains of Queen Min—reportedly consisting of the bone of one of her fingers—ceremoniously buried. (Of course, they had no understanding of the importance and weight of official burial rights for such a legendary figure.) Again the diplomats had to turn out before dawn, courtesy of Kojong's early-rising astrologers, along with 5,000 soldiers, 650 police, 4,000 lanterns, hundreds of testaments to the queen born aloft on scrolls, giant wooden horses for her later use, a procession that took hours—all followed by days of wailing and beating the ground by countless Korean mourners.[69]

Kojong now fancied himself a power broker able to feed one tidbit of Korean sovereignty to one power, a second tidbit to another. He doled

time or by the hindsight that came with the arrival of Soviet troops in Korea after World War II. Lensen has a sober analysis of Russian aims in Korea, arguing that the Czars never were willing to do much to get from Korea the infamous "warm-water port" that subsequent generations assumed to have been the daily goal of Moscow's diplomacy, and no longer desired it at all after leasing Port Arthur on the China mainland (pp. 850–54).

68. Lensen (1982), pp. 630–34.

69. Lensen (1982), pp. 642–44, has a colorful description.

out Korea's resources as if from a Chinese menu: column A—gold mines, railroads, a new electric system for Seoul—went to Americans; column B—banks and timber rights—he divided between Britain and Russia; meanwhile, Japan was still by far the most active commercial nation in Korea. Its Daiichi Ginkō was virtually the central bank, with branches all around the country. More than two hundred Japanese businesses now operated in Korea, compared with about fifty from other countries. Foreigners from all over ran the Korean customs service and other agencies at the nexus of Korea's new contacts with the world economy. In the meantime, all sorts of Koreans were taking upon themselves the tasks of modernity.

Many landlords had prospered after 1876, because of the rising export trade and new markets for Korea's rice. Aristocrats now began to translate landed wealth into commercial property, men like Kim Chong-han: from a wealthy family, he passed the prestigious *munkwa* exams in 1877, became a civil servant, and in the 1890s founded the Hansŏng Bank and the first Bank of Korea. Others, like Pak Ki-jŏng, pulled themselves up by their bootstraps. Born in Pusan in 1839 and lacking a formal education, Pak picked up Japanese, became an interpretor at Pusan House, prospered as external trade grew, and eventually helped open one of the Korean railway companies.[70]

Korean reformers influenced by the West, like Phillip Jaisohn (Sŏ Chae-p'il, he had studied in the United States) and Yun Ch'i-ho launched, an "Independence Club" in 1896 to promote Westernization and used the vernacular *han'gŭl* in their newspaper, the *Tongnip* (Independent), alternating pages of *han'gŭl* with English. The club included many Koreans who had studied Western learning in Protestant missionary schools, and for a while they influenced not only young reformers but elements of the Korean court; one of the reformers was Yi Sŭngman, otherwise known as Syngman Rhee (1875–1965, first president of the ROK). They made some advances in advocating civil and political rights, and doing whatever a small, elite club could by way of moving Korea toward parliamentary democracy. The club was soon repressed, however, by combinations of government police and irregular hoodlums (often itinerant peddlers), and collapsed after two years. Although many historians claim that the club was a champion of Korean independence and an avatar of democracy and modern civil society, its leaders were as captured by the rhetoric of American progressivism—right down to the denigration of the achievements of their own people—as the 1884 coup leaders had been by Japanese reformism.[71]

70. Cumings (1991), p. 18.
71. Michael Shin, seminar paper (University of Chicago, April 1994).

Yun Ch'i-ho, the president of this group, was born in 1865, into a prominent family, which by 1910 had founded one of Korea's first textile firms (the Kyŏngsŏng Cord Company). He studied in Japan in the early 1880s, then in Shanghai, where he attended the Anglo-Chinese College, then in the United States, where he attended a Methodist college until 1893. He returned to Korea in 1895 and edited the *Tongnip,* while participating in the politics of the Independence Club. A founder of the Seoul YMCA and many other new institutions, Yun was imprisoned in 1911 with 104 other men, implicated in a plot to assassinate the colonial governor-general. He later collaborated with Japan, however, and became a peer in the House of Lords. In 1945 he retired to his old family residence in Kaesŏng, and not long thereafter he died. (Many claimed he committed suicide, but his family said he had a stroke.)[72] Yun Po-sŏn, a well-known opposition leader in the 1960s, came from the same family.

Korean society was showing unaccustomed vigor, but the state was still incapable of mobilizing this latent energy. The only question now was which imperial power would colonize Korea. Japan found a champion in Theodore Roosevelt, who like many other Westerners saw Japan as a model of Asian modernization; the British were even more awestruck, as everyone from royalists to Fabians lauded Japan's progress. Phillip Lyttleton Gell, for example, wrote in 1904, "I shall turn Japanese for they at least can think, and be reticent! [Witness] their organization, their strategy, their virile qualities, their devotion and self-control. Above all, their national capacity for self-reliance, self-sacrifice, and their silence!"[73] In 1902 England established an alliance with Japan and, along with the United States, gave Japan a free hand in Korea.

To the north Russia was also expanding, developing the railway system in Manchuria and exploiting forests and gold mines in the northern part of Korea. Americans, too, were particularly active. Horace Allen, the first American doctor-missionary in Korea, embodied the tryptic of American expansion all by himself: missionary, diplomat, and businessman extraordinaire, he secured for James R. Morse Korea's best gold mine through a concession from Kojong, and arranged other concessions for rail and trolley lines (Seoul's first streetcars), Seoul's waterworks, and its new telephone network. Allen was a man with a quick answer at the ready when Kojong asked him, in 1887, how he might interest the United States in Korea as a way of balancing Chinese influence: "Give the gold mining franchise to an American company."[74] That didn't hap-

72. Rutt, in Gale (1972), p. 73.

73. Quoted in Colin Holmes and A. H. Ion, "Bushido and the Samurai: Images in British Public Opinion, 1894–1914," *Modern Asian Studies* 14 (1980): 304–29.

74. Harrington (1944), p. 130.

pen, however, until 1895. Allen also founded the first Western hospital and medical school in 1885, which still operates in Seoul, now called Severance Hospital. (Fortunately there is a great book about this remarkable man, Fred Harvey Harrington's *God, Mammon, and the Japanese.*)

American interests in Korea also included electric power lines and the main power plant in Seoul, a virtual monopoly by Standard Oil on kerosene for the lamps of Korea, plus an oil storage facility on Wŏlmi-do. Russia had coaling stations on Choryŏng and Wŏlmi islands, timber concessions along the Yalu, and smaller gold mines; England used Kŏmun Island as a coaling station and, with the (American) Morgan interests, also got a gold mine at Unsan. Japan had coaling stations on Yŏngdo, off Pusan, and also on Wŏlmi, and built the first Seoul–Pusan railway.

During Yüan Shih-kai's residency Chinese merchants flocked to Korean treaty ports, and although they often outdistanced the Japanese with their mercantile skills (helped along by Yüan's many soldiers), they behaved little better than Japanese carpetbaggers, by then a common bane of Koreans' existence. When they had trouble getting permission for travel outside the treaty zones, Yüan issued them passes just as he pleased. The Chinese sold silk, cotton, kerosene, herbs, and Western clothes and cosmetics, and bought hides, soybeans, gold, and Korean ceramics. By the mid-1890s imports from China were almost as valuable as those from Japan (Mexican $2.06 million vs. $2.6 million).[75]

Japan made far greater inroads in Korea than did China, however. Yüan's residency was the last gasp of a dying order; Japan's merchants, the cat's feet of the new movement. In 1880 a new treaty port had opened in Wŏnsan, midway up the peninsula on the east coast. A narrow cape curving outward from the shore created one of the best natural harbors in East Asia—deep, capacious, and ice-free the year around. Wŏnsan had been a local market town for centuries, selling rice, red pepper, garlic, tobacco, cotton and hemp cloth, and a few precious items from China. By 1883 it was home to the offices of Mitsubishi, Sumitomo, and the Daiichi Ginkō, or First Bank of Japan. Two steamships, the *Tokyo maru* and the *Satsuma maru,* carried merchandise between Wŏnsan and Vladivostok, calling at the port once or twice a month. The Wŏnsan customs service was directed by a Dane, J. F. Oiesen, assisted by several Englishmen with Chinese and Japanese wives. A small Japanese business community, serviced by a consular office, lived alongside Russian and Chinese traders. Much of the import trade was in textiles, not Japanese but reexported British calicos and shirts. Now Korea exported hides, soybeans, wheat, traditional items like ginseng and fish products, and,

75. Han (1974), pp. 389–91, 400–401; Lee (1984), pp. 288–89. (Mexican currency was frequently used in East Asian trade.)

above all, rice, which was often two-thirds of the export total. Korea's substantial deposits of gold encouraged a lot of prospecting and freebooting, and gold poured out of the country in an unregulated trade that probably exceeded all other exports in value.[76]

A few years later James Gale was appointed to the new Presbyterian mission post in this port city, and he embarked by pony and sedan chair from Seoul to Wŏnsan along the dirt path connecting the two cities (Wŏnsan was more of a town, having only two thousand thatched homes), a distance of some 135 miles, which took a week to cover. A Korean bannerman in blue coat and black felt hat, with "a scarlet oxtail attached," cleared the way for the entourage; "the roadsides were in bloom with hawthorn and sweet white honey-suckle, and the air was full of skylarks' song." The few roadside inns were full of fleas and mice; one night a tiger snatched a pig from the front yard of an inn and "the whole village turned out with flares and gongs" to scare it off. Life in Wŏnsan was slow and bucolic, save for the occasional tiger strolling through the Gales' front yard, or the errant lepers "who might at any time seek the traditional cure for their complaint, the flesh of children."[77]

AN "UNSPEAKABLE GROOVINESS": WESTERN IMPRESSIONS OF KOREA

We can close this chapter with a look at some first Western impressions of Korea, as the ancien régime creaked to a halt. They were generally bad, as attested to by all too many late-nineteenth-century writings; still, the accounts are often fascinating for the glimpse of a West thoroughly confident of itself and mostly incapable of comprehending what it saw in Korea. For those who remained to get beyond first impressions—usually for three yen per day at Mme Sontag's hotel,[78] where most foreigners stayed—initial dismay often gave way to appreciation. The main point is that from this encounter of progressive, enlightened Westerners and benighted, decrepit old Korea, one could never have predicted Korea's position in the world today.

Isabella Bird Bishop, an intrepid adventurer who visited and wrote about many exotic places in the world, began by calumniating all Koreans and ended up returning to the country out of fascination with it. "It is into this archaic condition of things, this unspeakable grooviness," she wrote in 1897,

76. Deuchler (1977), pp. 79–82; Gale (1972), p. 23; Han (1974), p. 399.

77. Gale (1972), pp. 22–24.

78. Imperial Japanese Government Railways, *An Official Guide to Eastern Asia, vol. 1, Manchuria and Chōsen* (Tokyo, 1913), p. 267.

> this irredeemable, unreformed Orientalism, this parody of China without the robustness of race which help to hold China together, that the ferment of the Western leaven has fallen, [on] this feeblest of independent kingdoms, rudely shaken out of her sleep of centuries, half frightened and wholly dazed. . . .

Arriving in Pusan, she recoiled in horror:

> Its narrow dirty streets consist of low hovels built of mud-smeared wattle without windows, straw roofs, and deep eaves, a black smoke hole in every wall 2 feet from the ground, and outside most are irregular ditches containing solid and liquid refuse. Mangy dogs and blear-eyed children, half or wholly naked, and scaly with dirt, roll in the deep dust or slime, or pant and blink in the sun. . . .

Seoul wasn't much better, although it stirred her to onomatopoeia:

> I shrink from describing intra-mural Seoul. I thought it the foulest city on earth till I saw Peking, and its smells the most odious, till I encountered Shao-shing! For a great city and a capital its meanness is indescribable.

Koreans were so backward commercially, Ms. Bishop thought, "that 'trade' in the ordinary sense has no existence in a great part of central and northern Korea, i.e., there is no exchange of commodities between one place and another, no exports. . . ." Furthermore, she found but two social classes, "the Robbers and the Robbed"; the yangban were "the licensed vampires of the country," and the other four-fifths of the nation "supply the blood for the vampires to suck." But just as we are ready to conclude that Isabella herself is an "irredeemable, unreformed Orientalist," Korea melts her heart:

> The distaste that I felt for the country at first passed into an interest which is almost affection, and on no previous journey have I made dearer or kinder friends. . . . I saw the last of Seoul in snow in the blue and violet atmosphere of one of the loveliest of her winter mornings. . . .[79]

Bishop was by no means alone in her terrible first impressions, which came from taking the surface squalor of a system in terminal decay for the substance. But then the American capital, Washington, was nothing to write home about in the nineteenth century: it had open sewers, piles of garbage, scruffy animals running through its dirt roads and paths, little if any sanitation.

The way foreigners recoiled often began with Korean sartorial display.

79. Bishop (1897), pp. 22, 27, 40, 304–5, 448, 459.

George Kennan, elder cousin to our George Kennan, and a person who took appearances for reality, excoriated Koreans for wearing "the fantastic and unbecoming dress of the Ming Dynasty," thus looking "so much like clowns in a circus."[80] He was right; it was indeed Ming dress, brought to Korea by a Taoist monk in 1380, with the hope that it would become Korea's favorite costume. This change coincided with the introduction of cotton from China, together with spinning jennies to weave it.[81] Before long, Koreans became known as "white people" *(paengmin)* and remained that way down to the Korean War, when American soldiers thought that Korean peasants went around in "white pajamas." Still, James Gale had a much better rendering of this outfit than did George Kennan:

> When the writer came to this country, the first thing that completely bowled him over, speaking metaphorically, was the manner of dress. Men walked in the streets in long tinted robes made of the finest silk, with a girdle across the chest of blue or green or scarlet. Nebuchadnezzar himself was surely never so adorned. The wide sleeves hung down on each side, deeper and more capacious than Aunt Miranda's pocket. Sometimes this robe was divided at the back, sometimes at the sides; sometimes it was a complete roundabout, or *turumagi*. . . . Over his eyes was a huge pair of spectacles, much like those Americans affect today, though more stunning in appearance. Back of his ears were gold buttons or jade; under his chin a lovely string of amber beads; in his right hand a waving fan; on his feet the daintiest pair of shoes mortal ever wore, wedded to a pair of socks white as Malachi's fuller never dreamed *[sic]*, the only really beautiful footgear in all the world. As he walked along with measured tread, the lengthy robe adding inches to his height, he was indeed one of the most startling surprises that the eye of the west ever rested upon.[82]

By comparison Kennan's observations merely dwelled upon the misleading visible edge of Korean civilization, and indulged in the widespread turn-of-the-century assumption that race was an indelible mark, a permanent attribute standing in the way of progress. This combination produced commentary/dysentery like this:

> So far as my limited observation qualifies me to judge, the average town Korean spends more than half his time in idleness, and instead of cleaning up his premises in his long intervals of leisure, he sits contentedly on his threshold and smokes, or lies on the ground and sleeps,

80. For Kennan's views see "Korea: A Degenerate State," *Outlook*, Oct. 7, 1905; also Kennan, "The Korean People: The Product of a Decayed Civilization," *Outlook*, Dec. 21, 1905.
81. Gale (1972), p. 228.
82. Gale (1972), p. 58.

> with his nose over an open drain from which a turkey-buzzard would fly and a decent pig would turn away in disgust.

Here Kennan merely recapitulates judgments that a German, Herr Kämpfer, had made about Japan in 1690. Miserable peasants lived in awful, stinking, low-lying hovels; he thought (wrongly) that the country was at war with itself, with forts and soldiers everywhere; gibbets and tortured bodies lay along the routes he traveled. Furthermore, there is classical authority behind such travelers' observations—Herodotus thought that the Egyptians were not a pretty sight, prostrating themselves in the open street toward one another, "lowering their hands to their knees" like dogs.

Kennan's "limited observation" did not keep him from knowing the answer to Korean problems: "The government officials corrupt and demoralize their subjects by setting them examples of untruthfulness, dishonesty, cruelty, and cynical brutality in dealing with human rights that is almost without parallel in modern times." He suggested that "a hundred intellectual samurai policemen and twelve or fifteen police inspectors" be brought over from Japan to remedy this predicament.[83]

William Griffis, a somewhat less caustic traveler, was taken aback by the centrality of Seoul: "If, as the French say, 'Paris is France,' then Seoul is Corea. An apparently disproportionate interest centres in the capital. . . . Three thousand official dignitaries are said to reside in the capital, and only eight hundred in all the other cities and provinces." Surrounded by walls "of crenellated masonry of varying height, averaging about twenty feet, with arched stone bridges spanning the watercourses," the city was above all centered on the king: "the high roads of the eight points of the compass start from the palace, through the city gates." Griffis summed up a lot of late-nineteenth-century history as Westerners understood it, when he wrote that "the fires of civilization" were starting to "smoke out the hermit," and that "the worn out dogmas of Chinese statecraft must pass away . . . and Corea be allowed to work out her career as a sovereign state, in the line pointed out by progressive Japan and democratic America."[84]

It got better with Percival Lowell, of the prominent family from Lowell, Massachusetts, a scientist and astronomer who became famous as the discoverer of the "canals" on Mars, and who wrote several books on East Asia that remain interesting today; he was the first to use "Land of the Morning Calm" as the translation for the title of his 1888 book, *Choson.* Completely captured by the rampant progressivism of the day, he thus

83. Kennan, "Korean People."
84. Griffis (1889), pp. 189, 233, 420, 459.

assumed that Korea had been stagnant for centuries: "Change knew them not, and time stood still . . . a most remarkable phenomenon, a living fossilification."[85] Lowell was an observant and sensitive soul, however, and made a comment on Korean commerce in the 1880s that thousands of New Yorkers made in the 1980s: on fruit stands in the markets, each item was carefully polished and then "gathered into little heaps":

> So symmetrical are the heaps that my curiosity was once piqued into counting them; and on doing so, I discovered that each heap contained exactly the same number of units as its fellows of the same kind of fruit. Three chestnuts were invariably to a pile, seven walnuts to another . . . each pile was for sale for half a farthing.[86]

Lowell also had the best appreciation in the Western literature of the lovely, flowing roof lines of Korean homes:

> It is unique. No dome, no minaret, no steeple that I have ever beheld, is, to my eyes, so simply beautiful. It is not in its ornament; for though it possesses its share of decoration, this rather takes away than adds. The charm lies in its grace of form. I had almost said Arcadian shape; for I mean it in the sense . . . of being in some sort born of Nature. Two corresponding curves, concave toward the sky, fall away on either hand from the central ridgepole. The descent is at first abrupt, but grows less and less so till it ends at the eaves. In small houses the roof is single; but in larger ones there are many slopes, of different degrees of curvature, that overlap and lie like festoons in tiles, one above another.[87]

A curious German, Paul von Moellendorff, squints out of 1880s portraits wearing the robes and accoutrements of a high Korean official except for his horn-rimmed spectacles. Something of a linguistic genius, he mastered both Chinese and Korean, went around in Korean dress, lived in the Korean style, and everywhere gave help to Koreans struggling to adapt to a new international order. Moellendorff organized and ran the Korean customs service, recommended the adoption of *han'gŭl* for all written communication, and started many reforms in education, commerce, finance—especially taxation—and industry. He urged upon Kojong a railroad-building campaign, a machine industry, and the export of Korean products to the world. Although the yangban officials were, in

85. Lowell (1888-A), p. 7. Lowell was a great scientist but not much of an economist: why should merchants sell different amounts of chestnuts for the same half a farthing? After twenty-five years in the East Asian field, my physicist friend Engelbert Schücking was the first to mention Lowell's work to me—for which I am grateful.
86. Lowell (1888-A), p. 222.
87. Lowell (1888-A), p. 277.

his view, merciless in exploiting the people, he "was convinced that the Korean people were superior to the Japanese and might surpass the islanders in the learning of Western sciences."[88]

Other visitors also stayed long enough to form more subtle impressions of Koreans. Henry Savage-Landor was so taken with some of the aristocrats he met that he appropriated them for his own race: he was amazed to find among Koreans "people almost as white and with features closely approaching the Aryan, these being the higher classes of the kingdom." He added,

> Notwithstanding the fact that it is not uncommon to hear Coreans being classified among barbarians, I must confess that, taking a liberal view of their constitution, they always have struck me as being extremely intelligent and quick at acquiring knowledge. To learn a foreign language seems to them quite an easy task. . . . They possess a wonderfully sensible reasoning faculty, coupled with an amazing quickness of perception.[89]

By the turn of the century some Westerners were observant enough to mark the important changes that Korea's early modernization had wrought; their views help us to understand the common Korean judgment that Japanese colonialism did nothing for Korea except retard a progressive drive already well under way before 1910. Angus Hamilton, for example, found Korea to be "a land of exceptional beauty" and Seoul much superior to Beijing. Seoul was the first city in East Asia to have electricity, trolley cars, a water system, telephones, and telegraphs all at the same time. Most of these systems were installed and run by Americans: the Seoul Electric Light Company, the Seoul Electric Car Company, the Seoul "Fresh Spring" Water Company, were all American firms. Hamilton counted one hundred Americans living in Seoul, sixty-five at Unsan and thirty-five in P'yŏngyang; Korean imports from the United States included Standard Oil Company kerosene, Richmond Gem cigarettes, California fruit and wine, Eagle Brand milk, Armour's canned meats, Crosse & Blackwell canned foods, flour, mining machinery, cotton, railway goods, and clothing. Hamilton seemed to speak of a city different from the one Kennan reviled at the same time:

> The streets [of Seoul] are magnificent, spacious, clean, admirably made and well drained. The narrow, dirty lanes have been widened; gutters have been covered, and roadways broadened. . . . Seoul is within measurable distance of becoming the highest, most interesting, and cleanest city in the East.

88. Lee (1988), pp. 60–61.
89. Savage-Landor (1895), pp. 45, 291.

The first trolley car wends its way through Seoul. *Courtesy of Carlo Rosetti.*

There was for him "no question of the superiority" of Korean living conditions, both urban and rural, to those in China (if not Japan). Kojong, Hamilton thought, was a progressive monarch.[90] Schools of every description abounded in Seoul—law, engineering, medicine. He noted that Kojong wanted personally to supervise all public business. The period since the opening of the country, he remarked, had afforded Koreans countless oppportunities "to select for themselves such institutions as may be calculated to promote their own welfare."[91]

Hamilton admired the activity and energy of Korean women: "her diligent integrity is more evident in the national life than her husband's industry. She is exceptionally active, vigorous in character, resourceful in emergency, superstitious, persevering, indomitable, courageous and devoted." Korea's peasants had an unlimited capacity for work and were "supremely and surprisingly hospitable" to a visitor like Hamilton. They evinced "profound reverence for everything beyond their own understanding, and [an] amazing sense of the beautiful in nature." In the region of Paektusan, however, he found hamlets of astonishing "poverty and squalor," populated by spiritless people; they were, he thought, "completely paralyzed by the exactions of the officials . . . knowing only too well that an immunity from the demands of the *Yamen* is found only in a condition of extreme poverty."

Hamilton was on hand to record a rare view of the royal procession, a few years before the ritual ended:

> The procession, which preceded the passing of the Emperor, seemed almost unending. At every moment the sea of colour broke into waves of every imaginable hue, as one motley crowd of retainers, servants,

90. It turns out that Hamilton was right, at least about Kojong's direct role in restructuring and developing Seoul. For more information see Yi Tae-jin, "The Nature of Seoul's Modern Urban Development during the 18th and 19th Centuries," *Korea Journal* 35, no. 3 (Autumn 1995): 15–24.

91. Hamilton (1904), pp. 8, 11, 24, 26, 33, 59, 150–51. On Seoul as the most modern city in East Asia outside of Japan, see also Lautensach (1945), p. 294.

King Kojong *(left)*, with his son, circa 1903. *Courtesy of Carlo Rosetti.*

musicians and officials gave place to another. Important and imposing officials in high-crowned hats, adorned with crimson tassels festooned with bunches of feathers and fastened by a string of amber beads round the throat, were pushed along, silent and helpless. Their dresses were glaring combinations of red and blue and orange; they were supported by men in green gauze coats and followed by other signal marks of Korean grandeur, more banners and bannermen, flags decorated with feathers, servants carrying boxes of refreshments, small tables, pipes

> and fire. . . . Imperial servants with robes of yellow silk, their hats decorated with rosettes; more medieval costumes, of original colour and quaint conception; a greater multitude of waving flags; a group of silken-clad standard-bearers bearing the Imperial yellow silk flag, the Imperial umbrella, and other insignia. Then a final frantic beating of drums, a horrid jangling of bells, a fearful screaming of pipes, a riot of imperious discord mingled with the voices of the officials shouting orders and the curses of the eunuchs, and finally the van of the Imperial *cortège* appeared, in a blaze of streaming yellow light, amid a sudden silence in which one could hear the heart-beats of one's neighbor. The voices died away; the scraping of hurried footsteps alone was audible as the Imperial chair of state, canopied with yellow silk richly tasselled, screened with delicate silken panels of the same colour and bearing wings to keep off the sun, was rushed swiftly and smoothly forward. Thirty-two imperial runners, clad in yellow, with double mitres upon their heads, bore aloft upon their shoulders the sacred and august person of his Imperial Majesty, the Emperor. . . .[92]

Kennan may have thought the progressive Japanese were the answer to Korea's problems, but Hamilton provided a much more believable portrait, one characteristic of colonialism the world over, namely, that often the worst of metropolitan nationals migrated to the colonies. "The scum of the Japanese nation" has come to Korea, he wrote, accounting for the "extreme animus" of Koreans against them. With their "puffed-up arrogance," the Japanese were sowing the seeds of future disaster. The colonizers "think might is right," and "master and man alike terrorize the Koreans. . . . [A]ny Japanese coolie thinks he's the better of them." The Japanese settlements in the treaty ports, he said, are

> at once the centre of business, and the scene of uproar, riot and confusion. In the comparative nakedness of the women, in the noise and violence of the shopkeepers, in the litter of the streets, there is nothing to suggest the delicate culture of Japan. The modesty, cleanliness, and politeness, so characteristic of Japanese, are conspicuously absent in their settlements in this country.[93]

Japanese traders sold kerosene in cans exactly duplicating Standard Oil's, trying to catch up with its control of the world petroleum market; meanwhile, Japanese textiles were now completely dominant in the Korean market. Japanese firms sold 4,154,533 pounds of yarn and 685,462 of piece goods in 1902, compared with 111,333 piece goods for

92. Hamilton (1904), pp. 39, 44, 68–70, 114–15, 248–49.
93. Hamilton (1904), pp. 129–31.

Britain and 39,356 piece goods for colonial firms in India. British cotton shirts, however, were still way ahead with 389,730 pieces imported into Korea, compared with about 19,000 Japanese.[94]

James Scarth Gale walked from one end of Korea to the other in the early 1890s, filling his diaries with pungent descriptions of old Korea seen through the eyes of a frosty Scottish Calvinist. On the road from Seoul to Haeju he witnessed corpses lying alongside the road, some of them with their heads cut off. Pusan, by then one of three Korean treaty ports, was "a heap of ruins, nothing more than a hamlet composed of mud-huts and mat-sheds." P'yŏngyang was filthy, the northwest border town of Ŭiju was "a poor little Asiatic Antwerp," with "a wilderness of demons, rags, dogs, unburied dead, vermin, squalor, filth and what not." Manchurian towns, Gale thought, were likewise grotesque and squalid, but the Chinese seemed more industrious to him than the Koreans.[95]

Gale stayed long enough in Korea to get well beyond these superficial impressions; indeed, he was the greatest scholar among the foreign missionaries in Korea. We can let him have the last word on Western imaginings of Korea at the turn of the century:

> With what face can we talk to the oriental about anything we have, or anything we do, or have ever been? Let's cover our lips with sackcloth, never mention the west again, but rather enter into a life of silence and prayer, and see if we cannot render the east a better helping hand than heretofore.[96]

CONCLUSION

Under an imperial impact that began in earnest with Korea's opening in 1876, the Chosŏn dynasty faltered and then collapsed in a few decades. How, therefore, can we account for its extraordinary, five-century longevity previous to this? In essence the traditional system was adaptable, even supple in the marginal adjustments and incremental responses necessary to forestall or accommodate domestic or internal conflict and change. The old agrarian bureaucracy managed the interplay of different and competing interests by having a system of checks and balances that tended over time to equilibrate the interests of differ-

94. Hamilton (1904), pp. 150–51, 304.

95. Rutt, in Gale (1972), pp. 14–16, 19–20, 25. The observation of Pusan comes from another missionary with whom Gale traveled, Bishop Charles Corfe. The Japanese routinely said similar things, even in Korean tourist guides: "The ordinary houses all over Chōsen . . . are low straw-thatched huts, most of them scarcely fit for human habitation." See *Official Guide to Eastern Asia,* vol. 1, *Manchuria and Chŏsen,* p. 228.

96. Gale (1972), p. 79.

ent parties. The king and the bureaucracy kept watch on each other, the royal clans watched both, scholars could criticize ("remonstrate") from the moral position of Confucian doctrine, secret inspectors and censors went around the country to watch for rebellion and assure accurate reporting, landed aristocrats sent sons into the bureaucracy to protect family interests, local potentates influenced the county magistrates sent down from the central administration.[97] The Chosŏn dynasty was not a system that modern Koreans would wish to restore or live under, but in its time it was a sophisticated political system, adaptable enough and persistent enough to give unified rule to Korea for half a millennium.

This civilized order was broken up and laid low by the Western impact in the late nineteenth century, when Korea could not withstand the full foreign onslaught of technically advanced imperial powers with strong armies. But this experience left important legacies for the present. As a small power Koreans had to learn to be shrewd in foreign policy, and they had a good example of that in China. Koreans cultivated the sophisticated art of "low determines high" diplomacy, seeking to use foreign power for their own ends, wagging the dog with its tail. Thus both South and North Korea strike foreign observers as rather dependent on great-power support, yet both not only claim but strongly assert their absolute autonomy and independence as nation-states, and both are adept at manipulating their great-power clients. North Korea until the mid-1980s was masterful both in getting big powers to fight its battles and in maneuvering between two communist giants to get something from each and to prevent either from dominating the North. Much like the traditional period, the North's heart has been with China.

The soft spot that Koreans have in their hearts for China is still not the main characteristic of Korea's traditional diplomacy: that is isolationism, finally to the point of exclusionism. For three centuries after the Japanese invasions of the 1590s, Korea isolated itself from Japan, dealt harshly with errant Westerners washing up on its shores, and kept the Chinese at arm's length. Thus the Western name "Hermit Kingdom" was not so misleading; Koreans have always respected hermits, and the term expresses the pronounced streak of obstinate autonomy toward foreign power and the deep desire for independence that marked premodern Korea. Ethnocentric and obnoxious to foreigners, a self-contained, autonomous Korea not besmirched by things foreign remains an ideal for many Koreans. North Korea has exercised a Hermit Kingdom option by remaining one of the more isolated states in the world; it is really South Korea that, since 1960, has been revolutionary in the Korean context by pursuing an open-door policy toward the world market and seek-

97. This is a major theme of Palais (1975).

ing a multilateral, varied diplomacy. But calls for self-reliance and the expelling of foreign influence will always get a hearing in Korea; this is one of its most persistent foreign policy traits.

It is hard for us moderns to understand that in spite of Korea's well-earned Hermit Kingdom moniker, it had a diplomacy. When we look back, we say—scholars say[98]—that Korea was stubbornly committed to an obsolescent Sinic order and could not grasp modern international relations. "If inadaptability is used to characterize China," Mary Wright wrote, "what word is left for Korea?"[99] Yet it is not clear, if war is the worst thing that can happen to a people, that the modern system has been better for Korea than the ancient and venerable East Asian system. Think about it: since that system died, Korea has experienced a war on its territory in four of the past ten decades, and fought a war elsewhere (in Vietnam) in two more. For four of those decades Korea was colonized, and for six more it has been divided. By contrast, the wars of old Korea we number in centuries—essentially three major wars (with Mongols, Japanese, Manchus) in the eight centuries of Koryŏ and Chosŏn. We can all quibble about these generalizations, but they may begin to sensitize us to the virtues and not just the vices of the old system.

98. For example, Deuchler (1977), p. 85 (Korea "refused to accept the principles of international relations"); see also Duus (1995).
99. Wright (1958), p. 364.

CHAPTER THREE

Eclipse, 1905–1945

There are neither two suns in the sky
nor two kings in one country.
—The Book of Rites

After Albert Einstein fled Nazi Germany in the 1930s, a former university colleague visited his home in Princeton. "Tell me about German physics," Einstein asked. "There is no German physics," the man replied. I am tempted to say the same thing about twentieth-century Korean history. For very different reasons, Japanese and Korean historians have shied away from writing about the period after 1910, using the basic stuff of doing history: primary sources, archival documents, interviews. Pick up any of the major histories of Korea, and you will see that nearly all treat the twentieth century as an afterthought. Why?

For one thing, many documents are still classified—almost all of them in postwar North and South Korea, but Japan has also shown a surprising reluctance to open prewar archives in spite of the 1945 break with militarism. But the causes go much beyond that; closed archives are themselves symptomatic of deeper problems. For Korean historians the colonial period is both too painful and too saturated with resistance mythologies that cannot find verification in any archive. North Korea has concocted whole tapestries of events that exist only in the hagiography of Kim Il Sung. In the South one particular decade—that between 1935 and 1945—is an empty cupboard: millions of people used and abused by the Japanese cannot get records on what they know to have happened to them, and thousands of Koreans who worked with the Japanese have simply erased that history as if it had never happened. Even lists of officials in local genealogical repositories (county histories, for example) go blank on this period. The history of divided Korea since 1945 is even more biased or nullified because of the national division. Not one good thing could be said about Syngman Rhee in the North or about Kim Il Sung in the South; to do so was to get a jail sentence. The question "Who started the Korean War?" has but one right answer, depending on which side of the demilitarized zone (DMZ) you find yourself.

In Japan, a unitary and free country, the unwillingness of most historians honestly to assess their imperial history is a constant insinuation that the imperial impulse may still not be dead. Regarding Japan's record in China, perhaps there is some sincere reflection. There is almost none in regard to Japan's activities in Korea. The twentieth century began with Japan's defeat of Russia and its slow rise toward global stature, which also drew Japan toward disaster like a moth toward a flame. England and America were the Pacific powers of the first half of this century, and they welcomed Japan as a junior partner but not as a hegemon. In the new century Japan has lingering apprehensions about its ability to live comfortably with the rest of the world, and those apprehensions are nowhere greater than among its near neighbors. Japan is Icarus, flying toward the sun.

Korea was Oedipus, blinded by Japan's swiftly rising glitter. Gazing for centuries toward the pleasant, benign sun that had always set over the Middle Kingdom, over the yellow tiles of the Forbidden City and the golden tints of Beijing's loess foothills, Koreans turned around to face an ascendant country strong and determined enough to take its measure, for the first time in recorded history. Their subsequent aversion is perhaps explained by Nietzsche's comment "When after a forceful attempt to gaze on the sun we turn away blinded, we see dark-colored spots before our eyes, as a cure."[1] At the beginning of another century we can say that Koreans have by no means gotten over this experience. Japanese imperialism stuck a knife in old Korea and twisted it, and that wound has gnawed at the Korean national identity ever since. That is the fundamental reason why so little modern history is written: and that is what so dignifies those few Koreans and Japanese who have stood outside this death urge toward silence and written good history anyway.

Why should Japan and Korea have a shared modern history so daunting and unnerving? It is because their relationship is more akin to that between Germany and France or England and Ireland than to that between Belgium and Zaire or Portugal and Mozambique. Colonialism is often thought to have created new nations where none existed before,

1. Friedrich Nietzsche, *The Birth of Tragedy and The Case of Wagner*, trans. Walter Kaufmann (New York: Random House, 1967), p. 67.

drawn new boundaries and brought diverse tribes and peoples together, out of a welter of geographic units divided along ethnic, racial, religious, or tribal lines. But, as we have seen, all of this existed in Korea for centuries before 1910. Korea had ethnic and linguistic unity and long-recognized national boundaries well before the peoples of Europe attained them. Furthermore, by virtue of their relative proximity to China, Koreans had always felt superior to Japan at best, or equal at worst.

Instead of creation the Japanese engaged in substitution after 1910: exchanging a Japanese ruling elite for the Korean yangban scholar-officials, most of whom were either co-opted or dismissed; instituting colonial imperative coordination for the old central state administration; exchanging Japanese modern education for the Confucian classics; building Japanese capital and expertise in place of the incipient Korean versions, Japanese talent for Korean talent; eventually even replacing the Korean language with the Japanese. Koreans never thanked the Japanese for these substitutions, did not credit Japan with creations, and instead saw Japan as snatching away the ancien régime, Korea's sovereignty and independence, its indigenous if incipient modernization, and, above all, its national dignity. Unlike some other colonial peoples, therefore, most Koreans never saw Japanese rule as anything but illegitimate and humiliating. Furthermore, the very closeness of the two nations—in geography, in common Chinese cultural influences, indeed in levels of development until the nineteenth century—made Japanese dominance all the more galling to Koreans and gave a peculiar intensity to the relationship, a hate / respect dynamic that suggested to Koreans, "there but for accidents of history go we."

THE END OF THE CHOSŎN DYNASTY

Russia and Japan both exercised more direct power in Korean affairs in the 1890s than any of the other powers, with Japan warring against China and then sponsoring epochal reforms, and Russia offering King Kojong the shelter of its legation and for a time involving itself in Korean politics. Several negotiations between Tokyo and Moscow sought to divvy up their respective interests in Korea, the main idea being a division of the peninsula into spheres of influence. The negotiations failed, however, and the rivalry evolved into war in 1904 when Japan launched a successful surprise attack on the Russian fleet at Port Arthur. It proceeded to electrify all of Asia by becoming the first nonwhite nation to subdue one of the "great powers."

Russia recognized Japan's paramount rights in Korea under the peace treaty signed in 1905, brokered by Theodore Roosevelt in a conference at Portsmouth, New Hampshire, and for which he won the Nobel Peace Prize. Diplomatic notes exchanged between Roosevelt and the Japanese (the Taft-Katsura agreement) acknowledged a trade-off between the Philippines and Korea: Japan would not question American rights in its colony, and the United States would not challenge Japan's new protectorate. Horace Allen tried to get Roosevelt to prevent the Japanese from taking Korea, but the president paid no attention; if anything, he was much more open to the racist views of George Kennan that we sampled in the preceding chapter.

Japan had a "free hand" in Korea after 1905, as the diplomatic historians say, because of its victories over China and Russia and because of British and American support (the Anglo-Japanese Alliance had been concluded in 1902). As long as the direction of Japanese imperialism was toward Korea and Manchuria, which pushed it away from the Philippines or the many British colonies, it had the blessing of London and Washington.[2] Secretary of State Huntington Wilson responded to Japan's announcement of the annexation in this way:

> While I am constrained by the great importance of the interests of American citizens in Korea to make all necessary reservations of their rights and privileges, I beg to inform Your Majesty that the Government of the United States is gratified to note the assurances already given by the Imperial Japanese Government concerning matters relating to foreigners and foreign trade in Korea.[3]

If Japan had a free hand, it also had a helping hand. It is a sad fact, but a fact, that almost every Westerner supported Japan's "modernizing role" in Korea, from callous diplomat to earnest scholar and Christian missionary. Richard Rutt wrote that "few missionaries lifted their voice in protest" of the annexation.[4]

Tyler Dennett, a historian who wrote texts that influenced generations of American students, said Korea was an errant skiff that Japan needed to tow to shore; Korea was not capable of striking a blow in its own defense, Dennett thought. Some American scholars were virtual cheerleaders for Japan's enlightenment project. George Trumbull Ladd, a professor from Yale, was close to Itō Hirobumi and was quick to assure his readers of Itō's beneficent and civilizing role.[5] An American named

2. Akira Iriye, *Pacific Estrangement: Japanese and American Expansion, 1897–1911* (Cambridge: Harvard University Press, 1972), pp. 47–48.
3. Quoted in Timothy Lincoln Savage, "The American Response to the Korean Independence Movement, 1910–1945" (M.A. thesis, University of Hawaii, 1994), p. 10.
4. Rutt, in Gale (1972), p. 49.
5. Dennett (1922); George Trumbull Ladd, *In Korea with Marquis Ito* (New York, 1909).

Durham Stevens was Ladd's friend and also advised Itō; when he landed in San Francisco in 1908 and began expounding on what a great job Japan was doing, Chang In-hwan and Chŏn Myŏng-un emptied their revolvers into him—only to provoke a Berkeley professor into long-winded disquisitions on "the Oriental races" and their violence (indeed, the assassination convinced him of a coming "race war").[6]

The "progressives" of the time were no better—or maybe worse. Beatrice Webb, perhaps with her husband, Sydney, not the most discerning of Fabian socialists in foreign lands, wrote in 1904 that Japan was a "rising star of human self-control and enlightenment." On her trip to East Asia in 1911 she found the Chinese to be "a horrid race," the Koreans also "a horrid race" (for Sydney these were "lowly vertebrates" who "show us, indeed, what homo sapiens can be if he does not evolve"). But Beatrice liked the "innovating collectivism' of Japan and its "enlightened professional elite" with its "uncanny" purposefulness and open-mindedness. Here was the "benevolent bureaucracy of the future socialist state."[7] Japan was the enlightened, anointed bearer of white civilization in the curious guise of a "yellow people"; nothing to do but pat such good boys on the back.

Why were English of all stripes lauding Japan in the first decade of the twentieth century? The answer is simple: British decline and German and Japanese advance; Germany was a threat, and Japan was the British ally after 1902. After two great waves of industrialization lasting a century and a half, England found itself beset by newly risen industrial powers, and by an obsolescent industrial base. Fervent soul-searching therefore marked most debate, with the watchword being efficiency: "give us efficiency or we die." Alfred Stead entitled his 1906 book *Great Japan: A Study of National Efficiency.* English pundits wished to discover models of efficiency and productivity and looked to a Japan that, it was thought, "afforded lessons from which the British might learn to solve their internal problems."[8] (Readers will not need prodding to remember the same Japanophilia developing in the United States in the 1970s.)

With this kind of international support, the die was cast for a quick colonization of Korea. Japan established a "protectorate" in 1905, taking control of Korean diplomacy, putting its police in the streets, running the telegraph system, and the like. Itō Hirobumi, among the greatest of Meiji

6. Alexis Dudden, seminar paper (University of Chicago, April 1994).

7. Holmes and Ion, "Bushido and the Samurai," p. 320; also J. M. Winter, "The Webbs and the Non-White World: A Case of Socialist Racialism," *Journal of Contemporary History* 9 (Jan. 1974): 181–92.

8. Holmes and Ion, "Bushido and the Samurai," pp. 314, 328.

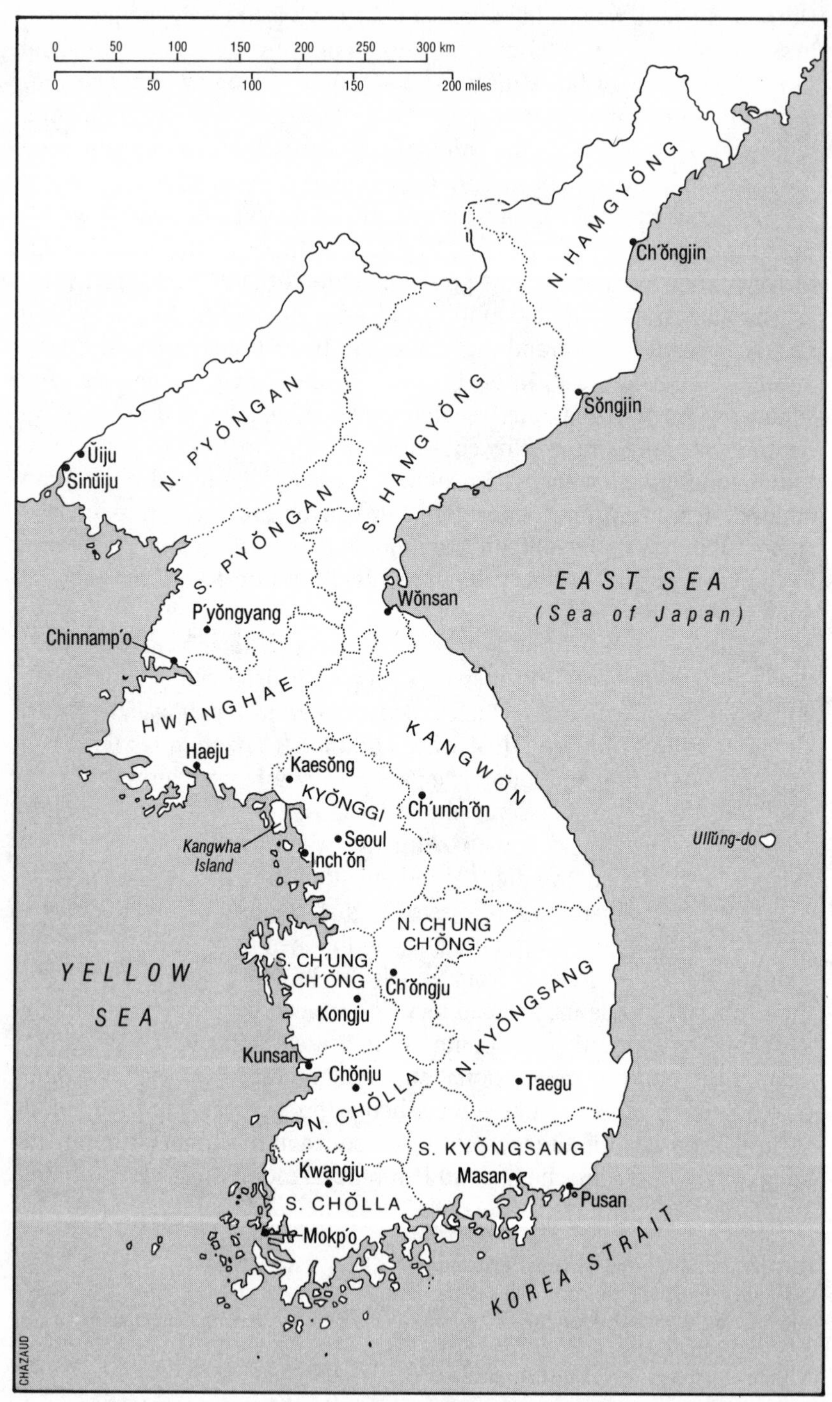

Korea in the early twentieth century, with provincial boundaries

leaders, was resident-general during the protectorate; he had established it at the point of a gun in November 1905, entering Kojong's palace escorted by Japanese troops and forcibly seizing the Foreign Ministry's seal to affix Korea's assent to the documents. It looked like another offer Koreans could not refuse, but many did.

Min Yŏng-hwan, the leading military aide-de-camp to Kojong, committed suicide, as did a number of other high officials. Kojong opposed the Protectorate Treaty publicly in early 1906 and appealed to the powers to save Korea's independence; in 1907 he dispatched three Koreans to the Second Hague Peace Convention, a milestone in global attempts to substitute diplomacy and the rule of law for the military rivalries of the big powers, but the convention ruled that Kojong was no longer sovereign over Korea's foreign relations. One of the three envoys, Yi Chun, committed suicide at The Hague. He and his friends succeeded, however, in generating enough publicity that the Japanese forced Kojong to abdicate, in favor of his mentally retarded son, Sunjong. When Itō disbanded the old Korean army, a total of about nine thousand troops, the commander of the First Infantry Guards, Pak Sŏng-hwan, committed suicide while his men and many from the Second Infantry Guards fought Japanese troops in the streets of Seoul. The Korean forces retreated from the city and joined "righteous armies" *(ŭibyŏng)* of guerrillas in the countryside.[9]

After Kojong abdicated, Yi Wan-yong became prime minister and ran the government at Japanese behest. A mob burned Yi's house down shortly thereafter, and in December 1909 a young Korean named Yi Chae-myŏng stabbed him in an assassination attempt. In May 1910 General Terauchi Masatake became the new resident-general, formulated the terms of the Treaty of Annexation with Prime Minister Yi Wan-yong, and got the latter's signature on the final document on August 22, 1910. Yi Wan-yong had enjoyed sharing sushi and sake with Itō and Terauchi, as each penned poems to the future of Japan-Korea amity: I once saw a scroll written in Yi's hand, which consisted of odes written by him, Itō, and Terauchi to the "sweet spring rain" and "new beginning" that augered the coming merger of "two peoples under one house."

Itō did not live to see the final amalgamation, though; An Chung-gun assassinated him at Harbin station on October 26, 1909. Finally on August 29, 1910, Sunjong yielded the throne and Korea became a colony of Japan. August 29 would become the darkest day of any subsequent year for Koreans, and Yi Wan-yong the darkest name in Korean history. Japan thereby extinguished Korea's hard-fought independence, which had first emerged with the Silla and Koguryŏ resistance to Chinese pres-

9. Lee (1984), p. 312.

sures. Japanese colonizers and *pied noirs* may have strutted like peacocks in the streets of Seoul thereafter, but they should have remembered the story about the tortoise and the hare. The first race went to the swift, but it was not the only race.

Strong Korean resistance to the annexation continued throughout the early years of colonization. Most important were the *ŭibyŏng* irregulars and guerrillas, who bedeviled the Japanese from 1907 through 1910. Most of them were demobilized soldiers and patriotic literati, who went into the countryside and accumulated peasant adherents; in many cases peasant militias sprang up spontaneously, no doubt drawing on the roots of the Tonghak movement. Most were bands of less than a hundred, although one whole garrison of troops revolted in Wŏnju under Min Kŭng-ho and had several thousand men under Min's command at one point. A force of nearly 10,000 penetrated to within eight miles of Seoul in 1907, and the scale of *ŭibyŏng* operations extended to the following provinces: Chŏlla, Kyŏngsang, Kangwŏn, Kyŏnggi, and Hwanghae—that is, the most populous districts in the country. Japanese estimates of guerrillas under arms were 69,832 in 1908 with nearly fifteen hundred clashes between them and Japanese troops; the number dropped to about 25,000 in 1909 and to under 2,000 in 1910; by that time many insurgents had run off to Manchuria.[10]

And what of our "Hongian legacy"? There in the middle of the *ŭibyŏng* was Ch'oe Ik-hyŏn, leading insurgents in Chŏlla Province and writing this about the reasons why an aged scholar of the very aged old school risked his life to organize militias against Japan:

> The four oceans have been filled with foul smelling barbarians. Nevertheless only our country, situated in the Eastern corner, could preserve a piece of superior, pure land; and it looked as if what was said of *yang*—that at the extremity of its wane it would wax again and that *yang* would alternate with *yin*—became a reality. Who would have reckoned that inferior, icy element would now make its way and overwhelm the superior, Pure Land? This is to be likened to the single topknot remaining atop the head, becoming the sole target for all of the arrows in all-under-heaven.[11]

Ch'oe's resistance did not last long; he was captured and thrown into a prison on Tsushima Island, where he died of hunger in 1906. He left his own epitaph: "I was unable to repel the traitors, dispose of our nation's enemies, restore our nation's sovereignty, recover our territory, or hold

10. Lee (1984), p. 316–17.
11. Quoted by Chai-sik Chung, in Wells (1995), pp. 68–69.

back our four thousand year long righteous Way of Chinese civilization from falling to the ground."[12]

Many more Hongians took their own lives at the annexation, an act that reverberated as strongly in Korea as the self-sacrifice of Islamic militants in a jihad, and resistance continued thereafter. The Japanese arrested as many as 50,000 Koreans in 1912 and 140,000 in 1918. One of these cases, known as the Korean Conspiracy Trial of 1912, involved 105 people accused of trying to assassinate the governor-general, and became famous for "the blatant fabrication of the criminal charges against the accused and for the vicious torture to which they were subjected."[13]

Our narrative is far too one-sided to this point, however: it was not the traitor Yi Wan-yong against a mass of patriots. Japanese progress attracted many Koreans before 1905 and enticed or subverted all too many thereafter; colonial officials always used divide-and-rule tactics, although more so after 1919 than before; far more Koreans did service to the colonial dictatorship than almost anyone likes to admit, and far too many Koreans came to model their behavior on Japanese practice after 1945 for this to have been a completely hostile and unbridgeable relationship. In the first decade of this century a Japan rapidly bringing itself to the world's attention was flypaper for many Asian progressives. Sun Yat-sen, founding father of Chinese nationalism, and many other eager young Chinese flocked to Tokyo, as did many Korean students and young people. Within Korea an organization called the Ilchinhoe, or Unity and Progress Society, enrolled large numbers of Koreans in a new mass organization that backed Japan's policies; one scholar wrote that this was Korea's first modern political organization, uniting leaders and led and mobilizing the masses.[14] That generalization is a bit of a stretch, but so is the subsequent attempt by nationalist historians to pretend that the Ilchinhoe's members were few, with each one devoted to selling Korea to Japan. The annexation wiped out remnant hopes of progressives that their country might retain its independence while marching in tandem toward modernity with the Japanese, but Japan did not squelch the dreams of other Asian modernizers until its famous "twenty-one demands" during World War I, and the subsequent May Fourth movement in China touched off by the demands.

12. Quoted in Dennis MacNamara, "Survival Strategies: Korean Solidarity in a Hostile World" (paper presented to the Annual Meeting of the Association for Asian Studies, April 1994).

13. Lee (1984), p. 314.

14. Henderson (1968), pp. 67–71.

ADMINISTRATIVE COLONIALISM: MODERNIZATION OR EXPLOITATION?

Korea escaped the Japanese grip only in 1945, when Japan lay prostrate under the American and Russian onslaught that brought World War II to a close. This colonial experience was intense and bitter, and shaped postwar Korea deeply. It brought development and underdevelopment, agrarian growth and deepened tenancy, industrialization and extraordinary dislocation, political mobilization and deactivation; it spawned a new role for the central state, new sets of Korean political leaders, communism and nationalism, armed resistance and treacherous collaboration; above all, it left deep fissures and conflicts that have gnawed at the Korean soul ever since.

Japan held Korea tightly, watched it closely, and pursued an organized, architectonic colonialism in which the planner and administrator was the model, not the swashbuckling conqueror; the strong, highly centralized colonial state mimicked the role that the Japanese state had come to play in Japan—intervening in the economy, creating markets, spawning new industries, suppressing dissent. Politically Koreans could barely breathe, but economically there was significant, if unevenly distributed, growth. Agricultural output rose substantially in the 1920s, and a hothouse industrialization took root in the 1930s. Growth rates in the Korean economy often outstripped those in Japan itself; recent research has suggested an annual growth rate for Korea of 3.57 percent in the period 1911–38, a rate of 3.36 percent for Japan itself.

The huge Oriental Development Company organized and funded industrial and agricultural projects and came to own more than 20 percent of Korea's arable land; it employed an army of officials who fanned out through the countryside to supervise agricultural production. The colonial Bank of Korea performed central-banking functions, such as regulating interest rates, and provisioned credit to firms and entrepreneurs—almost all of them, of course, Japanese. Central judicial bodies wrote new laws establishing an extensive, "legalized" system of racial discrimination against Koreans, making them second-class citizens in their own country. Bureaucratic departments proliferated at the government-general headquarters in Seoul, turning it into the nerve center of the country. Semi-official companies and conglomerates, including the big *zaibatsu* such as Mitsubishi and Mitsui, laid railways, built ports, installed modern factories, and, in fine, remade the face of old Korea.

Among Koreans today, North and South, the mere mention of the idea that Japan somehow "modernized" Korea calls forth indignant denials, raw emotions, and the sense of mayhem having just been, or about to be, committed. For the foreigner even the most extensive cataloging of

Japanese atrocities will pale beside the barest suggestion of anything positive and lasting that might have emerged from the colonial period. Koreans have always thought that the benefits of this growth went entirely to Japan and that Korea would have developed rapidly without Japanese help anyway. Meanwhile, on a sojourn in Taiwan as late as 1970 a scholar found nostalgia for the Japanese era at every turn, and during the 1950s heyday of modernization theory, American political scientists lauded the colonial effort as a model.[15] So, if we find that Japan brought modern facilities to its colonies, do we place them on the ledger of colonialism, or of modernization? The Korean answer is "colonialism," and the Japanese and Taiwanese answer is "modernization."

Tim Mitchell has a better answer to this question, which is to address "the place of colonialism in the critique of modernity": "Colonising refers not simply to the establishing of a European presence but also to the spread of a political order that inscribes in the social world a new conception of space, new forms of personhood, and a new means of manufacturing the experience of the real." Following Michel Foucault, Mitchell examines British colonialism in Egypt as a matter of a "restrictive, exterior power" giving way to the "internal, productive power" demanded by modernity, a disciplining that produces "the organized power of armies, schools, and factories," and, above all, "the modern individual, constructed as an isolated, disciplined, receptive, and industrious political subject."[16]

If we put things this way, with a conception of Foucauldian power and Foucauldian modernity, then there is no fundamental distinction between Japanese colonialism and the modern industrial project itself, and thus no basic distinction between Japanese colonialism, American hegemony, and South Korean, North Korean, or Taiwanese modernization. At the least, none of these national accounts of modernity can tell you why the precise timing of the factory punch clock or the railway timetable or the policeman's neighborhood beat is bad; they just differ over the auspices of their introduction and their effects on national sovereignty. Every political entity just mentioned, but above all Japan itself, put its citizens through a regimen of public education that seemed perfectly designed to develop the industrious political subject, with the vices of self-surveillance and repression that Mitchell analyzed for Egypt. The strong colonial state, the multiplicity of bureaucracies, the

15. Examples: "Taiwan under the [Chinese Nationalist] pigs is hell," compared with its prewar state. Douglas Mendel, *The Politics of Formosan Nationalism* (Berkeley: University of California Press, 1970), p. 7. Barclay wrote that "Taiwan . . . developed into one of the most successful colonial programs in the world . . . a success that would satisfy most of the countries striving for modernization today." Barclay (1954), p. 7.
16. Mitchell (1988), ix, xi.

policy of administrative guidance of the economy, the use of the state to found new industries, and the repression of labor unions and dissidents that always went with it provided a surreptitious model for both Koreas in the post-1945 period. Japan showed them an early version of the "bureaucratic-authoritarian" path to industrialization, and it was a lesson that seemed well learned by the 1970s.

The historian Thomas C. Smith wrote of Japan's Meiji state that in pursuing industrialization, it had no choice "but to act as entrepreneur, financier, and manager. . . . [C]apital was too weak, too timid, and too inexperienced to undertake development."[17] This was even more true of Korea, where Japan quickly installed a "developmental" colonial regime. Portugal may have been content to hold Angola as its colony for four hundred years and merely stitch a modern fringe along its coast while extracting coffee beans from the interior, but Japanese colonizers were state capitalists and Korea was their incubus: it should do what it is told, serve the metropolitan economy, and keep quiet. The Meiji Restoration's success grew out of the agrarian and commercial changes of the Tokugawa period, it was "endogenous" to Japan's modern history; the colonial state, however, was exogenous, its source being the metropole, and so the distortions attendant to a strong role for the state in development were, of course, all the more acute in the Korean case.

Japan did not send to Korea conquerers like Cecil Rhodes, but chose the civil service bureaucrat as the model overlord: the archetype would be a man like Gotō Shimpei, a colonial administrator in Taiwan and later active in Korea and Manchukuo, a man in black Western suit and top hat with developmental plans in his briefcase. From 1910 onward Japanese civil servants brought administration to Koreans far more often than a policeman brought the knout, and they had a tremendous advantage: the yangban aristocracy, however sublime its scholars and its arts may have been, was a class apart from ordinary Koreans—with the added insult that the yangban thought the ordinary people owed them a living. We saw it in the stirring rhetoric of the Tonghak movement: take off our P'yŏngyang hats! Take us for human beings! The great sociologist Robert Michels once wrote that a landed gentry whose members appealed only to others of their own class or who presented themselves to the people "by declaring to them that [they] did not regard them as capable of playing an active part in influencing the destinies of the country," such a gentry would evince incomparable sincerity but political insanity. The yangban displayed precisely this combination: sincere to a

17. Thomas C. Smith, *Political Change and Industrial Development in Japan: Government Enterprise, 1868–1880* (Stanford: Stanford University Press, 1955), p. 102.

fault, and bereft of a clue as to how to mobilize the very people they had so long exploited, and thus to resist Japan.

One thing the Japanese did not destroy from the Chosŏn dynasty, however, was this same aristocracy. Centuries of aristocratic legitimation would work to the colonizers' advantage, if the Japanese could secure cooperation from the old elite. Colonial administrators knew a great deal about Korea; after the annexation they pensioned off about 84 aristocrats and some 3,645 civil service officials, "with a detailed knowledge of the Korean upper class."[18] The higher scholar-officials were replaced by Japanese, but Korean landlords were allowed to retain their holdings and encouraged to continue disciplining peasants and extracting rice for export. These policies rooted Korean landlords more firmly to the localities by snipping their web of connections to political office in Seoul and using their traditional power and legitimacy to extract rice from peasants for the export market, more stably and effectively than if the Japanese had done it themselves (although many Japanese families did come to Korea and buy up land, too). Shortly after the Japanese took over, the traditional landholding system was put on a modern or rational-legal basis through new contract laws and a full cadastral survey. This was "the most ambitious and important task attempted by the Japanese" in the first decade of their rule, taking nine years and ¥20 million to complete. Now contractual property rights solidified the hold of yangban landlords who knew how to get their land registered, but led to the dispossession of traditional tenancy rights and land rights for many illiterate peasants.[19]

World War I was a wash for Japan, which was the only uninvolved big power; its exports predictably soared, transforming it from a debtor nation with a labor surplus to a creditor nation with abundant capital (a ¥2.7 billion surplus in 1920) and full employment.[20] This rapid growth led to a tripling of rice prices in Japan. Suddenly investment was available for Korea, and Korean landlords did very well, too, allowing them to buy additional land. One brother of Kim Sŏng-su, for example, held 1,800 acres of land in 1918, of which 90 percent was in rice paddies, worked by more than one thousand tenants. The main estate of the clan ran to 3,185 acres.[21] Agrarian tenancy systematically deepened through-

18. Cumings (1981), p. 11.

19. Hatada (1969), p. 113. For a corrective to critical accounts of this survey (which often exaggerate the number of Koreans who were dispossessed), see Gragert (1994), pp. 71–110.

20. Woo (1991), p. 23.

21. Eckert (1991), p. 26.

out the colonial period; by 1945 Korea had a tenancy system with few parallels in the world. Most landlords were content to sit back and let Japanese officials increase output. Japan had a budding cadre of colonial specialists who had been in Taiwan, like Gotō and Togō Minoru (a specialist in colonial agriculture), and they thought Koreans ought to go along to get along, as most Taiwanese had done and as most Korean landlords did. But it was not to be so. By 1945 Korean yangban were widely viewed as treacherous collaborators with the Japanese, and strong demands emerged for them to share out their land to the tenants.

In the first decade of their rule Japanese colonizers pushed a heavy-handed "military policy" *(budan seiji),* mainly because of the sharp resistance at their accession to power in the period 1905–10; even classroom teachers wore uniforms and carried swords. The government-general stood above Korean society, exercising authoritative and coercive control. Its connections were only to the remnant upper class and colonial parvenus, and even these were tenuous, designed to co-opt and thwart dissent, not to give Koreans a meaningful role in the state apparatus. The Japanese unquestionably strengthened central bureaucratic power in Korea, demolishing the old balance and tension with the landed aristocracy; operating from the top down, they effectively penetrated below the county level and into the villages for the first time, and in some ways neither postcolonial Korean state has ever gotten over it: Korea today is still a country with remarkably little local autonomy. Added to the old county-level pivot of central magistrate, local clerks, and landed families was a centrally controlled, highly mobile national police force, responsive to the center and possessing its own communications and transportation facilities. For decades black-coated policemen kept order and helped "bring in the harvest," manning the ramparts of the rice production circuit from paddy field to middleman to storehouse to export platform, and thence to Japan. Here is how Patti Tsurumi described this new, multifunctional police system devised in Taiwan by Gotō Shimpei, a model later transferred to Korea:

> Under Gotō the police became the backbone of regional administration. In addition to regular policing duties, the police supervised the collection of taxes, the enforcement of sanitary measures, and works connected with the salt, camphor and opium monopolies. . . . They superintended road and irrigation improvements, introduced new plant specimens to the farmers, and encouraged education and the development of local industries.[22]

22. E. Patricia Tsurumi, "Taiwan under Kodama Gentarō and Gotō Shimpei, "in *Papers on Japan,* vol. 4 (Harvard University, East Asian Research Center, 1967), pp. 117–18.

The Japanese governor-general on an inspection tour in the early years of the colony.

About 40 to 50 percent of this police force was Korean, depending on the decade.

Japan also stationed a big army in Korea, both for control and with an eye to security on the Asian mainland. Every governor-general was a military man throughout the colonial period: the first one, Terauchi, had been recommended for his post by the Meiji leader Yamagata Aritomo, who liked to pick colonial leaders from among his powerful Chōshū military clique. In 1894 the Japanese army established its main base at Yongsan, on the outskirts of old Seoul; it remains an American military base today, except that now it is a gigantic complex smack in the middle of a an enormous, sprawling, bustling city—contemporary Seoul. (I can't think of another capital city quite like it, where you turn a corner and suddenly see a mammoth swatch of land given over to a foreign army.)

Added to the Japanese army was a horde of bureaucrats. By the last decade of the colonial period some 246,000 Japanese civil servants and professionals ruled about 21 million Koreans; about 46 percent of the colonizer population was in government service. In 1937, by way of comparison, the French ruled a Vietnamese population of 17 million with 2,920 administrative personnel and about 11,000 regular French troops, and the British had even smaller administrative and military forces in most of their colonies (in proportion to the populations).[23] The

23. Cumings (1981), p. 12.

The Seoul railway station, shortly after its completion; its architecture mimicked European styles and bears close comparison to the railway stations that the Japanese also built in Harbin and Taipei.

majority of Japanese officials worked at one of the many government ministries in Seoul, a capital city that (in this century) has combined administrative and commercial centrality, and which still has a few vintage examples of Japanese colonial architecture—itself modeled on European Beaux Arts, neo-Renaissance, and imperial styles. In 1912 Seoul had a population of 277,711, of which 238,499 were Koreans, 38,397 Japanese, 770 Chinese, and around 100 Americans. By contrast P'yŏngyang had a mere 41,167 and Pusan 38,217, of which 21,928 were Japanese.[24] By the end of period Seoul had more than 500,000 people; Pusan, about 200,000.

THE RISE OF KOREAN NATIONALISM AND COMMUNISM

The colonial period brought forth an entirely new set of Korean political leaders, spawned both by the resistance to and by the opportunities of Japanese colonialism. The emergence of nationalist and communist groups dates back to the 1920s; it is really in this period that the left-right splits of postwar Korea began. The transformation of the yangban aristocracy also began then. In the 1930s new groups of armed resisters, bureaucrats, and (for the first time) military leaders emerged. Both North and South Korea remain profoundly influenced by political elites and political conflicts generated during colonial rule.

In 1919 mass movements swept many colonial and semicolonial countries, including Korea. Drawing upon Woodrow Wilson's promises of self-determination, a group of thirty-three intellectuals petitioned for

24. Imperial Japanese Government Railways, *An Official Guide to Eastern Asia,* vol. 1, *Manchuria and Chōsen* (Tokyo, 1913), pp. 260, 271, 302. This source puts the number of Americans at 13, but Donald Clark suggested to me that the figure had to be closer to 100.

The Beaux Arts and German-influenced colonial Bank of Korea.

independence from Japan on March 1 and touched off nationwide mass protests that continued for months. Japanese national and military police could not contain this revolt and had to call in the army and even the navy. At least half a million Koreans took part in demonstrations in March and April, with disturbances in more than six hundred different places. In one of the most notorious episodes, Japanese gendarmes locked protesters inside a church and burned it to the ground. In the end Japanese officials counted 553 killed and over 12,000 arrested, but Korean nationalist sources put the totals at 7,500 killed and 45,000 arrested.

Once again, Koreans had provided a stark contrast with Japan's other colony, in Taiwan. Even after the rebellion in Korea and the watershed May Fourth movement in China, an observant American traveler noted that quite a few Taiwanese wore Japanese clothes, whereas he could not "recall ever having seen a Korean in *geta*s and kimono." There was a big "independence question" in Korea, he wrote, but "independence, if it is ever considered at all in Taiwan, is evidently regarded as hopeless, not even worth thinking about."[25] Perhaps the most revealing remark ever made about the differences between colonial Taiwan and colonial Korea was one official's statement that "what can be done with incentives in Taiwan must be done with coercion in Korea."[26]

25. Franck (1924), pp. 183–84.
26. Myers and Peattie (1984), p. 230.

Stung by Korean resistance, Wilson and Lenin, and general foreign reproach, Japanese leaders suddenly understood that they were colonizers in the wrong century: wanting always to be "modern," they found their repressive rule condemned as out of date. So mid-1919 marked the start of the imperial "cultural policy" *(bunka seiji),* of tutoring Koreans for a distant day of independence. The new policy inaugurated a period of "gradualist" resistance to colonialism, in which Koreans took advantage of relaxed restrictions on their freedom of speech and assembly to organize a variety of nationalist, socialist, and communist groups, some openly and some clandestinely. Now Korean newspapers could be bought once again, and many other Korean-language publications appeared in the early 1920s. Writers like Yi Kwang-su became famous for novels in a nationalist vernacular, and others like Chŏng In-bo and Ch'oe Nam-sŏn deepened studies of Korean history, examining the Tan'-gun legend and the historical "soul" of Korea.[27]

A hopeful political development occurred in 1927, with the formation of the Sin'ganhoe, a coalition of moderate nationalists and a few left-wingers. The Japanese encouraged it, hoping thereby to corral, co-opt, or simply moderate independence activists of left and right. By 1929 it had 138 branches and nearly 37,000 members, and supported studies of the Korean language, more freedom of expression, and the like. Unfortunately it did not last or put down roots; one historian merely commented, "This organization was never very effective."[28]

By no means were all nationalists inside Korea in the 1920s. Shin Ch'ae-ho was similar to Chŏng and Ch'oe, but he remained in exile. Shin was born in 1880 and learned the classics as a child at a village *sowŏn* run by his grandfather, near Taejŏn. He edited the *Hwangsŏng sinmun* (Capital gazette) in 1905 and went into exile in China in 1910, working with An Chang-ho, an important nationalist who later lived for many years in the United States. Shin devoted himself to the study of Korea's ancient history and frequently visited the Yalu border—pondering the fate of his homeland from the other side of Paektusan. He joined the Korean Provisional Government in Shanghai in 1919 and set up another exile government, in Vladivostok in 1923, advocating armed struggle against the Japanese. He grew interested in anarchism, representing Korea at a meeting of Asian anarchists in Tianjin in 1927, and later founded a Korean anarchist group in Beijing. Japanese agents arrested him when he attempted to visit Taiwan, and he spent ten years in prison before dying of a cerebral hemorrhage in 1936.[29]

27. The best account of the post-1919 changes is Robinson (1988).
28. Han (1974), pp. 485–86.
29. *Korea Times,* Dec. 3, 1994.

American missionaries were divided in their judgment of the March First movement. All of them were appalled at the violence of the colonial authorities, but many also blamed radicals and agitators for provoking the violence. Most applauded the new "cultural policies" after 1919 and echoed Japanese justifications for the new course. The resident bishop of the Methodist Episcopal Church, Herbert Welch, wrote in May 1920 that while many Koreans still demand immediate independence, "some of the most intelligent and far-seeing" Koreans "are persuaded that there is no hope of speedy independence, and that they must settle down for a long period to build up the Korean people, in physical conditions, in knowledge, in morality, and in the ability to handle government concerns. . . ."[30]

This, of course, was the Japanese premier Hara Kei's justification for the new "cultural policy," to prepare Koreans "in due course" (Hara's words) for a distant day of independence. A colonial administrator, Nitobe Inazō, explained the rationale this way in 1919:

> I count myself among the best and truest friends of Koreans. I like them.. . . I think they are a capable people who can be trained to a large measure of self-government, for which the present is a period of tutelage. Let them study what we are doing in Korea, and this I say not to justify the many mistakes committed by our militaristic administration, nor to boast of some of our achievements. In all humility, but with a firm conviction that Japan is a steward on whom devolves the gigantic task of the uplifting of the Far East, I cannot think that the young Korea is yet capable of governing itself.[31]

Christian opposition to the Japanese is both a fact and a legend. The churches were sanctuaries in times of violence, like that of the 1919 independence movement, and many Western missionaries encouraged underdog and egalitarian impulses. But the post-1945 image of Syngman Rhee and other pro-American politicians as great Christian leaders and resisters to colonialism is false:

> Men like Syngman Rhee and Kim Kyu-sik went to missionary schools like Pai Chai less for their Christianity than to look for political position through English. Enrollment at Pai Chai declined when English was de-emphasized; in 1905, within a day or two of enrollment, "half the school had gone elsewhere in search of English."

It is the humble among Koreans who have truly been drawn to Christianity: at the turn of the century, "conversions among the 30,000 of Seoul's

30. Quoted in Alleyne Ireland, *The New Korea* (New York: E. P. Dutton, 1926), p. 70.
31. Quoted in Stefan Tanaka, *Japan's Orient: Rendering Pasts into History* (Berkeley: University of California Press, 1993), p. 248.

outcast butcher class soon became 'one of the most remarkable features of evangelical efforts.' "[32] The hierarchy of Korean society pushed commoners toward the egalitarian ideal of everyone the same before God.

If Christian and liberal ideas marked Korean reformers at the turn of the century, socialist ideas spread among young Koreans in the 1920s, again with the humble as the main subject of the movement. Like their counterparts in China, young Koreans turned their backs on Confucianism and their own history, in a rush to embrace science, democracy, and socialism. Here is the seed of the radical rejection of the past that gained far greater force in both Koreas after World War II; old Korea seemed to have no usable past either for capitalist reformers like Park Chung Hee or for radical nationalists like Kim Il Sung. They ran rushing to a future, the past of which they could not escape. Western missionaries deplored any radicalism save that implied by Koreans adopting Christ or fashioning liberal institutions, but not always without sharp observation: James Scarth Gale wrote,

> Whereas the Korean of thirty years ago was a scholar, the young Korean of today is in many respects an ignoramus. He has a smattering of western knowledge, and some little idea of his own tongue; but his knowledge of the ancient literature of his people is practically non-existent. Therein lies a great danger. That literature contains all the idealism of his race.[33]

Socialists and communists were always Korean nationalists as well, of course, but the nationalists were also split between those who remained in Korea and those who went into exile abroad; and at home nationalists divided into radicals and "gradualists," the latter urging a path of preparing Koreans for independence through cultural and educational activities. Exiles were further split between people who favored militant, armed struggle and those who urged diplomatic methods for securing Korean independence. We see this vividly in one of the great memoirs of the colonial period, Kim San's *Song of Ariran.* Writing of the "American group," made up of people like Syngman Rhee who pounded the pavement in Washington, buttonholing Foggy Bottom diplomats, Kim San said, "These were all 'gentlemen.' Most of them spoke good English. They actually expected to get Korean independence by being able to speak persuasive English!"[34] Kim threw his lot in with the revolution in China, hoping to build up enough force there eventually to liberate Korea from colonialism. Like many other Koreans, he participated

32. Henderson (1968), p. 207.
33. Gale (1972), pp. 67, 69.
34. Kim and Wales (1973), p. 114.

in the Northern Expedition, the disorders in Shanghai in 1927, and the subsequent uprising in Canton, known as the Canton commune. In the 1930s he made the "Long March" with the Chinese Communists, ending up in their base area at Yenan.

The largest split, however, brought Korea into the mainstream of world history after World War I: it was between liberal idealism and socialism, between Wilson and Lenin. Liberals had the advantage of association with Wilson's ideals of self-determination, and the disadvantage that the United States was not interested in supporting Korean independence; furthermore, their social base within Korea was very slim. The socialists had the disadvantage of Japanese police action, which targeted and walked off to jail anyone espousing "Bolshevik" ideas, and the advantage of a potentially large mass base and a spirit of sacrifice on behalf of Korea, so that by the end of the 1920s they were leading the Korean resistance movement. As the preeminent scholar of Korean communism, Dae-sook Suh, put it, leftists and communists

> succeeded in wresting control of the Korean revolution from the Nationalists; they planted a deep core of Communist influence among the Korean people, particularly the students, youth groups, laborers and peasants. Their fortitude and, at times, obstinate determination to succeed had a profound influence on Korean intellectuals and writers. To the older Koreans, who had groveled so long before seemingly endless foreign suppression, communism seemed a new hope and a magic touch.. . . For Koreans in general, the sacrifices of the Communists, if not the idea of communism, made strong appeal, far stronger than any occasional bomb-throwing exercise of the Nationalists. The haggard appearance of the Communists suffering from torture, their stern and disciplined attitude toward the common enemy of all Koreans, had a far-reaching effect on people.[35]

Korean militants in China and the USSR founded early communist and nationalist resistance groups. The Korean Communist Party (KCP) was founded within Korea in 1925; a man named Pak Hŏn-yŏng was one of the organizers, and he became the leader of Korean communism in southern Korea after 1945. Various nationalists groups also emerged during this period, including the exiled Korean Provisional Government (KPG) in Shanghai, which included Syngman Rhee and another famous nationalist, Kim Ku, among its members. However, Chinese Nationalists consistently undercut the independence of the KPG by commanding it to accept Sun Yat-sen's Three People's Principles, refusing to train Koreans in the Nationalist military because of Japanese protests, half-

35. Suh (1967), p. 132.

heartedly supporting the small KPG army after the war began, but then taking away the right of the KPG to command this army in 1941; within two years the KPG "was in chaos," and then in 1944 Chiang Kai-shek finally saw it in his interest to give the KPG a modest form of recognition as the de facto government of postwar Korea. When the Nationalists themselves could not unify China after the Japanese surrender, the KPG "practically dissolved."[36]

Sharp police repression and internal factionalism made it impossible to sustain radical groups over time. Many nationalist and communist leaders were thrown in jail in the late 1920s and early 1930s, only to emerge in 1945. When Japan invaded and then annexed Manchuria in 1931, however, a strong guerrilla resistance embracing Chinese and Koreans emerged. There were well over 200,000 guerrillas (all loosely connected, and including bandits and secret societies) fighting the Japanese in the early 1930s; after murderous but effective counterinsurgency campaigns the numbers declined to a few thousand in the mid-1930s. Korean resistance in Manchuria was very strong; a recent Chinese source found that Koreans constituted a much higher percentage of resisters as a proportion of population than any other ethnic group, including Han Chinese.[37]

It was in this milieu that Kim Il Sung (1912–94, originally named Kim Sŏng-ju) emerged. He was a significant guerrilla leader by the mid-1930s; the Japanese considered Kim one of the most effective and dangerous of guerrillas. They formed a special counterinsurgency unit to track him down, and put Koreans in it as part of their divide-and-rule tactics.

There are ridiculous myths about this guerrilla resistance in both Koreas today: the North claims that Kim single-handedly defeated the Japanese, and the South claims that Kim is an imposter who stole the name of a revered patriot. Nonetheless, this experience is important for an understanding of postwar Korea. The resistance to the Japanese is the main legitimating doctrine of the DPRK; the North Koreans trace the origin of the army, the leadership, and their ideology back to this founding moment. Today the top North Korean leadership still includes core leaders who fought the Japanese in Manchuria, even if most of the others have died by now.

The mythology about Kim and his allies can be sorted out through the lenses of unimpeachable documentation, of which there is a growing amount. There is a rare study by two Japanese Kwantung Army colonels in 1951, for example, men who tracked Kim in Manchuria and who pro-

36. Susuki Masayuki, in Suh and Shultz (1990), pp. 130–38.
37. Changyu Piao, in Suh and Shultz (1990), p. 64.

vided Americans with their experience and their judgments on how to fight Korean guerrillas during the Korean War. They depicted Kim Il Sung as "the most famous" of Korean guerrilla leaders in the late 1930s: "Kim Il Sung was particularly popular among the Koreans in Manchuria. It is said that there were many Koreans who praised him as a Korean hero and gave him, secretly, both spiritual and material support."

Although Kim and other Korean guerrillas cooperated with Chinese leaders like Yang Ch'ing-yü, they were under no one else's effective command. Nor were they run by the Kremlin: "They did not care about the relation of their command organ with the Soviet Army or the Chinese Communist [army]." They ran back and forth across the Soviet border to escape counterinsurgency units, but the Soviets provided little weaponry or material aid.

The guerrillas never established permanent positions and fought in small units of fifty or a hundred, something that was termed "natural" because larger groups would be much more liable to attack and capture. Instead, they "always make [a] surprise attack on the enemy with resourceful plans and tactics." "When they were attacked by a subjugation unit, they had to move like monkeys through the woodmen's paths in the dense forest." Local police "were at the complete mercy" of the guerrillas until 1939, when extraordinary counterinsurgency campaigns began. Even the Japanese army sustained major losses in 1938–39: "not infrequently, units under the command of the Kwantung Army . . . were annihilated by bandit [guerrilla] ambush." Entire convoys and companies were destroyed in the spring of 1939. The guerrillas got the aid of the local Korean population time and again; Ch'ientao, the home of hundreds of thousands of Koreans, was "a very safe place for Korean bandits." The Japanese officers described the local Korean population as "depraved, rebellious, and anti-Japanese." There were "only a few good people" among this "rebellious, crafty and lazy," indeed "very discontented race"; those few supported the Japanese. The nasty habits of the Koreans included appearing "very gentle outwardly," while they nonetheless "harboured ill feeling against Japan." They would give no information on guerrillas to the Japanese, another index of their general depravity, one assumes.[38]

If you visit the modern history museum in P'yŏngyang, you will find an entire room devoted to a mock-up of the Battle of P'och'ŏnbo in 1939, complete with lights punctuating the action and myriad sound effects. Outside of North Korea hardly anyone has heard of this clash, but it consisted of a brief takeover of the town by Kim and his guerrillas.

38. National Archives, Army Chief of Military History manuscripts, box 601, "Military Studies on Manchuria," bk. 4, chap. 9, "Bandits and Inhabitants" (Tokyo: FEC, 1952).

P'och'ŏnbo held one of seven branch agricultural stations that Japanese technicians used to improve farming; this one dealt especially with fire-field farming,[39] a group of peasants that was very important to Kim's slim base among Koreans in Manchuria. They were among the poorest but also the freest of Koreans during the Japanese period, escaping into the mountains to live a hardy existence. *Hwajŏn* (fire-field) farmers sometimes worked extremely steep slopes, where even tilling by hand would be difficult; but they still put a yoke of oxen up the slopes. They worked the fields for three to five years and then moved on. They grew millet, barley, and soybeans, sometimes potatoes and buckwheat. They usually had exhausted their harvest by spring, and lived all summer "on berries, nuts, mushrooms, herbs and roots."[40]

DEVELOPMENTAL COLONIALISM

In the 1930s a scholar observed that Koreans were still "poor merchants" and that Korea's cities still did not have a commercial bustle:

> The cities of Korea . . . are largely centers of administrative activity. . . . Not a single city in Korea is busy and brisk like a trading center of the Western world, or Tokyo or Shanghai; Seoul, the largest, has a population of less than 370,000, and even here everything seems at a standstill and quiet.[41]

The few seats of commerce were the new railway centers and rice-exporting seaports, and as they grew they slowly eroded the ancient hostility to commerce that had marked Korea.

At first Japan was determined to have Korea's commerce for itself. Colonial authorities passed laws in 1910 inhibiting the formation of Korean firms, with limits on how much paid-up capital could be Korean; this came at a time when Japanese capital was already quite predominant. Japanese-owned firms accounted for 70 percent of the total, Japanese-Korean firms for 10.5 percent, and purely Korean firms for only 18 percent. Under the "cultural policy" of the 1920s, however, Korean commerce began to grow. One source argued for "a tremendous increase in the number of Korean entrepreneurs," but by the end of the decade Koreans still had only about 3 percent of the total paid-up capital. Most Korean capitalists were still wholesalers, brokers, and merchants dealing in grain or grain-based liquor transactions, with such activity mushrooming in the new ports.

39. Lautensach (1945), p. 402–3.
40. Lautensach (1945), p. 228.
41. Lee (1936), p. 195.

The most important fruit of the cultural policy for Korean industry was the integral role it soon had in Japan's "administrative guidance" of the entire Northeast Asian regional economy. Now Korea was to play a part in plans linking the metropole with hinterland economies, and it is from this point that we can date Japan's specific brand of architectonic capitalism that has influenced Northeast Asia down to the present.[42]

Japan entered a period of economic stagnation in the 1920s and pursued free-trade policies, and Westerners then and thereafter lauded Japan for its liberal institutions. This period of "Taisho democracy" was for modernization theorists the progressive culmination of the Meiji success story, marred later by the aberration of the decade of militarism, 1936–45.[43] Japan girded its loins at home for trade competition, inaugurating tendencies in its political economy that remain prominent today; here was an early version of what is now termed "export-led development." Both Chalmers Johnson and William Miles Fletcher III date the origins of Japan's national industrial strategy and "administrative guidance" from the mid- to late 1920s, and the Americans and the British were most receptive to Japan's outward-turning political economy.[44] The Export Association Law of 1925 marked an important watershed, stimulating industrial reorganization, cartels, and various state subsidies to exporters.[45]

Also visible at this early point was the developmental model of state-sponsored loans at preferential interest rates as a means to shape industrial development and take advantage of "product cycles" yielding firms whose paid-in capital was often much less than their outstanding debt. Businessmen did not offer shares on a stock market, but went to state banks for their capital. Strategic investment decisions were in the hands of state bureaucrats, state banks, and state corporations (like the Oriental Development Company), meaning that policy could move "swiftly and *sequentially,*" and in ways that influenced South Korea in the 1960s and 1970s.

By the mid-1930s this sort of financing had became a standard prac-

42. Cumings (1984).

43. See John W. Dower's introductory essay in Dower, ed., *Origins of the Modern Japanese State: Selected Writings of E. H. Norman* (New York: Pantheon Books, 1975).

44. Johnson (1982); Fletcher, *The Japanese Business Community and National Trade Policy, 1920–1942* (Chapel Hill: University of North Carolina Press, 1989).

45. Gō Seinosuke, formerly head of the huge Oji Paper Company and director of the Tokyo Stock Exchange for twelve years, drafted a report in 1929 recommending, among other things, "a new national committee . . . to rationalize industrial production in order to 'aid industrial development' "; "Go endorsed the principle of export planning—selecting products that might sell well abroad and fostering their growth." The plan led to the Export Compensation Act of May 1930 and other measures to aid export industries. Fletcher, *Japanese Business Community,* pp. 59, 61–62.

tice; the key institution in this model was the Korean Industrial Bank (Chōsen Shokusan Ginkō), the main source of capital for big Korean firms (by the end of the colonial period about half of its employees were Korean). Meanwhile, the Bank of Chōsen played the role of central bank and provisioned capital throughout the imperial realm in northeastern China. It had twenty branches in Manchukuo, served as fiscal agent for Japan's Kwantung Army, and had an office in New York to vacuum up American loans for colonial expansion. On the side it "trafficked in opium, silver and textile smuggling" and participated in the ill-famed Nishihara loan, designed to buy off Chinese opposition to Japan's "twenty-one demands" (about nineteen of which bit off pieces of Chinese sovereignty).[46]

Most important for Korea, however, was the Industrial Bank's role under Ariga Mitsutoyo (1919–37) in "jump-starting Korea's first industrial and commercial entrepreneurs, men such as Min T'ae-shik, Min Kyu-sik, Pak Hŏng-sik, and Kim Yŏn-su."[47] We see the kernel of this logic in the government-general's industrial commission of 1921, which for the first time called for supports to Korea's fledgling textile industry and for it to produce not just for the domestic market but especially for exports to the Asian continent, where Korean goods would have a price advantage. This was by no means a purely "top-down" exercise, either, for Koreans were part of the commission and quickly called for state subsidies and hothouse "protection" for Korean companies. The nurturing of a Korean business class was a necessity if "gradualism" was to have any meaning, and this was in effect its birthday party—although a controversial one (three days before the commission opened, two bombs had been lobbed into the government-general building).[48] That Japan had much larger ideas in mind, however, is obvious in the proposal for "General Industrial Policy" put before the 1921 conference:

> Since Korea is a part of the imperial domain, industrial plans for Korea should be in conformity with imperial industrial policy. Such a policy must provide for economic conditions in adjacent areas, based on [Korea's] geographical position amid Japan, China, and the Russian Far East.

One of the Japanese delegates explained that Korean industry would be integral to overall planning in Tokyo and would require some protection if it were to accept its proper place in "a single, coexistent, coprosperous Japanese-Korean unit."[49]

46. Woo (1991), pp. 23–30.
47. Woo (1991), pp. 29–30.
48. Eckert (1991), pp. 44, 82–84.
49. Quoted in Eckert (1991), pp. 115, 128.

Government-general subsidies to Kim Sŏng-su's Kyŏngbang Textile Company began in 1924, amounting to 4 percent of its capital, and continued every year thereafter until 1935 (except for the depression year 1932–33), by which time they accounted for one-quarter of the firm's capital. Kim Sŏng-su got loans from the Industrial Bank of ¥80,000 in 1920 and one triple that size in 1929, allowing a major expansion of his textile business. For the next decade Kyŏngbang obtained several million yen worth of loans from this bank, so that by 1945 its ¥22 million outstanding debt was more than twice the company's worth.[50]

Japanese textiles had long been dominated by technology supplied by the famous Pratt Brothers in England.[51] With Japan's new-found preeminence in textile machinery, however, it was time to find a buyer for obsolescent machinery: why not find it in Japan's near reaches? Soon the giant firm C. Itoh was fobbing off its machines on Korean textile producers, who could match the older technology to lower labor cost and markets for cheap clothing in China, not to mention military uniforms. (See, for example, the use of surplus Japanese machinery in a new yarn and cloth mill set up in Taejŏn in 1942).[52]

In other fields Japan remained dependent on the United States and England. The Japanese allowed Americans to continue to run Korean gold mines until 1939, because they needed American technology. Japan occupied "an intermediate position" in mining, being an imperial power with mines, but lacking the advanced technology required to exploit them.[53] The Chōsen Oil Company set up a refinery in Wŏnsan, using American oil company "blueprints and consultations," a reflection of American dominance in the world oil regime of the 1930s.[54] Kim Sŏng-su also invested in this refinery, considered "the king of the peninsula's oil world" and of critical importance to Japan's war industry after American bombing of its home islands began, since the Wŏnsan plant produced high-quality lubricating oil.

The Japanese were and are great builders of railroads, as an integral part of their industrial architecture. To leave Tokyo station on a bullet train and whistle to Kyoto is still one of the great travel experiences in the world. Before 1939 you could board an express train in Pusan and travel all the way to Europe—through old P'yŏngyang, across the Yalu,

50. Eckert (1991), pp. 85–86.

51. Cumings (1994), p. 85.

52. Eckert (1991), p. 118.

53. Foster Bain, "Problems Fundamental to Mining Enterprises in the Far East," *Mining and Metallurgical Society of America* 14, no. 1 (Jan. 1921): 1–34.

54. MacArthur Archives, Norfolk, Va., Record Group 6, box 78, Allied Translator and Interpreter Service, issue no. 23, Feb. 15, 1951, quoting original documents captured in Wŏnsan.

into Harbin, thence via the Trans-Siberian railway on to Moscow, a day in Leningrad, on to Prague, Berlin, and then Paris. Korea and Manchuria were stitched together by rail networks, webs drawn by colonial spiders on a determined southeast (Japan) to northwest (Asian mainland) axis, thus to shrink space and time and to spill Korean rice and Manchurian soybeans all along the wharfs looking out to the Sea of Japan, then to bring back fruit-of-the-Toyoda-loom cotton clothes for the waiting backs of Koreans and Chinese. What the colonizers called "a mighty trio" of railway, highway, and sea transport drew the colonial peoples into new forms of exchange, not just with Japan but with the world market system.

The rails had penetrative and integrative effects, hastening the commercialization of agriculture and replacing the A-frame carrier, oxcart, and meandering path with the most up-to-date conveyances. As much as any other Japanese institution, the railroad network provided the people of Korea and Manchuria with a harbinger of unprecedented change and a symbol of Japanese power. Villages like Taejŏn became key railroad junctions, and remote outposts like Najin, near the Russian border, became entrepôts of a huge export trade. (Najin grew from 500 people in 1927 to 26,000 a decade later; nearby Ch'ŏngjin grew from 100 people in 1900 to 72,353 in 1938, making Ch'ŏngjin by 1940 the leading port on the Sea of Japan.) Korea's traditional isolation was broken; now White Head Mountain had black trains whistling through high tunnels on their way to China.

It was not the Harrimans and the Hills who built these railroads but a state company, the South Manchurian Railway Company (SMRC). Set up in 1906, it was the first of the great companies organized to promote Japanese interests on the continent. The big Japanese banks supplied its capital, and the bureaucrats supplied everything else. To quote from an early SMRC handout: "The traveler journeys in the company's cars and stops at the company's hotels, which are heated by coal from the company's own electric works. . . . If unfortunate enough to fall sick on the way, [the traveler] is certain to be taken to one of the company's hospitals."[55] After 1931 the SMRC took over Chinese and Russian rail lines and in 1933 the Korean rail lines (which had been run by a separate colonial company); within ten years it had doubled the rail lengths, to more than 10,000 kilometers in Manchukuo and over 6,000 in Korea. By contrast China, which had a population about eight times larger than Korea's and whose rail lines were heavily concentrated in Manchuria, carried only about twice the number of total passengers per year as the Korean rail-

55. Japan Times, *Economic Development of Korea and Manchuria* (Tokyo: Japan Times Publishing, 1923), p. 250.

The port of Ch'ŏngjin in the 1930s.

roads in the 1940s. Meanwhile, Vietnam had one rail line meandering from Hanoi down through Hue to Saigon. The colonizers were also road builders: until this century Korea was "one of the most roadless countries in the world," but by 1945 it was estimated to have 53,000 kilometers of auto and country roads, compared with perhaps 100,000 kilometers of "serviceable" roads in all of China.[56] In short, by 1945 Korea had a much better-developed transport and communications infrastructure than any other East Asian country save Japan; this sets Korea off from China and Vietnam and helps explain the different fate of rural political movements in postwar Korea.

Japan's closed-door policy in the 1930s had clear Keynesian pump-priming goals—farm village relief, a military buildup, and a "big push" in heavy industries, in order to pull Japan and its colonies out of the depression. Ugaki Kazushige was governor-general of Korea from 1931 to 1936; he was "an ultra-nationalist, [who] deeply believed in the need for a Japanese imperium of economic autarky and industrial self-sufficiency." Korea was industrialized out of the depression, with growth rates in manufacturing averaging more than 10 percent annually; unlike

56. V. T. Zaichikov, *Geography of Korea,* trans. Albert Parry (New York: Institute of Pacific Relations, 1952), pp. 82–83; Cumings (1981), p. 16.

Japan, Korea was a "capitalist paradise," with minimal business taxes and little regulation of working conditions and business practices. The *zaibatsu,* of course, got the best treatment of all; Mitsubishi, Mitsui, Nissan, and Sumitomo were all heavily involved in Korea in this period and had by 1940 become more important than the colonial state's companies, accounting for 75 percent of total capital investment.

Perhaps the model *zaibatsu,* however, was Noguchi Jun's "new" one, a very close model for postwar South Korea's *chaebŏl.* Noguchi, who was known as the "king of Korean industry," had his own little empire in the colony, accounting for more than one-third of Japan's total direct investment in Korea and including firms dealing in magnesium, coal, oil, explosives, aluminum, and zinc, in addition to his major firms in chemicals. He also built 90 percent of Korea's electric resources, including the great Suiho dam on the Yalu, second in the world only to Boulder Dam. Noguchi founded Nippon Chisso, the second-largest chemical complex in the world, and which provided the starting point for North Korea's postwar chemicals industry (which was integral to its self-reliant industrial policy). Noguchi explained at another industrial commission in 1936 how he integrated Korean workers into his industrial combine:

> The Koreans I employed as workers [at first] were generally graduates of higher common school. But Russian communism was rampant in North and South Hamgyŏng Provinces, and scores of arrests were carried out around this time. On each such occasion many of the criminals came from my factory. . . . I decided from that time on never to employ any higher common school graduates in my factories. . . . [T]he higher common schools are spending a good sum of money on producing people not very useful to business.[57]

Noguchi's main plant, the Chōsen Nitrogenous Fertilizer Company, was at Hŭngnam; it made ammonium sulfates and phosphates, most of which went to Japan. In 1936 its production was one-eighth of that in the whole German empire—and Germany was the largest producer of chemicals in the world. Noguchi was able to build this huge complex because of nearby hydroelectric facilities that provided cheap energy, especially the Chōsin (Changjin) reservoir.

In agriculture Koreans were to eat millet from Manchuria while exporting rice to Japan, just as in textiles they were to make rough clothes for the Manchurians while Japan produced the fine silks and cottons preferred by metropolitan consumers. Meanwhile, wage rates were set such that even though their skills were the same, Japanese

57. Eckert (1991), pp. 119, 149; Cumings (1990), p. 30.

workers in Korea got over 2 yen per day in 1937, a Formosan worker 1 yen, and a Korean worker .66 yen. Rarely has the typically tripartite segmentation of global capitalism into core, middling, and peripheral economies been so clear.[58]

Manchukuo was established on March 1, 1932, the date chosen precisely to stick in the Korean craw. Modeled on the Korean colony, the new puppet state was not going to have anything so disagreeable as another March First movement. Instead, Manchuria got something far worse, a skeleton of modernized cities and new industries, and an interior that became a quagmire of revolt and violence for the Japanese army. As the historian Ienaga Saburō was among the first to point out,[59] it was the army's failure to pacify Manchuria and (subsequently) North China that deeply influenced the military's critical July 1941 decisions to turn south and, four months later, to attack Pearl Harbor.

Manchuria was also an arena of opportunity for Koreans, however, as the Chōsen Business Club knew when it held a celebration of the new Manchukuo regime in Seoul in May 1932, with many important Korean business leaders attending.[60] Manchukuo was a frontier for Korean rice farmers, bureaucrats, soldiers, and businessmen. Nearly one and a half million Koreans were there by 1940, including the large population just across the Yalu River and deeply hostile to Japanese imperialism, but also the thousands of Korean families that the Japanese settled there because, so they thought, they were better rice farmers than the Chinese (apparently true in many cases).[61] Koreans also served in the Japanese police and military organizations in the puppet state, as did many of the most important civil servants in postwar South Korea—for example, Ch'oe Kyu-ha (interim president in 1980–81). Kyŏngbang Textiles even opened a spanking new subsidiary in Manchuria in 1944, just in time to lose it to incoming Soviet forces, which carted off $45 million worth of spindles and looms.[62]

In 1936 heavy industry accounted for 28 percent of total industrial production, and more than half a million Koreans were employed in industry, a figure that had tripled by 1945. Industry expanded in Korea at double or triple the rate in Taiwan:

58. Cumings (1981), p. 30; for the tripartite theory, see Immanuel Wallerstein, *The Modern World-System* (New York: Academic Press, 1974).

59. Ienaga (1976), pp. 65–71.

60. Eckert (1991), p. 169.

61. Koreans in the state of Parhae first brought wet paddy rice farming to Manchuria, and then revived it again in the twentieth century. Changyu Piao, in Suh and Shultz (1990), p. 55.

62. Cumings (1981), p. 55; Eckert (1991), pp. 162, 178–79.

KOREANS EMPLOYED IN INDUSTRY WITHIN KOREA, 1923–1943[63]

YEAR	NUMBER OF PERSONS	INDEX OF INCREASE
1932	384,951	100
1936	594,739	154
1940	702,868	183
1943	1,321,713	343

This table excludes mining and transportation, which employed tens of thousands more, and does not count the millions of Koreans working outside the country in the 1940s. By 1943 the production ratio between Korea's heavy and light industry had become equal. Nor was it really the case that the North of Korea had all the heavies and the South only light industry; the South surpassed the North in machine building, electric machinery, heavy vehicles, mining tools, and the like.[64] Thus Korea's industrial revolution began in earnest during the last fifteen years of Japanese rule.

One observant scholar was much impressed by the rapid development of Korea in the late 1930s. Here was an "obvious, indeed astonishing success," even if the development was "oriented toward the needs of the empire." This combined with a succession of excellent harvests in 1936–38, yielded the idea of a "Korean boom": with "the rapid development of all of Korea's economic capacity . . . a certain amount of prosperity is beginning to enter even the farmer's huts."[65] The northeast corner of Korea, long backward, was "experiencing an upswing unlike any other part of Korea," mainly because of its incorporation into Manchukuo trading networks.[66]

Some Korean scholars have argued that a "national bourgeoisie" began to develop in the 1920s, as part of a growing Korean nationalism. Although in my view no class of national bourgeois arose, the appearance of important individuals representing this tendency was critical. All kinds of new lines of activity opened up at home and abroad for enterprising and idealistic young Koreans: urban commerce, journalism, study abroad, and political organizing. Each line developed a fissure that would later play upon liberated Korea: independent businessmen versus collaborators, resisters against the Japanese who stayed at home versus those who went abroad, gradualists versus radicals, and, among all of them, those who called themselves nationalists pure-and-simple versus

63. Government-general statistics, in Cumings (1981), p. 26.
64. Woo (1991), pp. 31, 34–36, 41.
65. Lautensach (1945), pp. 383, 386–87.
66. Lautensach (1945), pp. 204–7.

those who became revolutionary nationalists and, often, communists.

The most important group in Korean commerce in the colonial period, Korea's first *chaebŏl* (*zaibatsu*, or conglomerate) was born among landlords who became entrepreneurs in the southwestern Chŏlla provinces, sometimes called the Honam area, made up of rich, double-cropped rice paddies fully involved in the export trade through big ports like Kunsan and Mokp'o and other, smaller ones along the southwest coast. Kim Sŏng-su was the core figure in a group of Honam people who got very rich in the colonial period and later played major roles in postwar South Korea. Kim was born into a wealthy, aristocratic family that possessed something more like a plantation of rice paddies than the typically small farms that dotted Korea. The ancestral spread was near the coast in Koch'ang, where North and South Chŏlla come together and where the family's influence is still strongly felt.

Kim founded the *Tonga ilbo* (East Asia daily), the leading Korean newspaper after 1920, and the Kobu School in Chŏlla and Posŏng College, later Korea University—where his statue stood until the 1980s, when radical students demanded that it be removed. Besides landholdings, the core of this fortune was the Kyŏngbang Textile Company. His brother Kim Yŏn-su ran this enterprise, which by the 1940s had become Korea's first multinational firm, with its new plant in Manchuria. Its interests included three ginning factories, a huge factory for spinning and weaving in Yŏngdŭngp'o, a bleaching and dyeing factory, and silk thread and cloth factories; it was also involved in ball bearings, brewing, gold mining, real estate, metal, oil refining, and even aircraft industries.[67]

By the 1930s many other Honam landlords were getting into urban commerce, like Chŏng Yong-ch'ŏl of Mokp'o, who founded a rubber company, and Kim Sŏng-gyu, who helped establish the Kwangju Agricultural and Industrial Bank and was said to have the largest landholdings in the Mokp'o region. This group was the basis for much of the political leadership in postwar South Korea: Kim Sŏng-su and his associates founded and led the Korean Democratic Party after 1945, provided many officials in the American occupation (1945–48), and structured the moderate opposition to the Syngman Rhee (1948–60) and Park Chung Hee (1961–79) governments.

Other Korean entrepreneurs came up the hard way socially and the easy way colonially: they traded commoner or outcaste backgrounds for the money to be made working with the Japanese. The key figure here was the much reviled but very wealthy Pak Hŭng-sik, another of Korea's capitalist pioneers. Pak's first venture was a small printing shop in Yong-

67. Eckert (1991), p. 58.

gang, not far from P'yŏngyang. By the age of twenty he had enough money to buy the Hwasin department store in Seoul, which he soon made as famous in Korea as Macy's in New York or Carson-Pirie-Scott in Chicago. Along with Kim Sŏng-su he became one of Korea's first *chaebŏl* owners (and each invested heavily in the other's ventures), with interests in an enormous variety of industrial ventures, including the Chōsen Aircraft Company near Seoul, and a joint venture with Mitsui in building kamikaze aircraft in the last year of the war.[68]

After the liberation you could hardly open a book or a newspaper without seeing someone single Pak out as a collaborator, if not an arch-traitor. Perhaps it occurs only to outraged nationalists to expect politically principled behavior from capitalist magnates. A blatant Japanophile (of whom there were many more than Koreans can now remember), Pak Hŭng-sik was widely thought to be the richest man in Korea in the late 1940s, and was brought to trial as a collaborator by the 1948 National Assembly. Among other charges it appeared he never paid a ¥10 million fine levied against him in 1945 for accepting a ¥20 million bonus payment from the departing Japanese—for services rendered, such as devoting his airplane parts factory near Suwŏn to the war effort. In April 1949, however, this shameless but wily entrepreneur coughed up a one million won bail note and never saw the inside of a jail again. What is more important to remember is that people like Kim Sŏng-su and Pak Hŭng-sik were unheard of in many colonies (for example, in Java, Burma, or Vietnam); some Koreans may not like them any more than I would the American robber barons of the late nineteenth century, but in the 1930s they were harbingers of radical change.

What was the alternative for talented Koreans in this colony? To miss their life chances through renunciation, to resist and end up dead or in jail, or to participate. One who took the latter course rose to become the first Korean judge in the Japanese government. In due time he was confronted with the necessity to levy a death sentence against a fellow Korean. That he did, but the experience so vexed him that "he simply left office and became a candy peddler," wandering the countryside until he lodged with monks in the Diamond Mountains. He later became, under the Buddhist title Hyobong *sŭnim,* one of the great Sŏn masters of his time. He died in 1966, at the age of seventy-eight.[69]

That is one story and a moving one, but it is, in typical human-all-too-human fashion, a rare one. Far more representative of Korean collaboration with the Japanese is the case of Kim Tong-jo, who began his career

68. Cumings (1981), p. 22.
69. Buswell (1992), pp. 91–92.

as a National Police officer, spying on his fellow Koreans, and never looked back. He traveled between Japan and Korea frequently during World War II, informing to the Japanese on Korean resistance among the multitude of Koreans mobilized for work in Japan. Later the Japanese moved him up, making him a responsible official in wartime rationing of food and other provisions to Koreans.

After 1945 he worked for the American occupation, also in provisions and supplies to the Korean population; after Rhee became president he entered the new Foreign Ministry, advancing to vice-minister before leaving the government. He came back after the military coup in 1961, as a foreign affairs adviser to the ruling party and the Korean CIA. After helping to negotiate Korea's normalization with Japan in 1965, he became the first ROK ambassador to Tokyo. In that role "he acquired a notorious reputation among Korean residents as a bag man who made payments to Japanese politicians"; soon (1967) he was appointed ambassador to the United States. A few years later, however, he ran afoul of an employee who blew the whistle when he observed Ambassador Kim preparing for a visit to Capitol Hill by stuffing envelopes full of $100 bills into his briefcase (see chapter 9).[70]

Neither Kim Tong-jo nor Hyobong *sŭnim* is a tragic figure. The tragedy of Korean collaboration can be seen in a person like Ch'oe Rin, a key leader of the March First movement, who by 1938 was giving speeches lauding "the Yamato people" and "the eternal, single-family lineage of the [Japanese] Imperial Household,"[71] or in a great modernizer and nationalist like Yun Ch'i-ho, who accepted a position in the House of Peers, or in leaders of business like Kim Sŏng-su who quickly threw their lot in with the big Japanese *zaibatsu* and profited from the war. These were people who would have been natural leaders of an independent and self-confident Korea, harbingers of a middle-class revolution. But because of their collaboration (under tremendous Japanese pressure, to be sure, but then others continued to resist in spite of that) the Japanese succeeded in compromising the emergence of a modern, liberal elite, and in many ways we are still waiting for it to appear.

As Korean growth rates took off in the 1930s, a small urban middle class began going to the movies, listening to the radio, buying cosmetics, and dressing in the latest fashions.[72] This is evident in observations by the scholar-missionary James Scarth Gale in the late 1920s. When he

70. All information from Boettcher (1980), pp. 292–93.

71. Eckert (1991), p. 231.

72. Lecture by Michael Robinson, University of Chicago, May 1992. Dr. Robinson is preparing a book on the Korean urban middle class in the 1930s.

was about to retire, he lamented what he saw before him in Korea, in words that deserve lengthy quotation and pondering (in part because they seem so contemporary):

> We weep over old Korea, a victim, not so much of political agencies, as of the social and intellectual revolution that has come from the west.
>
> We have unwittingly brought about the destruction of East Asia, in which Korea is involved. To her the west evidently does as it pleases, why should she not? The west has no barriers between the sexes, why should she have? In everything that she has seen of the west, religion counts as nothing: why should she bother about it? Labour-unionism, communism, socialism, bolshevism, and anarchism express the real mind of the western nations; why should she not take them up and be the same? Why should she sing in falsetto when the west sings with the whole throat wide open. . . . Why not go whirling off for joy-rides, boys and girls? Why not be divorced at pleasure? Why not be up-to-date as the west is up-to-date? This wild dream . . . well expresses the mind of the advanced youth of the city of Seoul in these days of confusion.
>
> Let us glance once more at the Korea that is gone, "the land of the superior man," as China long ago called her; land of the scholar, land of the book and writing-brush, land of the beautiful vase and polished mirror; land of rarest, choicest fabrics; land of poems and painted pictures; land of the filial son, the devoted wife, the loyal courtier; land of the hermit, the deeply religious seer whose final goal was God.[73]

It is a statement in three parts: an old, upright gentleman lamenting a lost past; a testament to his love of Korea, where he lived for forty years; and a sign that he had his finger on the pulse of Seoul. All of what he and his elder Korean friends held dear had been turned upside down, lock, stock, and barrel, or so it seemed, by young people who were in open rebellion against their society, against the Japanese, their parents, and old Korea, rushing off toward an unknown future.

THE COLONIAL PRESSURE COOKER

The most important characteristic of Korea's colonial experience may have been the manner in which it ended: the last decade of a four-decade imperium resembled a pressure cooker, building up tensions that exploded in the postwar period. The colonial situation built to a climax, abruptly collapsed, and left the Korean people and two different great powers to deal with the results.

In the mid-1930s, as we have seen, Japan entered a phase of heavy

73. Gale ends his book with this passage and a poem from Kim Yun-sik (1972), pp. 319–20.

industrialization that embraced all of Northeast Asia. Unlike most colonial powers, Japan located heavy industry in its colonies, bringing the means of production to the labor and the raw materials. Manchuria and northern Korea got steel mills, auto plants, petrochemical complexes, and enormous hydroelectric facilities; the region was held exclusively by Japan and tied together with the home market to such a degree that national boundaries became less important than the new transnational, integrated production. These changes were externally induced and served Japanese, not Korean, interests. Thus they represented a kind of *overdevelopment*.

The same changes fostered *underdevelopment* in Korean society as a whole. Since the changes were exogenous, the Korean upper and managerial classes did not blossom; instead, their development was retarded, or it ballooned up suddenly at Japanese behest. Among the majority peasant class, change was greatly accelerated. In the 1930s the combined effect of the depression and the industrialization of the peninsula shifted large populations off the farms and into new cities and industries; when Japanese imperialism expanded dramatically after 1937 and began mobilizing everyone in its sphere, the Korean population movement turned into a hemorrhage. Koreans became the mobile human capital used to work the new factories in northern Korea and Manchuria, mines and other enterprises in Japan, and urban factories in southern Korea. From 1935 to 1945 Korea began its industrial revolution, with many of the usual characteristics: the uprooting of peasants from the land, the emergence of a working class, urbanization, and population mobility. It is just that in Korea the process was telescoped, giving rise to remarkable population movements, when considered comparatively.

These effects were so powerful that few if any other agrarian societies were ever subject, in such a short time, to the immense population shifts and dislocations of Korea in the last decade of Japanese rule. This was all the more disruptive because of the ancient stability of provincial population distributions. By 1944 fully 11.6 percent of all Koreans were residing outside Korea, "a proportion unequalled by other Far Eastern populations and rarely matched in other parts of the world." About 20 percent of all Koreans were either abroad or in provinces other than those in which they were born; when we learn that most of these were in the fifteen-to-forty age group, it may mean that 40 percent of the adult population was part of this uprooting.[74] Meanwhile, even by Japan's 1945 exit a mere handful of Taiwanese (thirty thousand, most not forcibly mobilized) had left the island, or even their native village.

74. Glenn Trewartha and Wilbur Zelinsky, "Population Distribution and Change in Korea, 1925–1949," *Geographical Review* 45, no. 1 (Jan. 1955): 14; Cumings (1981), pp. 53–55.

This new work force came from the surplus peasant population, which had been hard hit by the depression and by a rapid increase in the concentration of landownership.[75] The most populous provinces were in southern Korea, such as the Kyŏngsang and Chŏlla provinces, and had the biggest migrations of population; North Kyŏngsang, in particular, lost hundreds of thousands of people, while North Hamgyŏng, never a populous province, gained 260,000 people in 1940 alone.[76] The vast majority of Koreans who went to Japan also came from southern provinces. Peasants left the countryside looking for work because they had none in home villages, or because they looked for wage income to supplement family budgets. In the depression years per capita rice consumption was 77 liters (in 1929, for example), compared with 124 liters in 1914 and 198 liters in Japan.[77] Peasants lost land or rights to work land only to end up working in unfamiliar factory settings, doing the dirty work for a relative pittance.

This was, by and large, a forced or mobilized movement; although some peasants were unquestionably attracted by the hope of better jobs or higher wages in earlier years, by 1937 the mobilization of labor was coming from above, as Japan opened a war in North China and thereafter sought to organize every aspect of Korean life to serve the war effort. By 1942 labor was simply drafted or conscripted. Korean laborers became the human capital moved hither and yon according to the dictates of Japan's industrial and military expansion. Koreans, like the Japanese home population, were subject to the National General Mobilization Law, various forms of conscription, and forced participation in work details, "patriotic" organizations, and the like. Japanese and Koreans now were to come together in forced assimilation, through the *naisen ittai* policy, making the two peoples into "one body" (*ilch'e*, in Korean).

As the war took on regional and global dimensions, Koreans for the first time had military careers opened to them. Although most were conscripted footsoldiers, a small number achieved officer status and a few even attained high rank. Japan's far-flung war effort also caused a labor shortage throughout the empire. In Korea this meant that bureaucratic positions were more available to Koreans than at any previous time; thus a substantial cadre of Koreans got administrative experience in government, local administration, police and judicial work, economic planning agencies, banks, and the like. That this occurred in the last decade of

75. The best study is Gragert (1994).
76. Cumings (1981), p. 58.
77. Lautensach (1945), p. 400.

colonialism created a divisive legacy, however, for this was also the harshest period of Japanese rule, the time Koreans remember with greatest bitterness.

In 1937 the Korean League for the General Mobilization of the National Spirit was established, with branches at province, county, township, and workplace levels. The next year a special volunteers corps gathered youths for military service, while the Korean Anti-Communist Association had branches in every province, local offices in police stations, and associated groups in villages, factories, and other workplaces. Participation in anticommunist "spiritual" discussions became compulsory in the workplaces and schools, a measure of the degree to which communists were resisting the Japanese. Recalcitrant Koreans, whether leftists or intellectuals or nationalists, had "impure" ideas winnowed out of their heads by totalitarian methods of interrogation until they were ready to confess their political sins in writing and join groups for those who had "reformed their thoughts" (with branches in every province). These practices deeply poisoned the wells of South and North Korea after 1945. (Both countries indulge in programs of political "thought education," the North doing more of it, of course, but the South doing much more than is usually recognized: "unconverted" political prisoners from the Korean War remained in South Korean jails until the early 1990s.)

After Pearl Harbor the general mobilization for the Greater East Asia Co-Prosperity Sphere was quickened; budget expenditures in 1942 quadrupled what was spent for mobilization in 1937, and they doubled again in 1943. Colonial authorities also set up some 3,245 "youth organizations" at all levels, with a total membership of 2.5 million. Here was born an organizational form that led to the widespread use of political youth groups in the postwar era. Most of all, however, the Japanese wanted Koreans for labor in Japan, northern Korea, and Manchuria. The far-flung efforts of Japan in the Pacific War, eventually stretching from Burma around to Manchukuo, left labor shortages in every industry.

In 1941 some 1.4 million Koreans were in Japan, of whom 770,000 were in the labor force: 220,000 were in construction work, 208,000 in manufacturing, 94,000 in mining, and the remainder in agriculture. Yet at least half a million more were sent to Japan thereafter, such that by the end of the war Koreans made up one-third of the industrial labor force in Japan; 136,000 worked the mines, often in the harshest forms of labor. Mining had been shunned like butchery in Korea, Japanese mines used little machine power, and the dirtiest work was in the pits—where Koreans, including women, who were forced to work bare-breasted, formed 60 to 70 percent of the pit force, working twelve-hour days from dawn to dusk.[78] Similar conditions obtained in Manchukuo, where more hundreds of thousands of Koreans were sent.

Colonial authorities established quotas for mobilized laborers, including so-called comfort girls. Postwar accounts assume a parallelism between ethnicity and position in the colonial years, but that was never strictly true, and by the 1930s the coincidence of ethnicity and position was waning dramatically because of divide-and-rule techniques and labor shortages that pushed Koreans up in the bureaucracy to fill openings. Koreans could no longer blame just the foreign race for the misfortunates that befell them, since the regime often presented itself in the person of a Korean official.

A number of memoirs of the colonial period, written in fictionalized form, depict Koreans in the police force or pushing Koreans around at the bidding of the Japanese. Kim Ronyoung, for example, writes in *Clay Walls* of a relative of hers who was caught by the police for anti-Japanese activities, only to end up being tortured by an interrogator named Okada, whose real (Korean) name was Yun.[79] Some 40 to 50 percent of the National Police were Korean, and Koreans were even used fairly widely as police in Manchukuo, where they acquired "an especially bad name for brutality and venality." Mobile units used to suppress Chinese and Korean guerrillas "were particularly dreaded, since they were usually composed mainly of Japanese soshi, or thugs, and low class Koreans."[80] There is nothing unusual about this in colonial practice; the French used Algerians and Africans in Vietnam for similar purposes. That still makes the practice no less nauseating.

The process of selection for mobilization was harsh and divisive: although each province got a quota according to population, after that selection was haphazard, depending on local officials and police. The Japanese mostly stuck to supervisory roles, so that it would "appear to be a Korean operation." Labor mobilization offices, usually in local police stations, picked laborers from among poor people and disadvantaged clans: "these same Korean officials were the most hated men in their communities."[81] A Korean village elder and former county chief told an interviewer, "He, as a village leader, had to bow to pictures of the Japanese emperor at school or any public meetings. He had to supply men for labor in Japan, the South Pacific, or elsewhere in Korea to work in factories, mines and similar projects." In the period 1942–45 he sent

78. Cumings (1981), pp. 28–29.

79. Kim (1984), p. 123. There is also a Captain Yamamoto in this novel, who turns out to be Korean.

80. Cohen (1949), p. 33.

81. Based on U.S. Army "Operations Reports," cited in Cumings (1981), p. 29.

Korean schoolgirls sent to Nagoya as "comfort women." *Courtesy of* Tonga ilbo *(Seoul), in Hicks,* The Comfort Women *(New York: Norton, 1995).*

fifteen people to Japan to work in coal mines; every one of them returned after liberation, whereupon the village elder retired, claiming "gastric difficulties."[82]

Here we begin to understand the true horror of the "comfort women" issue, why it was covered up by Japan and also left alone for so many years by the South Korean government: to open up inquiry on this sexual slavery would be to find that many women were mobilized by Korean men. Japan fractured the Korean national psyche, pitting Korean against Korean with consequences that continue down to our time.

Somewhere between 100,000 and 200,000 Korean women were mobilized into this slavery, along with smaller numbers of Filipinos, Chinese, and a handful of Westerners. Pae Pong Gi was the first Korean woman to come forward and tell her story with her identity unprotected. She did this in Yamatani Tetsuo's 1979 film, *An Old Lady in Okinawa.* "Like so many other comfort women," George Hicks writes, she "remained in the same role with the American Occupation Forces" on Okinawa. Yun Chong Mo's novel, *My Mother Was a Military Comfort Woman,*" was inspired by the sight of a drunken American soldier dragging a Korean girl by the hair down a street in Seoul. Here is the story of Kim Pok Tong:

82. Eugene Knez, "Sam Jong Dong: A South Korean Village" (Ph.D. diss., Syracuse University, 1959), pp. 46–48.

> Kim Pok Tong came from a well-off land-owning family with six daughters. On her father's death, the family lost most of its property, to settle his debts. . . . Her mother, who was illiterate, was prevailed on in 1941 to seal a form of approval for her daughter's recruitment to the Voluntary Service Corps by a Korean local official, and a Korean in Japanese uniform. The family was given to understand that Pok Tong would do three years of factory work.
>
> She was taken, with about twenty other girls, similarly recruited, to Taiwan. They were kept idle there for some months. . . . Finally they were taken to Canton, where she was forcibly stripped for an examination by an Army medical officer. This both humiliated and bewildered her. She was completely innocent of the facts of life.
>
> Pok Tong was then taken to a comfort station. . . . She was expected to provide service from her second day there. On resisting, she was beaten and denied food, so she yielded. The usual daily total of men was fifteen, rising to fifty or more over weekends. All bought condoms and tickets, which were handed over nightly to the Japanese manager. The women received no money, being told that they would be paid when Japan won the war. . . .
>
> When the war ended, Pok Tong was among fifty women from various "clubs" who were assigned as nursing aides to the 16th Army hospital in Surabaya. . . . After more than a year's internment . . . Pok Tong found her mother at home, left alone by the departure of the rest of the family for Japan. None of the returning women admitted having been comfort women. . . .
>
> Gradually, her secret came out. She began running a bar. Some of her wartime friends had remained in prostitution as the only means of survival. She herself eventually married a man whose first marriage had failed. . . . She [was] unable to have children; medical treatment had proved ineffective. After her husband's death . . . [she] resumed the bar business.[83]

In late 1944 Japanese authorities mobilized some seven thousand Koreans to build a huge, labyrinthine underground bunker near Mount Fuji for the imperial household and other high officials of government; it was preparatory to the "decisive battle for the Homeland" that never came, and was completed just before Japan surrendered. An untold number of Koreans died during the hasty, pell-mell blasting out of tunnels and caves, with little or no precaution for their safety. At least one

83. Hicks (1995), pp. 159, 176–77, 195, 247–48. As Hicks acknowledges, the seminal study on this subject was Kim Il-myŏn's *The Emperor's Forces and Korean Comfort Women*. Yun Chong Mo's book, mentioned in the text, was also a milestone, as were Yoshida Seiji's revelations in *My War Crimes: The Forced Draft of Koreans* (Tokyo, 1983).

The Shinto shrine on South Mountain in Seoul.

thousand Koreans died during the construction period, and persistent rumors claim that those laborers who constructed the emperor's inner sanctum were later killed because they might lead the enemy into it. (When the war ended, local residents plundered the bunker's "luxurious fittings.") Here, too, women were thrown into a comfort station, "housed in a refitted silk-worm workshop," which the police rented from its owner.[84]

Japanese propaganda in this last, harsh period harnessed Neo-Confucian habits of mind to authoritarian politics. The overarching buzzword was *kokutai,* meaning something like national body or essence. The character compound combines *koku* (country) and *tai* (*ch'e,* in Korean), a term meaning basis (of philosophy) or essence, that is, what makes Japan different from other countries. The emperor and the rulers were to govern "with the real significance of Kokutai as the centre, in every national affair and in perfect order." The people were to let "every thought, idea, and action have Kokutai as its principle and clearly display the principle in national life." The ideology drew contrasts between Western individualism and Japan's "Way of *musubi*"—the former indulging in selfish material desire, whereas the latter united everyone in the common effort to advance the "national polity," as *kokutai* was often translated. Emperor Hirohito was the father of Japan, in commu-

84. Hicks (1995), pp. 108–9.

nion with the sun, and all Japanese could become members of the great national family through "the Way of *musubi.*"[85]

Korean culture was simply squashed, and Koreans were expected to mouth this eccentric Japanese blather. They were for the first time required to speak Japanese or to take Japanese names. The colonizers even forced Koreans to worship at Shinto shrines, although Shinto was a strictly Japanese religion, imbued with nationalist and essentialist ideas. Korea in the 1940s had many Shinto shrines, approached by straight roads lined with cherry trees and stone lanterns. The biggest shrine was to the legendary founder of Japan, Ameterasu, and the Meiji emperor; called the Chōsen Jingū, it sat on South Mountain in Seoul. There were 58 *jingū* in all, and 322 smaller shrines around the country, plus 310 prayer halls.[86]

For all of this colonial activity, Korea remained fundamentally an agrarian society in 1945. More than that, it was one in which Japanese and Korean landlords maintained relations with tenants that were not fundamentally different from those of the nineteenth century. Few Korean landlords were enterprising farmers, and a veritable army of Japanese experts increased yields through the application of new seeds, fertilizers, and irrigation equipment. Most Korean peasants remained subsistence farmers, living in what one anthropologist called "the round of time," hoping that the next year would be no worse than this one. Furthermore, nearly four out of five were tenants, renting all or part of the land they worked.

A system that fosters land tenancy is not inherently exploitative: farmers who rent can be prosperous and productive. It is exploitative when there is insecurity of tenure, widespread debt and usury, uncompensated labor, and general penury, and when landowners make little contribution to the production process. In Korea many landlords were absentees, working through agents who collected rents; many were also Japanese, who had little interaction with their Korean tenants. So-called big landlords were people owning more than 50 *chŏngbo* (approximately 123 acres); in 1942 there were 2,173 Koreans and 1,319 Japanese in that category of landownership; 184 Japanese and 116 Koreans held more than 500 acres.[87] Scholars who studied Korean land conditions, like Yi Hungu and Andrew Grajdanzev, thought the first order of business after Japanese colonialism ended should have been a thorough reform and renovation of Korean land conditions, both for egalitarian reasons and to

85. *Kokutai No Hongi: Cardinal Principles of the National Entity of Japan,* trans. John Gauntlett (Cambridge: Harvard University Press, 1949), pp. 102, 186.
86. Lautensach (1945), p. 391.
87. Cumings (1981), p. 46.

stimulate production; Grajdanzev argued forcefully that land should have been redistributed to those who worked it without recompense to the owners, whom he terms "an almost purely parasitic group of the population."[88]

In this period the Korean majority suffered badly at the precise time that a minority was doing well. This minority acquired the taint of collaboration and could never shuck it off. Korea from 1937 to 1945 was much like Vichy France in the early 1940s: bitter experiences and memories continue to divide people, even within the same family; it was too painful to confront directly, and so it amounts now to buried history. Nonetheless, it continues to play upon the national identity.

When the colonial system abruptly terminated in 1945, millions of Koreans sought to return to their native villages from these far-flung mobilization details. But they were no longer the same people: they had grievances against those who remained secure at home, they had suffered material and status losses, they had often come into contact with new ideologies, they had all seen a broader world beyond the villages. It was thus this pressure cooker of a final decade that loosed upon postwar Korea a mass of changed and disgruntled people who deeply disordered the early postwar period, and the plans of the Americans and the Soviets.

World War II ended with at least ten thousand Koreans annihilated in Hiroshima and Nagasaki—most of them dragooned laborers in war industries. This awful insult to the human fodder that Japanese leaders moved hither and thither in their empire was not the final one, however; after the war the last irradiated survivors anyone cared about were the Koreans, written off on racial grounds by Tokyo and given no help from a Seoul government ashamed of their existence.

Many Korean A-bomb survivors scattered into the mountains of the Chŏllas. In 1972 one of them, Yu Chun-sŭng, was living with his four family members in a tiny *ondol* room next to the kitchen of a farmer's thatched-roof hut. Born in Chŏngŭp in 1917, he was drafted in 1944 to labor in a naval engineering operation. He and another Korean laborer, Shin T'ae-ryŏng, arrived at Hiroshima station at 8:05 A.M. on August 6, 1945. Mr. Yu looked at his watch just as a hot, blinding flash enveloped him:

> He ran desperately toward Mt. Futuba behind the station. He kept running while stumbling over the rails and iron fence of the station. . . . He reached the foot of Mt. Futuba, spent the night in a half-ruined farm-

88. Lee (1936), p. 171; Andrew Grajdanzev, *Modern Korea* (New York: Institute of Pacific Relations, 1994), chap. 10.

> house, and on the following day was carried by a rescue truck to the navy hospital in Kure. He lay with gauze dipped in oil on his burned face, and after a few days maggots hatched on the burns. . . .
>
> Around 1950 he started to vomit blood and have bloody stools. . . .

A few years later Yu's wife bore a child, Dong Su. The lower half of his body never developed. Another child had the same small lower body but a head twice as big as that of a normal baby. He died after three months. Yu had some success as a greengrocer, but around 1968 he again fell ill. By 1972, when he was but fifty-five, he could not move from his tiny hovel, "thin as a ghost" and with a "wax-white face": "He suffered attacks at intervals of about one minute, and when he did, his limbs and entire body writhed, and he gnashed his teeth which he closed to endure the pain." Yu died a few months later. As Dong Su reached puberty, he tried to commit suicide three times. After his father passed away, he went insane and refused to eat, dying within a year.[89]

Colonial Korea was full of powerless victims like Yu Chun-sŭng, but also estimable heroes like Yi Yuk-sa (1904–44). Yi may have come close to setting a record by getting thrown in jail seventeen times for political crimes against Japanese rule, and he perished in prison in 1944, never living to see a Korea free of the colonizer. We can commemorate his sacrifice and close this chapter by attending to his poem "The Wide Plain":

> On a distant day
> When heaven first opened,
> Somewhere a cock must have crowed.
>
> No mountain ranges
> Rushing to the longed-for sea
> Could have dared invade this land.
>
> While busy seasons gust and fade
> With endless time,
> A great river first opens the way.
>
> Now snow falls,
> The fragrance of plum blossoms is far off.
> I'll sow the seeds of my sad song here.
>
> When a superman comes
> On a white horse down the myriad years,
> Let him sing aloud my song on the wide plain.[90]

89. Kuak Kwi Hoon, "Father and Son Robbed of Body and Soul," in *The Atomic Bomb: Voices from Hiroshima and Nagasaki*, ed. Kyoko and Mark Selden (Armonk, N.Y.: M. E. Sharpe, 1989), pp. 200–204.
90. Translation by Peter Lee, in Lee (1990), p. 78.

CHAPTER FOUR

The Passions, 1945–1948

There is a Korean word, sinparam, *that expresses the pathos, the inner joy, of a person moved to action not by coercion but by his own volition.* Param *is the sound of the wind; if a person is wafted along on this wind, songs burst from his lips and his legs dance with joy. A* sinparam *is a strange wind that billows in the hearts of people who have freed themselves from oppression, regained their freedom, and live in a society of mutual trust. This word, redolent with a shamanistic mystique, has a talisman-like appeal for Koreans.* —*Chung Kyungmo*

The crucible of the period of national division and opposing states that still exists in Korea was the years from 1943 to 1953. Nothing about the politics of contemporary Korea can be understood without comprehending the events of this decade, which we will examine in the next two chapters. Here was the breeding ground of the two Koreas, of a catastrophic war, and of a reordering of international politics in Northeast Asia. In these events the United States had a major role, in many ways the predominant role among the big powers, and yet for most Americans and for many histories of the period, U.S. involvement in Korea is an afterthought or a footnote until the war that came in 1950.

Many Americans express surprise to learn of the U.S. occupation, in which Americans operated a full military government from 1945 to 1948. A. M. Rosenthal, a former editor and columnist of the *New York Times,* wrote in 1986 that "the Government of Korea" functioned throughout the peninsula in 1945, but was undermined by Americans who stupidly let the Russians come into the North. This is exactly backwards. An ostensible Korean government did exist within a few weeks of Japan's demise; its headquarters was in Seoul, it began in mid-August with the Committee for the Preparation of Korean Independence, and by September it was becoming anchored in widespread "people's committees" in the countryside. But its name was also changed in September, to the Korean People's Republic (Choson Inmin Konghwaguk, formed September 6, 1945), and the incoming Americans predictably shunned it. It was the Soviets, who began fighting the Japanese in Korea on August 8, who "let" the Americans come into the South (some of their soldiers came south of the thirty-eighth parallel, but they withdrew after August 15) and who supported the people's committee network. The American political preference was for a group of exiled nationalists and some domestic conservative politicians who formed the Korean Democratic Party (KDP) in September 1945. With Koreans choosing up sides and Washington and Moscow reinforcing the choices, within a few months Korea was effectively divided—long before the establishment of the two republics in North and South in 1948.

There was no historical justification for Korea's division: if any East Asian country should have been divided it was Japan (like Germany, an aggressor). Instead Korea, China, and Vietnam were all divided in the aftermath of World War II. There was no internal pretext for dividing Korea, either: the thirty-eighth parallel was a line never noticed by the people of, say, Kaesŏng, the Koryŏ capital, which the parallel cut in half. And then it became the only line that mattered to Koreans, a boundary to be removed by any means necessary. The political and ideological divisions that we associate with the Cold War were the reasons for Korea's division; they came early to Korea, before the onset of the global Cold War, and today they outlast the end of the Cold War everywhere else.

Perhaps because of this half century of conflict, a Cold War narrative is all too imbedded in American histories of the liberation period (Koreans call August 15, 1945, *haebang,* meaning liberation from Japan). The accounts begin with Japan's surrender, move quickly to the December 1945 agreements on Korea with the Soviets and the two U.S.-Soviet "joint commissions" of 1946 and 1947 that followed them; they then detail the United Nations's role in sponsoring elections that established the Republic of Korea in 1948, and conclude with the war in 1950. The literature lays most of the problems in these five years at the door of Soviet obstructionism or Korean political immaturity. In fact, Koreans were the prime historical actors in this period, shaping American and Soviet power to their ends and generally ignoring all the "externals" I have just mentioned, unless they appeared to serve Korean purposes. The national division, however, was not their doing: it is Americans who bear the lion's share of the responsibility for the thirty-eighth parallel.

THE DIVISION OF KOREA

In the days just before Koreans heard the voice of Emperor Hirohito for the first time, broadcasting Japan's surrender and Korea's liberation on August 15, 1945, John J. McCloy of the State-War-Navy Coordinating

Committee (SWNCC) directed two young colonels, Dean Rusk and Charles H. Bonesteel, to withdraw to an adjoining room and find a place to divide Korea. It was around midnight on August 10–11, the atomic bombs had been dropped, the Soviet Red Army had entered the Pacific War, and American planners were rushing to arrange the Japanese surrender throughout the region. Given thirty minutes to do so, Rusk and Bonesteel looked at a map and chose the thirty-eighth parallel because it "would place the capital city in the American zone"; although the line was "further north than could be realistically reached . . . in the event of Soviet disagreement," the Soviets made no objections—which "somewhat surprised" Rusk.[1] General Douglas MacArthur, the hero of the Pacific campaigns, issued General Order Number One for the Japanese surrender on August 15, including in it (and thus making public) the thirty-eighth parallel decision. The Russians accepted in silence this division into spheres, while demanding a Russian occupation of the northern part of Hokkaido in Japan (which MacArthur refused).

American officials consulted no Koreans in coming to this decision, nor did they ask the opinions of the British or the Chinese, both of whom were to take part in a planned "trusteeship" for Korea. Instead, the decision was unilateral and hasty. Still, it grew out of previous American planning. The United States had taken the initiative in great-power deliberations on Korea during the war, suggesting a multilateral trusteeship for postwar Korea to the British in March 1943, and to the Soviets at the end of the same year. President Franklin D. Roosevelt, worried about the disposition of enemy-held colonial territories and aware of colonial demands for independence, sought a gradualist, tutelary policy of preparing colonials (like the Koreans) for self-government and independence. He knew that since Korea touched the Soviet border, the Russians would want to be involved in the fate of postwar Korea; he hoped to get a Soviet commitment to a multilateral administration, to forestall unilateral solutions and provide an entry for American interests in Korea. Korean independence would come only at an appropriate time, or "in due course"—a phrase famous to Koreans, having been used in the 1943 declaration of the Cairo conference (where Roosevelt had met with Winston Churchill and Chiang Kai-shek) and by Prime Minister Hara Kei to justify Japan's "cultural policy" after the March First movement in 1919. The British and the French resisted Roosevelt's trusteeship idea because it threatened their empires; so did the Korean people, who were humili-

1. *Foreign Relations of the United States* (*FRUS*, 1945), vol. 6, p. 1039. For a detailed reconstruction of the period 1943–1951 with American and Korean archival documentation see Cumings (1981, 1990). I draw on that study in the next two chapters and cite a portion of the archival materials I consulted.

ated by the prospect of yet more great-power "tutelage." Stalin made no commitments to the policy, but seemed to enjoy watching Roosevelt and Churchill wrangle over the future of empire in the postwar world. Stalin was mostly silent in wartime discussions with Roosevelt about Korea, tending either to humor FDR and his pet trusteeship projects (which Stalin no doubt considered naive) or to say that the Koreans would want independence.

Roosevelt rarely consulted the State Department, but Foggy Bottom planners began worrying about the implications for Pacific security of Soviet involvement in Korea as early as 1942, within months of Pearl Harbor, and questioned whether a trusteeship would give the United States enough influence in Korean affairs. They feared that the Soviets would bring with them Korean guerrillas who had been fighting the Japanese in Manchuria, the numbers of which they grossly exaggerated (to as many as thirty thousand).[2] Afraid that a trusteeship might not work, various planners began to develop ideas for a full military occupation that would assure a predominant American voice in postwar Korean affairs. It might be a short occupation, or it might be one of "considerable duration"; the main point was that no other power should have a role in Korea such that "the proportionate strength of the U.S." would be reduced to "a point where its effectiveness would be weakened."[3]

This thinking was utterly new. No previous administration had the slightest interest in American involvement in Korean affairs, and Congress and the American people knew nothing about the proposed commitments. Several of these planners were Japanophiles, however, who had never challenged Japan's colonial prerogatives in Korea and now hoped to reconstruct a peaceable and amenable postwar Japan. They worried that a Soviet occupation of Korea would thwart that goal and therefore harm the security of the Pacific. The thirty-eighth parallel decision also, in my view, reflected the absence of President Roosevelt's experienced hand (he died in April 1945). His idea was always to involve the Russians in a joint administration of Korea, to embrace them and their interests in a country that touched their borders, thus to give them something while containing their ambitions. Division was a much cruder device, abjuring diplomacy and simply drawing a line in the dirt. Indeed, from that thoughtless point of line-drawing onward, no international

2. During the war Kim Il Sung had also come to the attention of the State Department's only Korean expert, George McCune. See Cumings (1981), p. 37. From 1941 to 1945 Kim Il Sung and other guerrillas were given sanctuary in Sino-Russian border towns near Khabarovsk, as we have seen; but they numbered in the hundreds, not the thousands.

3. "Korea: Occupation and Military Government: Composition of Forces, March 29, 1944," in *FRUS* (1944), vol. 5, pp. 1239–42; also "Briefing Book Paper," State Department, *Conferences of Malta and Yalta, 1945*, pp. 358–59.

diplomacy worked to solve any serious problem in Korea until the U.S.–DPRK nuclear agreement in October 1994 (an agreement based on post–Cold War premises). A diplomat named William W. Rockhill wrote at the turn of the century, "Korea is the place . . . there you will see diplomacy in the raw, diplomacy without gloves, perfume, or phrases." It was the same in 1945.

American forces in the Twenty-fourth Corps of the Tenth Army that had finally defeated fierce Japanese resistance on Okinawa under the war hero General John Reed Hodge (often called the Patton of the Pacific) got the nod for occupation duty in Korea because they were the closest substantial force—and then their embarkation date was moved up three times because of high-level fears of Soviet expansion, and Japanese worries that "communists" and "independence agitators" would take advantage of the vacuum of power inside Korea. On August 29 the colonial government-general radioed to Okinawa,

> Local Japanese authorities eagerly await the arrival of the Allied Forces . . . and urgently desire that the Allied forces will fully take into consideration the actual conditions on the spot before proceeding with the disarmament of Japanese forces and the transfer of administrative organs from the Japanese hand.

Hodge hearkened to this Japanese propaganda, later using it to justify "that scramble move" from Okinawa to Seoul.[4]

The Twenty-fourth Corps convoy of twenty-one ships (including five destroyers) weighed anchor in typhoon-like weather off Okinawa on September 5 and proceeded in five close columns under blackout conditions toward Inch'ŏn, plowing through its treacherous tides on September 8, the kind of warm, clear, late summer day that renders Korea especially beautiful and makes one think the sky is nowhere higher. It was, so it happened, the first of two Inch'ŏn landings, the second to come five years later (nearly to the day), when another victorious general would snatch (North) Korean defeat from the jaws of victory. American troops disembarked while black-coated Japanese police on horseback held Korean crowds at bay, with the total numbers of American troops and "civil service teams" approaching 25,000 within a few weeks. America's "black ships" had arrived, and Korea began the most anomalous period in its history since A.D. 668: the era of national division.

The period from 1943 to 1947 represented an internationalist phase in high U.S. diplomacy, reflected in the trusteeship policy and Washington's desire to place a still-unified Korea under temporary multilateral

4. Cumings (1981), pp. 125–27.

American soldiers marching away from the Government-General Building in central Seoul, September 9, 1945. *Courtesy of U.S. National Archives.*

administration, in cooperation with other great powers, including the Soviets. The policy was first to occupy Korea and then to see if a trusteeship might be worked out with the Russians, the British, and the Chinese. The United States gained Soviet adherence to a modified version of the trusteeship idea at the foreign ministers' conference in December 1945, an important agreement that eliminated irrelevant British and Chinese influence, while suggesting that the two powers might ultimately come to terms on how to reunify Korea. Roosevelt, basing himself on the experience of American colonialism in the Philippines, had argued that a Korean trusteeship might last as long as forty or fifty years, but the December 1945 agreement shortened the period of great-power involvement in Korean affairs to no more than five years and called for a unified provisional government of Korea. But even by that early date the agreement was still too late, because the de facto policies of the two occupations had identified the Soviets with Kim Il Sung and the people's committees, while the Americans backed Syngman Rhee and opposed the committees and widespread Korean demands for a thorough renovation of colonial legacies. Washington's internationalist policy was undermined not so much by the Soviets as by the determination of Americans on the scene in Korea to begin an early version of the Cold War "containment" doctrine.

The American military command, along with such high-ranking emissaries dispatched from Washington as John J. McCloy, tended to interpret resistance to U.S. desires in the South as radical and pro-Soviet. In particular the United States saw the "People's Republic" as part of a

Soviet master plan to dominate all of Korea. Radical activity, such as the ousting of landlords and attacks on Koreans in the colonial police, was usually a matter of settling scores left over from the colonial period, or of demands by Koreans to run their own affairs. But it immediately became wrapped up with Soviet-American rivalry, such that the Cold War arrived in Korea in the last months of 1945.

The key organizer of the Korean People's Republic in Seoul was Yŏ Un-hyŏng (known to Americas as Lyuh Woon-hyung), and he was far from being a communist. Yŏ was born in 1885 into a family of poor yangban in Yangp'yŏng, not far from Seoul. He entered the Paejae School at fourteen and went to China when he was twenty-nine. He participated in the founding of the Korean Provisional Government (KPG) in 1919 and two years later went with Kim Kyu-sik to the Congress of the Toilers of the Far East in Moscow (and came back appalled at the poverty of Russia, compared with Korea). After his return to China he served as a propagandist during the Northern Expedition and met Sun Yat-sen and Mao Tse-tung at that time. He avoided Chiang Kai-shek's terror in Shanghai in 1927 by posing as a Westerner, but in 1929 Japanese agents captured him in Shanghai and returned him to Taejŏn prison, where he served three years for anti-Japanese activity. Upon his release he assumed the editorship of the *Chungang ilbo* (Central daily). Like other prominent Koreans, Yŏ was pressured to collaborate in the Japanese war effort. He resisted, telling the Japanese at one point that he had fought them to the death and that there was nothing left for them but to kill him.

Yŏ's political views were a mixture of Christianity, Wilsonian democracy, and socialism. Always willing to work with the left, he never joined the Communist Party and said he could not believe in the materialist view of history. He was much more of a populist, a favorite of common people who enjoyed contrasting the simple generosity and unrewarded toil of Korea's peasants with "the so-called intelligentsia, the intellectual stratum that knows ideographs, which for 500 years has paralyzed the spirit of our people." He was known for his oratorical skills and robust good looks, and his easy charm drew many Americans to him. An occupation historian, Albert Keep, once wrote of Yŏ, "What an amazing Korean he was . . . grey fedora, grey tweed overcoat, grey flannel trousers, well-taylored tweed coat, blue shirt with clean collar and neatly tied foreinhand *[sic]* looking for all the world as tho' he were off for a date at the Greenwich Country Club."

Yŏ was a tireless advocate of coalescing the left and right ends of the Korean political spectrum and eliminating North-South division, and for his efforts he was beaten in August 1945, almost lynched in October 1946 (when he returned from a meeting with Kim Il Sung), had his home partially destroyed by a grenade in March 1947, and was then finally murdered in July 1947. Yŏ was a man for many seasons, but not for the season of divided Korea and the Manichaean political world that eventually destroyed him.[5]

Once the American occupation chose to bolster the status quo and resist a thorough reform of colonial legacies, it immediately ran into monumental opposition from the mass of South Koreans. Most of the first year of the occupation, 1945–46, was given over to suppression of many people's committees that had emerged in the provinces. This provoked a massive rebellion that spread over four provinces in the fall of 1946; after it was suppressed, radical activists developed a significant guerrilla movement in 1948 and 1949. They also touched off another major uprising at the port of Yŏsu in October 1948. Much of this disorder was owing to the unresolved land problem, as conservative landed elements used their bureaucratic power to block redistribution of land to peasant tenants. The North Koreans, of course, sought to take advantage of this discontent, but unimpeachable internal evidence shows that nearly all of the dissidents and guerrillas were southerners, upset about southern policies. Indeed, the strength of the left wing was in those provinces most removed from the thirty-eighth parallel, in the southwestern Chŏllas, which had historically been rebellious, and in the southeastern Kyŏngsang provinces, which had felt Japanese colonialism the most.

"SEVERAL HUNDRED CONSERVATIVES": AN EARLY ALLIANCE

Within one week Americans in Seoul, who had never met a Korean, decided that they knew which Korean political leaders they liked. We can trace this astonishingly rapid choice in the reports of Cecil W. Nist, head of Twenty-fourth Corps intelligence. He and other officers welcomed Koreans to conversations and interviews with them in their "billet" at the Bando ("Peninsula") Hotel, which had long been a favorite of Japanese travelers and which used to stand across from what later became the American embassy building (a building owned by the Mitsui *zaibatsu* before 1945). By September 15 Nist's judgments were embodied in a report that H. Merrell Benninghoff, State Department political adviser to General Hodge, sent back to Washington:

> Southern Korea can best be described as a powder keg ready to explode at the application of a spark.

5. Cumings (1981), pp. 474–75, 535.

> There is great disappointment that immediate independence and sweeping out of the Japanese did not eventuate.
>
> [Those Koreans who] achieved high rank under the Japanese are considered pro-Japanese and are hated almost as much as their masters. . . .
>
> All groups seem to have the common idea of seizing Japanese property, ejecting the Japanese from Korea, and achieving immediate independence. Beyond this they have few ideas.
>
> Korea is completely ripe for agitators. . . .
>
> The most encouraging single factor in the political situation is the presence in Seoul of *several hundred conservatives* among the older and better educated Koreans. Although many of them have served the Japanese, that stigma ought eventually to disappear. Such persons favor the return of the "Provisional Government" and although they may not constitute a majority they are probably the largest single group.[6]

Not bad for a week's work. The diplomatic historian Herbert Feis later called this "a farsighted description and analysis of the situation,"[7] and in a sense it was: these conservatives included Kim Sŏng-su and his brother Yŏn-su, Song Chin-u, Cho Pyŏng-ok, Yun Po-sŏn, Chang T'aek-sang, and many other Koreans who later became well known. Dubbed the Korean Democratic Party (Han'guk Minju-dang, KDP) at a meeting of party initiators on September 16 (with strong sponsorship by the Americans), this was to be the "Liberal Democratic Party" of Korea, that is, a ruling conservative party such as later emerged in Japan. The KDP has structured the opposition from that time right down to the present, when one of its stalwarts finally became president: Kim Young Sam. He and Kim Dae Jung both trace their political roots back to this group; Chang T'aek-sang was Kim Young Sam's mentor. What these conservative figures would have been without this early anointing by the occupation, however, is another question.

The problem was that Korean society had no base for either a liberal or a democratic party as Americans understood it; it had a population the vast majority of which consisted of poor peasants, and a tiny minority of which held most of the wealth: landowners, who formed the real base of the KDP. The elite of Korean society during the colonial period, nearly all of them were widely perceived to have fattened under colonial rule while everybody else suffered. The historical documentation could

6. Benninghoff to State Department, Sept. 15, 1945, in *FRUS* (1945), vol. 6, pp. 1049–53 (emphasis added).

7. Feis, *The Atomic Bomb and the End of World War II* (Princeton: Princeton University Press, 1966), p. 166n.

not be clearer: the United States intervened on behalf of the smallest group in Korea, not Nist's "largest single group," and helped to perpetuate its privileges thereafter.

This decision also went directly against the occupation's instructions, whether those from the State Department warning against involvement with any political group or those of the "Joint Army-Navy Intelligence Study number 75" that the Americans carried with them, which warned about the unequal land situation and the collaboration of landlords with the Japanese.[8] Nist, Benninghoff, and Hodge liked such people because all the alternatives seemed worse, especially any political group thought to be left of center (as an American would define it). Much later General Hodge came to understand what Korean political conditions were really like, as opposed to the knee-jerk reactions of Colonel Nist. In late 1947 he captured in his homespun way the essence of the American dilemma, as it fluctuated between the unhappy poles of supporting people whose one virtue was anticommunism and opposing native leftists, while hoping for a liberal outcome for which Korean society had no base:

> We always have the danger of Fascism taking over when you try to fight Communism. It is a very difficult political situation that we run into. Germany was built up by Hitler to fight Communism, and it went to Nazism. Spain the same thing. On the other hand, when the Communists build up—when Communism builds up—democracy is crushed, and the nation goes Communist. Now, what is the answer on the thing? How in the dickens are you going to get political-in-the-middle-of-the-road out of the mess. Just bring[ing] it up for discussion. I don't know the answer. I wish I did.

There was no middle in Korea, thanks to the Japanese, and there would not be until the 1980s.

The main problem for the conservatives was their lack of nationalist credentials. Therefore they wanted to bring back some of the exiled nationalists who had resisted the Japanese, while keeping the far more numerous exiled communists at bay. They succeeded in convincing Hodge that Syngman Rhee in the United States and Kim Ku in China (still in the wartime capital of Chungking with Chiang Kai-shek) should be brought back to head the southern conservatives. With Rhee there was no problem, since he had befriended wartime intelligence people in Washington and they were already trying to bring him back to Seoul. The most important of these was M. Preston Goodfellow, who had been deputy director of the Office of Strategic Services (forerunner of the CIA)

8. See Cumings (1981), p. 129.

under William "Wild Bill" Donovan and had a background in army intelligence; like Donovan, he was known for his interest and expertise in clandestine warfare. Goodfellow thought Rhee had more of "the American point of view" than other Korean leaders, and arranged to deposit him back in Korea in October, with MacArthur's support (but over the objections of the State Department, which had long disliked Rhee). Goodfellow then arrived in Korea himself, seeking to set up a separate, anticommunist southern government. Rhee flew into Korea on MacArthur's personal plane on October 16, 1945, and four days later General Hodge introduced him to the Korean public.

In October 1945, as it happened, both military commands sponsored welcoming ceremonies for two returned exiles: Rhee was allowed to give a strongly anticommunist speech with Hodge sitting at his side, and Soviet officers stood behind Kim Il Sung, introduced as a hero of the resistance to Japan on October 14, 1945. Did a Soviet "Goodfellow" deposit Kim back in P'yŏngyang? Apparently not. Original research in five languages[9] has suggested that just before the Manchurian guerrillas returned to Korea, the top leaders such as Kim Il Sung, Kim Ch'aek, Ch'oe Hyŏn, Kim Il, and Ch'oe Yong-gŏn agreed among themselves to promote Kim Il Sung as the maximum figure, for reasons that included his wider reputation and his personal force. By some indexes the others outranked him; Kim Ch'aek and Ch'oe Hyŏn stood higher than Kim in the Chinese Communist hierarchy. In any case, they did support Kim after he and his guerrilla group made its way back to Korea on September 19, and with an unstinting loyalty for the rest of their lives.[10] Along with other Manchurian guerrillas they became the core of the North Korean hierarchy.

Within a few months Kim Il Sung and Syngman Rhee were the dominant political figures in the two zones. Rhee was a septuagenarian who had lived in the United States for nearly four decades, had a Ph.D. from Princeton, and had taken an Austrian wife; a patriot well known for devoting his life to Korean independence, he was also a willful man of legendary obstinacy and strong anticommunist beliefs. Kim Il Sung, as

9. Professor Wada Haruki is the leading historian of modern Korea in Japan and teaches at Tokyo University. His work is available only in Japanese and Korean. See *Kin Nichisei to Manshu konichi senso* (Kim Il Sung and the Anti-Japanese War in Manchuria) (Tokyo: Heibonsha, 1992).

10. Kim and some sixty guerrillas in his band tried to return to Korea through Sinŭiju on the Chinese border, but bombing had blown the bridges and so they left from Vladivostok on the Russian ship *Pugachev,* disembarking at Wŏnsan on September 19. Although a Soviet transport deposited these men in Korea, they returned independently of Soviet authorities. Wada, *Kin Nichisei,* pp. 341–43.

we have seen, had begun armed resistance in the Sino-Korean border region shortly after Japan established the puppet state of Manchukuo in 1932, and was fortunate enough to survive a rugged guerrilla war that had killed most of his comrades by 1945. Kim was thirty-three years old when he returned, and represented a younger generation of revolutionary nationalists filled with contempt for the failures of their fathers and determined to forge a Korea that could resist foreign domination—while at the same time opportunistically allying with Soviet forces. Although both leaders had the support of the respective superpower, neither was an easily malleable person, let alone a puppet.

Just at the time Rhee returned, a political adviser to General MacArthur, George Atcheson, informed Hodge, "We should commence to use some progressive, popular and respected leader, or small group, to act as a nucleus of an organization which in cooperation with and under the direction of our military government could develop into an executive and administrative governmental agency." Atcheson suggested the names of three men: Rhee, Kim Ku, and Kim Kyu-sik.[11] The latter two were still in Chungking with the KPG group, but soon Hodge determined to bring them back and to move forward with a separate government for the South.

The State Department instantly objected to favoring one group over another, but McCloy (who visited Korea in November) sided with Hodge, saying that if the United States did not "build up on our own a reasonable and respected government or group of advisors," communists would seize the government instead.[12] Goodfellow was in Korea by this time and unquestionably influenced Hodge in this direction, as did Rhee; by the third week of November, Hodge and his advisers had come up with a plan that would supplant trusteeship: a "governing commission" to be formed under Kim Ku at Hodge's direction, which would quickly integrate with the military government (known as the U.S. Army Military Government in Korea, or USAMGIK) and soon thereafter succeed it (with Hodge retaining veto power over its activities). The memorandum alluded to an ongoing plan to organize, train, and equip "Korean military and naval forces." As for the Russians, they would be "informed in advance" and encouraged to send people to join the commission, "but if Russian participation is not forthcoming plan should be carried out for Korea south of 38th parallel." The person who wrote this memo, William Langdon (another State Department adviser to Hodge) thought that a southern government thus constituted would be good for foreign interests:

11. *FRUS* (1945), vol. 6, pp. 1091–92.
12. *FRUS* (1945), vol. 6, pp. 1122–24.

> The old native regime internally was feudal and corrupt but the record shows that it was the best disposed toward foreign interests of the three Far Eastern nations, protecting foreign lives and property and enterprises and respecting treaties and franchises. I am sure that we may count on at least as much from a native government evolved as above. . . .[13]

All this meant bypassing not just cooperation with the Russians in seeking a unitary independent Korea but also trusteeship, as Langdon acknowledged. The trouble was, trusteeship was the existing American policy, urged upon the Allies since 1943 and then being discussed with the Russians at high levels.

Kim Ku and some of his supporters in the KPG group returned to Korea on November 23, as an element of this planning. Kim was born in 1875 in Haeju, just above the thirty-eighth parallel. After failing the civil service exams, he joined the Tonghak movement in 1892 and became one of its minor leaders. When he heard about Queen Min's murder in 1896, he grabbed the first Japanese he could find and strangled him, leaving the body in an inn with his name—"Kim [Number] Nine"—scrawled in blood on the wall. This act led to an apocryphal story that he had killed the queen's assassin with his bare hands. In 1909 the Japanese arrested and tortured him on suspicion of involvement in the assassination of Itō, handing him a fifteen-year jail sentence. By 1919 he was out of jail and in Shanghai, where he joined the KPG and became its leader in 1926.

Kim Ku achieved wide notoriety for engineering the terrorist attack on April 29, 1932, in Shanghai that killed Kawabata Teiji, head of the Japanese Resident's Association, and that maimed Shigemitsu Mamoru, Japanese minister to China. He lost his leg, which caused him to limp aboard the USS *Missouri* as foreign minister, to offer the Japanese surrender to MacArthur in Tokyo Bay. After the 1932 attack Kim Ku's star rose with Chiang Kai-shek, who began supporting his faction and looking to Kim as a China-aligned leader for postwar Korea. When he returned to Korea, Kim was widely called "the Assassin" for his exploits in China; he traveled around with "a bevy of concubines" and "a flotilla of paid gunmen," according to the military government historian Richard Robinson.[14]

Hodge was less than impressed with Kim Ku, however, since his first major act was to show he had earned his title by engineering the assassination of the head of the Korean Democratic Party, Song Chin-u, and his

13. *FRUS* (1945), vol. 6, pp. 1129–33.

14. Biographical information from Ralph Keating Benesch, "Kim Ku: A Study of a Nationalist" (M.A. thesis, University of Washington, 1964); and Richard Robinson, "Betrayal of a Nation" (unpublished manuscript given to me by Dr. Robinson).

second was to mobilize mass demonstrations against trusteeship when the results of the foreign ministers' conference were published in late December, and his third was to attempt a coup d'état. The three acts were connected: when Hodge learned on December 29 that an agreement on a modified trusteeship had been concluded with the Russians, he called in various political leaders to prepare them for the news. Song Chin-u was one of them: in Hodge's words, he "went out and told his friends that he was ready to act sensibly and the next morning he was dead."[15] This assassination was the most important event since the liberation among the non-leftist groups, for it revealed that the political fault line was not right versus left, but patriot versus collaborator. Song Chin-u, like his lifelong friend Kim Sŏng-su, was a wealthy man who made many unfortunate compromises in the colonial period.

On New Year's Eve, Kim Ku issued a series of proclamations that amounted to a direct attempt to take over the government. This gambit was easily repulsed, however, and on New Year's Day 1946 Hodge called Kim Ku on the carpet and gave him a "going over" that became the talk of the occupation; Hodge told Kim he would "kill him if he double-crossed me again," and Kim responded by threatening to commit suicide. Thereafter, "the *coup d'etat* fizzled."[16]

General Hodge had contrived to violate established American policy at several levels, only to find his most cooperative politician dead and the secretary of state signed on to a deal with the Russians. In this political context he wrote a remarkable report on the first three months of the occupation:

> [There] is growing resentment against all Americans in the area including passive resistance. . . . Every day of drifting under this situation makes our position in Korea more untenable and decreases our waning popularity. . . . The word pro-American is being added to pro-Jap, national traitor, and collaborator.

If by "occidental standards Koreans are not ready for independence," they nonetheless want their independence immediately. Were this to happen, Hodge thought, southern Korea would be "extremely fertile ground for the establishment of Communism":

> The approximate international influences and our occupation policies of insuring all freedom and maintaining property rights and order among liberated oriental people favor Communistic activities.
>
> Koreans well know that the Russians have a force locally of about 4

15. Cumings (1981), p. 219.
16. Cumings (1981), p. 221.

> to 1 to Americans and with the usual oriental slant are willing to do homage and are doing homage to the man with the largest weapon. On the part of the masses there is an increasing tendency to look to Russia for the future.
>
> In summary, the U.S. occupation of Korea . . . is surely drifting to the edge of a political-economic abyss from which it can never be retrieved with any credit to United States prestige in the Far East. Positive action on the international level or the seizure of complete initiative in South Korea by the U.S. in the very near future is absolutely essential to stop this drift.

Hodge urged that trusteeship be abandoned; if no "positive action" were to follow upon that, U.S. and Russian forces should withdraw from Korea, thus to "leave Korea to its own devices and an inevitable internal upheaval for its own self-purification."[17]

With fifty years of hindsight—or even five, in 1950—we can imagine a cauterizing fire that would have settled Korea's multitude of social and political problems caused by the pressure cooker of colonial rule and instant "liberation," a purifying upheaval that might have been pretty awful, but nothing like the millions of lives lost in 1950–53, or the thousands in the April Revolution of 1960 or the Kwangju Rebellion of 1980. Had the Americans and the Russians quit Korea, a leftist regime would have taken over quickly, and it would have been a revolutionary nationalist government that, over time, would have moderated and rejoined the world community—as did China, as Vietnam is doing today. But we have to imagine this, because Americans do not understand the point of social revolutions, never having had one themselves; to allow this to happen would have meant that Hodge and many other Americans would have occupied Korea only to "turn it over to the communists." Indeed, this is exactly what Harry Truman's friend Edwin Pauley told the president in an important report after his tour of Korea in May 1946:

> Communism in Korea could get off to a better start than practically anywhere else in the world. The Japanese owned the railroads, all of the public utilities including power and light, as well as all of the major industries and natural resources. Therefore, if these are suddenly found to be owned by "The People's Committee" (The Communist Party), they will have acquired them without any struggle of any kind or any work in developing them. This is one of the reasons why the U.S. should not waive its title or claim to Japanese external assets located in Korea until a democratic (capitalistic) form of government is assured.[18]

17. *FRUS* (1945), vol. 6, pp. 1144–48.
18. *FRUS* (1946), vol. 8, pp. 706–9.

The Americans would not turn Korea over to the Koreans, and so they got on with the "positive action" necessary to create an anticommunist South Korea. Korea thus became a harbinger of policies later followed throughout the world—in Greece, Indochina, Iran, Guatemala, Cuba, Nicaragua—where Americans came to defend any group calling itself anticommunist, because the alternative was thought to be worse. And fifty years later the Korean problem remains unsolved.

The establishment of official organizations for the South alone went on apace. The ROK was not proclaimed until August 15, 1948, but the southern political system was built in the first few months of the occupation, and did not substantially change until the 1960s. In November and December 1945 Hodge and his advisers chose to take four steps: first, to build up an army to defend the thirty-eighth parallel; second, to buttress the Korean National Police (KNP) as the primary political weapon for pacifying the South; third, to strengthen the alliance with rightist parties; and fourth, to suppress Koreans who didn't like such policies. An army that occupied Korea to disarm the Japanese was now intensively shaping a containment bulwark in South Korea.

An office of "national defense" had already been formed in the middle of November (1945), and in spite of subsequent Joint Chiefs of Staff disapproval, the military government established an English-language school for potential officers in December, and then the Korean Military Academy, which by the fall of 1946 had graduated two classes. The second class included the future ROK president Park Chung Hee and his eventual assassin, Kim Chae-gyu, both of whom had been officers in the Japanese armed forces. The prime minister in the early years of the Roh Tae Woo government (1987–92), Kang Young Hoon, was also a veteran first of the Japanese and then the U.S.-sponsored army. Hodge called it a "constabulary" to get around Washington's objections, but this became the mother organization of the ROK Army. As Hodge later put it,

> I was very interested in establishing a Korean Army from the beginning of the Occupation, not only to relieve American troops of many details in handling Korean security, but to get a start for the future when we accomplished our mission of setting up a Korean Government. I met much opposition at higher levels.[19]

The reason for the opposition "at higher levels," of course, was that the United States had no mandate to build up a Korean military, under either official U.S. policy or international laws governing foreign occupations.

19. Hodge's letter of March 18, 1952, quoted in Robert K. Sawyer, *Military Advisors in Korea: KMAG in Peace and War* (Washington, D.C.: Office of the Chief of Military History, 1962), p. 21.

In the first military class the Americans brought in twenty officers from the former Japanese army, twenty from the Japanese Kwantung Army, which had been in Manchuria, and twenty from the KPG's "Restoration Army," which had been in China. Few of the latter were willing to work with Koreans who had been on the opposite side during the war, however, so the South Korean army became the preserve of those Koreans who, one would have thought, chose the wrong side during their nation's moment of maximum trial.

SWNCC's "Basic Initial Directive" for the occupation in Korea had called particular attention to rooting out collaborators in the hated colonial police force. The Supreme Command, Allied Powers (SCAP) in Tokyo, which had command over Hodge, said in its initial reports that the police had been "thoroughly Japanized and efficiently utilized as an instrument of tyranny." But by that time (early October), leaders of the KDP were already running the KNP, especially Cho Pyŏng-ok (national director) and Chang T'aek-sang (director of Seoul's police force), both of whom had been handpicked by Americans (Cecil Nist and others). The occupation began retraining this force on October 15, 1945, at the old Japanese police academy. About 85 percent of the Koreans who had served in the Japanese force were employed in the KNP by this time, and the figures were little different a year later: in November 1946 Colonel William Maglin, the American director of the KNP, gave this breakdown of former colonial police officers still on the force:[20]

Position	11/1946 Total	In Colonial Police	%
Superintendents	1	1	100
Division Chiefs	8	5	63
Provincial Chiefs	10	8	80
Inspectors	30	25	83
Captains	139	104	75
Lieutenants	969	806	83

These figures included police who had fled to the South from northern Korea, fearing reprisals.

Americans have resisted a national police force throughout their history, and in Japan MacArthur broke up the Japanese version as an obstacle to the twin occupation goals of demilitarization and democratization. In Korea, however, Hodge and his advisers set this national, self-contained police force against the main political opposition, the Korean People's Republic formed in Seoul in September 1945 and the many rural

20. Maglin, Nov. 1, 1946, briefing, in Cumings (1981), p. 166.

committees, labor unions, and peasants' associations connected with it. Hodge "declared war" on the KPR on December 12, 1945, and later said this: "Flatly stated, one of our missions was to break down this Communist government outside of any directives and without benefit of backing by the Joint Chiefs of Staff or the State Department."[21]

SOUTH KOREA'S LEFT AND RIGHT WINGS

The effective opposition to the developing southern system was almost wholly on the left, mainly because Japanese policies had left Korea with such a tiny middle class. A mass popular resistance from 1945 to 1950 mingled raw peasant protest with organized labor union activity and, finally, armed guerrilla resistance. I have written much about this elsewhere,[22] but we can see the general picture in some of the first CIA reports on Korea. In one 1948 document, CIA analysts wrote that South Korean political life was "dominated by a rivalry between Rightists and the remnants of the Left Wing People's Committees," which the CIA termed a "grass-roots independence movement which found expression in the establishment of the People's Committees throughout Korea in August 1945," led by "Communists" who based their right to rule on the resistance to the Japanese. The leadership of the right, on the other hand,

> is provided by that numerically small class which virtually monopolizes the native wealth and education of the country. . . . Since this class could not have acquired and maintained its favored position under Japanese rule without a certain minimum of "collaboration," it has experienced difficulty in finding acceptable candidates for political office and has been forced to support imported expatriate politicians such as Rhee Syngman and Kim Koo. These, while they have no pro-Japanese taint, are essentially demagogues bent on autocratic rule.

Thus, "the extreme Rightists control the overt political structure in the US zone," mainly through the agency of the National Police, which had been "ruthlessly brutal in suppressing disorder." The CIA went on to say,

> The enforced alliance of the police with the Right has been reflected in the cooperation of the police with Rightist youth groups for the purpose of completely suppressing Leftist activity. This alignment has had the effect of forcing the Left to operate as an underground organization

21. Quoted in Cumings (1981), p. 194.
22. Cumings (1981), pp. 193–201, 293–379.

since it could not effectively compete in a parliamentary sense even if it should so desire.

Although membership in communist and left-wing organizations was ostensibly legal under the American occupation, "the police generally regarded the Communists as rebels and traitors who should be seized, imprisoned, and sometimes shot on the slightest provocation."

Meanwhile, according to the CIA, the structure of the southern bureaucracy was "substantially the old Japanese machinery"; the Home Affairs Ministry, an agency which E. H. Norman had described as a base for forces of the darkest reaction in prewar Japan, exercised in South Korea "a high degree of control over virtually all phases of the life of the people." With crucial support from the director of the KNP, Cho Pyŏng-ok, whom many thought to be the most powerful Korean after Syngman Rhee, the Korean Democratic Party "built up its membership within the ranks of the police and local governments." (Some Americans disliked Cho "for harsh police methods directed ruthlessly against Korean leftists," but most found him to be a capable and intelligent official, the CIA said.)[23]

General Albert Wedemeyer reported much the same evidence during his tour of Korea in late 1947. The KDP, he wrote, held "the active membership or tacit support of the large majority of the administrative officials of the interim government." It was the party of "the land-owning community," led by Kim Sŏng-su, "one of the greatest landholders" in the southwest, and by Chang Tŏk-su, Kim's inseparable companion and the "dominating intellect" of the KDP—albeit a person somewhat constrained in public by his "strong support" of the Japanese regime. As a political party, however, the KDP left much to be desired: "it is not organized in the provinces, except in the leading cities." Wedemeyer found in conversations with Koreans that many had turned to the left because they could not stomach pro-Japanese collaborators, not because they were communists. The notable litterateur Chŏng In-bo told the general that communists had their hold on people not because of northern intrigue but because of the lingering memory of their anti-Japanese patriotism: "communism here has been nurtured with the fertilizer of nationalism." Furthermore, Chŏng observed pointedly, for decades "only Russia, contiguous to us, shared our enmity against Japan."

Younghill Kang, a New York novelist (see chapter 9) and an anticommunist, wrote to Wedemeyer that "Korea was one of the worst police states in the world"; the struggle in Korea, he said, was "a fight between

23. National Records Center, CIA, "The Current Situation in Korea," ORE 15-48, March 18, 1948; and CIA, "Communist Capabilities in Korea," ORE 32-48, Feb. 21, 1949.

A Korean village, nestled amid foothills in the southeast; the gate was last reconstructed in 1709. It was first built to hold back the Hideyoshi invasions by the governor of Mun'gyŏng, Sim Kil-wŏn; he and his men fought to the last man in 1592. *Courtesy of Joo, Myong-dok.*

the few well-fed landed and the hungry landless. These few today control [the KDP] and the mass of people want to rectify these ancient wrongs." Kang predicted that Rhee wanted the blessing of the United States and the United Nations so that he could then "kick the Russians out of the north." Several other prominent Koreans told Wedemeyer that the inevitable result of Korea's stalemated politics would be civil war.

An experienced observer of Korea, the Yale anthropologist Cornelius Osgood, made many analogous points in trying to get Army Secretary William Draper to comprehend the situation in Korea in late 1947. He remarked on the patriotic aura surrounding leftists and communists, the similarity between stated American objectives and Soviet reforms of land and labor conditions in the North, and the way in which "a hated group . . . is taking advantage of the Military Government with the same classical self-interest characteristic of Yi Dynasty politicians"—having learned "an added cunning developed by subservience under the Japanese." Most Koreans, especially the majority in the villages, never saw Americans, but only the local elite of Koreans (in many cases the same elite as during colonial rule). Reunification was what Koreans cared most about,

Osgood related, and they would never support a separatist policy. The only course for the United States, he argued, was quickly to eliminate police who had served the Japanese, carry out land reform, and move toward "a strongly supported 'middle' in politics."[24]

At the same time that American officials publicly praised (as free or democratic Korea) and privately censured the southern regime, they nonetheless misconstrued the reality. The South did have a police state, and it was an agent of a small class of landlords. But it was more than that, or it could not have survived even to June 1950. The landlord class held both obtuse reactionaries and vibrant capitalists. Korean capitalism may not have had articulate proponents, but it had impressive practitioners, of which the Kim Sŏng-su group was the most formidable. This was hardly the visionary entrepreneur, however, looking for the main chance; the main chance had been the Japanese regime and the opportunities that close alliance with it brought to this, Korea's first *chaebŏl.* Americans found this sort of capitalism hard to dignify or legitimate, as did Koreans, seeing little virtue in business that hewed close to the state. But it was a source of dynamism in the Korean economy, this state-led capitalism implanted by a Japanese "developmental" colonialism. It laid the foundations for the economic growth of the 1960s. However, it did not fit a textbook description of capitalism.

Just as it is wrong to underestimate the economic resources of the Korean right, so it would be wrong to misconstrue its political resources. It is a curiosity of Korean politics going back several centuries that the yangban and landowning class was capable of marginal change and adjustment in the long-run interest of preserving its position, but was weak and brittle when faced with external challenge. When observed in comparative perspective, Korea offers a remarkable example of internal strength and external weakness, of indigenous stasis and exogenously induced change. This same pattern marked the postwar period. By 1950 the South Korean state impressed observers with its relative stability, especially as the first glimmerings of economic dynamism appeared. Yet in 1950 a well-placed military thrust demolished the regime overnight. In the late 1970s various pundits likened the ROK to another Japan in glowing accounts of its economic prowess and political stability. Yet an assassin's bullet, combined with mass unrest in Kwangju and elsewhere, caused the temporary collapse of the southern system. Most of what held the system together was at the top: the central state in Seoul, its executive, and its claim of legitimacy. It is only when this is lopped off

24. National Archives, RG335, Secretary of the Army file, box 56, Osgood to Draper, Nov. 29, 1947.

that the disintegration begins. The Korean superstructure—state, culture, ideology—is remarkably tenacious. It has great staying power if not challenged from without by dynamic social and economic forces.

Syngman Rhee and Kim Sŏng-su embodied the old system in their concern for organizing the elite in Seoul and not worrying much about the masses. After 1945, however, Korea for the first time had a "modern" politics in which charismatic leaders of left and right developed huge mass constituencies. Such leaders in the South drew upon the same sources of strength as did leaders in the North, an appeal to complete unity at home and resistance to penetration from abroad, and an assertion of a Korean essence against all the rest. These would include self-described rightists like Yi Pŏm-sŏk, leader of the powerful Korean National Youth (KNY), and An Ho-sang, Rhee's first minister of education. Their ideal of a self-contained Korea was similar to Kim Il Sung's, except that they did not support a social revolution.

In 1947 a mass politics of the right emerged in the South and gave new strength to the system, resting on a myriad of youth groups, an incipient corporatist organization of the working class, and a set of Korean political ideas that amounted to a kind of home-grown fascism. The occupation-supported and -funded KNY melded Chinese influences with Japanese methods of dealing with political recalcitrants. Its leader, Yi Pŏm-sŏk, was a fierce Korean nationalist—except where the Chinese Nationalists were concerned. Born in 1899 in Kyŏnggi Province, he went to China during World War I. He fought the Japanese as a guerrilla along the Sino-Korean border in the early 1920s. In 1933 he visited Germany to study military affairs; later he worked with German and Italian advisers to the Nationalists in China. By 1937 he was in the Office of the Chief of Staff of the Nationalist's Fifty-first Army and by 1938 a company commander at the Nationalist Military Academy in Hangchou. He was widely known in Korea as a follower and admirer of Generalissimo Chiang Kai-shek.[25]

Chiang and his secret police chief, the unsavory Tai Li, organized a youth wing called the Blue Shirts in the 1930s, a fascist-style paramilitary force that chose the color blue, it would appear, because brown, black, and green were already spoken for. Yi worked with this group and later (1947) wrote that the Germans and the Italians were "pioneers" in youth movements, and also cited Chiang's good experience with youth groups. He originally termed his own youth group the Blue Shirts, and the KNY, as an American delicately noted, had "distinctive blue uni-

25. National Records Center, RG94, USAMGIK Special Reports, "Biographic Reports on the Cabinet of the Korean Republic," Aug. 11, 1948, compiled from State Department Intelligence & Research Department files.

forms."[26] Yi became known for his use of the Chinese slogan, "*minjok chisang, kukka chisang,*" meaning nation first, state first. He got the slogan in China, which probably got it from Germany.

In Yi Pŏm-sŏk's mind nation and race were synonymous, just as they were in Hitler's; the difference was that in Korea the distinction between race and nation was minimal, with the term *minjok* (ethnic people) often connoting both. His writings in 1947 and 1948 are interesting for their anachronisms, their "untimely" quality; coming two years after the Holocaust it is a bit much to hear someone prattling on yet again about race, nation, and bloodlines. At one point he lauds the Jews for preserving their identity for centuries; at another he remarks that "the exclusion of the Jews was quite efficacious for [German] unity." In classic corporatist fashion, he called upon Koreans to forget class conflicts or distinctions between superior and inferior and to unite as one family. He even used the term "Juche" *[chuch'e]*, by which he meant something like being ever subjective where things Korean are concerned, always putting Korea first. This is the cornerstone of Korean nationalism, just what one would expect from an ancient people prizing ethnic homogeneneity and long subject to outside threat. For the American who has rarely had to think about how to preserve a nation surrounded by predators, such views are bloody-minded, solipsistic, recalcitrant, obnoxious, unreasonable at every turn.[27] But these are popular ideas in Korea, and in the 1940s a realm where left met right.

Often, of course, South Korea's ubiquitous youth groups were little more than gangs arrayed around a tough tyrant. One such leader, Ko Hŭi-du, got himself arrested in 1948, and the next day his wife picked up his "tortured corpse" at the police station. An embassy officer discovered this analysis in the diary of the head of the Korean Counter-Intelligence Corps (CIC):

> Ko Hŭi-du was the Chairman of the Wŏnnam-dong Association, the Chairman of the Tongdaemun [East Gate] Branch of the Civil Defense Corps, the Chairman of the Supporting Society for the Tongdaemun Police Station and the Chairman of the Judicial Protection Committee. Such were the titles he had on his name card. Ko was the representative of the stallkeepers operating along the bank of the Ch'ŏnggyech'ŏn

26. Cumings (1990), p. 195; see also Lloyd Eastman, *Seeds of Destruction: North China in War and Revolution, 1937–1949* (Stanford: Stanford University Press, 1984).

27. In 1950 the CIA termed Yi "a man of little imagination and mediocre intelligence," possessing a forceful personality, "great political ambitions, and an intensely nationalist viewpoint." He thought and acted "like a traditional Chinese war lord" and remained deeply under the influence of Chiang Kai-shek. (CIA, "National Intelligence Survey, Korea.")

> streamlet under the jurisdiction of the Tongdaemun Police Station. He was the virtual leader of thousands of young men. In some respects, the man who holds the control of Tongdaemun and Ch'ŏnggyech'ŏn can be regarded as the practical dominator of Seoul.

This judgment erred in one respect: "Gang and boss were less dominators than they are the instruments of domination in government's confrontation with the masses."[28] The Northwest, or Sŏbuk, Youth was the most virulent political organization; U.S. intelligence pronounced it "a terrorist group in support of extreme right Wing political figures"; at its inception "the members had all been refugees from North Korea, with real or imaginary grievances against the Soviets and the Korean Communists."

Roger Baldwin, for many years the head of the American Civil Liberties Union, toured Korea in May 1947. "The country is literally in the grip of a police regime and a private terror," he wrote to friends; "you get the general impression of a beaten, discouraged people." He saw a prison where one thousand people were held for having organized labor unions and strikes. Koreans "want all foreigners to get out and let them build their nation." He thought that, were the Americans to pull out, however, a civil war would result. But after the American G-2 (intelligence) chief showed him political reports on the countryside, Baldwin concluded that "a state of undeclared war" already existed in Korea. He interviewed Yŏ Un-hyŏng, who told him that the government was "full of Quislings" and "toadiers to the Americans"; it was the American retention of the colonial police, Yŏ thought, that was the key to the "present chaos."[29]

On a quiet, sultry afternoon a few weeks later, Yŏ picked up the editor of the *Independence News,* Ko Kyŏng-hŏm, and motored over by the ancient Ch'anggyŏng'wŏn Palace to meet another American, Edgar Johnson. Johnson later recalled,

> I remember how impatiently I waited, with my interpretor, that afternoon of July 19, 1947. I had been told by messenger that Lyuh would come about four o'clock. Four o'clock came, four thirty, and then a furiously driven car swerved into the muddy lane leading up the hill to our house. . . . [A] man jumped out and ran stumbling up the hill. Breathlessly he told me that Lyuh had been assassinated less than half a mile from my house.[30]

28. Henderson (1968), pp. 233–34.
29. Cumings (1990), p. 205.
30. Edgar A. J. Johnson, *American Imperialism in the Image of Peer Gynt* (Minneapolis: University of Minnesota Press, 1971), p. 168.

The driver had slowed to negotiate the Hyehwadong traffic rotary, when the murderer mounted the running board and pumped three bullets from a .45 automatic into Yŏ Un-hyŏng's head, killing him instantly. G-2 investigators pinpointed the site "within a stone's throw of a police box," but said that police "made no effort to apprehend the assassin."[31] His daughter, Yŏ Yŏn-gu, told me that Chang T'aek-sang, head of the Seoul police force, ordered the murder. The police either arranged his assassination or looked the other way so that it could happen.[32]

Yŏ had reflected the aspirations of the great majority of the Korean people in 1945, as well as the peculiar class structure of Korean society as it emerged from the Japanese grip: at home with the vast peasantry, he also had a bit of the bourgeois gentleman about him. He was an ardent nationalist, too, and the most vocal critic of the retention of hated Korean police who had done Japanese bidding. As the CIA later acknowledged, he was the only noncommunist southern leader capable of challenging Syngman Rhee for power. Yŏ Un-hyŏng remains one of the few politicians from the 1940s who is honored in both South and North Korea.

American policy, of course, never set out to create one of the worst police states in Asia. The Korean problem was what we would now call a Third World problem or a North-South problem, a conflict over how best to overcome the debilities of colonial rule and comparative backwardness. In the Cold War milieu of the time, however, it was always seen by Americans as an East-West problem. The Soviets, we might say, pushed the North-South angle as a way of besting the United States in the East-West conflict on the peninsula. That is, they stayed in the background and let Koreans run the government, they put anti-Japanese resistance leaders out front, and they supported radical reforms of the land system, labor conditions, and women's rights—all of which were pushed through by the end of 1946. Although very active behind the scenes, the Russians made it seem that Kim Il Sung was in charge—especially after they withdrew their troops from Korea in late 1948.

THE INAUGURATION OF THE REPUBLIC OF KOREA

The Americans could not withdraw their troops so easily, because they were worried about the viability of the southern regime, its dictatorial tendencies, and its oft-stated bluster about marching north. But much more important was Korea's growing importance to American

31. G-2 Weekly Summary no. 97, July 13–20, 1947.
32. Thames Television interview with Yŏ Yŏn-gu, P'yŏngyang, Nov. 1987.

global policy, as part of a new, dual strategy of containing communism and reviving the Japanese industrial economy as a motor of the world economy, but one now shorn of its previous political and military clout. In early 1947 officials in Washington decided to revive Japanese heavy industries and end the purges of wartime leaders, a policy long known as the reverse course. They all thought the solution to the sluggish European and Japanese recovery lay in lifting restrictions on heavy industry and finding ways to combine Germany and Japan with their old providers of raw materials and markets. William Borden wrote that Germany and Japan thus formed "the key to the balance of power," and shrewdly observed that whereas Germany was merely "the pivot" of the larger Marshall Plan program, "the Japanese recovery program formed the sole large-scale American effort in Asia."[33]

Secretary of State George Marshall scribbled a note to Dean Acheson in late January 1947 that said, "Please have plan drafted of policy to organize a definite government of So. Korea and *connect up [sic]* its economy with that of Japan," a stunning mouthful. A few months later Secretary of the Army William Draper said that Japanese influence may again develop in Korea, "since Korea and Japan form a natural area for trade and commerce."[34] Acting Secretary of State Dean Acheson remarked in secret congressional testimony in early 1947 that the United States had drawn the line in Korea, and sought funding for a major program to turn back communism there on the model of "Truman Doctrine" aid to Greece and Turkey. Acheson understood containment to be primarily a political and economic problem, of positioning self-supporting, viable regimes around the Soviet periphery; he thought the truncated Korean economy could still serve Japan's recovery, as part of what he called a "great crescent" linking Japan with Korea, Taiwan, Southeast Asia, and ultimately the oil of the Persian Gulf. Congress and the Pentagon balked at a major commitment to Korea, however, and so Acheson and his advisers took the problem to the United Nations, in order to reposition and contain Korea through collective security mechanisms. It was at this time, in early 1947, that Washington finally got control of Korea policy from the occupation; the effect was essentially to ratify the de facto containment policies that the occupation had been following since September 1945 (and that some in the State Department, like John Carter Vincent, had long opposed).

33. William S. Borden, *The Pacific Alliance: United States Foreign Economic Policy and Japanese Trade Recovery, 1947–1955* (Madison: University of Wisconsin Press, 1984), p. 15.

34. National Archives, 740.0019 file, box 3827, Marshall's note to Acheson of Jan. 29, 1947, attached to Vincent to Acheson, Jan. 27, 1947; RG335, Secretary of the Army File, box 56, Draper to Royall, Oct. 1, 1947.

The United Nations, dominated by the United States at the time, agreed to form a committee (the United Nations Temporary Commission on Korea, or UNTCOK) to observe democratic elections in Korea. Its members included representatives of the Philippines and Nationalist China, who could be counted on to follow American directions, and representatives from Australia and Canada, who, although more recalcitrant once they got a taste of South Korean politics, came from allied governments subject to American influence and pressure. The North Koreans and Soviets opposed UNTCOK and refused to participate in such elections.

Most of the UNTCOK members did not like what they found in Korea when they arrived in early 1948. They soon discovered, for example, that twelve of fifteen members of the original National Election Committee were either KDP members or close associates of Kim Sŏng-su; when new nominees were added to balance them off, they always seemed to be described as "conservative" or "rightist." Brigadier General John Weckerling, the key officer in USAMGIK dealing with UNTCOK, hectored and lobbied the various delegates. When he found out that the Syrian delegate was partly responsible for a clause stating that UNTCOK would observe the elections only if a "free atmosphere" prevailed, Weckerling retorted, "Have you been instructed to find them [conditions in Korea] not free?" On March 10 the Australian delegate wrote a resolution that in effect would have denied both the UNTCOK function and the validity of any elections: "it appears that the elections are now under the control of a single party," the KDP, the resolution said; moreover, conditions were not suitable in either North or South to hold an election. The UN General Assembly "should not be drawn into a position where it may be held responsible" for an election in the South alone. He recommended that UNTCOK leave Korea and report this to the UN. The resolution, of course, was not adopted.[35]

The UNTCOK-observed elections in May 1948 presaged the final emergence of a separate southern government and thus raised the issue of Korea's permanent division. For that reason, and because of the right-wing cast of the Rhee government, virtually all the major politicians and political parties to the right of Rhee refused to participate—including Kim Kyu-sik, a rare Korean centrist, and Kim Ku, a man probably to the right of Rhee.[36] The election went forward even though the outcome,

35. Cumings (1990), pp. 72–77.

36. The CIA predicted in late 1947 that "the rightist leadership is so single-mindedly bent on dictatorial control that following its accession to power," the moderates would "join the leftist camp." This proved true, except that the moderates joined the leftists before the election was held. See Truman Library, PSF, box 253, CIA, "Implementation of Soviet Objectives in Korea," ORE 62, Nov. 18, 1947.

according to several members of UNTCOK, was a foregone conclusion. The National Police and associated right-wing auxiliaries organized the voting, requiring that peasants have their food ration cards stamped at the polls (if they did not vote, they would lose their rations). On May 10, 1948, the ROK's first National Assembly was elected, composed mostly of supporters of Rhee or Kim Sŏng-su.

The ROK was inaugurated on August 15, 1948, with General MacArthur on the podium—it was only the second time he had left Japan since September 1945. Soon the Truman administration replaced the military government with the 500-man Korean Military Advisory Group (KMAG), established an aid mission (known as the Economic Cooperation Administration, or ECA), pushed big aid bills through Congress to get the Korean economy moving and to equip an army capable of defending South Korea, and arranged for KMAG to retain operational control of the Korean police and military as long as American combat troops remained. The State Department successfully delayed the final withdrawal of American troops until June 30, 1949, mainly because of worries about South Korean security.

The ROK Army (ROKA) was born at this time, growing out of the constabulary that Hodge had set up in December 1945 and that Koreans always referred to as "national defense forces." Constabulary "detachments" were renamed "brigades" in 1948 and then "divisions" in 1949, but there were few changes in actual organization. Right-wing youth groups contributed many members to the army; often they just folded their members into it. After the May 1948 elections enlistments for the constabulary suddenly ballooned, as twenty thousand young men a week joined up. At Rhee's August 15 inauguration, tens of thousands of soldiers marched by reviewing stands, ripping off the constabulary insignia and proclaiming themselves members of the Army of the Republic of Korea.[37]

There were six divisions in the ROKA at the start, led exclusively by officers who had served the Japanese—the most flamboyant of whom was Kim Sŏk-wŏn. Kim had tracked Kim Il Sung in the Manchurian wilderness in the late 1930s as the head of the "Special Kim Detachment" in the Japanese army. He was known then as Kaneyama Shakugen; Emperor Hirohito had decorated him with the Order of Merit for "bravery" in campaigns in the war against China. On June 2, 1948, Kim led twenty-five hundred Korean veterans of the Japanese army through the streets of Seoul, their wartime uniforms now shabby but their goose-stepping smartness still impressive.

37. *Seoul Times*, June 5, Aug. 17, 1948; RG335, Secretary of the Army file, box 56, Coulter to State, Nov. 12, 1948.

Americans knew they had a volatile charge in the new president, Syngman Rhee, and his relations with the embassy were often tempestuous. In small doses, Rhee came off as a handsome, warm, charming gentleman; he was a past master of flattery and disarming, endearing use of the democratic symbolism that stirs American hearts. It took a measure of experience with Rhee to disabuse Americans of their first impressions of him. Hodge knew him best, and by 1948 Hodge thought of Rhee about what "Vinegar Joe" Stilwell thought of Chiang Kai-shek. Hodge's politics in the abstract were similar to Rhee's; he had a typical American's visceral disgust for anything that looked like communism. But he was an honest, unpretentious career military officer who, though he occupied the palatial governor-general's residence (thereafter known as the Blue House, because of its blue tile roof),[38] moved several of his staff in with him and was well known for hard work and plain living. Within a year of his arrival in Korea, if not earlier, he developed a profound disgust with and distrust for Rhee; it is the measure of his bone-hard pragmatic anticommunism that he backed him anyway, having no alternative.

Hodge had long, emotional sessions with Rhee where these two hard-bitten men went at each other without restraint. As Hodge put it once, "Rhee cannot get through his thick skull (he is aided and abetted by his wife in this) that in negotiating with me, he is negotiating with the U.S. Government." When Rhee assumed power Hodge remarked that Rhee and Francesca ("particularly the latter") retained "all the bitter hate fixation for me that they have ever had." After the May 1948 elections Hodge had asked MacArthur to relieve him as quickly as possible, saying he would soon be "persona non grata," and did not want to be around anyway when Rhee "bring[s] in his gang of carpet baggers from the States, Hawaii, and China." Rhee and his wife, the joint chiefs of Korea's "Capone Gang" in Hodge's eyes, reciprocated by telling incredulous listeners that Hodge was a communist. Unlike Stilwell, Hodge did not have the experience with Asian politics to threaten to remove American support as a way of disciplining Rhee; perhaps he was more realistic than Stilwell in thinking that Washington would not back him up.[39]

In seeking a moderate alternative to Rhee, Hodge actually sought to

38. This residence housed Korean presidents from Rhee through Kim Young Sam, until the latter tore it down and built a new presidential mansion. Still called the Blue House, it now has a flowing blue Korean-style roof. President Kim also demolished the old government-general building, which stood at the center of government until 1994. A German architect designed this building in 1915 to form the first character of Nippon when seen from above, and Koreans long thought the colonizers purposely situated it to destroy the *p'ungsu*, or geomancy, of downtown Seoul and two mountains that stand above it.

39. Cumings (1990), p. 226.

get the aged Philip Jaisohn (Sŏ Chae-p'il) to return to Korea and run for president, something that still seems hard to believe. Jaisohn had spent half a century in the United States after his early exploits in the attempted coup d'état of 1884 and with the Independence Club in the 1890s; he went to medical school, became thoroughly Americanized, and served as a local draft board physician during World War II. He arrived at Inch'ŏn in July 1947, getting off to a bit of a bad start by telling assembled reporters that Koreans did not know how to make a simple bar of soap; how could they expect to have an independent government? He served as a personal adviser to Hodge, who wanted him to run against Rhee in the 1948 elections. But Jaisohn was already ill with the cancer that took his life shortly after his return to the United States.[40]

The most important American influence on Rhee was really his "kitchen cabinet" of longtime associates, who were almost all either Americans or Koreans who had spent many years in the United States. The CIA thought that if any group succeeded in influencing this solitary president, it was the kitchen cabinet. Robert Oliver wrote many of Rhee's speeches, as did another longtime Rhee associate, Harold Noble; Oliver had far easier access to Rhee's office than did most of his cabinet ministers or, indeed, the American ambassador. Noble, from a missionary family in Korea, had been in army intelligence; he frequently served as a go-between in Rhee's negotiations with Ambassador John Muccio. Rhee was not simply dependent on the embassy and the State Department, in other words. He reached outside the official network of relations to his paid American advisers, or to General MacArthur, or to Chiang Kai-shek, or to Republican congressmen, or to allies in American intelligence like Preston Goodfellow; this was no one-way street. Yet, at the same time, Rhee often seemed like a tethered hound, constantly straining at the official American leash until he nearly strangled. So this was a bizarre relationship that defies easy categorization: the American giants sought to throw a net on this Korean Lilliputian, still worried that he would get free. Hand-wringing overlords scrutinized a palsied gambler, none knowing for sure what was happening today, what might happen tomorrow.

A CIA "personality" study of Rhee—the first the CIA ever prepared on a foreign leader—stated,

> Rhee has devoted his whole life to the cause of an independent Korea with the ultimate objective of personally controlling that country. In pursuing this end he has shown few scruples about the elements which he has been willing to utilize for his personal advancement, with the

40. *Seoul Times*, July 3, 1947; RG335, Secretary of the Army file, box 57, Hodge to State, April 1, 1948.

> important exception that he has always refused to deal with Communists. . . . Rhee's vanity has made him highly susceptible to the contrived flattery of self-seeking interests in the US and Korea. His intellect is a shallow one, and his behavior is often irrational and even childish. Yet Rhee, in the final analysis, has proved himself to be a remarkably astute politician.

The conclusion of this study was prophetic: "The danger exists . . . that Rhee's inflated ego may lead him into action disastrous or at least highly embarrassing to the new Korean Government and to the interests of the U.S."[41]

To the extent that there was an opposition to the Rhee regime, it came from the Korean Democratic Party. From its inception until the early 1970s, when younger leaders untainted by the Japanese era came to maturity (such as Kim Dae Jung), the original set of leaders who were prominent in the 1940s formed the backbone of this tepid opposition even though the party changed its name from time to time. In the literature on the ROK, the KDP is often depicted as an advocate of basic freedoms and human rights, and of parliamentary prerogatives against Rhee's dictatorial executive power. Many Americans remember Cho Pyŏng-ok and Chang T'aek-sang in the 1950s as good, well-spoken liberals, when they frequented Seoul cafés and tearooms as stalwarts of the Rhee "opposition."

Behind the formal democratic façade of the First Republic, however, traditional politics motivated the political elite. The KDP was the organ of landed wealth and local power, and like the old yangban aristocracy from which most of its members came, it fought with central executive power over the allocation of resources and the control of wealth. The tension between Rhee's presidency and the KDP mimicked James Palais's analysis of state-society conflicts in the Chosŏn dynasty, with Rhee playing the king and the legislature aggregating the interests of the landed nobility; it was, in typical Korean conservative fashion, old wine in new bottles. For those in the KDP who had cut their tie to the land and invested in industry, this tension was not as great, because the state bureaucracy was their ally in distributing vested properties and erecting walls of protection to incubate native industry through a nascent import-substitution industrialization program. But wealth still required a state guarantee or bureaucratic tie, as in the past, and in any case most KDP industrialists were like Kim Sŏng-su, interested in combining the traditional privilege and status of landed power with the greater returns of industrial investment.

41. CIA, "Prospects for the Survival of the Republic of Korea," ORE 44-48, Oct. 28, 1948, Appendix A, "Personality of Syngman Rhee"; CIA, "National Intelligence Survey, Korea."

The relationship between Rhee and the KDP was during the First Republic what it had been in 1945: a tempestuous marriage of convenience. As the CIA put it in the autumn of 1948, KDP leaders "dare not overthrow him but must maintain an uneasy coalition with him since they need his political prestige," the latter a reference to the collaborationist background of most KDP leaders and Rhee's role in protecting them; "at the same time, since [Rhee] requires their money and ability, he cannot ignore their demands."[42] From that point onward, South Korea has had in effect two parties: a ruling party seeking to manage a one-party regime, going under the name Liberal Party (in the 1950s), Democratic Republican Party (in the 1960s and 1970s), or the Democratic Liberal Party of the 1990s. The opposition has had some version of the original Democratic Party, going under that name or something close to it, from the 1940s into the 1990s. After 1948 the KDP continued to penetrate the commanding heights of the state bureaucracy, just as it had during the occupation. A listing of provincial governors, city mayors, and county magistrates in early 1949 shows remarkable continuity with lists of local officials in 1945–46; the same people were switched around to different locales through the old "law of avoidance," which operated at a higher velocity in Korea than in China.[43]

Rhee's position on the independence of the legislative branch, called for in the 1948 constitution, was conflicted and contradictory. He tolerated a good bit of noisy debate and interpellation, within the narrow limits of the parties and individuals who made up the National Assembly. The CIA was right to see the National Assembly as "the locus of democratic spirit" in the ROK, with legislative debate often bringing heated exchanges with government officials, but also right that it did not "approximate any typical democratic Western legislature" and was no obstacle to "Bonapartism," since it possessed no effective checks on executive power.[44] It was a legislature whose precarious perch within the political system was like a rowdy ski lodge on the slopes of an avalanche-prone mountain.

In late 1949 thirteen members of the National Assembly were arrested under the National Security Law. Ernst Fraenkel, formerly with the USAMGIK Justice Department and then serving in the ECA mission, said that those assembly members indicted ran afoul of an article of the law making it illegal to join a group having the purpose of "disturbing the

42. CIA, "Prospects for the Survival of the Republic of Korea," ORE 44-48, Oct. 28, 1948; CIA, "National Intelligence Survey, Korea."

43. National Archives, 895.00 file, box 7127, March 17, 1949, trip by McDonald and Rozier through the provinces.

44. CIA, "Prospects for the Survival of the Republic of Korea," ORE 44–48, Oct. 28, 1948.

Syngman Rhee at Chang Tŏk-su's funeral in late 1947, front right, with Francesca next to him; Kim Sŏng-su is visible over Rhee's left shoulder. *Courtesy of U.S. National Archives.*

tranquility of the nation." In their trial the judge refused to call witnesses nominated by the defense, since "these witnesses might make false statements in an effort to protect the accused"; the bias of the presiding judge, Fraenkel said, was obvious "time and again," and the prosecutor relied on confessions extracted by torture. Among other things, the accused assemblymen had sought to express to UNTCOK opinions critical of Rhee, called for the withdrawal of American troops, and, according to the indictment, opposed the "invasion of North Korea by South Korean forces."[45]

THE CHEJU AND YŎSU REBELLIONS

The critical background to the establishment of separate governments in Korea was not in the realm of political parties, however, but in the social and political conflict between left and right throughout the peninsula. This conflict went on at the national level in 1945 and at the provincial and county levels in 1946, as local people's committees controlled county seats and fought with their antagonists. The suppression of the

45. *New York Times,* March 14, 1950; National Archives, 795.00 file, box 4299, Drumwright to State, March 22, 1950, enclosing Fraenkel's analysis of the trial.

massive autumn harvest uprisings in 1946[46] consolidated state control in the county seats, making the seizure of power by county people's committees unlikely thereafter. Villages continued to be isolated from central power, however, and leftists therefore migrated downward through the bureaucratic reaches of the system in search of space for organization.

By 1947 most leftists were members of the South Korean Labor Party (SKLP). This party was always indigenous to the South, drawing its members especially from the southwest and southeast, but it was more independent of northern or Soviet influence in 1947 than after the formation of the Rhee government. Only vague and unreliable evidence existed on northern or Soviet provision of funding for the party, and American intelligence sources did not believe that the North directed the activity of the SKLP—instead that the two worked toward common goals.

It appears, however, that by mid-1948, if not earlier, the party was under northern guidance. Intercepted instructions from the North urged members to infiltrate into "all important bureaus" of the Rhee government, to secrete food and other supplies for guerrillas in the mountains, and to "infiltrate into the South Korean Constabulary and begin political attacks aimed at causing dissension and disorder." Up until the Korean War, however, it cannot be said that southern communists were mere creatures of Kim Il Sung, and there was much conflict between the two parties and their leaders (Pak Hŏn-yŏng was the southern communist head).

Rhee and his allies formed counterorganizations at the village level to fight the left. Roy Roberts of the Associated Press wrote in August 1947 that U.S. intelligence got an average of five police reports a day, "telling of fights in villages, fights between villages, beatings of rightists, beatings of leftists, burning of granaries, attacks on village officials, attacks on police, stoning of political meetings." An account of one of these battles, dated August 19, 1947, from a small town near Masan along the southeast coast, is representative. Some one thousand peasants gathered to hear officials talk about the military government's rice collection program and then

> became hostile and started stoning the speechmakers. The police present were forced to fire into the mob, to give the township officials a chance to retreat across the rice fields. The retreating policemen passed a police box, and stopped long enough to secure additional rifles and ammunition. The mob overran the police box, seized documents and

46. For a full account of this rebellion see Cumings (1981), pp. 351–79; more generally on peasant protest, see Shin (1996).

> demolished the box completely. They then split into two parts, one part erecting road blocks, and the other destroying telephone communications.

Soon police reinforcements arrived from Masan and T'ongyŏng; they fired into the mob, dispersing it and leaving four peasants dead.[47]

These village battles occurred in regions of previous people's committee strength; an American intelligence survey in September 1947 found "an underground People's Committee government" still existing "in certain parts of south Korea." South Chŏlla was "perhaps the most Leftist area"; the survey estimated that 15 to 20 percent of the communities visited "were openly hostile to the Americans. Leftist activity all over was evident. . . ." Leftists were also strong in the southwestern Kyŏngsang provinces, Kangwŏn along the upper east coast, and, above all, Cheju Island off the southern coast.[48]

Before 1950 no place suffered the political conflicts of liberated Korea like Cheju, a beautiful island covered with black volcanic rock, where guerrilla war began in 1948. The effective political leadership on Cheju until early 1948 was provided by strong, rooted people's committees that first emerged in August 1945; as General Hodge once put it, Cheju was "a truly communal area . . . peacefully controlled by the People's Committee without much Comintern [i.e., Soviet] influence." An official investigation by the USAMGIK judge Yang Wŏn-il conducted in June 1948 found that "the People's Committee of Cheju Island, which was formed after the liberation . . . has exercised its power as a de facto government." He also found that "the police have failed to win the hearts of the people by treating them cruelly." Shortly thereafter another USAMGIK investigation estimated that "approximately two-thirds of the populace" on the island were "moderate leftist" in their opinions. The chairman of leftist organization, a former Cheju governor named Pak, was "not a Communist and [was] very pro-American." The people were deeply separatist and did not like mainlanders; their wish was to be left alone.

The survey determined, however, that Cheju had been subjected to a campaign of official terrorism in recent months. According to CIC information, the current governor, Yu Hae-jin, was an "extreme rightist," a mainlander with connections to two right-wing youth groups; he was "ruthless and dictatorial in his dealing with opposing political parties."

47. USAMGIK, G-2 Weekly Summary no. 103, Aug. 24–31, 1947. There are many, many other such incidents of violence reported in this issue and subsequent ones through Sept. 1947.

48. National Archives, 895.00 file, box 7124, Jacobs to State, Oct. 21, 1947. He does not say who conducted this survey.

Governor Yu had filled national police units on the island with mainlanders and North Koreans, who worked together with "ultra rightist party terrorists." When Americans interviewed Governor Yu in February 1948, he acknowledged that he had utilized "extreme rightist power" to reorient the Cheju people, "the large majority" of whom were leftist. He justified this by saying that "there was no middle line" in Island politics; one supported either the left or the right.[49]

After a March 1, 1948, demonstration against the separate elections on the mainland, the police arrested 2,500 young people, and islanders soon fished the dead body of one of them out of a river: he had been tortured to death. But the affair that most inflamed the island population was the unleashing of the Northwest Youth. In late 1947 the American Counter-Intelligence Corps had "warned" this group about its "widespread campaign of terrorism" on Cheju. But under the American command, these same youths joined the police and constabulary in the Cheju guerrilla suppression campaigns. As a subsequent Korean press investigation put it,

> Since the coming of a youth organization, whose members are young men from Northwest Korea, the feeling between the [island] inhabitants and those from the mainland has been growing tense. . . . They may have been inspired by the Communists. Yet, how shall we understand how over 30,000 men have roused themselves to action in defiance of gun and sword. Without cause, there can be no action.

The Northwest Youth Corps was said to have "exercised police power more than the police itself and their cruel behavior has invited the deep resentment of the inhabitants."[50] All this helped to touch off a guerrilla rebellion.

The guerrillas generally were known as the *inmin-gun*, or People's Army, estimated to be 3,000 to 4,000 strong. But they were not centrally commanded and operated in mobile units of eighty or a hundred people who often had little connection with other rebels. The Japanese had left a honeycomb of caves, tunnels, and defensive bunkers on the island; caches of small arms were also left in some of the caves, which the guerrillas utilized. They hid in these emplacements, striking from mountains that commanded the coastal road and low-lying villages. By early

49. USFIK 11071 file, box 62 / 96, transcript of Hodge's monologue to visiting congressmen, Oct. 4, 1947; RG332, XXIV Corps Historical file, box 20, "Report of Special Investigation—Cheju-Do Political Situation," March 11, 1948, conducted by Lieutenant Colonel Lawrence A. Nelson.

50. G-2 Weekly Summary no. 116, Nov. 23–30, 1947; *Seoul Times*, June 15, June 18, 1950. These issues reported the results of a survey by a team of journalists from Seoul.

June 1948 most villages in the interior were controlled by the guerrillas; roads and bridges were destroyed throughout the island.

By the end of 1948 ROK authorities had recorded 102 battles, more than 5,000 combatants on both sides, nearly 6,000 islanders in custody, and a claimed total of 422 dead insurgents. By April 1949 some 20,000 homes on the island had been destroyed, and one-third of the island population (about 100,000) was concentrated in protected villages along the coast. In the same month the American embassy reported that "the all-out guerrilla extermination campaign . . . came to a virtual end in April with order restored and most rebels and sympathizers killed, captured, or converted." Some American sources thought that 15,000 to 20,000 islanders died in the conflict, but the ROK news agency cited an official figure of 27,719; the North Korean figure was 30,000. The governor of Cheju, however, privately told American intelligence that 60,000 had died and that as many as 40,000 had fled to Japan; officially 39,285 homes had been demolished, but the governor thought "most of the houses on the hills" were gone: of 400 villages, only 170 remained. In other words, one in every five or six islanders had perished and more than half the villages been destroyed.[51]

As the Cheju insurgency progressed, one event attracted much more attention: a rebellion at the port city of Yŏsu that soon spread to other counties in the southwest and southeast and that for a time seemed to threaten the foundations of the fledgling republic. The cause of the uprising was the refusal on October 19, 1948, of elements of the Sixth and Fourteenth regiments of the republic's army to embark on a mission against the Cheju guerrillas. By dawn on October 20, the rebels (numbered then at two thousand) had seized control of Yŏsu; some elements then entrained for the nearby town of Sunch'ŏn and seized it by the early afternoon, overwhelming police reinforcements. Soon rebels spread out to nearby towns. Within hours of the regimental revolt, large numbers of people were parading through Yŏsu, waving red flags and shouting slogans; at a mass meeting on October 20 the town people's committee was restored and "people's courts" proceeded to try and execute a number of captured policemen, as well as some other government officials, landlords, and "rightists." Speakers called for a "Korean People's Republic," using the 1945 term rather than the DPRK designation used in the North. (But some demonstrators also showed the DPRK flag, and pledged loyalty to Kim Il Sung.) People's committees were also restored

51. "The Background of the Present War in Korea," *Far Eastern Economic Review*, Aug. 31, 1950, pp. 233–37; this account is by an anonymous but knowledgeable American who served in the occupation. See also RG349, FEC G-2 Theater Intelligence, box 466, May 23, 1950, G-2 report on Cheju, which has the governor's figures.

in numerous small communities and islands near Yŏsu. Rebel leaders told followers that the thirty-eighth parallel had been done away with and that unification with the North would soon follow.[52]

Rhee and his American backers immediately charged that North Korea had fomented the rebellion, but it was in fact an outburst dating back to the frustrated goals of local leftists over the previous three years. A rebel newspaper referred to a "three-year fight" against the American occupation and demanded that all Americans leave Korea forthwith. It announced that all agencies of government should be handed over to the Yŏsu People's Committee, and called for land redistribution without compensation to landlords, a purge of police and other officials who had served the Japanese, and opposition to a separate government for the South.

The suppression of the rebellion was organized and directed by Americans and carried out by young Korean colonels, even though the occupation had ended and the United States ostensibly had no mandate to intervene in Korean internal affairs. But secret protocols placed operational control of the ROK military in American hands, and American advisers were with all ROK Army units. American C-47 transports ferried Korean troops, weapons, and other matériel; American intelligence organizations worked intimately with army and KNP counterparts. Meanwhile, during the rebellion the thirty-eighth parallel was quiet for the longest period in recent months, suggesting that North Korea did not want the fighting to spread.

The revolutionary terror of the rebels left hundreds of policemen, officials, and landlords dead; as many as five hundred members of the KNP may have been murdered, often brutally. But American G-2 sources nonetheless reported that the attacks on the police met with "the satisfaction of a large portion of the [local] population." Students of the Sunchŏn middle school avidly joined in the assaults on police.[53] After the rebel defeat loyalists predictably took their awful retribution. American sources reported that "loyal troops were shooting people whom they had the slightest suspicion . . . of giving cooperation to the communist uprising." James Hausman, a key figure who helped organize the suppression, reported that police in Sunch'ŏn were "out for revenge and are executing prisoners and civilians. . . . Several loyal civilians already killed and people beginning to think we *[sic]* are as bad as the enemy."[54]

52. USFIK 11071 file, box 65 / 96, XXIV Corps G-3 section, "History of the Rebellion of the 14th Regiment and the 6th Regiment of the Korean Constabulary," Nov. 10, 1948; also RG332, XXIV Corps Historical file, box 35, report by "Special Agent no. 9016"; also USFIK 11071 file, box 77 / 96, "223rd report on Yŏsu," Oct. 27, 1948.
53. Cumings (1990), pp. 259–67.

OFFICIAL ESTIMATES OF CASUALTIES FROM THE YOSU REBELLION [55]

loyalist soldiers dead	141	rebels killed	821
missing	263	rebels captured	2,860
civilians dead	1,000 +	still guerrillas	1,000 +

The Yŏsu rebellion was a fierce tempest for a week or so, but ultimately it was a tempest in a teapot that Rhee utilized to clamp down upon any resistance to his rule; a spontaneous and hasty mutiny by disgruntled soldiers, it merely incurred more repression. Internal American data on political prisoners under the U.S. occupation placed 21,458 in prison in December 1947, compared with 17,000 in southern Korea in August 1945; two years later, 30,000 alleged communists were in Rhee's jails and proceedings against suspected communists constituted 80 percent of all court cases. "Guidance camps" held those additional prisoners unable to be housed in the grossly overcrowded prisons; the U.S. embassy estimated that 70,000 people were in these camps. "Repentance" campaigns in November 1949 were followed in December by "extermination weeks," in which as many as 1,000 people a day were rounded up. An embassy political officer summarized this as follows:

> The suppression of Communism appeared to be increasingly successful. The government had mobilized its forces in many ways. Security forces were ruthlessly stamping out the Communist party organization and guerrilla resistance, using whatever methods were considered necessary. . . . The Great Korean Youth Corps [Taehan Youth] and Student's National Defense Corps were instilling patriotism and teaching military drill. Agents were everywhere watching actions and conversations; every organization had its watchers for communist behavior.[56]

54. "Yŏsu Operation, Amphibious Stage," report by "Special Agent no. 9016," G-2 Intelligence Summary no. 166, Nov. 5–12, 1948; USFIK 11071 file, box 76 / 96, Roberts to PMAG, Oct. 25, 1950; "message from Hausman," Oct. 25, 1950. Carl Mydans witnessed the execution of twenty-two rebels in Sunch'ŏn, writing that loyal troops "were as savage as the Communists had been." *Time,* Nov. 8, 1948.

55. National Archives, 895.00 file, box 7127, Drumwright to State, Dec. 10, 1948, giving Yi Pŏm-Sŏk's official ROK figures as of Dec. 7; G-2 Intelligence Summaries nos. 166, 167, Nov. 12–26, 1948; RG332, box 22, staff conference, Oct. 26, 1948; F0317, piece no. 76258, Seoul Embassy to FO, Jan. 7, 1949.

56. Truman Library, PSF, NSC file, box 205, CIA, "Review of the World Situation," Dec. 16, 1948; ibid., box 257, CIA, "Communist Capabilities in South Korea," ORE 32-48, Feb. 21, 1949; National Archives, 895.00 file, box 7124, Langdon to State, Dec. 12, 1947; ibid., box 7128, Muccio to State, Dec. 10 1949; ibid., Embassy to State, Dec. 10, 1949.

Writing many years later, a U.S. State Department official described the "National Guidance Alliance," which Rhee set up in 1949, as an "ingenious device" put to good use in "the drive against Communists."[57] In fact, it was a way to set up concentration camps for political prisoners, to do "conversion" and "reeducation" work among anyone at all suspected of leftist activity. The alliance frequently made claims that it was converting as many as 3,000 people per week, as many as 10,000 converts per province. Its chief, Pak U-ch'ŏn, explained to an embassy officer how the process worked:

> In order to be sure that conversions are sincere and complete, each individual upon surrendering himself to the Alliance is required to prepare a complete written confession. . . . Most important, he must set down the names of all individuals who served in the same cell. . . . For a period of one year confessions are subject to constant recheck, largely by matching name lists. If a confession proves false or deficient at any time during the year, the person who made it becomes liable to the full legal penalty for his action and for his leftist affiliations.[58]

When observers criticize the continuous autocratic harshness with which the ROK has dealt with the left wing and with communists over the past fifty years, they should remember that the United States has been tacitly supportive of and complicit in it since the founding of the system. Such measures were thought justifiable, given the threat posed by the regime to the north—and to which we now turn.

NORTH KOREA

When the Korean War broke out, few people knew anything about North Korea, but generally assumed it to be a typical Soviet satellite, a "people's democracy" like those in Eastern Europe. The Red Army occupied the territory, rode herd on the emergence of a socialist state with a planned economy, and installed Kim Il Sung as its handpicked puppet: what else could it be? Recent studies based on a treasure trove of documents seized when United Nations forces occupied North Korea,[59] however, support different interpretations, which we can summarize as follows. First, North Korea evolved an indigenous political system in the

57. Macdonald (1992), p. 106.
58. National Archives, 895.00 file, box 7127, Muccio to State, Nov. 7, 1949; ibid., Muccio to State, Dec. 2, 1949.
59. Mainly Record Group 242, "Captured Enemy Documents," declassified by the National Records Center in 1977; but also some recent Chinese and Russian archival materials. Scholars who have used this collection to produce new interpretations include Charles Armstrong, Wada Haruki, Pak Myong Lim, and myself.

late 1940s, and its basic structure has never changed substantially, so that in the fundamentals what you see in 1949 or 1950 is what you get in the 1990s. Second, the closest comparisons to North Korea were Romania and Yugoslavia—not the states under complete Soviet hegemony, such as East Germany. Third, Soviet influence competed with Chinese influence, and both conflicted with indigenous political forms and practices. The Democratic People's Republic of Korea (DPRK) was and is a divergent case among postwar Marxist-Leninist systems, representing a profound reassertion of native Korean political practice—from the superordinate role of the leader to his self-reliant ideology, to the Hermit Kingdom foreign policy.

For years many people also speculated that if the Soviets did not control Korea, a group of "Soviet-Koreans" did. A retrospective State Department study, based on captured North Korean records, asserted that a group of some forty-three Koreans who were born in or resided in the Soviet Union, most of them members of the Soviet party in 1945, constituted the core of the Soviet-Korean group; but even according to this official account, they played only "secondary roles" until after the Korean War, with Kim Il Sung's main competition coming from native communists and China-aligned groups. Although Soviet-Korean power rose briefly in the early 1950s, according to this study the group was "virtually eliminated" by 1956. The head of this group was Hŏ Ka-i, a proponent of Soviet models of organization described as "a disciplinarian in the best Bolshevik tradition," working closely with the Soviet embassy. The CIA put great emphasis on Hŏ Ka-i, viewing him as a key liaison between the Soviets and the Koreans, and an "enormous" behind-the-scenes influence.[60]

Recent, careful scholarship suggests a different picture. The leading authority on Soviet-Korean relations found that among Stalin's large grouping of international communists in Moscow, not a single Korean communist or nationalist existed who clearly "was a trusted Soviet man." In 1937 Stalin ordered the forced deportation of some 200,000 Koreans from the Soviet Far East to Central Asia, on the racist grounds that they might harbor pro-Japanese seditious elements. "At the same time all Korean communists who were working in the Comintern were arrested and killed as [potential] agents of Japanese militarism." The Soviets may also have subjected Kim Il Sung and other Korean guerrillas to investigation and interrogation when they moved back and forth across the Soviet-Manchurian border in the 1940s, keeping them under surveillance for a long time. In extant Soviet studies of Manchuria under

60. Evelyn McCune "Leadership in North Korea: Groupings and Motivations" (State Department, Office of Intelligence Research, 1963).

the Japanese, Kim Il Sung is usually not mentioned—distinctly short shrift for an alleged Soviet puppet.[61]

From the time of the czars Korea has been a concern of Russian security. As we have seen, the Russo-Japanese War of 1905 was fought in part over the disposition of the Korean peninsula. It has often been surmised that the Russians saw Korea as a gateway to the Pacific, and especially to warm-water ports. Furthermore, Korea had one of Asia's oldest communist movements. Thus it would appear that postwar Korea was of great concern to the Soviet Union; many have therefore thought that its policy was a simple matter of Sovietizing northern Korea, setting up a puppet state, and then directing Kim Il Sung to unify Korea by force in 1950. The problem is that the Soviets did not get a warm-water port out of their involvement in Korea, even with their full occupation of half the peninsula.

The number of Soviet advisers was never very high in the North, even in the military. British sources estimated that Soviet advisers to the central government dropped from 200 in 1946 to a mere 30 in April 1947, the greatest number of those, predictably, being in the Ministry of the Interior. The South Korean defense minister put the number of Soviet military advisers at only 120 before the war, which accords with intelligence estimates after the war began, saying the Soviets used "approximately fifteen advisory officers per NK division," there being fewer than ten divisions before June 1950. There were only fifteen Soviet advisers to the Korean Air Force. Advisers went down to the battalion level, the Americans liked to say, something that sounds impressive. But there were three regiments to each division, and three battalions to each regiment. If the total number was around 120, or 15 per division, then a battalion would have had only 1 or 2 Soviet advisers.[62] This Soviet presence simply cannot be compared to fully functioning satellites in Eastern Europe, which had thousands of Soviet staff people and advisers and where Soviet officials sometimes held important governmental posts.

Some internal reports said similar things at the time. R. S. Milward of the British Foreign Office wrote in mid-1948 that North Korea had

> an apparent similarity to the more autonomous western Communist states such as Yugoslavia. Kim Il Sung . . . was built up during the war

61. Wada Haruki, "The Soviet Union and North Korea" (paper presented at the Korea Seminar, University of Washington, 1984).

62. FO317, piece no. 69940, Milward to Crossley, March 17, 1948; KMAG G-2 Periodic Report no. 274, March 3–6, 1950; RG349, box 462, G-2 report on Hŭngnam explosives plant, Dec. 29, 1950; CIA, "Prospects for the Survival of the ROK," ORE 44-48, Oct. 28, 1948; G-2, Intelligence Summaries—North Korea, no. 39, June 30, 1947; KMAG G-2 Periodic Report no. 176, Sept. 2–6, 1949, all of which agree that Soviet advisers are not below the battalion level.

> into an almost legendary guerrilla hero . . . a Korean Tito. The Russians moreover are proposing to withdraw their forces from Korea, seeming to trust their puppets . . . [to] rule the land in the interests of Russia without direct Russian interference.

This "facade of autonomy," Milward thought, was more pronounced "than in almost any other country in the Russian orbit." A CIA study one year later made sharp distinctions between the Euro-Mediterranean region and East Asia, citing "a generally detached attitude" toward communism in East Asia in 1945–49. The Soviets' looting of Manchuria, the CIA thought, suggested that they did not want to build a dependent economic complex and had problems controlling Asian nationalism and "Titoism."[63]

North Korea was never simply a Soviet satellite in the 1940s, but evolved from a coalition regime based on widespread people's committees in 1945–46 to one under relative Soviet dominance in 1947–48, thence in 1949 to one with important links to China, which in turn enabled the DPRK to maneuver between the two communist giants. Kim Il Sung was not a handpicked Soviet puppet, but maneuvered politically first to establish his leadership, then to isolate and defeat the communists who had remained in Korea during the colonial period, then to ally with Soviet-aligned Koreans for a time, then to create a powerful army under his own leadership (in February 1948) that melded Koreans who had fought together in Manchuria and China proper with those who remained at home.[64]

From August 1945 until January 1946, the Soviets worked with a coalition of communists and nationalists, led by a Christian educator named Cho Man-sik. They did not set up a central administration, nor did they create an army. In retrospect their policy seems more tentative and reactive than American policy in the South, which did move forward with plans for a separate administration and an army in the South; Soviet power in the Far East was flexible at that time and resulted in the withdrawal of Soviet troops from Manchuria in early 1946. Whether in response to American initiatives or because most Koreans despised the trusteeship agreement negotiated at the end of 1945, in early 1946 separate institutions also began to emerge in the North.

In February an interim people's committee led by Kim Il Sung constituted the first central government, and in March the land reform ensued, dispossessing landlords without compensation. In August a powerful

63. FO317, piece no. 69945, R. S. Milward, "Communism in Korea," June 7, 1948; HST, PSF, Intelligence File, box 249, CIA, "Relative US Security Interest in the European-Mediterranean Area and the Far East," ORE 69-49, July 14, 1949.
64. Cumings (1981), pp. 382–426; Cumings (1990), pp. 291–94.

political party (called the North Korean Workers' Party—NKWP) came to dominate politics, and in the fall of 1946 the rudiments of a northern army appeared. Central agencies nationalized major industries (they had, of course, been owned mostly by the Japanese) and began a two-year economic program on the Soviet model of central planning and the priority of heavy industry. Nationalist and Christian leaders were ousted from all but pro forma participation in politics, and Cho Man-sik was placed under house arrest. Kim Il Sung and his allies dominated all the political parties, ousting people who resisted them. The Korean People's Army (KPA) was the backbone of Kim's dominance; although not founded until February 8, 1948, it was in formation from mid-1946 onward and was led by one of his close allies, Ch'oe Yong-gŏn.

The Communist, or Workers', Party in fact had its social base in the vast peasantry. The party apparatus recruited a mass following for Kim's rule, in an open-door policy that allowed almost anyone to be a party member, regardless of class background. This brought masses of poor peasants into the party ranks. Membership in the party gave them position, prestige, privileges, and a rudimentary from of political participation. Even among party leaders, a poor peasant background was common. In a secret compilation of data on some 1,881 "cultural cadres" in late 1949, about 66 percent came from a poor peasant background and 19 percent from a proletarian background. Fully 422 of these cadres had experience in the Chinese Communist Eighth Route Army.[65]

We also see this pattern in individual biographies. Kim Chu-suk was born into a poor peasant family in 1920, and worked as a tenant farmer during the war. In 1946 she joined the party and the women's league (as a "propagandist"). The next year she attended the provincial party cadre school and on graduation became a statistician in a township party branch office. By 1950 she had been promoted to the county level. Kim Ch'ŏl-gŭm fits the pattern of many other mobilized worker-peasants. Born into a poor peasant family in 1910 in Sihŭng, near Seoul, he farmed as a tenant and became responsible for the family when his father died in 1925; during the depression the family suffered greatly and his mother also died. He took his sister to northern Korea after industrial jobs started opening up. He got work on Japanese fishing trawlers as a boiler-room man, suffering "contemptuous treatment" at the hands of the colonizers, but managing to learn some skills. In 1942 he was forcibly drafted and sent to Singapore, where he worked in merchant shipping for three years. In April 1945, with British aircraft attacking every day, he decided he "did not want to die for the Japanese" and ran away. Three days later

65. Data from Record Group 242, courtesy of Pang Sun-joo.

he was caught and thrown into a military prison. After the war he returned to Wŏnsan; he joined the NKWP in 1946, as did four of his remaining five relatives in Wŏnsan.

Tong Hak-jŏng, from a family whose entire extended clan consisted of poor tenants, was also a typical worker-peasant of the 1940s. During the depression his father could not sustain a farming livelihood, and so when he was thirteen Hak-jŏng went with the family from Myongch'ŏn County, in North Hamgyŏng Province, to Ch'ientao, in Manchuria, where they remained until 1945. While his father worked in a Japanese textile factory, he labored in a mine. The son went to Seoul in 1946, hoping to get into high school. Failing to do so, he returned to Susang and joined a public peacekeeping unit (*poandae,* a forerunner of the army) in October 1946. After two months' training in 1947, he became a deputy detachment chief in the *poandae.* By 1950 he was a KPA officer.[66]

In the first year after liberation there were a number of noncommunist parties and groups—nationalists, Christians, and followers of the native Ch'ŏndogyo religion. The Kim leadership adopted a "united-front" policy toward two major parties, the Chosŏn Democratic Party (CDP) and the "Friends Party" of the Ch'ŏndogyo religion. In national people's committee elections in November 1946, the CDP elected 351 members, the Chŏngu-dang 253, and the NKWP 1,102, with 1,753 of those elected listed as belonging to no party.[67] Kim Il Sung publicly justified the presence of these parties in the united front by saying that the CDP opposed foreign interference in Korea and thus was anti-imperialist; the Chŏngu-dang "consists largely of peasants, and therefore we can always maintain a coalition with this party."[68] But this united-front policy gave no real power to these parties. It did take account of the rootedness in the peasantry of the Ch'ŏndogyo religion, and the significance of urban Christian power, especially in P'yŏngyang. But the regime subjected these parties to the same top-down control everyone else got.

Kim Il Sung installed his guerrilla friend Ch'oe Yong-gŏn as the leader of the CDP. Ch'oe gave one of his first major speeches on Christmas Day, 1946; in it he berated CDP members for being insufficiently active, for not sending enough reports to the party center, for "petty-bourgeois" attitudes, and for the "disease of our nation"—factionalism. He urged the members to get rid of "bad, feudal influences"—an example of which

66. RG242, SA2010, item 3 / 107, *"kanbu iyŏksa"* (cadre biographies), most of which were dated in early 1950.

67. Cumings (1990), p. 317.

68. Kim's speech to the Second Plenary Session of the NKWP, Jan. 24, 1948, quoted in G-2 Weekly Summary no. 125, Jan. 30–Feb. 6, 1948.

was CDP criticism of the NKWP. Businessmen and merchants in the party should strive to develop the national wealth, rather than their own; profiteering, he said, posed a major threat to the economy. Members should reflect on all this and criticize their bad ways.[69] The Kim regime wanted the CDP to be the never-victorious class representative of landlords and capitalists, who would slowly put their own class out of business by reflecting on their transgressions and rectifying their thoughts.

The CDP by this time was merely a transmission belt for the regime's policies, another of the ubiquitous organizations that did the bidding of the center. That is why the regime prodded CDP members to be more active, rather than less—the opposite of what would happen in a competitive party system. A secret NKWP investigation of a CDP branch in Namp'o in 1947 found that members did hardly anything to bolster membership, get out the vote, or organize more branches. "Democratization" of the party was taken to mean weeding out landlords and pro-Japanese, not getting it mobilized. This report said that the backgrounds of local members were uniformly bad ("every one of them was a pro-Japanese") and several had been removed from local people's committees just for that. Christians joined the CDP exclusively, the report said, and most of them were from landlord backgrounds. Thus "democratization" of the CDP had proved difficult: "bad landlords" and "Christian believers" were not being "purged." This investigation included "top secret" data on the class background of CDP members in Namp'o, showing that of some 2,974 members, 625 were workers, 486 were peasants, 493 were clerks or bureaucrats, and 1,365 were "others," which in the individual breakdowns tended to mean landlords, teachers, lawyers, businessmen, and persons in other professional occupations. Only 187 women were members of the CDP, whereas women often constituted one-quarter or more of NKWP rosters.[70]

Christians were particular targets of the regime. Christianity took hold in Korea in a way that it did not in Japan or China, and even if the proportion of believers in the general population was not more than 2 percent in 1945, they were numerous and influential in P'yŏngyang. American sources thought Christian churches formed the strongest opposition to the regime, and many pastors were imprisoned in the late 1940s—including the Reverend Sun Myung Moon, who ran a sect called

69. RG242, SA2005, item 7 / 81, CDP, Sixth Enlarged Central Committee Meeting, Dec. 25, 1946.

70. RG242, SA2012, item 8 / 70, secret investigation of Namp'o CDP branches by Kim Kyŏng-sŏk, who was head of the Namp'o branch of the NKWP. This file includes detailed background accounts of many CDP members.

the Israel Church and who was imprisoned on charges of fornication and adultery in 1948 and 1949 (according to subsequent South Korean sources). In one particularly bloody incident police fired on a crowd of Christian protesters in Sinŭiju, killing twenty-three people; Ham Sŏkhŏn, later a famous Quaker human rights figure in the South, was then in the provincial people's committee. He was beaten and arrested after this incident. Kim Il Sung visited Sinŭiju after this atrocity, seeking to mend rifts between communists and Christian nationalists.[71] Christian churches remained open until the war, and worship was allowed, but Christian political activities were ruthlessly stamped out.

Press freedom had ceased to exist in the North by the end of 1946, with all newspapers—central and local, communist and noncommunist—carrying essentially the same news, with some local coloring thrown in. Furthermore, Soviet-aligned Koreans tended to predominate in the cultural organs; all three of the editors of the party journal were "Soviet-Koreans" (usually meaning Koreans who had lived in the USSR, or followed the Soviet lead) in 1945–50.

Through such means the North Koreans soon eliminated all nonleftist political opposition with a draconian thoroughness. A couple of united-front noncommunist parties were still allowed to exist, but they had no power. The intent was the same as that of the right wing in the South, to squash alternative centers of power. But the northerners did it much more thoroughly, because of their superior organization and the general weakness of the opposition. Neither North nor South had qualms about using violence for political ends, but the North tended to be more discriminating, in part because its enemies were numerically small classes and groups, and also because of a political practice, perhaps growing out of the Korean leadership's experience with Chinese communism, of seeking to reeducate and reform political recalcitrants.

Those who did not go along with the regime's will or those thought to be lagging ideologically—which meant just about everybody—were required to engage in small-group criticism and self-criticism sessions much as in China; these political groups were also conduits of regime policies, and therefore occupied significant amounts of almost everyone's time. Internal party documents and party newspapers show a ubiquitous group life, with constant attention to holding meetings at all levels—in government offices, workplaces, schools, villages. The documentation suggests less a totalitarian atmosphere, and more the mundane problems of getting people to come to meetings, be punctual, speak up, and the like. Group leaders spent a lot of time combatting "liberal-

71. Haruki Wada, "Soviet Union."

ism," defined as skipping meetings, coming late or leaving early, "going out at night," remaining silent—doing what one pleased, in other words. Through these total methods, the regime achieved the result that almost everyone became a member of some organization, subject to the ever-present group life.[72]

The regime did not engage in massive slaughters of its enemies, however, such as those carried out in the USSR in the early 1930s, or in China and Vietnam in their bloody land reform campaigns. Landlords were allowed to flee south or to work small plots of land in other counties, and leadership purges before the war were usually neither fatal nor permanent. O Ki-sŏp, for example, was purged from the political leadership in 1948 but soon headed a joint stock company and came back to a relatively high position in the mid-1950s.

POLICE AND INTELLIGENCE

The North Korean security apparatus, judging by captured internal documentation, was an agency of revolutionary justice and a thorough, often total system of control and surveillance. Within a year after liberation the North Koreans had completely eliminated Koreans who had served the Japanese from the forces of order, in a thoroughgoing renovation of the most hated and feared of colonial institutions. They did not replace it with a system that any American would wish to live under. Those who staffed and benefited from it believed it to be a vast improvement over the previous system; those who suffered from it thought it to be a draconian network that denied all freedom to the individual. Both were probably right.

The security apparatus was very large in the North. An "extremely secret" document on the people's committee administrative structure shows that the intelligence section of each provincial committee always had more members than any other section (about twenty per province, with the provincial staff totaling 353 to 362, depending on the region). City committees had 55 members of the Ministry of the Interior attached to each committee, which varied in size from 141 members in Nanam to 185 in Sinŭiju, excluding the capital, which had 341 members. At the county level, out of a total of 10,499 staff more than one-third (3,732) were Interior Ministry people. These personnel included ordinary neighborhood police, and even the intelligence function encompassed routine things like control of narcotics and poisons—that is, it was not just ori-

72. Cumings (1990), p. 317.

ented to political cases. Furthermore, the total numbers of police were much smaller than in the South.[73]

A secret report in 1947 by Pak Il-u of the Department of Peace Preservation showed that political cases were matters of utmost concern. Pak admonished province chiefs that their "struggle against profiteers and evil capitalists" (also termed "political criminals") was quite weak. The chiefs should be sure "to examine the class background and the thoughts" of all neighborhood leaders in their jurisdiction and bring problem cases to the attention of the people's committee. The class enemy, needless to say, was given next to no rights under this system. Pak also commented on the weaknesses policemen were sometimes prone to, and urged them to repent: "Everyone has an appetite for food, and loves the opposite sex. But this is something that the patriot conquers. Debauchery, indolence . . . are just for the benefit of one's self, and are in opposition to patriotic thought."[74]

Internal documents on the training regimen for police personnel show similar emphases. Police recruits were urged to get rid of the old attitudes of "high-handedness, arrogance, selfishness, and self-aggrandizement"; recruits "must respect human rights," and "beatings, torture, and other inhuman evils must not be used." All policemen should be "models of respect for the law as a guide to the people." Among the virtues of a good policeman, these materials said, were loving to serve, "mutual comradely love," purging "unclean" things from one's life, and being disciplined, resourceful, and willing to face hardship. In North Korea the police must "serve the people"; otherwise it cannot be called a people's state. Security personnel must defend "the people" and fight against the enemy—defined here as "traitors and pro-Japanese."[75] This evidence cannot be dismissed as propaganda, since it is taken from secret internal documents. At a minimum it suggests that, whatever the excesses of individual police, the leadership sought to change some of the worst abuses of the old system.

However virtuous these new policemen tried to be, their functions included a total system of thought control and surveillance that would horrify a believer in basic political freedoms. The regime organized secret networks on a grand scale to report political statements, including rumors and hearsay, both as a means of checking on citizens' loyalty and

73. RG242, SA2009, item 9 / 113, North Korean people's committee, *to, si, kun, inmin wiwŏn-hoe chigu chŏngwŏn mit samu punjang* (district administrative staff and duties in province, city, and county people's committees), "extremely secret," no place, no date.

74. RG242, SA2005, item 6 / 11, *saŏp kwan'gye sŏryu* (work documents), "secret."

75. RG242, SA2009, item 6 / 72, DPRK Naemusŏng, *Haksŭp chaeryojip* (materials for study), no date.

of providing the leadership with rudimentary information about public opinion. One internal directive from the occupation of the South in August 1950, which can be assumed to be representative of North Korean practice (if in wartime conditions), said the following:

> The most important mechanism for impressing the masses with the correctness and superiority of people's sovereignty is the question of grasping what their opinions are, and how they can be changed. Therefore, it is of the utmost importance to strengthen the organized collection network . . . and through it broadly to collect and report mass opinion, so as to sweep away antidemocratic phenomena and incorrect thoughts among the village people.

The document called for the organization of inspection networks that would ascertain the names, addresses, class backgrounds, party affiliations, pre-liberation activities, and good and bad attitudes of everyone—to be reported as they were, without editorials by the compilers.

One example was a report on a "small landlord," Yi P'an-gŭn. He was ecstatic that big landlords had their land confiscated, but felt that there was no reason to take any of his land, since he worked it himself.[76] Similar reports on mass opinion in Haeju, marked "absolutely secret," gathered comments of various citizens, such as one who responded to a South Korean propaganda leaflet barrage by saying, "Sons of bitches! They're always dropping leaflets, to no purpose. I hope they're used by people to blow their noses." A group of workers were heard to say that "peaceful unification" will never work; Rhee rejects everything we offer, so "we'll have to attack." Some other documents reported opinions as to whether Kim Il Sung was an imposter or not, and quoted one man as saying, "Ch'oe Yong-gŏn is a superior man to Kim Il Sung." A laborer lamented, "If I don't work on a farm, I have to work in the factory, and either way my problems are so bad I might as well die—so why should I participate in elections? I just have to die."[77] With such materials the leadership got feedback and complaints from citizens. One hesitates to ask what a citizen got for denigrating Kim Il Sung.

People who had suspect backgrounds were subject to routine surveillance of all their activities. These included dispossessed landlords, former officials of the colonial regime, capitalists, and especially families with relatives in the South. Among nineteen people under surveillance in Anju County, several were members of local people's committees;

76. RG242, SA2010, item 4 / 46, Yi Min-yŏng, head of the North Ch'ungch'ŏng People's Committee, directive on "the collection of views and the organization of an inspection network for public opinion," Aug. 5, 1950.

77. RG242, SA2010, item 2 / 76, documents from the Haeju area, most dated in 1949 and 1950.

thirteen had a poor-peasant or proletarian class background, and sixteen were members of the NKWP. Reasons given for the surveillance included relatives who went south, and unspecified "reactionary activity." Obviously "good" class background or party membership did not provide an escape from supervision.[78]

Individual records of people under surveillance show a similar pattern. Kim Chae-gi, for example, was a former agricultural laborer who became chief clerk in a township people's committee and then a party member; no reason was given for classifying him, the father of three children then in school, as a man requiring "top-grade surveillance." Another person in the same category was Chang Myŏng-nyŏng, a laborer in a Kap'yŏng factory from 1934 to 1943 who became a people's committee official in Ch'ŏrwon. He had a brother in the South, which, combined with his position in a town near the thirty-eighth parallel, probably made him untrustworthy. Another case involved a township committee secretary, Yi Sŏng-hi, who was under surveillance because he had been a township official in the Japanese regime; the report noted his "zeal for work." Chŏng Wŏn-mo, a tenant farmer and later a factory worker before 1945, was a people's committee activist in 1945–47 and a minor government functionary in 1947–49. His surveillance was owing to his being a member of the Chosŏn Democratic Party. Although common criminals were watched, so was Sim Ki-sŏk, the finance chief of a county committee, born into poor peasant stock. His transgressions consisted of slurping 120 won worth of dog soup without paying for it at a local restaurant, and selling his wife's rubber shoes on the black market. These documents routinely listed the names of every relative of those under supervision.[79]

CONCLUSION

The passions of liberation produced the two very different Koreas that are still with us today. The Democratic People's Republic of Korea was proclaimed on September 9, 1948, three weeks after the Republic of Korea was formed in Seoul; like the South, the North invited MacArthur to be present at this creation (he ignored the invitation). Kim Il Sung was named premier, a title he retained until 1972 (when under a new constitution he became president). At the end of 1948 the Soviets withdrew their occupation forces from North Korea, a decision that contrasted strongly with Soviet policies in Eastern Europe, where in

78. RG242, SA2010, item 8 / 106, data on clerks in the county government.

79. RG242, SA2012, item 8 / 16, raw data on people under surveillance by the Ch'ŏrwŏn police.

countries such as East Germany, Poland, and Czechoslovakia Soviet divisions remained until the fall of the Berlin wall in 1989. But no Soviet troops were again stationed in Korea. At the same time, tens of thousands of Korean soldiers who fought in the Chinese civil war filtered back to Korea. All through 1949 tough, crack troops with a Chinese, not a Soviet, experience returned to be integrated with the KPA. This little-known but important episode carved out some breathing space for P'yŏngyang. Stalin was a consummate realist who had once asked how many divisions the pope could deploy; he would be forced to recognize that the return of these Korean troops would inevitably turn North Korea toward China. At a minimum it enhanced Kim's bargaining power and enabled him to maneuver between the two communist giants, something he became a master at after the Korean War. Like Syngman Rhee, he aimed to unify his country. Unlike Rhee, he had by 1950 assembled the wherewithal to do it.

CHAPTER FIVE

Collision, 1948–1953

The country at this time took ye Alarm and were immediately in Arms, and had taken their different stations behind Walls, on our Flanks, and thus we were harassed in our Front, Flanks, and Rear . . . it not being possible for us to meet a man otherwise than behind a Bush, Stone hedge or Tree, who immediately gave his fire and went off.

—A British officer at Lexington, 1775

Koreans have a quite remarkable attachment to the pine tree and to the many pine-covered mountains that range across the peninsula. Wang Kŏn's Koguryŏ ancestors believed in the geomantic legend that "if they planted pine trees on Mt. Song'ak, thus making the mountain green, and then moved their house to a site near the southern slope, a hero who would unite Korea . . . would emerge from among their descendants." When he united Koryŏ, Wang wrote in the fifth of his *Ten Injunctions,* "I carried out the great undertaking of reunifying the country by availing myself of the latent virtue of the mountains and streams. . . ."[1]

The thirty-eighth parallel not only cut through the center of Kaesŏng, the old home of the Koryŏ aristocracy and its capital, but ran along the southern slope of Mount Song'ak—perhaps right through the ancestral home of the Wangs, or through the royal residence that Wang Kŏn built on the same spot and called Manwŏldae, or Full Moon Palace. In 1987 I strolled through the streets of Kaesŏng in the early morning hours and finally came to a spot where I could gaze upon Mount Song'ak in its fullness: and there on its face were forty-year-old pockmarks, still easily visible, made by the pounding of southern artillery. The shells fell all during the Korean War (1950–53), but they fell all during the summer and fall of 1949 as well, when the thirty-eighth parallel was still the

1. Lee (1984), pp. 108, 112.

dividing line between the two Koreas (the post-1953 DMZ put Kaesŏng well inside North Korean territory).

The Korean War did not begin on June 25, 1950, much special pleading and argument to the contrary. If it did not begin then, Kim Il Sung could not have "started" it then, either, but only at some earlier point. As we search backward for that point, we slowly grope toward the truth that civil wars do not start: they come. They originate in multiple causes, with blame enough to go around for everyone—and blame enough to include Americans who thoughtlessly divided Korea and then reestablished the colonial government machinery and the Koreans who served it. How many Koreans might still be alive had that not happened? Blame enough to include a Soviet Union likewise unconcerned with Korea's ancient integrity and determined to "build socialism" whether Koreans wanted their kind of system or not. How many Koreans might still be alive had that not happened? And then, as we peer inside Korea to inquire about Korean actions that might have avoided national division and fratricidal conflict, we get a long list indeed.

A Korean War was inconceivable before the division of Korea in August 1945. But because of that division, it has been conceivable ever since—right down to the still-volatile present. The first inklings of a North Korean invasion came not in 1950 but in the spring of 1946 when General John Hodge told Washington that an attack might be imminent. The first evidence that powerful figures in both Koreas contemplated a war of reunification emerged in this same early period, a mere six months after the end of the Pacific War. However, neither the United States nor the Soviet Union would back military action to do away with the hated thirty-eighth parallel as long as their troops were likely to be drawn into it, so we can date the onset of the "hot" civil war in Korea from early 1949, when Soviet troops were out and American troops were on their way out. Nineteen forty-nine was also the year of Chinese Communist victory, which had a tremendous effect on both Koreas and on American and Soviet policy toward the peninsula. Of course, anyone familiar with Korean history would have expected that a China strong enough finally to throw off imperial subordination might have an impact on its near neighbor.

NORTH KOREA AND CHINA

Before the entry of Chinese forces into the Korean War in October 1950 (usually taken to be the date of renewed Chinese involvement in Korea), China had an important influence on the North—mainly through tens of thousands of Koreans who fought in the Chinese civil war, establishing a reciprocal call on Chinese assistance later on. Kim Il Sung sensed the immense strategic blessing of a Chinese Communist victory (an impregnable "rear" unimaginable in 1945), and therefore in early 1947 he began dispatching tens of thousands of Koreans to fight with Mao and to swell the existing Korean units to division size, a "volunteer" army that prefigured the Chinese "volunteers" that returned the favor in the fall of 1950. This came at a time of crisis for the Chinese Communists, especially in Manchuria. According to William Whitson, in March 1947 People's Liberation Army (PLA) morale was "very low because of a succession of defeats and heavy losses in all theaters"; aggressive Nationalist offensives meant that "the fate of the entire war seemed to hang in the balance."[2]

American intelligence paid close attention to troop and matériel movements across the Sino-Korean border in early 1947; North Korean military forces had expanded rapidly in late 1946 within Korea, preparing for a spring offensive in Manchuria. Some 30,000 Koreans under the command of Kim Ch'aek reportedly moved into Manchuria during April 1947, by which time 15 to 20 percent of the Chinese Communist forces in Manchuria were Koreans. From that point onward until the winter of 1950, American intelligence designated these soldiers as "Chinese Communist Forces" (CCF) or "CCF Koreans" (something that made it hard to identify truly Chinese soldiers when they entered the Korean War).

R. S. Milward, a perspicacious British Foreign Office observer, remarked in mid-1948 that Koreans were gaining a good deal of battle experience in China. British intelligence reported that the entire North Korean rail network was devoted to the movement of CCF troops in December 1946 and January 1947 and that North Korea was a "reliable rear area" for the CCF, providing grain and other materials, rest and recreation, and the quartering of large numbers of troops. G-2 sources in Seoul said that "during the period of the deepest Chinese Nationalist penetration into Manchuria, North Korea was a secure zone of communications for the CCF." In May 1947 the PLA used northern Korea to billet soldiers and exchanged Korean grain and minerals for Chinese manufactured goods. Most of the output of the big Hŭngnam explosives plant was shipped to China, especially dynamite and blasting fuses.

Korean forces in China originated from various units that fought in Manchuria or Yenan in the 1930s. The two units that survived into the late 1940s were the Korean Volunteer Army (Chosŏn ŭiyong-gun—KVA) and the Yi Hong-gwang Detachment (Yi Hong-gwang chidae—YHD). (The Yi Hong-gwang Detachment was named for a Korean guerrilla who died in Manchuria in 1935.) Some sources say the KVA dropped its name

2. William W. Whitson, with Chen-hsia Huang, *The Chinese High Command: A History of Communist Military Politics* (New York: Praeger, 1973), pp. 87–88.

in April 1946, to be integrated into Korean units in the Northeast United Democratic Army (NEUDA), a title similar to ones used in the 1930s; but use of the name KVA continued after that date. The KVA apparently was inaugurated in 1941, but until August 1945 it had probably no more than 300–400 members. Its ranks swelled rapidly, however, as Korean soldiers demobilized from the Japanese army came in and as civil war grew in China; G-2 sources cited Chinese Nationalist abuses of the local Korean population, including lumping them together with the Japanese for postwar reprisals, as "one of the costliest errors of the civil war," bringing many Korean recruits to the Communists.[3]

G-2 sources identified Mu Chŏng, the Korean guerrilla leader who joined Mao Tse-tung and Chu Teh's fledgling Red Army in 1928 and who made the Long March, as Korean chairman of a joint military council that included six Koreans, six Chinese, and two Soviets. It controlled all movements of troops and matériel across the Sino-Korean border. American military attachés estimated that fully 70,000 Koreans were fighting in Manchuria by this time. One intelligence document quoted a pregnant statement by Ch'oe Yong-gŏn, given to the Americans by an informant who said he was present at a meeting of Korean CCF leaders on May 10, 1947:

> Korea will soon be ours. At present there is not a single unit in the United Democratic Forces now driving the Kuomintang from Manchuria that does not have my troops in it. At the end of the Manchurian campaign these troops will be seasoned, trained veterans. When the Americans and the Russians withdraw, we will be able to liberate [South] Korea immediately.[4]

Ch'oe Yong-gŏn became the first KPA commander, presiding over the founding of the Korean People's Army at its inaugural meeting, on February 8, 1948.

In the KPA veterans of the China fighting, not Soviet-aligned Koreans, dominated the officer ranks; U.S. Army G-2 sources in Seoul thought upwards of 80 percent of the KPA officers had served in China. Mu Chŏng was the most prominent China fighter, but he did not hold high position until the war began, because of the political threat he posed to Kim Il Sung, given his long anti-Japanese record and his close ties to high Chinese Communist leaders. Mu Chŏng was a northern version of Kim Ku, a dedicated patriot of rough mien and little apparent political acumen. Pak Il-u, the DPRK interior minister and a confidant of Kim Il Sung, spent much of his life in China. He was deputy head of the Korean

3. Cumings (1990), pp. 357–64.
4. Cumings (1990), p. 359.

military-political school at Yenan, and later helped Mu Chŏng reorganize the KVA. The top leaders of the KPA's Third Division in April 1948—Pang Ho-san, Wang Cha-in, Hong Rim, and No Ch'ŏl-yong—were all China veterans. Pang Ho-san later played a critical role in the early phases of the Korean War. He had attended the famous Whampoa Military Academy in the 1920s and been a member of the Chinese Communist Party since at least 1933. After serving as an instructor at a Yenan military school, he fought extensively in Manchuria and North China with the YHD and other units, and came to command the 166th division of the PLA, which was mostly made up mostly of Koreans; the 166th later formed the basis of the KPA Sixth Division. American sources described Pang as an intelligent, systematic military man, highly respected within KPA ranks.

Kim Ŭng was another CCF commander who had studied at Whampoa; the military historian Roy Appleman called him "a spectacular soldier," "energetic and harsh," and the ablest of KPA commanders in the Korean War. Ch'oe Tŏk-jo led the KPA's western command, headquartered at Chinnamp'o; he was an officer in Mao's Eighth Route Army, and his chief of staff, Kwak Tong-sŏ, was a KVA veteran. Other North Korean army leaders with CCF experience included Yi Ho, Han Kyŏng, O Hak-yong, Ch'i Pyŏng-hak, Ch'oe A-rip, Kim Kwang-hyŏp, Yi Ik-sŏng, and Ch'oe Kwang. Ch'oe Kwang was the KPA commander in the mid-1990s; like Ch'oe and Kim Il Sung, most of these officers were in their thirties when the Korean War began.[5] This list does not include the Manchurian guerrillas from the 1930s who also worked with the Chinese, such as Kim Ch'aek, Ch'oe Yong-gŏn, Kim Il, and, of course, Kim Il Sung. With these people added, we have now named almost the entire high command of the Korean People's Army in 1950, all veterans of Sino-Korean joint fighting.

From 1948 until the autumn of 1950, Korean units that had fought in China filtered back home. The total numbers were somewhere between 75,000 and 100,000. Intelligence estimates in the late 1940s, primary documents from the time, and retrospective information gotten from POWs identify several waves: a unit 10,000 strong from the YHD returned for the initial formation of the KPA in February 1948; 30,000–40,000, in July–October 1949; 40,000–50,000, in February and March 1950. Koreans in the 164th and 166th Divisions of the PLA crossed the border in July 1949 and formed the basis of the KPA Fifth and Sixth divisions. Many reports of arriving returnees came through intelligence networks in October 1949; the 155th Division of the Sixteenth Army returned to Korea in February 1950, to become the Seventh KPA Divi-

5. Cumings (1990), pp. 359–60.

sion; irregular units from China returned and constituted the new Tenth Division in March 1950. Meanwhile, still more Korean soldiers fought all the way down to the "last battle" for Hainan Island in May 1950 and were not back to Korea before the war began in June.[6]

Diaries of Korean soldiers captured during the war show their mix of Chinese and Korean experience.[7] One had pictures of Mao and Chu Teh plastered against the front and back; as the soldier moved from China to Korea in the spring of 1950, his diary entries changed from Chinese to Sino-Korean script. He inscribed pledges of loyalty to the DPRK and to Kim Il Sung (while complaining that Korean officers were less egalitarian than Chinese):

> I, as a citizen of the DPRK, have solemn duties to my Motherland. Thus I will enter the KPA and faithfully devote myself to the homeland, the people, and the democratic people's government. I pledge this solemnly before our great forefathers. If I disobey any of my pledges, I will be dealt with mercilessly by a people's court.

The pledges went on: "serving the people is the most glorious task"; we "fight for our Republic's freedom and our beloved and respected supreme leader *[suryŏng]*, General Kim Il Sung."

One Fourth Field Army soldier, Kim Ho-il, joined the CCF in June 1947 and fought from Beijing down to Canton; assigned to Changsha, in Hunan Province, in February 1950, he then received orders to march north. He crossed the Yalu at Antung on March 17, 1950, changing his uniform that night. He was captured during fighting in northern Korea on October 17, 1950. Chŏn Chae-ro fought in China and then returned to P'yŏngyang, where he studied with 1,200 other KPA members at the Second Central Political School, located at Kim Il Sung's birthplace, Man'gyŏngdae. Upon graduation the students received commissions as second lieutenants. Chŏn was stationed with the KPA Fourth Division at Chinnamp'o until June 16, 1950, when the division marched to Yŏn-

6. For a fuller account see Cumings (1990), pp. 357–69. Shu Guang Zhang offers similar evidence in a new book. Citing recently released Chinese documentation, he estimates that 90,000 Koreans fought with anti-Japanese forces in China; he does not give figures for the Chinese civil war, but says that three waves of Korean soldiers totaling 28,000 officers and men returned to Korea in the period Jan.–Sept. 1949, followed by 14,000 more in early 1950. Zhang (1995), pp. 44–45. Other new Chinese sources, however, estimate that 62,942 Koreans from Manchuria joined the civil war on the side of the Communists; this figure does not count tens of thousands who came from North Korea, beginning in the spring of 1947, when Mao's forces were hard pressed in Manchuria by Chiang Kai-shek's army. See Changyu Piao, in Suh and Shultz (1990), p. 66; Chae-Jin Lee, in Suh and Shultz (1990), p. 96.

7. Cumings (1990), pp. 361–62.

ch'ŏn, near the thirty-eighth parallel, arriving on June 20. He was captured during the Pusan perimeter fighting in mid-August.

Later the reader may ask why North Korea did not respond to southern provocations during the summer of 1949 with an invasion, one that would have been far more difficult to interpret as unprovoked. The answer, I think, is simple: crack soldiers were still fighting in China, soldiers who subsequently became the main shock forces of the June invasion.

GUERRILLA WARFARE IN SOUTH KOREA

Organized guerrilla warfare on the Korean mainland dates from November 1948, after more than a thousand Yŏsu rebels fled to the Chiri mountains in South Chŏlla Province and joined up with guerrillas and bandits already in the hills. This movement began the armed conflict on the peninsula, carrying the urban political turmoil and rural peasant protest of 1945–47 to the level of unconventional warfare. In early 1949 the CIA estimated that the total number of guerrillas in the South was somewhere between 3,500 and 6,000, not counting several thousand more on Cheju Island. Some were armed with rifles, mostly Japanese and American, but many just carried clubs and bamboo spears. Food and other supplies came from foraging, contributions in villages, or theft of rice stocks. KMAG advisers thought overall strategy was in North Korean hands, passed through the South Korean Labor Party headquarters in Haeju, just across the thirty-eighth parallel. One team of 60 guerrillas was known to have been dispatched from the North, and defectors estimated that another 1,000 or so were undergoing training for missions in the South.

The Chŏlla and the Kyŏngsang provinces, the Americans said, "have been noted for extensive leftist activities since the liberation." Here,

> the People's Republic and its People's Committees were strongest. It was in those rich, rice-producing provinces that the Japanese had most exploited the peasants. It was in those provinces that the Communist-directed All Korea Farmer's Union was able to organize swiftly and, apparently, well during the first years of the American Occupation.

Two embassy vice-consuls toured the provinces in early 1949 and found that in South Chŏlla "the government has lost control outside of the cities and larger towns." Police stations in the province were "universally protected by huge stone walls of recent construction or by high mounds of sand bags. . . . Each police box resembles a medieval fort." The authorities had carried out extensive tree cutting in the hills to deny cover to the rebels, and all travel at night was prohibited. The province governor said there were 100,000 refugees from the guerrilla fighting in the province, many of them created by authorities who emptied villages to deny support to the guerrillas. In North Kyŏngsang, investigators found much ill feeling between the police and the local populace; Taegu was tightly controlled and curfewed every night. Kyŏngju, the ancient Silla capital, was "a mountainous area infested by Communists who hide in the hills and make frequent raids on the villages." An American account of a survey of North Kyŏngsang in July 1949 related, "Small attacks and ambushes punctuated by larger attacks characterized almost every locale. Police boxes were barricaded to the roof, trees everywhere were cut down with 100 meters of the roads, local officials and policemen felt compelled to move nervously from house to house at night."

Except in remote and underpopulated places, guerrillas were not able to hold several towns at the same time, or to create protected base areas outside the mountains. They would enter a village at night, call out the population, give speeches, recruit soldiers, and secure food and other supplies. Attacks on police stations were the most common sort of activity, both because hatred for the National Police was widespread and because records of leftist families were kept at stations. The guerrillas operated in small units, running hither and thither in the heavily wooded terrain. Hong Sun-sŏk, aged twenty-four, led one unit; Kim Chi-hwi, twenty-three, and his wife (a nurse from Cheju) led another. As their situation got more desperate, especially as winter dawned in 1949, guerrillas attacked whole villages and laid them waste in search of supplies.[8]

Walter Sullivan of the *New York Times* was almost alone among foreign journalists in seeking out the facts of this guerrilla war. Large parts of southern Korea, he wrote in early 1950, "are darkened today by a cloud of terror that is probably unparalleled in the world." In the "hundreds of villages across the guerrilla areas," local village guards "crouch in pyramided straw shelters," and nights "are a long, cold vigil of listening." Guerrillas make brutal assaults on police, and the police take the guerrillas to their home villages and torture them for information. Then the police shoot them and tie them to trees as an object lesson. The persistence of the guerrillas, Sullivan wrote, "puzzles many Americans here," as does "the extreme brutality" of the conflict. But Sullivan went on to argue that "there is great divergence of wealth" in the country, with both middle and poor peasants living "a marginal existence." He interviewed ten peasant families; none owned all their own land, and most were tenants. The landlord took 30 percent of the tenant produce,

8. National Archives, 895.00 file, box 7127, Drumwright to State, enclosing report of a two-week tour by Vice-Consuls John W. Rozier and Donald S. MacDonald, March 17, 1949.

but additional exactions—government taxes and various "contributions"—ranged from 48 to 70 percent of the annual crop.[9]

In the spring of 1949 Syngman Rhee dispatched a young colonel of Japanese army background named Chŏng Il-gwŏn to command a suppression force of 3,000 men, of whom about half were regular ROKA troops. Colonel Chŏng (who later became the ROK prime minister under Park Chung Hee) set up a pass system requiring citizens in the area to hold identity cards, and established a civilian defense corps in each village, posting sentries in village watchtowers, armed with bamboo spears. He told his troops not to requisition supplies without payment and not to molest local peasants, especially not women. On March 12 Chŏng began an all-out offensive against the Chiri Mountain guerrillas with four battalions of soldiers; within a month they had succeeded in killing Hong Sun-sŏk and capturing Kim Chi-hwi's wife. By May the embassy thought that Chŏng had achieved a big victory, in suppressing guerrillas if not in keeping his troops in line.[10] But the success was short-lived, as guerrilla strength grew all during the summer of 1949.

There was little evidence of Soviet or North Korean support for the southern guerrillas. In April 1950 the Americans found that the North Koreans had supported guerrillas in Kangwŏn and the upper coast of North Kyŏngsang with weapons and supplies, but that "almost 100 percent of the guerrillas in the Cholla and Kyongsang Provinces ha[d] been recruited locally." No Soviet weapons had ever been authenticated in South Korea, except near the parallel; most guerrillas had Japanese and American arms. Another report found that the guerrillas "apparently receive little more than moral support from North Korea."[11]

The principal source of external involvement in the guerrilla war was, in fact, American. Americans usually perceive an important gap between the withdrawal of U.S. combat forces in July 1949 and the war that came a year later, such that the question becomes, Why did the Americans suddenly return to defend the ROK? In reality they never left. American advisers were all over the war zones in the South, constantly shadowing their Korean counterparts and urging them on to greater effort. The man who distinguished himself in this was James Hausman, one of the key organizers of the suppression of the Yŏsu rebellion, who spent the next three decades as a nexus point between the American and Korean mili-

9. *New York Times,* March 6, 15, 1950.

10. National Archives, 895.00 file, box 7127, Embassy to State, March 25, 1949, transmitting a report on the guerrillas by Colonel J. W. Fraser; Muccio to State, April 18, 1949; Muccio to State, May 13, 1949; Drumwright to State, May 17, 1949.

11. CIA, "Communist Capabilities in South Korea," Feb. 21, 1949; State Department 795.00 file, box 4262, Drumwright to State, April 15, 1950, enclosing a report titled "Guerrilla Strength and Activity."

taries and their intelligence outfits. A wily operator who hid his skills behind the mannerisms of an Arkansas hayseed, he was the Edward Lansdale of Korea, without the latter's concern for civic action. Hausman called himself the father of the Korean Army in an interview, which was not far from the truth. He said that everyone knew this, including the Korean officers themselves, but could not say it publicly.[12]

At the end of September 1949 the the KMAG chief, General W. L. Roberts, said that it was of the "utmost importance" that the guerrillas "be cleared up as soon as possible," and asked Washington to dispatch more infantry officers to work with the ROK Army. Every division in the army, he told General MacArthur, was being diverted in part or in full from the parallel to the interior and "ordered to exterminate guerrilla bands in their zones." Roberts later said that 6,000 guerrillas had been killed in the November 1949–March 1950 period, in what he called an "all-out mop-up campaign [that] broke the backbone of the guerrilla movement."[13] Internal reports as of mid-April put the total guerrilla dead since October 1 at 4,996, so Roberts's figure seems plausible. The ROK claimed to have engaged a total of 12,000 KPA soldiers and guerrillas in January 1950, killing 813 and losing but 51.

If the Rhee regime had one unqualified success, viewed through the American lens, it was the apparent defeat of the southern partisans by the spring of 1950. A year earlier it had appeared that the guerrilla movement would only grow with the passage of time; but the suppression campaign begun in the fall of 1949 resulted in high body counts and a perception that the guerrillas could no longer mount significant operations when they would be expected to—when the spring foliage returned in early 1950. Both Secretary of State Dean Acheson and George Kennan (head of Policy Planning) saw the suppression of the internal threat as the litmus test of the Rhee regime's continence: if this worked, so would American-backed containment; if it did not, the regime would be viewed as another Kuomintang, as "little China." Preston Goodfellow had told Rhee in late 1948, in the context of a letter where he referred to his "many opportunities to talk with [Acheson] about Korea," that the guerrillas had to be "cleaned out quickly . . . [E]veryone is watching how Korea handles the Communist threat." A weak policy will lose support in Washington, Goodfellow wrote; handle the threat well, and "Korea will be held in high esteem."[14] In May and June 1950, guerrilla incidents

12. Interview with Thames Television, Feb. 1987. A reader of this manuscript pointed out that the entire first generation of ROK Military Academy graduates considered Hausman to be their mentor.

13. For a fuller account of this guerrilla movement, on which I draw below, see Cumings (1990), pp. 268–90, 398–406.

14. Goodfellow Papers, box 1, draft of letter to Rhee, no date (but late 1948).

tapered off remarkably, reaching in early June "a new low." The last report filed before the war began said small guerrilla bands of fifteen to thirty still operated in various areas, but were generally quiet. Walter Sullivan, however, had concluded from his observations that the optimistic reports of a thorough guerrilla defeat were wrong. Cold weather was the main reason for the abatement of guerrilla activity, and thus the 1949–50 winter offensive had failed.

THE BORDER FIGHTING IN 1949

The war that came in June 1950 followed on the guerrilla fighting and nine months of battles along the thirty-eighth parallel in 1949. Border conflict lasted from early May until late December, taking hundreds of lives and embroiling thousands of troops. The reason that war did not come in 1949 is at once simple and essential to grasping the civil origins of the Korean conflict: the South wanted a war then, the North did not, and neither did the United States or the Soviet Union. A year later this had changed. During this period Rhee rapidly expanded his army. Two new divisions (the Capital and the Eighth) were activated in June 1949; army strength was at 81,000 by the end of July and 100,000 by the end of August.[15] By then it was much bigger than the accepted order-of-battle strength of the North Korean Army; the subsequent buildup and the return of China-linked soldiers could thus be viewed as the North's attempt to establish a balance (U.S. intelligence thought it had 95,000 soldiers in June 1950, but its strength was certainly above 100,000).

Rhee also brought into the army officers who had served the Japanese and who were refugees from the North, at the expense of patriotic figures who had fought with the Chinese Nationalists. The main reason was Rhee's desire to surround himself with military people who owed everything to him, and who could be counted on not to mount a coup (as well as to loathe communists). Two Paek brothers, Sŏn-yŏp and In-yŏp, led a northwest faction in the army, which also included Generals Yang Kuk-jin and Kim Sŏk-bŏm and many former members of the Northwest Youth Corps. Both Paeks were born in P'yŏngyang a few years after Kim Il Sung and had been officers in Japan's Kwantung Army. Chŏng Il-gwŏn, also an officer in the Japanese Army, led a powerful northeast (or Tongbuk) faction in the southern army. Chŏng was thirty-two, and Paek Sŏn-yŏp thirty, in 1950.[16]

Although the South launched many small raids across the parallel before the summer of 1949, with the North happy to reciprocate, the

15. Sawyer (1962), p. 58.
16. Kim, (1971), pp. 46–63.

important border battles began at Kaesŏng on May 4, 1949, in an engagement that the South started. It lasted about four days and took an official toll of 400 North Korean and 22 South Korean soldiers, as well as upwards of 100 civilian deaths in Kaesŏng, according to American and South Korean figures.[17] The South committed six infantry companies and several battalions, and two of the companies defected to the North. Months later, on the basis of the defectors' testimony, the North Koreans claimed that several thousand troops led by Kim Sŏk-wŏn attacked across the parallel on the morning of May 4, near Song'ak Mountain.[18] Kim was the commander of the critically important First Division; he was also from northern Korea and, as we have seen, had tracked Kim Il Sung at Japan's behest in the Manchurian wilderness in the late 1930s.

On the last Sunday in June 1949, heavy fighting opened up in the dawn hours on the Ongjin peninsula; three days later the South sent about 150 "Horim" (forest tiger) guerrillas on a long foray across the parallel. They roamed around causing problems in the area above and to the east of Ch'ŏrwŏn for a few days, but were wiped out by July 5.[19] The Sunday, June 26, battle bears some scrutiny because the UN Commission on Korea (UNCOK) sent a delegation to Ongjin after hearing reports of "heavy fighting." It arrived courtesy of an ROK naval vessel and was guided around by ROKA personnel. UNCOK members remained on the peninsula for a day or so and then returned on Monday evening to Seoul, from which they then filed a report to the UN blaming "northern invaders" for the trouble.[20] It is probable that the North was to blame, but what is remarkable is UNCOK's failure to investigate and report upon provocations by the South as well. After all, just before this incident Kim Sŏk-wŏn gave UNCOK a briefing in his status as commander of ROKA forces at the thirty-eighth parallel: North and South "may engage in major battles at any moment," he said; Korea has entered into "a state of warfare." "We should have a program to recover our lost land, North Korea, by breaking through the 38th border which has existed since 1945"; the moment of major battles, Kim told UNCOK, is rapidly approaching.[21]

The worst fighting of 1949 occurred in early August, when North Korean forces attacked ROKA units occupying a small mountain north of the thirty-eighth parallel. It went on for days, right through an important

17. National Archives, 895.00 file, box 7127, Muccio to State, May 13, 1949; Drumwright to State, June 13, 1949.

18. *Nodong sinmun* (Worker's news) (P'yŏngyang), Feb. 6, 1950.

19. *New York Times,* June 28, 1949; Thames Television interview with Han Jin Hyong, P'yŏngyang, Nov. 1987.

20. *New York Times,* June 29, 1950.

21. UN Archives, BOX DAG-1/2.1.2, box 3, account of briefing on June 15, 1949.

summit conference between Syngman Rhee and Chiang Kai-shek. In the early morning hours on August 4 the North opened up great barrages of artillery and mortar fire, and at 5:30 A.M. some 4,000 to 6,000 North Korean border guard soldiers attacked, seeking in Roberts's words, "to recover high ground in North Korea occupied by [the] South Korean Army." The North claimed that southern elements from the *paekkol* [white bone] unit attacked northward from Ŭnp'asan on August 4; in any case the mountain was in northern territory, and the North cannot be blamed for wanting to recover it. The southern side was "completely routed," according to Ambassador Muccio; two companies of ROKA soldiers in the Eighteenth Regiment were annihilated, leaving hundreds dead and the North in occupation of the mountain.[22]

After this fighting, Ambassador Muccio penned two long memoranda of critical importance:

> Captain Shin stated that the reports from Ongjin reaching military headquarters on the morning of August 4 were most alarming. These reports indicated that the [South] Korean forces on the [Ongjin] peninsula had been completely routed and that there was nothing there to stand against the northern onslaught. He went on that in studying the situation with the general staff . . . the military were insistent that the only way to relieve pressure on Ongjin would be to drive north. The military urged mounting an immediate attack north towards Charwon [*sic*—Ch'ŏrwŏn].
>
> In line with the advice given by General Roberts, Captain Shin decided against attack and took immediate steps to send limited reinforcements into Ongjin.
>
> Captain Shin went on that as soon as the Prime Minister [Yi Pŏm-sŏk] returned from the Rhee-Chiang meeting at Chinhae he called Captain Shin and remonstrated with him that he should have had more courage, should have attacked the North. That General Lee [Pŏm-sŏk] took this position does not surprise me especially. It did surprise me, however, when Captain Shin went on to say that upon his return from Chinhae the following day President Rhee also told him that he should not have decided against attacking Charwon.

On August 16 Muccio went on to relate that Rhee, in a conversation with Muccio,

> threw out the thought that . . . he might replace [Chief of Staff] Chae [Pyŏng-dŏk] with General Kim Suk Wan [Kim Sŏk-wŏn]. . . . Kim Suk

22. MacArthur Archives, RG9, box 43, Roberts to Department of the Army, Aug. 1, 9, 1949; *New York Times*, Aug. 5, 1949; *Nodong sinmun*, Feb. 6, 1950.

> Wan has long been a favorite of President Rhee. Last fall prior to Yŏsu Rhee mentioned to General Coulter and myself that Kim had offered to "take care of the North" if he could be supplied with 20,000 rifles for Korean veterans of the Japanese Army who were burning with patriotism. The Minister of Defense, the Korean general staff and American advisors are all against General Kim. They do not consider him a good soldier but a blusterer. They have called my attention to his propensity for needling northern forces in his sector of the front, for resorting to Japanese banzai attacks and for deploying all his forces in a most hazardous manner right on the front without adequate reserves. They particularly object to his ignoring headquarters and going direct to President Rhee.[23]

General Roberts did indeed order southern commanders not to attack and threatened to remove KMAG if they did; British sources said that ROKA commanders' heads "are full of ideas of recovering the North by conquest. Only the American Ambassador's stern warning that all American aid would be stopped . . . prevented the Army from attempting to attack across the parallel at another point when the Communists attacked at Ongjin."[24]

When we now look at both sides of the parallel with the help of some new (if scattered and selective) Soviet materials, we learn that Kim Il Sung's basic conception of a Korean War was quite similar to Rhee's, and was influenced deeply by the August 1949 fighting: namely, attack the cul de sac of Ongjin, move eastward and grab Kaesŏng, and then see what happens. At a minimum, this would establish a much more secure defense of P'yŏngyang, which was quite vulnerable from Ongjin and Kaesŏng. At a maximum, it might open Seoul to his forces. That is, if the southern army collapses, move on to Seoul and occupy it in a few days. And here we see the significance of the collapse of the ROK Second and Seventh divisions, June 25–27, 1950, which opened the historic invasion corrider and placed the Korean People's Army in Seoul on the twenty-seventh, and why some people with intimate knowledge of the Korean civil conflict have speculated that these divisions may have harbored a fifth column.[25]

23. National Archives, 895.00 file, box 946, Muccio, memos of conversation on Aug. 13 and 16, 1949.
24. Niles Bond told Australian officials that Muccio and Roberts "were constantly warning the Koreans that such a step [an attack northward] would result in the stoppage of American aid, the withdrawal of the Military Mission," and other measures. See Washington to Canberra, memorandum 953, Aug. 17, 1949; also British Foreign Office (FO 317), piece no. 76259, Holt to FO, Sept. 2, 1949.
25. Cumings (1990), pp. 572–73, 582–85.

The critical issue in the Soviet documents[26] is a military operation to seize the Ongjin peninsula. According to these documents, Kim Il Sung first broached the idea of an operation against Ongjin to the Soviet ambassador to P'yŏngyang, Terenti Shtykov, on August 12, 1949, right on the heels of the August 4 battle. Like southern leaders, Kim Il Sung wanted to bite off a chunk of exposed territory or grab a small city—all of Kaesŏng, for example, or Haeju just above the parallel on Ongjin, which southern commanders wanted to occupy in 1949–50. We also see how similar the Russians were in seeking to restrain hotheaded Korean leaders, including the chief of state. When Kim spoke about an invasion of Ongjin, two key Russian embassy officials "tried to switch the discussion to a general theme." The Soviet documents also demonstrate the hard-won, *learned* logic of this civil war by late 1949, namely, that both sides understood that their big-power guarantors would not help them if they launched an unprovoked general attack—or even an assault on Ongjin or Ch'ŏrwŏn. A telegram from Shtykov to Moscow in January 1950 has Kim Il Sung impatient that *the South* "is still not instigating an attack" (thus to justify his own), and the Russians in P'yŏngyang tell him once again that he cannot attack Ongjin without risking general civil war.

Thus the 1950 logic for both sides was to see who would be stupid enough to move first, with Kim itching to invade and hoping for a clear southern provocation, and hotheads in the South hoping to provoke an "unprovoked" assault, in order to get American help—for that was the only way the South could hope to win. Kim already had begun playing Moscow off against Beijing, too; for example, he let Shtykov overhear him say, at an apparently drunken luncheon on January 19, 1950, that if the Russians would not help him unify the country, "Mao Zedong is his friend and will always help Korea." In general these materials underline that the victory of the Chinese revolution had a great influence on North Korea and that the latter's China connection was a trump card Kim could play to create some breathing room for his regime between the two communist giants.

Although an attack in early August was aborted, by the end of the month Muccio described the situation as follows:

> There is increasing confidence in the Army. An aggressive, offensive spirit is emerging. Nerves that were frayed and jittery the past few months may now give way to this new spirit. A good portion of the

26. See documents II through VI, translated and reprinted in *Cold War International History Project Bulletin,* no. 5 (Spring 1995): 6–9.

> Army is eager to get going. More and more people feel that the only way unification can be brought about is by moving North by force. I have it from Dick Johnston [*New York Times* reporter] that Chiang Kai-shek told Rhee that the Nationalist air force could support a move North and that they discussed the possibility of the Nationalists starting an offensive move against Manchuria through Korea! There is some feeling that now is the time to move North while the Chinese communists are preoccupied. I doubt whether Rhee would actually order a move North in his saner moments. Captain Shin, I know, is dead against it. Lee Bum Suk would love it. However, should we have another Kaesong or Ongjin flare-up, a counter-attack might lead to all sorts of unpredictable developments.[27]

On August 23 the ROK sent several naval patrol boats right up the Taedong River to Mongŭmp'o, sinking four North Korean ships in the 35- to 45-ton class; Inch'ŏn harbor was reinforced in case of a counterattack (which did not materialize). At the end of September, Rhee again made clear his desires to march North. In a letter of September 30, 1949, from Rhee to his adviser Robert Oliver (the authenticity of which the United States denied during UN debates in the fall of 1950, but which Dr. Oliver validated many years later), Rhee said,

> I feel strongly that now is the most psychological moment when we should take an aggressive measure and join with our loyal communist army *[sic]* in the North to clear up the rest of them in Pyongyang. We will drive some of Kim Il-sung's men to the mountain region and there we will gradually starve them out. Then our line of defense must be strengthened along the Tuman and Yalu River [i.e., the Sino-Korean border].

The point is not that North Korea was an innocent party to this fighting but that both sides were at fault—and according to several statements by General Roberts, the KMAG commander, the South started more of the battles than did the North. He said that in the numerous clashes in August, "each was in our opinion brought on by the presence of a small South Korean salient north of the parallel. . . . The South Koreans wish to invade the North. We tell them that if such occurs, all advisors will pull out and the ECA spigot will be turned off." Roberts went on to say that both North and South were "at fault" in the back-and-forth "needling" along the parallel.[28] But according to captured docu-

27. National Archives, 895.00 file, box 946, Muccio to Butterworth, Aug. 27, 1949.
28. Roberts to Bolte, "Personal Comments on KMAG and Korean Affairs," Aug. 19, 1949, Xeroxed document held by the archivist Robert Taylor, National Archives, room 13W.

ments sent to the United Nations by North Korea, in an August 2, 1949, meeting with ROKA divisional commanders, Roberts said, "Almost every incident has been provoked by the South Korean security forces," a stronger allegation.[29] Also important is the opening of the fighting in the Ongjin and Kaesong areas, for this is where the war began a year later. A tantalizing detail is that after ROK defenses collapsed at Ongjin in early August, ROK commanders considered not just an attack north against Ch'ŏrwŏn but also a very rapid pullback of the army—perhaps all the way to an offshore island.

The veteran journalist A. T. Steele captured the flavor of all this in a remarkable account written in October 1949: "An unadmitted shooting war between the Governments of the U.S. and Russia is in effect today along the 38th parallel. . . . It is smoldering throughout the territory of the new Republic of Korea. . . . Only American money, weapons, and technical assistance enable [the Republic] to exist for more than a few hours." The ROK is "dedicated to liberty," Steele wrote, but it is "a tight little dictatorship run as a police state." Its jails overflow with prisoners, 30,000 according to his estimate; "torture of captured political antagonists is commonplace," and "women and children are killed without compunction" by both sides. Americans on the scene "are almost evangelical in their fervor for Korean revival," but, Steele thought, "once the American props are withdrawn, South Korea will fall beneath the weight of Communist Asia."[30]

After the 1949 border fighting died down, both Syngman Rhee and Kim Il Sung sought backing from their big-power guarantors for a major assault on the other side. Rhee did this primarily through his "kitchen cabinet" of American advisers, especially Preston Goodfellow, and Kim did it through at least two secret visits to Moscow and others to Beijing in early 1950. Both expected that the summer of 1950 would open as did the summer of 1949, and both wanted to settle the hash of the other side once and for all. Kim was apparently the more successful, getting new equipment from Moscow and Stalin's seeming acquiescence to his plans, and direct support from Mao in Beijing.

In late February 1949, Kim Il Sung left P'yŏngyang for his only official, publicized visit to the Soviet Union before the Korean War. When he returned in March, Kim brought with him an economic and cultural

29. National Records Center, USFIK 11071 file, box 62/96, G-2 "Staff Study," Feb. 1949, signed by Lieutenant Colonel B. W. Heckemeyer of Army G-2. The North Koreans sent a host of captured documents to the UN in photostatic copy in late 1950, but UN archival authorities seem to be unable to find them. The reference in the text is to the *Daily Worker*, Dec. 4, 1950.

30. *New York Herald-Tribune*, Oct. 30, 1949.

agreement and, intelligence rumor had it, a secret military agreement.[31] In 1948 the Soviets left quite a bit of surplus military equipment behind for the North Koreans (as did the Americans when their troops pulled out), but in 1949 the Soviets made the Koreans pay for everything, including a 220 million-ruble loan at 2 percent interest, which was about what mortgages returned to American banks in 1949—that is, there was profit in it. A January 1950 document shows Stalin appearing to be more interested than at any previous point in Kim Il Sung's invasion plans for South Korea, without a hint of what Stalin's own strategic thinking might be.[32] Meanwhile, the North engaged in public bond drives to buy more and more equipment from Moscow.

Rhee, however, got a clear message from Washington that he would get American support only if South Korea were attacked without provocation. Goodfellow suddenly flew to Seoul in September 1949, saying that a war was imminent. As he later told Taiwan's ambassador to the United States, Wellington Koo, "he had been hurriedly sent for by R[hee] early last September and arrived at Seoul to hear that the N. Koreans were scheduled to attack on [the] 19th." (There had been American intelligence warnings that an attack might come around this time.) Goodfellow told Koo that by now (he met Ambassador Koo in January 1950) the momentum for attack had shifted:

> It was the South Koreans anxious to go into N.K., because they were feeling sharp with their army of well-trained 100,000 strong *[sic]*. But U.S. Govt was most anxious to restrain any provocation by the S.K. and Goodfellow had gone there lately to do just that. I asked how great was the possibility or danger of war breaking out in Korea. G[oodfellow] said U.S. Govt. position is this: avoid any initiative on S. Korea's part in attacking N.K., but if N.K. should invade S.K. then S.K. should resist and march right into N.K. with III World War as the result but in such a case, the aggression came from N.K. and the Am[erican] people would understand it.[33]

When Wellington Koo, years later, was asked by an interviewer to reflect on the outbreak of the Korean War, he referred first to this episode with Goodfellow.[34]

31. A rumor that appears to have been wrong, according to the materials ibid.
32. Document VII, Stalin's telegram to Shtykov on Jan. 30, 1950, translated and reprinted in *Cold War International History Project Bulletin,* no. 5 (Spring 1995): 9.
33. Wellington Koo Papers, Columbia University, box 217, Koo Diaries, entry for Jan. 4, 1950. Goodfellow arrived in Seoul on Sept. 27, 1949 (National Archives, 895.00 file, box 7127, Muccio to State, Oct. 7, 1949). He went back in Dec. 1949, which is the recent visit referred to in the quotation.
34. Wellington Koo oral history, Columbia University.

THE EVE OF THE WAR

American influence in the South had reached new heights by 1950. The British minister Vyvyan Holt eloquently captured this a few weeks before the war broke out: "Radiating from the huge ten-storied Banto Hotel," American influence "penetrates into every branch of administration and is fortified by an immense outpouring of money." Americans kept the government, the army, the economy, the railroads, the airports, the mines, and the factories going, supplying money, electricity, expertise, and psychological succor. American gasoline fueled every motor vehicle in the country. American cultural influence was "exceedingly strong," ranging from scholarships to study in the United States, to several strong missionary denominations, to "a score of traveling cinemas" and theaters that played mostly American films, to the Voice of America, to big-league baseball: "American is the dream-land" to thousands if not millions of Koreans.[35]

At this time South Korea was getting more than $100 million a year from the United States most of it in the form of outright grants. (The entire southern national budget for 1951 was $120 million.) The ECA aid mission and the KMAG contingent were the biggest of their type in the world. The U.S. Information Service had, by its own testimony, "one of the most extensive country programs that we are operating anywhere," with nine centers in Korea, parlaying libraries, mobile units, a variety of publications, films, and Americanism before the Korean people. American officials ran Kimp'o International Airport, controlling the entry and exit of American citizens. Besides the official presence, private Americans often advised or directed private industry.

The ECA lauded South Korean economic growth in 1950, and KMAG's work in training the ROK Army also seemed highly successful. In some exuberant interviews with the intrepid journalist Marguerite Higgins just before the war, Roberts said, "KMAG is a living demonstration of how an intelligent and intensive investment of 500 combat-hardened American men and officers can train 100,000 guys to do the shooting for you." The countryside had been "in a perpetual uproar" until recently, he said, but was now under control thanks to American advisers "at every level" who "live right there with [the Koreans] . . . and stay with them in battles." Higgins cited rumors that French counterinsurgency officers had arrived to learn about KMAG techniques for "export" to Indochina. In sum, Roberts opined, "the American taxpayer has an army that is a fine watchdog over the investments placed in this country and a force that represents the maximum results at minimum cost." He discounted

35. British Foreign Office, FO317, piece no. 84053, Holt to FO, May 1, 1950.

threats about an invasion from the North, saying, "At this point we rather invite it. It will give us target practice."[36]

The UN Commission on Korea had not liked its role in the summer of 1949, sandwiched between an indifferent United Nations and a bubbling civil war, and it wanted out. But it did not get out. It is of signal importance that the decision to install the military observers, who later reported on the outbreak of the war, grew out of worries about aggression emanating from the South more than from the North. In September 1949 Egon Ranshofen-Wertheimer, an important and knowledgeable UNCOK staff member, wrote to Undersecretary of State Philip Jessup urging that UNCOK be replaced by a UN high commissioner, who would seek to open talks among all sides—thus to prevent a unification of Korea by force. The North might "strike a decisive blow" against the South, he feared, although in September 1949 he did not think that was likely:

> On the other hand, the ROK might feel that its chances of absorbing the North are diminished from month to month in view of the growing strength of Kim Il Sung's armies. . . . The temptation for Rhee to invade the North and the pressure exerted upon him to do so might, therefore, become irresistible. The top military authorities of the Republic . . . are exerting continual pressure upon Rhee to take the initiative and cross the parallel.[37]

At the same time Walton Butterworth of the State Department told the British that "there had been a good deal of fighting and that there was a hot-headed element in the South, possibly composed of northern Koreans"; thus Butterworth thought it important for UNCOK to have military men on the scene, the implication being that they, like Roberts, would restrain the *South* Koreans.[38] It is exceedingly doubtful that the Americans bothered to inform the United Nations of this fact, however. But it did not escape the attention of the North Koreans, who reported accurately that the decision to post UN military observers grew out of two months of private discussions in Seoul, from September to November, about the possibility of a war along the parallel; they said publicly that the military observers were an American ploy to "legalize" interference in Korean affairs,[39] but it is clear that they understood that UNCOK

36. *New York Herald-Tribune*, May 30 and June 5, 1950.

37. National Archives, 895.00 file, box 7127, Ranshofen-Wertheimer to Jessup, Sept. 22, 1949.

38. FO317, piece no. 76259, conversation between Butterworth and Dening, Sept. 14, 1949.

39. *Nodong sinmun*, Feb. 15, 1950; it cited an undated UPI report on the discussions in Seoul. Earlier the party newspaper had said UNCOK's military observers would help Rhee

was expected to restrain the South while also monitoring the North.

In October 1950, KMAG officers finally succeeded in getting Rhee to remove Kim Sŏk-wŏn from his command along the parallel. British sources in the spring of 1950, however, indicated that KMAG advisers were still "seeking the removal of over-aggressive officers in command positions along the parallel"; in the interim until they were removed, the report said, "a border incident . . . could precipitate civil war." The British thought this would not happen as long as American officers controlled the situation. This judgment is correct and gives great weight to the absence of Generals Roberts and W. H. S. Wright and other high KMAG officers in late June 1950. (Roberts was on his way home to retirement, and Wright was in Tokyo.)[40]

UNCOK military observers did not arrive in Korea until May 1950. The two observers completed a survey of the parallel on the afternoon of June 23, 1950. They reported this to UNCOK on Friday and set about "the shaping up of the report" on Saturday, not out of a sense of urgency "but because it was something nice and tangible" to do on a lazy weekend. The observers slept mainly in Seoul and went up to the parallel on nine of the days between June 9 and 23. They returned to Seoul from the parallel on June 17, and stayed in Seoul until the twenty-first. But they were on the Ongjin peninsula from the twenty-first to Friday morning, the twenty-third, and that is where the war began on Sunday.

A few weeks before the South had held its second National Assembly elections. The result was a disastrous loss for the Rhee regime, bringing into the assembly a strong collection of middle-of-the-roaders and moderate leftists, several of them associated with Yŏ Un-hyŏng's political lineage, and most of them hoping for unification with the North. The Korean ambassador to the United States, John Chang, informed American officials of a resulting crisis in his regime in early June, prompting John Foster Dulles (then an adviser to Truman) to decide to visit Korea on his way to see MacArthur in Tokyo.[41]

During Dulles's visit to Seoul (which began on June 18), Rhee not only pushed for a direct American defense but advocated an attack on the North. Dulles invited along with him a favorite reporter, William Mathews, editor of the *Arizona Daily Star;* Mathews wrote just after the meeting between Rhee and Dulles, "He is militantly for the unification of Korea. Openly says it must be brought about soon . . . Rhee pleads justice of going into North country. Thinks it could succeed in a few

with his plans to touch off a war and called it an "aggressive tool" of the United States (*Nodong sinmun,* Jan. 24, 1950).

40. Cumings (1990), p. 477.

41. Cumings (1990), pp. 500–502.

days. . . . [I]f he can do it with our help, he will do it." And Mathews noted that Rhee said he would "do it," even if "it brought on a general war." All this is yet more proof of Rhee's provocative behavior, but it is not different from his threats to march North made many times before. Rhee hoped that a military alliance with the United States would come out of his meetings with Dulles, but got only some pro forma reassurances of U.S. support. In P'yŏngyang, Dulles's long-standing pro-Japan positions raised the gravest suspicions. But the Dulles visit merely brought out the vintage Rhee: there is no evidence that Dulles was in collusion with him, as the North Koreans have always claimed—while featuring a famous photo of Dulles peering into the North, across the thirty-eighth parallel.[42]

It may be, however, that Chinese Nationalists on Taiwan were willing to collude with Rhee. Taiwan was a hotbed of intrigue in June 1950. From New Year's Day onward, American and British intelligence agencies predicted that the "last battle" of the Chinese civil war would come in June 1950. In January, British Foreign Office sources predicted an invasion of Taiwan "by the end of June." Interestingly enough, Guy Burgess, infamous spy for Moscow and director of the Far Eastern Office of Britain's Foreign Office in 1950, watched this situation closely. In April, Burgess said the invasion would come in May–June or September–October.[43] Some Americans wanted to defend Chiang's regime, while others were hoping to say good riddance—President Truman among them, or so the newspapers said. MacArthur hoped that Dulles's visit would bring a change in U.S. policy in the Far East, especially in regard to Taiwan (which he thought should be defended). Chiang Kai-shek hoped that the high-level talks in Tokyo would herald an American commitment to his regime. In Moscow, the Kremlin would monitor the journey to the East of the very personification of the "Wall Street master."

William Pawley, Charles Cooke, and other Americans with intelligence backgrounds had organized an "informal" military advisory group in the autumn of 1949 to help with the defense of Taiwan. Pawley later became a key CIA operative, influential in the overthrow of the Arbenz regime in Guatemala in 1954, and the Bay of Pigs adventure in 1961. Pawley and Cooke operated outside the established channels of American foreign policy, seeking to retrieve Chiang and his regime from their impending demise. Chiang Kai-shek also faced maturing plans by American clan-

42. Mathews Papers, box 90, "Korea with the John Foster Dulles Mission," June 14–29, 1950.

43. FO317, piece no. 83297, comment or "minute" on Gascoigne to FO, Jan. 13, 1950; piece no. 83243, memo on invasion of Formosa, Jan. 25, 1950, minute by Burgess; piece no. 83247, report on Formosa, April 14, 1950, minute by Burgess.

destine officers for a coup d'état against him, something that has long been shrouded in secrecy. Like the Rhee regime, the Chiang regime was gravely at risk in June 1950. In May the Nationalists seemed to have played out their string; even American partisans of Chiang's regime appeared to draw back after the Nationalists failed to defend Hainan Island. Intelligence estimates continued to predict an invasion in June; the American consul, Robert Strong, reported from Taipei on May 17, "Fate of Taiwan sealed, Communist attack can occur between June 15 and end July."

In an interview the late Dean Rusk said that some elements of the Nationalist military were preparing to move against Chiang on the last weekend in June 1950, but then the Korean War intervened. In fact, Rusk was a key mover in this coup attempt and met with several important Chinese figures at the Plaza Hotel in New York on June 23, seeking to get them to form a government to replace the Kuomintang. Just after the war broke out, Kennan told a top-secret NSC meeting that "Chiang might be overthrown at any time."[44] Guy Burgess read everything coming in from Taiwan in May and June 1950, it would appear, including unclassified press reports. The British chancery in Moscow had earlier noted that Soviet newspapers took an inordinate interest in any scraps of information on the Taiwan question. Burgess's judgment on June 24, 1950, was that "the Soviets seem to have made up their minds up that the U.S.A. have a finally decided policy [not to defend Taiwan]. This *we [sic]* have never quite come to believe."[45]

For over a decade I have been trying to get documents on this episode and various others through the Freedom of Information Act, including Preston Goodfellow's odd return to the U.S. military just before the war. A few have dribbled out of the U.S. government, indicating that Goodfellow was called to active military duty in military intelligence on May 2, 1950, as an "executive officer" for an unknown assignment at Fort Eustis, Virginia. He was fifty-nine years old at the time.[46] We still lack critical documents on the coup against Chiang, on American intelligence-gathering overflights of North Korean and Chinese territory that began before June 1950, and the signals intelligence that the United States collected on North Korea, China, and the USSR. We still do not know why the Pentagon approved and distributed in the week of June 19, 1950, a war plan known as SL-17, which assumed a KPA invasion, a

44. For a full account of this *coup* planning see Cumings (1991), pp. 531–44.

45. FO 317, piece no. 83250, Burgess comments on FC1019/198, June 20, 1950. Burgess and his fellow spy Kim Philby were both immersed in following events in Northeast Asia before and during the Korean War. See Phillip Knightly, *The Master Spy: The Story of Kim Philby* (New York: Vintage Books, 1988), pp. 166–67.

46. Cumings (1990), p. 567.

quick retreat to and defense of a perimeter at Pusan, and then an amphibious landing at Inch'ŏn.[47]

With all this bubbling activity, the last weekend in June 1950 nonetheless dawned on a torpid, somnolent, and very empty Washington. Harry Truman was back home in Independence. Acheson was at his Sandy Spring country farm, Rusk was in New York, Kennan had disappeared to a remote summer cottage without so much as a telephone, Paul Nitze was salmon fishing, the Joint Chiefs of Staff were occupied elsewhere, and even the United Nations representative, Warren Austin, was not at his post.

INCIDENT AT ONGJIN

Most accounts of the outbreak of fighting in June 1950 leave the impression that a North Korean attack began all along the parallel at dawn, against an enemy taken completely unawares. But the war began in the same, remote locus of much of the 1949 fighting, the Ongjin peninsula, and some hours later spread along the parallel eastward, to Kaesŏng, Ch'unch'ŏn, and the east coast. As an official American history put it,

> On the Ongjin Peninsula, cut off from the rest of South Korea, soldiers of the 17th Regiment stood watch on the quiet summer night of 24–25 June 1950. For more than a week, there had been no serious incident along the 38th parallel. . . . Then at 0400, with devastating suddenness . . . [artillery and mortar fire] crashed into the ROK lines.

The North's official radio had it differently. It said (on June 26) that South Korean forces began shelling the Ŭnp'a Mountain area (scene of several 1949 battles, especially the big one on August 4) on June 23 at 10 P.M. and continued until June 24 at 4 A.M., using howitzers and mortars. A unit commanded by Kang To-gŏn was defending Turak Mountain on Ongjin in the early hours of June 25, when it was attacked by the Maengho, or "fierce tiger," unit of the ROK's Seventeenth Regiment, which it proceeded to destroy. By 2:30 P.M. on June 25, the unit had advanced as far as Sudong, on the Ongjin peninsula; meanwhile, guerrillas sprang forward to disrupt South Korean police stations and units in Ongjin.[48]

South Korean sources asserted, on the contrary, that elements of the Seventeenth Regiment had counterattacked and were in possession of Haeju city, the only important point north of the thirty-eighth parallel

47. Cumings (1990), pp. 614–15.
48. For a full account see Cumings (1990), pp. 568–85, on which I rely below.

claimed to have been taken by the South's army. Chae Pyŏng-dŏk announced this at 11:00 A.M. on June 26, a timing that would account for numerous newspaper articles saying that elements of the ROKA had occupied Haeju, articles that have since been used to suggest that the South might have attacked first.[49] The Seventeenth Regiment was not just another unit in the ROK Army. It was directly commanded by one of two brothers who headed the Northwest, or Sŏbuk, faction in the army, Paek In-yŏp, who had brought many Northwest Youth members into it; the other brother, Paek Sŏn-yŏp, commanded the ROKA First Division. Both were crack units of the South's army. Regional loyalties structured most units of the army, and this one was full of northerners with a virulent hatred of communism.

Fighting began at Ongjin around three or four in the morning of June 25 and began rippling eastward across the parallel by five. Kaesŏng was the only point on the parallel where an American officer was present that morning. Joseph Darrigo, KMAG adviser to the ROK Twelfth Regiment, was just below Song'ak Mountain, the bottom of which was in ROK territory but the peak of which was north of the thirty-eighth parallel and occupied by North Korean artillery units. At five that morning artillery fire jounced him out of bed, and he hopped into a jeep and headed south toward a ROK military base near Kaesông, as he had done on many other mornings. Darrigo later reported that "the volume of fire indicated an enemy attack." An American missionary in Kaesŏng heard the artillery, and heard Darrigo's jeep roar by his home, but both were such common occurrences that he rolled over and went back to sleep. Darrigo spotted no enemy troops, until he saw North Korean units disembarking at the railway station in the center of town. The missionary later woke up to find KPA soldiers peering in his window. The Thirteenth and Fifteenth regiments of the sixth KPA Division had opened their main attack at 5:30, and the town fell by 9:30 A.M. with almost no resistance.

At the border town of Ch'unch'ŏn, farther east from Kaesŏng, the South Koreans unquestionably had advance knowledge of fighting to begin on June 25, which southern and American sources say, of course, was advance knowledge of the North Korean attack. Thomas D. McPhail, an American intelligence officer, had gotten "a wealth of information" from South Korean agents whom he sent into northern territory. On Thursday, June 22, such information caused him to go down to Seoul from his position near Ch'unch'ŏn, to warn G-2 officials that the North

49. The *New York Times,* the *New York Herald-Tribune,* and the *Washington Post* reported on June 26 that two companies of the Seventeenth Regiment had occupied Haeju. The UK military attaché in Tokyo cabled on June 27 that two battalions of the Seventeenth occupied Haeju (FO317, piece no. 84057, Gascoigne to FO, June 27, 1950).

had moved citizens away from the parallel and had secreted camouflaged tanks and artillery in "the restricted area," which refers to land just north of the parallel. McPhail's information caused the 6th Division commander to cancel all passes "and fully man defensive positions for the week-end." Because of this "preparedness," "the initial attack was repulsed."[50] On the east coast the South's Eighth Division also gave a good account of itself. Here, too, no Americans were at the parallel; Koreans awakened the KMAG adviser George D. Kessler at 5 A.M. and told him the North had attacked.

The decisive North Korean assault, according to Roy Appleman, came when KPA forces south of Ch'ŏrwŏn at the parallel attacked the First Regiment of the ROKA Seventh Division, dealing it heavy casualties; it gave way and at some unspecified later point the Third and Fourth KPA divisions, with an armored brigade, crashed through and began a daunting march toward Seoul. MacArthur's command reported through the UN at the end of July that at the eastern and western portions of the parallel the North attacked with reinforced border constabulary brigades, at Kaesŏng and Ch'unch'ŏn with a division each (but, as we have seen, not at the start), and ran through the Ŭijŏngbu corridor with 8,000 to 10,000 troops and fifty tanks—in other words a total force of about 38,000. Thus the initial attacking force was not terribly large; the KPA had mobilized less then half its forces on June 25. Arrayed against them were five ROKA divisions located near Seoul or north of it, some 50,000 troops.

The official American position has always been that the Soviets and the North Koreans stealthily prepared an attack that was completely unprovoked, one that constituted an all-out invasion.[51] On June 26, Kim Il Sung, on the contrary, accused the South of making "a general attack" across the parallel. Rhee had long sought to touch off a fratricidal civil war, he said, having "incessantly provoked clashes" at the front line; in preparing a "northern expedition," he had "even gone so far as to collude with our sworn enemy, Japanese militarism." Some of these charges were true, but the charge of making a general attack across the parallel is false: the North attacked, and all along the parallel, by 6 A.M.

50. Ridgway Papers, box 19, Thomas D. McPhail to Ridgway, April 15, 1965. (McPhail finished his career as head of the U.S. Military Advisory group to Nicaragua under Somoza; he once wrote to Matthew Ridgway, "The old Guardia [National Guard] members who fought with the Marines against Sandino still talk about General Ridgway.")

51. For a rehabilitation of this position by means of some new Soviet and Chinese documentation, see Goncharov, Lewis, and Xue (1993). Since that book appeared, however, other documentation from the communist side has come out which challenges many of their points—something inevitable, no doubt, given the scattered and selective nature of the released communist documentation to date.

at the latest. The book still cannot be closed on the possibility that the South opened the fighting on Ongjin, with an eye to seizing Haeju, but there is no evidence that it intended a general invasion of the North on June 25.

The evidence that scholars now have (there is much more to come from unopened archives) is compatible both with an unprovoked North Korean invasion (one prefigured in North Korean and Soviet planning as we have seen) and with an interpretation linking the summer of 1949 to June 1950: that the North, like the South, wanted to seize the Ongjin peninsula and Kaesŏng and then see what happened next, but waited until it had the majority of its crack soldiers back from China, and the support or acquiescence of Stalin and Mao. It positioned its troops to take advantage of the first southern provocation in June 1950 or merely to attack and claim a direct provocation. (As we saw, new Soviet documents show Kim anxious for the South to make a move.) Kim Il Sung bears the grave responsibility for raising the civil conflict in Korea to the level of general war, with intended and unintended consequences that no one could have predicted. To say that this was the culmination of previous struggles and that Rhee wanted to do the same thing is true, but does not gainsay Kim's responsibility for the horrible consequences.

Scattered Soviet materials have shown that Soviet involvement in preparing and planning an invasion after Stalin gave his reluctant endorsement in January 1950 was higher than previous writers had thought, but we still know too little to determine the respective North Korean, Soviet, and Chinese roles in initiating the June fighting.[52] Even when we have every document the Soviets ever produced, we will still need the South Korean archives, the North Korean archives, the Chinese archives on both sides of the Taiwan Strait, and the American intelligence, signals, and cryptography archives before we will be able to argue on truly solid ground the question we ought all try to forget, namely, "Who started the Korean civil war?"

Whatever happened on or before June 25, it was immediately clear that this war was a matter of "Koreans invading Korea"; it was not aggression across generally accepted international lines. Nor was this the point at which the civil conflict began. The question pregnant with ideological dynamite "Who started the Korean War?" is the wrong question. It is not a civil war question; it only holds the viscera in its grasp

52. Shu Guang Zhang (1995) has the best information on the Chinese side, but as he acknowledges, it is not enough to determine China's level of involvement with Kim Il Sung prior to the war. His evidence suggests that China was more involved with Vietnam, supplying Ho Chi Minh with the same advisers, planning, and matériel that the Soviets supplied P'yŏngyang with in the spring of 1950. But no one yet knows if this was a planned division of labor or not.

for the generations immediately afflicted by fratricidal conflict. Americans do not care any more that the South fired first on Fort Sumter; they do still care about slavery and secession. No one wants to know who started the Vietnam War. Someday Koreans in North and South will reconcile as Americans eventually did, with the wisdom that civil wars have no single authors. It took Americans about a century to do so; it is therefore not surprising that Korean reconciliation is still pending after fifty years.

FROM SEOUL TO PUSAN TO INCH'ŎN: THE WAR FOR CONTAINMENT

Word of fighting in Korea arrived in Washington on Saturday night, June 24. In succeeding days Dean Acheson dominated the decision making that soon committed American air and ground forces to the fight. Acheson, along with Dean Rusk, made the decision to take the Korean question to the UN, before he had notified President Truman of the fighting (Acheson told Truman there was no need to have him back in Washington until the next day); at the famous Blair House meetings on the evening of June 25, Acheson argued for increased military aid to the ROK, American air cover for the evacuation, and the interposition of the Seventh Fleet between Taiwan and the mainland; and on the afternoon of June 26 Acheson labored alone on the fundamental decisions committing American air and naval power to the Korean War, approved that evening at Blair House. Thus the decision to intervene was Acheson's decision, supported by the president but taken before United Nations, Pentagon, or congressional approval.[53]

The military representatives at Blair House offered the only serious opposition to American intervention. General Omar Bradley supported Acheson's containment policy at the first Blair House meeting, remarking, "We must draw the line somewhere." But he questioned "the advisability" of introducing American ground troops in large numbers, as did Secretary of the Army Frank Pace and Defense Secretary Louis Johnson. At the second meeting on June 26, Generals Bradley and Lawton Collins again expressed the view that committing ground troops would strain American combat troop limits, unless a general mobilization was undertaken.

The United Nations merely ratified American decisions. In 1950 the General Assembly was a legislature more amenable to Truman's policies than the U.S. Congress was, so he got his war resolution out of the former. As an official Joint Chiefs of Staff study later put it, "Having

53. Cumings (1990), pp. 625–34.

resolved upon armed intervention for itself, the U.S. Government the next day sought the approval and the assistance of the United Nations." Truman called his intervention in Korea a "police action" so that he would not have to get a declaration of war; this inaugurated the pattern for the subsequent conflicts in Vietnam and the Persian Gulf, of war by executive decision rather than through proper constitutional procedure.

UNCOK's June 26 report blamed the outbreak of fighting entirely on the North and provided the slim information upon which the United Nations committed itself to the fighting. UNCOK's report said,

> Commission's present view on basis evidence is, first, that judging from actual progress of operations northern regime is carrying out well-planned, concerted and full-scale invasion of South Korea, second, that South Korean forces were deployed on wholly defensive basis in all sectors of the parallel, and third, that they were taken completely by surprise as they had no reason to believe from intelligence sources that invasion was imminent.

UNCOK's report was drawn together on the morning of June 26, then finalized in Japan on June 29, based exclusively on American and South Korean sources and on the military observers' report, on which some preliminary work had been done on June 24 before the hostilities commenced. On June 25 the two military observers reported that they "were having trouble getting information"; on June 27 all UNCOK members evacuated to Japan, on American military transport. Eight members arrived in Pusan from Tokyo on June 30. This means, of course, that UNCOK members woke up in Seoul on Sunday morning to a war, wrote a report based on the limited observations of two people and whatever the Koreans and Americans chose to tell them, and then were in the care of the American military for the next three days. They left all their archives behind in Seoul, making it impossible to examine the raw information UNCOK had at its disposal in making its report.

Acheson later said UNCOK's report was "of invaluable assistance" in confirming that South Korea was the "unprepared victim [of] deliberate assault." United Nations backing was crucial to the war of opinion, enabling Truman and Acheson to define the war as they saw fit, making their official story of what happened definitive and lasting. Member states were slow to commit forces to the battle, however. Ultimately the British made more of a stand than anyone else; by the spring of 1951 the totals showed about 12,000 British soldiers, 8,500 Canadian, 5,000 Turks, 5,000 Filipinos, and all other contingents (from eleven nations) below 1,000. The United States paid most of the bill for the allied troops.

Among the obscure and anomalous events still resistant to explanation and logic in the Korean decision, not the least is the Soviets' absence from the Security Council in June—thereby abjuring their much used and abused veto mechanism. Jacob Malik was boycotting the Security Council, ostensibly because the UN had refused to admit China, a boycott that had begun in February 1950. He was planning to return to Moscow for consultations on July 6. There is now evidence that Stalin explicitly ordered the Soviet delegation to stay away from the UN when the war began, in a message from Moscow that arrived on the morning of June 25. Why? The logic would suggest one of two possibilities: Stalin wanted to suck the United States into a war in peripheral Korea, hoping ultimately to pit the Chinese against American soldiers and thereby make Mao dependent on him; UN backing would greatly boost a policy of intervention. Second, Stalin may have hoped that cloaking American intervention in the flag of the UN would destroy this body or, at a minimum, reveal it to be an American tool. But it would have been a great help to the North Koreans if Stalin had exercised the veto.

When the war began, the Soviet information apparatus was silent for three days, except to repeat some of P'yŏngyang's statements verbatim and without comment. But from day one the Soviets made clear to Washington their determination to stay clear of the fighting. In the early morning hours of June 26, Russian ships that had sailed from the Soviet-controlled port of Dairen, in China, just opposite Korea, were ordered "to return to their own defense zone immediately." Soviet naval vessels also stayed clear of the war zone, and their submarines never, from June 25 onward, interfered with American shipping.[54] The Soviets also pulled back their advisers that had been with the KPA. All this was known to U.S. intelligence at the time, and daily field situation reports were generally negative on any direct participation by Soviet officers in the war, while occasionally citing evidence that Soviet advisers remained in the North with air and naval units.

There is no evidence of an upturn in Soviet military shipments to North Korea after June 25; if anything, a decrease was registered. By and large the only equipment the Americans captured that could clearly have been new equipment stockpiled for an invasion was trucks with low mileage on their odometers. In September 1950 MacArthur had "physical proof" of only ten military items delivered to the Koreans in 1949 and 1950—some machine guns, grenades, radio receivers, and the like. By early September 1950, intelligence sources told the *New York Times* that they had "no knowledge that the North Korean invaders actually received new supplies from the Soviet Union since the war began." We are thus left to reconcile the American assumption that Stalin started the

54. Cumings (1990), pp. 643–44.

war with the unambiguous evidence that he distanced Soviet prestige and armed might from the conflict.

The Chinese response was quicker than the Soviet, and less noncommittal. The official *People's Daily* published its first editorial on June 27, a day before the first Moscow editorial, and it said much more. The Chinese lambasted the Rhee regime as an American puppet, cited its many provocations of the North, and criticized American policy, following the North Korean line. They were particularly incensed, of course, by the Seventh Fleet's patrolling the Taiwan Strait. As the war and American involvement deepened, the Chinese took on a measure of responsibility for North Korea's fate that predated their actual intervention by months and that went quite beyond the Soviet position.

August 1 was Armed Forces Day in China, and the PLA commander, Chu Teh, used the occasion to assail American imperialism, calling the North Korean battle "completely just," and refering to the DPRK as "our good neighbor." In mid-August American authorities picked up the growing evidence of China's backing for the North. Intelligence sources later claimed that the Chinese pledged to furnish 250,000 soldiers for Korea in a high-level Beijing meeting on August 14,[55] and by the end of the month a huge Sino-Korean army was poised on the Chinese border with Korea. On July 21 Chou En-lai assured the Indian ambassador, K. M. Panikkar, that the Chinese had every intention of staying out of the Korean hostilities, but by late August he began the steady drumbeat of warnings that, in retrospect, clearly foreshadowed China's entry into the war.

THE DRIVE ON PUSAN

In the summer months of 1950 the North Korean Army pushed southward with extraordinary success and, until the American First Marine Division stiffened the defense, with one humiliating defeat after another of American forces. An army that had bested Germany and Japan found its back pressed to the wall by what seemed to be a hastily assembled peasant military, ill equipped and, worse, said to be doing the bidding of a foreign imperial power.

In the wake of the capture of Seoul, the KPA waited about a week to make its next big push, which resulted in the capture of Taejŏn in what military historians later considered one of the North's finest battles. In early July, American daily situation reports said KPA infantry was "first class," its armor and service "unsurpassed in World War II." Americans

55. This may refer to a Chinese Politburo meeting on August 4 (see below).

were especially impressed with the Sixth Division, formed entirely of "CCF Koreans" and led by Pang Ho-san, which participated in the initial fighting on Ongjin, swept southward along the coast through the Chŏllas, and then by the end of July abruptly turned east for a daunting march along the southern coast, occupying Chinju by August 1 and thereby directly menacing Pusan. But the initial delay south of Seoul, probably occasioned by the necessity of bringing up artillery and other supplies from the rear, gave MacArthur the essential time to organize a defense in the southeast.[56]

By the beginning of August, American and South Korean forces outnumbered the North's along the front, 92,000 to 70,000 (47,000 were Americans), but in spite of this the retreat continued. (MacArthur hid this from other American officials, claiming that his forces were outnumbered two or three to one.) In the first week of August, however, the First Marine Division went into action and finally halted the North's advance. The front did not change much from that point until the end of August.

The Pusan perimeter had its northern anchor on the coast around P'ohang, its southern anchor in the Chinju-Masan region, and its center just above the major city of Taegu. The latter became a symbol of the American determination to stanch the KPA's advance; for the North Koreans it was even more important, as a major stronghold of the southern left. But it was P'ohang in the North that was probably the key to stopping the KPA from occupying Pusan and throwing the Americans into the sea. The military historian Appleman wrote that the "major tactical mistake" of the North Koreans was not to press their advantage on the east coastal road. The North's Fifth Division worried too much about covering its flanks, instead of moving quickly on P'ohang and thence combining with the Sixth Division to form a pincer threatening Pusan.

Throughout the summer of 1950 northern troops were aided by guerrillas, most of them local but some coming from the North. From June 25 to August 31, guerrilla casualties running above an average of 100 per day were recorded, with total claimed losses of 67,228 killed, 23,837 captured, and 44,154 surrendered. (That is more than double the total number of Americans killed in action during the entire war.) During the weeks of the Pusan perimeter, "large tactical units, division [size] or larger," had to be diverted to secure rear areas infested with guerrillas.[57]

Americans first felt the combination of frontal assault and guerrilla warfare in the battle for Taejŏn. Local peasants, including women and children, would come running along the hillsides near the battle lines, as if they were refugees. "At a given signal, the 'refugees' snatched rifles,

56. For a fuller account see Cumings (1990), pp. 655–62.
57. Cumings (1990), pp. 686–90.

machine guns, and hand grenades from their bundles and brought down withering fire on the troops below."[58] The retreat from Taejŏn ran into well-organized roadblocks and ambushes, often placed by local residents. Americans thought anyone in "white pajamas," which they called the Korean native dress, might potentially be an enemy. From this point on, American forces began burning villages suspected of harboring guerillas, and in some cases burned them merely to deny the guerrillas hiding places.

In the midst of the massive push toward Pusan, thousands of Korean cadres, from North and South, set about restoring the people's committees disbanded in 1945–46 and redistributing land on a revolutionary basis. Through it all they beat the drum of Korean unification and independence. The North Korean occupation of the South is thus an essential experience in determining this war's origins, and what manner of war it was. Kim Il Sung called for the restoration of the people's committees in his first radio address after the war broke out, and American intelligence recognized the crucial importance to the North Koreans of the revival of this political form, "dissolved long ago by US Army Military Government." Propagandists referred to this history over and over again, and counterposed the committee form not to the politics of the ROK but to the reimposition of "the ruling organs of Japanese imperialism." In other words, from their point of view, the goal was to restore people's committees, which predated the reimposition of the colonial state, not to impose on the South the political forms of the North.[59]

The Seoul People's Committee formed quickly, led mostly by southerners. By early July it had confiscated all Japanese property, and that of the ROK government, its officials, and "monopoly capitalists." The KPA distributed stored rice stocks to poor people and left the administration of justice in the hands of local peace preservation groups, many of whose members had just gotten out of prison. In the early days prisoners released from Rhee's jails carried out a reign of terror against their former antagonists, mostly those in the police and youth groups. Otherwise, CIA studies found, North Korean officials ran a tight ship but without a lot of bloodshed.[60]

About sixty members of the ROK National Assembly remained in

58. MacArthur Archives, Norfolk, Va., RG6, box 60, G-2 report no. 2872, July 21, 1950; *New York Times*, July 21, 1950.

59. For the only account in the literature of the northern occupation of the South, see Cumings (1990), pp. 666–90.

60. Truman Library, Independence, Mo., PSF, NSDC file, box 3, CIA report of July 19, 1950; FO317, piece no. 84066, Korea mission to FO, Sept. 9, 1950. In 1951, the CIA said that a "large percentage" of the most prominent labor leaders in the South joined the North Koreans within ten days of the beginning of the war. See CIA, ibid., report of June 6, 1951.

Seoul, and toward the end of July forty-eight of them held a meeting expressing their allegiance to the North. Even one American did the bidding of the regime, whether voluntarily or not. "Seoul City Sue," the Tokyo Rose of the Korean War, broadcast appeals to American soldiers over the radio in an unmistakable native accent. She was Anne Wallace Suhr, a former Methodist missionary who married a Korean leftist. The occupation of the capital ended amid the crisis of the Inch'ŏn landing and the vicious battle for Seoul in September. Discipline broke down and many killings occurred. Many buildings were also burned, apparently by vagrants and children urged to do so by the KPA.

Throughout the rest of southern Korea, local people's committees reemerged, but not in the spontaneous fashion of 1945. The North Koreans exercised sharp procedural controls to assure that committee membership would conform to North Korean practice and discipline. A subsequent study by the forerunner of the RAND Corportion found that disadvantaged clans used the northern occupation to turn over the power structure in many villages, but also that single-clan yangban villages were in some cases impervious to North Korean attempts to change them.[61] The restoration of the committees was relatively easy, however, compared with the attempt to carry through revolutionary land reform in the midst of a war. But a confrontation with Korea's landed class, which had succeeded in blocking the reformist redistribution pushed on the ROK by the Americans, was taken to be the essence of the antifeudal, anticolonial character of the Korean revolution. The redistribution ensued in every province outside the Pusan perimeter, and even though it was hasty and done in wartime conditions, it cleared away class structures and power that later made possible Rhee's land redistribution program—because the Americans would not fight merely to restore land to this class, which had ruled Korea for centuries, and therefore required that Rhee finally carry through the reform that the National Assembly had passed in 1949. In this and many other ways, the war was a great equalizer for Korea at mid-century.

The North Koreans fought a war on all fronts: conventional war, guerrilla war, and a political war over the people's committees and land reform. In other words, this was also a people's war, and, like the subsequent war in Vietnam, it called forth an appalling American response. This has been a forgotten part of America's "forgotten war" in Korea, but in 1950 you could read about in the barbershop. Eric Larrabee, writing in *Harper's*, began by quoting an English captain who subdued the Pequot Indians in 1636: "the tactics of the natives . . . far differ from Christian

61. U.S. Air University, "A Preliminary Study of the Impact of Communism on Korea" (Maxwell AFB, 1951).

practice." He also recalled the reflections of a British officer at Lexington during the American Revolution, which are quoted at the beginning of this chapter. A Marine in Korea told Larrabee, "In Tarawa you could at least see the enemy. Here the gooks hide in the bushes." Larrabee argued that what was a limited war for Americans was a people's war for Koreans, and said it could not be fought with a "brutal and senseless display of technical superiority."[62]

Collier's began an article by saying, "Our Red foe scorns all rules of civilized warfare, hid[ing] behind women's skirts," and then quoted the following colloquy between American soldiers:

> The young pilot drained his cup of coffee and said, "Hell's fire, you can't shoot people when they stand there waving at you." "Shoot 'em," he was told firmly. "They're troops." "But, hell, they've all got on those white pajama things and they're straggling down the road." . . . "See any women or children?" "Women? I wouldn't know. The women wear pants, too, don't they?" "But no kids, no, sir." "They're troops. Shoot 'em."[63]

Reginald Thompson, a sensitive British war correspondent, wrote in his book *Cry Korea* that "there were few who dared to write the truth of things as they saw them." Journalists found the campaign for the South "strangely disturbing," very different from World War II in its guerrilla and popular aspect. Thompson witnessed an American Marine kill an elderly civilian as if in a fit of absentmindedness, showing no sign of remorse, and remarked that GIs "never spoke of the enemy as though they were people, but as one might speak of apes." Even among correspondents, "every man's dearest wish was to kill a Korean. 'Today, . . . I'll get me a gook.' " Americans called Koreans gooks, he thought, because "otherwise these essentially kind and generous Americans would not have been able to kill them indiscriminately or smash up their homes and poor belongings."[64]

Charles Grutzner, who reported the war for the *New York Times,* said that in the early going "fear of infiltrators led to the slaughter of hundreds of South Korean civilians, women as well as men, by some U.S.

62. Eric Larrabee, "Korea: The Military Lesson," *Harper's,* Nov. 1950, pp. 51–57.

63. Walter Karig, "Korea—Tougher Than Okinawa," *Collier's,* Sept. 23, 1950, pp. 24–26. General Lawton Collins remarked that Korea saw "a reversion to old-style fighting—more comparable to that of our own Indian frontier days than to modern war." See *New York Times,* Dec. 27, 1950.

64. Reginald Thompson, *Cry Korea* (London: MacDonald, 1951), pp. 39, 42, 54, 143, 150–51. It is often thought that "gook" emerged with the Korean War, since it sounds like *Han'guk* (South Korea) or *Miguk* (America). In fact, its usage began in the American war against the Philippine insurgency at the turn of the century.

troops and police of the Republic." He quoted a high-ranking U.S. officer who told him of an American regiment that panicked in July and shot "many civilians." Keyes Beech, another American correspondent, wrote, "It is not the time to be a Korean, for the Yankees are shooting them all. . . . [N]ervous American troops are ready to fire at any Korean."[65]

Reginald Thompson found himself sickened by the carnage of the American air war, with the latest machined military might used against "an almost unarmed enemy, unable to challenge the aircraft in the skies." In September 1950, "handfuls of peasants defied the immense weight of modern arms with a few rifles and carbines and a hopeless courage . . . and brought down upon themselves and all the inhabitants the appalling horror of jellied petrol bombs." Every enemy shot, he said, "released a deluge of destruction. Every village and township in the path of war was blotted out." In such warfare "the slayer needs merely touch a button, and death is on the wing, blindly blotting out the remote, the unknown people, holocausts of death, veritable mass productions of death, spreading an abysmal desolation over whole communities."

Perhaps the most daunting story is that, from the first days of the war, the Americans contemplated the use of atomic weapons in this "limited" war. On July 9—a mere two weeks into the war, it is worth remembering—MacArthur sent Matthew Ridgway a "hot message," which prompted the Joint Chiefs of Staff "to consider whether or not A-bombs should be made available to MacArthur." General Charles Bolte, chief of operations, was asked to talk to MacArthur about using atomic bombs "in direct support [of] ground combat"; some ten to twenty bombs could be spared without "unduly" jeopardizing the general war plan. Bolte got from MacArthur an early suggestion for the tactical use of atomic weapons, and an indication of MacArthur's extraordinary ambitions for the war, which included occupying the North and handling potential Chinese—or Soviet—intervention as follows: "I would cut them off in North Korea. In Korea I visualize a cul-de-sac. The only passages leading from Manchuria and Vladivostok have many tunnels and bridges. I see here a unique use for the atomic bomb—to strike a blocking blow—which would require a six months repair job. Sweeten up my B-29 force. . . ." At this point in the war, however, the JCS rejected use of the bomb.[66]

All sides in the war were guilty of atrocities. KPA forces executed several hundred American POWs, albeit in the traditional "humane" battlefield manner: one bullet behind the ear. (General Charles Willoughby called this the "typical Mongol-Slav manner" of killing prisoners.) Treat-

65. Keyes Beech, *Newark Star-Ledger*, July 23, 1950.
66. For a fuller account see Cumings (1990), pp. 747–53.

ment of ROK POWs was considerably worse, but there is little evidence on this. There were a number of brutal atrocities against civilians, especially as the occupation of the South ended. The United Nations archive contains well-documented accounts, verified by witnesses and relatives, of several mass murders of southerners by the northern occupiers, including a particularly ghastly one at Chŏnju. For what it is worth, captured North Korean documents continued to show that high-level officials warned against executing people. Several orders to stop any further executions were picked up on the battlefield; handwritten minutes of a party meeting, apparently at a high level, said, "Do not execute the reactionaries for [their] wanton vengeance. Let legal authorities carry out the purge plan."[67]

Roy Appleman alleged that the North Koreans perpetrated "one of the greatest mass killings" of the war in Taejŏn, with between 5,000 and 7,000 people slaughtered and placed in mass graves. Some Americans were included; in one incident six survivors, including two Americans, were found alive, feigning death under the light soil thrown on top of them. Mass burial graves were also found at many points in South Chŏlla, and Appleman wrote that the North Koreans "ran amok" in Wŏnju on October 2, killing between 1,000 and 2,000 civilians. Appleman, an officially employed historian of the war, did not mention any South Korean atrocities. What happened in the Taejŏn atrocity is not at all clear, however.

In early August, Alan Winnington published an article in the London *Daily Worker* entitled "U.S. Belsen in Korea," alleging that the South Korean police under the supervision of KMAG advisers had butchered 7,000 people in the village of Yangwŏl, near Taejŏn, during the period July 2–6. He found twenty eyewitnesses who said that truckloads of police arrived on July 2 and made local people build six pits, each two hundred yards long. Two days later political prisoners were trucked in and executed, both by bullets to the head and sword decapitation, and layered on top of each other in the pits "like sardines." The massacres continued for three days. The witnesses said that two jeeps with American officers observed the killings. North Korean sources said 4,000 had been killed (changing the number some months later to 7,000), composed mostly of imprisoned guerrillas from Cheju Island and the T'aebaek-san area, and those detained after the Yŏsu-Sunch'ŏn incident. They located the site somewhat differently.[68] The American embassy in

67. Handwritten minutes of a KWP meeting, apparently at a high level, Dec. 7, 1950, translated in MacArthur Archives, RG6, box 80, ATIS issue no. 29, March 17, 1951.
68. Cumings (1990), p. 669.

London called the Winnington story an "atrocity fabrication" and denied its contents. However, British officials in Tokyo said that "there may be an element of truth in this report."

There is undeniable evidence of South Korean massacres on a lesser scale. A *New York Times* reporter found an ROK policeman with forty civilians in his retinue, alleged guerrillas, observing him as he "crashed the butt of his rifle on the back of one after another." "We bang-bang in the woods," the policeman happily said, meaning that the prisoners "would be taken into the groves and executed after their backs had been broken." An Australian witnessed a similar incident, in Kongju, where twenty civilian prisoners were kneeling and being beaten by guards "on [the] least movement." On inquiry the guards said, "guerrillas, bang bang." A *Manchester Guardian* correspondent saw a truckload of sixty prisoners taken to the Kŭm River on July 12 and executed by ROK authorities. "Tiger" Kim had fifty North Korean POWs beheaded in August; when the Red Cross made representations to KMAG about it, KMAG officers said they "would not like to see it get in the hand of correspondents." The head of the National Police, Kim Tae-sŏn, acknowledged on July 14 that his forces had executed 1,200 suspected communists since June 25.[69] In recent years, as South Korea has democratized, investigations have revealed numerous killings of leftists and suspected collaborators with North Korea by the Rhee regime, often hundreds at a time.

James Cameron of London's *Picture Post* wrote about what he termed "South Korean concentration camps" in Pusan in the late summer of 1950:

> This terrible mob of men—convicted of nothing, untried, South Koreans in South Korea, suspected of being "unreliable." There were hundreds of them, they were skeletal, puppets of string, faces translucent grey, manacled to each other with chains, cringing in the classic Oriental attitude of subjection, the squatting foetal position, in piles of garbage. . . . Around this medievally gruesome market-place was gathered a few knots of American soldiers photographing the scene with casual industry. . . . I took my indignation to the [U.N.] Commission, who said very civilly: "Most disturbing, yes; but remember these are Asian people, with different standards of behavior . . . all very difficult." It was supine and indefensible compromise. I boiled, and I do not boil easily. We recorded the situation meticulously, in words and photographs.

69. *New York Times,* July 11, 1950; FO317, piece no. 84178, Sawbridge to FO, July 25, 1950; *Manchester Guardian,* July 13, 1950; National Records Center, RG338, KMAG file, Box 5418, report of Aug. 2, 1950.

> Within the year it nearly cost me my job, and my magazine its existence.

The *Picture Post* never published Cameron's story, causing a "mini-mutiny" on the magazine; shortly thereafter the *Post* "withered away, as it deserved."[70]

At the end of August KPA forces launched their last major offensive, making "startling gains" which in the next two weeks severely strained the American-Korean lines. On August 28 Pang Ho-san ordered his troops to take Masan and Pusan in the next few days; three KPA battalions succeeded in crossing the Naktong River in the central sector, P'ohang and Chinju were lost, and the perimeter was "near the breaking point," with KPA forces again pressing on Kyŏngju, Masan, and Taegu.

General Walton Walker moved Eighth Army headquarters from Taegu to Pusan, other high officials were evacuated from Taegu, and prominent Koreans began leaving Pusan for Cheju or Tsushima Island. On September 9 Kim Il Sung said the war had reached an "extremely harsh, decisive stage," with the enemy being pressed on three fronts; two days later General Walker reported that the frontline situation was the most dangerous since the perimeter had been established. Appleman wrote that by mid-September, "after two weeks of the heaviest fighting of the war [American forces] had just barely turned back the great North Korean offensive." American casualties were the highest of the war.

North Korea had brought its forces along the front to 98,000, but upwards of one-third of them were new, raw recruits. Guerrillas, including many women, were active in both the P'ohang and the Masan fighting. Still, the North Koreans were by then badly outnumbered. MacArthur had succeeded in committing most of the battle-ready divisions in the American army to the Korean fighting; by September 8 he had been sent all available trained army units except for the Eighty-second Airborne Division. By the time of the Inch'ŏn landing, some 83,000 American soldiers and another 57,000 Korean and British faced the North Koreans at the front.

THE WAR FOR ROLLBACK

In mid-September 1950 MacArthur masterminded his last hurrah, a tactically brilliant amphibious landing at Inch'ŏn that brought American armed forces back to Seoul five years after they had first set foot on

70. See "Cameron's Wars," *Guardian* (London), Sept. 5, 1982; also Halliday and Cumings (1988), which has some of the censored photos.

Korean soil. Inch'ŏn harbor has treacherous tides that can easily ground a flotilla of ships if the wrong time is chosen, but the American passage through the shifting bays and flats was flawless. American Marines landed almost unopposed, but then slogged through a deadly gauntlet before Seoul finally fell at the end of September. Admiral Arthur Dewey Struble, the navy's crack amphibious expert who led the landing operations at Leyte, in the Philippines, and who directed the naval operations off Omaha Beach during the Normandy invasion, commanded an enormous fleet of 261 ships in the Inch'ŏn operations, depositing 80,000 Marines with hardly a loss. Against this the North Koreans could do nothing. They were not surprised by the invasion, as the American mythology has it,[71] but could not resist it and so began what their historians call euphemistically "the great strategic retreat."

The first Korean War ended on September 30 as ROKA units crossed into the North, pressing a rollback against rapidly withdrawing KPA forces. The war for the South left 111,000 South Koreans killed, 106,000 wounded, and 57,000 missing; 314,000 homes had been destroyed, 244,000 damaged. American casualties totaled 2,954 dead, 13,659 wounded, and 3,877 missing in action. North Korean casualty figures are not known.[72] Now a new war began, a march to the Yalu River in the face of a combined army of Chinese and Koreans, waiting in the mountain fastness of the Sino-Korean border.

The North Korean thrust southward seemed immediately to stimulate American thinking of a thrust northward—or should we say, John Foster Dulles's thinking. Alvary Gascoigne has Dulles in late June saying, "in a desultory way," that the Korean incident might be used to go beyond the parallel. By mid-July, Dulles was a key advocate of rollback, assisted by Dean Rusk, John Allison, and John Paton Davies.[73]

Within three weeks of the war's start, key decision makers had turned containment logic on its head, a sleight of hand not without some black humor, in which the heretofore inviolable "international" boundary at the thirty-eighth parallel, which when crossed by Koreans of the northern persuasion had evoked talk of Hitler-style aggression, now was deemed permeable from the south. Everett Drumwright wrote Allison on July 10, "Once the rout starts it would be disastrous and stupid of us to

71. Captured documents show that KPA commanders in the Inch'ŏn region expected an invasion by late August and tracked the flotilla in the days just before the landing. See Cumings (1991), pp. 724–31.

72. National Archives, 895.00 file, Bix 5693, Embassy to State, Nov. 11, 195, giving official ROK figures; Ridgway Papers, Box 16, memo on official Department of Defense count of American casualties, Oct. 5, 1950.

73. Cumings (1990), pp. 709–15.

stop at the 38th parallel. . . . Our goal and the UN goal is unification." Allison was stimulated to prepare a top-secret memo, arguing that unlike the boundaries in central Europe, the parallel had no de jure significance (after all). The record, he said, showed "that this line was agreed upon only for the surrender of Japanese troops and that the U.S. had made no commitments with regard to the continuing validity of the line for any other purpose."[74] In other words, the parallel bisecting Korea was an internationally recognized boundary if Koreans cross it, but not if Americans do. Michael Walzer in his book *Just and Unjust Wars* notes that in justifying the march into North Korea the American ambassador to the UN called the thirty-eighth parallel "an imaginary line." Walzer comments, if the thirty-eighth parallel was an imaginary line, "how then did we recognize the initial aggression?"[75]

Dulles quickly gave Allison's paper to Rusk and the next day, July 14, penned a memo to Nitze, arguing explicitly for a march North. Soon Allison was heading the National Security Council study of rollback that resulted in the enabling document that appeared in September, NSC 81, embodying much of the language of Rusk, Allison, and Dulles in July. The Defense Department weighed in with its own paper, also arguing for rollback. The course of the war had now provided "the first opportunity to displace part of the Soviet orbit"; the paper was unusually frank in noting that "Manchuria, the pivot" of the Soviet Far East strategic complex, "would lose its captive status."[76]

General MacArthur always favored rollback, of course, and called for it on July 17. Three days later Louis Johnson tried to take credit for the new change in policy: he sent his aides scurrying off to the Nationalist embassy to spill secrets of the highest sensitivity: that the government had already decided to march North . . . at Johnson's insistence.[77] Truman approved a march north, according to the best evidence, at the end of August. The decision was embodied in NSC 81, written mostly by Rusk, which authorized MacArthur to move into North Korea if there were no Soviet or Chinese threats to intervene. It explicitly called for "a roll-back"; the enabling order to MacArthur, sent by Bolte on September 16, referred to "the pursuance of a rollback." MacArthur was to use only

74. National Archives, 795.00 file, box 4265, Drumwright to Allison, July 10, 1950; Allison, "The Origin and Significance of the 38th Parallel in Korea," July 13, 1950.

75. Michael Walzer, *Just and Unjust Wars: A Moral Argument with Historical Illustrations* (New York: Basic Books, 1977), pp. 117–23.

76. *Foreign Relations of the United States* (1950), 7: Dulles to Nitze, July 14, 1950, pp. 386–87; PPS draft memo, July 22, pp. 449–54; Allison to Nitze, July 24, pp. 458–61; Defense Department draft memo, July 31, 1950, pp. 502–10.

77. Cumings (1990), p. 711.

Korean units in operations near the Chinese border.[78] MacArthur was correct in telling senators in 1951 that the crossing of the parallel "had the most complete and absolute approval of every section of the American government," if we grant him the license of mild exaggeration owed to a person who had been badly blindsided by postwar reconstructions of these disastrous decisions.

The momentum of the Inch'ŏn landing carried UN forces across the parallel and deep into North Korean territory. It was also thought to have completely destroyed the North Korean Army. In early October ROK units swept up the east coast with next to no resistance. They were twenty-five miles above the parallel within two days, had four divisions in the North within a week, and captured the eastern port city of Wŏnsan on October 10. Thereafter they kept on rolling toward the Yalu, with the North Korean Army withdrawing ahead of them—an odd and heady new reality for an army that, a few weeks earlier, had been judged continual to "break" under North Korean pressure. After a week of marching in the North, a South Korean major kept repeating that he could not understand why the North "had been giving up beautiful natural defenses," causing a reporter to comment that the North Koreans "have not been fighting" and that the quality of their soldiers had clearly been overrated.[79] American forces faced stiffer opposition on the western side, but by mid-October MacArthur's headquarters announced "spectacular gains"; the Red capital was seized, causing SCAP (Supreme Command, Allied Powers) officers to claim that the war was over. The *New York Times* reported that the final phase of the war was at hand, and ran a banner headline saying, "UN Troops Race Unopposed toward the Manchurian Border." Hanson Baldwin thought the Russians must have decided to "cut their losses"; other commentators proclaimed a "smashing North Korean defeat," and cigars were lit all over Tokyo and Washington.[80]

In many ways, however, the Inch'ŏn victory was Pyrrhic. MacArthur and his advisers, fighting a guerrilla war as a conventional war, were drawn into a morass. Reginald Thompson wrote that "the North Korean Army had disappeared like a wraith into the hills. . . . The trap had closed, and it was empty." A discerning London *Times* account penned a phrase that would seem incomprehensible in the received wisdom on

78. See NSC 81 and the various drafts leading up to it in *Foreign Relations of the United States* (1950), 7. For Bolte's order, see Almond Papers, Army War College, Korean War General Files, X Corps, Bolte to MacArthur, Sept. 16, 1950; also Foot (1985), p. 74.

79. Truman Library, PSF, CIA file, box 248, CIA daily reports, Oct. 3–10, 1950; National Archives, 795.00 file, box 4268, Drumwright to Allison, Aug. 30, 1950.

80. *New York Times*, Oct. 15, 18, 22, 23,1950; on the atmosphere in UNC headquarters when P'yŏngyang was seized, see *Times*, (London), Nov. 16, 1950.

the post-Inch'ŏn fighting: "The aggressiveness of the rearguard suggests that there is a future Korean Mao Tse-tung in Kanggye." It went on that a "dangerous complacency" had overtaken American officers:

> The enemy's forces were declared to have been destroyed when elements of 12 divisions were identified. . . . [T]he intrinsic strength and pliability of Communist armies were forgotten. . . . Fears that large numbers of Communists and their followers withdrawing into the northern hills would wage a partisan war had been realized.

Among American reporters, only the Asia hand Walter Sullivan understood that many northern officers had fought with the Chinese and were now following "Chinese Communist" strategies of withdrawal and retreat, preparations for which had been made over the previous three months.[81] The high command retreated to Kim Il Sung's old guerrilla lair and set up its headquarters at Kanggye, which had been "a main base of Japanese power in northern Korea," with many military installations and tunnels.[82]

A captured notebook quoted Pak Ki-sŏng, chief of political intelligence in the KPA Eighth Division:

> The main force of the enemy still remained intact, not having been fully damaged. When they were not fully aware of the power of our forces, they pushed their infantry far forward . . . to the Yalu River. This indicated that they underestimated us. All these conditions were favorable to lure them near. . . .

A KPA officer captured at the time of the joint Sino-Korean offensive said that until late November the KPA had been "continuously withdrawing":

> One may think that going down all the way to the Pusan perimeter and then withdrawing all the way to the Yalu River was a complete defeat. But that is not so. That was a planned withdrawal. We withdrew because we knew that UN troops would follow us up here, and that they would spread their troops thinly all over the vast area. Now, the time has come for us to envelop these troops and annihilate them.

He said that combined KPA and Chinese forces striking from the front would be aided by "eight strong corps which will harass and attack the enemy from the rear." KPA forces had moved back as far south as Andong and Sangju, in North Kyŏngsang Province, to envelop UN troops.[83]

81. Appleman (1961), p. 658; Thompson, *Cry Korea,* p. 79; *Times,* (London), Nov. 16, 1950; Sullivan in *New York Times,* Oct. 2, 1950.
82. Lautensach (1945), p. 258.
83. Cumings (1990), p. 729.

After the Chinese came into the war, William V. Quinn, intelligence chief for the American Tenth Corps, grasped what had happened after Inch'ŏn. The enemy had "taken to the hills," he said, fighting necessary delaying actions while "relentlessly continu[ing] their northward withdrawal." Several different routes led to "the mountainous redoubt of Chagang-do." During the colonial period, he said, Kim Il Sung had acquired a reputation "as a skillful and ruthless guerrilla chief. . . . [H]is base of operations . . . was an area in the rugged terrain north and northwest of Hamhung." It may have been foresight, Quinn said, "or a safeguard against what has become inevitable"; in any case, in the spring of 1950 Kim carved out a new province in his old haunt, calling it Chagang. Natural boundaries, mountains and rivers, made it almost impregnable from the south, but "an adequate road grid laces the area together and provides access to Manchuria."

The North Koreans had established a system that, unlike the ROK's, did not rely on control of the capital, but penetrated to the villages in a way no previous Korean state ever had. Around October 10 DPRK party, state, and military leaders began to withdraw toward the Chagang area, taking with them local civil officials and "confirmed Communists." "Changjin and Kapsan were repeatedly mentioned as the assembly areas for withdrawing forces"; the east coast was left completely exposed, allowing the ROKA to cruise unassisted to the border. So rapid was the withdrawal that in many cases "the enemy completely broke contact" with UN forces (mostly ROKA forces in the east). On the western side, resistance was heavier to evacuate the capital; the assembly point was Kanggye, which they rapidly withdrew toward—while bombers blasted the escape route that Americans expected a conventional army to take, toward Sinŭiju, on the Chinese border. Quinn thought that with Manchurian resupply routes, guerrillas would be able to fight "for an indefinite period of time," being inaccessible to amphibious or air attack. When Chinese and Korean troops came into the war from Manchuria, major forces crossed the Yalu at Manp'ojin and moved through Kanggye, dealing the Americans their terrible defeat at the Changjin (Japanese name, Chosin) reservoir. Another large army crossed at Antung, eventually linking up with regrouped KPA units in the vicinity of Kapsan.[84]

Many partisans had been left along the route of the retreat. A long

84. Quinn Papers, Army War College, box 3, "The Chagang-do Redoubt," annex no. 2, periodic intelligence report no. 37, no date but post-Nov. 1950. The CIA said on Oct. 18, "There has been no evidence of any breakdown in the internal discipline of the North Korean communists. Their leaders have been through many years of adversity in China and Japanese-occupied Korea, and they probably will continue fighting in one way or another." See Cumings (1990), pp. 729–30.

listing of guerrilla activities south of the parallel for the last two weeks of October included the following: 15,000 guerrillas in possession of Yangyang, "strong concentrations" at Samch'ok, Uljin, and Kangnŭng, guerrillas in occupation of Kŭmhwa, Hwach'ŏn, and Koesan, 1,000 near Kwangju, 300 engaged near Mun'gyŏng, 300 attacked at Changsu by UN troops, 2,000 near Chŏngŭp, 2,000 to 3,000 near Mokp'o, and so on.[85] Of course, Inch'ŏn still represented a bad defeat for the North. Entire units in the Third Division panicked and collapsed, according to Appleman, and the Eighth Division suffered 4,000 casualties; the Twelfth was completely destroyed after fighting "stubborn delaying actions." Huge quantities of equipment were lost; the morale of troops and civilians was badly hurt. The retreat made the best of a bad deal that North Korea could do little about.

THE SOUTH OCCUPIES THE NORTH

Just as the North imposed its politics on the South, so the reverse happened. The effective politics of the southern occupation consisted mostly of the National Police and the rightist youths who came along with it. Cho P'yŏng-ok, now home minister, on October 10 announced that the KNP controlled nine towns north of the parallel, with a special force of thirty thousand being recruited for occupation duty. State Department officials had sought some mechanism for supervision of the political aspects of the rollback, "to insure that a 'bloodbath' would not result. In other words . . . the Korean forces should be kept under control."[86] Shortly the embassy's Everett Drumwright said the department's plans were "already outmoded by events," with some two thousand KNP across the parallel; he suggested that perhaps more local responsibility would result if police who originally came from the North could be utilized. By October 20, if not earlier, An Ho-sang had his rightist youth corps conducting "political indoctrination" in the North.[87]

The P'yŏngyang occupation was a disgrace. American civil affairs officers were "pathetically few" and barely experienced:

> The recruitment of a provisional city council for Pyongyang would have been farcical, if the implications were not so obviously tragic. It was rather like watching an Army sergeant selecting men for fatigue duty. As a result, weeks after the fall of the city there were no public utilities,

85. Cumings (1990), pp. 730–33.
86. National Archives, 795.00 file, box 4268, Durward V. Sandifer to John Hickerson, Aug. 31, 1950, top secret.
87. National Archives, 795.00 file, box 4268, Acheson to Muccio, Oct. 12, 1950.

law and order was evident only on the main streets during the hours of daylight, and the food shortage due to indifferent transport and distribution had assumed serious proportions.[88]

The British had by the end of October clear evidence that the ROK as a matter of official policy sought to "hunt out and destroy communists and collaborators," both from their own people and from experienced British correspondents like Louis Heron of the London *Times;* the facts confirmed "what is now becoming pretty notorious, namely that the restored civil administration in Korea bids fair to become an international scandal of a major kind." The Foreign Office urged that immediate representations be made in Washington, given that the ROK was acting under the name of the United Nations, and because this was "a war for men's minds" in which the political counted almost as much as the military. Ambassador Oliver Franks thus brought the matter up with Dean Rusk on October 30, getting this response: "Rusk agrees that there have regrettably been many cases of atrocities" by the ROK authorities and promises to have American military officers seek to control the situation.[89]

In mid-November, Cho Pyŏng-ok reported that 55,909 "vicious red-hot collaborators and traitors" had been arrested by that date alone, a total that was probably understated. Internal American documents show a full awareness of ROK atrocities; for example, KMAG officers said the entire North might be put off-limits to ROK authorities if they continued the violence, and in one documented instance, in the town of Sunch'ŏn, the Americans replaced marauding South Korean forces with American First Cavalry elements.[90]

Once the Chinese came into the war and the retreat from the North began, newspapers all over the world reported eyewitness accounts of ROK executions of people under detention. United Press International estimated that eight hundred people were executed from December 11 to 16 and buried in mass graves; these included "many women, some children," executed because they were family members of Reds. American and British soldiers witnessed "truckloads [of] old men[,] women[,] youths[,] several children lined before graves and shot down." A British

88. *Times* (London), Nov. 16, 1950.

89. British Foreign Office, handwritten FO notes on FK1015/303, U.S. embassy press translations for Nov. 1, 1950; piece no. 84125, FO memo by R. Murray, Oct. 26, 1950; FO piece no. 84102, Franks memo of discussion with Rusk, Oct. 30, 1950; Heron in *Times* (London), Oct. 25, 1950.

90. *Manchester Guardian,* Dec. 4, 1950; RG338, KMAG file, box 5418, KMAG journal, entries for Nov. 5, 24, 25, 30, 1950.

soldier on December 20 witnessed about forty "emaciated and very subdued Koreans" being shot by ROK military police, their hands tied behind their backs and rifle butts cracked on their heads if they protested.[91]

THE CHINESE ENTRY INTO THE WAR

The general conclusion of all American intelligence agencies was that China would not come into the war. On September 20 the CIA envisioned a possibility that Chinese "volunteers" might enter the fighting, and a month later it noted "a number of reports" that Manchurian units would be sent to Korea. However, it said "the odds are that Communist China, like the USSR, will not openly intervene in North Korea." On November 1 General Walter Bedell Smith, director of the CIA, accurately wrote that the Chinese "probably genuinely fear an invasion of Manchuria" and that they would seek to establish a cordon sanitaire for border security "regardless of the increased risk of general war." But on November 24, as MacArthur lunged forward, the CIA still found insufficient evidence to suggest a Chinese plan for "major offensive operations."[92]

The best-informed media in America were strongly behind the march to the Yalu, and just as incapable of judging Chinese intentions. The *New York Times* editorialized that it was incredible for China to feel threatened by "a free and united Korea"; as the final offensive began, James Reston assured his readers that Washington sources did not think the Chinese would intervene, and an editorial lauded American forces for refusing "to be deterred by Chinese Communist threats."[93] The Indian ambassador to the PRC, Sardar Panikkar, consistently warned that the Chinese would not tolerate a march to the Yalu. On September 26 the PLA chief of staff, Nieh Jung-chen, told him that China would have no option but to resist if the Americans continued to provoke them; when Panikkar said the experience of Korea had shown that the Americans would not spare "a single industrial establishment" in China from bombing, Nieh said that could not be helped. Chou En-lai and the Polish

91. National Archives, 795.00 file, box 4270, carrying UPI and AP dispatches dated Dec. 16, 17, 18, 1950; F0317, piece no. 92847, original letter from Private Duncan, Jan. 4, 1951; Adams to FO, Jan. 8, 1951; UNCURK reports cited in Truman Library, PSF, CIA file, box 248, daily summary, Dec. 19, 1950. See also *Times* (London), Dec. 18, 21, 22, 1950.

92. Truman Library, PSF, CIA file box 250, "Review of the World Situation," Sept. 20 and Oct. 18, 1950; box 248, CIA report of Nov. 1, 1950; CIA report of Nov. 24, 1950, cited in Willoughby Papers, box 10, "The Chinese Communist Potential for Intervention in the Korean War."

93. *New York Times*, Oct. 2, Nov. 19, Nov. 21, 1950.

ambassador to Beijing said similar things, convincing Panikkar that the PRC "had decided on a more aggressive policy, regardless of [the] consequences." A week later Chou called him in and told him China could not tolerate American soldiers' crossing the parallel. But no one was listening, because Panikkar was deemed unreliable. Jessup and Rusk thought him "temporarily following the Party line for ulterior motives"; his "Mephistophelian quality," they wrote, "was not limited to his spade beard."[94]

New North Korean and Chinese materials make clear that China did not enter the war as a defensive measure to protect its border, rather that Mao determined early in the war that if the North Koreans faltered, China had an obligation to come to their aid because of the sacrifice of so many Koreans in the Chinese revolution and the anti-Japanese resistance. On August 4, 1950, Mao told the Politburo of his intention to send troops to Korea "in the name of a volunteer army," should the Americans reverse the tide of battle; Mao decided to intervene immediately after the October 1 crossing of the thirty-eighth parallel, which caused him a sleepless night. The next day he informed Stalin of the decision.[95] In other words, the rollback strategy itself led to the Chinese intervention, not the subsequent arrival of American troops at the Yalu River.

When the first contingents of Chinese soldiers entered Korea, PRC sources cited the Korean volunteers in the Chinese civil war, likening them to Lafayette and his French soldiers in the American revolution, and the Abraham Lincoln Brigade in the Spanish civil war. "We can never forget the Korean people . . . [who] not only participated in the war of liberation but also in the Northern expedition of 1925–27, in the land reform war of 1927–37, and in the anti-Japanese war of 1937–45." Reciprocity thus came first and the defense of the border second; of course, the two would mingle inextricably, reinforcing each other. A third important consideration would be the decisive supplanting of Soviet influence that would follow upon this intervention, a motive unlikely to turn up in documents from the time, but clear in retrospect.

On October 22, KMAG advisers had said that only scattered pockets of resistance were being encountered in the North; the KPA was no longer capable of "an organized defense." Within a few days, however, "fresh, newly equipped North Korean troops" struck the UN front lines savagely, with tanks and air support; ROKA units went reeling back in disarray. Combined Sino-Korean units came roaring out of the mountains at Unsan on October 26, site of the old American gold mine concession, and badly bloodied American forces; the same day KPA attacks

94. F0317, piece no. 83306, High Commissioner to India to FO, Sept. 29, 1950.
95. Cumings (1990), pp. 738–45; Zhang (1995), pp. 63–64, 71–72, 77–78, 81–82.

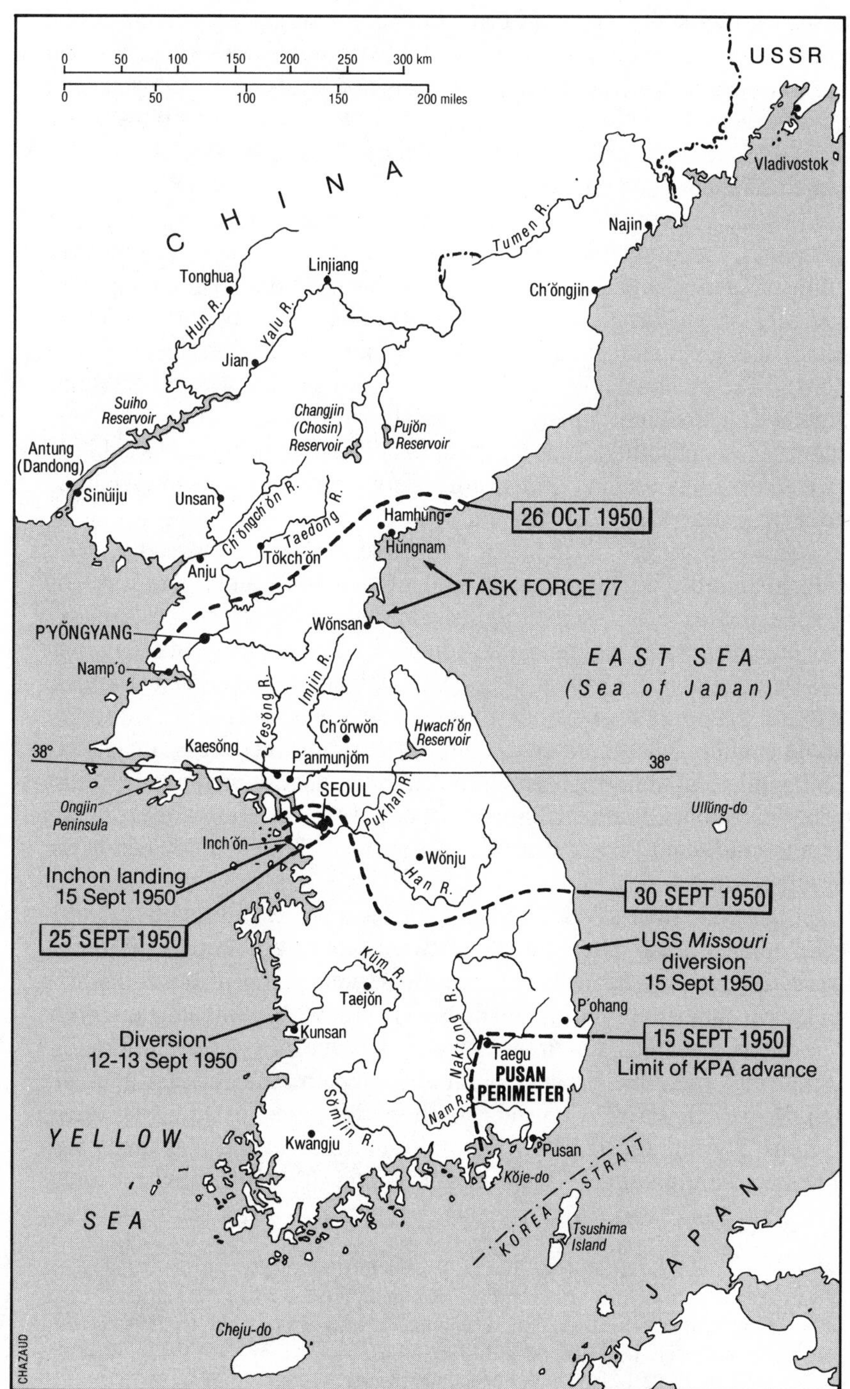

The shifting tide of battle in the Korean War

destroyed the ROKA Second Corps, thus crippling the right flank of the Eighth Army. Edward M. Almond wrote that, on October 26, attacks on the ROK Second Corps caused its "complete collapse and disintegration"; the attackers were "fresh, well organized and well trained unites, *some* of which were Chinese Communist Forces."[96] But shortly the enemy units disappeared again.

CIA daily reports this time caught the pattern of enemy rearward displacement, arguing that such withdrawals had in the past preceded offensive action and noting warily that there were "large, coordinated and well-organized guerrilla forces in the rear area" behind the allied forces, along with guerrilla occupation of "substantial areas in southwest Korea." But as late as November 20 the estimate was still mixed; some argued that the communists were simply withdrawing to better defensive points, and others that the pattern of "giving ground invariably in face of UN units moving northward" merely meant "a delaying action," not preparation for all-out assault.[97]

On November 24 MacArthur launched his euphemistically titled "reconnaissance in force," a general offensive all along the line. He described it as a "massive compression and envelopment," a "pincer" movement to trap remaining KPA forces. On November 25 he flew over the Yalu, dipping the wings of his "SCAP" plane at American troops in Hyesanjin. The offensive rolled forward for three days against little or no resistance, ROK units succeeding in entering the important city of Ch'ŏngjin. Lost amid the hoopla of American victory were reports from pilots that long columns of enemy troops were "swarming all over the countryside"—not to mention the retrieval of Chinese POWs from six different armies.

"Strong enemy attacks" began on November 27, through a "deep envelopment" that chopped allied troops to pieces. American forces were chased away from the Changjin reservoir, the ROK Second Corps collapsed again, and within two days a general withdrawal ensued. From December 3 to 10, G-2 sources noted many reports of guerrilla flanking and envelopment movements south of Hŭngnam. The "intense guerrilla activity which ha[d] occurred in these localities in the past three months" by regrouped KPA units and guerrillas in the rear areas was now coordinating attacks with other KPA and CCF units, their thorough

96. See MacArthur Archives, RG6, box 9, Walker to CINCFE, Nov. 6, 1950 (emphasis added). The best account of these battles from the Chinese side is in Zhang (1995), pp. 101–6. (Some of the dates differ in his account because of time zone differences between Washington and Seoul.)

97. Truman Library, PSF, CIA file, box 248, daily reports, Nov. 9–27, 1950.

General Douglas MacArthur lights his pipe on a run up to the Yalu in his personal plane; the date is November 24, 1950, as his "reconnaissance in depth" began. *Courtesy of U.S. National Archives.*

knowledge of the countryside being "invaluable to attacking CCF units."[98]

By December 6 communist forces occupied P'yŏngyang, and the next day the allied front was only twenty miles above the parallel at its northernmost point. The combined Sino-Korean offensive cleared North Korea of enemy troops in little more than two weeks from its inception. Almond wrote, "we are having a glut of Chinamen." He hoped he would have the chance later "to give these yellow bastards what is coming to them." By the end of December, Seoul was about to fall once again.

As American forces rushed pell-mell back down the peninsula, observers at the time wondered why they were moving so fast, often breaking contact with an enemy not necessarily pursuing them. On December 15 a British military attaché wrote, "The withdrawal continues without any major enemy pressure." There were no signs of defense lines being used to halt the enemy march; it looked like "a phony war," or "a great hoax."[99] British military attachés said in early December that

98. Ibid., daily reports, Nov. 27–Dec. 16, 1950; Almond Papers, "Korean War, Historical Commentary," Almond letters to H. E. Eastwood, Dec. 27, 1950, and W. W. Gretakis, Dec. 27, 1950; MacArthur Archives, RG6, box 68, intelligence summaries nos. 3007–14, Dec. 3–10, 1950.

99. F0317, piece no. 84074, Adams to FO, Dec. 6, 11, 12, 15, 17, 1950.

the numbers of Chinese were quite exaggerated, with "very few confirmed contacts with the Chinese"; furthermore, it was often impossible to judge the nationality of enemy units. The number of Chinese POWs being taken did not indicate huge numbers of troops.

In fact, the Chinese did not, in November and December 1950, commit the enormous forces that Americans then and since have thought they did. The total force was probably around 200,000, not much bigger than the newly recommitted KPA. Of course, the shock effect of Chinese intervention was the critical element in destroying the American rollback into North Korea. But the Korean contribution to the outcome, both in strategy and in fighting power, was also important and has been completely missed in the literature. The evidence makes the indictment of MacArthur's generalship even more devastating. He not only ignored the palpable Chinese threat but got badly outmaneuvered by the KPA generals, who operated with a fraction of MacArthur's matériel—especially Kim Ch'aek, who died of "paralysis of the heart" in February 1951, leading the North Koreans to rename the city of Kanggye for him. Acheson later called this the worst American defeat since Bull Run.

THE PANIC IN WASHINGTON

It is commonly remarked that the Cuban Missile Crisis was the worst and most dangerous of postwar crises; sometimes another one is suggested—for example, President Carter termed Afghanistan the worst of emergencies since 1945. But the defeat of the rollback in northern Korea occasioned the greatest danger, because it bore down upon two axes: the grand global conflict between communism and capitalism, and the internal struggle for the American state between Truman, Acheson, and their substantial opposition, which looked upon MacArthur as a hero. Whether they knew it or not, China and North Korea had perfect aim, decisively reversing the first and greatest attempt to displace a communist state, and simultaneously exploding a temporary and unstable coalition in America that advocated rollback. As 1950 drew to a close, panic gripped the highest levels of government in Washington, and the leaders sought to reverse their crushing defeat by contemplating the use of nearly every weapon in the U.S. arsenal.

The minutes of Truman's cabinet meetings are laced with the grave tension of the moment. The day after the Sino-Korean offensive began, the situation was thought capable of developing into "complete involvement in total war"; by December 9 Truman wrote, "I've worked for peace for five years and six months and it looks like World War III is here. I hope not—but we must meet whatever comes—and we will." Three days later he told the cabinet, "We are faced with an all-out situation," with "total mobilization" and the declaration of national emergency under consideration. National Security Council minutes show a similar alarm, Truman stating that the United States "would not surrender to these murderous Chinese Communists."[100]

Acheson saw an "unparalleled danger" in China's action, calling it "a fresh and unprovoked aggressive act even more immoral than the first," back in June. The next day Truman rattled the atomic bomb at a news conference, saying the United States might use any weapon in its arsenal;[101] it was a threat based on contingency planning to use the bomb, rather than the faux pas so many assumed it to be. It prompted the British prime minister, Clement Attlee, to bolt to Washington and deeply worried Stalin (who later read about the Truman-Attlee meetings, thanks to his well-placed spies).[102] According to a high official in the KGB at the time, Stalin expected global war as a result of the American defeat in northern Korea; fearing that consequence, he favored allowing the United States to occupy all of Korea: "So what?" Stalin said. "Let the United States of America be our neighbors in the Far East. . . . We are not ready to fight."[103] Unlike Stalin, the Chinese were ready, but only to fight down to the middle of the peninsula, rather than to start World War III. Thus within months the war front stabilized. General Ridgway's astute battlefield generalship eventually stiffened the allied lines below Seoul, and he then led gallant fights back northward, recapturing the capital. By the spring of 1951 the fighting stabilized along lines similar to those that today mark the Korean DMZ.[104]

That was where the war ended after another two years of bloody fighting, most of it positional and reminiscent of World War I. But the December crisis also led to the use of, or to the threat to use, what Washington called "weapons of mass destruction": atomic, chemical, and biological weapons.[105] Short of atomic weapons, America rained a fiery destruction from the air with another new weapon, napalm, and later broke massive dams to flood Korea's northern valleys. This is the most

100. Truman Library, Connelly Papers, box 1, cabinet notes, Nov. 28, Dec. 12, 1950; Truman, "Longhand Notes" file, box 333, note for Dec. 9, 1950; PSF, NSC file, box 220, 74th NSC meeting, Dec. 12, 1950.

101. *New York Times,* Nov. 30, Dec. 1, 1950.

102. *New York Times,) Nov. 30, Dec. 1, 1950; see also Modin (1994), pp. 182–84.*

103. Modin (1994), p. 183; Rhodes (1995), pp. 447–48.

104. For the complexities of this stabilization, see Cumings (1990), pp. 751–57; also Zhang (1995), pp. 121–43.

105. American use of biological weapons in Korea has never been proved, but recent Chinese accounts document that Chinese and North Korean leaders certainly thought they faced germ warfare, yielding enormous public health campaigns to inoculate their populations, stamp out vermin, and protect troops with special clothing and gas masks. See Zhang (1995), pp. 7, 181–86.

disturbing aspect of the Korean War, difficult to write and read about; it is what accounted for the remarkable civilian death toll of more than two million.

On November 30, the day of Truman's news conference threatening use of the atomic bomb, Air Force General George Stratemeyer sent an order to General Hoyt Vandenberg that the Strategic Air Command be put on warning "to be prepared to dispatch without delay medium bomb groups to the Far East. . . . [T]his augmentation should include atomic capabilities." Curtis LeMay remembered correctly that the JCS had earlier concluded that atomic weapons would probably not be useful in Korea, except as part of "an overall atomic campaign against Red China." If the orders were now changed, however, LeMay wanted the job: he told Stratemeyer that his headquarters was the only one with the experience, technical training, and "intimate knowledge" of delivery methods. The man who directed the firebombing of Tokyo was again ready to proceed to the Far East to direct the attacks.[106]

Prime Minister Attlee sensed that Truman was serious about using the bomb, and amid "grave perturbation" in London he left immediately for Washington. He knew that the United States had a strong advantage in atomic weaponry over the Soviets at this time, it possessed about 450 weapons and the Soviets 25. There was general disagreement between the British and American representatives in several days of meetings; according to Foreign Office records the Americans pushed for a "limited war" against China, including air attacks, a blockade of the coast, and covert introduction of anticommunist forces in southern China; General Marshall, however, had doubts about the "efficacy and success" of such a program. Attlee sought a written promise that the bomb would not be used in Korea, but Truman would give him only oral assurances. Attlee told the French prime minister that he thought American threats to use the bomb would suggest that "Europeans and Americans have a low regard for the value of Asiatic lives," and that such weapons should be reserved for times when "desperate measures" were warranted—"certainly not [in] a conflict in which the U.S. were confronted with a Power like Korea."[107]

MacArthur on December 9 said that he desired commander's discretion to use atomic weapons; on December 24 he submitted "a list of retardation targets" for which he needed twenty-six atomic bombs. He also wanted four to drop on the "invasion forces" and four more for "critical concentrations of enemy air power." In interviews published

106. Vandenberg Papers, Library of Congress, box 86, Stratemeyer to Vandenberg, Nov. 30, 1950; LeMay to Vandenberg, Dec. 2, 1950. See also Rhodes (1995), pp. 444–46.
107. Cumings (1990), p. 749.

posthumously, he said he had a plan that would have won the war in ten days: "I would have dropped between 30 and 50 atomic bombs . . . strung across the neck of Manchuria." Then he would have introduced half a million Nationalist troops at the Yalu, and then "spread behind us—from the Sea of Japan to the Yellow Sea—a belt of radioactive cobalt . . . [which] has an active life of between 60 and 120 years. For at least 60 years there could have been no land invasion of Korea from the North." He expressed certainty that the Russians would have done nothing: "my plan was a cinch."[108]

Cobalt 60 has 320 times the radioactivity of radium. One 400-ton cobalt H-bomb, Carroll Quigley wrote, could wipe out all animal life on earth. MacArthur sounds like a warmongering lunatic in these interviews, but if so he was not alone. Before the Sino-Korean offensive, a committee of the JCS had said that atomic bombs might be the "decisive factor" in cutting off a Chinese advance into Korea; initially they could be useful in "a 'cordon sanitaire' [that] might be established by the U.N. in a strip in Manchuria immediately north of the Manchurian border." A few months later Congressman Albert Gore complained that "Korea has become a meat grinder of American manhood," and suggested "something cataclysmic" to end the war: a radiation belt dividing the Korean peninsula. Although Ridgway said nothing about a cobalt bomb, in May 1951 he renewed MacArthur's request of December 24, this time for thirty-eight atomic bombs.[109] It was not approved.

The United States came closest to using atomic weapons in early April 1951, precisely the time that Truman removed MacArthur. It is now clear that Truman removed MacArthur not simply because of his repeated insubordination but because he wanted a reliable commander on the scene if Washington decided to use nuclear weapons: that is, Truman traded MacArthur for his atomic policies. On March 10, 1951, MacArthur asked for a " 'D' Day atomic capability," to retain air superiority in the Korean theater, after the Soviets moved thirteen air divisions to the vicinity of Korea and put two hundred Soviet bombers into airbases in Manchuria (from which they could strike not just Korea but American bases in Japan), and after the Chinese massed huge new forces near the Korean border. On March 14 Vandenberg wrote, "Finletter and Lovett alerted on atomic discussions. Believe everything is set." At the end of March, Stratemeyer reported that atomic bomb loading pits at Kadena

108. Cumings (1990), p. 750; Willoughby Papers, box 8, interviews by Bob Considine and Jim Lucas in 1954, printed in *New York Times*, April 9, 1964.
109. Carroll Quigley, *Tragedy and Hope: A History of the World in Our Time* (New York: Macmillan, 1966), p. 875; Quigley was President Bill Clinton's favorite teacher at Georgetown University. See also Cumings (1990), p. 750.

air base, on Okinawa, were operational; the bombs were carried there unassembled, and put together at the base—lacking only the essential nuclear cores. On April 5 the JCS ordered immediate atomic retaliation against Manchurian bases if large numbers of new troops came into the fighting or, it appears, if bombers were launched against American assets from there.

That same day Gordon Dean, chairman of the Atomic Energy Commission, began arrangements for transferring nine Mark IV nuclear capsules to the air force's Ninth Bomb Group, the designated carrier of the weapons. General Bradley (JCS chairman) got Truman's approval for this transfer of the Mark IV's "from AEC to military custody" on April 6, and the president signed an order to use them against Chinese and North Korean targets. The Ninth Group deployed out to Guam. "In the confusion attendant upon General MacArthur's removal," however, the order was never sent. The reasons were two: Truman had used this extraordinary crisis to get the JCS to approve MacArthur's removal (something Truman announced on April 11), and the Chinese and the Soviets did not escalate the war. So the bombs were not used. But the nine Mark IV's remained in air force custody after their transfer on April 11. The Ninth Bomb Group remained on Guam, however, and did not move on to the loading pits at Kadena AFB, on Okinawa.[110]

The JCS again considered the use of nuclear weapons in June 1951, this time in tactical battlefield circumstances, and there were many more such suggestions as the war continued to 1953. Robert Oppenheimer went to Korea as part of Project Vista, designed to gauge the feasibility of a tactical use of atomic weapons. In early 1951 a young man named Samuel Cohen, on a secret assignment for the Defense Department, observed the battles for the second recapture of Seoul and thought there should be a way to destroy the enemy without destroying the city. He became the father of the neutron bomb.[111]

Perhaps the most daunting and terrible project, however, was Operation Hudson Harbor. It appears to have been part of a larger project involving "overt exploitation in Korea by the Department of Defense and covert exploitation by the Central Intelligence Agency of the possible use of novel weapons." This project sought to establish the capability to use atomic weapons on the battlefield, and in pursuit of this goal lone B-29

110. Cumings (1990), pp. 750–51; Rhodes (1995), pp. 448–51.

111. Samuel Cohen was a childhood friend of Herman Kahn; see Fred Kaplan, *The Wizards of Armageddon* (New York: Simon and Schuster, 1983), p. 220. On Oppenheimer and Project Vista, see Cumings (1990), pp. 751–52; also David C. Elliot, "Project Vista and Nuclear Weapons in Europe," *International Security* (Summer 1986): 163–83.

bombers were lifted from Okinawa in September and October 1951 and sent over North Korea on simulated atomic bombing runs, dropping "dummy" A-bombs or heavy TNT bombs. The project called for "actual functioning of all activities which would be involved in an atomic strike, including weapons assembly and testing, leading, ground control of bomb aiming," and the like. The project indicated that the bombs were probably not useful, for purely technical reasons: "timely identification of large masses of enemy troops was extremely rare."[112] But one may imagine the steel nerves required of leaders in P'yŏngyang, observing a lone B-29 simulating the attack lines that had resulted in the devastation of Hiroshima and Nagasaki just five years earlier, each time unsure whether the bomb was real or a dummy.

The record also shows that massive use of chemical weapons against Sino-North Korean forces was considered. In penciled diary notes written on December 16, Ridgway referred cryptically to a subcommittee on "clandestine introduction [of] wea[pon]s of mass destruction and unconventional warfare." I know nothing more about this item, but it may refer to his apparent request of MacArthur that chemical weapons be used in Korea. The original of Ridgway's telegram is unavailable, but MacArthur's reply on January 7, 1951, reads, "I do not believe there is any chance of using chemicals on the enemy in case evacuation is ordered. As you know, U.S. inhibitions on such use are complete and drastic. . . ." The transcript of a conference the next day with Almond and others says, "If we use gas we will lay ourselves open to retaliation. This question has been taken up with General MacArthur for decision. We have requested sufficient quantities to be shipped immediately in the event use of gas is approved."[113]

Without the use of "novel weapons"—although napalm was very new at the time, introduced just at the end of the World War II, and unprecedentedly big conventional bombs were dropped—the air war nonetheless leveled North Korea and killed millions before the war ended. From early November 1950 on, MacArthur ordered that a wasteland be created between the front and the Chinese border, destroying from the air every "installation, factory, city, and village" over thousands of square miles of North Korean territory. On November 8, seventy B-29's dropped 550 tons of incendiary bombs on Sinŭiju, "removing [it] from off the map"; a week later Hoeryŏng was hit with napalm "to burn out the place"; by November 25 "a large part of [the] North West *[sic]* area between Yalu

112. Cumings (1990), p. 752.

113. Ridgway Papers, box 20, MacArthur to Ridgway, Jan. 7, 1951; memo of Ridgway's conference with Almond and others, Jan. 8, 1951.

River and southwards to enemy lines . . . [was] more or less burning." Soon the area would be a "wilderness of scorched earth."[114]

This was all before the major Sino-Korean offensive. With that, the air force on December 14–15 hit P'yŏngyang with seven hundred 500-pound bombs, napalm dropped from Mustang fighters, and 175 tons of delayed-fuse demolition bombs, which land with a thud and then blow up at odd moments, when people are trying to rescue the dead from the napalm fires. Ridgway ordered the air force to hit P'yŏngyang "with the goal of burning the city to the ground with incendiary bombs," in two strikes on January 3 and 5. At about the same time American B-29's dropped "tarzon" bombs on Kanggye; these were enormous new 12,000-pound bombs never tried before. As Americans retreated below the parallel, the scorched-earth policy of "torching" continued, burning Ŭijŏngbu, Wŏnju, and other small cities in the South as the enemy got near them.[115]

From Wŏnsan southward guerrillas had established themselves in many places, as we have seen, and the air war was extended to root them out through the creation of free-fire zones. Ridgway on January 5 "desired that consideration be given to the napalming of villages" on the axis of the enemy advance. Almond put the rationale as follows on January 16:

> We know that guerrilla bands with which we are now contending are going to be in our flanks and rear continuously, and we must fight them by every means available. Air strikes with napalm against those guerrilla bands wherever found is a most effective way to destroy not only the bands themselves, but the huts and villages in the areas they retire to.

The guerrillas hole up in villages in the day, he said, "and come out at night." Thus he "instituted a campaign of burning these huts."

General Barr flew over the vicinity of T'anyang on January 18, giving this description:

> Smoke from flaming villages and huts has filled valleys [in the] vicinity [of] Tangyang *[sic]* with smoke three thousand feet deep and blinded all my observations and created [a] flying hazard. . . . Methodical burning of dwellings is producing hostile reaction. . . . People cannot understand why US troops burn homes when no enemy present. . . . Methodical burning out poor farmers when no enemy present is against the grain of US soldiers. From house burning we already have estimated

114. Cumings (1990), p. 753.

115. Cumings (1990), pp. 753–54; *New York Times,* Dec. 13 1950, Jan. 3, 1951; Blair (1987), p. 603.

> 8000 refugees and expect more. These are mostly the old, crippled, and children.

Thus Barr recommended to Almond "selective" rather than "methodical" burning. Almond responded that Barr's orders were not to burn indiscriminately, but "to select and burn out those villages in which guerrillas or enemy forces were being harbored, willingly or unwillingly . . . and those habitations forward of front line positions or in isolated mountain fastnesses from which guerrillas could not otherwise be barred." Almond did not seem to understand that his orders amounted precisely to what Barr had observed, a free-fire zone against anything that moved. In any case, on January 25 he continued to defend the firing of villages, carrying the logic through to its conclusion: the local population was being killed, true, but "the meager population remaining appears sympathetic to and harbors the enemy."[116]

A bit later George Barrett of the *New York Times* found "a macabre tribute to the totality of modern war" in a village north of Anyang:

> The inhabitants throughout the village and in the fields were caught and killed and kept the exact postures they held when the napalm struck—a man about to get on his bicycle, fifty boys and girls playing in an orphanage, a housewife strangely unmarked, holding in her hand a page torn from a Sears-Roebuck catalogue crayoned at Mail Order No. 3,811,294 for a $2.98 "bewitching bed jacket—coral."

Acheson wanted censorship authorities notified about this kind of "sensationalized reporting," so it could be stopped. Ridgway later had second thoughts about the firing of towns:

> I have been struck by those areas I have visited which had formerly been occupied by the CCF [Chinese]. There appeared to have been little or no vandalism committed. . . . You have my full authority [to safeguard your troops]. . . . [T]his does not, however, extend to the wanton destruction of towns and villages, by gun-fire or bomb, unless there is good reason to believe them occupied.[117]

This did not seem to make much difference in policy. By 1952 just about everything in northern and central Korea was completely leveled. What was left of the population survived in caves, the North Koreans creating an entire life underground, in complexes of dwellings, schools,

116. Ridgway Papers, box 20, highlights of conference with Ridgway, Jan. 5, 1951; box 17, Almond to Ridgway, Jan. 16, 1951, and Almond to Ridgway, Jan. 25, 1951; Almond Papers, "General Files, X Corps," Barr to Almond, Jan. 18, 1951; Almond to Barr, Jan. 19, 1951.
117. Cumings (1990), p. 755.

hospitals, and factories. In spite of World War II bombing studies showing that such attacks against civilian populations only stiffened enemy resistance, American officials sought to use aerial bombing as a type of psychological and social warfare. As Robert Lovett later put it, "If we keep on tearing the place apart, we can make it a most unpopular affair for the North Koreans. We ought to go right ahead."[118] The Americans did go right ahead and in the final act of this barbaric air war hit huge irrigation dams that provided water for 75 percent of the North's food production.

On June 20, 1953, the *New York Times* announced the execution of Julius and Ethel Rosenberg at Sing Sing Prison; in the fine print of daily war coverage the U.S. Air Force stated that its planes bombed dams at Kusŏng and Tŏksan in North Korea, and in even finer print the North Korean radio acknowledged "great damage" to these large reservoirs. By this time agriculture was the only major element of the economy still functioning; the attacks came just after the laborious, backbreaking work of rice transplantation had been done in the spring of 1953. The air force was proud of the destruction created: "The subsequent flash flood scooped clean 27 miles of valley below, and the plunging flood waters wiped out [supply routes, etc.]. . . . The Westerner can little conceive the awesome meaning which the loss of [rice] has for the Asian—starvation and slow death."

Many villages were inundated, "washed downstream," and even P'yŏngyang, some twenty-seven miles south of one dam, was badly flooded. According to the official air force history, when the high containing wall of the Tŏksan reservoir collapsed, the onrushing flood destroyed six miles of railway, five bridges, two miles of highway, and five square miles of rice paddies. After the war it took 200,000 man-days of labor to reconstruct the reservoir. The Pujŏn River dam was also hit; it was built in 1932, designed to hold 670 million cubic meters of water, and the pressure gradient was 999 meters; the dam station generated a 200,000-kilowatt capacity from the water, which then flowed down into rice paddies for irrigation.[119]

There is no record of how many peasants perished in the assault on this and several other dams, but they were assumed to be "loyal" to the enemy, providing "direct support to the Communist armed forces." (That is, they were feeding the northern population.) The "lessons" adduced from this experience "gave the enemy a sample of the totality

118. Truman Library, Connelly Papers, "Notes on Cabinet Meetings," Sept. 12, 1952. I am indebted to Barton Bernstein for calling this reference to my attention.
119. Lautensach (1945), p. 202.

Korean People's Army Major General Chang Pyŏng-san leads the Sino-Korean negotiating team out of the truce talks at Kaesŏng, 1951. *Courtesy of U.S. National Archives.*

of war . . . embracing the whole of a nation's economy and people."[120] Tibor Meray was a Hungarian correspondent in North Korea during the war, and left Budapest for Paris after his participation in the 1956 rebellion against communism. When a Thames Television team interviewed him in 1986, he said that however brutal Koreans on either side might have been in this war, he "saw destruction and horrible things committed by the American forces": "Everything which moved in North Korea was a military target, peasants in the fields often were machine gunned by pilots who I, this was my impression, amused themselves to shoot the targets which moved." Meray had crossed the Yalu in August 1951 and witnessed "a complete devastation between the Yalu River and the

120. "The Attack on the Irrigation Dams in North Korea," *Air University Quarterly,* 6, no. 4 (Winter 1953–54): 40–51.

capital," P'yŏngyang. There were simply "no more cities in North Korea." The incessant, indiscriminate bombing forced his party always to drive by night: "We travelled in moonlight, so my impression was that I am travelling on the moon, because there was only devastation. . . . [E]very city was a collection of chimneys. I don't know why houses collapsed and chimneys did not, but I went through a city of 200,000 inhabitants and I saw thousands of chimneys and that—that was all."[121]

This was Korea, "the limited war." We may leave as an epitaph for this unrestrained air war the views of its architect, General Curtis LeMay. After the war started, he said,

> we slipped a note kind of under the door into the Pentagon and said, "Look, let us go up there . . . and burn down five of the biggest towns in North Korea—and they're not very big—and that ought to stop it." Well, the answer to that was four or five screams—"You'll kill a lot of non-combatants," and "It's too horrible." Yet over a period of three years or so . . . we burned down *every [sic]* town in North Korea and South Korea, too. . . . Now, over a period of three years this is palatable, but to kill a few people to stop this from happening—a lot of people can't stomach it.[122]

CONCLUSION

When the war finally ended on July 27, 1953, the North had been devastated by three years of bombing attacks that hardly left a modern building standing. Both Koreas had watched as a virtual holocaust ravaged their country and turned the vibrant expectations of 1945 into a nightmare. The point to remember is that this was a civil war, and, as a British diplomat once said, "every country has a right to have its War of the Roses." The true tragedy was not the war itself, for a civil conflict purely among Koreans might have resolved the extraordinary tensions generated by colonialism, national division and foreign intervention. The tragedy was that the war solved nothing: only the status quo ante was restored, only an armistice held the peace. Today the tensions and the problems remain.

121. Thames Television, transcript from the fifth seminar for "Korea: The Unknown War" (Nov. 1986); Thames interview with Tibor Meray (also 1986).

122. J. F. Dulles Papers, Princeton University, Curtis LeMay oral history, April 28, 1966.

CHAPTER SIX

Korean Sun Rising: Industrialization, 1953–Present

Ch'ŏl ŭn kungnyŏk *(Steel = National Power)* —*Park Chung Hee*

The Korean state has moved from a dependent, penetrated status to one of relative autonomy by positioning itself astride the flow of foreign capital, refracting capital in a prismatic fashion to fund rising industries, create mammoth firms, buttress its social support, and in dialectical fashion wrest national autonomy from the external system. —*Jung-en Woo*[1]

With that observation we can perhaps begin to explain the unexpected outcome of a Republic of Korea that, as this is being written, has a gross national product about the size of Spain's. This republic was dependent, almost completely so. First it was a colony, then it was occupied by a foreign army, then the United States retrieved it from oblivion in the summer of 1950. It was penetrated, not least by an American general commanding its army and full divisions of foreign troops. Lacking much domestic capital, the state found a way to use foreign capital and earnings both to reward its friends and to promote efficient production. It fostered one rising industry after another, starting with simple assembly operations and ending with gigaflop microprocessors etched in infinitesimally small lines upon silicon wafers. It created from scratch octopus-like firms now known to the world as *chaebŏl* (the Korean pronunciation of the characters for *zaibatsu*). In conditions of often stunning political and social dislocation, it worked effectively to build support and slowly to legitimate its hell-bent-for-leather development program. Ultimately it will wrest from the great powers that divided it a unified Korea which will be among the advanced industrial nations of the next century.

This industrial success is not something that the elder George Kennan or our good Fabian Beatrice Webb would ever have predicted. Nor was

1. Woo (1991), pp. 6–7.

it something any Japanese or American predicted before 1960 or so. But it happened, making for a sharp break, another rupture, both in Korean history and in our understanding of it. As it happened, much of our understanding of what it takes to build a strong capitalist system was thrown into question, Western conceits get mirrored back to ourselves, and pundits scratch around for something to explain it: must've been a miracle.

One scholar locates several causes of this growth that somehow did not occur to anybody else, or hardly anybody;[2] that Korea grew precisely *because* it lacked a class of capitalists, local versions of which kept getting in the way of growth in Latin America, for example; that Japanese imperialism not merely took but gave—"a colonially bequeathed strong state," among other things; that "Confucianism," Protestant or work ethic, and other cultural factors neither hindered nor helped this process; that "foreign capital," which one radical after another condemned since the first banker made a loan to a foreign country, was systematically put to good and different use by precisely the central government bureaucrats whom Republican free marketeers rail against; not to mention that Korea grew by the bureaucrats' endeavoring to "get prices wrong," in Alice Amsden's wonderful phrase,[3] instead of letting free markets get them right. South Korea, truncated into half a country, with almost no natural resources, a thoroughly uprooted and aggrieved population, no domestic capital to speak of, a minuscule domestic market, and a work force long claimed to be lazy louts (a common Japanese refrain)—and still here is this industrial country, this "miracle on the Han." There you have it: no capitalists, no Protestants, no merchants, no money, no market, no resources, no get-up-and-go, let alone no discernible history of commerce, foreign trade, or industrial development, so on and so forth—and yet there it is.

Nonetheless, Korea enjoyed comparative advantages. As early as 1888 Percival Lowell remarked of East Asian education, as compared to that of the West, "if the peaks of intellect rise less eminent, the plateau of general elevation stands higher."[4] He was wrong about the "peaks," but right about the egalitarian belief, ultimately deriving from Confucian philosophy, in the inherent perfectibility of all humans. Translated into a compulsory school system through the elementary level in the 1950s and 1960s, and later including middle and high school levels, the broad Korean work force was better suited to industrial tasks than was the population of many other countries. The long tradition of bureaucratic

2. Woo (1991).
3. Amsden (1989).
4. Lowell (1888-B), p. 7.

governance by scholar-officials, reaching preindustrial peaks as high as anywhere else, was excellent background for a state-led development program. As Etienne Balazs has argued, such people were also technocrats: their speciality was statecraft above all, but also agriculture, irrigation, hydraulic control of everything from rivers to lakes and reservoirs, military technology (armaments), even rockets (where, for example, the Chinese excelled; the American rocket program was a combined German-Chinese effort).[5] The state was the embodiment of knowledge. Why should the state not play a major role in the economy?

Perhaps now we can begin, where we left off: with the war. What role did the war play in Korea's subsequent economic growth, other than dramatically to delay it? Both Koreas were shattered by this fratricidal conflict, although the North suffered much more destruction in three years of intensive bombing than the South did in the nine months of warfare before the front stabilized in 1951. What the Japanese had begun with their massive shifts of Korean population in 1935–45, what the national division had intensified, the Korean War completed: Koreans of all classes were now thoroughly displaced from their local roots. Everyone was jostled or pushed or thrown bodily out of his or her social niche.

Relatively wealthy refugee families from the P'yŏngan region in the North crowded together in Seoul after the war; Seoul's wealthy, who had spent many months sheltered behind the Pusan perimeter, now returned to the capital; masses of common people led a hand-to-mouth existence, moving hither and yon looking for work or lost relatives and trying to recapture whatever life they had before 1950. The one cohesive social class, perhaps, consisted of the absentee landlords whose property was based in the southwest Hŏnam region. The radical land reform in the summer of 1950 and the reformist distribution of 1951 dispossessed many of them, but also gave many a continued advantage through disguised tenancy (which experts estimated at 20 percent of the arable land total in the South), the state bonds they had been given for their land, or the social prestige that was still accorded the aristocracy and that expressed itself in the educational and cultural institutions of the capital. Their political power, however, was now mostly gone. Above all, their capacity to control the people "below them," in clan, clientele, and tenancy lineages, and their continuous tendency to control markets and stifle enterprise, was blasted to smithereens. People could no longer be frozen in place in rural settings: two successive wars had set them loose. In a country with such solidity of lineage and place, there now arrived

5. See Iris Chang, *Thread of the Silkworm* (New York: Basic Books, 1995), a biography of Tsien Hsüe-shen, who helped design American rockets at the Jet Propulsion Laboratory and then became the father of China's missile program.

the time of Thomas Hobbes's "masterless men," harbingers of anomie and modernity. Here is the deep meaning of the axiom that war is the great equalizer.

In place of the aristocracy came entrepreneurs who had built up wealth through the auxiliary supply of warfare, a small but growing middle class of people engaged in commerce or attached to the enormous foreign presence and its many organizations, and rough people who had prospered at the nexus of human despair through moneylending and corruption, or simply the provision of services otherwise scarce in wartime (clothing, shelter, food, drink, sex). All these people were fertilized by the inconceivable amounts of American cash that flowed into the country, down from the presidential mansion, through the bureaucracies civil and military, coursing through the PXs and onto the black market, into the pockets of a horde of people who serviced the foreign presence: drivers, guards, runners, valets, maids, houseboys, black-market operators, money changers, prostitutes, and beggars. Chŏng Chu-yŏng, later the billionaire chairman of the Hyundai Corporation, had run a small auto repair shop before the war, but got his big break by ferrying supplies to American bases on half-ton trucks or constructing billets. Many of the other *chaebŏl* groups got going at this time, with little connection to big enterprise before the war.

War is also a devil of heartbreak and an angel of destruction. Let's face it, the "modern" era is the throw-away era, a time for things that would never have occurred to a yangban aristocrat: planned obsolescence, unplanned obsolescence, innovative obsolescence, insured obsolescence, uninsured act-of-God obsolescence. Piled-up, useless inventories, tax incentives to recycle every twenty years, junked cars, abandoned houses, empty buildings, empty and homeless people. I remember asking Koreans who came to the United States in the 1960s what they most liked about America, and many said "used cars and yard sales." You can take a $35,000 Mercedes, put 75,000 miles on it, and then drop a perfectly good car, built to last a lifetime, on the market at give-away prices. Or you can outfit a complete household with a few mornings spent at the flea market or the "swap meets" that Koreans specialize in and that became part of the national vocabulary after the 1992 Los Angeles riots. For both South and North Korea the war renovated plant and industry in the flash of phosphorous, just as Curtis LeMay's bombers cleaned Japan's slate in 1944–45, making it possible to build up inventory again with the latest technology.

Standing above all the disorganization and human fragments of post-1953 Korea was a Korean military that had swelled from 100,000 in 1950 to well over 600,000 by 1953. It was now the strongest, most cohesive, best-organized institution in Korean life, and it would soon make its political power felt. Meanwhile, national conscription sent every male who could not bribe his way out through its brand of education: boot camps, drills, discipline, patriotism, anticommunism, and an authoritarian practice that chilled even the most hard-bitten American officers. The Korean military fought no more wars (save for some tens of thousands who went to Vietnam), but in the next thirty years it provided a school for industrial discipline. It was Max Weber, after all, who once likened the modern factory to a military organization, so the military's relevance to Korea's economic development is abundant.

Wealth came later, however. South Korea in the 1950s was a terribly depressing place, where extreme privation and degradation touched everyone. Cadres of orphans ran through the streets, forming little protective and predatory bands of ten or fifteen; beggars with every affliction or war injury importuned anyone with a wallet, often traveling in bunches of maimed or starved adults holding children or babies; half-ton trucks full of pathetic women careened onto military bases for the weekend, so they could sell whatever services they had. Even twenty years after the war ended Felliniesque residues of this tragedy remained, in the dreadful slums of Ch'ŏnggyech'ŏn in downtown Seoul or the packs of orphans who still begged in the streets or traveled in boxcars on the trains.

A woman from one of Seoul's wealthiest families once told me she had been able to save only a handful of diamonds when the war began in June 1950; her husband killed, she lived at the margins of Pusan's vast agglomeration of refugee camps, trying to feed several young children. Upon her return to Seoul she was able to reoccupy the family residence, only to find less than half of it still standing and refugees from the North living in what was left. The ordeal had been so shattering that she resolved, should another war come, simply to commit suicide. Ahn Junghyo, a well-known novelist in Seoul, wrote this about his family's existence in Inch'ŏn just after the war:

> My father worked as a carpenter at the American base . . . and Mother ran a small shop at a nearby intersection of a three-forked road. Every day I used to go to the garbage dump a little distance off from my house. Often my foot was cut by a used razor blade, on the sharp teeth of a broken saw or a jagged lid of a can, but the cuts were worth it because the whole family could feast on pig soup at dinner if I happened to find a piece of meat among the garbage. . . . Sometimes you would have good fortune and unearth oranges, Hershey chocolate wrapped in sleek brown paper or Brach's jelly candies of five different colors shining like jewels in their cellophane wrappers. One day the American soldiers dumped a heap of chicken legs that had quite a lot of meat still hanging. . . . Mother boiled a delicious soup with those

bones and meat and barley, even adding some precious rice. Where had I found all those chicken legs, Father asked me. I told him. That night, he took a rusty tin bucket from the kitchen and asked me to show him the way to the dump.[6]

WORKING UNCLE SAM

This story, wrenching as it is, nonetheless suggests that the South was a place for creative enterprise in the 1950s, which quite reasonably consisted of sucking the American teat for all it was worth. Every single American, from GI to ambassador, possessed more than virtually any Korean. Americans of modest income could amass fortunes just by trading cigarette cartons for Koryŏ celadon vases or Yi dynasty mahogany chests. Koreans therefore attached themselves to Americans by any means necessary, hoping against hope to get to America—uniformly conceived as a country where the streets were paved with gold, a fabulous PX in the sky. This is by no means an exaggeration, since the American post exchanges were the main supply line for the Korean black market and since the American military commander controlled the entire U.S. aid program from 1951 to 1959.[7] As late as 1972, middle-class friends would ask me to buy scarce items for them with hard currency at the foreigners' commissary.

The common subject of discussion among American expatriates in the 1950s was what a bizarre and muddled octogenarian Syngman Rhee was, especially when it came to the economy. He would waste money building fences around the refugee camps in Pusan, as if thereby no one would know they were there. He was expected to explain how every American aid dollar was spent, but kept the embassy in the dark, not to mention the members his own cabinet, who had never heard of this rule. Inflation, the crippling fever of the business cycle, was nothing to him—call the mint and print some more *hwan*. It is quite amazing to discover that while Kim Il Sung was positioning Pang Ho-san's crack division above Haeju and Paek Sŏn-yŏp was redeploying the ROK Army from the guerrilla zones to the thirty-eighth parallel, the State Department was complaining all through the spring of 1950 about inflation. No doubt it thought if inflation worsened Rhee would go the way of Chiang Kai-shek, but then Chiang never had a small army of American nannies looking over his shoulder and putting candy in front of him every day.

What was Syngman Rhee's political economy? In a nutshell, it was

6. Ahn Junghyo, *White Badge* (New York: Soho Press, 1989), p. 54.
7. Macdonald (1992), p. 114.

"Give us everything Japan has and give it to us tomorrow." Rhee wanted a full-blown industrial economy, with the young industries incubated behind a wall of protection—above all, protection from Japan. In this he was by no means alone. I remember a conference once when Linda Lim, a fine scholar from the University of Michigan, was asked if Malaysia was following the Korean model. Heavens no, she exclaimed, "the Koreans are Marxists, they want everything, but Malaysia will look for export niches that it can fill." And by that she meant that Rhee and his successors, like Joseph Stalin, wanted a full-blown, self-reliant industrial base with steel, chemicals, machine tools, and the electric energy to run them. Since a combination of Japanese investment in the 1930s and Stalinist investment to rebuild North Korea in the 1950s had given Kim Il Sung the same thing, Rhee's desires were completely overdetermined: South Korea had to be another Japan.

What did the United States want? A Republican administration wanted to cut back on the money going to people like Rhee and the immense outflows to defend them, in the form of American troops—at least that is what Treasury Secretary George Humphrey wanted, saying so in several memorable NSC outbursts. But that is not the whole story. The United States was willing to indulge certain countries, especially places like Korea sitting on the fault lines of the Cold War, so that they could become self-supporting and compete in world markets. If that meant hothouse protection for their cement industry, so be it. The Joint Chiefs of Staff had still other ideas: posting huge armies like that in South Korea along these same fault lines, in order to contain communism. (The doctrine of containment may have been formed in the mind of George Kennan, but it was the army that had to build the dikes and plug the holes around the world.) The 600,000-man armies in Korea and Taiwan were expensive, to be sure, but they were the sandbags holding back the onrushing waters for a disarmed Japan and a stretched United States.

Thus you hardly got free-market economics in the 1950s, in spite of a Republican administration. Rhee followed what specialists call "import substitution industrialization," or ISI, with nearly full American support. If he couldn't get the State Department to go along, General James Van Fleet would intervene and get it done: after all, the ROK was also our courageous Free World ally:

> Korea was a "client" state, led nevertheless by a recalcitrant, putative nationalist. It had a political system where autocracy commingled with party politics and semifascist mobilization, thriving on a system-wide corruption, but this pastiche still carried the U.S. cachet of liberal democracy. Said to be an economic failure, the ROK was still an unac-

countably expensive one, making unprecedented inroads on the U.S. Treasury in the form of billions of dollars in aid.[8]

Syngman Rhee was a past master at this business, wheedling so many direct grants out of the United States that by the end of the 1950s they accounted for five-sixths of all Korean imports. That was the "legal" or registered total. Meanwhile, immense cases of corruption unfolded under Rhee, whether it was the tungsten export case of 1952, the cotton import case of 1954,[9] or many similar scams. Apparently Rhee and his wife took little for themselves, but they did make effective arrangements to enrich cabinet officials, political friends, and cronies. Indeed, almost every major business project in the 1950s would have to pass through his office. There was thus method to his madness, as Jung-en Woo has argued.

But what an affront this was to liberal and free-market American virtues! Syngman Rhee was "an Oriental bargainer," a "master of evasion," said John Foster Dulles, while Eisenhower complained about Rhee's "blackmail." Richard Nixon once called him either a gambler or a communist or both, giving the Republicans a lesson in bluffing and brinkmanship. Rhee extracted "maximum 'rents' from the global hegemon," using the ROK's immense geopolitical leverage granted by the Cold War and his own inveterate skills as a tough poker player willing to cash in the whole game, knowing the United States had no one else to rely on but him.[10] Like the comedian Richard Pryor, Syngman Rhee knew there was a place for money in this world: in his pocket. That it happened to be American taxpayers' money was the least of his worries. Was this irrationality or Woo's "method to his madness"? With such mind-boggling flows of cash, why should Rhee have done anything else but figure out more ways to wheedle dough out of Eisenhower?

Official sources say that about $12 billion of the American treasury went to Korea in the years 1945–65.[11] We have seen that aid funds alone amounted to 100 percent of the ROK government budget in the 1950s. We always hear that Korea in 1960 had a per capita income of $100. If so, with about 20 million people in the country, you just add two zeroes and get a figure of $2 billion for national income. Official figures show $12 billion going to Korea over twenty years, that is, $600 million per year in official transfers alone. Using different figures, another analyst comes up with an annual American per capita assistance figure of $600

8. Woo (1991), p. 44.
9. On the former see Cumings (1990), pp. 469–71; on the latter see Macdonald (1992), p. 178.
10. Woo (1991), p. 44.
11. Ogle (1990), p. 35.

from 1945 to 1976—that is, $600 for every Korean man, woman, and child for thirty years. One high point was 1957, when Korea drew $383 million in economic assistance from the United States, as against $456 million in domestic revenue. But then there was an additional $400 million in military aid in 1957, and another $300 million for the costs of U.S. troops in Korea. The military aid figure is considerably higher than that for all of Europe and four times that for all of Latin America.[12] These are simple calculations, but the magnitudes are amazing. The figures leave out what there is no way to count—namely, the hundreds of thousands of Americans who spent money in Korea for one thing or another, nor can they account for the informal but often gargantuan exchanges of the curb money market and the black market, really a complete underground economy that makes a figure of $100 per year in per capita income grossly uninformative.

Ike and his secretary of state were flummoxed at their point of least resistance, the defense budget. Knowing they loved Korea's forward "containment" posture, Rhee got the money and used it to thwart their ideological preference for a liberal, democratically sound, dependent state. American liberals were by no means any smarter. Arthur Bloomfield, an economist with the Federal Reserve Board of New York, recommended to Rhee that he create "a genuine central bank" and lodge responsibility for bank borrowings "where they properly belong, namely, in the National Assembly."[13] Bloomfield called this "privatization," but all it would have done was add one more step to Rhee's standard operating procedure—now he would also have to call in the head of the assembly's banking committee, and tell him what to do. Needless to say, Rhee paid him no mind.

Was this ISI program "irrational"? Rhee knew perfectly well that the unvoiced American strategy for South Korea was to restitch its economic relations with Japan; by substituting Korean industries for Japanese, duplicating them if need be, the seams for the stitching would no longer be there. Korea again to be the handmaiden of Japan's growth? Better to be "another Japan" than a dependency. This was the sterling logic behind Rhee's policies. Eisenhower, for example, told General Van Fleet in 1954 that he was going to tell Rhee, "We have got to get Japan backing up Korea as a 'big brother,' " but soon Rhee shot this back to Ike: "What [aid coordination with Japan] means is that [Korean] recovery is slowed as we are expected to buy more from Japan, and accordingly to use less to build up our own productive facilities. This has an immediate effect

12. She estimates $15 billion in economic and military aid from the United States and Japan from 1946 to 1976, a conservative figure. See Woo (1991), pp. 45–6.
13. Woo (1991), pp. 48–50.

of once more placing our economy at the mercy of the Japanese."[14]

The easiest way to promote import substitution was an overvalued exchange rate for the *hwan* (later renamed *wŏn*), which increased the value of dollars received and maximized aid imports, while keeping the cost of imported capital and intermediate goods low. Furthermore, the ROK's exports were mostly primary products then, like rice and tungsten, with inelastic prices. The United States succeeded in obtaining a devaluation in 1953 and 1955, but no official reduction occurred thereafter until 1960.[15] The beneficiaries of import substitution were people like Samsung's Yi Pyŏng-ch'ŏl, to whom Rhee gave remarkably favorable purchase prices on former Japanese industries, like Cheil Chedang (sugar) and Cheil Mojik (textiles); Samsung was supposed to remember such favors and return them at election time. Not a forgetful man, Yi Pyŏng-ch'ŏl was later accused of dropping 64 million *hwan* on Rhee's Liberal Party. The U.S. Army presence also made possible ISI, military-style. The hands-down winner for milking the Rhee regime and the U.S. Eighth Army was Cho Chŏng-hun, head of the Hanjin Company and, later, Korean Airlines. All through the 1950s he had transportation contracts with the U.S. military, amounting to $2.28 million annually by 1960; he also got surplus buses from the same source, allowing him to set up a bus line between Seoul and Inch'ŏn.[16] Nowadays Americans see Hanjin containers, one after another, sitting piled up at our ports or traveling along our major highways and railroads.

Whatever historians might say about commerce under the ancien régime, in post-1953 South Korea gigantic urban markets were beehives animated by the human propensity to truck and barter. For many foreigners Seoul's great markets—especially those at East Gate and South Gate—still hold tremendous fascination, twisting through labyrinthine streets and alleys, exotic smells tantalizing or assailing the nostrils, sea urchins frying on the griddle of a small cart, bean paste fermenting in the sun, feasts for the eye (a boar's head here, a bull's penis there),[17] and around the corner and down the stairs some Tropicana orange juice with the date still fresh, a tent full of used suits, a bicycle repair shop big enough for three bikes and three repair boys, mechanics who can fix absolutely any problem on an old Honda motorcycle, a claque of old ladies smoking long pipes while sitting on their haunches chanting "chang-a money" to the Yankee (who can thereby obtain a reasonable exchange rate for once), old men throwing sticks on the ground and

14. Quoted in Woo (1991), p. 57.

15. Woo (1991), pp. 63–64.

16. Woo (1991), pp. 68–69.

17. Both of which the author has been served in Seoul restaurants.

betting on the layout, little kids running in and out of a tiny storefront, naked except for a shirt, beautiful silks piled by the doorstep, in the middle of the alley a paraplegic strapped to a leather casing on top of a wooden platform with skate wheels, playing the accordion for donations while the shopkeeper shoos him away, and everywhere rising above the din, the endless haggling preparatory to buyer meeting seller at the right price. In the past the only time the din died down was just prior to the midnight curfew (a device to catch communists, but also to let the hagglers collapse). The merchants withdrew to a three-by-six-foot *ondol* room for five hours sleep, and then it was up in the morning, washing their face in a bucket and then throwing the water on the alley to hold down the dust. The great markets were the gathering place for peasants become entrepreneurs (grouped according to home region), an incubator of capitalism every bit as good as the Harvard Business School, and the post–Korean War launching pad for any number of immigrant business families now prospering in Los Angeles or New York.

Capitalism, after all, is not a matter of Protestant ethic and Confucian virtues. It is a system of exchange in the marketplace: if a butcher takes off his P'yŏngyang hat and offers a good steak at the right price, an aristocrat will buy it; if Hyundai offers a car that runs like a top at a low price, Americans will desert their Toyotas and buy it. Business is amoral. Any child on the short end of a bad deal knows the feeling in the pit of the stomach: just an amoral exchange, nothing more. If a destitute Korean woman finds an African-American soldier in the insouciant darkness of Tongduch'ŏn, that is capitalism. When she marries him and goes to the States, and they raise seven children and she ends up directing all the registered nurses at a large urban hospital,[18] that is survival, hard work, ethical conduct, maybe even a remnant of Confucian virtue.

MIRACLE ON THE HAN

In the period 1945–60 it was rare to find any American official who thought the ROK would become "economically viable," in the stock phrase, without unification or a very close connection to Japan. This was George Kennan's judgment right in the middle of the worst fighting at the Pusan perimeter in August 1950. Japan, he told Acheson, was "the most important single factor in Asia," but at the moment it was "too weak to compete." However, "with the revival of her normal strength and prestige," Japan would be able to regain her influence in Korea: "It is important that the nominal independence of Korea be preserved, for *it provides a flexible vehicle* through which Japanese influence may

18. Reported in a Korean women's magazine in 1990.

someday gradually replace Soviet influence without creating undue international repercussions."[19] That is an unusually frank statement, but it is essentially what Acheson and many American officials after him believed; some considered the ROK useful as a "buffer between Japan and Communist Asia," but not for much else. One official reported that in 1960 "only one or two of the score of officials" in the Eisenhower administration involved in planning for Korea thought that South Korea could become "economically viable" short of reunification.[20] As late as the mid-1960s some scholars still wrote as if South Korea were more or less a basket case. Even specialists on East Asia had trouble seeing South Korea's future in this period, so wrapped up were they in the previous two decades' perception of economic stagnation and dislocation. Thus James W. Morley wrote in 1965 that South Korea had still not "taken off": "[it] has made little progress. It has remained politically unstable and economically prostrate. . . . The day when it can be more than a ward of the United States not only has not dawned but cannot now be foreseen." American economic and military aid still accounted for about 75 percent of the South's military budget, 50 percent of the civil budget, and nearly 80 percent of the available foreign exchange, Morley wrote; meanwhile, North Korea was growing and industrializing rapidly, with its people better fed and housed than ever before.[21]

W. W. Rostow had stimulated an enormous debate with his 1960 book, *The Stages of Economic Growth* (subtitled *A Non-Communist Manifesto*), which inaugurated the new, Kennedy-style concern with "nation-building" and economic development. Rostow had been teaching at Massachusetts Institute of Technology, which had prepared policy papers for the incoming administration that quickly began to influence policy.[22] Rostow was named national security adviser to President Kennedy, and he hit the ground running. Within weeks of the inauguration he and his close associate Robert Komer had taken a close look at South Korea and argued that in spite of its truncated and isolated condition, it had strong human resources and was an ideal place to develop light industries for export. In a March 15, 1961, memo called "Action in Korea," Komer outlined "the major thrust of U.S. effort[s] over the next decade": (1) "crash economic development," (2) "creation of light labor-intensive industry,"

19. Truman Library, Acheson Papers, box 65, memoranda, Kennan to Acheson, Aug. 21, 1950 (emphasis added).
20. Macdonald (1992), pp. 26, 28–31.
21. James W. Morley, *Japan and Korea: America's Allies in the Pacific* (New York: Walker, 1965), pp. 40, 48–49, 52.
22. Woo (1991), p. 70; Macdonald (1992), pp. 26–27.

and vigorous U.S. action "in directing and supervising ROK economic development." Komer and Rostow thought Korea had one great, underutilized resource: its people.[23] A major revision of U.S. Korea policy in 1965 embodied the new American judgments. Although it restated Korea's utility as a strategic backstop for Japan, it now also touted the ROK as an example, like Taiwan, that "the non-Communist approach to nation-building pays off." Among eight policy goals, number two was "economic growth averaging at least six percent per year" over the five years from 1966 to 1971. Nor was the United States unhappy with the strong role of the state in the Korean market: it wished to promote "whatever appears to be the most effective division between the public and private sectors."[24]

Park Chung Hee was a stolid son of Korea's agrarian soil who, like Kim Il Sung, had come of age in Manchuria in the midst of depression, war, and mind-spinning change. In this radicalized milieu he had witnessed a group of young military officers organize politics, and a group of young Japanese technocrats quickly build many industries—including Kishi Nobusuke, who later became prime minister of Japan.[25] The Korean officers who took power in 1961 were simultaneously anticapitalist and desperate to build up Korea's national strength:

> The junta leadership . . . [had] a peasant's suspicion of the wealthy. When they thought of capitalism, they thought of a conspiracy of the rich; when they entertained the notion of economic development, they thought of a rich nation and a strong army, and wartime Japan came to their minds; and when they awakened to the need for domestic resource mobilization, they badgered the rich and forced citizens through campaigns and edicts, to salt away chunks of their salaries. Joseph Schumpeter knew the type, and he called them mercantilists.[26]

In Park's first book after the coup, *Our Nation's Path*, regime scribes lauded the Meiji Restoration as a great nation-building effort; but it was really the Manchurian model of military-backed forced-pace industrialization that Park had in mind.

Latin America was then the continent of import substitution. Inaugurated in the depression as a way to survive in a collapsed world economy and having a certain intimacy with the Iberian, corporate politics of

23. Woo (1991), pp. 76–77. Komer was with the CIA Office of National Estimates in the 1950s, but moved to the NSC in 1960.

24. Macdonald (1992), pp. 31–32.

25. Chalmers Johnson rightly called attention to this Manchukuo group in his seminal *MITI and the Japanese Miracle* (1982).

26. Woo (1991), p. 81.

the region, and given that World War II passed this continent by, import substitution lasted far longer there than anywhere else. Behind walls of protection the people and firms involved with production for domestic markets built up extensive networks of personal and political ties, as the scholar Guillermo O'Donnell has shown. Therefore, when all the world told these nations in the 1960s that they had to begin exporting and dropping their barriers to trade, the question was how to break the thick nexus of interests that had grown up around the previous strategy. Here military coups have advantages: General Pinochet used his emergency powers to push the Chilean economy onto a totally different "free trade" track. But a decade earlier Park Chung Hee had shown how to break this same nexus. The junta arrested the import-substituting businessmen who had fattened at Syngman Rhee's trough and marched them through the streets Cultural Revolution–style, with dunce caps and sandwich placards displaying "I am a corrupt swine," "I ate the people," and other such appetizing slogans.

Soon the junta had lined up a large group of "illicit profiteers," those who had made a lot of money courtesy of Syngman Rhee. Chief among them was Yi Pyŏng-ch'ŏl, chairman of Samsung. Making himself chairman of the accused businessmen-swine-people eaters, he went to General Park and suggested that instead of hewing close to the government in order to glom onto Japanese properties as in the past, the businessmen should be encouraged to seek foreign capital to get the economy moving. Samsung, Goldstar, and other firms had begun to saturate Korea's small domestic market, so why not see if they could succeed in exporting? Park was no revolutionary, in spite of what some Americans thought. He listened to Yi Pyŏng-ch'ŏl, and soon he called in ten major business leaders, including Yi, and made a deal with them: he would not jail them, and they would make good on their "fines" by investing the money in new industries, donating "shares" to the government. The new industries would learn to sell in foreign markets.

Soon every year Korea held "Export Day," a national celebration at which President Park would give guidance, laud a new export target overfulfilled, cut a ribbon on a Hyundai ship, try out some new slogans, and make a speech. None other than Kim Yŏn-su, founder with his brother of Kyŏngbang Textiles, got Park's "Gold Pagoda Industrial Medal" in 1971, as the nation's most successful exporter.[27] On November 1973's Export Day, Park gave voice to the values behind the "Factory Saemaŭl movement" (a bit of a contradiction in terms, since the Saemaŭl, or New Village, movement had been started in 1970 to refurbish rural villages); the new slogan was "Treat employees like family":

27. Eckert (1991), p. 254.

> The Saemaul Movement as practiced in offices and factories is nothing different . . . for its basic spirit remains the same: diligence, self-help and teamwork. . . . There should be close labor-management cooperation, with the company president making an utmost effort to improve pay and welfare, and the later fulfilling their duties with a sense of responsibility and sincerity, doing factory work like their own personal work. . . . In such a corporation, productivity will be high, thanks to the family-like atmosphere. . . . Thereby complete harmony between employees and employers would be made possible. . . .[28]

Park sought to draw upon the old virtues of obedience and loyalty, family values and filial piety, and the leader as father of the nation. Foreign experts, hearkening to rhetoric like this, thought Korea was moving along quickly behind Japan toward lifetime employment, the company uniform and song, and "harmony" between worker and owner: "Korea, Inc."[29] The next chapter, however, will show that neither Confucianism nor Japanese industrial practices worked very well in promoting worker-owner solidarity.

In the early 1960s the labor cost saving for firms in the United States willing to move to Korea was a factor of 25, since workers were paid one-tenth of American wages but were 2.5 times as productive. How was this possible? Let an expert explain:

> In transistor assembly operations, for example, given wage rates ⅒ of those of equivalent operators in the U.S. (for the same firm), the machinery is run at physical full capacity, that is, 6 days, three shifts a day, which is 20 percent above the U.S. equivalent. . . . In spite of the greater use of labor, productivity per worker seems to be higher partly due to the fast learning process . . . but mainly to the greater discipline and attentiveness on the assembly line throughout. For example, in one firm the difference in speed of assembly on identical equipment yields a 30 per cent differential in output. . . . These greater speeds of operation, either due to faster machines or operator pacing, are once again accomplished by putting additional women into more intensive testing, inspection and repair efforts than in Japan or the U.S.[30]

Economic planning was another wrinkle that Park borrowed either from the Japanese in Manchuria in the 1930s or from the North Koreans thereafter; successive five-year plans unfolded from the hallowed halls

28. Quoted in Choi (1989), pp. 182–83.
29. See, for example, Ronald Dore, "South Korean Development in Wider Perspective," in *Korea: A Decade of Development*, ed. Chang Yun-shik (Seoul: Seoul National University Press, 1980).
30. Gustav Ranis, "Industrial Sector Labor Absorption," *Economic Development and Cultural Change* 21 (April 1973):402–3.

of the Economic Planning Board (EPB), known as Korea's MITI, after Japan's Ministry of Trade and Industry. The First Five-Year Plan was to run from 1963 through 1967, but Americans in the Agency for International Development (AID) mission did not like it, and refused to certify it for foreign lending. It never really got off the ground. The Second Five-Year Plan (1967–71) was more to their liking, but the Koreans had also learned how to muddle American minds: when Joel Bernstein, director of the AID mission in Korea, complained that Korean future projections were much too optimistic, the Koreans quoted back to him his boss, Walt Rostow, who headed the State Department's Policy Planning Staff. Bernstein wrote to Rostow,

> You are being quoted as saying that conventional economists always underestimate demand for the products needed in a growing economy, that Korea should not worry about overcapacity because demand is always underestimated, that estimates of requirements should be made in the ordinary way and then everything should be doubled, and that economic development is too serious a matter to leave to economists who do not understand it adequately.

The Koreans, Bernstein thought, had a "damn their torpedoes" attitude, and still lacked understanding of "the principle of marginal utility."[31] Rarely have we had a better example of conventional American economics confronting neomercantilism; Bernstein did not win, of course, because the Koreans were right: Rostow was just as Schumpeterian as they were.

MECHANICS OF FINANCE: THE GNOMES OF SEOUL

Here is one of the secrets of finance: most of us would rather not think about it, giving a conscious minority a grip on our jugular. The highly conscious agents of the miracle on the Han were state bureaucrats willing to hand out something for something: no-cost money if you put it to good use, building up another industrial prodigy. Policy loans for export performance, they were called, and they showed that sometimes there is a free lunch in capitalist economics.

What does it mean, this term "policy loan"? Until recently, money *was* different in Korea. In the United States you get exactly three White Castle hamburgers for one dollar, whether you are in Chicago or LA. In Korea, however, as the old women at the East Gate market could tell you much better than I, four currencies circulated: the American dollar at the official exchange rate, the American dollar at the East Gate rate, the "mil-

31. Quoted in Woo (1991), p. 99.

itary payment certificate" (MPC), a dollar euphemism useful at the PX, and the unconvertible Korean won at rates constantly changing against the other three. (Unconvertible means that 10 million won outside of Korea won't buy you one White Castle hamburger.) The authorities sought from time to time to control the informal markets, for example, by top-secret plans to replace all MPCs in circulation with new bills (which would somehow leak to the money changers just before the deadline). Now, of course, there is another problem with money, any kind of money: it degrades instantly; you either use it or lose it.

If you think back to our discussion of obsolescence, even money obsolesces under capitalism if you let it sit idle for a moment—which is why bankers lodge our money in their overnight accounts before reluctantly shifting it to our accounts the next morning. "Time is money" said the new slogans in 1980s Shanghai, replacing the Maoist dictum "A socialist train running late is better than a capitalist train on time"—and everyone knew that China had changed. The clock ticking against money is the interest rate. In Korea, once again, you had several interest rates: the officially set, nationally owned central bank rate; the *kye* rate, a longstanding institution in which women would pool money and then draw lots to see who gets the pot each month; the "curb rate," which is what the claque of money changers will give you and through which a truly mind-boggling amount of money sloshed around. Of course, the "curb" was not just the old women squatting at East Gate market. Often the only source from which households could get loans outside the state-controlled banks, the curb loan market was in 1969 estimated at 82 percent of the M1 money supply, and during the difficult years of 1969–71 as much as 70 percent of its loans were to corporations. The rest went to farms and urban households.[32]

Then there was so-called negative interest: that was the rate Park Chung Hee would give you on a few million dollars, if you would throw it into electronics or steel. In Korea the state deployed money in the magical way that Joseph Schumpeter imagined,[33] as a mysterious poof of energy for the incessant innovation that he saw as the motive force of growth. A man goes to a bank with an idea for a better mousetrap, the banker signs a piece of paper, greenbacks pour out like cheese in Wisconsin, and all the mice run for cover. In the American system it is typically the private bank and the entrepreneur whose symbiosis creates this energy, but Schumpeter said that other institutions could perform this function—which they did in Korea, even if *chaebŏl* coupling with the

32. Woo (1991), p. 113.

33. This is derived from many conversations with Meredith Woo-Cumings, a rock-ribbed Schumpeterian.

finance ministry isn't quite as romantic as the entrepreneur looking for the main chance. It isn't too hard to imagine the incentive, however, if the bank rate is 20 percent per annum on loans, and the state gives you one for 10 percent, or even 5. People come running for money like that, but they had to perform to keep it coming.

Here's the deal: I will arrange for, say, a bank in Japan to give you $10 million at below-market interest rates to make 12-inch black-and-white TVs, and guarantee the loan to the bank. I will set aside property for you in our free-export zone, build the roads to your plant, give you heat and electricity at preferential rates, and set aside American surplus cement for your buildings. I will find a foreign firm with established markets, know-how, and channels of distribution, which will sell your TVs everywhere in the United States, even in grocery stores. I will guarantee a steady supply of educated and disciplined labor at a set price (also well below market), outlaw unions, and send in the army whenever dangerous combinations emerge at the workplace. I will decide how many competitors you will have, give you annual targets for production (with bonuses for going beyond them), and make sure there's room enough for all of you to grow. (Not to mention the fact that you are my wife's brother, etc.)

If this system worked intermittently in the 1960s, it worked like clockwork in the 1970s and became the essence of the "Korean model." With huge amounts of petrodollars sloshing through world markets after the OPEC-induced quadrupling of oil prices, and thus with bankers begging people to take loans, the Korean state mediated that flood of money, pointing it toward the immensely expensive "six industries" of Park's "big push." For the next fifteen years, Korea borrowed abroad at Latin American rates: foreign debt rose 42 percent shortly after the oil shock, but investment also shot up, to a historic high of 32 percent of the GNP in 1974. By the end of the decade Korea was among the big four debtors in the world, led by Brazil; its foreign borrowing from 1976 to 1979 placed it third, behind Mexico and Brazil, but in the decade 1967–78, Korean debt grew fifteenfold, twice the rate of all less-developed countries and well ahead of Mexico's and Brazil's. Korea also, however, grew by an average of 11 percent from 1973 to 1978, with heavy industry accounting for 70 percent of total manufacturing investment. To get the big loans of that period, though, you had to be big already—a *chaebŏl*. To keep getting them, you "had to be gigantic."[34]

The central element in the Korean model, then, is finance: and "the main goal of Korea's finance was to hemorrhage as much capital as possible into the heavy industrialization program":

34. Woo (1991), pp. 149–53.

> The financial policy of *Yushin* was this: the government set financial prices at an artificial low to subsidize import-substituting, heavy, chemical, and export industries. . . . The political economy of this bifurcated financial system was illiberal, undemocratic, and statist. . . . Every bank in the nation was owned and controlled by the state; bankers were bureaucrats and not entrepreneurs, they thought in terms of GNP and not profit, and they loaned to those favored by the state.[35]

The average cost of such loans through much of the 1970s was minus 6.7 percent, whereas even the curb rate was positive—well above the inflation rate, in fact. Not bad, somebody paying you nearly 7 percent to take his money. The result was that each favored *chaebŏl*, "for all practical purposes, was a private agency of public purpose."[36] The public purpose, of course, was to herd them into specific, selected industries that would build the "rich country, strong army" of Park's dreams.

If this sounds like a capitalist heaven, it was: South Korea was a cornucopia of state supports to business. But so were many other poor countries, and they are still poor. The question for Korea is how a state bureaucracy could allocate credit resources efficiently, that is, rationally; and how could officials be wizards of finance, gnomes of Seoul, when every political calculation would push in the direction of rewarding friends and benefactors at the expense of the commonweal. The answer to this question comes in four Korean parts.

First, political leaders pay attention not to efficiency and rationality but to political and, in this case, national efficacy.[37] All kinds of risks disappear when a company knows that a long-term investment has the backing and the resources of a highly nationalistic political leadership (like, let's say, the American aerospace industry in the 1960s) and politicians who will sink or swim with the investment. Second, the Korean ideal and tradition of the civil servant does produce many well-educated people devoted to what is best for their country and government, and by the 1960s many were also foreign-trained technocrats who knew how to plan and allocate resources. Third, there *were* many rewards for friends, as one "slush fund" scandal after another has shown.

The firms that got policy loans were quasi-state organizations that had common interests with the government, that sank or swam by following government dictate, and whose leaders were personally connected (often by marriage, as we will see) to the ruling elites. This third element led to a kind of rational or efficacious corruption, in which relatives in the government lent money to relatives in business, piling money upon

35. Woo (1991), p. 159.
36. Woo (1991), p. 169.
37. Woo (1991), p. 11.

growth expectations and growth upon money expectations, somewhat like a chain letter or crap game that worked year in and year out as long as the pie kept expanding. The carrot and stick that the government always held was the big firms' complete dependency on it for capital. If performance was poor or the firm did not do what the state wanted, it could be bankrupted the next day. This gave the state tremendous influence on investment patterns, mobility into new industries, and simple day-to-day corporate performance.[38]

The last Korean difference is that the proof of success was export performance in the hothouse of international competition—something that in the 1960s was simultaneously a discipline on firm performance *and* easier than the same thing today, because the world economy was much less crowded with other exporters in the 1960s. South Korea was nicely placed in the 1960s to receive declining light industries from the United States or Japan (textiles, footwear, transistor radios, black-and-white TVs, wigs, small appliances) and to export them to the low end of the American market. Because it had such a small market of its own, however, Korean firms were precariously poised in the flows of global commerce, very vulnerable to recessions and slowdowns—another reason for the Korean government to be a good partner, benefactor in good times and insurance agent in bad times.[39] South Korean interests frolicked for years in the yawning maw of the American market (usually in cooperation with American firms that had moved to Korea for coproduction), long before China, Indonesia, or Thailand got into the act.

NORMALIZATION WITH JAPAN AND THE VIETNAM WAR

From 1947 onward, as we have seen, a cardinal element of U.S. foreign policy was to bring Japanese economic influence back into Korea. Syngman Rhee ran South Korea's foreign policy out of his Kyŏngmudae office, ignoring his Foreign Ministry and trying his best to ignore the State Department. His position on Japan was considered completely recalcitrant by Americans, since he always seemed to suggest a negotiating stance that would guarantee failure. Rhee loathed the Japanese with a passion, which nonetheless did not stop him from developing economic ties with Japan when it was under MacArthur's tutelage. Rhee also found his usual cloud of anti-Japanese rhetoric useful in deflecting attention away from the many collaborators who served in his government.

Japan in the 1950s was not inclined to assuage Korean sensibilities,

38. Woo (1991), pp. 10–13.
39. Woo (1991), p. 13.

either; in 1953 the chief Japanese delegate in negotiations with Seoul, Kubota Kanichirō, told his opposites that everything the United States had done since 1945—the repatriation of Japanese nationals from Korea, the disposition of Japanese properties to Koreans, even the establishment of an independent Korean state prior to the peace treaty with Japan—had violated international law. For good measure he added that the Cairo declaration referring to Korea's "enslavement" at the hands of Japan was so much wartime hysteria and that "Japan's compulsory occupation of Korea for 36 years was beneficial to the Korean people." The Korean side publicized Kubota's remarks, and his subsequent, obligatory "apology" did little to improve the atmosphere of total distrust.[40] (This pattern continues even today; many Japanese leaders cling to the idea that they did wonders for Korea during the colonial period, while issuing apology after apology to China for Japan's wartime behavior.)

No significant progress in Korean-Japanese relations occurred before Kennedy was inaugurated, or before the 1961 military coup. After that, however, Washington pushed hard for normalization, with Rostow and Robert McNamara in effect reviving Acheson's strategy of pushing Japan toward a regional economic effort in Northeast Asia. Within three months of Park's 1961 coup, after some initial misgivings Ambassador Samuel Berger gave a strong endorsement to the junta, reporting to Secretary of State Dean Rusk that it was "moving on all fronts, especially economic, with lightning speed, and by and large in the right direction." Berger called this a "genuine revolution from the top." American economic aid quickly increased by nearly 50 percent, from $192 million in 1961 to $245 million in 1962.[41]

For its part the Park regime included many people who had willingly learned from Japan in the 1930s and were ready to do so again. They also had the coercive power to stifle any dissent; one decree issued in 1962 threatened to punish anyone who called attention to inconvenient facts—even if they were true. Several business leaders from the colonial period were instrumental in re-forming ties with Japanese business. In October 1961 Kim Chŏng-p'il came to Japan for consultations, amid a stream of public and secret visitors going back and forth between Seoul and Tokyo. A month later Park Chung Hee accepted an invitation from Prime Minister Ikeda (a visit that had been brokered by Dean Rusk) and spent long hours in personal discussions with Ikeda and other Japanese leaders (including Kishi). Ikeda then assured Rusk that "normalization would only be a matter of time." By 1963 imports from Japan had reached $162 million, 30 percent of Korea's total imports and four times

40. Macdonald (1992), p. 129.
41. Woo (1991), pp. 79–80.

the highest level under Rhee. Nor were the Japanese stingy when it came to doing their political share for Park and Kim: according to U.S. CIA information, Japanese companies provided two-thirds of the ruling party's budget from 1961 through 1965, with six firms contributing a whopping total of $66 million.[42] Still, there was no normalization.

The breakthrough came in 1964 under strong American pressure: "after years of urging on our part," according to one report from the embassy in Tokyo, including personal letters from John Kennedy to Ikeda and Park.[43] Kim Chŏng-p'il again came to Tokyo to clear up the amount of the claims settlement, the Koreans wanting reparations, the Japanese willing to give a bundle of grants and loans only if it were not called "reparations." On April 3, 1965, Korean and Japanese representatives initialed agreements on all the outstanding issues, and the ROK National Assembly ratified the treaty on August 14, 1965. This treaty did wonders for the Korean economy, but the settlement remains controversial today because it ended the possibility of future claims against Japan. Meanwhile, revelations like those involving the "comfort women" have raised the issue of more claims (in late 1994 the Japanese Diet voted to give each woman who could verify her status a payment of $20,000).

Nearly twenty years after the empire collapsed, visitors from Japan slowly began trickling into Korea again. The great film director Oshima Nagisa spoke of his bittersweet feelings after touring Korea for several months in 1964:

> Many people I met expressed a sincere desire for their nation to develop a harmonious relationship with Japan. They emphasized, however, that the relationship must always be that of two equals. They said that when they considered the disparity in the economic strength of the two nations, they felt oppressed by Japan's economic power. When I travelled through a small fishing village in South Korea, I met a man who wept when he saw me, saying that I was the first Japanese he had seen in twenty years. When I asked him if he didn't feel hatred for the Japanese, he responded that he did feel hatred and bitterness, but also nostalgia. Hatred and bitterness alone are not enough to close the door on a future relationship.
>
> I am not worried about people like him, but how will it be for the children? I was thinking about this on the train from Masan to Pusan. I was looking at the youth sitting next to me, who had fallen asleep leaning against me, breathing softly and peacefully. He had no way of knowing I was Japanese. Feeling his warm breath, I thought: When will

42. Macdonald (1992), p. 133; Woo (1991), pp. 85–86.
43. Macdonald (1992), p. 134; Woo (1991), p. 86.

> the day come that two peoples as close as this can develop a truly friendly relationship? When this boy and my son grow up, will they help each other rather than try to kill each other?[44]

In the normalization the ROK received from Japan a direct grant of $300 million and loans of $200 million in 1965 dollars, and private firms put in another $300 million in investment. This was at a time when Korea's total exports were $200 million. Ultimately Park used this money and the latest Japanese technology to get the steel mill that the United States had denied him in the early 1960s, which he installed in P'ohang, not far from his hometown. When it came onstream in 1973, it was the most efficient integrated steel mill in the world.[45] Well before that money was spent, however, another bonanza came along in the form of the Vietnam War.

Lyndon Johnson consistently escalated the war in Vietnam in 1965 and 1966 and sought to get an allied commitment like that which had accompanied the American intervention in Korea. Park Chung Hee had already offered several times to send Korean troops to Vietnam, and a Korean MASH (mobile army surgical hospital) unit had been dispatched in mid-1964—a bit of an irony given that the most popular American television sitcom for many years was "M*A*S*H," a program set in Korea but always alluding to Vietnam—a program that ROK officials hated because it recalled war-torn Korea and was much too sympathetic to the communist enemy.

In April 1965 Henry Cabot Lodge, American ambassador to Vietnam, came to Seoul with Lyndon Johnson's personal message to Park asking for Korean combat troops. After several months of negotiations, the Koreans squeezed a large pile of cash and aid commitments out of Washington, estimated at $7.5 million per division. The operative document was the so-called Brown memorandum of March 4, 1966, under which about $1 billion in American payments went to Korea in the period 1965–70. Scholars estimated that this arrangement annually accounted for between 7 and 8 percent of Korea's GDP in the period 1966–69 and for as much as 19 percent of its total foreign earnings.[46]

Soon nearly 50,000 Korean soldiers were fighting in Vietnam, and by the time they withdrew in 1973, as many as 300,000 Koreans had served there. Vietnam became a frontier for Korean enterprise, as many firms, especially construction companies, got contracts to support the Ameri-

44. Annette Michelson, ed., *Cinema, Censorship and the State: The writings of Nagisa Oshima, 1956–1978*,. trans. Dawn Lawson (Cambridge: MIT Press, 1992), pp. 62–63.
45. Woo (1991), p. 87–88.
46. Macdonald (1992), p. 110; Woo (1991), pp. 93–96.

can effort. Vietnam absorbed 94 percent of Korea's total steel exports and 52 percent of its export of transportation equipment.[47] For Koreans it was a welcome irony, since Japan had gotten its economy off the mark through allied procurements in the Korean War, something that one scholar called "Japan's Marshall Plan."[48] All this underlines the way in which warfare in East Asia was handmaiden to economic growth in the period 1935–75.[49]

THE BIG PUSH

At his New Year's press conference in January 1973, Park announced a program of "heavy and chemical industrialization," with steel, autos, ships, and machines projected to be 50 percent of the 1980 export totals. The target was $10 billion in exports and $1,000 per capita income within a decade. This was the press conference Park had wanted to give a decade earlier but could not; it was always his dream to make steel the symbol of his industrialization drive, and not shoes or wigs. Steel meant national power, he often said; North Korea turned out thousands of tons of the stuff, an essential part of its armaments industry and just about everything else.[50] The Pittsburgh of Korea was to be P'ohang, a small port city virtually erased during the Korean War because of its location along the shifting lines of the Pusan perimeter. Steel, however, was just one of six great industries to be built virtually overnight: the others were chemicals, automobiles, shipbuilding, machine tools, and electronics.

American advisers and multilateral institutions like the IMF were less than impressed. The world market had too much capacity in most of these industries, and the Korean domestic market was too small to absorb them. Their conduit of influence within the government was the EPB, which wanted to continue leading from Korea's comparative advantages in light-industrial exports. Park therefore centralized the Third Five-Year Plan team in the Blue House. The Economic Secretariat of the Presidential Palace was the brains and the "Corps for the Planning

47. The best book on the Korean effort is a novel, Ahn Junghyo's *White Badge*. The figures are from Woo (1991), pp. 95–96.

48. Johnson (1982).

49. The Korean soldier's experience in Vietnam was like the American GI's, with lots of postwar trauma. Robert Buswell, who lived for years in a Korean Buddhist monastery in the 1970s, said he was "astonished" by the number of monks he met who had been in Vietnam. "These events opened their eyes . . . to a suffering inherent in ordinary life and prompted them to search for alternatives." Buswell (1992), p. 70.

50. Park (1993), p. 31. General Van Fleet had led a delegation of American steel makers to Korea in 1962, but the U.S. AID mission refused to support the project. See Woo (1991), p. 134.

and Management of Heavy and Chemical Industries" the horse for this gallop, this end run around foreign and internal opposition on the Schumpeterian basis that incremental, marginal utility was not the name of the game: how about a great leap forward, on the grounds that every future estimate of demand should at least be doubled—or tripled, or quadrupled? The Blue House became a hothouse for neomercantilists, of which the biggest was President Park himself. Much as the Manchukuo mafia industrialized Japan out of the world depression, the Blue House team industrialized Korea out of the 1970s miasma of stagflation and oil shocks.

The economists' estimates of future demand should have been multiplied by the hairs on their legs. P'ohang Steel came onstream in 1973 at an annual capacity of 1 million tons; 2.6 million tons of crude steel were pouring out of the mill by 1976, 5.5 million by 1978, and 8.5 million by 1981. In a decade Korea's steel capacity grew fourteenfold.[51] Who bought all this steel? Korean shipbuilders who had no factories in 1970, Korean automakers who weren't supposed to be needed by the world market, American manufacturers who bought Korean steel delivered to the Midwest well below the posted price in Pittsburgh or Gary. Sometimes there were problems: P'ohang girders used for a new football stadium in Seattle buckled during construction, for example, but the Koreans provided new ones with the proper tensile strength free of charge. Steel is an industry with all sorts of linkages to other industries. About a third of the cost of an automobile, for example, is for steel, and Korea's oil tankers "guzzled thick steel plates."[52] A steel and chemical industry also guarantees, of course, independent capability for the manufacture of all sorts of weaponry and armaments.

It was the "big push" that created Korea's big firms, now known by their names or logos all over the world. It is amazing to realize that this Korean business phenomenon is only as old as Park Chung Hee's early 1970s program: Daewoo did not exist until 1967, and the other big *chaebŏl* did not go into heavy industry until this formative period. Nor was this a matter of technocrats' conducting market surveys and testing the waters: Park would call in the *chaebŏl* leaders and tell them what to do. At one point, so the story goes, Park heard that there was a big global demand for oceangoing tankers, mainly because of the OPEC shake-up in the global oil market, and the widespread use of tankers for oil storage. He summoned Chŏng Chu-yŏng and exhorted him to start building ships.

Chŏng flew off to Greece and landed two contracts for 260,000-ton

51. Woo (1991), p. 134.
52. Woo (1991), p. 135.

oil tankers, by promising cheaper and quicker delivery than any other company. He didn't bother to mention that he had no shipyard to build them. He then put the two orders in front of Barclay's Bank, and it lent him enough capital to build the shipyards. No Korean knew how to do this, so Chŏng sent sixty engineers to Scotland to learn how. Two years later the tankers were finished, before the deadline.[53] The story is a bit unlikely; shipbuilding was an industry in which Korea had much experience, going back to Yi Sun-shin's turtle ships, with many fine shipbuilding artisans in the old days. It had none, however, in chemicals.

For any country lacking access to raw materials and energy sources, the chemical industry had always been the sine qua non of self-reliance, putting synthetics in the place of absent natural resources. It had been for Germany and Japan, as it was for North Korea; and since Japanese chemical plants had been built in the North, South Korea was completely dependent on imported fertilizers in the 1950s. In the first fifteen years of the Park administration, this industry grew dramatically, however, with production expanding by a factor of 180. Still, almost all of this production had been in joint ventures—with Dow Chemical, Gulf, Bechtel, Mitsui, and other firms—and many of the associations had been acrimonious (Dow left in a huff in 1982).[54] By 1973, however, an independent Korean chemical complex emerged at Ulsan, making polyethylene, methanol, and other materials. Very quickly Korea's dependence on imports of synthetic fibers for its textile industry nearly disappeared, dropping down to a 10 percent rate by 1975.

The pièce de résistance for Park was his new machine-tool complex, the industry that builds the machines for all the others, and the heart of an autonomous defense industry.[55] He stuck the Ch'angwŏn Machine-Building Industrial Complex in the harbor of Masan, on the southeast coast, as far from the DMZ as you can get and still be on the peninsula. This seemed to be the worst misallocation of resources in the eyes of economists, since Japan was then building a big lead in global machine tools and lots of threatened American manufacturers would be happy to relocate to Korea or sell machine tools at low cost. But, like Stalin (whose name means "steel"), Park thought an industrial sovereign did not rely on foreigners for the guts of an industrial base; what good was it for Korea to get on the daisy chain of multinational production just

53. This is a famous, perhaps apocryphal story, but every Korean knows it. See Ogle (1990), p. 70.

54. Woo (1991), p. 138–39.

55. See David Noble, *Forces of Production: A Social History of Industrial Automation* (New York: Knopf, 1984).

because some American-trained bureaucrats thought it should? In 1970 Korea had a remarkable 86 percent rate of dependency on foreign imports in machine tools, many of them from American firms, at a time when Nixon was cutting back on troop commitments to Korea. In spite of its new economic prowess, Korea still could not manufacture an internal combustion engine for its own automobiles, and many of the 2,500-odd parts that make up a car still had to be imported.

Park herded all the big firms into Ch'angwŏn to build more than one hundred factories and required foreign construction firms to source out their components in Korea (if it had the domestic capability to make them). Ch'angwŏn took off like a rocket, with machine building increasing an average of 36 percent per annum during the period of the Third Five-Year Plan. By 1977, domestic parts made up 90 percent of Korean autos. Park and his successor also assured that as more Koreans bought family cars, they would be Korean cars: today the market is so protected that it is as hard to find a foreign car in Seoul as it is to find someone walking at a measured pace (even the old people hustle through the markets now).

One big success piled on another, but no one—not even Schumpeter—would have expected Korea to rival Japan and the United States in high-technology electronics. By the mid-1980s, however, it became only the third country in the world to manufacture 286-bit silicon chips and lined the walls of American discount houses with low-cost 286-chip home computers. (As it had earlier done with TVs, Daewoo even sold Leading Edge computers in supermarkets.) It was a stunning success.

I have often thought that this simple fact must have dropped onto Kremlin foreheads in the mid-1980s like the proverbial "Chinese" water torture: how can the best Soviet and East German technicians not do what little old South Korea can do, a country that Soviet T-32 tanks rolled over so easily in 1950? I am not being facetious; the "Korean model" generalized to Southeast Asia and then to China broke the back of Stalinism as a model of development not just in North Korea but all over the world: by 1990 only a fool would still have believed that "socialism in one country" would one day catch up with a 1990s East Asian capitalism taking off like a Pasadena drag racer, or that "self-reliant" Third World development was the way to go (as nearly every postcolonial leader had thought a generation earlier).

Irony of all ironies, 86 percent-dependent South Korea somehow yanked industrial self-reliance from the jaws of the world economy: after the big push, it had the basis to go all they way and develop a comprehensive industrial structure. It was a grand success and a declaration of Korean independence. Ever since, Koreans have straightened their backs and walked with confidence; this is what still makes Park the most popular leader in postwar Korea (more than 70 percent of the population said so in a 1994 poll), in spite of all you will read in the next chapter. When the industrial sovereigns of the twentieth century are lined up—Andrew Carnegie, Henry Ford, Joseph Stalin, Chairman Morita of Sony—a Korean captain of industry will be among them. Most delightful of all, just about everybody won from the big push. In the old urban political machines of America the point of all deals was that "everybody makes money." In the 1970s just about everybody made money: blue-collar workers, engineers, technicians, car salesmen, computer discounters, the cities and towns of the southeast, above all the *chaebŏl,* which began their swift climb up the Fortune 500 list.

Park's one great mistake (completely predictable, given his political coalition) was to festoon his home region with all these new industrial complexes and to shortchange the Chŏllas. Of the six target industries, only one went to the southwest—the petrochemical factory in Yŏsu and Yŏch'ŏn, and this was only one part of the chemical complex; most of it was at Ulsan. Development means growth, no development means the status quo, but underdevelopment means a structural condition in which prospective development is retarded, or in which something happening elsewhere (cotton sales in England) deepens an obsolescent social formation (slavery in the American Deep South). In the Korean case the steel mills, auto plants, shipbuilding facilities, free-export zones, the capital to pay for them, the jobs they created, the new highways and sprouting cities they needed were all going with clockwork regularity to Korea's southeast, home to Park and just about everyone associated with him.

An industrial belt extended north and west from Pusan, linking the free-export zones in Masan and Ch'angwŏn with new industries in cities like Taegu and Ulsan. Little towns like Kŭmi and ports erased in the Korean War like P'ohang were transformed overnight into industrial cities because they were near Park's birthplace (next to Kŭmi) or were hometowns of one of his close associates (P'ohang). Tile roofs and television antennas sprouted on homes all over the Kyŏngsangs, while in southwest Chŏlla peasants living in thatched-roof huts continued their backbreaking agrarian toil at near-subsistence levels, or sent children off to Seoul in search of a job in a tearoom or a massage parlor. Park paid the price at Kwangju, as we will see.

THE BIG *CHAEBŎL*

What is a *chaebŏl*? Most simply it is "a family-owned and managed group of companies that exercises monopolistic or oligopolistic control in product lines and industries."[56] But that is just the technical definition. Many founders came from landed families and have held their *chaebŏl* tightly within the lineage. An early study found that of three hundred businessmen, 47 percent were from families of "large-to-medium landowners." The owners of the conglomerates spend a lot of time trying to convince their workers that they are all part of the same family, especially Samsung, which never saw a Japanese business practice that it didn't like. Strong Korean family ties are, indeed, important to the *chaebŏl*: mainly the founding family of the firm.

Every last one of the *chaebŏl* was started by a family group (just like Korean greengroceries in New York), and about 70 percent of them are still held by the founding family. Succession to the helm (which hasn't happened often, because most of them are so new) is a matter of high protocol and deep reflection worthy of King Yŏngjo and Prince Sado. Which son is the most talented, if the eldest is not? Fortunately the problems are not too severe for the *chaebŏl*: old Korea had only one king, but the conglomerates have many subsidiaries. Thus the founder of Hyundai turned over daily operations of the headquarters firm to his brother, while both put their sons in at the top of subsidiaries of this octopus-like corporation. The kingdoms of the *chaebŏl* are also easier to run than was old Korea: you don't have to worry about foreign invasions, fielding an army, training police, scratching taxes out of the people, educating workers, or legislating against combination at the workplace; the state does all that for you. So these large kingdoms, said to be run by men of unimpeachable morality and integrity in good Confucian fashion, expecting loyalty and distributing beneficence, prove Mel Brooks's adage even more than did the old court system: it is fun to be king.

A newspaper survey in 1989 reported that 60 percent of the founding-generation leaders of the top business groups own 80 percent or more of their companies' stocks.[57] Like aristocracies elsewhere, the *chaebŏl* groups also intermarry efficiently. According to one study, thirty-one out of the thirty-three largest firms have inter-*chaebŏl* marriage connections, with the connubial ties following the ranking by size of each group (that is, the sons of the biggest firms marry the daughters of the biggest, and so on down the line).[58] Samsung and Hyundai, for example, are linked by marriage alliances; often a *chaebŏl*-state alliance is also formed.

Let's look at some of the individual firms. Chŏng Chu-yŏng is Korea's most famous businessman and in 1992 was labeled Korea's Ross Perot when he ran for the presidency against Kim Young Sam and Kim Dae

56. Woo (1991), p. 149.
57. Kim (1992), pp. 49, 65; Jones and Sakong (1980), p. 224.
58. Kim (1992), p. 77.

Jung; like Perot, he was by then a billionaire, but at least twice as wealthy a one as Perot. A man of little formal education and no aristocratic pedigree, he came up the hard way. He began with auto mechanics and a small machine repair shop in the early 1940s. In 1947 Chŏng and his brother, Chŏng Sei-yong, set up a small construction company in Pusan to do work for the U.S. Army, and called it Hyundai (*hyŏndae*, meaning "modern" or "contemporary"). Then the war came along, and, sheltered by the Pusan perimeter, the Chŏng brothers piled deal upon deal building Quonset huts and refugee settlements, doing any kind of war-related construction, not to mention the reconstruction that occupied much of the 1950s. Chŏng Sei-yong spoke decent English, helping both to make key connections for American construction contracts, most of which were noncompetitive. Hyundai expanded rapidly within Korea in the 1960s, and also was a major contractor for American forces in Vietnam. By 1972 the company was worth $64 million and had split into six subsidiaries. It ranked 86th on the *Fortune* 500 list for 1994, with revenues of $27.5 billion.

Yi Pyŏng-ch'ŏl, founder of Samsung, always considered himself "a Japanese gentleman," and proved it by marrying a Japanese woman. Samsung ("Three Stars") is a play on Mitsubishi's "Three Diamonds," which probably modeled its logo on Mercedes's. Unlike many *chaebŏl* leaders, Yi got his start during the colonial period. From a landlord family, he began with a rice mill in Masan in the 1930s and then exported rice liquor from Taegu. His business expanded rapidly during World War II when he mobilized workers living in barracks on the grounds of his factories. Always hostile to unions, Yi often said, "I will have earth cover my eyes before a union is permitted at Samsung." Samsung was the most important light-industrial firm during the Rhee period, helped along by strategic purchases of Japanese factories at fire sale prices. By this time Yi was the richest man in Korea. During the big push, however, Samsung diversified into many other fields, including computers, consumer electronics, and shipbuilding. In 1994 Samsung got permission from the government to begin manufacturing automobiles at a new plant on Koje Island, which just happened to be President Kim Young Sam's birthplace.[59] The 1994 *Fortune* 500 list ranked Samsung 221st, with $14.6 billion in revenues.

In 1967 Kim Woo Chung borrowed $18,000 from his family and friends to found a small trading company, which he called Daewoo. Today it runs the largest textile mill and the largest shipyard in the world; entire city blocks in Seoul are often hidden by Daewoo construction fences, on which have been drawn pastoral mountain or floral spring

59. Ogle (1990), p. 126.

scenes. In 1987 Daewoo had 100,000 employees in twenty-five affiliated companies. With revenues of $50 billion, it stood 52nd on the *Fortune* 500 list for 1994.

Lucky-Goldstar was begun by Ku In-hoe, the son of a landlord who went into textile production in the colonial period. Ku started a cosmetics firm in 1947, selling toothpaste and brushes. A decade later he was producing transistor radios and refrigerators for the home market. For some time this firm has been run by Ku's son, Ku Cha-gyŏng. Known for its emphasis on "harmony" among staff and workers, it has had few labor problems. A strike in January 1989 at three electronics plants was settled quickly with 19 percent wage increases and a reduction to a forty-four-hour workweek. Chairman Ku personally stepped in to arrange the settlement.[60] In 1995 it purchased the Zenith television company.

The *chaebŏl* firms also know how to put people into the government: one-third of the fathers-in-law of *chaebŏl* owners "are high-ranking officials in the three government branches." President Roh Tae Woo (1988–93) married two children into the owning families of *chaebŏl*, making fathers-in-law of Chey Jong Hyun, who ran Sunkyung, and of Shin Myung Soo, owner of the Dong-A *chaebŏl*. Probably this did not hurt when the Roh government awarded the rights to Korea's second mobil-telephone franchise to Sunkyung, until a barrage of criticism forced its cancellation.[61] Roh Tae Woo appointed another relative by marriage to be minister of commerce and industry, while a well-known political figure and another in-law, Pak Ch'ŏl-ŭn, became minister of political affairs.

The Korean military is a kind of *chaebŏl* all by itself, with responsibility for defense and coercion. President Roh also had a relative by marriage there, too, Lieutenant General Kim Pok-dong, who led a "Pine and Nut Club," made up of hundreds of retired military officers. When all else failed in knitting together the state and business elite, there were always the graduates of North Kyŏngsang Senior High School in Taegu, which both Chun Doo Hwan and Roh Tae Woo attended. In Roh's years alums of that school held the "six most powerful positions" in the government, including the head of the Agency for National Security Planning, the top general in the army, the chief of the National Police, and the commissioner of the National Tax Administration. Other alums had portfolios as well, however, including the Ministries of Finance, Defense, Justice, and Home Affairs, and the presidencies of several state banks.[62]

60. Ogle (1990), pp. 141–42.

61. Park (1993), pp. 140–41. The Washington lobbyist Richard Allen, long a friend of Korea's rulers, remarked, "Nowhere else in the world do I know of anything like this existing." *Wall Street Journal*, Aug. 21, 1992.

62. Research by Cho Kap-jae, cited in Park (1993), p. 189.

This was nothing new for the Roh government; the Park and Chun governments also drew heavily from the same region.

Shin Hyŏn-hwak, for example, was born in North Kyŏngsang and graduated from this same Taegu high school and then from Keijo Imperial University. In 1943 he passed the Japanese higher civil service exam. In 1959 he was the youngest cabinet member in the Rhee regime (as rehabilitation minister) and later was a stalwart of the Park regime, rising to be deputy prime minister in the late 1970s. Shin was by no means alone: a 1989 survey found that people of Kyŏngsang origin accounted for twenty-three of the fifty biggest *chaebŏl* owners, nine of twenty-four cabinet ministers, and half of the board members of the central bank. Many individuals were willing to grant that their provincial origin had much to do with their success during the period 1961–92.[63]

In the mid-1990s, after much talk about scaling down the *chaebŏl* and diversifying the economy, the ten largest firms still accounted for about 60 percent of all production, and the big four did 40 percent all by themselves. As George Ogle points out, that means that ten families controlled 60 percent of the miracle on the Han.[64] Some scholars speculated that the Korean state will shrink as time goes by, giving over more and more tasks to the private sector (but then if the private sector is made up of *chaebŏl* groups, the state will be handing functions over to the parastate). Little of that has happened, although the conglomerates became more self-reliant in generating capital. That didn't stop the Kim Young Sam government from giving them yet another interest rate break in late 1993, dropping preferential loan interest by a full one percentage point. Any number of proposals to rein in the conglomerates were tabled or even legislated, but few were implemented.[65] The Kim Young Sam government tried to make more loan money available to small and medium-size industries; this did not stop loans to the *chaebŏl* from growing in absolute terms, but it did somewhat lessen the percentage of loans given to them.[66] In 1995 a huge scandal engulfed Roh, Chun, and most of the big *chaebŏl* leaders; the two former presidents landed in jail and at least twelve captains of business faced trials, all for providing Chun with upwards of $900 million and Roh with at least $650 million in political "campaign" funds; several hundred millions of dollars also managed to end up in special accounts managed by close associates of Chun and Roh after they left office.

63. Kim (1992), pp. 42–43.

64. Ogle (1990), p. 53.

65. These would include limitations on *chaebŏl* real estate speculation, control of mass media companies, internal trade between their subsidiaries, "inter-subsidiary mutual warranty for loaning," and the like. See Park (1993), p. 233.

66. *Korea Times*, June 7, 1993.

The Korean model of strong state-business coordination, huge concentration in the economy, policy lending, and cheap-labor cost advantages advanced Korean development for decades. In a 1992 German-Swiss survey of the comparative advantages of several industrial nations (three big ones, Japan, Germany, and the United States, and three smaller ones, Italy, Spain, and Korea), Korea was rated at 100 out of 100 on wage rates (whereas Japan was at 24 and the United States at 28) and 100 on tax burden or lack thereof (with Spain the next highest at 71, and the United States third at 55).[67] In other words, the Korean state still provided a relative capitalist heaven for the big business groups.

CRISIS AND REFORM

Toward the end of 1997 the worst economic crisis since the Korean War hit the ROK, not only upending its march toward advanced industrial status but also raising questions about its entire developmental program. Beginning with a run on Thailand's currency in the early summer, the contagion spread through one Asian economy after another, until it struck Korea like a force-10 typhoon in November. With the economy essentially bankrupt by early December, the International Monetary Fund stepped in with a $57 billion bailout—but before doing so it signaled that this bailout, unlike earlier ones, would come at a high price: a thorough restructuring of Korea's political economy. By the time the crisis had run its course, the ROK currency had depreciated to one-half of its former value, and its GNP ranking among the world's developed economies had dropped from eleventh place all the way back to seventeenth. It was a cruel blow coming at the end of a tumultuous century and nearly four decades of sustained growth, but the cruelest cut of all was the role played by prominent American officials in attacking the Korean economic model and in working closely with IMF officials to try to reform basic elements of Korean political economy.

During the Cold War, as we have seen, South Korea had a kind of sheltered economy (as did Japan), with American policy turning a blind eye toward, or even indulging, a state-led neomercantilist program of protectionism at home and export-led growth abroad, which relied above all on the openness of the vast American market: here was the essence of the "Asian developmental state." These economies were to be engines of economic growth by any means necessary, because of the great value they had in providing an alternative model of development in the global struggle with communism. During the Cold War, as a key ally and frontline state, South Korea would have gotten its bailout with an immediate

67. This study was in *Wirtschafts Woche* in Dec. 1992, quoted in Park (1993), p. 180.

and overriding emphasis on issues of security—as it did in 1983, when President Reagan and Prime Minister Nakasone arranged a $4 billion package for Seoul, amounting to 10 percent of its entire outstanding debt. Now that the bipolar struggle was over, however, the issue of their "fit" with a new era of free markets and "neoliberalism" came to the fore—to the surprise and shock of Koreans. The deep meaning of the 1997–98 Asian crisis therefore lay in the American attempt to ring down the curtain on "late" industrial development of the Japan/Korea type.

This kind of foreign interference—a form of economic intervention by remote control—was possible because the strong, nationalistic neomercantilism of postwar South Korea was propagated in the soft soil of semisovereignty; South Korea always had a strong state vis-à-vis its own people, but a weak state vis-à-vis the United States. Moreover, the American reformers paradoxically had willing accomplices in the Korean people themselves, and especially in strong labor unions, which had long sought to reform or nullify this same political-economic model. Perhaps most important, the depth of the crisis struck just as Koreans were electing Kim Dae Jung president, a man who had been on record for at least two decades in opposition to the central nexus of government, finance, and *chaebŏl* that defined the Korean model. This odd and utterly unpredictable turn of events became the key to riding out the crisis and returning the ROK to high rates of growth.

In late 1997 the IMF proved to be little more than the creature of U.S. Treasury Secretary Robert Rubin and his deputy secretary, Lawrence H. Summers.[68] Rubin and Summers, along with Federal Reserve Chairman Alan Greenspan, had been the three leaders of "Clintonomics," a term reflecting not simply the return of the United States to sustained economic growth but also a very active foreign economic policy seeking to enmesh developing economies in Asia and Latin America into a host of American-influenced multilateral organizations (like the Asia-Pacific Economic Cooperation group—APEC—and the North American Free Trade Association—NAFTA), and an oft-repeated mantra about the virtues of free trade, free and open markets, "transparency" in economic exchange, and "the rule of law." When the liquidity crunch hit Northeast Asia in the fall of 1997, the influence of these three officials was critical first in deflecting Japan's attempt to create an "Asian fund" to bail

68. See, for example, the column by David Warsh of the *Boston Globe*, reprinted in *Chicago Tribune*, Dec. 14, 1997; also Sebastian Mallaby, "In Asia's Mirror: From Commodore Perry to the IMF," *National Interest*, no. 52 (Summer 1998): 14; also Richard W. Stevenson and Jeff Gerth, who wrote that "the United States is the fund's largest shareholder, at 18 percent, and effectively wields a veto over major programs and policies," and also said that the IMF "is pushing far more deeply than ever before into the day-to-day operations on a foreign economy—the Korean one." *New York Times*, Dec. 8, 1997.

out threatened banks, and then in demanding far-reaching restructuring in return for IMF bailouts, along the lines of their "mantra."

To say that South Korea's finances "lacked transparency" at this time was an understatement, if not a joke; the highest officials were panicked and covered up the dire nature of the situation. In November the Bank of Korea governor said that short-term nonperforming loans totaled only $20 billion, whereas private analysts were placing the figure as high as $80 billion; he said foreign reserves were at $31 billion, when in fact Korea had but $6 billion in reserves left, and all of it was committed in the near term. In other words, the country itself was bankrupt: Seoul was "burning through its reserves by as much as $2 billion a day to help banks that needed cash."[69] However, the Kim Young Sam government was desperate to avoid an IMF bailout before the December 19 presidential elections and sought Japanese help instead; in mid-November the South Korean finance minister, Lim Chang Ryul, openly pleaded with Japan to intervene: "If the Korean economy goes wrong, so does the Japanese economy." Washington, though, wanted a quick bailout *during* the electoral campaign, so that all candidates would be committed to it—or alienated from it, if they chose that option.

The critical moment came when Treasury Secretary Rubin gave up his Thanksgiving vacation to huddle with Alan Greenspan, and then dispatched two senior officials to Seoul, including Larry Summers (later called "a modern version of Gen. Douglas MacArthur, reshaping Asia in America's interest"), who told reporters that "financial support . . . should only be provided in the context of an IMF [reform] program."[70] After an all-night negotiating session on December 1 and 2 between the finance minister and the IMF team, agreement was reached on a $57 billion bailout package made up of $21 billion in standby credits from the IMF, $10 billion from the World Bank, and $4 billion from the Asian Development Bank, with the United States, Japan, and other countries anteing up an additional $22 billion.

In return for the $57 billion package, the IMF demanded drastic restructuring. The classified text of the IMF agreement aimed directly at the Korean developmental model: it had a "highly leveraged corporate sector that lacks effective market discipline," with such high debt-to-equity ratios that most *chaebŏl* were technically bankrupt at any given time; easy credit had led to "excessive investment in certain sectors such as steel and

69. Even the $6 billion in usable reserves left on Dec. 2 was in jeopardy because of $6.2 billion in committed forward contracts to sell dollars at a set price at a future date. See *Wall Street Journal*, Dec. 10, 1997.

70. *New York Times*, *Wall Street Journal*, Nov. 20, 1997; *Washington Post*, Nov. 21, 1997: *Korea Herald*, Nov. 22 and 26, 1997; *Wall Street Journal*, Dec. 8, 1997 (where Alan Murray quoted a German analyst on Summers as MacArthur).

autos." Korea had to "restructure and recapitalize the financial sector and make it more transparent, market-oriented, and better supervised." It would have to cut its 1998 growth rate projection by half (6 percent to 3 percent), lift ceilings on foreign investment in Korean firms from 26 percent to 50 percent, facilitate foreign mergers and acquisitions, open domestic markets (especially the capital and auto markets), and create flexibilities in the labor market that would allow enormous layoffs. Large financial institutions should now be audited by internationally recognized firms, and the vastly diversified conglomerates should stop intersubsidiary loan guarantees and other kinds of internal deals. Rubin personally held up the agreement for ten hours while he pushed for new, "transparent" standards of accounting. For their part, Korean officials pleaded to include anti-labor provisions in the reform package.

From the perspective of December 1997 it is instructive to glance back at the rather different situation exactly one year before. President Kim Young Sam had proudly announced that South Korea had come of age as an advanced economy by joining the Organization of Economic Cooperation and Development, or OECD, a group of top industrial nations. To polish Korea's application Kim had abolished the EPB, which had been the Korean locus of "administrative guidance." Under severe pressure from big business throughout his term to reduce labor costs and restore comparative export advantage, President Kim and his ruling party in December 1996 rammed a new labor law through the National Assembly at dawn, with no notice to the still-sleeping opposition members. The new law retained the Korean Federation of Trade Unions (KFTU), a large, state-controlled trade union, as the only officially approved labor organization for five more years, leaving the independent, 500,000-strong Korean Confederation of Trade Unions (KCTU) out in the cold, tarred as "illegal"—even though it is one of the strongest unions in the world. The same law gave Korean business the legal right to lay off workers and the leeway to replace strikers with scabs.

Because Korea has no unemployment compensation or safety net, the new law severely undercut workers' interests. Korea never had "lifetime employment" like Japan, but for decades workers had traded reasonably good job security for the absence of independent representation and the right to work the longest hours in the industrial world at wages barely able to sustain one's family. But after the dictatorship ended in 1987 Korean labor organization expanded dramatically, especially in the flagship heavy industries: steel, automobiles, shipbuilding, and chemicals. Severe repression of labor under three decades of American-supported dictatorships finally gave way to modest improvement in wages and working conditions over the decade 1987–97, but according to Kim Young Sam, in 1996 Korean labor was supposed to pay the cost of business excesses, thus to restore Korea's global competitiveness.

The response to the new labor law was not long in coming: in January 1997 hundreds of thousands of Korean workers occupied the streets of Seoul for weeks on end, in what approached a general strike for days at a time, until the government finally relented and agreed to shelve the law. Come the December crisis, and the IMF adopted the task of doing what the Kim government could not: to try to enforce millions of layoffs. This could be done without too much distress, the IMF said, if Korea enacted unemployment compensation laws. But how was this supposed to happen when the government was virtually bankrupt?

The massive labor protests in early 1997 shocked the Korean elite and turned Kim Young Sam into a lame duck for the remainder of the year (Korean presidents can serve only one five-year term). Kim Young Sam's lame-duck status and the disappearance of the EPB meant that Korea's usually astute economic planners did not have the political backing to take the measures necessary to head off the ballooning debt and liquidity problems, which were then vastly accelerated by panicked foreign investors.

After the IMF bailout, influential analysts inveighed against a model of development that had been the apple of Washington's eye during the decades of authoritarianism in Korea. Deputy IMF Director Stanley Fischer said true restructuring would not be possible "within the Korean model or the Japan Inc. model." "Korean leaders are wedded to economic ideals born in a 1960s dictatorship," an editorial in the *Wall Street Journal* said, leading to "hands-on government regulation, ceaseless corporate expansion, distrust of foreign capital and competition"; the thirty largest *chaebŏl*, accounting for a third of the country's wealth, were "big monsters" that "gobbled up available credit" and relied on "outdated notions of vertical integration for strength." The chief economist at Deutsche Morgan Grenfell, Ed Yardeni, heaped scorn on Seoul: "the truth of the matter is that Korea, Inc. is already bankrupt. . . . All that's left is to file the papers. This is a zombie economy."[71] If the economy wasn't a "zombie," the crisis certainly cut it down to size. In November, South Korea ostensibly had a GNP of almost $500 billion and a per capita GNP of about $11,000; it accounted for about 6 percent of total world GDP (compared with 2.5 percent in 1980) and ranked eleventh among industrial countries. By January per capita GNP had fallen to $6,600 and GNP to $312 billion, or seventeenth place (behind Mexico, India, and Russia).[72]

71. Editorial by Joseph Kahn and Michael Schuman, *Wall Street Journal*, Nov. 24, 1997; Fischer quoted ibid., Dec. 8, 1997; Yardeni's "zombie" remark was broadcast widely on CNN News; see the full quotation in *Washington Post*, Dec. 11, 1997.

72. *World Development Indicator*, 1997; Asian Development Bank, *Key Indicators of Developing Asian and Pacific Countries*, 1996 (GNP figures assume purchase-power parity, or PPP; 1995 and 1996 figures are multiplied by 1996 and 1997 growth rates); 1998 figures from LG Economic Research Institute, reported in *Korea Herald*, Feb. 21, 1998.

Former Prime Minister Lee Hong Koo expressed the obvious conclusion: "The model is now clear. . . . It's not Japan, it's the West. The current crisis has convinced almost all people that the old style doesn't work."[73]

By the New Year, Rubin and other U.S. officials had neatly accomplished three goals: to stop a run on Korean (and Japanese) banks, to rewrite the rules of Korea's political economy as prelude to the (still ongoing) struggle to do the same in Japan, and to maintain American hegemony in the region. Alan Greenspan was ecstatic in his testimony before a Senate panel: the result of the Asian crisis was "a worldwide move toward 'the Western form of free market capitalism.'" Another analyst exclaimed that "Wall Street won."[74] As we will see in the next chapter, however, it was really the Korean people, and the democratic movement that they had long developed, that enabled the ROK to reform itself and to make a quick return to high growth.

HAN'S MIRACLE

Kim Woo Chung, founder of Daewoo, was long known for a work ethic that sounds more like self-flagellation: eighteen-hour days for years without a vacation or even more than an occasional day off. He was the most energetic of the high-energy *chaebŏl* leaders. Below the level of the conglomerates, however, there are many similar stories—among small and medium industries, not to mention workers themselves. But they are typical business history cases, I think; they show nothing peculiar to the "Korean model." For example, one of the largest bicycle manufacturers in Korea spent the 1990s in a fierce race to keep ahead of the "product cycle" curve, working enormously long days, weeks, and months; Korean workers were now organizing unions, putting upward pressure on wages, and the opening of China and the rapid growth in exporting by Southeast Asian countries like Thailand and Indonesia put yet a lower floor on wages, and so their bicycles quickly became competitive with Korea's. Unlike quasi-state firms like Daewoo, however, this man got little or no help from the state. We can call him Mr. Han.[75]

Bicycle technology is relatively easy to master at the low end of the scale, and it does not change much over time; for that reason competition is intense, virtually cutthroat. Furthermore, as China came onstream in the world economy, along came a nation of hundreds of millions of

73. Nicholas Kristof, "Asian-Style Capitalism Giving Way to the Free Market," *New York Times*, Jan. 17, 1998.

74. Alan Murray in *Wall Street Journal*, Dec. 8, 1997.

75. The following is based on several conversations with the owner of this Korean bicycle firm.

bike riders, riding machines of (Maoist "self-reliant") native manufacture. For years Mr. Han had a contract to supply Sears, Roebuck with bikes. One day the Sears man said sorry, Charlie, we're now buying bikes from China. So Mr. Han went into a joint venture with Schwinn in Chicago, only to watch Schwinn soon switch to lower-cost production in Southeast Asia—and then go bankrupt in spite of that. So Mr. Han flew off to Italy and Eastern Europe, looking for a comanufacturing deal with upscale, higher-technology gear—"yuppie bikes," as he called them—and a budding middle class to buy them. Soon he was manufacturing middle-range bikes and selling them in Hungary and the Czech Republic.

To get capital for a new factory, he signed another joint venture with an American bicycle firm. Mr. Han and his staff built the factory with a number of original Korean innovations in production design and manufacturing technology. As soon as the American company had figured out what these innovations were, it broke its contracts with him and stole the innovations. He lost about $2 million, he told me. Question: "Why didn't you sue them?" Answer: "I didn't want to get a bad business reputation, and life is short." So he took the $2 million hit and, left without a coproducer for the American consumer, found a way to grab nearly 10 percent of Canada's market while keeping his European sales up and relying on a growing domestic market in Korea for stable sales.

This is not a Korean story, I think. This sort of breakneck competition, self-reliance, innovative brilliance, vital energy, and drive to work fingers to the bone is a universal story of entrepreneurship. Mr. Han puts nothing on his back, lives without ostentation, and is totally devoted to his business. Every time I see him, Mr. Han is wearing the same blue suit, and often the same red tie. He treats his employees fairly and works every bit as hard as they do. He operates in the harsh, pitiless glare of a global bicycle market and rides the business cycle of creation and destruction like a rodeo man trying to tame a bucking bronco. Joseph Schumpeter would be proud. True, lately Mr. Han has tried to slow his pace by meditating for thirty minutes every morning after he rises at dawn. "Sŏn [zen] Buddhist techniques?" I asked him. "No, T.M." (transcendental meditation).

NOT SO MIRACULOUS

The year 1988 was of great significance in Korea, as the Summer Olympic Games came to Seoul and the Republic of Korea put its best foot forward. It would be difficult to overestimate the importance of the Olympics to the Chun and the Roh governments of the 1980s, since this was to be the coming-out party for the miracle on the Han, just as the 1964 Olympics brought Japan's economic prowess to the world's attentions. It is also doubtful that Roh Tae Woo would have made the dramatic announcement about direct elections on June 29, 1987, had the Olympics not been pending.

The games went off with only the North Koreans and Cubans boycotting; for the first time since 1976 the Americans and the Russians were both there, and the competition was splendid. The opening ceremony was a magnificent homage to Korean culture, both the high if constricted one of the Confucians and the low but diverse and vital one of the masses. The organic choreography of masses of people was worthy of a Kim Il Sung extravaganza (and often like it). Predictably the herd of foreign journalists who descended for a look at Korea did not like what they saw: too noisy, too spicy, too proud, too nationalistic, these people. Thus the commentary ranged from the blatant racism of P. J. O'Rourke in *Rolling Stone* to the more subtle aversions and aspersions of Ian Buruma in the *New York Review of Books*.[76]

Michael Shapiro also went to Korea in the Olympic year, and wrote a fine book about it. If you stand on a street corner in Seoul, you are not likely to see Chŏng Chu-yŏng or Kim Woo Chung. You will see cab drivers honking in the gridlocked traffic, shoeshine boys, tearoom waitresses hustling by with a take-out order, grandmothers selling apples, young office workers in black pants and white shirt, bus girls in blue uniforms leaning out of the back door of a bus to announce the destination, old men heaving along under A-frames or pulling two-wheeled carts, women with sleeping babies strapped to their backs trying to maneuver enormous sidewalk vending wagons festooned with hats and wigs, delivery boys balancing ten auto tires behind the seat of their motorbike, scooting in and out of traffic. Mr. Shapiro wrote about these people.

One man named In-sŏk had not done badly, graduating from a regional college and then getting an office job in Seoul. But he "hated his job, hated having to stay late at the office . . . hated the drudgery of his paper-shuffling assignment." There was also In-sŏk's domineering mother, who fretted so mightily about her son's unmarried status that she surreptitiously sprinkled ground antler horns in his breakfast, thinking he might be impotent. Chung Hee idled her life away in a dead-end job in a small-town coffee shop, thirty-eight years old and divorced; it was her tenth town in two years. Then there was Sammi, a textile worker who one day wrote, "I am sick of life, struggling for my liveli-

76. O'Rourke did a sort of racist potpourri/travelogue in *Rolling Stone* (Oct. 1988), dwelling on Korean facial features that he found outlandish (for example). Buruma compared the 1988 games to those Hitler sponsored in 1936; after visiting Korea's Independence Hall, he asked if his "revulsion" against Korean nationalism was "a sign of decadence" or was there something "to the idea of the rise and fall of national, even racial vigor?" See Buruma, "Jingo Olympics," *New York Review Books*, Nov. 10, 1988.

hood. I want to die." On another day, however, she had met a nice young man; she wasn't sure he liked her:

> As I was leaving the street, roses were dying. It was nice when the roses were blooming. Somehow I feel empty. Could it be because I compared them to a person? People are the same. Even after showing burning love, they separate with the pretext of some problem. I look forward to the ideal and set sail with hope and dreams.

"What is it I am thinking of," she wrote; "[the] future . . . when I think of the future, I get a terrible headache." She worked at the Greenhill Textile Company, located upstairs from a poolroom in a suburb of Seoul. One night a fire broke out in the factory, while the women from the day shift were sleeping in the firm's dormitory. The gate had been locked to keep drunken young men from entering, but it also kept twenty-two women from escaping, including Sammi. Her diary was retrieved from somewhere among "the soot-black sewing machines."[77]

AMORAL FAMILISM[78]

When we look at a corner vegetable store in New York City, displaying shiny apples and oranges, bright green lettuce, and glossy cabbage, the lights on twenty-four hours a day, we do not necessarily realize that an entire extended family is often employed in this enterprise, or that the enterprise is not an end in itself but an avenue to upward mobility—the suburbs and a Mercedes for the parents, Harvard for the kids.

Those Koreans who find their fortunes in America are beneficiaries of a large economic unit called the family. If you stop and think about it, there is no reason why it has to be an individual entering the marketplace to truck and barter—why not send a son down to the Fulton fish market to barter, another to truck the fish back to the store, a father to manage the store, a son to watch for shoplifters, a daughter who can speak English to sell the fish, Mom behind the cash register, eyeballing the accounts, grandmother home watching the other kids?

Economic historians never thought of this "advantage of backwardness," but whether it is Koreans in New York or Hong Kong Chinese in the electronically wired commercial archipelago running from China through Southeast Asia and Taiwan ("island China") up to LA, San Francisco, Seattle, and Vancouver, the family unit is the entrepreneur,

77. Shapiro (1990), pp. 40, 61–67, 91–94.

78. This term was originally used by Edward Banfield to describe southern Italian peasants. Dongno Kim, however, used it to analyze Korean business families in a brilliant article, "The Transformation of Familism in Modern Korean Society." *International Sociology* 5 (1990):409–25.

Schumpeter's innovator, Friedman's rational actor looking for the main chance. For Asian families this is the equivalent of the European discovery of the New World, except that today there is much more opportunity and much more wealth to go around. This New World offered a lateral move unavailable in the old society, namely, migration or immigration; it broke down the hermetic unit that was Korea. Furthermore, the questions that have so bedeviled people since the time of Smith, Bentham, Marx, and Weber—By what right does the capitalist accumulate so much wealth? What is the justice of this system of unequal gain?—these questions need not occur to a Korean family. The justice inheres in doing right by one's relatives, providing for children, remembering obligations to elders or ancestors, or simply to the poor parents who bled their knuckles so you could go to the New World.

CONCLUSION

The Korean model of development had its heyday during Park's years from 1961 to 1979, and as they ended the economy briefly ran into a period of crisis. The economy lost 6 percent of the GNP in 1980, and exports did not really rebound until 1983. For the first time Japan proved willing to step in and help bail the ROK out of its debt crisis with a $4 billion package in early 1983 (which was about 10 percent of Korea's outstanding debt and more than 5 percent of its GNP). The package consisted of $1.85 billion in governmental loans and $2.15 billion in Japanese Export-Import Bank loans at preferential interest rates. This, combined with American support and visits by Kishi Nobusuke and David Rockefeller, helped South Korea escape its economic crisis. The price Chun Doo Hwan paid was to begin to open Korean markets to American and Japanese service industries like banks and insurance companies, and to American agricultural exports of rice, wheat, tobacco, and fruit.[79]

The big push, which had contributed to the late 1970s economic difficulties (especially through idle plant capacity), became a great boon to the Korean economy in the mid-1980s as Korean exports of heavy-industrial goods took off and the economy grew by more than 12 percent per year from 1985 through 1988. Growth "dropped" to about 7 percent in 1989 and 9 percent in 1990. Inflation was relatively low (2 to 5 percent per annum), and unemployment hovered in the 2 to 4 percent range. Korea's unionization rate has remained low by international standards; about 12 percent in 1985, it was up to 18 percent by 1990—about the American rate of unionism, but much lower than European rates. Com-

79. Woo (1991), pp. 185–88.

pany assets and the stock market began to be more important sources of *chaebŏl* capital than state-mediated loans, although there were still many of the latter. The total value of the stock market increased 28-fold in the period 1980–89; that value was only 9 percent of Korea's GNP in 1985, but nearly 57 percent by 1988. In the early 1990s Korea was the ninth-largest market in the world, and predicted to be the fourth largest by the year 2000.[80] Meanwhile, the *chaebŏl*, tired of new generals coming in and seizing their property or telling them what industries to invest in, clearly moved in the same direction as the middle class, toward democratic elections and the rule of law. Their ideal was the Japanese model of stable one-party democracy. But that is for the next chapter.

It is a useful thing to keep in mind when evaluating South Korea's remarkable spurt of growth, and its relative position vis-à-vis other industrial countries and North Korea, that until the early 1990s its GNP was not as large as the annual total sales of Japan's pachinko parlors. This sounds absurd, but it is true: in 1993 the total pachinko business was estimated at $175 billion, but that was a recession figure; earlier the estimate had gone as high as $250 billion, that is, equal to the ROK's GNP circa 1992. Many Korean residents in Japan are pachinko parlor owners, and by and large their loyalty is to the North.[81] This is just one more reason not to believe the pundits who speak of "miracles" on the Han, or those who think the half-century competition between South and North is over. Koreans in the South have worked their fingers to the bone to create the industrial country that we now see; to say there was no miracle is merely to give this vast, talented population its proper acknowledgment.

80. Woo (1991), pp. 200–201.

81. *Time* estimated that upwards of $1 billion annually may go to the DPRK from pachinko operators in Japan, but I think the total is a good bit higher than that. Like many other American publications, *Time* treated this as hot news, when in fact the practice was in place at least by 1955, if not earlier. See "Kim Il Sung's Money Pipeline," *Time*, June 13, 1994.

CHAPTER SEVEN

The Virtues, II: The Democratic Movement, 1960–Present

What is violence? Bullets, nightsticks, and fists are not the only forms of violence. It is also violence when people ignore the fact that infants are starving in one corner of our city. A nation with no expression of dissent is a nation in ruins. Who would dare keep order through violence? . . . I think that in the past exploitation and barbarism were at least uncontrived. Those "educated" people who read Hamlet and shed tears over Mozart's music perhaps have lost the capability to weep over the desperate suffering of their neighbors? . . . To rule is to provide work for the people, to enable them to appreciate their own heritage, and to make their life meaningful lest they wander empty and aimless in the wasteland about them.

—*Cho Se-hŭi*[1]

In the early 1990s I was happy to receive an invitation to a conference on "development and democracy" sponsored by the International Economics Association, mainly because it was to be held in Barcelona. In the middle of our discussions, an American political scientist dissented from what he had just heard, a comment that political upheaval often follows on the heels of industrial development. "Korea has had a very smooth development, hasn't it, while growing by double digits almost every year. Hasn't it? Well, hasn't it? Don't we have a Korea expert here?" The two of us had not yet met, and I remained silent in order to see what more he might say.

It is not a surprising judgment, and may be one held by many readers of this book. The miracle on the Han was the most highly touted developmental success story in the world, until other "tigers" in East and Southeast Asia came to people's attention; Korea was supposed to be a haven of cheap and disciplined labor, talented technocrats, high GNP growth, egalitarian distribution of wealth, and citizens who never said,

1. Writers like Cho Se-hŭi have written movingly about Seoul's sweatshops and the travails of Korean factory workers, trying to give them voice. In this extract Cho examines his own society in 1976, through the eyes of his brother; it is from "A Dwarf Launches a Little Ball," trans. Chun Kyung-ja, in Lee (1990), p. 346.

"Yankee, go home." Yet every Korean republic until the one elected in 1992, under Kim Young Sam, began or ended in massive uprisings or military coups. The longest one, the Third Republic under Park Chung Hee (1961–79), began with a coup and ended with Park's murder at the hands of his own intelligence chief. The next-longest, under Chun Doo Hwan (1980–87), began and ended with popular rebellions that shook the foundations of the system.

In contrast to our Barcelona political scientist, one could just as easily argue that South Korea has had one of the most unstable political systems in the world. The touchstone of that disorder, in the recent period, was the Kwangju Rebellion in May 1980, Korea's Tiananmen nightmare in which students and young people were slaughtered on a scale the same as or greater than that in "People's" China in June 1989.[2] Kwangju is the capital of South Chŏlla Province, and like the Tonghak rebellion, the autumn harvest uprisings in 1946, and the guerrilla struggle in the Korean War, the 1980 disorders expressed the problems of underdevelopment and disenfranchisement that have haunted the old Paekche territory in the modern period. But the movements for democracy and labor rights were nationwide, and as they grew through several decades of struggle the words "Yankee, go home" became stock phrases in the dissident arsenal.

Those who praised South Korea's development rarely spoke of this dark side and all too often tended to justify the authoritarian politics of successive regimes in terms of the harsh requirements of development and security vis-à-vis North Korea, or the Confucian tradition, or the immaturity of Korean politics. A fine American secretary of state, George P. Shultz, arrived in May 1986 to praise Chun for "moving fast" toward democracy, while insulting Koreans with talk about their political immaturity compared with Filipinos—who had just vanquished the Marcos dictatorship and accomplished their "Yellow Revolution" under the leadership of Corazon Aquino.[3]

We will now examine these movements, grouped again among "the virtues" not because the members were necessarily more virtuous than those whom they opposed (although often they were) but to suggest how the moral order that Koreans thought they left behind in the twentieth century still activates their minds, the special role that students and the well-educated still play in Korean society, the dignity and valor of

2. Although dissidents in both countries argue that thousands were massacred, it appears that about 700 protesters were killed in China. In Korea the exact number has never been established; the Chun government claimed about 200 died, but recent National Assembly investigations have suggested a figure no lower than 1,000.

3. Shim Jae Hoon, "Left Out in the Cold," *Far Eastern Economic Review*, May 22, 1986, p. 14.

the rough people who built modern Korea, its massive force of blue-collar laborers, and, above all, to learn that democracy is not a gift or a political regime that one is born with but something that must be fought for every inch of the way, in every society. In this sense, the Korean struggle has been so enduring that there may be no country more deserving of democracy in our time than the Republic of Korea.

THE APRIL REVOLUTION

During some congressional hearings in the 1980s, a specialist on Korea testified that student protests drew upon wellsprings of Confucianism that demanded or even required the educated to be moral exemplars, conscientious sentinels of the nation. Representative Stephen Solarz (Democrat of New York), who during his time in Congress was a stalwart human rights advocate, responded that this was a most interesting point; he had always heard that Confucianism was a buttress of authoritarianism. In fact, the overthrow of Syngman Rhee in 1960 by phalanxes of college students and professors was the best example of the Hongian legacy in contemporary Korean political culture.

Other special circumstances also prevailed, however. College and high school enrollments had nearly quadrupled in the period 1948–60; a far higher percentage of the populace attended college in Korea than in England (by 1965, 1 of every 280 Koreans was in college, compared with 1 in 425 people in England).[4] Meanwhile, South Korea had a listed per capita income of $100 in 1960, compared with England's $1,200, a good indication that such figures often do not make for fruitful comparisons. Furthermore, most universities and certainly all of the best ones were in Seoul; sending one's son "up to Seoul" for school was a national ambition, and when the sons got there they holed up in ubiquitous *hasuk*, or boardinghouses—outside the discipline of the family. Korean universities, like those in Japan, also did not require a whole lot of their students—or for that matter their professors, who were swamped with students and frequently skipped classes. Korean students worked their tails off in high school and graduated with skills at about the level of American college juniors; Koreans got the education they needed for their careers mostly in high school; Americans, mostly in college. Yet there was a strong incentive to stay in college, and then in graduate school, since jobs were often unavailable upon graduation, particularly for liberal arts majors. When all of these things are combined, as they were in Seoul in 1960 and thereafter, it is a combustible mix indeed.

Seoul also had, and has today, a vibrant intellectual atmosphere. The

4. Henderson (1968), p. 170.

leading intellectual journal, *Ch'angjak kwa Pip'yŏng* (Creation and criticism) has a circulation of 18,000, far larger than comparable American publications. Other, less critical or exacting political journals and magazines circulate in far greater numbers. In 1960 the intellectual journal was *Sasanggye* (World of thought), one of the best in East Asia and frequently subject to closure for its criticism of the government. The number of newspapers and reporters soared in the late 1950s; by the time Chang Myŏn was in power, one survey counted 100,000 people claiming to be journalists, most of them concentrated in Seoul.[5] Meanwhile, hundreds of "tearooms" (*tabang*) had sprouted up, offering everything from a quick breakfast to your favorite music to a quick encounter with one of the waitresses; above all, people gathered there to gossip about politics. Seoul was still small enough that everybody seemed to know everyone else, and to have an opinion. Some of my earliest memories of Seoul are tearoom conversations with recent acquaintances who would proceed to excoriate every politician, parlay every rumor, and gossip endlessly about the high and mighty.

This took concentrated form in clandestine student groups, often consisting of a handful of political science or philosophy majors from the same college and the same class, meeting to exchange drinks, criticism of the regime, and oaths of loyalty. Faculty members frequently advised the group. I had an experience of this in 1972, when a student friend invited me to a meeting of his "philosophy club" held on a rooftop in one of Seoul's tangled, impenetrably dense neighborhoods near Korea University—I could never have found the place again without a chaperone. The meeting began with each member introducing himself to me, by reciting a long academic curriculum vitae and often his family's academic pedigree as well. Then I heard about how they were all committed to dying for democracy. If this seems quaint or funny, it is important to remember how many of them did just that.

President Rhee had continued to rule as an autocrat after the war, and was at his absolute worst in 1960, when he was eighty-five years old. A congenitally suspicious man, obtuse and stubborn beyond measure, he remained convinced of his own messianic importance. Ten years earlier the CIA had labeled him "senile," "indomitably strong-willed and obstinate" with "great powers of persuasion," possessing an "absolute and uncompromising" fear and hatred of communism, and devoid of patience for the idea of a legitimate opposition. Rhee, in the CIA's view, had "not hesitated to use such totalitarian tactics as stringent censorship . . . police terrorism, and . . . extra-governmental agencies such as youth corps and armed 'patriotic' societies to terrorize and destroy non-

5. Henderson (1968), p. 172.

Communist opposition groups and parties."[6] Rhee may have been many of these things, but he was not senile and he was not crazy (as several Americans thought). His adviser Robert Oliver remembered Rhee possessing in the late 1950s the same mixture of calm lucidity and mercurial eruption that had always characterized him. If the CIA thought him monumentally obstinate in 1950, so did Koreans who knew him in the 1920s. Rhee was a strange hybrid, thoroughly Korean to Americans and thoroughly alien to many Koreans, because of his long residence abroad and his Austrian wife.[7]

His personality, however, does seem modal for elderly Korean men of responsibility. It is quite common to witness in the same person, sometimes on the same day, ineffable charm and outrageous crudity—an icy Confucian demeanor of utter self-control and dignity at one point, giving way to a show of raging insanity or puerile inanity. This is often what it takes to maintain a patriarchy whose legitimation is purely traditional. As for his obstinacy and willfulness, a people that has survived for centuries under an arbitrary rule and a perennial foreign threat will have many Syngman Rhees, just as shrewd, just as Machiavellian, just as willful.

Rhee formally dominated the administration and sought to centralize everything in his own office; most officials cringed before him and feared doing anything without his approval, from major decisions to daily items like the issuance of passports, which Rhee or his close associates reviewed. Rhee personally appointed most officials at the national and provincial levels, operated a highly centralized and nepotistic spoils system, and, the CIA said, treated the prime minister like his own executive assistant.[8] But all this does not mean that everyone marched in lockstep at Rhee's order. The facade of top-down control masked a fractured regime that frequently splintered into competing clusters of power, and it is not true that Rhee was in thorough control, even if that was his goal. He sheltered his own actions from real and presumed antagonists, and they did the same to him.

Ambassador Muccio surmised that "Rhee really trusted no one—not even his wife." But it would appear that Rhee had reason to mistrust her, since she had the habit of tipping Muccio to Rhee's actions: "She quite frequently telephoned just to tip me off that he was about to do something that she thought I should know about." A Catholic, Francesca also

6. CIA, "Prospects for the Survival of the Republic of Korea," ORE 44-48, Oct. 28, 1948, Appendix A, "Personality of Syngman Rhee"; CIA, "National Intelligence Survey, Korea."
7. Oliver interview, Aug. 1985. Koreans used to apologize to Oliver for having to work for a Korean president with a foreign wife.
8. CIA, "National Intelligence Survey, Korea."

passed information to Muccio through the apostolic delegate, Father Patrick Byrne. Muccio explained this by saying she felt alone and afraid as a "white Austrian" in Korea, but he did not grasp the implications of such behavior. Perhaps he would have if Bess Truman had been in the habit of ringing up the British ambassador or the archbishop of Canterbury to let him know when old Harry was about to go off the deep end. This is just another vignette of the American habit of treating as perfectly natural their desire to monitor Rhee's every action; after all, it was the Russians who ran the *bunraku* show in Korea.[9]

American policymakers played several times during the war with the idea of replacing Rhee, by various means. After China came into the Korean War and Rhee dissolved into another foaming fit, Muccio cabled Dean Rusk, asking him to send John Chang (Chang Myŏn), the ambassador to Washington, hurrying back to head a War Cabinet, thus "to guide the Princetonian" (Muccio's moniker for Rhee). Actual planning for a coup against Rhee materialized in 1953, when he obstructed armistice negotiations by releasing anticommunist prisoners of war. Mark Clark was the main mover behind "Operation Everready," with General Paek Sŏn-yŏp the designated replacement for Rhee. But the old man outmaneuvered the Americans and remained in office.

In the middle of the war, during the temporary remove of the government to the southeast, Rhee declared martial law and suspended the National Assembly. After more squabbling with the tepid opposition over whether Korea should have a presidential system (like the United States) or a parliamentary system (like England or France), a debate that began in the 1940s and continues today, Rhee in May 1952 declared martial law, arrested twelve assemblymen, censored the press, threatened to dissolve the assembly entirely (which he had no legal power to do), and in that way intimidated the assembly into approving an amendment for direct presidential elections (which Rhee thought he could control). The murder of four American soldiers was the pretext he utilized to do this, blaming their deaths on communists; it is noteworthy that a declassified American study states that these soldiers "may have been sacrificed for the purpose [of the martial law decree] by the Koreans."[10]

The 1954 general elections gave Rhee's Liberal Party a landslide as testimony to his political controls and the weakness of the opposition. (Occasionally reports would surface, for example, that ROK commanding generals would deliver the votes of their entire divisions to the polls.)[11] He then tried to ram through a constitutional amendment giving himself

9. Truman Library, Muccio Oral History, Dec. 27, 1973, p. 29.
10. Macdonald (1992), p. 188.
11. See Macdonald (1992), p. 168.

a third term in office; he got one vote short of the necessary two-thirds majority, whereupon a mathematics professor offered some legerdemain known as the *sa-sa, o-ip* ploy (drop four tenths, add five), thereby enabling Rhee to promulgate the amendment.

Just before the 1958 National Assembly elections Rhee arrested Cho Pong-am and, after a rigged trial, executed him over strong worldwide protests. Cho had been his first minister of agriculture and was at best a tepid agrarian reformer, but he had won more than one million votes in 1956 under his "Progressive Party" banner, by advocating peaceful reunification, and thereby threatened both Rhee and the Democratic Party opposition. A month after that the Rhee government withdrew his party's registration, "under the authority of American Military Government Ordinance 55." At this time American Counter-Intelligence Corps agents were still monitoring Korean politics; they attended Cho's trial and interrogated some of the participants,[12] so perhaps Rhee didn't think the use of Ordinance 55 was as improper as did the U.S. embassy. (American officials surveilled Rhee's every move and sought by various ways to influence him to move in less dictatorial directions.)

In the winter of 1958–59 Rhee sought to amend the National Security Law, the essential constitutional loophole through which he and his successors drove any number of authoritarian measures in the postwar period (revised from time to time, it is still in effect as I write). The best study of this law estimates that 188,621 people were arrested in the first full year after its enactment in 1948. It was draconian enough to deal with people who could be accused of leftism or sympathy with the North, but it was apparently not effective enough in Rhee's eyes for use against the press and opposition political activity. Thus the third revision of the law in 1958 mandated up to five years in jail for those who "knowingly disseminate false information or who distort facts and disseminate such facts to benefit the enemy."[13] Rhee's supporters passed the amendments in a three-minute session of the assembly on December 19, while opposition legislators were barricaded in a basement restaurant—prompting fistfights on the floor the next day, and a legislative deadlock that lasted into May 1959. (In that same month Admiral Felix Stump, former Seventh Fleet commander, presented Rhee with a leadership award from the Four Freedoms Foundation.)[14]

The Rhee regime announced in February 1960 that a presidential election would be held a few weeks later, in the middle of March. As the day

12. Macdonald (1992), p. 188.
13. Park Won-soon (1993), pp. 10, 15. This book is an English-language excerpt from Park's three-volume study of the National Security Law in Korean.
14. Macdonald (1992), p. 199.

drew near, the opposition candidate, Cho Pyŏng-ok, a good friend of the Americans who had led the National Police during the occupation, died of cancer while undergoing treatment at Walter Reed Hospital in Washington. That did not postpone the elections, and neither did campaign bribery or frequent beatings of those opposed to Rhee, all happening under the noses of American and United Nations observers. Much more fraud and abuse occurred on election day, March 15, with ballot stuffing, group voting, and the sudden disappearance of ballot boxes from opposition strongholds. All this swelled implausibly large majorities for Rhee and his running mate, Yi Ki-p'ung, now enfeebled with advanced locomotor ataxia. Rhee claimed to have won nearly 90 percent of the vote. Student protests that had started up before the election now escalated all over the country; in southwestern Masan police clashed with demonstrators, killing several students. The Korean Army asked the American commander, General Carter Magruder, for permission to dispatch troops; Magruder approved and Korean Marines landed at Masan to restore order.[15]

In an unusual action the State Department told reporters that it "deplore[d] any actions taken contrary" to the principle of free and fair elections. In response Rhee yet again urged a northern expedition to unify the country. Things quieted down for a time, until April 12 when the bloated body of Kim Chu-yŏl, a middle school student still clad in his uniform, was pulled out of Masan harbor. He had been missing since election day; grenade fragments stuck out of his eye socket. Masan, which had a strong left wing in the 1940s, erupted in mass demonstrations involving as many as forty thousand people. They attacked police and government offices, and the police fired into the crowds, causing unknown numbers of casualties. Again the American commander was asked for and approved the release of troops to restore order. But rebellion spread throughout the country, and the regime declared martial law. Soon events were completely out of hand.

On April 19, 1960—long since commemorated as *sa-il-gu* (4.1.9)—an enormous crowd of at least 100,000 students and young people converged on the presidential palace and demanded to see Rhee. Palace guards fired directly into the crowd, causing pandemonium in the downtown streets of Seoul. At least 115 young people died, and nearly 1,000 were injured. Finally regular army units moved in and secured order, aided by protesting students who now believed—rightly—that many soldiers sympathized with their protests.

That evening the American ambassador, Walter P. McConaughy, went to visit Rhee and found him mostly uninformed on what had happened

15. Macdonald (1992), p. 201. This fact was generally unknown at the time.

that day—but still recalcitrant. Two days later he saw Rhee again. Somewhat like Ferdinand Marcos in 1986, Rhee thought Chang Myŏn and the Catholic archbishop in Seoul were conspiring against him, with the State Department perhaps hiding in the wings.[16] Whatever the Catholic delegate might have been doing, Chang clearly was the American favorite. The embassy in Seoul had this to say at some point in 1958 (the document itself is still classified):

> The Democratic Party merits the attention of the U.S. as a strong force in present-day politics and as the possible administration after 1960. As the Party has grown stronger and come to play the major role in a two-party system, the Embassy has given it proportionate emphasis. . . . Increasingly careful attention and planning should be devoted to the Democratic Party . . . inasmuch as a Democratic victory would require and hold great potential for the exercise of American influence to effect a basic improvement in government in Korea.[17]

On April 25 several hundred university professors held a peaceful demonstration calling for Rhee's resignation, and that evening 50,000 demonstrators demolished Vice-President Yi's home. The next day when another 50,000 people turned out in the streets of Seoul, Ambassador McConaughy and General Magruder went to Rhee and urged him to resign; as they left the palace, assembled crowds gave them a resounding ovation. This action, the frequent meetings and press releases, and the release of Korean troops convinced many that the United States had arranged Rhee's departure; a few days later demonstrators put a large floral wreath on General MacArthur's statue, as tribute. Then suddenly the departure happened: in a slow procession along streets lined with people on April 29, Syngman and Francesca Rhee went off to exile in Hawaii. Many wept as they saw the back of an octogenarian who had witnessed all of Korea's modern history, while making quite a bit of it himself.

The April Revolution and the subsequent military takeover combined to finish off a good bit of the agenda left over from the liberation period. There were still about six hundred officers in the National Police who had served the Japanese, and nearly all of these were in key positions. Most of them quit or were fired in 1960–61, and some found themselves victims again of rough peasant justice. In several rural towns people settled scores with the police that went back twenty or more years, and in one case villagers boiled a colonial policeman in oil. The Korean military

16. Macdonald (1992), p. 204.
17. The document is quoted in Macdonald (1992), p. 161, but neither its date nor its locating numbers were released for publication.

still had high officers from the Japanese period, but the young colonels arrested, fired, or retired all but a handful. Still, there was no left wing and no labor union worthy of the name in South Korea; it maintained a remarkably narrow political spectrum. Rhee's Liberal Party soon disappeared without a trace; it had been a one-man vehicle and the driver was in Hawaii.

For the first time the opposition Democratic Party organized the government, with Chang Myŏn as prime minister. Chang was a well-educated man from a landed family who spoke English fluently, a devout Catholic (something of a rarity among Korean leaders), and the Korean ambassador to the United States when the war broke out. He was almost always described in American documents as intelligent, capable, reasonable and docile, lacking the strong nationalism that characterized so many other Koreans. It would seem that when he guided the government that followed Rhee's exit, known as the Second Republic, he hardly made an important move without consulting the embassy and the Seoul station chief of the CIA.[18] But, then, the opposition had wanted a weak executive; the inheritors of the old yangban aristocracy, they favored a weak president and a hamstrung central government. That is more or less what they got in 1960–61. Chang was a decent man and a sincere if anemic democrat; but his relations with Americans represented a classic example of *sadae* (serving the great).

The Second Republic was, however, South Korea's first democratic regime. True to its word, the opposition created a bicameral parliamentary system, with the cabinet responsible to the legislature; it weakened the extensive powers of the executive, turning the presidency into a titular office of little more than ceremonial use. The new National Assembly, elected on July 29, became a forum for diverse views, the press was free, and sophisticated schemes for building the economy came from Chang's economic planners. The more open the system got, the more bickering dominated the National Assembly, and the more independent thinkers began to call for a new approach toward reunification with the North. Few days passed without street demonstrations, and sometimes the students came into the National Assembly to browbeat cowering politicians. Then began the ordeal that sent shivers up the spine of Seoul's ruling groups, recalling the period before the war: an apparent move to the left.

By this time North Korea's industrial economy had overcome the war-

18. Chang's CIA biography describes him as more reasonable and less nationalistic than other Korean politicians (CIA, "National Intelligence Survey, Korea"); Peer de Silva, the CIA chief in Seoul in 1960–61, describes his relations with Chang in *Sub Rosa: The CIA and the Uses of Intelligence* (New York: Times Books, 1978), pp. 151–71.

time destruction and was steaming far ahead of the South. On August 15, 1960, Kim Il Sung had tabled a proposal for a confederal system of unification with a supreme committee made up of representatives of both regimes, and students began marching in the streets of Seoul or planning to meet counterparts from North Korea at P'anmunjŏm. Large numbers of students joined Mint'ong, short for the National Students Federation for National Unification, and organized out of Seoul National University's politics department. This terrified the right wing and the security forces. Furthermore, the agrarian economy was still desperately poor, and by the spring famished poor peasants ran out of food stocks and began foraging in the mountains. Korea's experiment with democracy thus foundered in an unfortunate combination that linked democracy with economic stagnation, dependency on the United States, political instability, and a drift to the left. As many observers have pointed out, the political atmosphere improved dramatically in the early part of 1961. But by then the military had its pretext for action.

MILITARY RULE

The hour of the colonels began shortly after midnight on May 16, 1961. Park Chung Hee and a handful of army and marine officers swiftly positioned armored units at strategic points in Seoul, securing the city, the national radio and press, and shortly thereafter the government—bloodlessly, with about 3,500 men and a dozen or so colonels out of an army of 600,000. Chang Myŏn was sleeping in his suite at the Bando Hotel, across the street from the American embassy; at 2 A.M. he got word of the coup and fled to Seoul's Catholic archdiocese. At 3:30 A.M. his army chief of staff, General Chang To-yŏng, asked the U.S. commander Magruder to mobilize American troops to put down the coup, but Magruder refused, while saying that the United States still supported the legally constituted government. That wasn't much help to the government or hindrance to the colonels. Prime Minister Chang called the embassy in the morning, still in hiding but now demanding that Magruder "take charge" of the situation. Magruder went to meet President Yun Po-sŏn, who was less than helpful to Chang's predicament; he told Magruder that "Korea needed a strong government," and Chang had not been a leader.[19]

The next day the prime minister was still hiding. Magruder cabled his estimate of the situation to the Joint Chiefs of Staff, saying that Chang seemed to have little support and that "all the powerful men in and around the Seoul government appear to have had knowledge of the plan

19. Macdonald (1992), p. 209–10.

for the coup and at least have not opposed it." The coup was not communist inspired, Magruder reported; he had operational control of the crack ROK First Army, but thought it inappropriate to use it to put down the rebellion "on his own authority only." By this time Park controlled the ROK Army, however, and he quickly moved two divisions into Seoul without consulting Magruder, "thus challenging his operational control of the Korean armed forces"[20] (and not for the first or last time). Magruder's action—that is, his inaction—persuaded Washington to acquiesce to the coup.

By May 17 a junta of thirty colonels and junior generals had closed the National Assembly and banned all political activity. A "revolutionary committee" issued a platform calling for the eradication of "all corruptions and social evils" and the creation of a new national spirit, while pledging anticommunism and close ties with the United States. The committee also called for a "self-supporting economy" and promised to return power to civilians once these goals were realized. "Like their spiritual predecessors, the young Japanese officers of the 1930s," one scholar wrote, "they had a messianic, self-styled patriotism that despised civilian politics and believed that direct, extremist action could perfect the world."[21]

The renegade colonels had instantly spread the word on May 16 that the United States supported the coup, thus disarming many opponents. Did it? In answering this and the same question in several other like episodes (in 1972, 1979, 1980, and 1987), we have to disaggregate "the United States." In Washington, you have the White House and the NSC, the State Department, the CIA, the Pentagon, the army, military intelligence, and other unnamed or even unnamable agencies; in Seoul you have the embassy, the U.S. Army command, the CIA station, military intelligence, and assorted others. Each agency has a network of contacts and friendships with Korean counterparts. The available (incomplete) evidence does not suggest that the Kennedy White House, the State Department, or the JCS had advance knowledge of the coup. No evidence on this episode has yet been declassified from the CIA, so far as I know. In Seoul the embassy does not appear to have had any advance warning. Magruder, however, seems to have accumulated a lot of information, very quickly, on what Seoul's "powerful men" thought. The CIA station chief, Peer de Silva, merely indicates a seamless web of transition between his frequent meetings with Prime Minister Chang and his equally frequent meetings with the junta leader Park; the insurrection does not seem to have surprised him. The veteran reporter Keyes Beech

20. Macdonald (1992), pp. 212–13.
21. Henderson (1968), p. 183.

Park Chung Hee presents awards to General George H. Decker, U.S. Army chief of staff, and an unidentified American admiral.

called James Hausman (the key liaison between the U.S. command and the ROK) immediately upon getting news of the coup, and Hausman gave him "to believe that he had prior knowledge of the action."[22] The consequence of this episode for Korean-American relations seems clear, however: in 1960–61 Americans deemed it okay for the ROK Army to put down Rhee's street opposition, but not okay to put down a military coup that breached military discipline and the protocols of United Nations and American operational control over the Korean military.

The year 1961 brought another point of rupture in modern Korean history. Military leaders ran South Korea until 1993, a watershed change that deeply affected Korean politics and society. Korea had long prided itself on civilian leadership, but it now had the military in the saddle: "Unlike Japan, the Korean variant of Confucianism long held the Man on Horseback in supercilious contempt and equated the ascendancy of praetorians with national degeneration."[23] Sons of peasants now rode herd on the sons of aristocrats; young students infused with the idea that they had the mandate of heaven, the moral right to rule, often found themselves on the short end of a baton.

Park Chung Hee was born to a peasant family in North Kyŏngsang

22. De Silva (1978), pp. 151–71; author's interview with the late Keyes Beech, Feb. 1987.
23. Woo (1991), p. 97.

Province and joined the Japanese military, a new route to upward mobility outside Korea's rigid class structure. Park trained at an officers' school in Japan, and later joined the Kwantung Army in Manchuria. A biography subsidized by his supporters noted how proud he was to get a gold watch from Emperor Hirohito as a reward for his services,[24] which may have included tracking down Korean guerrillas who resisted the Japanese. Park later graduated with the second class of the Korean Military Academy under the American occupation in the fall of 1946. During the Yŏsu-Sunch'ŏn rebellion he and his brother joined the insurgents; Park was arrested as a "communist," and, according to many unconfirmed reports, helped the authorities track down remnant rebel forces. He worked in military intelligence during the Korean War, but when he made his coup in 1961 his Yŏsu background turned up in CIA files, causing momentary worry that he might be a communist.[25]

Roger Hilsman, who ran the Office of Intelligence Research in the Kennedy administration, told the National Security Council that this might be one of the most cunning communist plots in history; Koreans claim Park had a speedboat waiting in the waters off Inch'ŏn on May 16, should his coup fail: the question was, Would the boat take him to Tokyo or P'yŏngyang?[26] Brief acquaintance with General Park, however, revealed a strong anticommunist and a determined man. Soon the Kennedy administration was delighted with Park's plans for developing the economy. At this time the cutting edge in studies of political and economic development was the idea of the military as a "nation builder," and stalwarts of that genre like the University of Chicago sociologist Morris Janowitz began making frequent trips to Seoul.

The colonels now set about "purifying" Korea. Park ran Korea for the next two years under an emergency junta, called the Supreme Council of National Reconstruction (SCNR), proclaimed by a June 1961 "extraordinary measures law," which suspended most provisions of Chang Myŏn's 1960 constitution. Within a week the junta had arrested more than 2,000 politicians, including Chang Myŏn, and within a few more weeks had arrested or purged some 13,300 civil servants and military officers. A "political purification law" in March 1962 banned 4,367 politi-

24. Michael Keon, *Korean Phoenix: A Nation from the Ashes* (Englewood Cliffs, N.J.: Prentice-Hall International, 1977), p. 45.

25. Park's participation in the rebellion is documented, but his role in tracking down rebels—including his own brother, as the story had it—cannot be documented except in newspaper accounts of questionable reliability. "Major Pak Chung Hi" is included in a list of field grade officers in the ROKA "confined for subversive activities" on Nov. 11, 1948. RG338, KMAG file, box 5412, W. H. Secor to PMAG Chief of Staff, Nov. 12, 1948.

26. The Hilsman story is true (as Kennedy Library files show); the Korean story cannot be verified.

cians from politicking for six years. Forty-nine of the sixty-four daily newspapers in Seoul were closed, and nearly 14,000 people were arrested under the catch-all category of "hooligans." The colonels even put dampers on Seoul's raucous life after dark, centered on the exuberant Myŏngdong district, neon signs ablaze and using almost as much precious electricity as Tokyo's Ginza. Park added an anticommunist law, to go along with the still-extant National Security Law, in June 1961; all socialist countries were defined as enemy states.[27]

We might pause to ask if there were justifiable reasons for this complete deactivation of political life. There were none that would accord with any definition of democracy. Nonetheless, the measures were not entirely unpopular. As Jung-en Woo argued, the only democracy Japan knew after 1952 or that South Korea knew in the 1950s, was a Schumpeterian circulation of elites where the state and business worked together, the bureaucrats posing and business disposing, while both kept the politicians happy and well bankrolled as long as they did not cause too much trouble in the legislature. A superficially broad political spectrum in Japan, including communists and socialists in the Diet, masked the dominance of a strong conservative coalition that kept the LDP in power for half a century. Japan in the 1950s, of course, protected basic freedoms, and its growth boom was difficult for anybody to argue with. Korea in the 1950s had neither. But the model of a one-party dominant system that could also call itself a democracy has been strong in Korea and eventually appeared to have been realized with the 1992 elections—only to founder again as the ruling party fell apart.

If, however, you had neither an effective bureaucracy nor an enterprising business community, no growth, and no political stability, with every politician thinking it his birthright to be supported and have his every opinion heard, above all a historically obsolescent landed class of would-be aristocrats who had lorded it over the common people for centuries and now claimed to be the principled democratic opposition—that is, the South Korean system in the 1950s—then one can understand how different the junta's dictatorship was from, say, a French junta shutting down parliament, why it was popular with many ordinary people, and why, far from paralyzing the streets in mass rebellion, the coup was almost entirely bloodless.

The garden-variety national assemblyman of the 1950s would rise in the morning and have breakfast while his driver warmed up his slick black war-surplus Jeep, dusted off the metal canopy on top, and straightened out the white linens on the seats. Soon they would motor down to the local tearoom for some serious gossiping; off they would go in a

27. Kim (1971), pp. 111–12; Henderson (1968), p. 184; Choi (1990), p. 30.

cloud of dust, various and sundry servants bowing low. After an hour or two of tea and capital scuttlebutt, it was off to the National Assembly building—but only to the Speaker's office, where your comrades were holding a sit-down strike to protest some outrageous measure by the ruling party. A brief comment for the journalists, a stroll into your office, the entire staff at attention, some alms for this bowing and fawning group and a bit of business, and then it was time for lunch at the mildly disguised Japanese restaurant with your stalwart opposition buddies, while *kisaeng* girls dropped sashimi into your mouth with their chopsticks at those rare moments when your jaw stopped flapping. By three in the afternoon it was time for the entourage to motor back to the legislature, and repeat the morning routine: but all too soon the sun had set over Seoul's mountains and it was time to head for festive Myŏngdong, for some Korean barbecue and *soju* (a kind of vodka) and more willing *kisaeng* girls. Or maybe there was a party at the American embassy, and the driver would go pick up your "temporary wife," the young and beautiful Ewha Women's University coed who spoke English well (unlike your dowdy old spouse) and who would duly impress the diplomats. This may sound like a harsh caricature, but I witnessed such things more than once, so average Koreans, struggling to support their families, must have seen them all too often. To move from autocratic patriarch to gallant democrat in a brief period of time is unquestionably hard; but to make this move back and forth every day, posturing all the while, is infuriating.

Gregory Henderson, a Korea hand if there ever was one, finely drew yet another distinction between Great Japan and the South Korea that often seemed to mimic it:

> The relationship of superior and inferior is relished less, even among the humble, than in Japan. . . . The government, politicians, youth groups, veteran's associations, gang leaders, beggars, one's own expanding household, one's children's school, and one's wide circle of poor relatives with their needs for weddings, schooling, and funerals all vie with each other for whatever a man has, some not without force and blackmail.[28]

Of course, relatives, schools, weddings, funerals all have worth. But what can be said for the politicians? A rational analysis might say that a certain insubordinate and even mutinous mentality is what we should expect in a poor economy with a seemingly endless zero-sum struggle, but then "the weapons of the weak," as the late historian E. P. Thompson called them, are also raised to an art form in Korean society. So, for

28. Henderson (1968), p. 230.

a nation of current and recent peasants to watch the political class cashiered for a few months or years, by someone instantly recognizable as a son of the peasantry, was doubtless met with much mirth and silent approbation.

In addition to his disciplined military spit and polish, Park's World War II experience in Manchuria served him well, as did his extensive ties with the Japanese right wing—including former "class A" war criminals like the politician Kishi Nobusuke, the rich man Sasakawa Ryoichi, and many other not necessarily savory characters. The real brains behind the coup, however, was Kim Chŏng-p'il, a graduate of the eighth class of the Military Academy in 1949 and a nephew of Park Chung Hee by marriage. Kim was the key builder of the two truly new political institutions of the Third Republic: the Korean Central Intelligence Agency (KCIA) and the political organization it set up, the Democratic Republican Party (DRP).[29] In founding the KCIA on June 13, 1961, he was helped by the U.S. CIA, although exactly what help the Americans gave remains mostly classified; in building the DRP, he took lessons from Chiang Kai-shek's Nationalist Party (Kuomintang), which had long operated on Leninist principles of internal organization (Soviet agents had advised the Chinese Nationalists in the 1920s). And when he couldn't raise enough money at home by hook or crook, he went to Japan and got $66 million, as we saw in the last chapter.

Kim became a legendary figure in South Korean politics, charming, affable, well organized, and effective. He was loyal to a fault to his classmates; the military class of 1949 turned out to have talents no one had quite discerned before: sixteen minister-level officials and twenty-four national assemblymen.[30] Kim was excoriated from time to time for corruption and forced into exile more than once. He was a survivor, though, and in 1994 was chairman of the ruling Democratic Liberal Party, still one of the "three Kims" that dominated Seoul's politics.

For a few years the DRP bid fair to be the first coherent and effectively organized noncommunist political party in ROK history. The Harvard political scientist Rupert Emerson helped prepare a new constitution in 1963, the drafting of which was handled by a committee within the KCIA, and his colleague Samuel Huntington lauded the DRP in his seminal 1968 book, *Political Order in Changing Societies*.[31] Huntington's argument was that nations undergoing rapid industrial development needed

29. Henderson (1968), pp. 305–6.

30. Park (1993), p. 152.

31. Huntington's book was probably the most important text in comparative politics for the next twenty years; on Emerson's role and the KCIA auspices, see Macdonald (1992), pp. 171, 220.

political institutions that could channel and accommodate newly "socially mobilized" citizens. The DRP seemed to be such a vehicle.

The Kennedy administration brought consistent pressure on General Park to return to civilian rule in the period 1961–63, including the suspension of development loans and public criticism of the constant backsliding in scheduling elections. After a sharp power struggle between Park and Kim Chŏng-p'il, Kim left Korea "for extended travel" and Park lifted political restrictions on 2,300 former politicians so that they could participate in election campaigning. Later, when it looked as if he might lose the 1963 election, Park threatened to declare martial law and prolong the junta for four more years, causing Ambassador Sam Berger to threaten open American opposition to Park's plans. Berger succeeded in keeping the elections on schedule. As an official study delicately noted, however, the assassination of Ngo Dinh Diem in Vietnam (with American support) caused some Koreans to draw "a parallel between U.S. attitudes toward Park" and the overthrow of the South Vietnamese government, giving Park the chance to exploit "explicit anti-Americanism" in his campaigning.[32]

From the start the colonels had bet on their anticommunism to stay the American hand if it came to outright intervention against them, and they were proved right. Park was able to arrest hundreds of America's close friends in the Democratic Party, destroy the representative institutions of 1960–61, violate the joint command, muzzle the press, and throw innocent people into jail wholesale, while continuing to slurp at the trough of the American taxpayer. Kim Chŏng-p'il built the KCIA into an elaborate, very well-funded organization employing tens of thousands of agents, combining the functions of the American CIA, the FBI, and a political machine worthy of Boss Tweed into an organization that dominated Korean political life right down to the point where its chief shot Park Chung Hee to death over dinner one night in October 1979. The KCIA became an alternative to the military as an avenue of upward mobility, and every KCIA chief became a rival to Park Chung Hee—including Kim Chŏng-p'il, who was frequently rumored to be hatching his own coup against Park.

The United States did succeed in getting Park to don mufti and run for election, through frequent threats to tie aid to the holding of elections. The KCIA-drafted constitution made for a weak, unicameral National Assembly whose legislative action was subject to the decrees of the SCNR. In spite of these new institutions and extensive KCIA involvement, in the October 1963 presidential elections Park only narrowly

32. Macdonald (1992), pp. 222–25.

defeated the opposition candidate, Yun Po-sŏn, but the ruling party was still able to dominate the weakened legislature after elections the following month, because of a new system of proportional gerrymandering. It got less than a third of the popular vote, but had 110 of 175 seats in the new National Assembly: 88 seats that its candidates had won and 22 that it arranged from the top through "proportional representation."

For the next two years the dominant issue was the normalization treaty with Japan. Large student demonstrations began in the spring of 1964, amid new threats to abolish the National Assembly and reinstitute martial law. Things came to a head in June 1964 when, once again, Park declared martial law and the American commander acquiesced to the use of two combat divisions of ROK Army troops to quell massive street demonstrations. Ambassador Berger thought Kim Chŏng-p'il was the main magnet for dissent, and succeeded in getting him to leave the country again, this time to attend Henry Kissinger's international seminar at Harvard University.[33] Things quieted down as the rhythm of another school term began in August, but started up again in April 1965, with incessant demonstrations continuing until August—but this time martial law was not invoked. The normalization of Korean relations with Japan, which did so much for the Korean economy, was thus accomplished only after massive demonstrations and political disorders lasting several years. In August 1965 the ruling party voted 110 to nothing to ratify the treaty, the opposition members having boycotted the National Assembly. In Japan LDP politicians used "blitzkrieg" tactics to push it through the Diet over Socialist Party opposition, and the treaty became valid in December 1965.[34]

The period from 1965 to 1971 was one of rapid economic growth and comparative political stability. Park ran for reelection in 1967, and by then the fruits of the export-led program had translated into political popularity. Park won by more than a million votes (again over Yun Po-sŏn) in a reasonably fair election; that the DRP and KCIA had literally tens of millions of dollars to throw around did not hurt, of course. In 1968 the KCIA kidnapped several Koreans living in West Germany and brought them back to Seoul for trial on charges that they were pro-North, an act that nearly brought the Bonn government to break off relations with Korea. Among those captured was the great opera composer Yun I-sang, who once told me that he encountered in his jail Korean students who had been kidnapped in the United States and returned to Seoul. On the whole, however, this period was one of relative freedom and growing

33. Macdonald (1992), p. 227.
34. Macdonald (1992), p. 135.

prosperity. I lived in Korea for part of that time, and its atmosphere was rather like the scene in the mid-1990s of relative press freedom, party competition, and endless bickering, mudslinging, boycotts, sitdown strikes, and other shenanigans in the National Assembly. On the other hand, if the duty of an opposition is to oppose, in the British phrase, the Korean version did precious little in the late 1960s. From 1967 to 1971 not one of 306 administration-sponsored bills was rejected in the National Assembly.[35]

THE YUSHIN SYSTEM

Dissent in the 1960s took much the same form that it had in the April Revolution, namely, an elite protest by students, intellectuals, and remnant aristocrats (like Yun Po-sŏn) who considered it their birthright and solemn duty to admonish the powerful—particularly if the powerful were untutored military men. Through their sacrifice and sporadic American pressure, South Korea seemed to have entered a fairly stable, if often raucous, form of limited pluralism, representing the still-small urban middle class. It was a politics remote from the still-substantial rural peasantry, and without political relationship to the growing blue-collar labor force. All that changed as the 1970s dawned, throwing Korea headlong into twenty years of deep crisis that shook the foundations of the system—in 1972, 1979–80, and 1987. Nevertheless, it came as a surprise when Park decided to batten down all the hatches in 1971–72, let the KCIA loose everywhere, and declare himself president for life. That decision killed him seven years later.

Since Gregory Henderson could not have known this in a book published in 1968, his judgment on the KCIA at that time is worth recalling:

> The [K]CIA replaced ancient vagueness with modern secrecy and added investigation, arrest, terror, censorship, massive files, and thousands of agents, stool pigeons, and spies both at home and abroad. . . . In [Korean] history's most sensational expansion of . . . function, it broadly advised and inspected the government, did much of its planning, produced many of its legislative ideas and most of the research on which they were based, recruited for government agencies, encouraged relations with Japan, sponsored business companies, shook down millionaires, watched over and organized students . . . and supported theaters, dance groups, an orchestra, and a great tourist center [Walker Hill].[36]

35. Kim Se-jin, "National Government and Politics in South Korea," in Kim and Cho (1976), p. 82.
36. Henderson (1968), p. 264.

The only thing missing from this long 1960s list is the KCIA's sponsorship of Sun Myung Moon's obscure religious sect, the Unification Church, which soon produced a globe-stretching organization.[37] If in the 1960s the KCIA was more restrained, in the 1970s its very lack of restraint seemed only to bring more problems for the head of the regime.

One bellwether, so to speak, of this changed era was the frequent wafting through Seoul of trailing wisps of acrid, burning gas—tear gas. Some reporters came to call Korea the "tear gas nation." During the protests over the normalization of relations with Japan in the spring of 1965, dissidents had accused the United States of supplying "poisonous chemical weapons" to the Park regime, whereupon it turned out that under its aid program, the United States had been supplying "standard riot control materials, such as tear gas," to the ROK Army for some time and continued to do so for many years thereafter.[38] By the 1980s the Koreans had taken over this technology, too; Han Yun-jo, the woman who owned Samyang Chemicals and wangled an exclusive contract to supply the gas, frequently paid the highest annual taxes of any business person in Korea ($3.4 million tax on a gross income of $7.3 million in one year).[39]

One day in mid-October 1971 I was studying on the campus of Korea University, the most prestigious private university in Seoul. The regime issued a "garrison decree," and suddenly armored columns of tanks burst through the campus gates and began spraying tear gas everywhere. Troops set up bivouac tents in the middle of the campus. I escaped with a woman professor who showed me how to climb a back fence onto the roof of a gas station; we descended to terra firma on a ladder. Having been gassed by American police during antiwar demonstrations in the period 1969–71, I can assure the reader that the Korean variety was a far more virulent kind of "pepper gas," excruciating to the eyes and nostrils. By the 1980s the whole process had become mechanized; as students

37. See Boettcher (1980), pp. 39–40. Robert Boettcher was the chief investigator for Congressman Donald Fraser's "Koreagate" inquiry. Pak Bo Hi, for many years Moon's right-hand man and translator, was a KCIA man in Washington in the early 1960s. The KCIA was also involved in the introduction from Japan of the Saenara automobile in the early 1960s, from which has grown an immensely tangled web of intrigue woven around the now deceased founder, Pak No-chong, and his widow, Pak Kyŏng-yun, who in 1994 was said to be a key link between the Unification Church and North Korea, and a broker for North Korean business deals in China. She is said to have personally escorted Pak Bo Hi to P'yŏngyang to attend the funeral of Kim Il Sung. See U Chong-ch'ang's report in *Chugan Chosŏn* (Seoul, Aug. 18, 1994), pp. 22–23, translated in United States Foreign Broadcast Information Service, "East Asia Report," FBIS-EAS-94-187, Sept. 27, 1994, pp. 49–50.

38. Macdonald (1992), p. 108. This was, of course, a secret program, but an opposition leader in Korea learned of it and forced the American commander in Korea, General Hamilton Howze publicly to admit its existence, on April 23, 1965.

39. Ogle (1990), p. 99.

would gather on the streets, Black Marias the size of tanks (but armored vans in fact) would roar into their midst, spewing out tear gas through yawning holes in their sides.

A month after the occupation of Korea University came emergency measures justified in terms of national security (see below), and a year later came martial law, thousands of arrests, and the proclamation of Park's famous "Yushin system." "Yushin" is the Korean pronunciation of the Japanese *issin*, used by the Meiji leaders in 1868. Not for the last time, Seoul's rulers made their incessant anti-Japanese bombast look empty and silly by taking yet another model from their former colonial ruler; as we saw in the last chapter, Park sought to use Japanese values and practices to make a big happy family of the workplace, and he justified his deactivation of the National Assembly in terms of "organic cooperation" between the executive and the legislature. Few Koreans bought this rhetoric, however, even if many foreigners did.

The changes were nonetheless deep and definitive. Park had his scribes write a new constitution removing all limits on his tenure in office and giving him powers to appoint and dismiss the cabinet and even the prime minister, to designate one-third of the National Assembly (reducing it to a rubber stamp and a cringing bunch of myrmidons), to suspend or destroy civil liberties, and to issue decrees for whatever powers the Yushin framers forgot to include.[40] Meanwhile, the National Security Law and the anticommunist law remained in place; still, emergency decrees flew out of the Blue House like bats at dusk in the early 1970s. One 1973 decree declared all work stoppages to be illegal, and the infamous no. 9 in 1974 more or less made any criticism of the regime a violation of national security.

What caused the turn toward full-blown, formal authoritarianism? Park justified the new course by reference to rapid changes in the international arena, and his reasons should not be dismissed as purely self-serving. In this period the Cold War in East Asia began to end, two decades before the fall of the Berlin wall. Dramatic changes in U.S. foreign policy deeply shocked Seoul and made it appear to be the last domino in Asia. Henry Kissinger's clandestine visit to Beijing in July 1971 and Richard Nixon's state visit the following February led to the "Shanghai communiqué" and an effective end to American support for the Republic of China on Taiwan. The "Nixon Doctrine" also clearly signaled a withdrawal without victory from the endless Vietnam War, thus jeopardizing Seoul's counterpart regime in Saigon. The ROK had concluded its own bloody war with China just eighteen years earlier, Taiwan was a

40. A good account can be found in C. I. Eugene Kim, "Korea at the Crossroads: The Birth of the Fourth Republic," *Pacific Affairs* 46 (Summer 1973): 218–31.

close anticommunist ally, and 50,000 Korean soldiers still fought in Vietnam. Furthermore, Nixon announced the withdrawal of a full division of American troops from Korea, reducing the total numbers from 62,000 to 42,000. Around this time a State Department official, Francis Underhill, "wrote a notorious memorandum" advocating "total military disengagement from South Korea."[41] A sense of crisis afflicted Seoul within and without, and the regime reacted with a complex mixture of rigid authoritarianism, dramatic change in the political economy (the "big push," which we surveyed earlier), and some quick footwork in foreign policy.

The Nixon administration did not try to rein in civil and human rights violations by the regime, acquiescing to and even supporting the transformations of the system in successive Octobers (1971 and 1972), which gave Park space to do what he wanted at home. Just as he ignored advice from American-trained technocrats on the Third Five-Year Plan, so he now justified his draconian measures as "Korean-style democracy" (*Han'guk-sik minjujuŭi*), an early elaboration of Singapore's theme that "Western-style democracy" is alien to capitalist Asia or of Deng Xiaoping's "socialism with Chinese characteristics." If Richard Nixon was declaring his independence of America's Cold War commitments in the region, Park would declare Korean independence in politics, economics—and national security.

It was at this time that South Korea embarked on an expensive, highly secret nuclear program to reprocess plutonium into weapons-grade fuel and build atomic weapons; a blistering cable from Kissinger shut down the direct weapons program, but the Park government still fooled with "heavy water and other hanky-panky," in the words of one American official, which included buying specifications and assembly equipment from an American firm for the Atlas Centaur missile.[42] (This experience helps to explain the North's mirror-image program, begun when it needed to match developments in the South and then revived when it had its back to the wall, after the collapse of the Soviet bloc in 1989.)

Meanwhile, Park hedged all his bets by dispatching his KCIA chief, Yi Hu-rak, on a secret mission to P'yŏngyang, where he held discussions with Kim Il Sung's brother, Kim Yŏng-ju; Kim Yŏng-ju came down to Seoul as well, and the two sides held many discussions. The public knew nothing about this when it happened, of course, but it resulted in a sensational press conference at KCIA headquarters in July 1972, where it was disclosed that both regimes had committed themselves to peaceful reunification and a "broad national unity" apart from the influence

41. Boettcher (1980), p. 35.
42. Quoted in Hayes (1991), p. 205.

of "outside forces." That the carefully orchestrated announcement came on the fourth of July seemed to be a joint declaration of Korean independence by both regimes, with P'yŏngyang distancing itself from Moscow then and for much of the 1970s. The North Korean press touted the agreement as follows:

> Korea is one. Twenty-seven years of division into North and South Korea. Through these years under the divided sky and land, tree rings of the people's suffering were etched and a whole new generation of people grew up. But who is to say he can slice a stream of water into two? Who is to say he can split the sky into two? Korea, which lived as one land through the 5,000 years of its history inheriting a single line of blood, is one.[43]

On July 4 one of the dissident students from the "philosophy club" came running over to see me. "I might become a communist!" he exclaimed. "Why?" "I just saw Kim Il Sung's face and he's very handsome!" Kim's photograph had been published for the first time in South Korea, which had always blocked it from appearing before—sometimes by the simple measure of splotching black ink over Kim's picture in international magazines like *Time*; of course, caricatures of his features were cartoon staples and festooned carnival effigies that people tried to smack at three baseballs for a quarter, often with a gigantic flea-infested boil on his neck added for good measure. (Kim had a large calcium deposit behind his right ear for decades, a common affliction from a malnourished youth that Koreans call a *hok*. North Korea never photographed him from that side, while South Korean sources flummoxed the Western press time and again with stories about its being a cancerous tumor.)

The United States knew about the secret talks, since it controlled the P'anmunjŏm truce area through which the black cars of both sides motored and since it monitored electronically Park's Blue House conversations (a fact that came out during the "Koreagate" scandal). In a little-noticed footnote in Kissinger's subsequent memoirs, he wrote that when he infiltrated himself into Beijing in July 1971, Foreign Minister Chou En-lai excused himself one evening to go and have dinner with Kim Il Sung. P'yŏngyang did not announce this visit, but ten years later when I mentioned this anecdote to one of my North Korean "travel guides," he showed no surprise and instantly shot back, "Do you think they talked?" Perhaps Kissinger did meet with Kim, perhaps not. But their joint presence in Beijing sent instant tremors through Seoul. President Nixon may have had a behind-the-scenes role in promoting inter-Korean talks, since

43. *P'yŏngyang Times*, July 15, 1972.

a unified Korea still friendly to the United States and China would fit perfectly the logic of his realpolitik vision, predicated on new warming with China and new pressures on Japan. I have seen no evidence that he did, however.

There was also a superficially simple explanation for Yushin: Park almost lost the 1971 election. The opposition candidate Kim Dae Jung outpolled Park with 46 percent of the vote, in spite of massive vote buying helped along by some $7 million from American oil firms (see below). Behind Kim's success were two new and transformative phenomena: Kim's mass politics, and the underdevelopment of the Chŏlla provinces.

Kim Dae Jung came from the port of Mokp'o in South Chŏlla, and he was no aristocrat like Yun Po-sŏn. In 1945 he did what every other patriotic and conscientious young man did in thoroughly left-wing Mokp'o—he joined a people's committee. Thereafter he worked his way up through the ranks of the Democratic Party, which was better organized in the Chŏllas than in any other rural area. By 1971 he was in his mid-forties and full of charismatic power. Americans who met him found a fairly stolid, unthreatening Confucian gentleman, but he could work a crowd better than any other politician. Kim took the legitimate grievances of an aroused Chŏlla population, left out in the cold by the miracle on the Han, and became their complete advocate, their champion, their unquestioned leader. When he could run for office, which was not often over two decades, he rolled up voting percentages in his home region that would shock political scientists (see below).

In the 1970s there were no elections after Kim got his 46 percent, but the Blue House continued to notice him: he was run over by a truck in 1971, kidnapped in 1973, put under house arrest until 1979, indicted in 1980 on trumped-up charges of having fomented the Kwangju Rebellion and nearly executed until the Carter and Reagan administrations (one leaving, one incoming) jointly intervened in late 1980, exiled to the United States in 1982, returned to house arrest again in 1985, and finally able to run in the 1987 direct presidential elections, only to lose when the opposition once again split and Kim Young Sam ran against him, thus electing Roh Tae Woo with a little over one-third of the vote. Kim's mass appeal sharply transformed Korea's pattern of authoritarianism and elite democracy.

Kim's abduction in August 1973 was known by Americans to have been a KCIA plot. Donald L. Ranard, former Korea Desk director in the State Department, told Kyodo News Service on May 16, 1979, that the KCIA was responsible; South Korean authorities, he said, had admitted to Ambassador Richard Sneider in January 1975 that Kim Tong-ŏn, the first secretary in the Korean embassy in Tokyo and a KCIA man, had taken part in the abduction. Ranard also cited a telegram from the U.S. ambassador to Seoul at the time, Philip Habib, dated August 21, 1973, and giving the same facts.

In 1972 I traveled extensively through the Chŏllas, mapping for myself the towns and counties struck by disorders in the 1940s. I rode on local buses, jerry-built with sheetmetal perched on old military half-ton trucks. Unlike people in Seoul, local people on the buses frequently stared at me with uncomplicated, straightforward hatred. The roads were still mostly hard-packed dirt, sun-darkened peasants bent over ox-driven plows in the rice paddies or shouldered immense burdens like pack animals, thatch-roofed homes were sunk in conspicuous privation, and old Japanese-style city halls and railroad stations were unchanged from the colonial era. At unexpected moments along the way, policemen would materialize from nowhere and waylay the bus to check the identification cards of every passenger, amid the sort of generalized sullenness and hostility that I had seen before only in America's urban ghettoes. The Chŏllas had been left alone to feed rice to Japan in the colonial period, and they were left alone again as the regime poured new investment into the southeast.

Jung-en Woo has argued that the change in hegemonic (that is, American) policy was more important than Kim's challenge, but that the overriding reason for Yushin was the big push in heavy industry, which Park had long dreamed about, along with a crisis in government-business relations over how to finance Korean growth that lasted for the two years before Yushin.[44] In 1969 thirty firms went bankrupt, sending them into receivership, Korean-style: the state took them over. Another ninety were about to go belly up, and most had been recipients of foreign loans. By 1971 the number of bankruptcies among firms getting foreign loans had reached two hundred, and Korea's external debt had climbed to 30 percent of the GNP. The International Monetary Fund (IMF) stepped in with a stabilization program, limiting Korea's appetite for foreign loans and requiring an 18 percent devaluation of the won in 1971. Business firms, unable to get subsidized state loans, were forced to turn to the market-rate loans of the "curb," which only increased bankruptcies, since the state could not bail them out.

Meanwhile, Park was agitated about Kim Dae Jung and labor was more restive than ever before, with 1,656 disputes in 1971. The ruling party had splintered into four personal fiefdoms, with Park and Kim Chŏng-p'il running the two most powerful cliques. Amid that turmoil, Woo writes, "business was the pivotal force that finally tipped the balance in favor of full-fledged authoritarianism." What did business want?

44. Woo (1991), pp. 109–15.

A massive state-sponsored bailout, the costs of which would fall upon someone else—the 210,000 Koreans who had their money invested in the curb market, at an average of about $2,900 apiece. Park caved in and dropped his bombshell on August 3, 1971: "an immediate moratorium on all payments of corporate debt owed to the private, domestic financial market—the curb." Small investers were "stunned and incredulous," unable to believe the news they watched on TV. Big business, however, "was thus resuscitated overnight."[45]

Here is how Woo summed up Korean state-business relations:

> The state has its hand on the tiller but business provides the motive force. The state is strong in that it can—and does—give and take life away from individual firms; but it is constrained by virtue of being a capitalist state whose survival is contingent on the health and contentment of the business class.[46]

It was a short move from August 3, 1971, to the garrison decree of October and to the Yushin system that evolved over the next year.

THE KCIA IN THE 1970S

How did a new Korean intelligence agency originate? A formerly classified State Department study states that by the mid-1950s "counter-subversion had become a major U.S. government concern throughout the Free World"; thus under a plan known as the "1290-d program," American authorities assisted ROK security agencies with "equipment and a modest training program" and tried to bring about better coordination among Korea's myriad intelligence groups. This, the study said, was the "sorcerer's apprentice" that led to the vast Korean Central Intelligence Agency, an organization "far transcending the advisers' intentions."[47]

Under Kim Chŏng-p'il the KCIA used "unbudgeted funds" for political purposes, which for a time tended to lessen generalized "corruption" because it so concentrated the process of funding political activities, and anything else Park and Kim wanted to support, at a central and higher level.[48] Although the claim cannot now be proved, many observers also thought heavy monies went to the opposition, which might account for its habit of dividing into two just before election time. (In 1995 investigations revealed that Kim Dae Jung had gotten $2.5 million in Blue House "slush funds" for his presidential campaign in 1992, and rumors persisted that Kim Young Sam also got large amounts from the same

45. Woo (1991), p. 113.
46. Woo (1991), pp. 111–13.
47. Macdonald (1992), p. 107.
48. Macdonald (1992), p. 179.

source in the 1987 campaign.) Certainly the KCIA constantly infiltrated agents into opposition parties, who acted as agents provocateurs or pushed for additional candidates to run for party leader, or for election. To call this "corruption" is perhaps misleading; this was the way politics worked through much of postwar Korean history. Foreign experts can be excused for wondering why Koreans seem to get so embarrassed every time another scandal is unveiled (as in 1995–96); it's a bit like Madonna complaining about a violation of her virtue.

Park's junta was a good bit more systematic than Syngman Rhee in requiring wealthy people to cough up, however, and the amounts grew by leaps and bounds. In August 1961 the regime simply announced that twenty-seven businessmen would be required to provide $37 million, or else their factories might be confiscated. In 1962 Kim and the KCIA acquired operating funds through "highly questionable commercial operations and in a blatant rigging of the Seoul stock exchange." The stock issue gambit alone netted $40 million, and that was just the tip of an iceberg.[49] Every large business firm was routinely expected to fork over small fortunes, and foreign firms like the Gulf Oil Corporation kicked in large amounts just before elections ($1 million from Gulf in 1967 and $3 million in 1971, plus another $4 million from Caltex Petroleum, according to Senate hearings in the mid-1970s; Americans called this "the J Factor" meaning "juice money," a political price of doing business in Korea).[50] No doubt much of this activity was brokered by American CIA operatives working with the Korean CIA, as in Italy and Japan in the early postwar period.

In the early 1960s the United States still spent $500 million a year to support the ROK,[51] which was occasionally brought to the attention of Korean leaders, especially after an abrupt currency conversion in 1962. American officials howled privately and now and again publicly over Kim Chŏng-p'il's shenanigans, but he used American protests to stimulate already rising nationalism, presenting himself as the victim of Yankee bullies. The embassy had been far happier with Cho Pyŏng-ok, Chang Myŏn, and others in the KDP group during the Rhee years, and many Americans in the official entourage, like the cultural attaché Gregory Henderson, later became vocal critics of the militarists who now governed in Seoul. By the same token the Democratic Party had learned to depend on American support, and tended to turn to the embassy in crises, thus undercutting its patriotic credentials. The result was that Park and Kim often convinced Koreans that they were defending Korean

49. Macdonald (1992), p. 218; Henderson (1968), p. 264.
50. Boettcher (1980), pp. 26–27, 92.
51. Macdonald (1992), p. 218.

sovereignty when they resisted American pressures or ran roughshod over the civil rights of people whom the United States had backed. Furthermore, Kim deftly played the embassy off against other Americans in the army and the CIA, a pattern that continued for the next thirty years. For every ambassador trying to rein in the Park regime, there was another American willing to defend it.

Allen Dulles, director of the CIA, invited Kim to visit Washington in September 1962 hoping "to expose him directly to Washington views and influence"; he also met with Bobby Kennedy, then the attorney general.[52] Kim quickly utilized this attention to show Koreans that he had strong backing in Washington (and in fact he did). In the State Department and the embassy, however, he was not appreciated. Assistant Secretary of State Averell Harriman directed the Far Eastern Office, and in 1963 he drew up plans for withdrawing American forces from Korea.[53] The question whether the plans would have been implemented became moot after the assassination of John Kennedy and the subsequent escalation of the Vietnam War, but Richard Nixon returned to them ten years later and succeeded in withdrawing a division of American combat troops. U.S. military forces had been continuously at a strength of two army divisions or more from 1945 until that point, with the exception of the period June 30, 1949–July 1950. They have remained at one army division and various air force, navy, and other supporting units, varying between 38,000 and 42,000 in total numbers, from the early 1970s down to this writing.

By the Yushin period the KCIA was a complete rogue institution, using its immense power at will to reward friends and punish enemies. In spite of power struggles within the KCIA, it was for all intents and purposes a smooth-functioning agency, with swift communications up and down its lines, and sideways with the National Police, the Army Security Command, district and local government offices, and many other agencies.[54] Its agents were everywhere, not just in all potentially oppositional political groups but in newspaper offices, radio and TV stations, company unions, college classrooms in Korea—even in college classrooms in the United States. One of my former students returned to an elite Korean university to teach and soon was made a dean. He once told me that during student demonstrations—meaning most of the time—he was reporting to seven different agencies on a weekly basis: the district police, the district government office, military intelligence, and several within or connected to the KCIA.

52. Macdonald (1992), p. 219.

53. A friend with access to Harriman's personal papers showed me a top-secret memorandum to this effect.

54. Choi (1990), pp. 97–98.

Another friend, now a professor at one of Seoul's best universities, wrote a dissertation at a foreign university on Korean politics during the period of the American military government. When he returned to Seoul in the mid-1970s, he was taken to the South Mountain headquarters of the KCIA, where interrogators hooked him up to electrical torture machines and began reading passages from his thesis, asking him why he had said this, why he had said that, each question punctuated by excruciating pain. The torturers also dialed up his wife, an artist, and left the phone off the hook so that she could hear her husband screaming. About five years later this man was a visiting scholar in the United States, and once asked me to drive him to the grocery store and then to the liquor store: he still could not sleep at night without first downing some whiskey. His wife had a psychogenic nervous ailment in her extremities, making it impossible for her to continue her career. Fortunately she recovered and resumed her career in the 1980s. This family was saved through powerful personal connections; others were not so fortunate.

A *New York Times* reporter wrote this about the KCIA in 1973: "The agents watch everything and everyone everywhere. . . . [T]he agency once put a telephone call through from Seoul to a noodle restaurant in the remote countryside where a foreign visitor had wandered on a holiday without telling anyone." Korean citizens believed that the best way to deal with KCIA surveillance was "not to talk about anything at all to anybody," even to members of one's family.[55]

The dreaded event was "the trip to *Namsan* (South Mountain)," the KCIA headquarters where the most important interrogations and tortures were conducted. George Ogle was taken there in 1974, for seventeen straight hours of the third degree. Yi Yŏng-t'aek, chief of the KCIA's sixth section, grilled him on how he could possibly defend eight men about to be executed for treason as socialists. Didn't he know that one of them, Ha Chae-wŏn, "had listened to the North Korean radio and copied down Kim [Il Sung]'s speech?" This seemed to be the main fact that convinced Yi that Ha was a communist. Then Mr. Yi "switched over into an emotional monologue": "'These men are our enemies,' he screamed. 'We have got to kill them. This is war. In war even Christians pull the trigger and kill their enemies. If we don't kill them, they will kill us. We will kill them!'"[56]

One day in the 1970s a Korean professor showed up at my office at the University of Washington, quickly entered, and closed the door. He was a visiting professor for a short time, he told me, in one of the science

55. *New York Times*, Aug. 20, 1973.

56. Ogle (1990), p. 52.

departments. He wanted to thank me for speaking out against the Park regime. Then he whipped out a history of his home county, more or less a genealogy, and showed me how one of his ancestors had fought against the Manchu invasions in the 1630s. If only he had the courage of his ancestor, he told me—but he had a family to support. When he left my office he looked both ways down the corridor and then quickly exited. In July 1973 Kim Dae Jung spoke at this university, in a classroom with no more than fifteen people present. A month later he was kidnapped in Tokyo by KCIA agents and nearly murdered. Seven years later when he was indicted for "treason," his criticism of the Park government at the University of Washington was included in the indictment, drawn from a tape of his remarks that one of the fifteen people had given to the KCIA. Meanwhile, one American university after another was accepting large grants from the "Korean Trader's Scholarship Foundation," a front for KCIA attempts to influence scholarly studies of Korea in the United States, as a congressional investigation proved.[57]

THE LABOR MOVEMENT

In the teeth of overwhelming repression the working class grew and gained steam all during the 1970s, moving strongly to affect politics in 1979–80 and finally maturing after the 1987 crisis into a central player in South Korean life. Labor was very active in the late 1940s, as we have seen, but after the Korean War the Rhee regime maintained No-ch'ong as a state-controlled "company" union, representing the interests of management and frequently intervening to break strikes and any hint of independent unions; it had a mosaic of small-enterprise unions under its control, a dispersal that also hindered horizontal solidarity among workers. After 1961 the KCIA reorganized labor from the top, retaining a single national center but creating bigger workplace unions by sector to accord with the developing industrial structure—textiles now had one national union, and so did transportation, chemicals, six metal-working industries, and so on. In ten days in August 1961, a KCIA-appointed "nine member committee" created twelve industrial unions and founded a new national labor federation, the centrally appointed representatives of which all pledged fealty to Park's "revolution." As the best study of Korean labor put it, this was "a purely top down process, exhibiting an order exactly the reverse" of the usual pattern of labor union emergence in industrializing societies. Within two years the junta had also outlawed labor union political activity—that is, when it was directed toward the opposition rather than in support of the ruling party.[58]

57. Boettcher (1980), pp. 351–52.
58. Choi (1990), pp. 30–32, 84.

In this period Korean labor was still formed by the absorption of poor peasants into the unskilled or semiskilled ranks of workers; the hierarchical, patron-client ties of rural society, continuing poverty and unemployment, the terrible cost paid by union organizers and strikers in the 1940s, and the widespread use of young female labor (often in the work force for only a decade or so before marriage) all combined to weaken unions, intimidate many workers, and account for the flocks of docile, disciplined, low-cost laborers in Korea's light industries in the 1960s. A decade later 600,000 women were employed in manufacturing, about 30 percent of the whole work force; 83 percent of all textile workers were women. This, of course, had been a pattern in textile industries around the world, and especially in Japan's; working conditions in the 1960s were as old as textile production in Korea, going back to the turn of the century.

Teenage women, drawn off the farm to earn some cash for their parents, formed a veritable army of low-skill workers in spinning, knitting, sewing, making footwear, assembling simple electronic devices, packaging food, or rote tasks like stamping nuts and bolts out of sheets of steel. Young women were truly the foot soldiers of the export-led "take-off" in the 1960s. Bulking into the 18–22 age group, having either a junior high or a grade school education, with nearly half living in company dormitories on company food with one day off per month, these women constituted a gold mine for exporters. (At the Bando Trading Company, four hundred women workers suffered frostbite in 1974 because their dormitory lacked heat.)[59]

Kim Chi Ha was the poet laureate of a protesting nation in the 1970s, for which he suffered several jail terms; he was prosecuted under the National Security Law for poems said to have promoted "class division, thereby allowing [poetry] to be manipulated as North Korean propaganda." In one poem he commemorated the myriad sacrifices of young women in Korea:

> *The Road to Seoul*
>
> I am going.
> Do not cry;
> I am going.
> Over the white hills, the black, and the parched hills,
> down the long and dusty road to Seoul
> I am going to sell my body.
>
> Without a sad promise to return,
> to return some time blooming with a lovely smile,

59. Choi (1990), pp. 60, 125; Ogle (1990), p. 80.

to unbind my hair,
I am going.

Do not cry;
I am going.
Who can forget the four o'clocks, or the scent
of wheat? Even in this wretched, wretched life, the
deeply unforgettable things . . .
and in countless dreams I return,
drenched with tears,
following the moonlight. . . .

I am going.
Do not cry;
I am going.
Over these parched hills that anguish
even the skies, down the long and dusty road to Seoul
I am going to sell my body.[60]

The foreign multinational firm was one source of employment for such women, often at a better wage than they could get elsewhere, but so was the Peace Market in Ch'ŏnggyech'ŏn, a vast warren of sweatshops to make Dante or Engels faint. In three- and four-story warehouses small garment manufacturers would create platforms about four feet high, and in every available space put a table, a sewing machine, and a young woman. Dust, dirt, heat, and cotton particles would blow through this small space, which had no proper ventilation. Ten to twenty young girls, unable to stand upright, would trundle in to squat in front of the whirring machines. Put a thousand of these shops together and you have the Peace Market, employing about 20,000 workers in all. A 1970 investigation had this to say:

> Young girls 14 to 16 years of age had to work kneeling on the floor for an average of 15 hours a day from 8 a.m. to 11 p.m. The workers were entitled to two days off per month, the first and third Sunday. When there was a great deal of work to do, they were forced to work throughout the night . . . [and] to stay awake . . . take stimulants [amphetamines].
>
> In 1970, the wages for such hard work ranged from 1,500 won to 3,000 won per month. . . . [t]heir daily wage was the equivalent of the price of a cup of coffee at a tea room. . . .
>
> Laborers who worked in the Peace Market area for more than five years suffered, without exception, from such afflictions as anemia, poor

60. Kim Chi Ha, *The Middle Hour: Selected Poems of Kim Chi Ha*, trans. David R. McCann (Stanfordville, N.Y.: Human Rights Publishing Group, 1980), p. 19.

digestion, bronchitis, T.B., eye problems, arthritis, neuralgia, and irregular menstruation.[61]

At Bangrim Cotton Textiles, Kim Yŏn-su's pioneer enterprise (see chapter 3) in Seoul's vast, undulating Yŏngdŏngp'o industrial area and a far better place in which to work than the Peace Market, 4,704 of 5,794 workers in 1979 were women, all pushed around by a male oligarchy of company union officers and shop floor foremen. In 1978 one of the Bangrim workers wrote,

> In the dark shadows of [Bangrim's] pride and glory, we, women workers, have for too long worked too hard, and experienced too much pain. Our one reason for working is to help our poor parents. We want to wear a student's uniform [i.e., go to school], but instead we have left our home town in the country and have come to the strange surroundings in Seoul to work in a factory. We came to earn money, but it has been more difficult than we thought possible.[62]

The Yushin system may have been seen by Park as essential to the solution of problems in his state-business coalition, as Woo argued, but it also created a mass labor movement for the first time. Such things are not made by opposition leaders like Kim Dae Jung. His party and the others in Korea's tepid opposition still, in the 1990s, had no real organization among laborers and common people. Labor protest and unionization thus arose largely outside the established political system. The first large-scale strike occurred in 1968, directed at the American electronics firms Signetics and Oak Electronetics Corporation; Oak, an Illinois firm that had been paying its workers $17 per week (low even by Korean standards), promptly pulled out of Korea.[63] Metal workers struck at Chosŏn Shipbilding in 1969, chemical workers staged a long hunger strike at Korea Pfizer in 1970, and auto workers struck General Motors–Saehan in 1971. The KCIA stepped in to break or to mediate several strikes, which Park saw as a direct threat to his "big push" program.

In 1970 there occurred a solitary act that, in retrospect, became the touchstone of the labor movement. A textile worker, Chŏn T'ae-il, immolated himself at Seoul's Peace Market on November 13, shouting as the flames consumed him, "Obey the labor standards act!" and "Don't mistreat young girls!" This suicide shocked the entire nation, much as the self-immolation of a Buddhist priest in downtown Saigon seven years earlier did so much to bring down the Diem regime. Chŏn's sacrifice spurred many groups to action, but perhaps his greatest legacy was the

61. *The Peace Market* (Philadelphia: American Friends Service Committee, 1970).
62. Choi (1990), p. 117; Ogle (1990), p. 82.
63. Ogle (1990), p. 24.

Ch'ŏnggye Garment Workers' Union, formed in the same month he died, led by his mother, Yi Sŏ-sun, and influential all through the 1970s in spite of terrible repression. Chŏn's self-immolation in 1970 and Kim Dae Jung's mass support in 1971 were key reasons for the Yushin system.

Shortly after the garrison decree of October 1971, the regime passed the "Law Concerning Special Measures for Safeguarding National Security," arrogating to President Park "almost unlimited emergency power . . . to restrict civil liberties, mobilize the whole populace for the purpose of national security and set wages and prices for economic needs." These measures were the "Yushin before Yushin," and they were immediately used to squelch industrial strikes and independent labor unions. Collective bargaining and collective action were now subject to the whim of the president; only the right to organize remained on the books.[64] In spite of—or perhaps because of—the draconian measures of the early 1970s, workers were still organizing. In 1974 some two thousand laborers rioted at the Hyundai Heavy Industries shipyard in Ulsan, in spite of their privileged status vis-à-vis almost all other industrial workers in Korea.

Korean churches were primary sanctuaries of resistance to the Park dictatorship, mainly because even the KCIA worried about knocking down the doors of churches with tanks (banging through university gates did not bother the KCIA). Latin American "liberation theology" had also migrated to Korea, influencing many Catholic leaders and yielding a Minjung movement that had tremendous influence in Korea for the next twenty years. (*Minjung* literally means "masses," but "common people" is a more accurate connotation.)[65] On Easter Sunday, 1973, the Reverend Park Hyŏng-gyu, a Presbyterian minister and a stalwart human rights activist, led a peaceful demonstration against the Yushin system. The "Christian Manifesto" issued that day included the following:

> 1. The present regime in Korea is a one-man dictatorship, and it rules the people by force. Such arbitrary rule is contrary to the will of God. Korean society has become a jungle where the weak are eaten by the strong.
>
> 2. The present regime is destroying freedom of conscience and freedom of religious belief. . . .
>
> 3. The present regime is using systematic deception, manipulation, and indoctrination to control the people. . . .

64. Choi (1990), pp. 88–90.
65. Ogle (1990), pp. 72–73; on the ramifications of the Minjung movement, see Kim (1993) Wells (1995).

> 4. The present regime has been employing inhuman and ruthless methods to destroy political opponents, intellectual critics, and innocent people. People are physically and mentally tortured by the agents of the Korean Central Intelligence Agency, which is similar to the Nazi's Gestapo or Stalin's KGB. Once the suspected person is seized by an agent, he disappears completely. We Korean Christians condemn such acts as murderous.
>
> 5. The present regime has been the government of the privileged few, for that class and by that class. . . .
>
> 6. The present regimes of South Korea and North Korea are using the unification dialogue only to prolong their own powers. . . .[66]

For many years the Urban Industrial Mission (UIM), an organization run by Christians, sought to make workers aware of their rights. George Ogle, a Methodist missionary who first arrived in Korea in 1954, worked with the UIM for twelve years until the Park regime deported him in 1974 (because Ogle had defended eight men who had been tortured into confessing that they were part of a communist conspiracy). Later he wrote that the Korean labor movement of the 1970s and 1980s played a major role in turning the Korean system away from harsh authoritarianism, much like the Solidarity movement in Poland. Unlike those of Solidarity, however, the sacrifices of Korean workers have been met in the West with a "stony silence."[67]

In spite of heavy intimidation, women workers made headway at the Dongil Textile Company in Seoul in creating an autonomous union. This touched off several years of sharp confrontation and amazing examples of human witness, reminiscent of the civil rights struggle in the American South in the early 1960s. The Reverend Cho Hwa-sun, a Methodist minister who had worked at the plant for two decades, was the key catalyst in forming the women's union, for which the KCIA jailed her in 1972 (on charges that she was a hidden communist). In February 1978 the women went to their union hall to prepare for elections and found everything covered with shit—literal, human excrement. Thugs who were hiding inside then smeared it all over the women, including their faces. As police now descended on the hall, about 70 women "stood nude, forming a human wall in front of riot police," as the thugs continued to throw shit at them, while pawing at their naked bodies. The company then fired 124 of the union women "for causing damage to company property."[68]

66. Quoted in Choy (1979), pp. 266–67.
67. Ogle (1990), pp. xiii–xiv.
68. Ogle (1990), pp. 85–86; Choi (1990), p. 139.

In 1979 the Korean economy ran into severe difficulties, caused first by sharp increases in oil prices during the "second oil shock" surrounding the Iranian revolution, second by idle assembly lines in the heavy industries of the big push (many of which were running at less than 30 percent of capacity), third by an enormous debt burden comparable to Argentina's ($18 billion in 1978, Korea's burden grew quickly, to nearly $44 billion by the end of 1983, when only Mexico's and Brazil's were higher), and finally by rising labor costs among skilled workers caused by the export of many construction teams to the Middle East (thus to recycle petrodollars). The growth rate fell by 5 percent in 1979, the economy lost 6 percent of the GNP in 1980, and exports were dead in the water from that point until 1983. As this crisis deepened, another event of great symbolic importance took place—the YH incident.

In early August 1979, young female textile workers at the YH Trading Company were holding a sit-down strike. YH was a medium-sized factory utilizing the skills of women workers to make wigs for export; located east of Seoul, this factory paid 220 won per day—like the Peace Market's, this wage was equivalent to a cup of coffee. YH had become the largest exporter of Korean wigs in the late 1960s, stitched together with the hair of Korean females by Korean women between the ages of eighteen and twenty-two. It was ranked fifteenth in export earnings in 1970. By the late 1970s, however, YH had lost its hold on wigs, and women were instead doing simple needlework behind sewing machines, in "execrable" working conditions.[69] On August 7 the owner abruptly shut the factory down, dismissed all employees, and closed their dormitories and mess halls. He then absconded to the United States with all the company's assets. Police evicted 170 women, beating many of them mercilessly. After consultations with Kim Young Sam, then chairman of the opposition New Democratic Party, the women escaped to party headquarters. Two days later a force of about one thousand policeman stormed the building, injuring scores of people and killing one woman worker. Park Chung Hee ordered the government to investigate the UIM, and called for "a thorough investigation into the true activities of certain impure forces which, under the pretense of religion, infiltrate factories and labor unions to agitate labor disputes and social disorder."[70] The controlled media also claimed that the UIM had communist connections and was bent on inciting class conflict. The Carter administration, however, denounced the government's actions as "brutal and excessive," which led the opposition party to step up its support of the workers.

The Park regime quickly unraveled from that point onward. In a few

69. Choi (1990), pp. 287–88.
70. Choi (1990), p. 289; Ogle (1990), p. 92.

weeks massive urban protests hit Masan and Pusan, as workers and students took to the streets of cities in the privileged southeast, shocking the Park leadership. For the first time since its inception in 1970, workers in the Mason free-export zone succeeded in organizing four labor unions, and some appeared in the other export zones in Iri and Kuro.[71] Students returned to their campuses and mounted large demonstrations, which, by October, found the regime's leaders at loggerheads over whether more repression or some sort of decompression of the Yushin dictatorship was the better remedy for the spreading disorders. This internal debate was the subject of conversation on October 26, 1979, when President Park went to a nearby KCIA safe house to have dinner with its director, Kim Chae-gyu. Kim, like Park, had graduated in the 1946 class of the American occupation's military officers' school. Sitting with Park at the dinner was his bodyguard, Cha Chi-ch'ŏl, a short, squat man without a visible neck, known for his ability to kill a man with his bare hands and, gossip had it, increasingly a strong influence on President Park.

At some point an argument broke out. Kim Chae-gyu drew his pistol, exclaimed, "How can we conduct our policies with an insect like this?" and shot Cha, who tried to crawl out of the room to mobilize his guard detail. And then, inexplicably (for it never has been explained), Kim also shot and killed Park Chung Hee. Pandemonium broke out among the power elite in the security services, extending well through the night until military forces under General Chŏng Sŭng-hwa took control and ordered Kim Chae-gyu arrested. When soldiers came for him on the morning of October 27, Kim reached for a revolver in a holster on his leg—but it was too late.

Two years after these events I visited North Korea for the first time. My guides did not know what to do with me in the evening, there being next to no nightlife at that time (a bit has appeared by now). So they showed me movies in a screening room in the hotel. At the end of one of them, a historical docudrama in wide-screen color with the (Korean) soul-soothing title "An Chung-gun Shoots Itō Hirobumi," the date of the act faded out slowly from the scene of the assassination at Harbin station: October 26, 1909. One of the guides looked at me and said, "When was Park Chung Hee shot?" I answered, "October 26, 1979." "Seventy years is not such a long time," he said, and then looked at the other guide with a self-satisfied grin. Later I wondered if this date had played a role in Kim Chae-gyu's motives, but probably it was just a coincidence.

In the aftermath of Park's assassination the Carter administration did little to support democracy in Korea. Worried instead about internal

71. Choi (1990), p. 103.

political disintegration and the military threat from North Korea, Carter sent an aircraft carrier to Korean waters while Secretary of State Cyrus R. Vance hurried to Seoul to express his "hopes for political stability." He pointedly refused to commit the United States to a democratic transition. Meanwhile, Pentagon sources told reporters that the best idea was to rely on the Korean military, which they thought was the only institution with effective power after Park's murder.[72]

The investigation into the assassination was headed by Major General Chun Doo Hwan (Chŏn Tu-hwan), who was then chief of the powerful Defense Security Command and a longtime acolyte and loyalist of Park Chung Hee. The next night of the colonels occurred on December 12, 1979, when General Chun and his close friend General Roh Tae Woo used the army's Ninth Division (commanded by Roh), Seoul's capital garrison, and various special forces—all nominally under American operational control—to execute a coup within the Korean military, which slowly brought to power the 1955 graduating class of the Korean Military Academy, of which both were members. According to a 1994 Seoul District Prosecutor's Office report, Chun and Roh met on December 7 and decided to make the twelfth their "D-Day." On that day they and thirty-six other officers arrested Chŏng Sŭng-hwa, the ROK Army chief of staff, and about forty other high officers. They mobilized armored units in front of the ROK Army headquarters, forcing its high officers to flee through tunnels to the American Eighth Army command across the street.

Reporters for the *New York Times* rightly called this "the most shocking breach of Army discipline" in South Korea's history and "a ploy that would have been a hanging offense in any other military command structure," but they found U.S. officials unwilling to comment publicly (while privately depicting themselves "at a loss" to do anything about it).[73] The 1994 Seoul report termed the events a "premeditated military rebellion" and a "coup-like event," but chose to suspend indictments against all thirty-eight officers, including the former presidents Chun and Roh—thus prompting the opposition party to boycott the National Assembly.[74] In 1996, however, both generals came to trial for this mutiny.

In the early months of 1980 the political atmosphere improved measurably, and Koreans met all over the country to discuss a new constitution. In February the interim government under Ch'oe Kyu-ha

72. *New York Times*, Nov. 4, 1979, sec. A; also Oct. 31, 1979 (Richard Halloran's article).
73. Henry Scott Stokes, in New York Times, Dec. 15, 1979; James Sterba, in *New York Times*, June 15, 1980 (News of the Week in Review).
74. *Korea Herald*, Oct. 30, 1994.

Looking toward the garden from a home Kangnŭng, 1980. *Courtesy of Joo, Mong-dok.*

(an all-purpose former official and diplomat) restored the political rights of Kim Dae Jung and other politicians and reinstated university professors who had been fired for political reasons. (One historian whom I know had left his office on a Friday, and returned Monday morning to find everything gone and his name erased from the door.) Expelled students came back to the universities, and in the spring demonstrators held a number of peaceful rallies, never venturing off the campuses.

In late April, however, miners took over a small town near the east coast, and Chun Doo Hwan used this as a pretext to make himself head of the KCIA, while keeping his post as head of the Defense Security Command. A few weeks earlier the American commander, General John Wickham, had given his blessing to the Korean military's role in politics—which included "being watchdogs on political activity that could be de-stabilizing, and in a way making judgements about the eligibility and reliability of political candidates."[75] After Chun's actions, demonstrators took to the streets all over the country. By mid-May tens of thousands of students and common people had flooded Korea's cities, with daily demonstrations of at least fifty thousand in Seoul. On May 17, 1980, General Chun tried to complete his coup: he declared martial law, closed the universities, dissolved the legislature, banned all political activity, and arrested thousands of political leaders and dissidents in the midnight

75. *Asian Wall Street Journal,* March 11, 1980, quoted in Ogle (1990), pp. 95–96.

hours of May 17–18. He also set up a special committee for national security measures, making himself head of its standing committee. With these emergency measures, Chun detonated the Kwangju Rebellion.

KWANGJU

On May 18 about 500 people took to Kwangju's streets, demanding the repeal of martial law. Elite paratroopers, widely thought to have been on drugs, landed in the city and began the indiscriminate murder of students, women, children—anyone who got in their way. One woman student was pilloried near the town square, where a paratrooper attacked her breasts with his bayonet. Other students had their faces erased with flamethrowers. By May 21 hundreds of thousands of local people had driven the soldiers from the city, which citizen's councils controlled for the next five days. These councils determined that 500 people had already died and that some 960 were missing.[76] The citizens' councils appealed to the U.S. embassy to intervene, but it was left to General Wickham to release the Twentieth Division of the ROK Army from its duties along the DMZ on May 22. A 1988 ROK National Assembly report alleged that the suppression forces waited for three days to enter Kwangju, until the U.S. aircraft carrier *Midway* and other American naval ships could arrive in Korean waters.

There may not have been an alternative to turning a cold shoulder to the citizens of Kwangju, since for the United States to deny Chun troops or to take the side of Kwangju's citizens would have been an intervention with no precedent since the 1940s. But American operational control under the United States–South Korean Combined Forces Command made U.S. responsibility inescapable, and the release of frontline troops made hash of Carter's human rights policies; the United States paid dearly for both in Korean attitudes thereafter. Like everything else in the Carter administration, Kwangju also fell between the stools of incessant NSC–State Department feuds between Cold Warriors and moderates, except that in this case Richard Holbrooke of the State Department also counseled a prudent silence; there was, he thought, far too much "attention to Kwangjoo [*sic*]" without proper consideration of the "broader questions" of Korean security and the like, which had not been properly addressed.[77] Holbrooke had also helped to reverse Carter's policy of

76. These figures were compiled in Sept. 1980 by the most important watchdog group in the United States, the North American Coalition on Human Rights in Korea, led by the Reverend Pharis Harvey. Japanese network television covered the entire rebellion closely, filming many of the worst atrocities. On Kwangju more generally, see Clark (1988).
77. *New York Times*, May 29, 1980.

withdrawing troops from Korea; after Reagan defeated Carter, Holbrooke became a well-paid consultant to the Hyundai Corporation.

Loudspeakers from helicopters warned Kwangju's citizens that the Twentieth Division would enter the city at dawn on May 27; all were to disarm and return to their homes. At 3 A.M. the soldiers came in shooting, killing scores more people who had refused to put down weapons they had seized from local armories. These units were disciplined, however, and quickly secured the city. Now Chun moved to complete the coup d'état he had begun on December 12, shutting down political activity completely, arresting Kim Dae Jung and blaming the rebellion on him, knocking together an "electoral college" under the barely disguised Yushin system, and thereby making himself president of the Fifth Republic. General Roh Tae Woo was one of his closest associates in the suppression of Kwangju and the seizure of power. It will probably never be known how many people died in the Kwangju Rebellion, but Kwangju's death statistics, which had had a monthly average of 2,300, soared to 4,900 deaths in May 1980.[78] In the mid-1990s official inquiries for the first time since 1980 examined what happened in Kwangju, how many died, and what crimes should be laid at the doorstep of the former presidents Chun and Roh (both of whom were indicted and jailed for their roles in the December coup and the Kwangju tragedy).

After a show trial in 1980 found Kim Dae Jung guilty, his execution was pending when American pressure was brought to bear to keep him alive. He was sentenced to life in prison, and President Ronald Reagan hurried to invite Chun to Washington as the president's first visiting head of state after his inauguration. His aides told reporters that the United States was anxious to shore up relations with Seoul, lest North Korea try to fish in troubled waters. Thereafter the Reagan administration sold Chun thirty-six F-16 jet fighters and added about four thousand Americans to the existing troop commitment, including new intelligence facilities.

In January 1981, just before his visit to Washington, Chun dissolved the Ch'ŏnggye Garment Workers' Union by administrative decree, thus smashing the union that had begun with Chŏn T'ae-il's suicide. In a desperate act, the garment workers went to the AFL-CIO's Free Labor Institute and took its American director hostage. Two demonstrators threatened suicide if the authorities tried to throw them out. Police stormed the building anyway, and two workers pitched themselves out of upper-story windows, committing suicide.[79] By this time Chun had created "white skull" (*paekkŏl*) strikebreakers, known for their martial

78. *Lost Victory* (1988), pp. 30–32.
79. Ogle (1990), p. 75; Choi (1990), p. 127.

arts skills: they would arrive at the scene on motorcycles, padded and shielded head to foot, and wade into the workers, breaking heads. In the early 1980s workers arrested under the National Security Law made up one-third of all political prisoners.

Chun had himself inaugurated president in February 1981. In the same year he purged or proscribed the political activities of 800 politicians and 8,000 officials in government and business. He also threw some 37,000 journalists, students, teachers, labor organizers, and civil servants into "purification camps" in remote mountain areas; some 200 labor leaders were among them. They were said to be boot camps for political miscreants, who would see the error of their ways after lots of push-ups, marathon running, small-group criticism and self-criticism, and ideological exhortation. Here is the testimony of one survivor:

> Right before supper we were beaten out of our minds and at suppertime we were given three spoonfuls of barley rice. Even though we offered thanksgiving for this, we were beaten again. For one laugh—80 lashings. In the morning there is a marching song period which is called a screaming time but we were so hungry we couldn't shout [so] then they beat us with clubs until we screamed. One friend of mine, a Mr. Chai, could not scream because of a throat infection and therefore, he was beaten to death. Another person, a Mr. Lee, was also beaten to death. Two out of the eleven in our group were killed.[80]

Any student wishing to find a good term paper topic can retreat into the library to examine American media commentary on South Korea in the early 1980s, and find many huzzahs for the "new era" of political stability that the Chun regime had achieved and for the ROK's return to world-beating economic growth (at least after 1983). Taking a page from North Korean practice, the KCIA (now renamed the Agency for National Security Planning, or ANSP) required newspapers to feature Chun's photo every single day. A comedian who was the spitting image of Chun, complete with bald pate, was forbidden to appear on television. Kim Young Sam began a hunger strike on the anniversary of Kwangju in 1983, demanding a return to democracy and fasting twenty-six days until the authorities took him to a hospital and force-fed him; that was an unusual and courageous event in this dark period. More typical was Kim Sang-hyŏp, the textile magnate Kim Yŏn-su's son and a politician long associated with the Democratic Party, who consented to become prime minister under Chun in 1982–83. This attempt at bipartisanship did not work, however; all political parties were regime controlled, and there was no letup in this dictatorship until pivotal National Assembly elections in February 1985.

80. Quoted in Ogle (1990), p. 55; see also *Lost Victory* (1988), p. 33.

Chun Doo Hwan was the most unpopular leader in postwar Korean history, reviled as much for his lack of imagination and his slavish attempts to mimic Park Chung Hee's politics as for his draconian measures. Since Kim Dae Jung was the choice of just about everyone in the southeast and since Kim Young Sam's political machine was running Pusan and much of the surrounding area, Chun was forced to do everything he could for his friends in the only sure base left to him, North Kyŏngsang Province and its capital at Taegu. Supporters from this area coalesced into the "Club of One Mind" (Hanahoe, that is, whatever was on the mind of President Chun), composed mostly of military officers from the region and known colloquially as the T-K Group (for Taegu and Kyŏngsang). Like the 1955 military school class, they also proved to have talents few had yet come to notice: "Under Chun's regime, *Hanahoe* members virtually monopolized politically sensitive positions . . . the Army Security Command, the Capital Garrison Command, the Special Forces Command, the Joint Chiefs of Staff, and the Ministry of National Defense."[81]

Meanwhile, slowly building up steam was a very different kind of opposition movement. With Kim Dae Jung out of the country (he was allowed to go into exile in the United States in 1982) and opposition politicians banned from politics, young people now began to leave the universities and their promising careers and go to work in the factories. Significant numbers of young people at great personal sacrifice took industrial jobs and sought to merge with Korea's burgeoning urban working class, leading the state to call them "disguised workers" (George Ogle estimated that as many as three thousand students went into the factories to organize workers.)[82] Furthermore, the new, heavy-industrial sector emerged as a main arena for such action; the labor movement "bec[a]me quite organically meshed with the radical student movement," leading to the decline of liberal labor rights groups like the Urban Industrial Mission. An enormous cultural and intellectual space opened through samizdat-like publications, and even overt dissemination; in the middle and late 1980s radicals openly and obsessively read Marx.[83]

Chun Doo Hwan came out of the military intelligence apparatus, of

81. Park (1993), pp. 157, 188.

82. Ogle (1990), p. 99.

83. Choi (1990). It is difficult to see this tendency in English-language materials. The Seoul magazine titled *Mal* (*Speech*) published many important articles and studies in the late 1980s, exemplifying radical trends in the period. I also benefited from reading Professor Choi Jang Jip's unpublished study "Political Cleavages and Transition in a Military Authoritarian Regime: Institutionalization, Opposition, and Process in South Korea, 1972–1986" (Nov. 1986).

course, and correspondingly expanded its function as a suppression force. He undertook a vast expansion of paramilitary riot police, numbering around 150,000 in the mid-1980s. They bore the main brunt of demonstrations, wearing a strange armor: black helmets, tight screens over the face, leather scabbard protecting the back of their neck, padded clothing, thick elbow, knee, and shin guards, heavy combat boots, and long metal shield in the left hand and riot batons in the right. These were the Darth Vader–like figures that showed up frequently in photos in the *New York Times*, often with no accompanying article (for none was needed). Actually most of them were young conscripts, not very different from the students they confronted.

A huge, extended strike at the Daewoo auto factory in 1985 shook the confidence of the regime, since now workers in the best, highest-paid new industries were organizing. Kim Dae Jung returned in February 1985, and I was fortunate to be part of an American delegation that accompanied him back to Seoul from exile in the United States, in hopes that our presence would prevent another airport murder like that which cut down Benigno Aquino on the Manila tarmac in 1985. The Koreans were too smart to do that, but stupid enough to cause a huge fracas at Kimp'o International Airport; a phalanx of KCIA thugs in brown windbreakers pummeled and threw to the floor prominent Americans (two congressmen were on the delegation), while roughly snatching Kim and his wife into a waiting car and subsequent months of house arrest.

When we got to the bus that would take us into Seoul, hundreds of Chŏlla people in tattered winter clothing milled around us, exclaiming that Kim was their "great leader." On the left side of the road leading into Seoul were thousands of riot police. On the right side were enormous numbers of Seoul's common people—workers in denims, students in black uniform, mothers in long skirts, little kids wrapped tightly against the wind, old men and women in traditional dress—with placards hailing Kim's return. It seemed as if the whole population had divided between the riot police and the demonstrators.

ANTI-AMERICANISM AND ANTI-KOREANISM

The radical tendencies of the 1980s also deepened the anti-Americanism that many Koreans had felt all along, but especially after the Kwangju Rebellion. Radicals linked Korea's internal repression to the history of American imperialism in Korea and elsewhere and thus drew upon deep wellsprings of nationalism. Kwangju brought all this to a head, but the soil of anti-Americanism was plowed up first and foremost by Americans themselves.

James Wade, an American expatriate who lived in Korea for decades, wrote a book in the 1960s that perfectly captures the atmosphere of Korean-American relations in the period 1945–80. He has every vignette right—he renders with accuracy and empathy every encounter in the streets, every visit to the U.S. military bases, the embassy, the Seoul Civilian Club, or the many other places where Koreans and Americans came into contact. The period during and after the Korean War was the worst, of course, because that saw America at its height and Korea at a depth it had never plumbed before. Wade records American soldiers complaining in the mid-1950s about "sensitivity" manuals that say Koreans were "proud and dignified." "All the people we've seen so far have been filthy beggars, or farmers living in huts worse than animals. They're not even civilized, let alone dignified or proud." Wade describes a scene at a railway stop in the 1950s, as an American troop train came to a rest and urchins crowded forward looking for candy bars. A girl of twelve or thirteen, with sores on her face, a torn dress, and hair shaved on one side of her head from a wound, walked up to the train.

"Say," one the soldiers called out, "here's one of those Gook women. . . . Ain't she a sexy sight, though?"

Amid catcalling and obscene guestures from the troops, the girl began dancing in circles, waving her arms, and howling. As the catcalls increased, she "pranced still higher, protruding her bloated belly suggestively." Suddenly an old Korean farmer ran up to the girl and slapped her in the face; she fell back against a pile of rice bags. He screeched at the other children, shooing them away. Soon the troop train lurched forward, leaving the girl on the platform—"weeping quietly beside the pile of straw sacks."[84]

Peace Corps groups got three months of training in "cross-cultural awareness" before going to Korea, learning how ancient the country was, how much Koreans revered their families, how Koreans would never steal a pin or a penny from a friend, and the like; then we got to Seoul, and within days my typewriter and my whole wardrobe had been stolen by what was known then as a "small thief"—by leaving a turd in the yard for the police to find, he identified himself as a petty criminal so that they wouldn't go too hard on him if he were caught. "Cultural awareness" also did not help much with the traumas of going to the bathroom. There were few indoor toilets outside of Seoul in the 1960s, and entering a filthy outhouse often required a long period of steeling the mind. One of my friends lived in a home with the outhouse over a pigsty; the pigs would grunt expectantly when they saw him coming. Six months later a black pig was born, which the family thought was auspicious and a manifestation of my friend's good work. We were all too

84. Wade (1967), pp. 105–7.

young to understand that the detritus of a terrible war still hung over the country, affecting everything and everybody. Wade captures the argot of an American captain in 1966, hulking over Koreans as if they were all his coolies: one of them had run an American flag up a pole, improperly:

> "God damn it!" he bellowed. "Look at that mucking flag. They've got it all bass-ackwards." Glaring wildly about, he continued shouting: "Hey! Where's Skoshi? Where's Boy-san? Somebody get over here on the double, hubba-hubba."[85]

Later on came the multitude of American economists, business pundits, and political scientists, who, for reasons that still escape me, thought it their solemn duty to extol Korean capitalism to the heights—not once but a thousand times. "Miracle" became the trope on everyone's lips, with "dynamic" not far behind. In September 1977 *Fortune* magazine had this to say about business in Korea:

> What positively delights American business men in Korea is the Confucian work ethic. . . . Work, as Koreans see it, is not a hardship. It is a heaven-sent opportunity to help family and nation. The fact that filial piety extends to the boss-worker relationship comes as a further surprise to Americans accustomed to labor wrangling at home.[86]

Korean labor was also said to be "weak," presumably another good thing (even if American business quickly found out that it wasn't so). It is one thing for *Fortune* to say such things; that is the job of its writers. I still do not understand why the immense sacrifice that the Korean people made to drag their country kicking and screaming into the twentieth-century rat race should merit such uncritical, well-nigh hysterical enthusiasm from academics who presumably are not paid for their views.

Koreans look upon Americans with far more subtlety and awareness than most of us look upon them, and they found ways to bear all the indignities that flowed from American misunderstanding with varying degrees of resignation, stubbornness, self-interest, daily resilience, or grin-and-bear-it good cheer, and usually to remain grateful to the United States for sharing its wealth and shedding the blood of its soldiers on Korean soil. Rarely if ever would a Korean put an American colleague in a position where he might be humiliated or lose face, and therefore the brashness and vigor with which young people condemned the Yankees in the 1980s was mortifying to the older generation. But it was a sign of Korea's return to itself, to self-awareness and assertion, and ultimately to national dignity.

85. Wade (1967), p. 259.
86. Quoted in Ogle (1990), p. 76.

Chun Doo Hwan and his wife visit Ronald and Nancy Reagan at the White House, February 1981.

What were the students protesting about? The touchstone was always Kwangju and the American reaction to it. Through his human rights policy President Jimmy Carter had built up hope that the United States might do something about Park's dictatorship, human rights violations, and the terror. He visited Korea in June 1979, in the midst of a growing crisis in politics and a rare downturn in the economy. But by then Carter's advisers had persuaded him to direct his human rights efforts toward Latin American and communist dictatorships, and not toward "strategic" allies like Korea and the Philippines. This policy blew up in Carter's face when his administration did nothing but make some idle protests about the bloodletting at Kwangju. One creative student poster put Chun's visage atop Mount Rushmore, with Jimmy Carter down below guarding the ramparts with an M-16, Ronald Reagan performing oral sex on Nancy, and the "three Kims" vacantly kibitzing by the side.[87]

U.S. officials often saw the student protests in a narrow empirical light: the students claimed American involvement in Chun's two coups, especially in supporting Chun's crackdown at Kwangju in May 1980. The embassy would respond that there was no such involvement, which as a matter of high policy in Washington may have been true, but which could not have been true in the dailiness of American-Korean relations.

87. Reprinted in *Sahoe wa sasang* (Society and thought) (Seoul, March 1989).

The United States maintained operational control of the ROK Army; Chun violated the agreements of the joint command twice, in December 1979 and May 1980: why did the United States not act against those violations? With his service in the Vietnam War and his position as chief of Korean military intelligence in 1979, Chun had to have a thick network of ties with American counterparts: had they stayed his hand, or did they even try? Above all, why did President Reagan invite this person to the White House and spend the early 1980s providing him with so many visible signs of support? There was no good answer to most of these questions, and especially not to the last one. The first of many anti-American acts was the arson of the Kwangju U.S. Information Service office in December 1980; by the mid-1980s such acts were commonplace, with many young people committing suicide for their beliefs.

I got sucked into the middle of all this, through no fault of my own—or so it seemed to me. As we have seen, Koreans pay attention and respect to scholars, no doubt far more than they deserve (but then, this is another thing Americans can learn from Koreans). In the mid-1980s the American embassy in Seoul had the hallucination that my work was one cause of the incessantly anti-American student demonstrations of the period. This is pure nonsense, but it flew back into my face so many times that the experience may be pertinent to our story. The first volume of my Korean War study circulated as an English-language samizdat in the early 1980s and then was translated (badly) by publishers who pirated the copyright, only to find the book banned by Chun Doo Hwan. Nonetheless, it was usually available in the right bookstores.

In 1987 and 1988 I kept getting calls from the Voice of America or the U.S. Information Agency, asking me for taped interviews that would then be broadcast in Korea. My work was being distorted by the students, they said, and I should clear the record. The American director of the Fulbright program in Seoul told me that I ought to come out to Korea and disabuse the students of their false impressions. Other American historians were invited under these or other auspices to travel to Korea and set the record straight on the Korean War and other things; a couple of them did not hesitate to please the powers that be by denouncing me as a radical if not a pro–North Korean sympathizer.

I never agreed to any of the official entreaties. Usually I would just not return their calls, but once or twice I opined that if Americans stopped backing dictators and began treating Koreans with dignity, the problems would go away and I would sink back into my ordinary obscurity. This probably struck them as self-righteous and accurate in equal measures, since any American who has ever spent time on the streets of Seoul quickly learns that plenty of Koreans do not like them. When I lived in a Korean home in the late 1960s, little kids in the neighborhood would tag along behind me sing-songing "mmmooooonkeeeee" (monkey) and shouting out various Korean epithets that took me a while to learn. One day I was strolling in a back street with a Korean friend and a man heaved out of a bar, spied me, and spit full in my face—to the overwhelming mortification of my friend, who later patiently explained that not all Koreans liked Americans.

A JUNE BREAKTHROUGH

In spite of the nationwide distaste for Chun's Fifth Republic, in 1987 he determined to handpick his successor and continue to hold power behind the scenes; he had importuned one big firm after another to set up a so-called Ilhae Foundation (Ilhae was Chun's pen name), from which he hoped to continue ruling the roost after he was no longer president. If the process of beating the bushes for political funds was nothing new, the amounts Chun vacuumed up were truly amazing: $900 million during his tenure in office, with at least $150 million remaining in coffers under his control after he left office.[88]

The circumstances in which the Chun regime fell, or entered crisis, bear comparison to those surrounding the demise of Latin American dictatorships and their transition to democracy—especially in Argentina; along with the "yellow revolution" in the Philippines a year earlier, Korea in 1987 was also a harbinger of mass democratization protests that helped to bring down the European communist regimes in 1989. The political scientists Guillermo O'Donnell and Philippe Schmitter have eloquently analyzed "the explosion of a highly repoliticized and angry society" in words that fit the Korean milieu in the 1980s perfectly:

> the resurgence of previous political parties or the formation of new ones to press for more explicit democratization or even revolution; the sudden appearance of books and magazines long suppressed by censorship; the conversion of older institutions, such as trade unions, professional associations, and universities, from agents of governmental control into instruments for the expression of interests, ideals, and rage against the regime; the emergence of grass-roots organizations articulating demands long repressed or ignored by authoritarian rule; the expression of ethical concerns by religious and spiritual groups previously noted for their prudent accommodation to the authorities. . . .[89]

88. These figures appeared in many newspaper articles in early 1996 leading up to Chun's trial.

89. Guillermo O'Donnell, Philippe C. Schmitter, and Laurence Whitehead, eds., *Transitions from Authoritarian Rule: Tentative Conclusions* (Baltimore: Johns Hopkins University Press, 1986), p. 49.

As the authors note, human rights organizations and churches were critical sanctuaries for dissidents, with the former relying on international support and the latter often being the only institution relatively immune from intrusion by the regime. Otherwise the Chun regime intruded everywhere: no visitor to Seoul in the mid-1980s could miss the warlike atmosphere of resistance and repression.

In the spring of 1987 another student was tortured to death by the Korean police; they claimed it was an accident, but the cover-up of the case unraveled and touched off nationwide demonstrations on June 10. Catholic fathers at the Myŏngdong Cathedral harbored students hunted by the authorities; those still protesting were subjected to merciless repression by riot police. In this atmosphere the ruling party nominated Roh Tae Woo to succeed Chun under the existing antidemocratic system, without any real presidential election. In the massive protests that ensued, middle-class people cheered and often joined protesters. From June 10 through 20, "all streets in urban areas were virtual battlefields."[90] A mass movement for democracy, embracing students, workers, and many in the middle class, finally brought a democratic breakthrough in Korea.

The Reagan administration now worried that a full-fledged revolution might topple the regime. It had already dispatched a career CIA officer to Seoul, James R. Lilley, to be the American ambassador; this was highly unusual but a reflection of fears in Washington that South Korea might unravel. In late June various Americans pressured Chun and Roh to change their policies. On June 29 Roh Tae Woo grabbed the bull by the horns and announced direct presidential elections for December 1987, an open campaign without threats of repression, amnesties for political prisoners, including Kim Dae Jung, guarantees of basic rights, and revision or abolishment of the current press law.[91] This watershed event showed Roh to be a far shrewder politician than Chun; by this simple stroke Roh made himself a plausible candidate in the next election and convinced many Westerners that he was the real champion of democracy in Korea.

The regime also removed controls on labor organizing in the summer of 1987. During the period June 1987–June 1988, unions increased their membership by 64 percent, adding 586,167 new members; some 3,400 labor disputes, strikes, and lockouts occurred from July through October 1987, involving 934,000 workers. Most labor actions were over wage rates, but this was nevertheless a historic advance for Korean labor.[92]

90. Park (1993), p. 49. English-language accounts usually do not do justice to the depth of the June 1987 events. In Korean an excellent source is *Yuwŏl minjuhwa tae t'ujaeng* (The great June [1987] struggle for democratization) (Seoul: Korean Christian Social Research Center, 1987).

91. Roh's declaration is in *Lost Victory* (1988), pp. 308–13.

92. Ogle (1990), p. 115; Park (1993), p. 107.

One would still not want to say that blue-collar labor was doing swimmingly in South Korea: fully 42 percent of the country's population lived in or near Seoul in 1989, and two million of Seoul's citizens lived in rented spaces giving families less than 180 square feet, with many of these containing up to three households, or about fifteen people.[93] Nor has any one of the major parties established a real coalition with labor by the mid-1990s. But since 1987 there has been vast improvement in wage rates and working conditions.

South Korea's middle class has been growing rapidly with industrialization and urbanization, but it remains difficult to specify its political tendency. Elements in it gave critical support to youthful dissidents in the June 1987 mobilization, but also faded from the streets once the elections terminated. Disaffected sectors of the middle class include small and medium-sized businesses run roughshod over by the state and the conglomerates, the regionally disadvantaged, families that cannot make ends meet and educate their children, parents observing the clubbing of students (theirs or others'), and the like. Much of the recent growth in Christian believers (now about 25 percent of the population in South Korea, with most of the growth since 1970) has come within this class or aspirants to it, and the witness and sacrifice of important church figures has doubtless galvanized parts of the middle class in favor of democratization. The middle class tends to be mostly salaried and bureaucratic, however, and has a slim basis for independent resistance against the state. Furthermore, it is a prototypical *nouveau* social formation, far more intent on making money than on contesting for power. The absence of effective political representation in the Park and Chun regimes was a basic issue for many middle-class citizens, and once they got it, they did not rush back into the streets to help the working class achieve the same thing.[94]

Meanwhile, the opposition groups managed to split yet again and to run both Kim Dae Jung and Kim Young Sam against the ruling party candidate in the December 1987 elections. This devastating failure allowed Roh Tae Woo to win the presidency with a plurality, in the most pronounced pattern of regional voting in Korea's history, and perhaps any other nation's history:[95]

93. Kim (1992), p. 79.

94. This is, of course, a typical pattern in democratic transitions elsewhere. See Dietrich Rueschemeyer, Evelyne Huber Stephens, and John D. Stephens, *Capitalist Development and Democracy* (Chicago: University of Chicago Press, 1992).

95. Park (1993), pp. 67–70.

	ROH TAE WOO	KIM YOUNG SAM	KIM DAE JUNG
Kwangju	4.8%	0.5%	93.4%
North Chŏlla	13.7%	1.5%	80.9%
South Chŏlla	8.0%	1.1%	87.9%
North Kyŏngsang	64.8%	27.5%	2.3%
South Kyŏngsang	40.4%	50.3%	4.4%
Total/all ROK	35.9%	27.5%	26.5%

(Kim Chŏng-p'il also ran in the election, getting 8 percent of the national vote and nearly a majority in his home province of South Ch'ung-ch'ŏng.)

As Park Kie-duck writes, "the election displayed strong regionalism that cut across every possible group identification line, including class." Furthermore, he rightly says, the enormous dissident movement of June 1987 had only one thing holding it together, and that was the full-throated demand for a return to direct electoral politics.[96] After that was pressured out of Roh Tae Woo on June 29, the middle class returned to its apolitical pursuits, and the radicalized young people and workers found themselves once again in the minority.

To save his own neck Roh Tae Woo scapegoated Chun Doo Hwan for the revolt of December 12, 1979, and for the Kwangju Rebellion, pretending once again that a totally new era had dawned in 1988. But he also did well by his longtime friend, protecting him from punishment or jail. Chun made like an honorable man, taking off to a remote Buddhist temple for some serious self-reflection. Although one powerful person did do some time in jail (Chang Se-dong, who had run the intelligence groups), not one active-duty military officer was punished for anything done in the 1980s. The political system under Roh, wrote one expert, was by no means "a civilian regime": "the military coexisted with the ruling bloc while it exercised veto power over opposition groups." When one courageous journalist, O Hong-gun, suggested clearing the military culture completely out of politics, agents of the Army Intelligence Command stabbed him with a bayonet.[97] The partial democratization that occurred in 1987–88 in South Korea also proceeded without dismantling the repressive state structures, like the ANSP.

President Roh's next political victory was handed to him on a platter by Kim Young Sam. Concerned that with such highly skewed regional voting patterns he would never be elected president in a three-way race (he assumed Kim Dae Jung would run every time), Kim brought his

96. Park (1993), pp. 67–70, 224.
97. Park (1993), pp. 161, 170–71.

splinter party together with the ruling group and Kim Chŏng-p'il's personal following, accomplishing a "three-party merger" that yielded in early 1990 the Democratic Liberal Party, or Minjadang. If this sounds close to Japan's Liberal Democratic Party, it is: you get it by transposing one character (Chamindang)—and by transposing all your Korean bleating about how terrible Japan is, into so much excess hot air.

As the party merger unfolded, it also gave Roh Tae Woo the freedom to arrest dissidents under the National Security Law (at the average rate of 3.3 per day for all of 1989) and to crush various ongoing labor strikes—on the grounds that unions were eating into Korea's exporting comparative advantage by bidding up wages. Businesses that granted wage increases, the government warned, would be excluded from policy loans. As one analyst noted, however, the recession in Japan and the United States contributed much more to the ROK's modest economic slowdown than did rising wages.[98]

With the 1992 elections and the accession to power of Kim Young Sam in February 1993, however, the military was finally retired to the barracks. President Kim removed Hanahoe bigwigs from key positions, and a number of well-respected scholars and former dissidents joined the new cabinet. Kim, like his friend Bill Clinton in the United States, was nonetheless elected with only slightly over 40 percent of the vote, and during periods of tension over the North Korean nuclear problem, there were persistent rumors of a restive "T-K" group that might once again intervene to destroy civilian electoral politics. In the aftermath of Kim Il Sung's death, President Kim spent most of the summer of 1994 placating this hard right wing by issuing calumny after calumny over Kim's dead body—thus driving North-South relations into the deepest freeze in years. Condolences would have gone a long way toward reconciliation between the two Koreas; failing that, simple silence would have done no damage. But then in November 1995, amid daily revelations of the enormous political "slush funds" that Chun and Roh had accumulated, Kim suddenly arranged to indict both of them for the coup in December 1979 and the bloodletting at Kwangju five months later. Unlike any other former military dictatorship in the world, the new democratic regime in Korea did not allow bygones to be bygones: Kim Young Sam jailed the two former presidents and launched official investigations of their crimes; it appeared that both would spend the rest of their days in prison. This was a fine moment for Korean democracy, and vindicated the masses of Koreans who had fought for democratic rule over the past fifty years.

But the National Security Law was still on the books and still was

98. Park (1993), pp. 208–9.

widely used to punish dissent—in spite of an unusual State Department entreaty (in August 1994) that Seoul do away with this anachronistic and draconian measure. Under the law any person who praises or encourages "anti-State activities" can be prosecuted, and North Korea remains defined as an "anti-state organization." The law embraces every aspect of political, social, and artistic life; in the summer of 1994 even a professor's lecture notes were introduced in court as evidence of subversive activity.[99]

The new ruling party of 1990 was meant to be Korea's "LDP," launching a decades-long run of stable one-party democracy. It did not last past the incarceration of Chun and Roh; Kim Young Sam retitled it, and soon it was merely his political machine. Why couldn't Korea be . . . more like Japan? The growing middle class would certainly have liked a long period of stability, since it now found its interests represented in the National Assembly and the Blue House. But labor was still excluded from the ruling coalition, still could not legally engage in open partisan politics,[100] and yet grew in numbers and power every year. Japan under LDP rule neither excluded labor from "peak" political arrangements nor had laws on its books (like the NSL) that canceled basic political rights. The legislature, while including many former dissidents and opposition figures, nonetheless remained basically "a conservative club,"[101] as it had been since its inception in 1948. The stark regional voting blocs also did not augur well for long-term single-party rule.

HOW KOREANS REWROTE THE RULES OF DICTATORSHIP AND DEMOCRACY

Perhaps the supreme irony of the 1997–98 financial crisis was that the worst economic crisis in the country's history should come just as the Korean people were about to elect the dissident Kim Dae Jung, who suffered under the previous dictators as much as any political leader in the world. But it wasn't an accident, because Kim embodied the courageous and resilient resistance to decades of dictatorship that marked Korea as much as its high-growth economy did. Paradoxically, this maturing civil society became a key enabling mechanism for Washington and the IMF to get their way in Korea. Why? Because Kim's election brought to power people who had long criticized the state-bank-conglomerate tie-up and who, like the new president, had long been its victims. The irony grows

99. Park Won-soon (1993), pp. 122–23.
100. Labor unions are prohibited by law from giving their funds to any parties or candidates, and from fielding candidates themselves. See Park (1993), p. 225.
101. Park (1993), p. 139.

in that the global managers feared Kim's election (he might be a radical or a "populist"), and Washington had long backed the dictators who tormented him. Insiders in Washington and Wall Street openly suggested that Kim was the wrong leader at the wrong time in the wrong place: a U.S. diplomat told a reporter, "We could be in a position in which Kim Dae Jung takes office in the midst of a financial emergency that is going to require a lot of pain and downsizing of South Korean businesses. . . . Almost no one thinks he will command the authority to pull it off."[102] In fact, no other conceivable political leader was better positioned than Kim to truly change the Korean system; he had called for reforms analogous to those of the IMF throughout his long career.[103]

Kim Dae Jung was never a radical, and did not have a strong base in labor, for two reasons: first, until 1998 it was illegal for labor to involve itself in politics; second, over the years Kim was much more a champion of small and medium business than of labor (and, of course, supporting labor was a ticket to political oblivion in Korea's McCarthyite political milieu). He was clearly more sympathetic to labor demands than previous leaders, however, and labor preferred him to the past run of dictators. But that isn't saying much, given the harsh anti-labor environment of the past fifty years. The KFTU was for decades the only legal union—because it was controlled by the state in the interests of owners, through what the late James West called "corporatism without labor" whereby the state, the conglomerates, and the banks worked hand in glove, but labor was systematically excluded. From 1970 to 1987 the state controlled the recognition of unions at foreign-invested companies, banning strikes and all unapproved union organizers—thus "to placate uneasy foreign investors."[104] The other large union is the Korean Confederation of Trade Unions (KCTU), which grew rapidly after 1987 but was illegal until early 1998. Both have about half a million members, but the KFTU was built upon an enterprise union base controlled from the top down, which allowed just one union per enterprise and thus dispersed horizontal solidarity across industrial sectors. The Trade Union Act in force for decades barred intervention in the workplace by "third parties" (anyone who is not an employed worker or manager) and banned political activities by unions—making support of a specific political party illegal. All unions had to be approved by the Ministry of Labor.[105]

102. Quoted by David Sanger, *New York Times*, Nov. 20, 1997.

103. In English, see especially Kim Dae Jung, *Mass-Participatory Economy* (Cambridge: Harvard East Asian Center, 1985).

104. James M. West, "South Korea's Entry into the International Labor Organization: Perspectives on Corporatist Labor Law during a Late Industrial Revolution," *Stanford Journal of International Law* 23, no. 2 (1987): 494–95.

105. KCTU, "Struggle for Labor Law Reforms Campaign News no. XXIV," Feb. 28, 1997.

In spite of all this South Korea was a remarkable country where even white-collar bank employees strapped on identical headbands saying "Down with IMF trusteeship!" and marched through the streets yelling slogans in unison. Students on the raucous campuses in the 1980s, they were now united with blue-collar workers in the KCTU. President Kim changed labor's position in the system with a master stroke in January 1998, however, one that augured a far-reaching political transformation: under his direction, for the first time in Korean history, labor leaders met with leaders of business and government to work out fair and equitable policies to deal with the IMF crisis, a kind of "peak bargaining" arrangement that represented labor's biggest political gain ever. After tough negotiations Kim got labor to agree to large layoffs, which would triple the precrisis unemployment rate, albeit from 2 percent to 6 percent (not a high rate by Western standards); eventually the unemployment rate reached 8 percent, but by 2001 had fallen again to less than 4 percent. In return labor unions got the right to exist legally and to participate in politics and field candidates for elections. The result was that labor unions shaped and conditioned the reform process, rather than seeking to destroy it.

In an interview shortly after he was elected, Kim Dae Jung blamed the financial crisis on military dictatorships that lied to the people and concentrated only on economic development to the detriment of democracy, leading to a "collusive intimacy between business and government." He said the way out of the crisis was to reform the government-business nexus, to induce foreign investment, and then to increase exports.[106] His *chaebŏl* reform package went along with IMF demands to eliminate inter-subsidiary loan guarantees, to lower debt-to-equity ratios, and to improve transparency. Early threats to dismantle the conglomerates, however, soon gave way to plans to break the nexus between the state and the firms. Kim Dae Jung indicated more than once that he had no plans to change the size or purpose of the *chaebŏl*.[107] Instead, he promoted a "big deal" in which the conglomerates would swap subsidiaries to concentrate on core businesses: for example, Samsung's automobile factory would go to Hyundai, in return for Hyundai's giving its semiconductor business to Samsung.[108] But the depth of the economic crisis ended up doing Kim's work for him: even the best of the conglomerates had such a towering level of bad debt that Daewoo went bankrupt, with its founder, Kim Woo

106. Mary Jordan's interview with Kim Dae Jung, *Washington Post*, Jan. 9, 1998.

107. Minister of Finance and Economy Lee Kyu-sung said Kim's reforms were aimed not at diminishing the power and size of the *chaebŏl* but at using various incentives and tax reductions to encourage restructuring (*Korea Herald*, April 10, 1998); President Kim told reporters he had no intention of breaking up the *chaebŏl*, but merely wanted them to "run their firms in the black" (ibid., June 2, 1998).

108. *Korea Herald*, July 11, 1998.

Chung, fleeing abroad in fear of prosecution; Hyundai continued to have massive troubles in returning to profitability and accommodating to strong unions; and only Samsung seemed to emerge from the crisis relatively unscathed. In effect, the financial crisis' intense pressure on the long-standing, jerry-built credit structure of the big *chaebŏl* was enough to break many of them up, without the government's doing anything.

Kim's decision not to try to dismantle the conglomerates was unsurprising, given their importance to Korean development, and the recent merger mania among many Western transnational corporations, as they sought to "get big" in the name of enhancing global competitiveness. But Kim also could not simply get rid of these firms, because they are also feudal industrial estates like the one maintained for centuries by the Du Pont Corporation in the small state of Delaware—namely, provisioners of their employees' needs in every way. The typical Hyundai worker drives a Hyundai car, lives in a Hyundai apartment mortgaged by Hyundai credit, gets health care from a Hyundai hospital, sends his kids to school on Hyundai loans or scholarships, and eats his meals at Hyundai cafeterias. This extreme form of corporatism is perhaps best seen in the masses of construction teams that Hyundai has long dispatched to the Middle East; every worker would depart in Hyundai T-shirts and caps carrying Hyundai bags, would live and eat in Hyundai dormitories, and would use Hyundai tools and equipment to build Hyundai cities in the desert. In the same way that Kim Il Sung built a Confucian-influenced hereditary family-state in North Korea and called it communism, the Korean *chaebŏl* have built large family-run hereditary corporate estates in Korea and called it capitalism. Korea's reformers thus had no alternative but to work within this *chaebŏl* system, and to concentrate on breaking the nexus between these firms, the state, and the big banks.

Democratic reforms proceeded rapidly under Kim Dae Jung. Kim Young Sam had done nothing to change Korea's ubiquitous ANSP, merely putting his own allies in control of it. The agency prosecuted hundreds of cases under the National Security Law in the mid-1990s, including the labor organizer Park Chŏng-yŏl, who was arrested in the middle of the night in November 1995 when ten men rushed into his home and dragged him off to an unheated cell, where for the next twenty-two days his tormenters beat him, poured cold water over him, and limited him to thirty minutes of sleep a day, all to get him to confess to being a North Korean spy—which he wasn't. A government official told a reporter such measures were necessary, explaining "We found the whole society had been influenced by North Korean ideology"; he claimed that upward of 40,000 North Korean agents existed in the South.[109]

109. Andrew Pollack, *New York Times*, Feb. 22, 1997.

A subsequent investigation proved that the ANSP had run an operation just before the election to tar Kim Dae Jung as procommunist, and incoming officials also gave reporters the list of KCIA agents who had kidnapped Kim in 1973. In February 1998 the *Sisa Journal* published for first time the full administrative structure of the ANSP, showing that it had more than 70,000 employees (and any number of informal agents and spies), an annual budget of around 800 billion won (about $1 billion), and almost no senior officials from the Southwest (three from among the seventy highest-ranking officials, one from among thirty-five section chiefs). It controlled eight academic institutes, including several that provide grants to foreign academics and that publish well-known English-language journals. The new government cut the "domestic" arm of the ANSP by 50 percent, reduced the rest of the agency's staff by 10 percent, fired twenty-four top officials and many lesser people, and reoriented the agency away from domestic affairs, toward North Korea. A top official said the ANSP "will be reborn to fit the era of international economic war,"[110] not a bad characterization of the contemporary world economy.

Kim Dae Jung's presidency thus achieved major changes in the economy, the political system, and, as we will see later, in relations with the North. South Korea's foreign exchange reserves were built up to unprecedented heights, near $100 billion, that is, about the level of reserves that enabled Taiwan, Hong Kong, and China to avoid runs on their currency in 1997. Within two years high growth rates had returned (over 11 percent in 1999 and 9 percent in 2000), even if the downturn in the American economy in 2001–04 reduced growth to the 5–6 percent range. Korea's civil society and democracy were both strong and vibrant, and no longer threatened by the military. It therefore turned out that a curious and paradoxical confluence of liquidity crisis, IMF reform, Washington's desire to rein in the Northeast Asian model of development, and Korean democratization served to put the ROK on a much better footing, both politically and economically, than it had at any point before 1997.

Kim Dae Jung and his close allies promoted Roh Moo Hyun to succeed him in office, a shock to the body politic since Roh was not part of Korea's political elite and a virtual unknown. Coming from a modest background, he had taught himself enough law to pass the bar exams, and in the 1980s courageously defended many dissidents and labor activists. Unlike any major politician, he had married a woman from a politically blacklisted family (her father, a member of the South Korean Labor Party, died in prison). Roh ran against Lee Hoi-chang, a former

110. *Korea Herald*, March 19, 1998.

judge and stalwart of the old ruling party. Everyone seemed to expect Lee to win, including the Bush administration, which feted him during a 2002 visit to Washington. But Roh won the election in December, and then in 2004 his party (the Uri-dang, or "Our Party") won a majority in the National Assembly—thus giving him a firm political base until the end of his term in 2008. Kim and Roh thereby achieved a thorough political transition away from the elites who had dominated the ROK since 1948.

Unfortunately this victory for democracy was not entirely welcome in Washington, because it appeared to have been part of a new wave of "anti-Americanism." Richard Allen, a Republican who was often registered as an agent of the ROK by the U.S. Justice Department,[111] wrote that Roh Moo Hyun's election made for "a troubling shift" in U.S. relations with the ROK. Korean leaders seemed now to have "stepped into the neutral zone" and had even gone so far as to suggest, in the current nuclear standoff, that Washington and P'yŏngyang should both make concessions: "the cynicism of this act constitutes a serious breach of faith." Maybe American troops should be withdrawn, Allen suggested, "now that the harm can come from two directions—North Korea and violent South Korean protesters."[112] Other Americans wondered how Koreans can criticize the United States, when "North Korea is rattling a nuclear sword"? A Pentagon official argued, "It's like teaching a child to ride a bike. We've been running alongside South Korea, holding on to its handlebars for 50 years. At some point you have to let go."[113] Another American military official in Seoul said of Roh's election, "There is a real sense of mourning here"[114]—i.e., on the military base. This remarkable combination of petulant irritability and grating condescension somehow seems unremarkable both to the people who say such things and sometimes to the reporters who quote them.

The media's use of the term "anti-American" to describe the discontent in Seoul was flawed and inappropriate. It would be closer to the truth to say that the policies of the Bush administration were as responsible as anything else for the upsurge in protest; it was really "anti-Bushism," and that hardly made Korea different from many other countries. When I observed demonstrations in Seoul in August 2001 and in December 2002, I was prepared to tell people I was from New Zealand, if asked. But no one bothered me in the slightest. Many Amer-

111. See Cumings, "The Korea Lobby," Japan Policy Research Institute, 1996.

112. Richard V. Allen, "Seoul's Choice: The U.S. or the North," *New York Times*, Jan. 16, 2003.

113. James Dao, "Why Keep U.S. Troops?" *New York Times*, Jan. 5, 2003.

114. Howard W. French, "Bush and New Korean Leader to Take Up Thorny Diplomatic Issues," *New York Times*, Dec. 21, 2003.

icans and Westerners participated in the massive, dignified, and impressive candlelight vigils held in Seoul on Saturday nights in the period leading up to Roh's election in late 2002. On December 14, 2002, I observed tens of thousands of young people, families with little children, painted protesters festooned with slogans, and a sprinkle of middle-aged and elderly people holding candles protected from the wind, moving slowly under billowing white banners calling upon the United States to support North-South reconciliation, reform the Status of Forces Agreement (SOFA), and move military bases outside of Seoul. It was serious and yet amiable, moving and dignified, and very well organized (both by the protesters and by the forces of order). The nonviolent tenor of these demonstrations differed markedly from the actual high point of (violent) opposition to U.S. policy, in the mid-1980s.

CONCLUSION

Through the decades-long sacrifices of countless individuals, South Korea now has a politics that does not nauseate its democratic friends and finally brought forth a democracy of which all Koreans can be proud. But at what price, necessary and unnecessary? Since it is commonplace for Americans to sympathize with those victims of authoritarianism who share their ideals and to fall silent about those who do not, it may be instructive to end with the story of Kim Sŏn-myŏng: emerging from a jail cell in August 1995 like Rip Van Winkle, he had been behind bars for so long that another long-term political prisoner, Kim Sŏk-hyŏn (who had gotten out earlier), had to instruct him in how to use a telephone and how to turn on the television; others gently informed him that his ninety-three-year-old mother believed he had died twenty years earlier. Who was this man?

In the fierce conflict raging across the peninsula in October 1950, American intelligence officers captured Kim Sŏn-myŏng, a southerner supporting the North, and turned him over to ROK authorities. They accused him of spying, which he denied; but he would not recant his political allegiance to P'yŏngyang. His jailers threatened him with execution and tortured him, seeking a confession; meanwhile, they executed his father and his sister in order to pressure him further. When he still would not recant, they threw Kim into solitary confinement in a tiny cell for the next forty-four years. Forbidden to speak to anyone, to meet relatives, or to read anything, beaten frequently and surviving somehow on a "prison starvation diet," he remained incarcerated because he would not "convert" and give up his political support of North Korea. "The guards would show me food, like a soup full of meat. And then they would just give me broth for dinner. They would say, 'if you want food, you better change your beliefs.'" He entered prison at twenty-nine and came out at seventy-three, still unrepetant.

The Kim Young Sam government probably released him because of embarrassment at holding in its jails the world's longest-serving political prisoner. Meanwhile, twenty-four more North Korean sympathizers remained in prison, each having served at least twenty years.[115] The reader should ask if this is a mere unfortunate remnant of interwar Japanese techniques of thought control and conversion of recalcitrants, or something that South Korea took quite beyond this foul point of origin; and if we can dignify with the word "democracy" a regime that continued to do such things.

115. Nicholas D. Kristof reported on Kim's release in the *New York Times*, Aug. 20, 1995.

CHAPTER EIGHT

Nation of the Sun King: North Korea, 1953–Present

What all men speak well of, look critically into; what all men condemn, examine first before you decide. —*Confucius*

The sun sheds light everywhere; even its least beam thoroughly brightens the obscure and small. Your vast kindness pervades all; its least wavelet thoroughly cleanses the false and the oppressed. Your benevolence covers both the living and the dead. —*A Korean memorial to the Ming emperor*[1]

The Democratic People's Republic of Korea (DPRK) evolved into a singular and puzzling nation that resists easy description. Because its leadership is secretive and unyielding to foreign attentions, many basic facts about the country are unknown. Onto this inkblot pundits are therefore able to project equally unyielding stereotypes (a Stalinist attempt at re-creating "1984," a renegade state, a socialist basket case, a Confucian/communist monarchy, Joan Robinson's economic miracle, Che Guevara's idea of what Cuba should eventually look like).[2] In the night of our ignorance, North Korea confirms all stereotypes. But closer familiarity confounds simple expectations.

During a visit in 1987 with members of a British film crew, I learned that they expected P'yŏngyang to be something like Teheran in the 1980s, where they had also filmed a documentary: the State Department called this a "terrorist" nation like Iran, and so they assumed that cars

1. Quoted in Peter H. Lee, "Versions of the Self in the *Storytellers' Miscellany* (P'aegwan chapki), in de Bary and Haboush (1985), p. 479.

2. The first several stereotypes animated much American discourse about North Korea during the 1990s nuclear crisis. Joan Robinson, a great socialist economist, proclaimed during a visit in 1965 that North Korea had accomplished an economic miracle, just as pundits would later claim for the South. See Joan Robinson, "Korean Miracle," *Monthly Review* (January 1965): 541–49. Che Guevara visited P'yŏngyang around the same time and told the press that North Korea was a model to which revolutionary Cuba should aspire.

filled with "revolutionary guards" would be careening through the streets, machine guns dangling out the windows. (They had put in for and received the equivalent of combat pay from their employer.) Or they thought it would be a poorer version of China, the masses pedaling to work on bicycles, clad in drab blue work clothes. They dreaded that creature comforts could only be harder to find there than in Moscow, where they had recently suffered.

They were ill prepared for the wide tree-lined boulevards of P'yŏngyang, swept squeaky clean and traversed by determined, disciplined urban commuters held in close check by traffic women in tight uniforms, pirouetting with military discipline and a smile, atop platforms at each intersection. They had not expected a population living in modern high-rise buildings, hustling out in the morning like Japan's "salarymen" to a waiting subway or electric bus. They were suddenly enamored of the polite waitresses who served ample portions of tasty Korean and Western food at hotels and restaurants.

In the 1980s P'yŏngyang was one of the most efficient, best-run cities in Asia, a mixture of the fastidiousness of Singapore and the bucolic quiet of Alma-Ata. Older utilitarian Soviet-style apartment houses and state office buildings mingled with grand new monumental architecture, lavished with marble and topped off with traditional Korean curved roofs. About two million people lived there, or 10 percent of the population. If the pickings were predictably slim among consumer goods, daily necessities were available and the traveler observed few queues (although resident diplomats said there were many lines for services). Well-tended parks dotted all sections of the city, through which two rivers flowed along willow-lined banks.

Smaller cities were less pleasing; many were unrelievedly ugly in their mimicry of Soviet proletarian architecture, the apartments all stamped from the same mold, sitting akilter along jolting, potholed roads. But then, most of them had been built since the Korean War (1950–53), when nearly every urban building of note was razed by American bombing. And always there was color, whether affixed self-consciously to storefronts and apartment balconies or leaping out from the ever-present political billboards.

North Korean villages were spartan, plain, clean, and evocative of the rustic atmosphere of the Korean past so lacking in the capital. They were linked by a network of hard-pack dirt roads, whereas cities are connected by extensive railways. Residents planted vegetables raised for home consumption or the small private market on every square meter of land, right up to the edge of streets; electric wires ran to all peasant homes, but television aerials were much less apparent than in the cities. As in South Korea, thatched roofs had given way to tile, signifying modernity (shortly before he died Kim Il Sung claimed that North Korea had realized the age-old dream of having everyone live in a tiled-roof home); so did the rice paddies, which no longer gave off the peculiar odor of human manure, because of the widespread use of chemical fertilizer. Signs urged self-reliance ("regeneration through one's own efforts") on the locals, no doubt a reflection of state priorities, which emphasized heavy industry, military preparedness, and the city.

In city, town, and village there was Kim Il Sung; everywhere there was Kim Il Sung, staring down from a billboard or in the subway or on the apartment wall: offering here a maxim for industry, there one for agriculture ("rice is communism"), or simply averring (in the National Folk Museum) that "Koreans can hardly be Korean if they don't eat *toenjang*" (fermented bean paste). The regime announced that the orchid *Kimilsungia* was blossoming around the country. In utterly predictable DPRK fashion, there was also *Kimjongilia*, a new begonia brought forth by state-controlled florists.[3] No leader in the twentieth century stamped a nation with his presence more than did Kim: born on the day the *Titanic* sank (April 15, 1912), in power for nearly five decades, he died of a heart attack on July 8, 1994—sending his kingdom into a state of shock.

Few police and military were visible to the traveler, in this, the most militarized country on the face of the earth. The one-won note was a tip-off, however, showing on its face a woman in bright traditional dress leaping forward with a pistol in her hand. This is a garrison state with one in twenty citizens in the military, compulsory military service for everyone, an army one million strong, millions more in militias, enormous military bases and arsenals built deep underground, subterranean subway stations with gigantic blast doors recessed into the walls, round-the-clock vigils for trouble along the DMZ, a dictator who sleeps in a different place every night for security reasons, and twenty-two million citizens each with a personal reliability rating.

In the late 1940s, as we have seen, the regime emerged within the bowels of Russian Red Army occupation and thus took its administrative and industrial structure from Soviet models (as did every socialist state in the period). The DPRK was proclaimed on September 9, 1948, but much of it was in place within a year after Japan's colonial rule ended in 1945, and many of the themes visible then remain features of the regime today. Above all this is a postcolonial state, still fighting the Japanese.

3. Korean Central News Agency (KCNA), April 11, 20, 1988. *Kimilsungia* is an orchid developed by an Indonesian botanist and given to Kim by Sukarno in Jakarta in 1965. In all his modesty Kim resisted having a flower named for him, regime scribes say, but the Korean people demanded it out of respect for their leader.

Hardly a day goes by when the controlled press does not rant on about a fifty-year-old Japanese atrocity, or warn about the imminent revanche of Japanese militarism. The resistance to Japanese imperialism is still so prominent that one would think the war had just ended; many signs exhort citizens to "live in the way of the anti-Japanese guerrillas," and young people go on camping trips that retrace their struggles. Kim's Korean guerrilla comrades structured the core or commanding heights of the regime, and now as they pass on their images remain for the ages in a stunning cemetery atop T'aesŏng Mountain, overlooking P'yŏngyang, each person's exploits memorialized with a stone and a life-size bronze bust.

The unique symbol/logo of the Korean Workers Party (KWP) places a writing brush across the hammer and sickle, indicating an inclusive policy toward the educated and the expert: Kim rarely if ever denigrated them, in contrast to Maoist China, and explicitly authorized their widespread introduction into positions of authority—scholar-officials, communist-style. The Koreans also established a vague category, *samuwŏn*, meaning clerks, small traders, bureaucrats, professors, and the like. This category served two purposes: for the regime it retained educated people and experts who might otherwise have fled south; for large numbers of Koreans it provided a category within which to hide "bad" class background.

Thus the Korean revolution, after polarizing the population into good and bad classes at its inception, soon pursued an inclusive, all-encompassing mass politics. The Koreans have envisioned their society as a mass, the gathered-together "people," rather than a class-based and class-divided society. The union of the three classes—peasant, worker, *samuwŏn*—excluded few but the landlords of the old period, who, after all, were much stronger in southern than in northern Korea. Probably the key factors explaining this would be the relatively industrialized character of the North, an inheritance from the heavy Japanese investment there, the opportunity for many capitalists and landlords to flee to the South, and chronic labor shortages, especially among skilled experts.

The Koreans also adapted typical postcolonial Third World policies to their indigenous political culture and to Soviet-style socialism: an economic program of rapid industrialization and a philosophy of subjecting nature to human will. They combined Lenin's program of national liberation and Stalin's autarky of socialism in one country (to become in Korea socialism in one-half a country and, now, as one wit remarked, socialism in one family). Autarky fit Korea's Hermit Kingdom past and answered the need for *closure* from the world economy after decades of opening under Japanese imperial auspices.

"THE GREAT SUN": NORTH KOREAN CORPORATISM

Karl Marx had no political model for a future socialist state, only a highly opaque set of prescriptions (mainly the *Critique of the Gotha Program* and some remarks on the dictatorship of the proletariat). It was Lenin who turned Marxism into a political theory and, some argue, transformed it into a voluntaristic doctrine that left open the possibility of the extreme statism of Stalin, in which politics from on high became the agency for engineering an entire economy and society. But the political vacuum in Marxism-Leninism also opens the way to an assertion of indigenous politics; this may even be demanded by the very paucity of political models; in any case, we see it in Russian, Chinese, and (perhaps more strongly) Korean communism. In an era of revolution that now looks almost archaic, Marxism-Leninism seemed to be a talisman that made all things possible, rapid and millennial change that wiped away the past. Recent history has demonstrated that Marxism-Leninism had far less transformative effect than either its proponents or its opponents cared to admit. We all know how hard it is to change old habits; when those accumulate into a general practice—a culture—they prove far more recalcitrant than revolutionaries can know. Thus twentieth-century revolutions were grafted onto existing, long-standing roots and, while seeking to transform the roots, were themselves transformed as peoples and societies rendered them intelligible to their lives.

This has proved truer in Korea, precisely because of the very alienness of the setting to this fundamentally Western set of ideas. Korea had a minuscule proletariat, the beginnings of capitalism, and far too much internationalism (capitalist-style) by 1945. It therefore took from Marxism-Leninism what it wanted and rejected much of the rest.

Over time a unique political system evolved within the Marxist-Leninist crucible and is fully in place today. It can best be compared to varieties of corporatism around the world or in the past, a kind of socialist corporatism. It is a tightly held, total politics, with enormous repressive capacity and many political victims—although no one really knows how repressive it is, how many political prisoners there are, and the like, because of the exclusionism and secrecy of the regime. (Some reports suggest as many as 100,000 people are held in prisons and reform-through-labor camps; if and when the regime falls, we will probably learn of larger numbers and various unimaginable atrocities, as with the other communist states.)

What is corporatism? It is not an easy concept to grasp. Most American intellectuals who do not work on Latin America or southern Europe seem bewildered when asked to define this political form. In the 1968 edition of *The Encyclopedia of the Social Sciences*, the entry "corporatism" merely says this: "See fascism." But the phenomenon has a long pedigree. One might say it is the preeminent antithesis of a liberal politics. It predated the emergence of liberalism, it fueled the romantics of the nineteenth and twentieth centuries who hated liberalism, and it sparks the dreams of utopians who envision a transcendence of liberalism. Liberal theory characteristically separates the political from other realms of human behavior, making politics just a part of one's existence, or a subdiscipline for study, whereas politics played an architectonic role for the ancients and is interconnected with society in corporatism.

If corporatism is known by what it rejects, it also comes in several varieties: traditional corporatism had three great themes—hierarchy, organic connection, and family—and three great images that corresponded to it—political fatherhood, the body politic, and the great chain. "The whole of the chain of being might be imagined as an immense organism, animated by its divine source."[4] For traditionalists, and later for fascists like Mussolini, the body politic was a living organism, literally corporeal.[5] All members of the body politic were interconnected and functional to the whole. The head (or king) was the father of the people, ruler and ruled were joined by "perfect love," and the paternal wisdom and benevolence of the leader "was to be relied upon and never doubted." The king would display loving solicitude and "fatherly care" for his subjects; in the words of the Earl of Strafford, "princes are to be the indulgent nursing fathers to their people . . . love and protection descending and loyalty ascending."[6] The most significant corporate body was the family; then came the church, which was seen in medieval times as the visible body of Christ.[7] The leader was the object of adulation: Henry VIII of England was thought to be "the sun of man."[8] This was a politics of the medieval society of estates and communal organizations that slowly disappeared in the solvent of capitalism. The traditional corporate ideal held fastest and longest in those countries where the Catholic church remained dominant.

Conservative corporatism sought to recapture this lost age and was a prevalent ideology in the nineteenth century among romantic anticapitalists and antiliberals. It idealized hierarchy, fixed social position, com-

4. Michael Walzer, *The Revolution of the Saints* (New York: Atheneum, 1970), p. 149. For a useful recent discussion see "The Material and Social Bases of Corporatism," in Bob Jessop, *State Theory: Putting Capitalist States in Their Place* (State College: Pennsylvania State University Press, 1990), pp. 110–43.

5. Walzer, Revolution, p. 171; see also Franz Neumann, *Behemoth: The Structure and Practice of National Socialism* (New York: Harper & Row, 1942), p. 358.

6. Quoted in Walzer, *Revolution*, pp. 172, 186.

7. Ibid., pp. 171, 188.

8. Newmann, *Behemoth*, p. 86

monly shared values, and closed communities. As Roberto Mangiaberra Unger has put it, "Forgetful of history, it proposed to resolve the problems of bureaucracy by reviving the very forms of social order whose dissolution created these problems in the first place."[9] Among twentieth-century dictatorships of the right, conservative corporatism provided an ideology and a set of slogans, but not much guidance in practice. The weak authoritarianism of late Franco Spain, the Salazar dictatorship in Portugal, and some of the interwar regimes in Eastern Europe adhered to this set of ideas, but never succeeded in establishing a real corporate hierarchy of groups and classes segmented according to work and station, and never really tried to do so.[10]

The pathological variant of corporatism is fascism, exemplified by Germany and Italy in the 1930s. Fascism gave corporatism the bad name that it still possesses. Fascists used the rhetoric of conservative corporatism for different ends: totalitarianism, breaking up the secondary associations that real corporatism would presumably wish to preserve, an aggressive militarism, and a mobilized politics of the street that corporatist regimes could never muster. Fascist regimes also relied on the charisma of a leader, whereas the corporate polities were led by more plodding, truly "fatherly" types. Neumann argued that in Germany, instead of organic connection, only the leader principle unified state and party, with the leader and various Nazi groups functioning to disaggregate people and leave them helpless: Nazism appealed not to organically rooted individuals but to the "least rational" stratum of the population.[11]

There was also a left-wing version of corporatism. Political theorists like Robert Michels, Vilfredo Pareto, and the Romanian Mihail Manoilescu moved from a sophisticated and interesting corporate conception of socialism to more or less egregious sympathy with 1930s fascist regimes. But they also developed a kind of neosocialist corporatism, which has interesting similarities with the North Korean system. Their fundamental departure from Marxism was to substitute nation for class and to develop a conception of a world system of advantaged and disadvantaged (or bourgeois and proletarian) nations. For Manoilescu, "the

9. Roberto Mangiaberra Unger, *Knowledge and Politics* (New York: Free Press, 1975), pp. 188, 249–50.

10. Juan Linz, "An Authoritarian Regime: Spain," in *Cleavages, Ideologies, and Party Systems*, ed. Erik Allardt and Yrjo Littunen (Helsinki: Academic Bookstore, 1964), pp. 291–341; Philippe C. Schmitter, "Still the Century of Corporatism?" in *The New Corporatism*, ed. Frederick B. Pyke and Thomas Stritch (Notre Dame: University of Notre Dame Press, 1974), pp. 85–131. George Kennan shows considerable empathy for the Salazar regime in his *Around the Cragged Hill: A Personal and Political Philosophy*, (New York: W. W. Norton, 1993).

11. Neumann, *Behemoth*, pp. 83–84, 96.

organic, 'productivist,' vertically structured metaphors of a harmonic political-economic order" at home had their corollary in a hierarchical world at large.[12] The international division of labor had distributed rich nations here, poor nations there; the "proletarian" nations of what we would now call the periphery should structure themselves vertically at home (to accumulate power) and horizontally abroad to redress their positions in the world economy.[13]

Other neosocialists thought no practical Marxism could continue to avoid the problems that nations and nationalism posed for class analysis: class was for the nineteenth century, whereas "the concept of the nation would be the key concept of political organization in the twentieth century."[14] Such thinking made neosocialists strong supporters of protectionism and the type of autocentered development associated with Stalinism in the 1930s. Neosocialist corporatism has had its most profound recent statement in the work of Unger, who proposed a movement toward a corporatism embodying equality of conditions, democracy, and the overcoming of liberalism and individualism through a new conception of organic groups.[15] Unger's proposals seek once again to introduce the family as either a refuge from liberal politics or a metaphor for transcending liberalism. Unger wrote that the family "comes closest to [the ideal of] community of life in our experience. . . . The modern family forever draws men back into an association that . . . offers a measure of individual recognition through love."[16] Thus we have come full circle: the logic of corporatist disgust with liberalism leads progressives to rediscover the family as a model for politics, something that the traditionalists never abandoned.

It has rarely occurred to Asian thinkers to abandon the family as metaphor or reality: only Mao's China during the Great Leap Forward assaulted the family structure, and even this monumental effort was dropped rather quickly. The family has been the centerpiece of Asian corporatism, the preeminent example of which is interwar Japan and its failed attempt to fashion a "family state." The three corporatist images

12. Philippe Schmitter, "Reflections on Mihail Manoilescu and the Political Consequences of Delayed Development on the Periphery of Western Europe," in *Social Change in Romania, 1860–1940*, ed. Kenneth Jowitt (Berkeley: Institute of International Studies, University of California, 1978), p. 120.

13. Daniel Chirot, "Neoliberal and Social Democratic Theories of Development," in *Social Change in Romania*, pp. 31–52; also Schmitter, "Reflections."

14. Zeev Sternhell, "Fascist Ideology," in *Fascism: A Reader's Guide*, ed. Walter Laqueur (Berkeley: University of California Press, 1976), pp. 352–55.

15. Unger, *Knowledge and Politics*, p. 250.

16. Ibid., pp. 252, 264; see also Christopher Lasch, *Haven in a Heartless World: The Family Besieged* (New York: Basic Books, 1977).

of political fatherhood, a body politic, and the great chain were pronounced in interwar Japan: the emperor was the father of all the people, the people were united by blood ties, and the blood "running through the veins of the race . . . has never changed" since time immemorial.[17] As one publicist put it, "It is only Nippon in which national society has ensured not merely horizontal union by dint of blood and land relations but also the blood-relation-center of the society itself . . . as the authority of national society."[18] The emperor was the center of blood relations extending through the whole polity and back through time—benevolent, august, solicitous, wise, eternal, and loving.

Masao Maruyama, seeking out the unique in what he called "Japanese fascism," settled on "the family system extolled as the fundamental principle of the State structure." Its basic principle was to view the state as "an extension of the family; more concretely, as a nation of families composed of the Imperial House as the main family and of the people as the branch family. This is not merely an analogy as in the organic theory of the State, but is considered as having a substantial meaning."[19] According to imperial officials, each Japanese family was "an independent animate body, a complete cell in itself." Radicals like Kita Ikki called Japan "an organic and indivisible great family."[20]

The ideology of Kim Il Sung resonated loudly with the history of corporatism. Kim's theories, just like Mihail Manoilescu's, substituted the nation for the proletarian class as the "unit" of historical conflict and argued that former colonies, dependencies, and peripheral socialist nations should unite horizontally in common cause.[21] But Kim did not have to read European or Japanese theories to arrive at a native conception: long before his time, Korean Neo-Confucians saw the human body as an organism that required a proper physiological harmony, of course; still, it was just one organism, an integral part of a unitary world:

> The body was simply one network of functional interactions within the cosmic pattern of interrelating and interdependent networks. Disharmony within the body's physiological processes could be either a reflection of disharmony in the cosmos at large, or it could itself be a cause of such disharmony.[22]

17. Chigaku Tanaka, *What Is Nippon Kokutai?* (Tokyo: Shishio Bunko, 1936), p. 95.
18. Ibid., appendix, p. 3.
19. Masao Maruyama, *Thought and Behavior in Modern Japanese Politics*, ed. Ivan Morris (New York: Oxford University Press, 1969), p. 36.
20. Ibid., p. 37.
21. Schmitter, "Reflections."
22. See Don Baker's chapter in the forthcoming *Cambridge History of Korea*, vol. 3.

This organic political thought was embodied in Kim's endlessly trumpeted "Juche idea," as P'yŏngyang renders it in English. *Chuch'e* seems at first glance to be readily understandable. It means self-reliance and independence in politics, economics, defense, and ideology; it first emerged in 1955 as P'yŏngyang drew away from Moscow, and then appeared full-blown in the mid-sixties as Kim sought a stance independent of both Moscow and Beijing. One can find uses of the term *chuch'e* before 1955 in North and South, but no one would notice, were it not for its later prominence. But at that time Kim's rhetoric rang with synonymous language; a variety of terms translating roughly as "self-reliance" and "independence" structured Kim's ideology in the 1940s: *chajusŏng* (self-reliance), *minjok tongnip* (national or ethnic independence), *charip kyŏngje* (independent economy). All these terms were antonyms of sadaejuŭi, which means serving and relying upon foreign power, which had been the scourge of a people who naturally inclined toward things Korean.[23] Added up, these ideas were the common denominators of what all the colonized peoples sought at mid-century: their basic dignity as human beings.

On closer inspection, however, *chuch'e*'s meaning is less accessible. The North Koreans say things like "Everyone must have *chuch'e* firm in mind and spirit"; "Only when *chuch'e* is firmly implanted can we be happy"; "*Chuch'e* must not only be firmly established in mind but perfectly realized in practice"; and so on. The second character, *ch'e* in the Korean pronunciation, is found in Li Hung-chang's term from the late-nineteenth-century self-strengthening movement, *t'i* of *t'i-yung*, meaning Chinese learning for the base (*t'i*) and Western learning for use; it is also the *tai* of *kokutai*, a concept promoted in Japan in the 1930s that meant, in essence, what it means to be Japanese as opposed to everything else, what is authentically Japanese. *Kokutai* was deeply identified with the prewar emperor system and with ultranationalism. Japanese scribblers would write on and on about "getting *kokutai* firmly in mind"; once you have it firmly in your mind, all else follows.[24] In the postwar period, *shutaisei* (*chuch'esŏng* in Korean) has been a common usage among Japanese intellectuals, on the central theme of how Japan can be modern and Japanese at the same time. The Koreans use *chuch'e* in similar ways—in their case with the goal of creating a subjective, solipsistic

23. On Shin Ch'ae-ho's opposition of *sadae* to *chuch'e* in the 1920s, see Michael Robinson, "National Identity and the Thought of Shin Ch'ae-ho: *Sadaejuŭi* and *Chuch'e* in History and Politics," *Journal of Korean Studies*, 5 (1984): 29–55.

24. Of course, *kukch'e*, or "national polity," was a term Koreans used well before Japan did in the 1930s—for example, in Korean debates in 1875 about whether to receive Japanese envoys or not.

state of mind, the correct thought that must precede and that will then determine correct action—but also as a means of defining what is simultaneously modern and Korean. The term is really untranslatable; the closer one gets to its meaning, the more the meaning slips away. For a foreigner its meaning recedes into a pool of everything that makes Koreans Korean, and therefore it is ultimately inaccessible to the non-Korean. *Chuch'e* is the opaque core of North Korean national solipsism.

Kim was always the major interpreter of Korean self-reliance. In July 1982 he gave a vintage exposition of his ideology. Korea should not become "a plaything of great powers," he declared, adding, "I say to our officials: if a man takes to flunkeyism [*sadaejuŭi*] he will become a fool; if a nation falls into flunkeyism, this nation will go to ruin; and if a party adopts flunkeyism, it will make a mess of the revolution." He went on, "Once there were poets who worshipped Pushkin and musicians who adored Tschaikovsky. Even in creating an opera, people patterned it on Italian ones. Flunkeyism was so rampant that some artistis drew foreign landscapes instead of our beautiful mountains and rivers. . . . [But] Koreans do not like European artistic works." Koreans, he said, should always "hold fast to independence."[25] It isn't very elegant phrasing, but long experience with colonized or dependent Korea explains why the North Koreans thought such admonitions were so necessary.

A kind of national solipsism expresses something you see all the time in North Korean materials: an assumption that Korea is the center of the world (it wouldn't occur to many non-Koreans to think this, but then look again at the *kangnido* map). Korea is the center, radiating outward the rays of *chuch'e*, especially to Third World nations that are thought by the North Koreans to be ready for *chuch'e*. (The regime funded *chuch'e* study groups all over the world for decades and treated their leaders like heads of state when they visited P'yŏngyang.) The world tends toward Korea, with all eyes on Kim Il Sung or Kim Jong Il. This is perhaps the most bizarre aspect of the DPRK, but also one of the most palpable. Its analogue is the Sinocentrism of the Middle Kingdom, this time writ small.

Few would have much guidance for how to get up every morning and "perfectly realize" *chuch'e*. Its real meaning might best be translated as putting Korean things first, always: it suggests a type of nationalism, in other words. It is closer to Neo-Confucianism than to Marxism. Let's pause here for a brief philosophical exercise: I hope the reader will stay

25. "Conversation of the Great Leader Kim Il Sung with the south Korean delegates to north-south the high-level political talks," KCNA, July 4, 1982. In this same discussion he referred to Soviet efforts to prevent Korea from collectivizing agriculture before mechanization was available, a frequent complaint of the Chinese as well.

with me, because our purpose is not merely to describe the behavior of North Koreans but to understand why they do the things they do—they are, after all, twenty-two million fellow human beings inhabiting this same earth. If one of our congressmen says, as many did during the nuclear crisis with the DPRK, "Those people think differently than we do," we ought to have an intelligent view of what it is they think, and why.

Here is Kim Jong Il, expounding on the theme "Abuses of Socialism."[26] After a tour through the history of socialism and the causes for its collapse in "some countries" (which happened mainly because of a failure to indoctrinate the young, in his view), Kim Jong Il says, "Consciousness plays a decisive role in the activity of a human being. . . . The basic factor which gives an impetus to social development must always be ascribed to ideological consciousness."

The Korean assumption is that "mind" is simultaneously "heart," as we saw earlier. Daily Korean body language locates the thinking mechanism in the breast. Second, the principle of human action is not an "if, then" premise about an a priori human being, whose external circumstances motivate him to act in a certain way (such as incentives that elicit rationally self-interested behavior): instead, the principle is an internal condition in the human being, premised on a state of mind. "Only if the *chuch'e* idea is firmly in your mind, will you know how to get up in the morning and be a good citizen of our state." But what, then, is the internal condition?

A good question: it is the question the Neo-Confucian philosophers always argued about. Without entering their arguments, let's take a passage from the work of Chŏng To-jŏn, architect of the fourteenth-century Chosŏn reforms. In his "Philosophical Rebuttal of Buddhism and Taoism,"[27] he says this (and even makes a passing comment on self-interested behavior, using a metaphor of squirming insects):

> Principle (*li*) is the virtue (*te*) endowed upon the mind (*hsin*) and is the cause by which material force (*ch'i*) comes into being.
>
> Ah! Profound principle
> That exists before heaven and earth
> Material force comes into being through the self
> So is mind also given. . . .
>
> The mind combines principle and material force to become master of the body. . . . [Principle] is also received by the mind and becomes virtue.

26. Kim Jong Il, "Abuses of Socialism," *Kŭlloja* (The worker), March 1, 1993, KCNA, P'yŏngyang, March 3, 1993.
27. Trans. John Duncan, in Lee (1993), pp. 454–58, 461.

> If there were only mind and no self,
> There would be only the race for worldly gain.
> If there were only material force and no self,
> There would be only a body of flesh and blood
> Moving like squirming insects
> And reverting to bird and beast. . . .

> This tells us that a human being is different from beasts because he has righteousness. If a human being has no righteousness, then his consciousness is no more than emotion, desire, and the selfishness of worldly gain [and] his activity is like a mass of squirming insects. . . . Principle is truly embodied on our minds.

In the same discourse, Kwŏn Kŭn says this:

> Only after one is able to embody humanity, make complete the virtue of his mind, and constantly maintain without fail the principle with which he is born, can he be called human without being embarrassed.

The "internal condition" is nothing other than *virtue*, embodied in *mind* (conceived organically as brain, heart, and body integrated); virtue-in-mind is what makes us different from animals. Not only that—it is the "cause by which material force comes into existence"! Now, that is a very complicated business: it doesn't mean that the human mind conjures up the external environment, the world. But if we make the "postmodern" stipulation that we are all subjective creatures (not objective rational actors), and that therefore we construct our own realities and call them things like history books, then Chŏng To-jŏn does seem to be saying that humans create their universe. But not just any human, only those humans who, through long study, have cultivated the virtues that are the sine qua non of having the capability to judge, to decide, to lead, to teach, and thus to create.

It is unquestionable that no class of scholars ever provided a better justification for Plato's injunction to "let philosophers be kings, and kings philosophers"; this is the Hongian legitimation. What sort of politics flows from this logic? to ask a Platonic question. An eleventh-century Sung scholar, Fan Tsu-yü, said that "order and disorder in the world all depend on the heart-and-mind of the ruler. If his heart-and-mind are correct, than the myriad affairs of the court will not be incorrect."[28] The formula is virtuous-mind-become-master-of-the-body. Now let the body be the body politic, and presto, the virtuous king becomes its master. How does he do that? Precisely by decades of reading the classics and tutoring by the philosophers, just as we saw with King Yŏngjo. The king

28. Quoted in Haboush (1988), pp. 9–10.

then becomes a perfected being, "the supreme mind of the nation," and woe to the person who challenges his authority or denies that he can walk on water. His power, however, is not absolute: he is still hamstrung by the scholars, the censors, the remonstrators; after all, they were and are his teachers.

Central to the North Korean version of corporatism is this philosophy, and it is one way to understand the position of Kim Il Sung and his son, and what many observers call the "personality cult" surrounding them. My position is that North Korea is closer to a Neo-Confucian kingdom than to Stalin's Russia. With its absurdly inflated hero worship and its nauseating repetition, the North Korean political rhetoric seems to know no bounds; to a person accustomed to a liberal political system it is instinctively repellent. But it has been there from the beginning.

Kim became the top leader when he chaired the North Korean Interim People's Committee in February 1946, and he held on to maximum power until he died. Within months of his accession to power, the evidence of a hagiographic and grandiose style was almost as palpable as it is today. Agents making forays into North Korea in 1946 reported that pictures and posters of Kim festooned telephone poles and the like with tales of how "wise, clear-sighted, spirited, wonderful" Kim Il Sung was. At the same time, articles appeared describing him as "the Sun of the Nation," "a beautiful new red star in the sky," wisely guiding everything with his "brilliant, scientific" methods.[29] In an important interview with Kim's first biographer in 1946, an unnamed member of his guerrilla unit promoted a Kim Il Sung line that remains the official history today. Kim set the following sort of example:

> This sort of person naturally has an extremely strong power of attraction to others. . . . And it goes without saying that a guerrilla organization with such a person at the center is incomparably strong. The sublime good fortune of our guerrilla detachment was to have at our center *the Great Sun*. Our general commander, great leader, sagacious teacher, and intimate friend was none other than General Kim Il Sung. Our unit was an unshakeable one, following General Kim and having General Kim as the nucleus. The General's embrace and love are like the Sun's, and when our fighters look up to and receive the General, their trust, self-sacrifice and devotion are such that they will gladly die for him.

29. G-2 Weekly Summary no. 99, July 27–Aug. 3, 1947; "General Kim Il Sung Is the Leader of the Korean People," *Podo*, no. 3 (Aug. 1947): 18–21. As Yŏ Un-hyŏng's followers moved in the wake of his bier in July 1947, they held up signs paying tribute to their dead leader as "the Sun of the Nation" (*minjogŭi t'aeyang*).

The soldiers' "philosophy of life" was their willingness to follow Kim's orders even to the death; "its strength is the strength deriving from uniting around Kim Il Sung . . . our guerrillas' historical tradition is precisely that of uniting around Kim as our only leader."

Kim loved and cared for his followers, according to this text, and they responded with an iron discipline for which "a spirit of obedience is needed, and what is needed for that is a spirit of respect": "Above all, the spiritual foundation [of our discipline] was this spirit of respect. And the greatest respect was for General Kim Il Sung. Our discipline grew and became strong amid respect and obedience for him."

The language used by this man is fascinating. It is all moral language, bathing Kim in a hundred virtues, almost all of which are Confucian virtues—benevolence, love, trust, obedience, respect, reciprocity between leader and led. The *Shu Ching* stated, "The Mandate of Heaven was conferred upon 'the sincere, intelligent and perspicacious among men' to establish [the] moral order." Koreans have always assumed, implicitly and often explicitly, that the fount of wisdom, the spark of philosophy, occurs in the mind of the king or the leader—that it resides in an exceptional person. One genius is at the core, one philosopher-king, and he tutors everyone else. But if Kim was at times an engineer from above, he also descended to the lower levels to observe his engineering through incessant "on-the-spot guidance." If he was often a remote emperor, protected by moats of security and mystery, he was also an emperor who pressed the flesh. Thousands of places in North Korea have plaques over their door giving the date of visits by Kim or his son, often both. Hardly a cornerstone could be laid, a tunnel dug, a building topped off, without the genius-leader being present to sanctify it. Always smiling, Kim seemed to have taken to heart the ancient injunction from the *Book of Changes* "Be not sad, be like the sun at midday." His teaching was studied over and over, everywhere, in inner sanctum-like rooms where a ghostly white bust presided, until it was established as a state of mind.

The high tradition of the Neo-Confucian patriarch also met the second tradition of matriarchal rearing, mother-child relations, and shamanism—"the woman-dominated religion of the lower classes." P'yŏngyang translates *obŏi suryŏng* as "fatherly leader," but *obŏi* is a familiar reference to both parents; by 1950 the North had also found a tenderhearted grandparent: not Joseph Stalin, but Karl Marx.[30]

The phrase "uniting around Kim" uses a term, *chuwi*, that literally means "circumference"; in a neighborhood it means living around a cen-

30. Armstrong (1994), pp. 196, 281. Charles Armstrong found the reference to "*Mark'ŭssŭ haraboji*" in a May 1950 children's story entitled "Children and Grandfather Marx."

ter, or *chungsim*, which literally means "central heart." This model of concentric circles is profoundly Korean and has also characterized the DPRK since 1946. Confucius wrote that "a government that stands on right principles is like the North Star that abides ever in its place, with all the other constellations circling round it."[31] The term "party center" was a euphemism for Kim and his closest allies, just as it became the euphemism for Kim's son in the 1970s when the succession to power was being arranged. In short, the North Korean system is not simply a hierarchical structure of party, army, and state bureaucracies (although it is that) but also a hierarchy of ever-widening concentric circles—somewhat like the old RKO radio signal as depicted in advertisements. At the center is Kim. The next circle is his family, the next the guerrillas who fought with him, then come the party elite.

This group forms the core circle, and it controls everything at the commanding heights of the regime. The core then moves outward and downward concentrically to encompass the bureaucracy, the military, and other elements of the population, and to provide the personal glue holding the system together. As the penumbra of workers and peasants is reached, trust gives way to control on a bureaucratic basis, and to a mixture of normative and remunerative incentives. Nonetheless, the family remains the model for all North Korean social organization and is the building block of the system (the DPRK constitution defines the family as the core unit of society).[32]

An outer circle marks off that which is Korean from that which is foreign. Yet the circle keeps on moving, as if to encompass foreigners under the mantle of Kim and his *chuch'e* idea. Kim, his flatterers say, is not only a modern sun king at home (referred to often as "the Sun of the Nation") but a beacon to the world as well. If so, he isn't alone among Koreans. For T'oegye, Korea's greatest philosopher, the universe was itself an organism, with stages of beginning, growth, and florescence. In explicating the universe, he began with a "Diagram of the Supreme Ultimate," represented as an upper white circle. Heaven itself was a "circle of wondrous coalescence"; he also spoke of "the circle of Heaven's imperative," in seeking to explain the unity of "principle and material force."[33]

The 1940s practice of burnishing Kim's image and "uniting around

31. Quoted in Gale (1972), p. 107. Gale called such sayings Korea's "coin of the realm," passed from mouth to mouth.

32. Article 63: "The State pays great attention to consolidating the family, the cell of society." *Socialist Constitution of the DPRK* (P'yŏngyang: Foreign Languages Publishing House, 1972).

33. Tomoeda Ryutarŏ, "Yi T'oegye and Chu Hsi: Differences in Their Theories of Principle and Material Force," in de Bary and Haboush (1985), pp. 251–54. On circles in Korean

him" also suggests an element of chivalry, of men and women bound together by oaths of fealty, duty, and obligation and possessing among them uncommon virtues of courage, daring, and sacrifice. It is the language of feudal warlords, and indeed Kim in the early period always used the title *changgun*, translated as "general," but using the same characters as the Japanese term *shogun*. Evelyn McCune was the first person to grasp the nature of this system, in a study done for the State Department in 1963. She correctly called the relationship between Kim and his close allies "a semi-chivalrous, irrevocable and unconditional bond . . . under iron discipline." It is a "deeply personal" system, "fundamentally hostile to complex bureaucracy." The 1946 interview cited earlier recommended the anti-Japanese guerrilla tradition as a good principle for party and mass organizations; he might have added that it would be the principle for the organization of the entire North Korean state (a leading scholar of North Korea, Professor Wada Haruki of Tokyo University, calls it a "guerrilla state"). Kim carried the armed struggle against Japan into Manchuria and then returned to claim power in P'yŏngyang: so did Yi Sŏng-gye in 1392. Kim and his allies were generalists, jacks-of-all-trades who could run the government or command the army, show a peasant how to use new seeds or cuddle children in a school, but then so were the scholar-officials of the Chosŏn dynasty. McCune thought that the powerful glue holding the guerrilla group together made it much more formidable than typical Korean political factions, which were based on weaker patron-client relations and given to splintering in power struggle and personal competition; thus it was able to assert dominance over rival groups rather easily.[34]

The term that the North Koreans translate as "to hold [Kim] in esteem," *urŏrŏ patta*, literally means "to look up to and receive," and is used religiously for receiving Christ. It is also used in the sense of esteeming one's father. The term "great sun" resonates with Western usages placing a king in communion with the sun, or by extension with God, and with Japanese usages regarding the emperor. To my knowledge, the first statue of Kim erected in the North was unveiled on Christmas Day, 1949, something that suggests a conscious attempt to present him as a secular Christ, or Christ-substitute.[35]

The seemingly bottomless North Korean capacity for indulging in hero

cosmology see also Don Baker's contribution to the forthcoming Cambridge History of Korea, vol. 3.

34. McCune, "Leadership in North Korea: Groupings and Motivations," State Department, Office of Intelligence Research, 1963. She also understood the concentric circle metaphor, providing in this report a chart of the leadership radiating outward from Kim.

35. See, for example, Tillyard (1942). On the statue, set up in Hŭngnam, see *Sun'gan t'ongshin*, no. 3 (Jan. 1950), daily record for Dec. 1949. The term "great sun" was used for

worship and venerating the individual qualities of the king is reinforced by, or may come from, Korean child-rearing patterns. The first son is both pampered and spoiled, by non-Korean standards, and given solemn responsibilities for rearing the other children. When Kim's son finally (and predictably) came forward to assume the mantle in the 1980s, traditional first-son patterns explained the careful rearing and unveiling; the universal line was that he, personally, was a genius—genetically, through blood ties with his father, a eugenic route to maximum power (but also something very old in Korea, where yangban elites, such as those of the early Chosŏn dynasty, legitimated themselves and their offspring by virtue of their "pure bloodline"). But such family patterns also tend to produce first sons who think they can be anything; it is often said that every first son wants to be president of Korea. Kim Il Sung and Kim Jong Il were first sons who got their wish.

Kim was only thirty-four years old when the veneration and walk-on-water rhetoric began, but no matter; King Sejong was thirty-one when he took power, and Kim would rule almost as long as King Yŏngjo, falling short by one year of reigning for half a century. Once Kim passed his sixty-year cycle, or *hwan'gap* (1972), a point beyond which Korean elders are venerated generally, he was venerated particularly—veneration that, by non-Korean standards at least, knew no bounds. In April 1972 the party journal said, "Comrade Kim Il Sung, a genius of revolution and great Marxist-Leninist, has lived his entire 60 years only for our people's freedom and happiness and the victory of the Korean and world revolutions. . . ."[36] At Kim's sixty-fifth birthday P'yŏngyang's scribes claimed, "Our whole society has become a big revolutionary family, all members of which are firmly united in one ideology and one purpose." They also described Kim as the "tender-hearted father" of the million or so Koreans living in Japan.[37] In November 1978, for the first time, to my knowledge, Kim was termed "the supreme brain of the nation,"[38] a formation used interchangeably with "great heart" (maŭm, a term that can mean "heart" or "mind," or both). Chŏng To-jŏn, architect of the early Chosŏn dynasty reforms, wrote,

> The mind of the king is the foundation of government. In discussing the ways of governance, if the mind of the king is not treated as the most

Kim as early as July 1946, when the first "Song of General Kim Il Sung" was published. See Armstrong (1994), p. 284.

36. *Kŭlloja* (The worker), April 1972, in KCNA, April 20, 1972. *Kŭlloja* at this time also carried paeans of praise from Kim's close allies Kim Il, Pak Sŏng-ch'ŏl, and Ch'oe Hyŏn, and Kim's brother Kim Yŏng-ju, who disappeared for many years and then came back into the leadership in 1994.

37. KCNA, April 17, 1977.

38. KCNA, Nov. 23, 1978.

fundamental consideration, is it not tantamount to leaving the source of a stream unclean and still expecting the water downstream to be pure?[39]

For Chu Hsi, too, the "mind-heart" (*insim*) was the master of the corporeal body or total human being, and therefore the king's mind was master of the body politic.

Long termed "the fatherly leader" (*obŏi suryŏng*), Kim after his sixtieth birthday became simply "our father," and the country the "fatherland" or "motherland." "Great son of the nation," "great sun of the people," a "fatherly leader of lofty benevolence and immense solicitude"—this is Korean political tradition, not communism. After Kim entered his "second life," every book or article had to begin with quotations from Kim's work; all successes were due to "the beloved and respected leader." It seems impossible that anyone actually reads the mind-numbing prose that the regime puts out in the millions of words, but the flavor of this politics can be gotten only through quotation:

> Only a man of great heart [*widaehan maŭm*] . . . possessed of rare grit and magnanimity and noble human love can create a great history. . . . His conception of speed and time cannot be measured or assessed by established common sense and mathematical calculation. . . . The grit to break through, even if the Heavens fall, and cleave the way through the sea and curtail the century [is his]. . . .
>
> His heart is a traction power attracting the hearts of all people and a centripetal force uniting them as one. . . . His love for people—this is, indeed, a kindred king of human love. . . . No age, no one has ever seen such a great man with a warm love. . . . Kim Il Sung is the great sun and great man . . . this great heart. . . . Thanks to this, great heart national independence is firmly guaranteed.

A 1989 article went so far as to demand that all citizens show "filial devotion" to Kim, "the tender-hearted father who gave a genuine life" to them: but then the reversion to filial piety became much more pronounced in the 1990s as Kim Jong Il rose to power. In one of the son's tracts we find this statement:

> The parental organization of man's socio-political integrity is the social community. . . . The Korean Communists were united firmly in one socio-political organism around the revolutionary leadership and set

39. Quoted in Chai-sik Chung, "Chŏng Tojŏn: 'Architect' of Yi Dynasty Government and Ideology," in de Bary and Haboush (1985), p. 69.

> the pattern for *close ties of kinship* based on collectivism between the revolutionary ranks and the people.[40]

If all this seems odd, if not abominable, at least it helps the reader with the rhetoric that leaps out from North Korean newspapers—or, for a time, from American ones: readers of the *New York Times* were frequently treated to full-page advertisements for the concept. Here you have the logic, the practice, the Kim worship, and the solipsism of North Korean ideology. It is Neo-Confucianism in a communist bottle, or Chu Hsi in a Mao jacket.

This corporate system and its hero worship are instinctively repellent to anyone who identifies with the modern liberal idea, or indeed with the modern Marxist idea. The DPRK's simple adherence to such ideas would be one thing, but by trumpeting them far and wide the regime merely provokes widespread disbelief and ridicule. All this is deeply embarrassing to many Koreans in the South, who understand all too well where it comes from, but would rather that foreigners not hear such foolish things. Nonetheless, the system is different, and once you understand its logic North Korean behavior becomes much more predictable than if you thought it were merely another "puppet of Moscow" (that one went out after 1991), "renegade state," or totalitarian nightmare imposed on a people groaning for Western freedoms. In the same way that the Nobel Prize–winning economist Milton Friedman's opinions are more or less predictable if you understand his thought, so Kim Jong Il's opinions are more or less predictable if you know his.

The resonance with Korea's past means that the DPRK often impresses foreign visitors precisely in its cultural conservatism: a Japanese visitor old enough to remember prewar Japan remarked on the similarities he found in the "antiquarian atmosphere" of North Korea. There is an egalitarian sameness about most people in the DPRK, at least to an external observer. They put on their "vynalon" (a synthetic fabric like nylon) suits, worker's caps, canvas shoes, and go off to work. What about the elite? Officials zip through the wide avenues of P'yŏngyang in Mercedes-Benz automobiles of different vintages and luxury; Mercedes mechanics spend six-month sojourns in North Korea to maintain the fleet. The officials wear tailored suits and foreign watches, and many get their hair cut in a circular downtown emporium that offers thirteen styles for men, a different set of styles for women. In 1981 I witnessed a blue Mercedes roar up to the door of this place; out bounded an official who needed a new coif. His driver sat waiting for him to finish up, never bothering to close the door that he left open.

40. Kim Jong Il, "Abuses of Socialism," *Kŭlloja*, March 1, 1993, KCNA, P'yŏngyang, March 3, 1993.

The antiquarian aspect of this regime thus extends to an elite that has the same sense of birthright and entitlement as the old yangban (and for a minority that travels abroad, a life of world-class privilege). There is a yawning chasm between elite prerogative and the difficult daily lives of nearly everyone else in North Korea. The regime put a floor on poverty, which was a major accomplishment, but it also built a ceiling that is probably relatively impervious to upward mobility. If tremendous mobility occurred in the 1940s and 1950s for cadres of peasant and working-class background, I imagine (we have to imagine, in the absence of all evidence except foreigners' observations) that these same cadres over time reestablished elite lineages through intermarriage and horizontal cohorts of region, age, education, and career that are very difficult to penetrate. For the past quarter century the key to maximum life chances was probably to form a relationship with Kim Jong Il or his close allies and move up with them, just as proximity to the crown prince was the sine qua non for career success in the ancien régime.

THE SUCCESSION TO KIM JONG IL

Systems like this, traditionally in East Asia and markedly in North Korea, seem to lack a political process (at least to any public scrutiny). Always it is the absence of conflict that the regime seeks to project, all for one and one for all, a much bruited "monolithicism." (Trotsky noted how appalled he and his Bolshevik allies were when Stalin began using this term, but the Koreans use it all the time.)[41] How can there be a political process, when the leader is perfect? What is the "political process" of the Japanese emperor system? This is one reason, perhaps, for the absence of much public conflict since 1946, a remarkable phenomenon even when Korea is compared to other communist states. But it is important to remember that there still is a politics to such regimes, because there has to be; we just cannot see it.

In 1980 came the blessed event in North Korea: Kim's son by his first marriage, Kim Jong Il, was publicly named at the Sixth Congress of the Workers' Party to the Presidium of the Politburo, the Secretariat of the Central Committee, and the Military Commission. In other words, he was openly designated successor to his father. Kim was reportedly born in 1941 in the Manchurian fastness near Khabarovsk, but the regime now claims he was born on the slopes of Paektusan. His mother, Kim Jong-suk, was a guerrilla activist who died in the late 1940s (and has

41. Leon Trotsky, *Stalin*, 2d ed. (New York: Stein and Day, 1967), p. 18.

had one honor after another granted posthumously).[42] By the time his father died, he ranked second in the leadership, behind his father and ahead of his father's old comrade-in-arms, O Chin-u (who died of cancer in early 1995). But from the time of his coming of age in the 1960s—or perhaps from time immemorial?—everyone in the DPRK had expected that Kim Jong Il was going to succeed his father, barring a conflict within the ruling family. A memorial on kingly succession in 1405 had this to say: "The heir-apparent is the foundation of the nation and the state of order and disorder is linked to him. The goodness [of the heir-apparent] depends on early instruction and teaching . . . [in] filial piety, benevolence, propriety, and righteousness. . . ."[43] A song from a Korean village in the 1970s expresses the typical way in which families treat their offspring:

> Silver baby, golden baby,
> Treasure baby from the deepest mountains,
> On the water, sun and moon baby,
> Patriotic baby for the nation,
> A baby with filial piety for his parents,
> A baby affectionate toward his family and kin.[44]

The "deepest mountain" connotes purity and preciousness; why not Kim Jong Il, "treasure baby from Paektu mountain"?

The ground was carefully laid for this succession throughout the 1970s: by 1973, specialists could already see Jong Il's presence in important campaigns at the grassroots level ("the Three Revolutions"), he was immersed in party organizational work, and his rise to power was carefully coordinated with party control. The year 1972 saw his public emergence, and it so happened that Jong Il was the same age as King Sejong's son Munjong, who was thirty in 1443 when the king began to transfer some of his work to him. (Thus began a long "process of apprenticeship" for the throne that Munjong inherited in 1450.)[45] People began displaying pictures of the son alongside the father in their homes. For years Jong Il was referred to as "the party center" (*tang chungang*)

42. King Yŏngjo loved his stepmother, Queen Inwŏn, with a rare devotion. He "heaped honors on her" to the point where she had nine different honorary titles. Her birthdays became the occasion for another of Yŏngjo's poems. Among the most grandiose was that done for her sixtieth birthday (*hwan'gap*), where he referred to her not just as his mother but also as "the mother of our nation." When she died in 1757, "Yŏngjo wailed and fasted for days." See Haboush (1988), pp. 52–53.

43. Quoted in Haboush, "The Education of the Yi Crown Prince: A Study in Confucian Pedagogy," in de Bary and Haboush (1985), p. 176.

44. Quoted in Janelli and Janelli (1982), pp. 66–67.

45. Haboush, "Education," p. 183.

and then "the glorious party center." When the glorious party center began visiting factories, external observers realized it was a person.[46] In the 1970s the top leadership included Pak Sŏng-ch'ŏl, O Chin-u, Kim Yŏng-nam, Yi Chong-ok, Chŏn Mun-sŏp, and Sŏ Ch'ŏl, all of whom supported the succession and all of whom were on hand after Kim Il Sung's death to assure that nothing untoward happened to the son.

All through the past thirty years rumors flew around that Jong Il was ill, or a drunk, or insane, or that some generals tried to run him over with a truck and that's why he dropped from view for a time, or that either he or his father was plotting coups and assassinations against the other. Most of these stories were manufactured out of Seoul's multitudinous intelligence groups, and the only way to refute them was to observe what happened over time—and time and time again, the rumors were proved wrong. (Only in the 1990s when the nuclear crisis bubbled along did the American media show interest in these tales, and they got their fingers burned over and over for hearkening to Seoul's ceaseless gossip.) One day we will learn of the pulling and hauling that occurred as Kim Il Sung prepared to have his son succeed him: it probably resembled court politics in the old days, and blood may have been spilled. Meanwhile, on the visible surface, the move toward familial succession seemed as inexorable as under any Chosŏn king.

The basic line was that the revolution, "started by the Father Marshal," must be carried through to completion "generation after generation." Editorials on "the glorious party" asserted that the KWP "can have no traditions except those established by the Leader," and that this tradition must be "brilliantly inherited" and passed on to future generations. At the leader's birthday in 1980 (a big national holiday every year), editorials called for "reliable succession" so that the Korean people will never forget Kim's "profound benevolence" generation after generation. As the party newspaper put it in 1984, "There will be no change in the tradition of loyalty to the leader of the revolution which was formed and has been carried forward historically. . . . We will glorify the history of loyalty under the leadership of the party center, too, cherishing this honor deep in our hearts."[47]

At the time of the Sixth Party Congress, in 1980, organic metaphors

46. The official Seoul monthly *Vantage Point*, carrying the views of approved North Korea watchers, called attention in Feb. 1979 to a long article on Jong Il's birthday (Feb. 16), referring to "the Party Center" and the "Three Revolutions Campaign," which it is leading; the publication noted that this was a reference to Jong Il. The article was entitled "The Revolutionary Spirit of Mt. Paektu is a Great Banner for Victory and Glory," and was carried in the party newspaper. See *Vantage Point*, March 1979.

47. KCNA, P'yŏngyang, April 17, 1984, carrying a *Nodong sinmun* (Workers' news) article of April 16, 1984.

Kim Jong Il gives advice to peasants at the Ch'ŏngsan cooperative farm, the model for all other cooperatives. The photo was probably taken in the early 1970s.

proliferated. Kim Il Sung's report to the congress referred to "the organizational will" of the party and the party's "pulsation," always felt by the masses; the party was called "one's own mother"; "infinite loyalty" to the party and the establishment of an "iron discipline" were expected of everyone, "under which the whole Party acts as one body under the leadership of the Party central committee. It is a fixed practice in our Party that all its organizations move like an organism according to the principle of democratic centralism."[48]

In the aftermath of the congress the party newspaper published sev-

48. KCNA, Oct. 14, 1980.

eral editorials and articles full of organic metaphors. "Father of the People" in February 1981 said the following:

> Kim Il Sung is . . . the great father of our people . . . possessed of greatest love for the people. Long is the history of the word father used as a word representing love and reverence . . . expressing the unbreakable blood ties between the people and the leader. Father. This familiar word represents our people's single heart of boundless respect and loyalty. . . . This love shown by the Great Leader for our people is love of kinship. . . . Our respected and beloved Leader is the tender-hearted father of all the people. . . . Love of paternity . . . is the noblest ideological sentiment possessed only by our people, which cannot be explained by any theory or principle or fathomed by anything.[49]

Another article argued that

> the blood ties between our Party and the people [mean that] . . . the Party and the people always breathe one breath and act as one. . . . The creed of the people [is] that they cannot live or enjoy happiness apart from the Party. . . . [T]oday our party and people have become an integrity of ideology and purpose which no force can break. The Worker's Party of Korea . . . is the Mother Party bringing boundless honor and happiness to the people. . . .[50]

The party, in other words, was the "motherly" source that had nurtured "Dear Leader" Kim Jong Il and everyone of his generation:

> O motherly Party, I will always remain true
> To you all my life.
> A baby gets to know its mother's face first
> It is most happy to see her. . . .
> The Party gives me a motherly image.
> I shall follow it all my life as a child longs for its mother
> O whenever I am at its side
> I feel happy.[51]

During the Kim Il Sung era, DPRK propagandists used only one untranslated word in their English publications, "Juche." With the rise of the son came another: "Chajusong." What does that mean? It is another synonym for "independence" and "autonomy." Just before the Korean War, the KWP Agit/Prop Department put out a guide for propagandists that began by referring to Korea's having "lost its *chajusŏng*" during the Japanese period and, in the post-1945 period, having constructed an

49. *Nodong sinmun*, Feb. 13, 1981; KCNA, Feb. 16, 1981.
50. *Nodong sinmun*, Feb. 4, 1981; KCNA, Feb. 7, 1981.
51. "Party of the Motherly Image," *Korea Today* (P'yŏngyang), Feb. 1987.

economic and political base "that firmly guarantees our nation's interests and *chajusŏng* on the world stage." The existence of the Soviet Union and other socialist countries was the external condition that guaranteed Korea's position, and the economic basis at home would "build a rich and strong state that can guarantee our nation's *chajusŏng*." The document said explicitly that central planning "was a means of guaranteeing the *chajusŏng* of a democratic state's economy and ensuring that it does not become subordinated to a foreign economy." In spite of praise for Soviet efforts in this document, it underlines the manner in which the Koreans took Japanese and Soviet state structures and ideas and turned them toward an autarkic conception of a self-contained national economy; it clearly referred to all foreign nations by using the term "foreign" instead of "imperialist." This document quoted Kim Il Sung many times on the necessity "to build our own democratic homeland independently using our own strength and our own assets." Korea must use "our own domestic resources and our own strength," in order to avoid dependency on external sources of supply: this, too, would guarantee "the *chajusŏng* of our national economy." Perhaps most important, this document dates the adoption of these "basic principles" (*wŏlli*) from 1949, signaling the break toward an independent trajectory that occurred after Soviet troops left Korea.[52] Here is the historical pedigree of Jong Il's new buzzword.

In the 1980s I happened to talk to a Soviet diplomat in P'yŏngyang, and asked him if the succession would be disruptive or might lead to a political crisis as any number of "P'yŏngyangologists" were always saying. No, he said, a new generation is tied to Kim Jong Il's inheritance and has been brought along with it; he controls all of them and their careers, and therefore everything will go smoothly: "You should come back in the year 2020 and see Jong Il's son inherit power." So far, that diplomat has been right.

THE NORTH KOREAN ECONOMY

Self-reliance is not a matter of mere rhetoric. North Korea offers the best example in the postcolonial developing world of conscious withdrawal from the capitalist world system and a serious attempt to construct an independent, self-contained economy; as a result it is the most autarkic industrial economy in the world. Unlike Albania in the socialist world and Burma in the "free world," two countries that "withdrew" to no apparent purpose as their economies idled along or got worse, North

52. National Records Center, 242, SA 2008, item 34, KWP Agit/Prop Department, "Se hwan'gyŏng kwa se chogŏn," pp. 1–3, 6, 16–18, 32–35.

Korea never idled but always raced. This was withdrawal with development, withdrawal for development. Self-reliance was also directed at the Soviet bloc, but with less perseverance; North Korea got a lot of economic aid and technical help from the USSR and China (although not remotely close to what the South got from the United States and Japan). Still, unlike nearly every other communist state, North Korea never joined COMECON, the socialist would-be common market.

The DPRK has had a socialist command economy with long-run plans (seven to ten years recently) and a bias toward heavy industry. It allows only a sharply limited role for market allocation, mainly in the rural sector, where peasants sell produce from small private plots. There is almost no small business. Like South Korea, it has sought a full, comprehensive industrial base; therefore it would seem to be a typical socialist system on the Stalinist model, and certainly it is in the emphasis on heavy industry first.

Although the Soviets gave aid and advice up to a point in the 1940s, skilled Koreans with experience in the Japanese period came to dominate the development of the economy. Chŏng Il-yong, termed the "king of North Korean industry" by State Department intelligence, had been an engineer under the Japanese. The same was true of another powerful figure, Chŏng Chun-t'aek. The First Two-Year Plan (1947–49) was drawn up under the direction of a former economics professor at Keijo Imperial University, Kim Kwan-jin. Yi In-uk, another key figure, had twenty-five years of experience in the construction of northern factories. Of ninety-three Koreans on a partial listing of the North's Industry and Engineering Federation in 1950, thirty-five had more than five years of experience, all with former Japanese industries. Japanese technicians who did not flee were also used throughout the economy; in 1947 some of them wrote home that industrial production was in full swing, expressing surprise at the Korean workers' "eagerness for production" as compared to the pre-1945 period.[53] Paradoxically, by accomplishing a quick postcolonial social revolution, the North was able pragmatically to use Korean and Japanese expertise from the colonial period with little criticism, whereas the South tended to employ Korean experts from the agencies of law and order, with no legitimacy and endless criticism.

A reporter for a northern newspaper told an American in mid-1947 that the regime rationed food in six categories, workers doing heavy labor getting the most and collaborators with Japan the least; wages varied from 950 to 3,500 won, with four categories: technicians, managers,

53. McCune, "Leadership in North Korea"; U.S. Army intelligence intercepted many letters in 1947 from Japanese technicians; see, for example, G-2 Weekly Summary no. 99, July 27–Aug. 3, 1947, and G-2 Weekly Summary no. 100, Aug. 3–10, 1947.

skilled workers, and ordinary workers. Employment centers all over the country recruited industrial technicians and workers. Women workers had increased rapidly, with "equal pay [for equal work] and special treatment." Some twelve hundred cooperatives distributed goods to workers and peasants; they bought 100 percent of the output of state factories, 90 percent of that from privately owned factories, with the remaining portion being sold on a free market. The average wage was low, "barely permit[ting] workers to live."[54] The result of this extraordinary effort to get the industrial economy functioning again was that, from the 1940s into the mid-1960s, minus the period of the war and recovery from it (1950–56), North Korea grew far more rapidly than did the South, as rapidly perhaps as any postwar industrializing regime.

Americans captured the top-secret text of the 1947 plan during the Korean War, giving a rare, full picture of the DPRK economy. About one-fifth of the total budget went for industrial construction and one-fifth for defense. Among top-grade experts, 105 of 1,262 were Japanese; 245 of the middle-grade experts were Japanese. No Russians were listed, but Soviet documents show that many Russian advisers were also present, often in the form of Koreans who had lived in the USSR before 1945. Seventy-two percent of all children were in elementary school, compared with 42 percent in 1944; some 40,000 adult schools across the country held basic literacy classes for workers and peasants. American data on the economy gotten from internal, classified North Korean sources show pig iron production going from 6,000 metric tons in 1947 to 166,000 in 1949, steel billets from 61,000 tons to 145,000, and common steel products from 46,000 tons to 97,000, with the latter two figures surpassing Japanese production in 1944, when Korean industry was pumping the war effort; industrial production rose 39.6 percent in 1949 and, interestingly, figures for 1950 show that northern industry had almost reached 1949 totals in the first three quarters, before the heaviest American bombing began. Indeed, targets for the first year of the Second Two-Year Plan were surpassed early in 1950, causing a revision upward of targets for the rest of the year.[55]

Some Americans detained in Chinnamp'o (now called Namp'o, this is the port of P'yŏngyang, at the mouth of the Taedong River) for three months in September 1949 reported that people were generally less well clad than in the South; pens, watches, and leather shoes were rare; shell-

54. Hugh Deane Papers, "North Korea," Aug. 1947.

55. MacArthur Archives, MacArthur Papers, RG6, box 79, ATIS Issue no. 24, Feb. 21, 1951. (Defense is assumed to be included in the budget line for "other expenditures.") See also a published copy of the plan in G-2, Intelligence Summaries-North Korea, no. 36, May 18, 1947; also 895.00 file, box 5693, Muccio to State, Dec. 3, 1950, enclosing an ECA study of the northern economy (both in the National Archives).

Children at play in North Korea in the late 1950s. *Courtesy of Chris Marker, Coréenes (Paris: Court-Métrage I., [1958 or 1959]).*

fish were abundant but meat was scarce; railroads were very active at night; electric power was abundant, as was coal, the latter being used even to power cars and trucks, since petroleum was in short supply; a steel mill in the port ran around the clock shifts, as did a coal yard; the streets were clean and well maintained, but sparsely populated, and few workers loitered as they usually do in port towns. This account is convincing and accords with my own observations of the port of Wŏnsan thirty-five years later.

A speech by Kim Il Sung in late 1949 cited many problems in the economy, in spite of strong growth rates. Referring to "complicated, troublesome difficulties," he said that by September 1949 some industries had increased production 50 to 60 percent over 1948 figures, but some grew by only 20 percent, and "worst of all" were small increases in critical industries like coal and metallurgy that did not meet planned targets. He said that many workers had been peasants just a few years before; they came in from the countryside and "would take any job they could get." Many had been "forced to work by the Japanese imperialist bastards," who had exploited labor at the lowest cost. The Japanese had starved people to the point that they had to work, he said, but now with no threat of starvation, workers consumed too much of the available surplus; some workers simply went back to their villages because agricultural conditions were good, and only a small supply of labor now came from the rural areas. Labor power was not fixed to the factory, so workers moved from place to place as they wished. Kim gave an example from the Hwanghae Iron Works, which got seven hundred new workers in August 1948, but could not supply more than three hundred of them with housing, so the rest left within a couple of days. Labor, therefore, "does not automatically supply itself."

What was to be done? First, in typical fashion, Kim called for better work with people, "a new style of leadership," and individual "rectification of work," using the Maoist characters *kai tsao* (*kaejo* in Korean). But "above all, we must correctly organize the wage system for workers, and stimulate production efficiency," fighting "a merciless struggle against the average wage system," that is, a system that would equalize all wages at the expense of proper incentives. "It is a principle that those workers who produce more must also receive more in wages."[56] There can be few better examples of the way in which Kim borrowed Maoist methods from China and materialist methods from the Soviet Union, always with a pragmatic eye toward what worked in the Korean context. The Koreans accepted the socialist principle "From each according to his ability, to each according to his work" and have never challenged it as the Maoist radicals later did (Lenin gave it a biblical flourish: "He that does not work, neither shall he eat"). An early statement of this principle argued that "our system is not one of general equality"; North Korea had political equality, equality of work and equality of rest, but "people work according to their abilities and are paid according to the quality and quantity of their work."[57] But they also accepted the Maoist principle that work with people, moral or ideological incentives, and mass rectification campaigns can also help to stimulate production.

The three-year plan that began at the end of the Korean War and the five-year plan that succeeded it (1957–61) both stressed the reconstruction and development of major industries devastated by the war, with consumer goods left at the bottom of the regime's priorities. This bias toward major industries, combined with unprecedentedly large amounts of aid from the Soviet bloc, however, pushed the economy forward at world-beating growth rates in the 1950s and 1960s. DPRK industry grew at 25 percent per annum in the decade after the Korean War, according to external observers, and about 14 percent from 1965–78.[58] Official figures put the average annual growth rate in industry at 41.7 percent for the three-year plan (1953–56) and 36.6 percent during the subsequent

56. Kim Il Sung, "Speech at the Meeting of Enthusiasts from the Industrial Branches of the Economy," Nov. 19, 1949, in *Sun'gan t'ongshin* 42 (Dec. 1949).
57. *Sae hwan'gyŏng*, pp. 40–41.
58. Joseph Chung, "North Korea's Economic Development and Capabilities," *Asian Perspective* 11, no. 1 (Spring–Summer 1987): 45–74.

five-year plan. The First Seven-Year Plan (1961–67) projected an average rate of 18 percent, but stoppages of aid from the Soviet Union in the early 1960s (owing to DPRK support for China in the Sino-Soviet dispute) caused the plan to be extended for three years. Still, for two decades after the Korean War the North's growth far outdistanced the South's, striking fear into the hearts of American officials, who wondered if Seoul would ever get off the mark.

By the early 1970s the DPRK clearly had exhausted the extensive development of its industry based on its own or prewar Japanese or new Soviet technologies, and it therefore turned to the West and Japan to purchase turnkey plants. These included a French petrochemical complex in 1971, a cement plant in 1973, and in 1977 a request that Japan sell an integrated steel mill to P'yŏngyang (which was denied). Even a complete panty hose factory was imported, suggesting more attention to consumer items. Ultimately these purchases caused North Korea to run into problems in servicing its external debt, which in the past twenty years has been estimated at between $2 billion and $3 billion. Later seven- and ten-year plans have failed to reach projected growth rates; still, a CIA study published in 1978 put the DPRK's per capita GNP at the same level as the ROK's in 1976, and another study estimated that the respective per capita rates were the same up until 1986.[59] DPRK per capita GNP probably kept pace at least through 1983, in part because of South Korea's 6 percent loss of GNP in 1980. The North's total production of electricity, coal, fertilizer, machine tools, and steel was comparable to or higher than South Korean totals in the early 1980s, even though its population was half that of the South. Such figures, however, do not indicate the quality of production in the North, where labor productivity is much lower and energy is routinely wasted. Still, one critic of the DPRK's economic performance puts its annual average industrial growth rate for 1978–84 at 12.2 percent, while noting how far North Korea fell short of its own planning targets.[60]

The South's economy revived by the mid-1980s and has forged well ahead of the North since then, although not as far ahead as its backers claim. Seoul's urban middle class does much better than all but a tiny elite in North Korea, but the living standards of the mass of South Korean citizens, while better, do not tower over those of average North Koreans. In 1979 Kim Il Sung claimed a per capita income of $1,900, and in the late 1980s the DPRK put the figure at more than $2,500; but it is

59. U.S. CIA, "Korea: The Economic Race between North and South" (Washington: CIA, 1978); Hwang (1993).
60. Hwang (1993).

not known if the figure is accurate, or how it was arrived at; furthermore, it has fallen dramatically since then. Published CIA figures in recent years place North Korea at around $1,000 in per capita income. For the past two decades the North has clearly fallen behind South Korea in what it wants to do—namely, race neck and neck or beat the South in industrial development. Transportation bottlenecks and fuel resource problems have plagued the economy, but above all it has missed out on the technological revolution of recent years.

The North did not do badly in goods of the second industrial revolution: steel, chemicals, hydroelectric power, internal-combustion engines, locomotives, motorcycles, various sorts of machine-building items. But it lags far behind in the "communications" technologies of the third industrial revolution: electronics, computers, semiconducter chips, telecommunications. (North Korea manufactures a Paektusan computer, probably with obsolescent technology; the state also imports the latest computers it can buy on the international market, while sharply limiting personal computers for individual or home use.)

There are departures and successes, however, that the "basket-case" scenario never talks about. Officials with the World Health Organization and other UN agencies praise the delivery of basic health services; North Korean children are better vaccinated against disease by far than are American children. United Nations data from the 1980s showed that life expectancy in this small and poor country is 70.7 years (compared with 70.4 in the ROK), not much less than the American figure. Infant mortality is 25 per 1,000 live births, compared with 21 in the South. About 74 percent of North Koreans live in cities, compared with 78 percent in the South (again according to UN data), meaning that both are quite urbanized and industrialized by world standards.

Agronomists from the UN determined that the North used miracle rice seeds by 1980 and had mostly replaced human manure (still in wide use then in the South) with chemical fertilizers in the fields. The delivery of goods and services is often decentralized to the neighborhood or village level, and several provinces are said to be self-reliant in food and consumer goods; foreign visitors see few long lines at stores and restaurants, although resident diplomats say little is available in the stores. Clearly the morale of the population is better than in the former Soviet Union, and both the cities and the factories give an appearance of efficiency and hard work. I stayed for several days in a Wŏnsan hotel in 1981 and was awakened all too often by construction going on around the clock in a big building across the street.

The North's dogged pursuit of relative autarky in a world of interdependence and mostly free trade has hampered its industrial growth, sacrificing economies of scale and closing the country off to the more developed capitalist economies (although it should be remembered that the United States mounted an economic blockade against North Korea from 1950 to 2000, when it was partially lifted for all but strategic and high-technology items.) But one unqualified success for self-reliance is DPRK energy policy, which has one of the lowest world rates for dependence on petroleum. It has substituted hydroelectric power and coal for oil, using petroleum products primarily for its military. About 10 percent of the energy North Korea consumed came from imports in the early 1990s, according to South Korean figures, yet per capita energy use was about the same in both countries. In an interview in 1978[61] Kim Il Sung told a Japan Socialist Party delegation that in the late 1960s some Korean scientists wanted to start up a petrochemical industry for refining petroleum (probably because Park Chung Hee had similar plans). However, Kim said, "our country does not produce oil," and the United States influenced the world oil regime: ergo "we are not yet in a position to depend on imports. . . . [To do so] means allowing a stranglehold on our jugular." Much of the extensive rail system is now electrified, as are city buses and subways, and the use of automobiles is minimal. In the early 1990s per capita energy usage was still estimated to be nearly as high as the South's, although consumers use a much higher total quantity of energy compared with the North, where most of it goes to industry.

The collapse of the socialist bloc deprived P'yŏngyang of major markets, leading to several years of declining GNP in the early 1990s. South Korean figures put these declines in the 2 to 5 percent range, and American government analysts thought that the worst was over for the North Korean economy by the end of 1993. But it was a general crisis for the leadership, to the degree that P'yŏngyang for the first time publicly acknowledged "big losses in our economic construction" and "a most complex and acute internal and external situation" at the Twenty-first Plenum of the Workers' Party, in December 1993. Most of the blame was attributed not to North Korea's ponderous socialist system but to "the collapse of socialist countries and the socialist market of the world," which "shattered" many of P'yŏngyang's trade partners and agreements.[62]

This crisis forced North Korea to think seriously about the future of its autarkic system, resulting in a host of new laws on foreign investment, relations with capitalist firms, and new zones of free trade. Many new

61. Report on an interview with Kim Il Sung, Dec. 22, 1978, in *Tokyo Shakaito*, March 1979, pp. 162–68 (U.S. Joint Publications Research Service translation #073363).
62. KCNA, Dec. 9, 1993.

banking, labor, and investment laws were promulgated.[63] Foreign businessmen have seen these new laws, at least on paper, as among the most liberal in East Asia in welcoming foreign investment, profit remissions, and ownership regulations. A relative of Kim Il Sung named Kim Jong U became head of the Najin-Sŏnbong free economic and trade zone in the northeast corner of the country and assiduously courted foreign investment in the early and mid-1990s. Several firms in Hong Kong, Japan, France, and South Korea have made commitments to open manufacturing facilities in the DPRK, and a consortium headed by a former executive from the Bechtel Corporation in the United States is leading the efforts to improve the transportation and communications infrastructure at Najin-Sŏnbong. The Shell Oil Corporation also invested in this zone in 1995.

If East Asian development in recent decades has demonstrated anything, it is that rapid capitalist growth is not incompatible with strong central state power. Thus it was quite predictable that Kim Jong U told reporters that P'yŏngyang "would like to take Singapore as a model"; it combines, in his view, "great freedom in business activities" with "good order, discipline and observation of laws."[64] Most of all, the deep interest of many South Korean firms in cheap but intelligent and disciplined North Korean labor may help South Korea recoup comparative advantages in the world market, while moving both Koreas slowly toward reunification. But the DPRK still has a long way to go to match the epochal outward-looking reforms in China or Vietnam.

North Korea's Hermit Kingdom policies of self-reliance were a response to a prolonged twentieth-century crisis in the country. Put in place to insulate the nation against the disasters of colonization, depression, and war, they seem irrelevant now. But one can imagine Kim Il Sung looking at his Politburo friends in 1989 when the Berlin wall fell, or in 1991 when the USSR collapsed, and asking them where North Korea would be if it had integrated with the Soviet bloc and participated in the international division of labor that Moscow fostered in Eastern Europe.

63. The laws are summarized in Eui-gak Hwang, "North Korean Laws for the Induction of Foreign Capital and Practical Approaches to Foreign Investment in North Korea," *Vantage-Point* (Seoul), March and April 1994. See also the relatively liberal labor regulations for foreign-funded enterprises, published by KCNA on Jan. 11, 1994.

64. *Far Eastern Economic Review*, Sept. 30, 1993.

LIFE ON THE FARM

Both Koreas now have an agrarian sector no larger than 30 percent of the population and 20 percent or less of GNP. Grain production, the U.S. CIA reported in 1978, has grown more rapidly in the North than in the South, living standards in rural areas "have probably improved faster than in the South," and "North Korean agriculture is quite highly mechanized, fertilizer application is probably among the highest in the world, and irrigation projects are extensive."[65] When I visited in 1981 and 1987, flying over from China in a propjet, I could see that the fields were a deep green and, when I visited villages, that every inch of land was carefully tended. But then, this was true in 1950 as well: a London Times reporter motored up to P'yŏngyang at harvest time in 1950 through "a countryside as trim and carefully husbanded as any in Asia," observing the neat, orderly placed rice mounds drying in the fields, preparatory to being bound and marketed.[66] In the 1980s the DPRK claimed to have the highest per hectare rice output in the world; although that claim cannot be proved, experts who visited the country did not question the North's general agricultural success. For years the DPRK has failed to reach its projected targets, however; Kim Il Sung called for the production of ten million tons of grain by 1986, but during the past several years of distress, North Korea has produced only a little over four million tons of grain, with foreign aid and international relief agencies providing another roughly two million tons, to reach the minimum target for feeding the population, of around six million tons of grain. Today South Korea's rural population lives far better than its northern counterpart.

North Korea's agrarian life, like so much else in the country, was dramatically transformed in the 1940s in order to return its people to something closer to the old agrarian routine, another "closure" after decades of Japanese opening. In March 1946 a quick and relatively painless land reform broke the back of the yangban aristocracy and did away with perennially high rates of tenancy. The reform did not compensate owners for the redistributed land, but involved comparatively less class violence than similar reforms in China and North Vietnam because the border to the South was still quite porous, and many landlords already resided in Seoul or Kaesŏng anyway. The regime also allowed landlords

65. U.S. CIA, "Korea: The Economic Race between North and South" (Washington: CIA, 1978).

66. *Times* (London), Nov. 16, 1950. This reporter remarked on the absence of a North Korean "scorched earth" program. Peasants were grateful that the KPA retreat from South Korea "remained unmarred by any attempt . . . to destroy his crops or paddy bunds. Stocks of rice were removed, but the earth was not scorched."

who wanted to work the land themselves to move to adjacent counties, where they were given the same amount of land as other farmers. This broke their political power at the roots, but left them with their lives (and a livelihood) in their accustomed agrarian habitat.

Peasants got land that could be inherited by their children but that was "socialized" in the sense that it could not be sold on the market. Collectivization of agriculture did not begin until after the Korean War, giving the reform a distinct "land to the tillers" flavor that had a big demonstration effect on the South. Mutual aid groups that had long engaged in reciprocal-help work at harvest time or in putting a new roof on a house and that were called *p'umassi-ban* formed the basis for a cooperative movement in 1954. Four years later all of the rural population lived and worked in some 13,309 cooperatives, with an average of seventy-nine households each. Still, this unit essentially corresponded to the old "natural village" and drew upon a long tradition of cooperative mutual aid and labor. In these cooperatives peasants continued to live in homes heritable by their children, but did not own the land they worked and were instead compensated according to the labor they contributed. The best study of North Korean agrarian conditions argues that the majority of poor peasants welcomed cooperativization, whereas richer peasants who held more than the usual three *chŏngbo* (about 7.5 acres) of land or who had prospered tended to resist it.[67]

In one particular village, an investigation revealed, three of seven landlords had moved to other communities after land reform, but four managed to remain by having only their rented land confiscated. In the mid-1950s these families were still wealthier than the rest of the village and "still farmed their large landholdings by seasonally employing poor villagers." When the cooperative movement began, the former landlords sought to establish their own cooperative apart from the local people's committee, offering loans of grain and cash to poor farmers if they would go along. Things came to a head in heated discussion among the hundred or so households involved, until the officially sponsored cooperative won out and the richer families joined—but only after "about two months of continuous effort."[68]

In the late 1950s a movement toward larger cooperatives amalgamated village farmers into bigger accounting units of perhaps three hundred households, and marked the first move beyond the old natural village. A primary reason for the larger units was the wish to regularize fields so that large farm machinery could be used; in the past many fields had

67. Lee (1976), pp. 26–29.
68. Lee (1976), pp. 30–32.

irregular and irrational boundaries, resulting from parceled-out inheritance through the generations. Still, most farmers continued to labor in work teams of fifty to a hundred or subteams of ten to twenty members, drawn from people in their own village. Village people collectively controlled their own destiny when it came to accounting for labor inputs and sharing out the work and its annual reward.[69] There is little evidence in North Korean history of the foolish haste, violence, and ultimate breakdown of agrarian society that occurred in China during the Great Leap Forward, resulting in a famine that killed millions. Scholars who have visited North Korea or interviewed refugees come away with the impression that much effort is taken to equalize conditions of work and production, as well as reward.[70]

The regime has always emphasized mechanization of agrarian work through the use of tractors, combines, and automatic rice-transplanting machines, as well as widespread application of chemical fertilizers from North Korea's big chemicals industry. How successful they have been is a matter of debate; when I visited several farming communities in 1987 I was struck by the absence of the characteristic smell of human fertilizer. I also witnessed large-scale and highly inefficient use of young children and old women for road-building and other construction projects (although it is fair to say that one sees the same thing in the South). Some Western newspaper accounts in the early 1990s spoke of semistarvation in more remote rural areas of North Korea, suggesting that the self-sufficiency in agriculture achieved by the late 1970s was no more, because of bad weather and a series of bad harvests throughout East Asia in the early 1990s, or because of grain hoarding and sales on the international market to earn foreign exchange. The regime said that floods in the summer of 1995 were the worst in this century, destroying much of the harvest and leaving hundreds of thousands of people homeless. For the first time, P'yŏngyang asked for Western and Japanese aid; by mid-1996 only a trickle had come in, and many analysts thought there would be little food available by the autumn.

The reform of agrarian conditions has not altered North Korean agrarian life to the extent suggested by the term "revolution"; it returned peasants to their natural village and their accustomed interactions, while stripping off the aristocratic social structure and the grinding tenancy arrangements of the past. But the social hierarchy was turned on its head, as young people now preferred to marry into the families of Workers' Party officials or the favored poor peasants, and resisted following

69. Lee (1976), pp. 34–35.
70. Lee (1976), p. 40.

the older path to upward mobility by marrying into a yangban family. Still, the superior education and inbred self-esteem of yangban families no doubt continued to give them important advantages in the new society.

In one case study, a man named Pak got drafted into the People's Army after working in a textile factory; during a rare furlough he sought to marry a woman from his village who seemed eligible. She checked into his family background and found out that his brother's wife was the daughter of a Korean policeman during the Japanese period and therefore came from a "reactionary family"; she refused to marry Pak. Through his elder brother's help, Pak found another possible mate, a schoolteacher, and after Pak's brother and the woman's brother arranged a meeting at the latter's home, the two agreed to be married. Now the local party committee objected to the marriage, for the same reason: a colonial policeman in the genealogy. Through the intercession of a willing official at a higher level—who argued that the sins of an uncle-in-law should not be visited on the nephew—the committee's objections were overcome and the wedding was duly consummated.[71]

FALLEN SUN KING

Kim Il Sung died of a heart attack on July 8, 1994. With Cable News Network cameras in P'yŏngyang, the world was able to watch an outpouring of grief that seemed, for such a reviled, renegade dictator, incomprehensible. Millions of people streamed into and through the capital city, tearing their hair, beating the ground, weeping uncontrollably. Many thought the regime staged the displays, but that seemed implausible given the sincerity of most people and their enormous numbers. Perhaps it was a case of mass hysteria: *Newsweek* seemed to think a national nervous breakdown was ensuing, with the DPRK now a "headless beast."[72] Now listen to Hendrik Hamel, writing in 1653: "As soon as one dies, his Kindred run about the Streets shrieking, and tearing their Hair."[73] Mourning for Kim lasted for one hundred days, and when it ended a government spokesmen said this:

> The loss of the great leader was the irretrievable loss of our people. At this shocking news, like the earth breaking apart and the sun falling, not only our party members and working people as well as the South

71. Lee (1976), pp. 133–35.
72. "Korea after Kim: The Headless Beast," *Newsweek*, July 18, 1994.
73. Hamel, in Ledyard (1971), pp. 220.

Korean people and overseas compatriots, but even the mountains rivers, plants, and trees wailed.[74]

P'yŏngyang's scribes began using an unfamiliar term to describe the new regime: Kim Jong Il now had the "mandate of heaven" (*ch'ŏnmyŏng*). Why? Because he inherited his father's line. Earlier, an article in the party newspaper had hailed Kim Jong Il's leadership qualities:

> The Dear Leader Comrade Kim Jong Il's iron will has become a boundless source of might to turn misfortune into a blessing. . . . The Great Leader Comrade Kim Il Sung has taught: Comrade Kim Jong Il has an invincible will, courage, outstanding strategy, and commanding art as befitting the supreme commander of the revolutionary Armed Forces. . . . The leader's will plays a decisive role in pioneering the destiny of one nation and in carrying out the socialist cause. . . . The leader is the *supreme mind* of the popular mass. . . .[75]

King Yŏngjo died at the age of eighty-three, fifty-two years into his reign. Kim Il Sung died at eighty-two, forty-nine years into his: the world will soon see if he succeeded with Jong Il where Yŏngjo failed with Sado. In any case we are now in the Kim Jong Il era:

> Ah! Immortal sunshine of February
> The bright and clear sunshine
> Shining over the whole world.
> From the jungle of the holy mountain of revolution
> The greatest man was finally born.[76]

Since the death of Kim Il Sung, the North has faced one terrible crisis after another. It was visited with two years of unprecedented floods (in 1995 and 1996), a near-collapse of its energy system (which then caused many factories to close), a summer of drought (1997), and a resulting famine that claimed the lives of more than half a million people. This is a textbook example of the calamities that are supposed to mark the end of the Confucian dynastic cycle, and North Korean citizens must wonder how much more suffering they will endure before the economy returns to anything like the relatively stable situation that foreigners like myself observed in the 1980s. Kim Jong Il waited out the three-year traditional mourning period for the first son of the king before assuming his father's leadership of the ruling party; on the fiftieth anniversary of the regime's

74. Korean Central Broadcasting, P'yŏngyang, Oct. 24, 1994, in Foreign Broadcast Information Service, East Asia Daily, FBIS-EAS-94-210, Oct. 31, 1994, p. 45.
75. *Nodong sinmun* (P'yŏngyang), Sept. 19, 1994, in Foreign Broadcast Information Service, East Asia Daily, FBIS-EAS-94-210, Oct. 31, 1994, p. 46 (emphasis added).
76. KCNA, April 17, 1984.

founding, in September 1998, he became the maximum leader, but chose not to become head of state (that is, president of the Democratic People's Republic of Korea)—probably because he appears to be uncomfortable in meeting foreign leaders. Kim Jong Il assumed the mandate of heaven (a term that the North Koreans used repeatedly after Kim Il Sung died) with the regime's future shaky and with his people still starving.

No one knows how many people have died of starvation and disease since 1995. Andrew Natsios, the vice-president of World Vision, told reporters in September 1997 that North Korea had lost five hundred thousand to one million of its citizens to famine, and if full information were at hand, the total might be closer to two million, that is, nearly 10 percent of the population.[77] Since that time newspaper reports have simply assumed that upward of two million have died. A survey in August 1997, conducted among some four hundred Koreans living in China and crossing the border into North Korea frequently, came up with an estimate that 15 percent of the population in towns along the northern border had died. In orphanages, from which have come many of the televised images of this famine, the figure was 21 percent; in poor mining towns in the far north, about 9 percent.[78]

Such figures do not apply to the whole country, however. Regional differentiation is great in North Korea, with 10 percent of the population living in the highly centralized and much privileged capital. Foreign travelers have not witnessed starvation conditions in P'yŏngyang, and an international delegation that visited the upper east coast, to break ground for the light-water reactors envisioned in the October 1994 nuclear framework agreement, did not see much evidence of famine and malnutrition.[79] The DPRK is a class society, and those families with homes (as opposed to apartments) in villages and small cities have small plots of land at their disposal, every inch of which is under cultivation. A *Los Angeles Times* reporter visited several families with small gardens, and found that such families did not need government rations and had enough to eat.[80]

If Mother Nature shares some of the blame for North Korea's recent travails, even in the best weather conditions the North's agricultural problems are irremediable, short of major reform. The collapse of the Soviet bloc left the DPRK's export markets in a lurch, exports that had

77. *Chicago Tribune*, Sept. 17, 1997.

78. Korean Buddhist Savior Movement, figures provided to me in Sept. 1997.

79. Nicholas Kristof, "A Ceremony in North Korea Breaks More Than Ground," *New York Times*, Aug. 20, 1997.

80. Teresa Watanabe, "In North Korea, Resilience in the Face of Famine," *Los Angeles Times*, June 8, 1997.

been exchanged at favorable rates for petroleum, coking coal, and other essential imports. A rapid decline in petroleum imports in the 1990s, in turn, hurt the national transportation network and the huge chemical industry, which provided so much fertilizer to the farms. For several years now industry appears to have been running at less than 50 percent of capacity. North Korea must find ways to export to the world market to earn the foreign exchange needed to import food, oil, and other essentials.

Any kind of coordinated reform seems difficult for the regime to accomplish, however. In the North Korean administrative system bureaucratic lineages and hierarchies often exist as independent kingdoms, and have trouble communicating with each other. Hard-liners in the military have clearly been at odds with those in the Foreign Ministry who want better relations with Washington and Tokyo (something that foreign diplomats have witnessed on occasion), but the problems go much beyond that. Relative bureaucratic autonomy, the practice of provincial self-reliance, a vast party apparatus organizing upward of one-third of the adult population, the privileged position of the military (gaining at minimum 25 percent of the annual budget), the death of the only leader the country ever had, intense generational conflict (between an increasingly small, but still influential, revolutionary old guard and people in their forties to sixties), and the piling on of externally generated crises have all resulted in a kind of paralysis and immobilism since 1994. Decisions are pushed upward through the hierarchy, and at the top no one seems capable of making the hard choices necessary to push the country on a truly new course. In the summer of 2002 the regime revalued its currency drastically and ended most of the rationing system, but those acts were still not part of a general top-to-bottom reform.

North Korea is neither muddling through toward some sort of post-communism, the way other socialist states did after 1989, nor is it seriously reforming like China and Vietnam. The leadership seems deeply frightened by the consequences of opening up the economy, preferring instead to open small enclaves (like the Kaesŏng export zone, funded mainly by South Korean firms). Still, for all the troubles that have come in recent years, there are few signs that any of them have threatened the stability of the top leadership. Instead, change is trickling up from below, as the population is forced onto rudimentary markets to try to make ends meet.

In recent years foreigners have observed a huge market in P'yŏngyang with more than two thousand vendors, and witnessed large barter markets operating every day along the riverbanks in Hamhŭng. Hard currencies, especially dollars, were in wide use and highly valued. The historically centralized, administratively planned delivery of goods and services by the state seemed almost completely broken down at the local levels, with many people getting no food rations.

The North's situation today is not as bad as in 1998, when its official news agency said that "the people are tapping all possibilities and reserves and eking out their living in reliance upon substitute food" (but claimed that "the Korean people are moving ahead merrily in the teeth of the present difficulties"). It also acknowledged the large amounts of relief grain coming in from China—which had rendered "free assistance" to North Korea "on several occasions for years."[81] Western sources, including the U.S. government, have given more than $500 million in aid to the North since 1995, and World Bank officials have arranged assistance from several European countries that would enable training of North Korean experts, saying that they wanted "to learn about capitalistic economic operations."

Unlike similar humanitarian emergencies around the world, however, this one has provided little evidence of a collapse of state power, except for the breakdowns at the local level. There have been few significant changes in the North Korean leadership since Kim died. There have been defections, many of them hyped in the South Korean press and the world media, but only one—that of the leading ideologue Hwang Chang-yŏp in February 1997—was truly significant, and although the regime was embarrassed and demoralized by Hwang's departure, he had never been a central power holder and the core leadership still appears to be unshaken. In August 2001 Kim Jong Il chose to spend three weeks on an armored train while traveling to Moscow and back, presumably a junket meant to indicate that his hold on power back home is now firm and secure.

Another curiosity is that North Korea suffers as if it were Somalia or Ethiopia, but has a much more developed and modern economy. The DPRK historically had a powerful industrial economy and remains relatively urbanized, and, as we have seen, until recent years international agencies found that life expectancy rates, child welfare, inoculation rates, and general public health conditions were all quite good in North Korea, comparatively speaking. Unlike other places afflicted by humanitarian disasters, this is not a peripheral, penetrated state with a weak government. North Korea has a notably strong central state, high state capacities, and the ability to reach its arms into the smallest communities. Serious reform could happen in North Korea once the key decisions were taken, because this is a country that can mobilize everyone for centrally determined tasks. With its well-educated and disciplined work

81. Korean Central News Agency, July 9, 1998.

force, North Korea could effectively exploit a comparative advantage in labor cost in world markets.

In this sense the suffering of the North Korean population is truly inexcusable, because something could be done about famine conditions and malnutrition if there was really a will to do so among the central authorities. Instead, they seem morbidly insecure and determined therefore to give the armed forces what they need, to the detriment of every other institution in society (Kim Jong Il has loudly talked about his "army first" policies since the mid-1990s, as if the Workers' Party no longer comes first—an anomaly for a communist regime, and a tragedy for the people).

CONCLUSION

In *Knowledge and Politics* Roberto Unger distinguished between an inner and an outer circle in contemporary politics. The inner circle represents power and domination, exercised everywhere by the few. The outer circle includes all the rest, and their search for community, decency, and participation through the architecture of politics. Nowhere has the problem of the inner circle been resolved, he argued, and therefore in the outer circle "the search for community is condemned to be idolatrous, or utopian, or both." In Unger's sense, the inner circle—the Kim family nucleus—is the critical problem in North Korea; in the absence of a nonfamily and impersonal principle for constituting the core, the outer circle is condemned to idolatry. It may be that the apparent stability of this state masks instability at its center, in the failure to constitute a politics that can extend beyond the circle of family and personal relations. Or perhaps the North Korean leaders know their people better than we do and, with their singular meld of premodern and corporatist politics, will weather the problems that bedeviled and finally destroyed other communist systems.

The strength and stability of the system has rested on marrying traditional forms of legitimacy to modern bureaucratic structures, with the peculiar charisma of Kim Il Sung, in good Weberian fashion, providing the transition and the glue between the two. The Achilles' heel of the system, whether the ancien régime or the North Korea of today, is that it does not have "great leaders" or philosopher-kings, but human beings of a certain subjectivity. Not everyone agrees on what the virtues are or who embodies them. Not everyone is virtuous. Squabbles burst out, factions fall out, violence breaks out, and a new reality not subject to human virtue disciplines everyone: the Machiavellian realm of power politics that someone like Queen Min knew in her bones. We can call this life, and remember that there are twenty-two million human beings who go about their daily lives in the kingdom of the Kims.

The world today seems more inhospitable to P'yŏngyang's policies than that at any other point since 1948. Yet this cloistered regime faced the death of its founding king and remained stable, while passing on the baton to Kim Jong Il—in spite of twenty-five years of predictions that Kim's death would lead to the collapse of the system. With party elders like Pak Sŏng-ch'ŏl and Yi Chong-ok leading the way for the younger Kim, the core of high politics again showed itself to be cohesive and strong. Meanwhile, the outer circle hangs in the balance, as the North Korean people put up with another "sun king" and a very different world closes in upon this modern Hermit Kingdom. What will happen to the DPRK? It's anybody's guess. But in the past foreign observers have gone wrong, in my view, by underestimating North Korea in nearly every way possible. In the meantime, predictions based on the idea that this regime draws deeply from the well of Korean tradition and anticolonial nationalism, and will therefore have staying power in the post–Cold War world, have so far been correct.

CHAPTER NINE

America's Koreans

Korean Americans know themselves to be individuals with roots and context, people with rich and complex histories, thoughts, feelings, and flamboyant dreams. But most Americans see us primarily through the lens of race; they see us as all alike and caring only about ourselves.

—Elaine H. Kim[1]

Elaine Kim gives eloquent voice to the heterogeneous complexity of thousands of individual Americans who happen to be of Korean extraction. Korea, as we have learned, is an ethnically homogeneous nation of about seventy million whose real history is as complicated and diverse as that of any other twentieth-century people. The perceived purity of the *minjok*, the ethnic people, gives to them a long, continuous history, culture, and durability of which Koreans are deeply proud. At the same time this solid ethnic identity presents the non-Korean with an easy, superficial, seductive, and profoundly misleading sameness. Our earlier discussion of DNA and race helps to make this point: in the same way that the relative purity and longevity of Koreans on one peninsula is belied by the DNA they share in such abundance with humans of distant races and regions, so the Korean face masks a diversity of personality as extensive as the human condition itself.

Koreans born in this country feel this tension between identity and perception acutely, in everyday life. A Spanish-American teacher will assume that a student named John Kim sitting in her class is Japanese; an African-American or Jewish-American student sitting next to him will say he's Chinese; the response that he is Korean is not quite right, either, because John Kim thinks of himself as an American—and, anyway, most Americans who are not of Asian extraction have trouble distinguishing

1. Elaine H. Kim, in Aguilar-San Juan (1994), p. 73.

Korea from Japan and China. Along comes a little knowledge of Korean difference, and things simultaneously get better and worse.

When Chan Ho Park became the first Korean to play major league baseball the *New York Times* headline read, "Bearing Kimchi, a Dodger Is a First." It reminded me of my earliest days in Korea, when I read about Vice-President Hubert Humphrey crowing that the American largesse accompanying Korean troops being dispatched to fight in Vietnam would include C-ration cans of *kimch'i,* or American soldiers calling a troubled situation "deep *kimch'i*" ("We're in deep *kimch'i* now!"). Thirty years later the Dodger announcer was not sure which was Park's family name and which his first, and Park gave up two runs in his debut inning, but the half million Korean-Americans living in southern California were ecstatic and agog anyway. Mr. Park is handsome and friendly, and doesn't forget those who helped him: when he signed for a $1.25 million bonus, he promptly gave 10 percent of it to the university in Seoul where he got his education. Elsewhere in the article Kye Young Park, an anthropologist at UCLA, said that "Koreans are a little sick and tired of hearing of themselves as gun crazy, merciless merchants." A Mexican-American fan told a reporter that "members of some minority groups tended to dislike Koreans without knowing them."[2] The Dodger manager Tommy Lasorda was the Branch Rickey of our era, bringing Mexican, Japanese, and Korean talent to a team in need of wins and a city that is now the site of America's great multiethnic and multicultural experiment in urban living—and not at all sure it is the better for it.

It is a common teaching experience these days to find wonderfully worldly and intelligent young Korean-Americans in the classes of our best universities (Korean-American youngsters often make up 10 percent of entering freshman classes, and a higher percentage in California schools). Yet this also is a problem, because it makes of them a "model minority"—a distinction in one sense, but in another just one more way that the dominant white majority divides American minorities among themselves, and into "good" and "bad." This "model minority" is riven by differences of class, wealth, generation, language, ethnicity (for mixed offspring), politics, religion, region of domicile both here and in Korea, city and suburb, and time of immigration,[3] just to name a few differences. In other words, they are Americans.

Most Korean-Americans don't think their lives are so easy, and many want to find role models of their own, rather than provide one for other minorities. *New York* magazine quoted an economist who called Koreans "New York City's most productive community," yet while seven hundred

2. *New York Times,* April 10, 1994.
3. Ablemann and Lie (1995), pp. 108–18 and passim.

Korean-owned stores opened up in 1994, another nine hundred closed down. The author of the article called Koreans "the city's super-immigrants," likening them to Jews in their concern for upward mobility through small business and their obsession with educating the young. Koreans, like Jews, handle vegetable stores or clothing shops in one generation, and provide violin players and Harvard graduates in the next. Some Korean-Americans even call themselves "Kews" to symbolize the success and the marginalization of both groups. "Everyone knows a Korean, and nobody knows a Korean":[4] stated from the perspective of the majority, this nonetheless summarizes the daily experience of Korean-Americans—in the society, but not of it.

Why are there so many Korean-Americans in the best universities? There is no single answer, but certainly education in the old country taught several generations that entry to the best schools was essential to the future material well-being of the entire family, and a hard lesson about what happened to those who could not afford college or failed the entrance exams: the worker bent over under a heavy load but still clad in his elementary school uniform is a common sight in Seoul.

Like other children of immigrants, Korean-American college students pose for themselves this question: what part of me is Korean, what part is not? It is a question I also ruminate on, not least because it is a question asked by my sons. The question is most insistently posed, however, by Koreans in Korea, who find it well-nigh impossible to fathom how young people can look Korean but cannot speak the language (and therefore cannot insert themselves into the culture); some determine that they must no longer be Korean, a view that provides emotional hardship for many Korean-American students who go to Seoul for travel or study. Many Koreans in the United States do not learn English and live cloistered in small "Koreatowns"; they, too, look askance at assimilation and, above all, at their own assimilated children. Thus the timing of one's immigration causes cleavages within the Korean-American community and deeply affects the majority view of the individual Koreans one may happen to meet. One day I was sitting in a Korean barbershop, watching my boy get a haircut. A Korean mother was sitting next to me, doing the same thing. Her child spoke native English to my son, while the mother spoke native Korean with the hairdresser. When she was finished, the mother brushed some hair off his forehead, put his coat around his shoulders, and walked out saying, "Yu arŭ mai sŭwit'ŭ ch'ocorat'ŭ p'ai" (You are my sweet chocolate pie).

But it still is a question, isn't it: what part of me is American, what Korean? We can begin to answer it by looking at the experience of

4. Jeffrey Goldberg, "The Soul of the New Koreans," *New York*, April 10, 1995, pp. 42–51.

Korean-Americans, which now covers about 40 percent of American history since the United States was founded. Koreans began to arrive in American territory shortly after the turn of the century, in the colony called Hawaii. White plantation owners heard that they were just as diligent as Japanese workers, but would come cheaper; soon several thousand men signed on with work teams and landed in Honolulu. About fifty Koreans were in the United States by 1903, students, diplomats, merchants, and laborers. But a multitude arrived in Hawaii between 1903 and 1905, about seven thousand Koreans in all, mainly to work in sugar plantations; American missionaries facilitated this emigration, convinced that sugar cane labor would enable Koreans "to improve their conditions and to acquire useful knowledge," just as plantation owners welcomed the Koreans since it was "utterly impossible for white men to work in the cane fields."[5] Horace Allen told Sanford E. Dole, governor of Hawaii, that Koreans were superior to Chinese—"a patient, hard-working, docile race, easy to control from their long habit of obedience."[6]

It was hardly an idyll in the Hawaiian tropics. Koreans worked ten-hour days, six days a week in the cane fields under a blazing sun, for fifteen dollars a month plus living quarters. One foreman directed 250 workers, gender-divided into 200 men and 50 women. An early immigrant, Lee Hong-ki, described the work to an interviewer in 1971, when Lee was ninety-five years old: "I got up at four-thirty in the morning and made my breakfast; I had to be out to the field at five o'clock. . . . [M]y lune [foreman] was German. He was very strict with us. . . . He treated us like cows and horses. If one violated his orders, he was punished, usually a slap on the face or flagellating without mercy." Workers were never called by their names, but instead got numbers; the men slept four to a room on hard wooden beds.[7]

Thereafter, especially when women were able to join them (often wives married husbands sight unseen), Koreans began migrating to the mainland, scattering up and down the West Coast from 1904 to 1907 and working mostly in agriculture, especially orange and lemon picking in the groves that stretched from Los Angeles out to Riverside in those years. There were still only about 650 Korean-Americans in Los Angeles in the 1930s, and as late as 1970 only about 8,900, or about 13 percent of the total Korean-American population of about 115,000.[8] But Los Angeles was then, and remains today, home to the largest community of Korean-Americans in the United States.

5. Patterson (1988), pp. 3, 76, 85.
6. Quoted in Choy (1979), p. 74.
7. Choy (1979), pp. 94–96.
8. Ablemann and Lie (1995), p. 99.

Korean immigrants picked fruit at harvest time, ran truck farms that they leased, and hoped to buy some land for themselves and set up a family farming business. White Californians enforced an apartheid regime against Koreans and other Asians: exclusionary laws in 1913 denied property rights to Chinese, Japanese, and Korean immigrants; a 1921 "quota law" allowed annual immigration equal to 3 percent of the foreign-born population of that nationality as of 1910, which meant only a trickle of new Korean immigrants.[9] This was followed quickly by the 1924 Immigration Act, directed particularly at Asians. Thereafter, Koreans came to the United States only in small numbers, mainly as students.

Missionaries in Korea often sponsored students for study at demoninational colleges in the Midwest. Yŏ Un-hong, the brother of the KPR leader Yŏ Un-huŏng, attended Wooster College in Ohio, and many other Koreans went to nearby Ohio Wesleyan. Some wealthy Koreans, like Chang Tŏk-su and Cho Pyŏng-ok, studied at Columbia University in New York; Cho had also gone to high school in Kingston, Pennsylvania. There was a virtual Korean mafia from Ohio State University, where Ben Limb (Rhee's first foreign minister) and several other Koreans close to Rhee studied. Kim Kyu-sik went to Roanoke College and always retained sharp memories of the racial discrimination he suffered in Virginia.

By 1924 there were perhaps three thousand Korean-Americans living in the United States, most of them in the Los Angeles area. It was difficult for them to rent a home or a farm, and they were denied service in restaurants, hotels, and barbershops. Occasionally a kindly white person would stand up for them as hardworking and clean-living people (usually by reference to some other racial group that was thought less so); a woman named Mary Steward famously armed her Korean orange grove workers against rioting white mobs trying to throw them off her land, during one of California's recurrent "yellow peril" uproars.[10]

Koreans did manage to lease or buy their own farms, however, and a minority of them became prosperous. Kim Jong-lim, for example, was known by 1920 as the "rice king" of the Korean community in the San Joaquin Valley, bringing grain to Korean wholesale markets in LA. Others ran small businesses that eventually netted them modest wealth, but the majority (more than 75 percent) were firmly in the working class.[11] A tiny archipelago of Korean merchants and professionals offered services to the community: one restaurant, one hotel, and two grocery stores in Los Angeles; a dentist named Lee Eug in Pasadena; a photographer on Sunset Boulevard named Soong Suk, who took the stolid, unsmiling pic-

9. Ablemann and Lie (1995), p. 53.
10. Choy (1979), pp. 108–9.
11. Choy (1979), pp. 126–29.

tures Koreans favor; Dew Jung, who ran Elite Produce on Aliso Street; plus a doctor in Whittier, a car repairmen in El Segundo, and so on.

Korean-Americans in Los Angeles spent a lot of time trying to distinguish themselves from the many Japanese-Americans living in LA's "Little Tokyo" before World War II. It was not easy; the colonizers gave them Japanese names on their passports (if they were lucky enough to get one), and few Americans knew enough about Korea's precolonial independence to tell the two peoples apart. Stanford University, for example, lists a person named Senoo Hachiro as its first Japanese graduate, but Senoo (Sŏnu) is a Korean, not a Japanese, name.

One little-known but very fine novel has preserved the details of Korean life in Los Angeles in this period, Kim Ronyoung's *Clay Walls.* The author's mother was a yangban woman who had the bad luck, from her point of view, to be married off to a lowborn man who then emigrated to the United States. To support the family she did housekeeping, laundry, cleaning other people's toilets, and the like, exclaiming all the while to her daughter that yangban weren't supposed to do things like this—nor were they used to the constant discrimination she encountered among white Americans. Like many other Asian-Americans, this family relied on the kindness of African-American strangers—their landlady was a black woman, who rented them a white bungalow with a red tile roof on Thirty-sixth Place; the boys grew up knowing how to "talk jive." Their daughter found a good friend in Bertha, a broad-faced, coffee-skinned neighbor, who always wore a dahlia in her hat: "Bertha was the only girl I knew who took hold of life and made things happen. 'Girl, don't you know anything?' she always said to me."[12] (Mary Paik, an early immigrant to the United States, also had many black friends in childhood, living side by side with them and sharing white discrimination. In her old age she still frequented a predominantly black church.)[13]

Mrs. Chun and her husband also spent time trying to sell fruits and vegetables from a cart:

> It had taken them several weeks to learn that if they were to make a profit, they would have to push their wagon from one place to another. In the early morning they were at Temple and Sunset selling apples to workers leaving for work. At mid-morning, they moved on to Grand Avenue to catch shoppers at lunch. In the afternoon, they made stops in residential districts on their way home. As the day wore on, the apples showed signs of ageing and were sold at reduced prices to children returning home from school.[14]

12. Kim (1984), p. 284.
13. Ablemann and Lie (1995), pp. 190–91.
14. Kim (1984), p. 13.

Slowly they prospered, joining the vast southern California middle class—but only in income. Once her son fought back in school after being called a "chink" and was disciplined by the principal. So Mrs. Chun decided to put him in a military academy, only to be told, "The Academy does not accept orientals." They were American citizens, she protested, born right here in LA. Ah yes, the colonel replied: but they are not "Anglo-Saxon, uh . . . Caucasian." She was enraged, but when she returned home her husband asked her what she expected to happen—"That's the way those sons-of-bitches are. You can't tell them anything."[15]

Mrs. Chun's daughter grew up to be a bobby-soxer in the halcyon days of La-Laland, before smog and traffic gridlock, before Pearl Harbor, and before tremors from the San Andreas Fault. She worried instead about her "pathetic, inadequate breasts"; her boyfriend was Willie Koo, from a San Joaquin Valley farming family:

> Being Willie's girl meant that I would be included when the boys took their girls bowling, or to movies, or to Simon's Drive-in for a hamburger. I wanted to be the kind of girl boys liked to be with so, while watching movies, I studied the way Hollywood stars walked and talked. I thumbed through magazines to see how starlets fixed their hair and dressed. . . . I even considered Ruth Johnson one of my best friends until she told me, "You know, Faye, I don't think of you as being Korean anymore," as if there was something wrong with being Korean.[16]

After Pearl Harbor she couldn't walk down the street without someone's yelling, "You stinkin' Japs. Go back where you came from." Some politicians wanted to run Koreans into the concentration camps along with Japanese-Americans, until Young-jeung Kim (a prosperous orange grove owner and longtime editor of the *Voice of Korea*) and other community leaders taught them a little history. The daughter watched as her bobby-soxer Nisei friends had to sell their homes and shops for a pittance, before the trains took them to the camps. Her mother thought the Japanese were getting what they deserved, but the daughter had a different idea: "Some things are just plain bad with nothing good about them at all."[17]

Koreans in Los Angeles were particularly proud of Philip Ahn, the son of An Chang-ho, who (in a nice turn of the screw) became a millionnaire playing evil Japanese officers in Hollywood movies. When the interroga-

15. Kim (1984), p. 51.
16. Kim (1984), pp. 231, 251.
17. Kim (1984), pp. 260–67. Kim edited and published the *Voice of Korea* for decades, closing it down finally in the early 1970s. The *Voice* is an excellent source on Korean-American history.

tor squinted his eyes at a downed American flyer and said, "We have ways of making people talk, GI," that was Philip Ahn talking. Today there is a boulevard named for him in one of the Korean sections of Los Angeles.

When the United States went to war in Korea in 1950, Koreans still could not emigrate to the United States under existing racial quotas, and the 3,000-odd Koreans who came to the country before 1924 but were not born there were still denied naturalization. Mary Paik Lee recalled that during the Korean War, in LA "most of the 'For Whites Only' signs on public restrooms, swimming pools, and so forth, were removed. But although there were no signs on barber shops, theaters, and churches, Orientals were told at the door that they were not welcome."[18] Fifteen states outlawed Korean-Caucasian marriages, eleven states refused to allow Koreans to buy or own land, and twenty-seven occupations in New York City were proscribed to Koreans.[19] Because of their lack of citizenship, moreover, several Korean-Americans paid a high price.

In Los Angeles in the late 1940s was a newspaper called the *Korean Independent,* its main attribute being a distaste for Syngman Rhee (based on long experience with him in America), support for An Chang-ho, and criticism of the politics of the American occupation in Korea from a left-liberal or New Deal point of view. The *Independent* dared to oppose U.S. intervention in the Korean War, and as a result got constant surveillance by the FBI and local police "red squads."[20] No doubt many of the Korean-Americans associated with the paper were left-wingers with maybe a communist here and there, but it had a tepid politics. One man from this group named Diamond Kim (Kim Kang) was deported by the FBI in the 1950s, and ended up in North Korea; a couple of others were not so lucky, the FBI returning them to the tender mercies of the Rhee regime, which imprisoned them and perhaps executed some of them.[21]

Another Korean-American was in San Francisco awaiting deportation when a friend got a lawyer to intercede, and he ended up working the rest of his career as a librarian at a prestigious women's college. In Seattle several Korean-Americans associated with the University of Washing-

18. Quoted in Ablemann and Lie (1995), p. 95.

19. *Nation,* Aug. 26, 1950.

20. Choy (1979), p. 183. The only relatively complete run of this newspaper, to my knowledge, is in the University of Washington Library in Seattle. Kim Ronyoung wrote about fights between Korean leftists and more conservative nationalists in LA as far back as 1923. Kim (1984), p. 40.

21. I base myself on discussions with members of this group who do not want to be identified; the last time I asked the FBI for papers on these Korean-Americans, they were still classified.

ton were turned in to the FBI by a leading American professor of Asian Studies; at least two were fired from their university positions, and one of them, who later became a well-known photographer, could not get a passport again until 1967.[22] It would appear that Kim Ronyoung's family was dealt the same hand; her mother had kept a plot of land in Korea, always thinking she would go back and live there, but then her relatives got caught up with Yŏ Un-hyŏng's People's Republic: " 'I guess Uncle Min won't be going back to Korea,' I said. [Mom] shook her head. 'What for? The South Korean government says the KPR is a communist group. We can't get into North Korea either. . . . [M]y land in Qwaksan is gone.' "[23] The novel ends with a moving passage on what it means to be a person of Korean ancestry living in the United States.

America's anachronistic racial exclusion laws ended only in 1965, at the height of the civil rights movement. According to U.S. Naturalization and Immigration figures (which probably understate the numbers quite a bit), there were but ten Korean immigrants to the United States in the year 1950, 1,507 a decade later, nearly 10,000 in 1970, and 32,158 in 1975. The 1970 census reported 8,881 Koreans in Los Angeles County, which other sources thought was less than 50 percent of the actual total. By 1975 there were also about 13,000 Koreans born in the United States, perhaps 10,000 of whom antedated the 1965 changes in U.S. laws that vastly speeded up Korean immigration. It is this new immigration that so enlarged the Korean-American community in the United States over the next thirty years, but it also deeply shaped the population of Koreans able to emigrate. The law gave preferences to highly skilled occupations and to those with money to invest in the American economy; this led to a "brain drain" from Korea that has begun to reverse itself only in recent years (through emigration back to Korea), as well as an outlet for the sons and daughters of wealthy Koreans who were not doing so well in the ROK's tough and demanding educational system. (The phenomenon of the Korean-American princess, or KAP, is now a fixture on American campuses.)

Koreans emigrated for other reasons, too, by no means the least being the repressive regimes of Park and Chun. (The peak period of Korean immigration was 1985–87, when 35,000 people emigrated annually, which coincided with the last throes of the military dictatorship; sociolo-

22. Interview with Seattle informant, 1987. The president of the University of Washington at this time was in frequent contact with J. Edgar Hoover, according to declassified materials in the Sigmund Diamond Papers at Columbia University Law School; among other things, Hoover gave him advice on how to handle a famous 1949 case in which several faculty were fired for refusing to say whether they had ever belonged to the Communist Party or not.

23. Kim (1984), p. 300.

gists later found that many cited Chun's repression as a key reason to leave.)[24] The vast disparity in wealth between America and Korea, visible at the American military "PX" exchanges in Korea, in the American television programs always available on AFKN (Armed Forces Korea Network), or in the Sears, Roebuck catalogs (called "moose manuals") that generations of GIs used to entice their girlfriends, led many Koreans to think that American streets were paved with gold. Women left to escape Confucian patriarchy, or because as Christians they had come to appreciate gender equality (54 percent of the recent immigrants were Christians, as opposed to 21 percent of the population of the ROK); small business men were squeezed out of an economy increasingly dominated by the *chaebŏl* groups; Chŏlla people emigrated in large numbers because of discrimination or lack of opportunity within Korea. Many were relatives joining family members who had come earlier; others merely wanted an easier life and a better opportunity to educate their children: "as late as 1986 South Koreans [still] worked the longest hours in the world and under terrible working conditions."[25]

In the mid-1970s about 85 percent of all Korean-Americans were in the working class, and only 5 percent were professionals; yet upwards of 70 percent of the Korean immigrants had been professionals back home. In southern California in the 1970s there were some six hundred immigrant physicians with no license to practice medicine, who found jobs as health care workers or hospital clerks. Recent studies do not suggest that these percentages have dropped that much; 33 percent of all Korean émigrés were professionals back home, compared with 8 percent for the general population, and 80 percent considered themselves middle or lower-middle class back in Korea.[26] Today there are more than a million Korean-Americans, living all over the country but with big clusters in Los Angeles and New York; many more may be professionals by now, living in the suburbs, but the majority of professionals who emigrated still do not work in positions commensurate with their skills and backgrounds, and the majority of the community is still working class.

This is important evidence, large grains of salt to take while you read about Koreans as a "model minority." A person with a college degree from Korea who brings his family to New York and runs a vegetable store for ten years—a very common phenomenon—is not going to be happy with his status; probably there won't be much he can do about his own, but he and his wife will work their fingers to the bone to assure that

24. Ablemann and Lie (1995), pp. 67–68.
25. Ablemann and Lie (1995), pp. 67–75.
26. Choy (1979), pp. 218–19, 226, 249–50; Ablemann and Lie (1995), pp. 108–18.

their offspring regain the status that the father had in Korea, namely, a college degree and a professional career. Maybe the family will be lucky and get a child into a top university; then they will encourage that child to specialize in the sciences, since in so many other fields there are "glass ceilings" that prevent Korean-Americans from getting top jobs—especially in American corporations, which at the top levels remain overwhelmingly segregated minorities of white males.

American stereotypes of Koreans have generally been far less flattering than the "model minority" fiction. During the Korean War the media depicted desperately poor people wrapped in thick cotton in endless refugee lines escaping the fighting in heavy snows, an image so strong that when I told my mother I was going to Korea in 1967, she responded, "Oh, no! There's a war going on there." (Later I learned that she was right. . . .) A druggist who had served in the war took me aside and warned me about what I would face: "Korea's nine hundred years behind us." Today it is hard for me to believe, but in the 1970s a Tacoma newspaper called upon me to explain why local Korean-Americans were upset about a column it had published, where the writer referred to Koreans as "the niggers of the Orient." Korean-American groups were protesting outside of the building, and generally up in arms. It turns out that this was a fairly common epithet, used mainly by white Americans who served in the Korean War. Tacoma had many problems with Korean wives and the GI soldiers they had married in Korea, now living on or near its military bases; divorces and suicides by the women were common, as were massage parlors, bars, and houses of prostitution. Children of mixed marriages acted up in Tacoma schools. It took weeks for the controversy over this slur to die down.

Americans who lived in Korea in the 1960s were convinced that all Koreans were thieves. Bob Hope would get huge belly laughs from American GIs by telling them that he was late for his tour of military bases "because slicky boys stole my landing gear." Nelson Algren, Chicago's favorite native-son writer, took a walk on the wild side of Pusan in the 1960s. In his *Notes from a Sea Diary,* he has fifteen pages on his experience:

> Four thousand years looks down, from that ancestral mountain, upon a race of hardluck aristocrats toting buckets of slopwater. . . .
>
> She lived in a little kimchi house with an earthen floor, where kimchi mice ran in and out in the light of a kimchi moon. Incense cut the odor of kimchi while she undressed in the dark. . . .[27]

27. *Notes from a Sea Diary: Hemingway All the Way* (New York: Putnam, 1965), cited in Wade (1967), p. 227.

In Ian Fleming's *Goldfinger,* written in the same period, a bullnecked Korean character named Oddjob makes an appearance, famous for his ability to fling his steel-ringed hat at someone's neck and take his head off. Koreans have "no regard for human life," Fleming wrote, and that's why the Japanese employed them: to get the "cruelest, most ruthless people in the world." In 1965, as the ROK entered its export-led take-off, C. D. B. Bryan wrote, "This is the foulest, goddamndest country I've ever seen!" The only thing that made Korea bearable, he thought, was "the availability of women."[28]

One of the many problems with such literary judgments is that Koreans are very much drawn to literature, and read them; I often found Koreans who had learned English to be better read in Western literature than most Americans. One day a young man stopped me on the streets of Seoul to ask me the meaning and symbolism of the rubber hose in the basement in Arthur Miller's *Death of a Salesman.* A wife and mother down the hall from an apartment where I once lived got engrossed in one Thomas Hardy novel after another. She was a woman of extraordinary dignity and charm, who worked at the Fulbright offices. I was reminded of her in James Wade's description of the ubiquitous Korean woman assistant, working in American offices: "the everyday aesthetician," he called her; always visible by her desk "a tiny bouquet or nosegay of flowers," put there with "unobtrusive artfulness." Under the glass on top of the desk were "English poems, uplifting quotations, literary fragments, and reproductions of great art."[29]

By the 1970s Korea had become the location for the most popular American television sitcom for many years running, "M*A*S*H," a program set in Korea but meant to depict the new sensibilities that came with the Vietnam War and the massive American opposition to it. Instead of snow-blown, pitiable refugees or "slicky boys," average Koreans seemed like normal human beings, whether those on our side or those on the other side. ROK officials hated "M*A*S*H" because it recalled war-torn Korea and was much too sympathetic to the communist enemy; they were happy when it went off the air—only to watch it come back as an eternally popular rerun.

The next stereotype of Koreans and Korean-Americans arrived with the Koreagate scandal: devious Orientals subverting our high-minded congressmen with their money, or our youths with strange doctrines—the Reverend Moon's "love-bombing." This was a thoroughly investigated "gate" scandal of the 1970s, at least by the U.S. House team under

28. Bryan, *P. S. Wilkinson* (1965), cited in Wade (1967), p. 231.
29. Wade (1967), pp. 248–49.

Congressman Donald Fraser, a Democrat from Minnesota (the Justice Department was much less enthusiastic in getting to the bottom of it). It had its origins in President Nixon's determination to withdraw a portion of the American troop contingent from Korea, as part of his "doctrine" of getting Asians to fight Asian wars, especially the Vietnam War, which he was systematically escalating with an eye toward eventually winding it down after the Hanoi regime had been duly terrorized. Park Chung Hee and his allies were absolutely appalled by Nixon's plans, and desperately sought to counter them. In early 1970, for example, Prime Minister Chŏng Il-gwŏn told the American ambassador, William Porter, that if Nixon tried to take U.S. troops out, he would lie down on the runway so the planes couldn't take off. "Do that, my good friend," Porter replied, "but let me take a picture before the planes begin to roll."[30] It was actually Vice-President Spiro Agnew who lowered the boom, however, in a bizarre six-hour meeting in August 1970 with Park Chung Hee in which Agnew was denied lunch, coffee, or even a trip to the men's room. One of Agnew's aides remarked that this grueling session was "brutal and absolutely offensive," a performance by a head of state "unlike any [he] had ever seen." It was all to no avail, however; three days later an entire division—about ten thousand American troops and many others in supporting capacities—rolled out of Korea. Shortly thereafter, in a meeting on August 26, 1970, Park started the influence-peddling ball rolling, hoping to make up in a Democratically controlled Congress what he had lost in the Nixon White House.[31]

Soon a retinue of KCIA-controlled individuals, operating out of the Korean embassy in Washington, the Unification Church, and other front organizations, began bribing influential Americans to build up Seoul's influence in the United States. The prime targets were sitting congressmen, and even the ambassador, Kim Tong-jo (whom we met earlier), got into the act, stuffing envelopes with $100 bills and distributing them on Capitol Hill; the immediate goal was to reverse Nixon's troop withdrawal policy or to assure that no more American troops would leave Korea. But there were many other targets, including several universities that housed critics of the human rights violations of the Park regime.[32]

30. Boettcher (1980), p. 91.
31. Boettcher (1980), p. 96. Years later newspapers revealed that American intelligence had monitored the August 26 Blue House meeting, sending Park into another fit of rage.
32. All the information in my discussion of Koreagate comes from Boettcher (1980) and the investigation that Boettcher ran under Donald Fraser's direction, with which I consulted at the time and which ultimately produced many published volumes of evidence and testimony (see the list in Boettcher's book, pp. 351–52). This information came under oath and under threat of perjury and is therefore much better than most other sources on Korean-American relations and on the Park regime and how it operated.

The key—and colorful—figure in this scandal was Tongsun Park, a rice merchant, lobbyist, and bon vivant who was under KCIA direction by 1971 if not earlier; Park had been a big man on the campus of a Tacoma high school, pictured in its 1950s yearbook with a white sportcoat and a pink carnation, a regular American if there ever was one. Pak Bo Hi was another key Koreagate operator; he was a regular KCIA officer if there ever was one, and later the Reverend Sun Myung Moon's right-hand man and translator.[33] This scandal never ended with full disclosure about what really happened; it just ended—because a new Democratic administration arrived in Washington in 1977, and all too many congressional Democrats were implicated in the scandal (starting at the top with Majority Leader Tip O'Neill, according to much unverified Washington scuttlebutt at the time).

If Koreans in America were dutiful, hardworking "Orientals" useful for sugar cane cutting at the beginning of this century and "slicky boys" in the middle, by its end they had become a model of bootstrapping your way to Horatio Alger success without help from the federal government or the welfare state.[34] None of these stereotypes have made Korean-Americans happy, because they lump a diverse population under a catchall rubric, but this one is decidedly preferable to the previous ones. Nevertheless, people who witness Korean success in America should know that there is another place where Koreans are still "the niggers of the Orient": Japan, which enforces a virtual apartheid system against Korean residents, many of them third and fourth generation. If you take the express bus to Narita Airport from Yokohama and can read Korean, you will at one point notice a high-rise apartment building in a working-class neighborhood that has on its roof large, red Korean letters. What they say, or said until July 1994, is "Long Live the Great Fatherly Leader Kim Il Sung." Japanese prejudice and the absence of opportunity long ago pushed hundreds of thousands of Korean residents to the left, and the North still runs a state-within-a-state in Japan: a full educational system in the P'yŏngyang curriculum, for example, taught in tens of elementary schools, a handful of high schools, and Chosen University in Tokyo.

We are not examining Koreans in Japan in this book, but Japan provides a good example of how racial stereotypes die so hard: many Japanese think of Koreans today in the stereotypical way that white Americans thought of Chinese a century ago—dirty, conniving, devious, criminal elements, generally up to no good. This adds up to one more

33. Boettcher (1980), pp. 214–15.

34. See many examples of the latter stereotype in Won Yong-Jin, " 'Model-Minority' Strategy and Asian-Americans' Tactics," *Korea Journal* 34, no. 2 (Summer 1994): 57–66.

reason not to think in racial terms, because Koreans cannot be a model minority in the United States, a deprived minority in Japan, or a hugely diverse population in Korea, and still be part of some quintessential thing called Korean. And then, of course, racism comes full circle to the point where you want to fall on your knees in shame: today Korean-Americans list African-Americans at the bottom of surveys indicating racial preference hierarchies; meanwhile, Koreans harbor the delusion that they come "right after whites" in America's racial pecking order.[35]

The latest model minority stereotype, combined with racism among Korean-Americans, has put them at loggerheads with African-Americans. Racial disputes have broken out between Koreans and blacks in New York, Chicago, Philadelphia, and many other places, but nothing was more disheartening than the example of poor Koreans arming themselves against poor blacks, Hispanics, and whites in the April–May 1992 Los Angeles riots that followed upon a Simi Valley courtroom's judgment that LA policemen were not guilty of beating Rodney King within an inch of his life.

The case of Soon Ja Du was an important prelude to the 1992 uprising. An immigrant shopkeeper with rudimentary English, she shot and killed Latasha Harlins in March 1991 in a dispute over a $1.79 bottle of orange juice, as the security cameras whirred. Over and over the television media played this videotape, inflaming black passions and shaming Koreans, while whites stood by watching as if uninvolved: "every time it played it made black people hate Koreans."[36] Soon a court acquitted Ms. Du of any wrongdoing. LA's "black-Korean conflict" was tailor-made for the towering cynicism of Hollywood writers, who in a film called *Falling Down* presented your stereotypical rude and crude Korean shopkeeper, who gets what he deserves from an enraged white man—a guy who's "not gonna take it anymore"—played by Michael Douglas. This film offers a perfect example of the divide-and-rule tactics that whites have long used, whether consciously or unconsciously, to assure that they do not face a unified multiracial opposition from below.[37]

The auto that police pulled Rodney King from in the most famous private video in recent American history was a Hyundai sedan; King was known to the police because of an earlier arrest for robbing a store owned by Korean-Americans. Those Koreans who run liquor stores or "swapmeets" in the Los Angeles ghetto are a mere step above poverty themselves, but (like Jews in the past) became a target of wrath just

35. Ablemann and Lie (1995), p. 34.
36. Lee (1993), p. 74.
37. Lee (1993), pp. 76–77.

because they are there and not in a pleasant suburb. Many African-Americans complain that Korean businesspeople are racists and do not treat them with dignity, which may well be true in many cases—but that makes Koreans no different from white Americans. Furthermore, many Korean-Americans have shared the poverty and racial degradation of American society, as *Clay Walls* showed, and often have much more sympathetic understanding of the African-American predicament than do whites.

The subsequent riots in the spring of 1992 were the worst experience imaginable for the growing numbers of Korean-Americans in the United States. They left an estimated 58 dead and 2,400 injured, nearly 12,000 arrests, and $717 million in property damages. These were urban America's first multiethnic riots, since many of the looters were Hispanic and some white; Nancy Ablemann and John Lie argue that it was a "Korean-Latino conflict," since Latinos constituted the majority of the arrested looters.[38] But that is not the way our media saw it.

Day after day the TV networks showed ruined Korean shops, young Koreans arming themselves against young rioters, enormously disproportional property losses (Korean businesses lost at least $350 million to $400 million, more than 50 percent of total losses and far more than any other group), and endless harping on the theme of black versus Korean, miscreant versus hardworking businessman, despised minority versus model minority. The Asian-American playwrite Frank Chin wrote, "The Alamo in Koreatown was a mini-mall. In the race war that's started, are we all going to choose up sides and appear at the appropriate mini-mall to man the barricades?"[39] Elaine Kim expressed the anguish that ran through the entire Korean-American community:

> It is difficult to describe how disempowered and frustrated many Korean Americans felt. . . . [They] shared the anguish and despair of the Los Angeles *tongp'o* [community] which everyone seemed to have abandoned—the police and fire departments, black and white political leaders, the Asian and Pacific American advocates who tried to dissociate themselves from us because our tragedy disrupted their narrow and risk-free focus on white violence against Asians. At the same time, while the Korean Americans at the center of the storm were mostly voiceless and all but invisible (except when stereotyped as hysterically inarticulate, and mostly female, ruined shopkeepers or gun-wielding male merchants on rooftops concerned only about their property), we repeatedly witnessed Americans of African, European and, to a slightly

38. Ablemann and Lie (1995), pp. 2–3, 161.
39. Quoted in Ablemann and Lie (1995), p. 1.

> lesser extent, Chinese and Japanese descent discussing publicly the significance of what was happening.[40]

Rarely if ever did any media pundit point out that the Koreans had bought their stores from African-Americans, who had bought them from Jews after the Watts riots a generation earlier; or that the Korean merchants were often the poorest segment of Korean businesspeople in the United States, doing a job and providing a service that most others would reject.

Warren Lee is a remarkable, but by no means unique, example of a Korean-American who grew up cheek by jowl with blacks in Los Angeles. His family lived on Vernon Avenue near Jefferson Boulevard in South Central LA, because restrictive housing clauses prevented them from living elsewhere. He talked jive and became a first-class basketball player, and thought of himself as black for many years. He also suffered from the diabolical inversions that a racist society conjures up in the mind of the oppressed, often unbeknownst to the white majority: "It created within me a burning, yearning, face-pressed-up-against-the-glass sexual and romantic desire for white women, especially blond-haired, blue-eyed ones."[41]

Another Korean-American woman, Elaine Kim, grew up being called "chink" and "Jap" and being exhorted to "remember Pearl Harbor"; all she wanted was "to be as American as possible" while going to football games, drinking beer, and dating the high school heroes:

> I drank a lot and tried to be cool. I had convinced myself that I was "American," whatever that meant, all the while knowing underneath that I'd have to reconcile myself, to try to figure out where I would fit in a society that never sanctioned that identity as a public possibility. Part of growing up in America meant denying my cultural and ethnic identity, and part of that meant negating my parents. I still loved them, but I knew they could not help me outside the home.[42]

Like many Korean-Americans, she finds the "model minority" stereotype maddening: first, because it is not true; second, because it pits Koreans (many of whom come from wealthy or middle-income families in Korea) against poor, uneducated blacks and Chicanos; and third, because it is true enough to defy denial—given their prominence today in American

40. Kim, in Aguilar-San Juan (1994), pp. 71–72. See also Elaine Kim, "Home Is Where the *Han* Is: A Korean American Perspective on the Los Angeles Upheavals," *Social Justice* 20, nos. 1–2 (Spring–Summer 1993).
41. Lee (1993), p. 12.
42. Kim, in Aguilar-San Juan (1994), p. 75.

universities, Korean-Americans will soon be widely visible professionals in all walks of life, far out of proportion to their numbers.

If we take the Koh family of New Haven, for example, we find two college professors who reared six children: five went to Harvard and one to Yale, and all went on to graduate work, yielding two Yale Law School professors, two professors at medical schools in Massachusetts, one professor of chemistry in Seoul, and one assistant dean at Yale (the youngest son). The protean mother also found time to earn a Ph.D., teach at Yale Law School, become one of the world's leading librarians and bibliographers of Korean materials, and publish several books and numerous articles on Korean women, the Korean-American community, and many other subjects.[43] Both Hesung Chun Koh and her late husband, Kwang Lim (a former Korean ambassador to the United States), are friends of mine and they have disposed of enormous resources of love and energy; at the same time, it is important to point out that they both come from prominent families in Korea and would never claim to have arrived penniless at Ellis Island. The reader who wants to pursue the stereotype of the "model minority" can read an article on the subject written (as the reader may already have guessed) by one of their sons—the distinguished Yale Law School professor Harold Koh.[44]

Highly favorable, unalloyed American images of Korea, of course, commingle with the coarse and one-sided ones. Korean-Americans have made stellar contributions to American music, beginning two decades ago with the recognition of Kyung-hwa Chung as a world-class violinist. Touring exhibitions of Korean art are now routine, and routinely praised by the critics (although the first important one, "5,000 Years of Korean Art," was as recent as 1979–81). Korean literature and film, however, are still remote from the mainstream of American culture, even when compared to their Chinese and Japanese counterparts; Korean literature in translation is becomingly increasingly available,[45] but no Korean feature film has ever, to my knowledge, gained commercial release in the United States. Namjune Paik's avant-garde work has been a Soho staple for years, though, and Korean-Americans now have their own journals and magazines. No doubt we will hear much more from them in the future.

American images of Korean cuisine, to the extent that they exist, are also changing. Only in the late 1970s did Korean restaurants begin to

43. Howard Kyongju Koh, ed., *Hesung Chun Koh: Essays in Honor of Her Hwegap: 1989* (New Haven: East Rock Press, 1992).

44. Harold Hongju Koh, "Looking beyond Achievement: After 'The Model Minority,' Then What?" *Korean and Korean-American Studies Bulletin* (Fall–Winter 1987).

45. Thanks to the efforts of Bruce and Ju-chan Fulton, Peter Lee, Walter K. Lew, David McCann, Marshall Pihl, Richard Rutt, and others.

proliferate, and most of them were rough-and-ready barbecue houses where English did not get a customer very far. Now American cities have excellent Korean cuisine, often in diverse regional varieties. One New York food critic found a restaurant worthy of two stars for "a cuisine quite accessible to the American palate but still largely unknown to it":

> When you walk into the room, your first impression is warmth and laughter. All around the restaurant, people are huddled over grills, drinking and talking and gesturing wildly as great gusts of fragrant steam go billowing toward the ceiling. Men scurry about with buckets of blazing coals, replenishing the fires at each table, and waitresses walk past bearing trays laden with vegetables as bright as jewels. The air smells of smoke and chilies and garlic, and the whole atmosphere is so inviting that you are irresistibly drawn into the center of the room.[46]

In 1994 American television viewers were treated to a new ABC sitcom, "All American Girl." The star, Cho Mo-ran, better known as Margaret Cho, got her start on Home Box Office's comedy hour; she is the daughter of a well-known bookseller in San Francisco, who emigrated to this country when Margaret was a young child. She is therefore a "one-and-a-half," born in Korea but reared in the United States. (Then there are pure "ones" and pure "twos," a basic difference being that "ones" speak Korean well and English badly, while "twos" speak English well and Korean badly or not at all.)

Margaret Cho is a very funny woman, but perhaps only one familiar with the Korean-American community can fully appreciate her humor. Much like the Yiddish vaudeville tradition and their successor comedians, still given full voice by Jackie Mason, or Dick Gregory and Richard Pryor in the African-American community, Margaret Cho's deft, knowing, foulmouthed sarcasm is a sign of the times; she is the stalking-horse for a quickly rising professional class of Korean-Americans who will soon, if they have not already, make their presence known in the boardrooms of American society.

Margaret Cho is a guide to their dilemmas, caught as they are between a mother shouting "Moooooaaaaa-Raaaannn!!" and desperately trying to find a nice Korean boy for her to date (while having done all the right things during childhood to get her into Harvard or Yale), a father who tries to be doting and protective, fearing the worst and knowing he will fail, a grandmother fully convinced that American society is a loony bin and that they should all pack their bags for Seoul forthwith, and an

46. Ruth Reichl, review of Kang Suh Restaurant, *New York Times*, Oct. 22, 1993.

America that none of their elders begin to understand, but that the young know intimately, in their bones—with the exception that they look different, and so whites are always saying things like "When are you going back to your country?" This is not to say that Korea is any easier for them. Should they dare to spend a summer in the old country, as many do, they will be told that they can't possibly be Korean, because they don't speak the language, or not well enough, that Korea is a far better place than America (judging by what they read in the newspapers), and . . .

Every answer to the question "What is Korean about me?" will be deeply personal, but mine is close to the one given by Sergeant Joker in Stanley Kubrick's film *Full Metal Jacket*—namely, that inside every Vietnamese (or Korean) is an American trying to get out. The lures of American mass culture are simply too powerful a solvent for the old Korean verities to have much of a chance. The first commendable example of this dissolution and the delightful Korean-American result, in my reading, is Younghill Kang's account of his life in 1920s New York, *East Goes West: The Making of an Oriental Yankee.* It is unlikely that most New Yorkers understood that in their midst was a person steeped in a Korean classical education and haute-family patriarchy who enjoyed tripping through the streets of Manhattan like a boisterous Thomas Wolfe, with a world-ranging, human-loving desire to be accepted as an equal—if a formidable equal. "I am a true New Yorker," he announced not long after his arrival:

> One of my favorite routes was along Broadway around 42nd Street where Broadway is democratic, not to say vulgar. But it has New York personality, plenty of it, and its own individuality. "What a sight!" I kept thinking. "Is it not the greatest pageant in the history of the world?" . . . To be a New Yorker among New Yorkers means a totally new experience from being Japanese or Chinese or Korean—a changed character. New Yorkers all seem to have some aim in every movement they make. (Some frantic aim.) They are like guns shooting off. How unlike Asiatics in an Oriental village, who drift up and down aimlessly and leisurely! But these people have no time, even for gossiping, even for staring. . . .
>
> Just to move in New York and not be ploughed under, man must provision and plan out. Free, factual, man is reasoning from cause to effect here all the time—not so much thinking. It is intelligence measuring, rather than intellect's solution. Prophets of hereafter, poets of vision . . . maybe the American is not so much these. But he is a good salesman, amidst scientific tools. His mind is like the Grand Central Station. It is definite, it is timed, it has mathematical precision on clear-

> cut stone foundation. . . . Every angle and line has been measured. How solid the steel framework of this Western civilization is![47]

All this from a Greenwich Village poet and intellectual, lover of jazz, and professor of comparative literature at New York University named Kang, who was a few years away from the turn-of-the-century village he memorialized in *The Grass Roof.*

I would like to close this chapter with excerpts from a poem by one of my former students, Julie Kim, entitled "Red and Yellow Dreams":

> I remember
> when I was a little girl of six or seven
> in old Korea
> I used to marvel at the huge icicles that hung
> heavy from our roof
> glistening from the bright sunshine.
> I would get my obba to break some off
> and we'd play sword-fights until they broke
> and our small hands were red with cold. . . .
> I remember our courtyard
> where brilliant yellow forsythias blazed every spring.
> Those little red flowers shaped like thin vases grew there too.
> Grandpa taught me how to suck at the bottom
> to taste the sweetness. . . .
>
> We left Korea before I finished the first grade.
> I grew up in the suburbs of Chicago, watching
> Scooby-doo and eating ham and cheese sandwiches
> with all-American ease.
> Korea grew up too
> and left my memories behind.
> They lay in my brain like dusty pictures
> losing their color with age.
> I have yet to see the new Korea.
> They tell me our old house was torn down.
> A condominium is standing on top of the spot. . . .
>
> My memories of Korea.
> They seem so strange sometimes
> like they are about someone else's childhood
> that I had stolen. . . .
> So I try to look for bridges
> to connect my two childhoods,
> to give meaning to my short existence in Korea
> before I became a hyphenated duality.

47. Kang (1937), pp. 162–63.

Someday I will go back to Korea
and look at my past in the face.
Try to reconcile my past and my present.
Figure out why my memories keep haunting me still and
maybe mourn for the person
I could have been if I had never been planted
somewhere else.
Grandpa used to tell me
those red flowers will taste just as sweet
in America.
I miss my grandfather a lot.[48]

48. Julie Kim, "Red and Yellow Dreams," *Kilmok: Korean American Perspectives Journal* 5 (University of Chicago, 1994): 12–13.

CHAPTER TEN

Korea's Place in the World

When the unified life of our country is cut in two . . . our country will be like a nail stuck in the flow of history.
—Paek Ki-wan

To visit either Korean state today is to encounter a past and a future that intermingle promiscuously: a white-coated yangban elder in horsehair hat playing cards in a park on Seoul's South Mountain, observed from the state-of-the-art exercise room of the Seoul Hilton; the skyscraper headquarters of the Daewoo Corporation towering over a raucous South Gate market that seems unchanged from the 1960s; a giant American military base at Yongsan now surrounded by an ever-expanding Seoul; peasants with backs bent carefully tending fields of red ginseng near the old Koryŏ capital at Kaesŏng; pedestrians in blue jackets and wide-brimmed worker's hats passing by the 105-story Yanggang Hotel in P'yŏngyang, a pyramid in the sky much like the TransAmerica building in San Francisco, allegedly erected to accommodate tourists in a country that admits as few as any in the world—and is therefore empty inside. (The Yanggang Hotel is the tallest skyscraper in East Asia, but reports say its interior has never been finished.)

If the internal milieu juxtaposes a century of contrasting images, externally the Korean peninsula is only beginning to emerge from two time warps. The Cold War was more frigid here than anywhere else in the world and has not ended: the peninsula is a museum of that world-ranging conflict. Added to that anachronism is a Second World War deep freeze: the Northeast Asian region remains locked in a 1940s settlement that easily outlived the end of American-Soviet rivalry and is best evidenced by the 100,000 American troops that continue to occupy Japan and South Korea. For these internal and external reasons, Korea cannot establish its own definitions of reality (and thus risks being misunderstood and misconstrued in the West, particularly in the United States), and the denouement to Korea's fractured modern history and its ultimate place in the world remains unresolved.

This chapter will return to the subject of Korea's relationship to the rest of the world, especially its relations with the United States and the persistence of Cold War structures; it will examine the defining crisis of the 1990s over North Korea's nuclear program and the eye-opening American reaction to that crisis; and it will take up the central question for the early part of the next century, namely, how the Korean peninsula might be reunified.

IMPENETRABLE BOUNDARIES?

Forty years after the Korean War ended, the two Koreas still face each other across a heavily fortified demilitarized zone, shaped by an errant decision fifty years ago to divide their country and by the civil war that followed. Both Koreas continue to be deeply deformed by the necessity to maintain an unrelenting struggle that might well have been ended with some abrupt and radical surgery in 1945. The Korean War itself solved nothing except to make another war an impossible route to reunification, but it did solidify armed bulwarks of containment, which the United States, the ROK, and the DPRK remain committed to, even in the post–Cold War world of the 1990s. Yet around the peninsula much has changed.

In great contrast with Europe, Northeast Asia was occupied unilaterally by the United States and Russia in 1945, a division followed within five years by a redivision corresponding to the bipolar structures of the Cold War. General Douglas MacArthur issued General Order Number One on August 15, 1945, excluding allied powers from the occupation of Japan, dividing Korea at the thirty-eighth parallel and Vietnam at the sixteenth parallel, and seeking to unify China under Chiang Kai-shek's rule by requiring Japanese soldiers to surrender to Nationalist forces. The Russians accepted the Korean division, while protesting their exclusion from the occupation of Japan and aiding local communists in coming to power in North Korea and Manchuria; but their troops promptly quite Manchuria in 1946 and left Korea in 1948. The only part of that 1945 East Asian division that did not hold was China, and as the Communists triumphed in 1948–49 a new division took place: that between Taiwan and the mainland. MacArthur ruled Japan as a benevolent emperor, while policing the fault lines of great-power conflict in Korea and China. The Pacific had become an American lake.

For a quarter century thereafter great-power strategic logic derived from the peninsula's promontory position in a world-ranging conflict. The bipolar fault lines bisected Korea; this small nation moved from the periphery to the center in the Cold War because its hot war began at the point where the two blocs intersected. The Korean War both solidified and vastly deepened the division of Northeast Asia. An undulating demilitarized zone replaced the thirty-eighth parallel and remains to this day the most heavily fortified line in the world; for a generation China was excluded from the postwar global system by threats of blockade and war. Japan also remilitarized, if modestly, as a result of the Korean War. Above all, the Korean War left an archipelago of American military installations throughout the noncommunist part of the region.

The long-term result of this history from 1945 to 1953 may be summarized as follows: the capitalist countries of the region tended to communicate with each other *through the United States,* a vertical regime solidified through bilateral defense treaties (with Japan, South Korea, Taiwan, and the Philippines) and conducted by a State Department that towered over the foreign ministries of these four countries. All became semisovereign states, deeply penetrated by American military structures (operational control of the South Korean armed forces, U.S. Seventh Fleet patrolling of the Taiwan Strait, defense dependencies for all four countries, military bases on all their territory) and incapable of independent foreign policy or defense initiatives. Horizontal contact between South Korea and North Korea or China was nonexistent, but was very much attenuated with Japan as well.

The capitalist countries "communicated" with the communist countries primarily through the American military, symbolized by the military talks at P'anmunjŏm, the developing war in Vietnam, chronic threats exchanged between the United States and the PRC, mini-crises like those over Quemoy and Matsu in the Taiwan Strait, periodic fracases with North Korea (the *Pueblo* in 1968, the EC-121 in 1969, and the "tree-cutting incident" in 1976), and all-around containment of the (relatively weak) Soviet position in Northeast Asia. There were minor demarches through the military curtain beginning in the mid-1950s, like low levels of trade between Japan and China, or Japan and North Korea. But the dominant tendency was a unilateral American regime heavily biased toward military forms of communication. Until the mid-1960s the political economy of the region, too, was primarily bilateral among the United States and its allies, with the smaller countries sustained by American aid grants (constituting five-sixths of ROK imports in the late 1950s).

The decade of the 1960s marked a watershed in beginning the transformation of the Northeast Asian system and bringing Korea back in touch with its neighbors. Thenceforth and to the present, economic exchange would be the driving force restitching ties among the nations of the region. As we have seen, the Kennedy administration was pivotal in this regard, inaugurating many policies directed toward drawing down the multifurcated military structures and bringing into play new economic relationships. In some ways this was a fulfillment of the original Achesonian "great crescent" conception of the late 1940s, linking Tokyo, "island Asia," and the Middle East, which was temporarily demolished by the North Korean invasion in 1950; and in others it anticipated changes later implemented by the Nixon administration—especially the Nixon Doctrine and his opening to China. The leitmotiv of Kennedy's strategy, one scripted by the national security adviser W. W. Rostow, as we have seen, was to bring Japan's economic influence back into the region. This resulted in the normalization of Japan-ROK relations in 1965, and both Taiwan and South Korea began industrializing under the banner of export-led development, with both learning much from Japan's combination of neomercantilism at home and oceans of exports to foreign markets. Richard Nixon opened relations with China in 1971, initially to draw down American involvement in the Vietnam War and to contain communism by communism, but after the normalization of U.S.-China relations and the epochal reforms instituted by Deng Xiaoping (both accomplished in December 1978), the economic character of China's interaction with East Asia and the world economy became the dominant tendency. Since the mid-1960s, in short, economic forces drove past or ran roughshod over the previously impervious security barriers hardened by the Korean War. However frozen its political division, Korea followed suit: today economic exchange is the main (and deepening) form of horizontal contact between the two Korean regimes, and between North Korea and the rest of the world.

If the Cold War ended in Europe only in 1989, the watershed changes in East Asian politics in the early and mid-1970s emptied Cold War logic of its previous meaning. With the emergence of the Sino-Soviet conflict, North Korea lost its joint backing by Moscow and Beijing and got instead a small war in 1969 between the big communist powers, just across its border along the Ussuri River. With Nixon's opening to China in 1971–72, both North and South Korea watched helplessly as their great-power benefactors cozied up to each other. With the conclusion of the Indochina War in 1975, obstacles to ending the Cold War throughout Asia seemed even fewer.

The new strategic logic of the 1970s had an immediate impact on

Korea. Originally the DPRK was the point country for a Sino-Soviet bloc that looked monolithic to outsiders. This was by far the best foreign policy alternative from P'yŏngyang's standpoint, lasting from 1949 to the early 1960s, when the Sino-Soviet conflict forced the DPRK to make a choice between Moscow and Beijing—and it predictably chose China. During the Cultural Revolution (1966–71) relations with China soured briefly, however, mainly because of "Red Guard" criticisms of Kim Il Sung's ample girth and abundant lifestyle. But Nixon's changes in 1971 energized both Seoul and P'yŏngyang; from 1972 through 1983 DPRK foreign policy sought a breakthrough in relations with the United States, as it tried to be the Korean beneficiary of Sino-American détente. The Nixon administration, as we have seen, withdrew one-third of the American troop contingent without heightening tension; instead, the North Koreans responded by virtually halting attempts at infiltration in the 1970s (whereas in 1968 more than one hundred soldiers had died along the DMZ and the American spy ship *Pueblo* had been seized) and by significantly reducing their defense budget. As we have also seen, both Koreas held secret talks, leading to the July 4, 1972, announcement on peaceful reunification. Within a year this initiative had effectively failed, but it remained as a reminder of what might be accomplished through enlightened and magnanimous diplomacy, and of the continuing salience of the unification issue.

Later on, American and Chinese policy shifted again, if less dramatically. When the Carter administration (1977–81) announced plans for a gradual but complete withdrawal of U.S. ground forces from Korea (air and naval units would remain deployed in or near Korea) and began assiduously playing "the China card" in world politics, a prolonged period of North Korean courting of Americans began. In 1977 Kim referred to President Jimmy Carter as "a man of justice," and the DPRK press momentarily dropped its calumny against the United States, including use of the term "U.S. imperialism." Kim gave interviews saying he was knocking on the American door, wanted diplomatic relations and trade, and would not interfere with American business interests in the South once Korea was reunified. The North Koreans also began using a term of opprobrium for Soviet imperialism, "dominationism" *(chibaejuŭi)*, their version of the common Chinese term used to vilify Moscow ("hegemonism"). P'yŏngyang also vastly deepened its relations with the Third World, sponsoring many exchanges with leaders of developing countries, and becoming a force in the nonaligned movement. By and large P'yŏngyang stayed close to the Chinese foreign policy line during the Carter years, while taking care not to antagonize the Soviets needlessly. When Vietnam invaded Cambodia in 1978, the North Koreans forcefully and publicly condemned the act, while maintaining a studied silence when China responded by invading Vietnam; thereafter Prince Norodom Sihanouk was a frequent guest in P'yŏngyang, developing a close friendship with Kim Il Sung that, no doubt, was aided by the villa and the cash subventions that Kim provided to him.[1]

The disorders in South Korea in 1979–80 and the emergence of the "new Cold War" on a world scale froze the Korean situation through much of the 1980s. The Carter administration dropped its program of troop withdrawal in 1979, after Carter's advisers finally succeeded in convincing him that it was a bad idea.[2] The Reagan administration invited the dictator Chun Doo Hwan to visit Washington in February 1981 as its first foreign policy act, something designed to bolster ROK stability. The United States committed itself to a modest but significant buildup of force and equipment levels in the South. In the early 1980s some 4,000 American personnel were added to the 40,000 already there, advanced F-16 fighters were sold to Seoul, and huge military exercises involving upwards of 200,000 American and Korean troops (called Team Spirit) were held toward the beginning of each year. Defense Secretary Caspar Weinberger declared in 1983 that Korea was "a vital interest for the United States,"[3] and also brought forward a five-year defense guidance, which suggested that what the document called "horizontal escalation" could mean that were the Soviets to attack in the Persian Gulf, the United States might respond by attacking at a point of its own choosing. Korea was such a point, the document said. This scenario truly horrified the North Koreans, and during the remaining Reagan years they shouted themselves hoarse in opposition to U.S. policy.

Sino-American relations warmed considerably in 1983, however, and

1. Sihanouk had the use of a villa sporting 200-square-foot bathrooms, with "heated floors to take off the chill in winter, and half a dozen bottles of toilet water, cream and deodorant—all marked 'Made in the D.P.R.K.' " (*New York Times*, July 22, 1980.) Sihanouk also directed a film in North Korea, in which he played an evil World War II Japanese officer seeking the virtue of a Cambodian maiden, played by his wife, Princess Monique. It was shot in Korean and dubbed in Cambodian. When the prince returned to his throne in Pnom Penh, Kim sent several hundred granite-faced Korean bodyguards as a permanent security detail.

2. Carter visited Seoul in June 1979 and, according to reporters who accompanied him, got so angry after a meeting with Park that he nearly overruled the reversal of the troop withdrawal policy that he had come to Seoul to announce. He sat arguing in the presidential limousine outside the U.S. embassy with National Security Adviser Zbigniew Brzezinski and Defense Secretary Harold Brown, their voices rising to the point that reporters knew something was wrong.

3. *Korea Herald*, April 17, 1983.

for the first time China said publicly that it wished to play a role in reducing tension in Korea; this was followed by a major DPRK initiative in January 1984 that called for the first time for three-way talks between the United States, the ROK, and the DPRK. Before this the DPRK had never been willing to sit down with both at the same time. (The Carter administration had made a similar proposal for three-way talks in 1979.) Right in the middle of this activity, however, a terrorist bombing in Rangoon, Burma, in October 1983 took out much of the South Korean cabinet (but narrowly missed President Chun) and demolished a Chinese diplomatic demarche on Korea. A Burmese court determined that North Koreans were behind the bombing, and that, combined with the Reagan buildup, made relations between Washington and P'yŏngyang as bad as in any period since the Korean War.[4]

From 1983 to 1987 P'yŏngyang tilted toward the Soviet Union. Relations warmed markedly, and Kim visited Moscow twice—his first visits in a quarter century. The Soviets upgraded the North Korean Air Force with MiG-23's, jet fighters that nonetheless reflected early-1960s technology. The advent of Mikhail Gorbachev, however, put a damper on this warming trend, as the Soviets systematically cut back on aid to P'yŏngyang or told it to use Soviet aid more wisely. A lot of criticism of the DPRK appeared in Soviet publications, the general idea being, Why should we give money to people who use it to build 105-story hotels for nonexistent tourists?

In the 1980s the DPRK became a significant actor in international arms trafficking, selling machine guns, artillery, light tanks, and other items to friendly countries such as Zimbabwe and Iran (North Korea traded weaponry for oil with Iran, accounting for as much as 40 percent of all Iranian arms imports during the long Iran-Iraq war). It also sold its own Scud rockets and transshipped Chinese Silkworm missiles to the Middle East, according to U.S. intelligence, although some analysts suggested that these might be Korean copies of this Chinese missile, since P'yŏngyang copied Soviet Scud missiles and even improved upon them. In spite of the Rangoon bombing and the tensions between the United States and North Korea, through most of the 1980s China encouraged Kim Il Sung to take the path of diplomacy and sought to sponsor talks between Washington and P'yŏngyang (talks that occasionally took place in

4. The Rangoon bombing remains something of a mystery, because it occurred just when Kim Il Sung was meeting with Deng Xiaoping in China, in search of a diplomatic breakthrough with the United States. Some observers therefore thought he had not approved it, and that someone else in the North Korean hierarchy had mounted this terrorist attack. Subsequent personnel changes suggested that this might well be true. But no one really knows.

Beijing between low-level diplomats). China also reached out to Seoul, and by the end of the 1980s had a much larger trade with South Korea than with North Korea, with freighters going back and forth directly across the Yellow Sea.

Until the 1970s DPRK foreign trade was almost wholly with the socialist bloc, but in the past two decades it has diversified imports and exports toward Japan, Western Europe, and various Third World nations. By the mid-1970s 40 percent of its trade was with noncommunist countries, and within the bloc only half was with the USSR; but by the late 1980s foreign exchange shortages and other difficulties left North Korea once again rather dependent on trade with the Soviet Union. Russian demands that it pay hard currency for oil and other items drastically hurt the DPRK's economy in the early 1990s. Exporting has been a regime priority for several years, although the North in no sense has an export-led economy like the South's. The focus on exports is to garner foreign exchange to import advanced technologies needed for further industrial growth, and to pay for imported oil; the exporting policy has not been successful to date.

Under Roh Tae Woo the Seoul government developed a "Nordpolitik" policy on the German model of "Ostpolitik," seeking to open talks and trade with P'yŏngyang. The founder of the Hyundai conglomerate, Chŏng Chu-yŏng, toured North Korea in January 1989 and announced a joint venture to promote tourism in the Diamond Mountains. Both sides offered to open the demilitarized zone to exchanges on the forty-fifth anniversary of liberation, in August 1990, but bitter wrangling between the two governments kept any exchanges from taking place, to great popular dismay. In the fall of 1990 for the first time prime ministerial talks were held—in Seoul in September, in P'yŏngyang in October. In 1991 both Koreas joined the United Nations, in spite of long-standing North Korean opposition to entering that body under two Korean flags. Roh's Nordpolitik appeared to achieve its greatest success on December 13, 1991, when the prime ministers of the ROK and the DPRK signed the Agreement on Reconciliation, Nonaggression, Cooperation, and Exchange at Seoul. Its twenty-five articles called for mutual recognition of the respective political systems, an end to mutual vilification and confrontation, "concerted efforts" to turn the Korean War armistice into a durable peace, guarantees of nonaggression, economic cooperation and exchange in many fields, and free travel through both halves of the country for the estimated ten million Koreans from families separated by the war. By the end of 1991 both sides had also signed an agreement pledging to make the Korean peninsula nuclear free. Even the Reverend Sun Myung Moon, a fervent anticommunist who had fled North Korea forty years earlier, showed up in North Korea in December 1991 to meet his relatives and to hold talks with Kim Il Sung.[5]

Shortly after the December 1991 agreement was signed, however, P'yŏngyang continued to denounce Roh Tae Woo as a "puppet," a "traitor," and the chieftain of "military fascist gangsters." Meanwhile, Seoul demanded a long prison term for a radical student leader arrested under Seoul's elastic National Security Law, charging him with "benefitting the enemy."[6] These events proved to be a better sign of future tendencies than the "epochal" December agreement, which, like the July 1972 accord, has never been implemented.

The reemergence of détente in the mid-1980s and the end of the Cold War as the decade closed provided a major opportunity to resolve the continuing Korean confrontation. South Korea has been much more effective than the North in exploiting these new opportunities. It pursued an active diplomacy toward China and the Soviet Union and various East European countries, saying it would favor trade and diplomatic relations with "friendly" communist regimes. This bore fruit in 1988 when most communist countries attended the Seoul Olympics, with only Cuba honoring the North Korean "boycott." The Soviets took the initiative in opening diplomatic relations with the South in September 1990; greeted with tremendous hype and fanfare by the ROK, the relationship between Seoul and Moscow has not progressed much since then—most of their exchanges have been economic, with Moscow mainly seeking huge amounts of aid. American-Soviet cooperation in reducing tensions and keeping the peace (for example, in the aftermath of the Iraqi invasion of Kuwait) raised hopes that their joint efforts might also be invoked in Korea, but the United States did not go nearly as far as the USSR in reaching out to the other side (it relaxed restrictions on travel and certain types of humanitarian trade with North Korea, but did little more than that). Once the Soviet Union disappeared in 1991, everyone understood the United States to be the major external player in the Korean situation. Meanwhile, the collapse of East European communism grievously damaged North Korean diplomacy, as Hungary, Yugoslavia, Poland, and other states opened diplomatic relations with Seoul. By 1992 Seoul had embassies in Moscow and Beijing, but the United States chose not to reciprocate by implementing the cross-recognition formula that it had so long advocated in the 1970s and 1980s. The main reason for this foot-

5. *Korean Report* no. 257 (Tokyo), Dec. 1991. Since then the Reverend Moon's close associates have visited North Korea many times, and his right-hand man and translator, the former KCIA operative Pak Bo Hi, attended Kim Il Sung's funeral in 1994. Many observers have speculated that Moon's operation has provided funding to P'yŏngyang.

6. KCNA, P'yŏngyang, Dec. 23, 1991.

dragging was Washington's concern with P'yŏngyang's nuclear intentions.

MYSTERIES AT YŎNGBYŎN

In the early 1990s the North Korean nuclear program and the American response to it stood in the way of further diplomatic progress in Korea. There is much to be said about this issue, [7] but for our purposes perhaps its greatest importance was to show just how volatile the Korean peninsula continues to be and how little most Americans still know about Korea, from the person in the street to the national commentators. Another Korean War nearly began in June 1994; had it happened, the mutual ignorance on both sides would not have been so different from that during the war in 1950: Washington and P'yŏngyang again stumbling blindly toward mutual slaughter over incomprehensible and incommensurable goals, once again with the peace of the world hanging in the balance.

Yŏngbyŏn is a relatively well-known Korean town about sixty miles north of P'yŏngyang. Its secluded geographic position led to its fortification at least by the early fifteenth century; later it became a scenic spot and pleasure resort for the yangban. Yŏngbyŏn had been a silk-producing town in the old days, and the North Koreans built a large synthetic-textile (mainly rayon) industry there, accounting for over 50 percent of the production in the area[8]—and leading some American intelligence observers to think that alleged nuclear reprocessing facilities observed by satellites might just be textile mills. Here is the way Lautensach described it in 1942: "Out of the way of the modern traffic routes the county seat of Yŏngbyŏn is concealed high above the meandering valley of the Kuryong River in a tremendous, well-preserved old Korean fortress sprawling out across the surrounding . . . dome-shaped granite mountains."[9]

By now viewers of American television news will have seen a stock film clip of the Yŏngbyŏn nuclear facility, but never have they been told the meaning of the ubiquitous slogan affixed to the roof: *charyŏk kaengsaeng,* a Maoist term meaning "self-reliance," literally "regeneration through one's own efforts." That was the North Korean justification for Yŏngbyŏn from the beginning—to substitute nuclear power in an energy

7. Peter Hayes has written many articles on the problem, but perhaps his best work is *Pacific Powderkeg* (1991). See also my articles on the North Korean nuclear issue in *Bulletin of the Atomic Scientists,* April 1992, *Nation,* Aug. and Nov. 1993, *Sekai* (Tokyo), Oct. 1993, and the Seoul publication *Dialogue,* Spring 1994.

8. *Korea Today* (P'yŏngyang), March 1979, pp. 41–43.

9. Lautensach (1945), p. 258.

regime dependent on domestic coal and imported petroleum. In other words, P'yŏngyang sought to do what Japan and South Korea have been doing for decades. It built a reactor that would utilize North Korea's substantial deposits of uranium; the problem was that such reactors produce plutonium from uranium, and plutonium, with a bit of refining, can become the high-grade fuel for nuclear weapons.

The DPRK obtained a small nuclear reactor for research purposes of perhaps 4-megawatt capacity from the USSR in 1962 and placed it under UN-watchdog International Atomic Energy Agency (IAEA) safeguards in 1977. It then built a 30-megawatt facility on the model of a 1950s-era British gas-graphite reactor known as the Calder Hall. Construction probably began around 1979, and it went into operation in 1987 at Yŏngbyŏn. No one paid much attention, including an IAEA that P'yŏngyang asked to come have a look—only to be told that North Korea had missed that year's deadline and would have to reapply for IAEA inspections. Subsequently, in 1989, American spy satellites monitored a 75- to 100-day shutdown of the reactor, while fuel rods were withdrawn and new fuel was added. The satellites picked up apparent evidence of another reactor, of 50- to 200-megawatt capacity, which some thought would come onstream in the early 1990s; government experts also claimed to have spied a building nearby that looked like a reprocessing facility (but which others thought might be a textile mill).[10]

Still no one paid much attention, until the Persian Gulf War came along and gave to the post–Cold War world a new category of international miscreant: the renegade or rogue state. From the American standpoint North Korea (if not Iraq) had always been a renegade state, outside the boundaries of any Western-defined international regime of control, but the collapse of the USSR also turned it loose as a rogue state. North Korea's sudden reemergence in American eyes thus came from its new prominence as a test case for other Third World problem countries, as the United States saw itself as the only superpower and found it necessary to monitor a Third World much more unruly than that of the defunct bipolar era: after all, the USSR policed its bloc even more assiduously than did the United States, preventing Iraq, Iran, North Korea, and many others from developing nuclear weapons (only China succeeded, and the USSR tried to block China when Khrushchev sundered nuclear sharing agreements and brought his experts home in 1959–60).

In the early 1990s I participated in a Carnegie Endowment study group on nonproliferation and the North Korean nuclear problem, with other scholars, congressional aides, and government officials (current and retired). Although those meetings were off the record, the discussions

10. *New York Times*, Nov. 10, 1991.

enabled me to evaluate the accuracy (more often, the inaccuracy) of press reports. Government observers were and are deeply divided on the DPRK's purposes at Yŏngbyŏn; some said it never constructed a bomb and perhaps did not want one, while others—particularly in the CIA—maintained a consistent estimate in the early 1990s that the North probably had one or two bombs and wanted the fuel to build many more. A small group thought the DPRK lacked the technology and know-how to manufacture a nuclear weapon, while another thought that it had no intention of developing atomic weapons and that its program was really focused on nuclear power generation. Their judgments relied upon the same satellite photography, infrared monitoring, and spy plane reconnaissance of Yŏngbyŏn that they all saw (but which they interpreted differently), and on broader estimates of the DPRK's scientific and technical capabilities.

The DPRK always denied that it had either the intention or the capability to produce nuclear weapons. Since the early 1980s it frequently called for the peninsula to be made a nuclear-free zone. But it also clearly played a dual game: when the USSR recognized Seoul in September 1990, P'yŏngyang's Central News Agency said ominously that this violated its 1961 defense treaty with Moscow, and therefore it might have to develop certain weapons it had theretofore relied upon its allies to provide. Although I think it unlikely that North Korea ever felt the comforting shade of a Soviet or Chinese nuclear umbrella, this public threat was not inclined to allay fears about its nuclear program. Furthermore, Washington insiders knew that in secret talks with the South in 1972, Kim Il Sung had abruptly blurted out that the two Koreas ought to work together to develop nuclear weapons.[11]

The DPRK probably decided in 1991, if not earlier, to develop a small-state deterrent for a country surrounded by powerful enemies, like Israel: to display enough activity to make possession of a nuclear device plausible to the outside world, but with no announcement of possession, in order to lessen the chance that those same enemies will determine to develop nuclear weapons (e.g., South Korea or Japan)—in short, to appear to arm itself with an ultimate trump card and keep everyone guessing whether and when the weapons might become available. (One expert documented South Korea's identical interest in the Israeli deterrent model.)[12] This is the only explanation for the Yoñgbyŏn facility's being built above ground, where it can be "seen" by spy satellites; if the North Koreans had not been interested in the world's discovering their

11. An apparently accurate transcript of these talks was leaked to a South Kŏrean magazine in 1989 (allegedly by the former KCIA director Yi Hu-rak); Kim's remarks caused a big stir.
12. Hayes (1991), p. 206.

program, they would have put it well below ground (as they have so much else, and as the Israelis did at their Dimona complex, where they reprocessed plutonium and built bombs eighty feet underground).[13]

If some worries were voiced from time to time in the late 1980s about the Yŏngbyŏn complex, the real clanging of alarm bells began just as the Persian Gulf War ended in 1991. Stanley Spector and Jacqueline Smith published an article in March 1991 entitled "North Korea: The Next Nuclear Nightmare,"[14] which encouraged Leslie Gelb to editorialize in the *New York Times* that North Korea was "the next renegade state," a country "run by a vicious dictator" with Scud missiles, "a million men under arms," and likely to possess nuclear weapons "in a few years." Another Iraq, in short.[15] It will be remembered that North Korea was not defeated in the Korean War: the 1953 settlement recognized a stalemate that merely restored the status quo ante. The United States and the DPRK remained technically at war thereafter (an armistice, not a peace treaty, closed off the hot war). This set of tropes was therefore quite amazing, instantly reconfiguring a North Korean enemy that Americans had been confronting at the DMZ for four decades into a different type of threat, where all the adjectives were new, but the Cold War demonization remained the same. The result was that "North Korea" became a Rorschach inkblot evoking Orientalist, anticommunist, racist, and outlaw imagery all in one neat package. Soon hardly a media mention of North Korea went unaccompanied by these same tropes. Furthermore, nearly every major media outlet, whether television or print, accepted uncritically various information about North Korea that had either been standard rhetoric for decades (and often that put out for foreign consumption by Seoul's intelligence services) or was demonstrably false.

Take this statement: "There's signs of a big buildup. . . . The [North Koreans] could be in Seoul in four hours if they threw in everything they have." James Wade got this in from an American engineer working for the U.S. Army—in 1960.[16] General Richard Stilwell, an old Korea hand and American intelligence operative, spent a good part of his adult life repeating the mantra that a Korean People's Army bellied up against the DMZ could be in Seoul within hours or days.[17] During the crisis over the

13. On this see Seymour Hersh, *The Samson Option: Israel's Nuclear Arsenal and American Foreign Policy* (New York: Random House, 1991), p. 196.

14. *Arms Control Today,* March 1991, pp. 8–13.

15. "The Next Renegade State," *New York Times,* April 10, 1991, op-ed page; see also *New York Times,* April 16, 1991.

16. Wade (1967), p. 23.

17. I had a local television debate with Stilwell in Pullman, Washington, in 1978 in which he argued that the United States needed "the guts to stand up to the commies in Korea."

seizure of the USS *Pueblo* in 1968, it was routine to read that 70 percent of the North Korean army was concentrated near the DMZ. Many similar claims were made during the hysteria in August 1976 over the North Koreans' having tried to trim a poplar tree in the DMZ (see below). Most American reporters in the 1990s had no immunity to such timeworn shibboleths, however, nor the inquisitiveness to ask what percentage of the South Korean Army was similarly "bellied up." (It is exceedingly rare ever to find a public statement that would answer this question, but in June 1994 *Time* magazine featured a map showing 90 percent of the ROK Army between Seoul and the DMZ.)[18]

For the next several years after the Persian Gulf War, "crises" between Washington and P'yŏngyang arose with predictable regularity: every November you could count on one, for example, since that was the month usually chosen for high-level confabs between the Pentagon and its Korean counterparts in Seoul. In November 1991 just before Defense Secretary Richard Cheney's visit to Seoul, the two capitals jointly cranked up the pressure, with an anonymous Defense Department official remarking to reporters that if North Korea "missed Desert Storm, this is a chance to catch a rerun," and an ROK Defense Ministry white paper saying the North's atomic bomb project "must be stopped at any cost."[19] At the time the *Chicago Tribune* twice called editorially for a preemptive strike on Yŏngbyŏn,[20] and most television and newspaper reporters accepted the CIA's estimate that North Korea was months away from having a nuclear weapon, if it had not made one already. Secretary of Defense Cheney soon visited Seoul and announced that the United States would put off previously scheduled American troop withdrawals until the North allowed IAEA inspections. Other reports in this November 1991 flurry, however, indicated that some U.S. government experts thought the DPRK was five to ten years away from producing a bomb; the real worry was that it might sell reprocessed plutonium to Middle Eastern states. Soon the spotlight on North Korea intensified again. George Bush made his obligatory, presidential belly-up-to-the-DMZ trip in January 1992, and unnamed officials traveling with him told reporters that they would require "a mandate to roam North Korea's heavily guarded military sites at will" before they could be sure of the DPRK's

18. *Time*, Dec. 13, 1993. My educated guess would be that this has been true since the internal guerrilla threat disappeared in the mid-1950s. Before and during the Korean War, however, large segments of the army were dispatched southward to fight interior guerrillas.

19. *Tribune*, Nov. 26, 1991; *New York Times*, Nov. 10, 1991.

20. *Tribune* editors, Nov. 26, 1991; Stephen Chapman, *Tribune* editorial writer, Nov. 14, 1991.

capabilities[21]—an astonishing statement, since for forty years Americans have gained access to North Korea only rarely, and then only for carefully chaperoned visits. Now American officials wanted to roam its military bases. The reasoning was this: the United States really had very little hard information on North Korea's nuclear program, but that only made matters worse; post–Persian Gulf War inspections of Iraq had taught experts how much can be concealed from satellites.

November 1992 found the media engrossed with presidential election news, but a year later another spate of scare stories dominated the American news (on the weekend of November 5–7, 1993, coinciding with Defense Secretary Les Aspin's visit to Seoul). The *Chicago Tribune* headlined its November 7 issue this way: "U.S. Fearful of N. Korean Attack on South." This wire service article quoted officials flying home from Korea with Aspin to the effect that North Korea was massing its troops along the border, probably had the bomb, and was led either by a "dying" Kim Il Sung or "a more radical and perhaps even psychotic" Kim Jong Il. The fine print at the end of the *Chicago Tribune* article, however, reported the exact opposite: sources at the State Department knew of no unusual troop movements or massing at the parallel; the *New York Times* had Aspin saying, "There was no evidence that North Korea was now producing or reprocessing plutonium."[22] The various sources expressed no opinion on the sanity of "the Dear Leader," but for the past twenty-five years of Kim's involvement in politics, the South Korean intelligence services have put out the line that he's dangerously unstable and probably psychotic.

Mimetic American broadcasting is a bit harder to excerpt, but on the same weekend (November 5–7, 1993), from CBS "Evening News" to the Fox Channel and even National Public Radio, wild charges circulated about crazed North Koreans readying an atomic bomb, forbidding access to international inspectors and concentrating 70 percent of their army on the border with South Korea—the implication being that they might attack at any minute. On Sunday, November 7, President Clinton told "Meet the Press" that "any attack on South Korea is an attack on the U.S.,"[23] and on November 18 CBS "Evening News" again ran a scare story saying North Korean nuclear weapons were the single greatest threat to world peace today. In trying to watch as much of this television coverage in the three years from 1991 to 1994 as I could, I did not once

21. Quoted in *New York Times*, Jan. 6, 1992. These officials were also quoted as saying, "What we don't know about the North is still terrifying. . . ."
22. *New York Times*, Nov. 4, 1993 (and also reported in the *Times* on Nov. 3, with the words put into the mouth of one of Aspin's aides).
23. *New York Times*, Nov. 8, 1993.

see a broadcast that went into what P'yŏngyang constantly spoke about, namely, the long history of American nuclear threats against it.

The disturbingly mimetic quality of print and TV stories on North Korea could be found across the spectrum of American journalism, from right to left and from the worst to the best. Over and over again the same unexamined facts and assumptions intruded every article. Here are two examples from the November 1993 war-scare episode. This is what *Newsweek* said:

> It is one of the scariest scenarios the post-cold-war world has produced: an economically-desperate North Korea, its leadership as isolated as ever, rejects every effort the West makes to persuade it to abandon its steadfast pursuit of a nuclear bomb. Instead, it issues warnings about the possibility of war, which are promptly echoed by a high-ranking U.S. Defense Department official visiting Seoul. North Korea's troops, 70 percent of which are gathered within sprinting distance of the Korean peninsula's tripwire demilitarized zone, go on combat alert and Communist Party officials gather at a hurriedly called meeting in Pyongyang, the North Korean capital. Last week in Korea, the nightmares all seemed to be coming true.[24]

Now read Charles Krauthammer, an editorialist for the *Washington Post:*

> There is a real crisis brewing in a place the cameras don't go. The single most dangerous problem, the impending nuclearization of North Korea, is not yet on the national radar screen. It will be. . . . None will sleep well with nukes in the hands of the most belligerent and paranoid regime on earth. The North Korean bomb would be controlled by either Kim Il Sung, the old and dying Great Leader, or his son and successor, Dear Leader Kim Jong Il. . . . [u]npredictable, possibly psychotic, [he] would be the closest thing to Dr. Strangelove the nuclear age has seen.[25]

Here is David Sanger, the main *New York Times* reporter covering the North Korean nuclear issue, writing at the end of 1992:

> One of the world's most menacing powers [is now] bereft of its cold-war allies and on the defensive about a nuclear-weapons project that ranks among the biggest threats in Asia. . . . "North Korea could explode or implode," said General RisCassi, the commander of the 40,000 U.S. troops who remain here. As the Stalinist Government of Kim Il Sung is driven into a corner, its economy shrinking and its people running short of food, General [blank] contends, "it is a debateable matter" whether the country will change peacefully or lash out as it

24. *Newsweek*, Nov. 15, 1993, p. 41.
25. Charles Krauthammer, "North Korea: The World's Real Time Bomb," *Washington Post*, reprinted in *Chicago Tribune*, Nov. 7, 1993.

> once did before. . . . One senior [blank] Administration official said last week that North Korea already had enough plutonium to build a crude nuclear weapon. . . . [t]his has helped fuel . . . fear that the country that has bombed airliners and tried to kill the South Korean cabinet would make one last lunge for survival.[26]

Sanger in the *New York Times,* six months later:

> Experts monitoring North Korea say they are increasingly concerned that the country may be preparing to use 50 tons of uranium now fueling a large reactor as raw material for nuclear weapons. . . . [t]he 50 tons would be enough to produce two or three nuclear bombs. . . . General RisCassi . . . said he was "increasingly concerned that North Korea could slide into an attack as an uncontrollable consequence of total desperation or internal instability."[27]

Sanger in the *New York Times,* November 1993:

> A top military officer . . . said tonight that the challenge posed by Pyongyang's continued refusal to allow international inspection "is in many ways much tougher and more dangerous than . . . Bosnia." . . . There is evidence . . . that North Korea has extracted plutonium from its nuclear waste in recent years, probably enough to build one or more crude weapons.[28]

Reporters, these and many others, routinely wrote that North Korea has refused inspections: yet at the time of the last excerpted Sanger article ("Pyongyang's continued refusal to allow international inspection"), North Korea had allowed six formal inspections of its Yŏngbyŏn site by the IAEA in the period May 1992–February 1993. North Korea is perhaps more jealous of its national sovereignty than any other postcolonial state, but under American pressure it still went ahead and opened itself to unprecedented inspections by the IAEA—an agency that routinely uses information gotten from U.S. intelligence through satellite reconnaissance of North Korean territory.[29] The day before he wrote this article, Sanger had reported one of Les Aspin's aides as saying, "We have no evidence that they are extracting or reprocessing plutonium." Sanger then added that in the past *the CIA* said "it suspects North Korea already has enough plutonium to make at least one crude weapon."[30] That is, a

26. David E. Sanger, *New York Times,* Dec. 16, 1992.
27. Sanger, *New York Times,* May 5, 1993.
28. Sanger, *New York Times,* Nov. 4, 1993.
29. A rare public admission of this fact came from the IAEA director Hans Blix, in an interview with Nayan Chanda of the *Far Eastern Economic Review,* Feb. 10, 1994. See also *Bulletin of the Atomic Scientists,* June 1993, p. 16, and *New York Times,* March 13, 1993.
30. Sanger, *New York Times,* Nov. 4, 1993.

CIA estimate one day is turned into Mr. Sanger's statement the next that "there is evidence" of this.

Each article and editorial (the difference between news stories and editorials often disappeared) assumed without question that North Korea is a nightmare regime, that it intends to and has the capability to develop nuclear weapons, that it probably has enough plutonium to do so already, that it has prevented inspections by the appropriate agency (the IAEA), that this is a major crisis for U.S. foreign policy, and that American officials are so reliable on the issue that the reporter need not question their judgment, but instead may make it his or her own. That North Korea is a menace has been a standard claim since 1946: Kim Il Sung came to power in February of that year, and the following month brought the first alarms about an attack on the South. That North Korea was teetering on the verge of collapse with a basket-case economy has been a stock line since the Berlin wall fell.[31]

The point is not that North Korea is a nice place, or that it is beyond suspicion, or that P'yŏngyang has a better media policy: quite to the contrary, its policy for half a century has been to pile lie upon lie, exaggeration upon exaggeration, even when it would be more convenient and helpful to its cause to tell the truth. But that is what we have learned to expect from communist regimes. What is the excuse for a lemming-like, mimetic, and ultimately ignorant media in a raucous democracy like that in the United States, in spite of its many (regrettably post facto) protests about how the Pentagon herded the media like cattle during the Persian Gulf War?

It is now commonplace to blame this media accommodation on the celebrity status of anchorpeople and op-ed-level reporters and the fleeting sound bites of daily television, leading journalists to seek not just the access they need but power and glory to go with it, and to shrink their prose to acceptable (that is, unacceptable) brevity. But the greatest problem is simply the asymmetry of America and Korea, a general problem of incommensurability—namely, that the United States for fifty years has meant everything to Korea, but Koreans mean so little to the United States. The media attention span for Korea is next to nil unless there is a crisis to discuss.

Koreans who favor the South may think it is politically useful when North Korea is demonized and caricatured, but they shouldn't take much satisfaction: it is a disturbing fact that mainstream American journalism was no more help in understanding the North Korean nuclear problem than in explicating black-Korean relations during the 1992 Los Angeles

31. See, for example, Nick Eberstadt, "The Coming Collapse of North Korea," *Wall Street Journal,* June 26, 1990.

riots. Does this not say something quite damning about how many Americans have come to any level of respect for Koreans and their history, fifty years after our daily involvement in Korean affairs began? (Distortions of the nuclear conflict are in fact more understandable, because the nature of the issue required deep knowledge of U.S.-Korean relations, the military balance on the peninsula, nuclear physics, and nuclear-capable weaponry.) Nor can Americans in general rest easy with a gullible and uninformed media: some fine morning they may wake up to find that their sons and daughters are fighting in Korea again, with no idea how the war might have started or what its real causes might have been; the Pentagon war machine would again deploy its democracy-blotting media regime ("Pentavision"),[32] and this time no one will be sure that the war might not escalate to a regional if not a global holocaust.

FROM NEAR-WAR TO RELAXATION

The most dangerous crisis involving Washington and P'yŏngyang since the Korean War came in early 1993 and lasted for eighteen months. It began for the American press on March 12, 1993, when North Korea announced that it would withdraw from the Nuclear Non-Proliferation Treaty (NPT). Once again Leslie Gelb (by then head of the Council of Foreign Relations) held forth, arguing that North Korea's nuclear activity would bring on "the next crisis," where another "bad guy" like Saddam might soon test the mettle of "the sane nation[s]."[33] For Congressman John Murtha (Democrat of Pennsylvania), chairman of the House Appropriations Subcommittee on Defense, North Korea had become "America's greatest security threat"; if it did not let its nuclear facilities be inspected, he said in March, the United States ought to knock them out with "smart weapons."[34] By this time it was routine for influential American analysts to argue that Kim Il Sung was evil or insane or both, that his regime ought to be overthrown, and that if necessary his nuclear facilities should be taken out by force.[35]

For North Korea, however, the crisis began on January 26, 1993, when the newly inaugurated President Bill Clinton announced that he would go ahead with the Team Spirit games, which George Bush had suspended a year earlier and then revived for 1993. In late February, General

32. See Cumings (1992).

33. *New York Times*, March 21, 1993, op-ed page.

34. *Chicago Tribune*, March 18, 1993.

35. A recent example is Fred C. Ikle, "Response," *National Interest* 34 (Winter 1993–94): 39.

Lee Butler, head of the new U.S. "Strategic Command," announced that he was retargeting strategic nuclear weapons (i.e., hydrogen bombs) meant for the old USSR, on North Korea (among other places). At the same time the new CIA chief, James Woolsey, testified that North Korea was "our most grave current concern."[36] By mid-March 1993, tens of thousands of American soldiers were carrying out war games in Korea again, and in came the B-1B bomber, B-52's from Guam, several naval vessels carrying cruise missiles, and the like: whereupon the North pulled out of the NPT. It is a basic principle of the nonproliferation regime that countries without nuclear weapons not be threatened by those that possess them,[37] and since the demise of the USSR, American war games in Korea aim only at the North. By threatening to leave the NPT, the DPRK played a strong card; implicitly it raised the specter of other near-nuclear powers' doing the same, when the current NPT was due for renegotiation in 1995 and major countries like Japan and India were unhappy about it.

Once Team Spirit was over, the North agreed to high-level talks with the United States and subsequently (on June 11, 1993) suspended its withdrawal from the NPT. That Team Spirit and other U.S. nuclear threats were what motivated the North could not be clearer from reading the North Korean press, which had since the fall 1992 American elections warned against resuming the games. Yet amid the usual frothy bombast against American imperialism, all during this "crisis" P'yŏngyang continued to call for good relations with the United States. The other issue that energized P'yŏngyang in early 1993 was the IAEA's demand to carry out "special inspections" of undeclared sites in North Korea, including one that the IAEA said was a nuclear waste dump. The IAEA had never before demanded such an inspection for any other country, but it was under international pressure for not having ferreted out several sites in Iraq, discovered after Baghdad was defeated. The North resisted these inspections on two grounds: first, that the IAEA utilized American intelligence to ferret out new sites to visit (which it did), and that since the United States was a belligerent in Korea this violated the mandate of the IAEA; second, that the IAEA has passed the results of its inspections on to the United States, and should the DPRK allow this to

36. *New York Times*, Feb. 24, 25, 1993.

37. This was expressed in UN Security Council resolution no. 255, March 7, 1968. In order to obtain the requisite votes from nonnuclear states to get the NPT through the UN, the United States, Great Britain, and the Soviet Union committed themselves to aid any "victim of an act or an object of a threat of aggression in which nuclear weapons are used." Quoted in Hayes (1991), p. 214.

continue, the United States would eventually want to open up all DPRK military facilities to the IAEA.[38] (As we saw above, that is precisely what some high-level American officials advocated.)

The desire for additional inspections grew out of a complicated and, on the basis of public information, unresolvable conflict between North Korea and the IAEA over the interpretation of data on samples of plutonium that the North extracted when it renewed the fuel in its reactor in 1989. P'yŏngyang claimed it reprocessed only a small sample of this fuel, whereas the American CIA claimed it processed as much as eleven kilograms (i.e., the entire fuel load removed in 1979), and the IAEA never declared its own preference between the American and the Korean positions: it just wanted to inspect the waste dump.

So, here was the intricately raveled knot of the disagreement in 1993–94, with the IAEA demanding inspection of an alleged waste site and the North Koreans claiming that this site was a military installation and therefore off-limits, while lambasting the IAEA for following the desiderata of the DPRK's sworn enemy, the United States, and for not demanding equal time to see what the United States might be doing at its many installations in South Korea. And as if someone had been trying to feed the paranoia of the North Koreans and tell them to summon even more of the blank recalcitrance for which they are justly famous, the *New York Times* featured an essay by a well-placed expert who referred darkly to "faddish and misguided notions" in Washington's new strategic war plans—such as "forming a nuclear expeditionary force aimed at China and the third world."[39] Little wonder that the DPRK worked assiduously on its medium-range (600 miles) missile, the Nodong 1, launching it well into the Japan Sea during a test in June 1993, banging the target precisely at a distance of 300 miles—and making no bones about its purpose this time. The Nodong 1 is a Scud missile with additional engines wrapped around its waist, giving it medium-range thrust; foreign experts are not sure whether the precise targeting of the missile was an accident or an indication of the North's technological prowess.[40]

38. KCNA, P'yŏngyang, Feb. 22, 1993. In fact, the IAEA had sent its plutonium samples to Washington for examination, since its technology was not good enough to determine how much reprocessing the North might have done. I do not know if P'yŏngyang was aware of this, but in my reading of the North Korean press, the regime never mentioned it.

39. Bruce D. Blair (a senior fellow at the Brookings Institution), "Russia's Doomsday Machine," *New York Times*, Oct. 8, 1993.

40. The KCNA referred in Sept. 1993 to a "regular missile launching exercise in the DPRK," which Japanese authorities were "making quite a noise about," wishing to add "a 'missile problem' to the 'nuclear problem,' " in order to block normalization of relations. It justified the missile test as a necessary measure of self-defense, given that Japan is dotted with American military bases of all kinds. See KCNA, DPRK Foreign Ministry statement issued Sept. 24, 1993. (It is highly unusual for KCNA to report any DPRK military exercise.)

Whatever the truth about North Korea's nuclear program, it played a masterful diplomatic game after its support from the Soviet bloc ended and the USSR collapsed. By its negotiations, confrontations, and prevarications with the United States and the IAEA, P'yŏngyang got one concession after another out of the United States—withdrawal of nuclear weapons from South Korea (in the fall of 1991), postponement of Team Spirit war games, and the first high-level U.S.-DPRK talks ever. If we assume that P'yŏngyang's real goal was to build weapons, it had solid justifications for going nuclear: after all, it could easily make the classic argument that it is merely engaged in deterrence—that once both sides have nuclear weapons, the resulting Mexican standoff negates the possibility of use, and that a DPRK weapon returns the peninsula to the status quo ante 1991. Nearly all the American press commentary ignored this simple fact: the DPRK was the target of periodic nuclear threats and extended nuclear deterrence on the part of the United States for decades, yet until now it has possessed no such weapons itself.

THE BACKGROUND TO AMERICAN NUCLEAR POLICIES IN KOREA

After the Korean War ended, the United States introduced nuclear weapons into South Korea, in spite of the armistice agreement, which prohibited the introduction of qualitatively new weaponry. It took this drastic step primarily to stabilize the volatile civil war. In 1953 Syngman Rhee had opposed any armistice settlement, refused to sign the agreement when it was made, and frequently threatened to reopen the war. In November 1953 Vice-President Nixon visited Korea "and sought to extract written assurances from President Rhee 'that he is not going to start the war up again on the gamble that he can get us involved in his effort to unite Korea by force.' " He got no such written assurance, but in the absence of it the American commander was directed, in a highly secret "annex" circulated only to a few American leaders, to secure "prompt warning of any decision by Rhee to order an attack" and to prevent its issuance or receipt by ROKA field commanders.[41] The implication, of course, was that American intelligence would monitor activity in the presidential mansion and intercept new orders for war.

In spite of being hamstrung in this way, Rhee well knew that there were Americans who supported his provocative behavior and that they were critically placed people who advocated the use of nuclear weapons, should the war be reignited and the act clearly laid at the communist door. Among them was the chairman of the JCS, Admiral Arthur Rad-

41. Macdonald (1992), pp. 18–20.

ford, who at a conference between the State and Defense Departments in September 1956 had "bluntly stated the military intention to introduce atomic warheads into Korea."

On January 14, 1957, the NSC Planning Board, at the instruction of President Eisenhower, "prepared an evaluation of four alternative military programs or Korea." A key question was "the kinds of nuclear-capable weapons to be introduced, and the question of storage of nuclear warheads in Korea." In the ensuing six months of discussions, Secretary of State Dulles agreed with the Joint Chiefs of Staff that such weapons should be sent to Korea. There were two problems, however: the armistice agreement and Syngman Rhee. A subparagraph in the agreement (section 13d) barred both sides from introducing new types of weapons into the Korean theater. Radford simply wanted unilaterally to suspend section 13d, since in his view it could not be "interpreted" to allow nuclear weapons. Dulles, ever the legalist, conditioned his support of the JCS proposal on the provision of "publishable evidence confirming Communist violations of the armistice sufficient to justify such action to our Allies and before the UN." The problem was that the "publishable evidence" was not satisfactory, because the communist side had not seriously violated section 13d. It had introduced new jet aircraft, but so had the United States, and neither innovation was considered a radical uprading of capabilities. Nuclear weapons were quite a different matter. This bothered the British, but the United States went ahead in spite of their worries and in June 1957 relieved itself of its section 13d obligations.[42]

There remained the problem of Syngman Rhee. Unverified intelligence reports in February 1955 "spoke of meetings in which Rhee told Korean military and civilian leaders to prepare for military actions against north Korea." In October came reports that he had ordered plans for the retaking of Kaesŏng and the Ongjin peninsula, firmly in North Korean territory since the armistice, and in 1956 came more alarms and diversions. Meanwhile, no doubt unbeknownst to Rhee, the Eisenhower administration in August 1957 had approved NSC 5702/2, a major revision of Korea policy that approved the stationing of nuclear weapons in Korea and, in what one official called "a small change," allowed for the possibility of "U.S. support for a unilateral ROK military initiative in response to a mass uprising, Hungarian style, in north Korea."[43] This is an amazing mouthful. It may have been a response to rumors around that time that a North Korean general had tried to defect across the DMZ with his whole division in tow, or it may merely have been a harbinger of the thinking

42. Macdonald (1992), pp. 23, 78–79.
43. Macdonald (1992), pp. 23–24, 80.

that subsequently led to the Bay of Pigs fiasco in Cuba (a small provocation might touch off a general uprising against communism). It was, however, exactly what Rhee and his allies were looking for; who knows if they got wind of it, but John Foster Dulles certainly did.

Dulles was the man, it will be remembered, who famously eyeballed Kim Il Sung across the thirty-eighth parallel a week before the war started. He appears to have spent the rest of his life with unsettling whispers from that sudden Sunday, as if Banquo's ghost were shaking his gory locks. At an NSC meeting in 1954 he worried that the North might start the war up again—and in a rather creative fashion: Dulles "thought it quite possible that the Communists would launch their attack by infiltrating ROK units and staging an attack on the Communist lines in order to make it appear as though hostilities had been started on ROK initiative."[44] At several other high-level meetings Dulles worried aloud that the United States would not know how a new war might start in Korea, and that Rhee might well start it. At the 168th meeting of the NSC, in October 1953, Dulles had warned that "all our efforts" must be to forestall a resumption of war by Rhee; in 1957, at the 332d meeting, he still worried that Rhee might "start a war"; two weeks later he said that "if war were to start in Korea . . . it was going to be very hard indeed to determine which side had begun the war."[45]

It is in this specific context that Dulles lent his agreement to the JCS's desire to place nuclear weapons in Korea. Pursuing the civil war deterrent that Acheson had applied to Korea before the war, he wanted to restrain both sides. Hotheads like Rhee and Kim Il Sung would think twice before starting a war that would rain nuclear destruction on the peninsula. Rhee had not shrunk from advocating the use of the H-bomb to have his way; he shocked even his Republican supporters by calling for its use in a joint address to Congress in 1954. But Dulles's nukes would be kept under exclusive American control and would be used only in the event of a massive and uncontainable North Korean invasion.

In January 1958 the United States positioned 280-mm nuclear cannons and Honest John nuclear-tipped missiles in South Korea, and a year later the air force "permanently stationed a squadron of nuclear-tipped Matador cruise missiles in Korea." With a range of 1,100 kilometers, the Matadors were aimed at China and the USSR as well as North Korea.[46] By the mid-1960s Korean defense strategy was pinned on routine plans to use nuclear weapons very early in any new war. As a 1967 Pentagon war game script put it, "The twelve ROKA and two U.S. divisions in South

44. Eisenhower Library, Anne Whitman file, NSC, 179th Mtg, box 5, Jan. 8, 1954.
45. Ibid., boxes 4 and 9.
46. Hayes (1991), p. 35.

Korea had . . . keyed their defense plans almost entirely to the early use of nuclear weapons." In January 1968 the North Koreans seized the U.S. spy ship *Pueblo,* capturing the crew and keeping it in prison for eleven months: "the initial reaction of American decisionmakers was to drop a nuclear weapon on P'yŏngyang. . . . [T]he fact that all the U.S. F-4 fighter planes held on constant alert on Korean airfields were loaded only with nuclear weapons did not help the leaders to think clearly."[47]

U.S. atomic demolition mines (ADM) were defensive weapons designed to be used in South Korea, "to contaminate an advance area and to stop an armored attack," as one ADM engineer put it; ADMs weighed only sixty pounds and yet had a 20-kiloton explosive force; "you could get two weeks worth of contamination out of it so that an area was impassable."[48] The ADMs were moved around in jeeps and placed by special teams who carried them in backpacks; meanwhile, U.S. helicopters, as the *Washington Post* pointed out in 1974, routinely flew nuclear weapons near the DMZ. That one of them might stray across the DMZ during a training exercise (as a small reconnaissance helicopter did in December 1994) and give P'yŏngyang an atomic bomb was a constant possibility. Meanwhile, foreward deployment of nuclear weapons bred a mentality of "use 'em or lose 'em"; even a small North Korean attack might be cause enough to use them, lest they fall into enemy hands.[49] In 1975 Richard "Dixie" Walker, later the American ambassador to Korea during the Chun Doo Hwan regime, wrote this:

> The presence of American conventional and even tactical nuclear forces in Korea helps to confirm strategic guarantees for Tokyo and to discourage any Japanese thoughts about a French solution: a force de frappe of their own. This is a fact well understood by leaders of many political persuasions in Tokyo and also appreciated in Peking.[50]

In other words, Korean lives were hostage to an American policy of dual containment: containing the communist enemy and constraining the Tokyo ally.

The commander most enamored of nuclear weapons for both defensive and offensive use was General Richard Stilwell, who originated the Team Spirit war games, which began in the late 1970s and continued into the 1990s. Team Spirit exercises were the largest in the world, often including 200,000 troops, of which about 70,000 would be Americans—those already in Korea and others flown in for the games. In Stilwell's

47. Hayes (1991), pp. 47–48.
48. Quoted in Hayes (1991), p. 49.
49. Hayes (1991), pp. 50, 58.
50. Quoted in Hayes (1991), p. 59.

strategy, the games were "a dry run for a retaliatory attack on the north and a precursor of the Airland Battle doctrine" of the 1980s, emphasizing offensive strikes behind enemy lines.[51] A famous August 1976 incident illustrated the extraordinary "trip wire" nature of the DMZ confrontation, where a new war could occur on almost any day. Some American and Korean soldiers had entered a forbidden zone of the DMZ near P'anmunjŏm to "trim a poplar tree," which the United States said was obstructing its vision northward. (The poplar stood alone by itself; anyone who has been to P'anmunjŏm knows that the surroundings are largely denuded of trees, since the area took such a pounding in the war.) A North Korean team confronted the trimming team, and in the fight that ensued a North Korean grabbed an ax from one of the Americans and then killed two American soldiers with it. This was an unfortunate incident, but a completely predictable one given the ratcheted-up tension of this insanely militarized "demilitarized zone."

General Stilwell put U.S.-ROK forces on high alert (for the first time since 1953) during this confrontation, and festooned the Korean theater with American force—an aircraft carrier task force came to Korean waters, and a phalanx of nuclear-capable B-52's lifted off from Guam and flew up the peninsula toward the DMZ, "veering off at the last moment." According to one analyst, Stilwell asked permission from the Pentagon (and received it) to delegate to his subordinates the authority to initiate artillery and rocket fire, should they lose communications with him and be unable to consult, yielding the possibility that tactical nuclear weapons might be used without central command and control. Now a joint U.S.-ROK task force entered the joint security area, with seven helicopter gunships escorting another twenty helicopters carrying a full rifle company protecting them. They proceeded finally to chop down the offending limbs on the poplar tree.[52] Meanwhile, another Washington informant, whom I cannot name, told me that it was actually Stilwell who exercised "restraint" in this episode; he was fearful that back in Washington Henry Kissinger might want to start a war, in order to further the lame-duck Gerald Ford's chances in the upcoming elections.

In 1991 I heard a high-level, retired official and former commander of U.S. forces in Korea give an off-the-record presentation of U.S. strategy as it had developed by the 1980s: (1) The United States planned to use tactical nuclear weapons in the very early stages of a new Korean conflict, at "H + 1," or within one hour of the outbreak of war, if large masses of North Korean troops were attacking south of the DMZ. This

51. Hayes (1991), p. 60.
52. Hayes (1991), pp. 59–62.

he contrasted with the established strategy in Europe, which was to delay an invasion with conventional weapons and then use nuclear weapons only if necessary to stop the assault. The logic was that we dared not use nuclear weapons in Europe, because the other side had them, except in the greatest extremity, but we could use them in Korea because it didn't. South Korean commanders, he said, had gotten used to the idea that the United States would use nuclear weapons at an early point in a war with North Korea.

(2) The "AirLand Battle" strategy developed in the mid-1970s called for early, quick, deep strikes into enemy territory, again with the likely use of nuclear weapons, especially against hardened underground facilities (of which there are many in North Korea). In other words, the strategy itself implies "rollback" rather than simple containment of a North Korean invasion.

(3) Neutron bombs—or "enhanced radiation" weapons—might well be used if North Korean forces occupied Seoul, in order to kill the enemy but save the buildings.

(4) North Korean forces both expanded and redeployed in the late 1970s as a response to the AirLand Battle doctrine. The redeployment led to the stationing of nearly 80 percent of their ground forces near the DMZ. American and South Korean sources routinely cite this expansion and redeployment as evidence of North Korea's aggressive intent, as we have seen; in fact, it was done so that as many soldiers as possible could get into the South (regardless of how a war started), to mingle with ROK Army forces and civilians before nuclear weapons would be used, thus making their use less likely.[53]

This harrowing scenario became standard operating procedure in the 1980s, the kind written into military field manuals; the annual Team Spirit military exercises played out AirLand Battle games.[54] These implied an initial containment of a North Korean attack, followed by thrusts into the North, ultimately to seize and hold P'yŏngyang and topple the regime. (In December 1993 the *New York Times* detailed such plans in a front-page article, erroneously stating that they had just been developed.) Such war games were also conducted in Korea because in the early 1980s NATO governments and strong peace movements would not allow similar exercises in Europe.

The Persian Gulf War, however, again according to this source, caused a reevaluation of the role of nuclear weapons. With "smart" bombs that reliably reach their targets, high-yield conventional weapons are more useful than nuclear warheads with their messy and uncontrollable

53. This point is also made in Hayes (1991), pp. 148–49.

54. Hayes (1991), p. 91.

effects. The army, he said, wanted out of battlefield nuclear weapons as soon as possible. Thus American policy reached a point where its own interests dictated withdrawal of obsolescent nuclear weapons from Korea in the fall of 1991. (The weapons removed included forty 203-mm and thirty 155-mm nuclear artillery shells, plus large numbers of ADMs. Official spokesmen were silent, however, about some sixty nuclear gravity bombs for F-4 and F-16 bombers, reported in 1985 to be stored at an American air base at Kunsan.)[55] The perceived success in deploying large masses of troops halfway around the world for the Persian Gulf War would also make it much easier, the general thought, to respond to pressures (mainly from cost-cutting congressmen) to withdraw American ground forces from Korea. But, of course, 38,000 American troops remain in Korea today.

From the Korean War onward, North Korea responded to this nuclear blackmail by building enormous facilities underground or in mountain redoubts, from troop and matériel depots to munitions factories, even to subterranean warplane hangars. American control of the air in that war illustrated a deterrence principle supposedly developed only with "smart" weapons—namely, that "once you can see the target, it is already destroyed."[56] The North Koreans have long known this and have acted upon the principle. In the mid-1970s P'yŏngyang faced more threats as the Park Chung Hee government sought to develop nuclear capabilities, ceasing the activity only under enormous American pressure, while retaining formidable potentialities. The ROK went ahead with its clandestine program to develop "indigenous ability to build ballistic missiles" capable of carrying nuclear warheads. South Korea also garnered a reputation as a "renegade" arms supplier to pariah countries like South Africa and to Iran and Iraq during their war.[57] Much of this reads as if it were written about North Korea, not South Korea, and puts P'yŏngyang's activity into perspective: much of it was in response to U.S. pressure and ROK initiatives.

TOWARD RELAXATION

When it took office in 1993, the Clinton administration was stuck with Bush's decision to renew Team Spirit, and it immediately faced a crisis over P'yŏngyang's threat to withdraw from the NPT. In spite of much

55. Hayes (1991), pp. 94–95.

56. President Clinton's defense secretary William J. Perry is quoted to this effect in Paul Virilio, *War and Cinema: The Logistics of Perception*, trans. Patrick Camiller (New York: Verso, 1989), p. 4.

57. Janne E. Nolan, *Trappings of Power: Ballistic Missiles in the Third World* (Washington, D.C.: Brookings Institution, 1991), pp. 48–52.

provocation to do otherwise, it took the road of negotiation and accomplished several things no previous administration ever did. First, Defense Secretary Les Aspin publicly admitted what insiders had known for some years, that government experts are deeply split over how to interpret North Korea's nuclear activity. Second, it opened direct, high-level talks with North Korea not just on nuclear weapons but on a wide range of policy issues. Third, it proffered a number of possible concessions to the North, including an end to Team Spirit, a pledge that it would not use force against North Korea, and an upgrading of diplomatic relations (including the opening of liaison offices in both capitals). Fourth, the administration mobilized various governments and the United Nations to warn North Korea of the dangers to the world as a whole, should it withdraw from the NPT, while offering to help North Korea with less threatening kinds of nuclear power generation. For once, in other words, the United States used deft diplomacy to defuse a Korean crisis, instead of sending a hailstorm of B-52's, F-4 Phantoms, aircraft carriers, and troop alerts to face down Kim Il Sung, as all previous presidents had done. The Clinton administration deserves much credit for this sober and artful effort.

It wasn't easy, and much mutual misunderstanding delayed a settlement. In July 1993 the North Koreans proposed that their entire nuclear program, based in graphite reactors and the natural uranium that it has in abundance, be replaced by American-supplied light-water reactors, which are much less prone to weapons proliferation but which would also require that P'yŏngyang become dependent on external supplies of fuel. This unexpected proposal moved the discussion forward, and in November 1993 P'yŏngyang tabled a package deal to resolve the issue—one that was similar to the eventual provisions agreed upon in October 1994.

For a complex of reasons agreement did not come, however, and in May 1994 P'yŏngyang forced President Clinton's hand by shutting down its reactor for the first time since 1989, withdrawing some eight thousand fuel rods and placing them in cooling ponds. This called Washington's bluff and left officials with no apparent room for maneuver; predictably this act also occasioned another irresponsible media blitz about a new Korean War. In this case, however, the alarms were warranted, unbeknownst to the media: the United States and North Korea came much closer to war at this time than most people realize. Former President Jimmy Carter had been invited to visit P'yŏngyang some years before and, alarmed by what he had learned of the depth of the crisis from briefings by Clinton administration officials, decided to take matters into his own hands.

Carter flew off to P'yŏngyang in June 1994 and by a sleight of hand that depended on Cable News Networks' simultaneous transmission of his discussions with Kim Il Sung on a boat in the Taedong River (direct TV mediation that short-circuited the ongoing diplomacy), he broke the logjam. He suggested that P'yŏngyang freeze its Yŏngbyŏn facility in return for light-water reactors and a new relationship with the United States, gaining Kim Il Sung's apparent assent with the TV cameras to record it. President Clinton appeared in the White House press room and declared that if P'yŏngyang were to freeze its program (that is, leave the fuel rods in the cooling ponds and halt ongoing construction on new facilities), high-level talks would resume—which they did on July 8 in Geneva. That was what made possible the real breakthrough that was consummated in October 1994.

This was not a one-way street of American concessions to P'yŏngyang, as often reported. In recent years North Korea has also made many concessions, diplomatic and otherwise, that have gone generally unremarked in our press. It agreed to join the United Nations in 1991, in spite of extant resolutions branding it the aggressor in 1950. It allowed the International Atomic Energy Agency to conduct seven regular inspections of its nuclear facilities, a fact many American newspapers ignored, but also one that would have been unthinkable for P'yŏngyang during the heyday of the Cold War. It passed several unprecedented joint venture laws and tax-and-profit regulations and had numerous ongoing projects with foreign firms, including many from South Korea. South Korean newspapers were filled with reports of business interest in the North, but relations between Seoul and P'yŏngyang were still sufficiently bad that much potential business activity between the two Koreas remained blocked. P'yŏngyang also conducted normalization talks with Japan for several years. It has consistently called for better relations with the United States and has welcomed a wide range of American visitors (including the Reverend Billy Graham, who preached in P'yŏngyang in 1992 and again in early 1994).

The October framework agreement promised P'yŏngyang that in return for freezing its graphite reactors and returning to full inspections under the NPT, a consortium of nations (including the United States, Japan, and South Korea) would supply light-water reactors to help solve the North's energy problems; the consortium also agreed to extend long-term loans and credits to enable P'yŏngyang to purchase the new reactors, valued at about $4 billion. In the meantime the United States would supply heating oil to tide over the DPRK's energy problems and would begin a step-by-step upgrading of diplomatic relations. In early 1995 the North balked at accepting South Korean light-water reactors because of fears of dependency on the South, but high-level negotiations in May solved that problem, essentially by re-labeling the reactors. The framework agreement was predicated on mutual mistrust, and therefore both sides had to verify compliance at each step toward completion of the agreement, which will not come until at least the year 2008, since constructing the reactors and bringing them on-line will take years.

Shortly after Jimmy Carter's salutary intervention, Kim Il Sung died and the world watched to see if the succession to power of his son went badly or well. But there was nothing to indicate an unstable transition, although Kim Jong Il had not taken up all of his father's posts and continued to be called *yŏngdoja* rather than *suryŏng*, as his father had been (both terms translate as "leader," but *suryŏng* is the higher rank). When the North signed the October 1994 agreement, it was said to be at Kim Jong Il's explicit instruction. Today the top leadership in P'yŏngyang is a collective one, of elders united around the younger Kim. Meanwhile, Russian specialists from the highly secretive Soviet operation that embalmed Lenin and Ho Chi Minh, among others, were called in to preserve Kim Il Sung's cadaver. It now lies on display in the Mansu Mausoleum in P'yŏngyang.

After the nuclear crisis seemed to have been resolved, North Korea (and Korea in general) receded from the attention of the American media, which now comes only when a department store collapses or a Korean company takes over another American firm or the psychotic playboy Kim Jong Il inherits another title from his deceased nutcase/father. I have no idea what the average American must think about a media that carried on for years about North Korea's evil intentions, only to have been proved completely wrong in its estimates, thence to sink into silence. Since I read the P'yŏngyang and Seoul press and North Korea has been familiar to me for two decades, I cannot put myself into the shoes of Americans who read this yellow journalism, especially since the majority were born after the Korean War. But I do know that through this drumbeat of media disinformation, a few people who have long studied our problems with North Korea were proved right in arguing that P'yŏngyang was sincere in saying that it would give up its nuclear program in return for better relations with the United States. They include Anthony Namkung of the Rockefeller Foundation, Dae-sook Suh of the University of Hawaii, Steven Linton of Columbia University, and the author of this book—but, above all, Selig Harrison of the Carnegie Endowment, who was by far the most important private citizen involved in bringing Washington and P'yŏngyang together, thus helping to avoid another terrible war.[58]

In the mid-1990s none of the great powers saw profit in conflict on the

58. It was Mr. Harrison who first got Kim Il Sung to think about freezing the Yŏngbyŏn facility, during a meeting in P'yŏngyang in May 1994.

Korean peninsula, none wanted to be involved in a new war, most sought relations with both Koreas, and so the fault lines of Cold War conflict no longer cut across Korea. In this situation the United States finally moved toward a more evenhanded policy toward the two Koreas, trying to play the role of honest broker while retaining its alliance with the South. Continued American troop commitments at pre-1989 levels underlined Washington's strong support for Seoul, but the United States no longer lets Seoul dictate the pace of engagement with the North.

THE SUNSHINE POLICY

Kim Dae Jung's most far-reaching changes involved North Korea and culminated in the P'yŏngyang summit of June 2000, where the two Korean heads of state shook hands for the first time since the country's division in 1945. At his inauguration in February 1998 President Kim pledged to "actively pursue reconciliation and cooperation" with North Korea, and declared his support for P'yŏngyang's attempts to better relations with Washington and Tokyo—in complete contrast with his predecessors, who chafed mightily at any hint of such rapprochement. He soon underlined his pledges by approving large shipments of food aid to the North, lifting limits on business deals between the North and southern firms, and calling for an end to the American economic embargo against the North in June 1998, during a visit to Washington. Kim explicitly rejected "unification by absorption" (which was the de facto policy of his predecessors) and in effect committed Seoul to a prolonged period of peaceful coexistence, with reunification put off for twenty or thirty more years.

Both governments are now committed (on paper) to a staged confederal process of reunification. The North first tabled its confederal plan in 1960, as we have seen, and Kim Dae Jung's scheme also calls for a prolonged period of confederation, the first stage of which would involve "close, cooperative" relations while maintaining two different systems, states, militaries, and foreign policies. The two sides would manage relations between each other through various inter-Korean organizations, pending the second stage when, after a fairly long period of preparation, formal unification would occur under a federal system of one people, one nation, one political system, but two autonomous regional governments; the federal government would run Korea's diplomacy, defense, and major domestic policies. (In his inaugural address Kim had cited a practical need to respect the pride of the North Koreans and the necessity to govern the North Korean region separately for a considerable time, under a regional autonomous government.) The third stage would be real unification under a central government. All of this would be done with the consent of the people through a democratic process.

North Korea waited a year to test Kim Dae Jung's resolve, and a couple of submarines and several dead infiltrators washed up on the South Korean coast—suggesting that hard-liners might be trying to disrupt North-South relations. But by mid-1999 it was apparent that P'yŏngyang viewed President Kim's "sunshine policy" as a major change in South Korea's position. Its attitude toward Washington also began changing. Long determined to get the United States out of Korea; at least some North Korean leaders apparently wanted American troops to stay on the peninsula, to deal with changed international power relations (especially a strong Japan and a strong China), and to help P'yŏngyang through its current economic difficulties.[59] Former Secretary of Defense William Cohen seemed almost to echo such views in June 1998, when he declared that American troops would stay in Korea even after it was unified.

In late August 1998 a hailstorm of alarmist press reports claimed that North Korea had sent a long-range, two-stage missile arcing over Japan, leading to virtual panic in Tokyo—as if the missile had barely cleared the treetops in Tokyo. North Korea's press, however, had spoken for weeks of little else but preparations for the celebration of the fiftieth anniversary of the regime. P'yŏngyang announced, though, that its three-stage rocket had put a satellite in orbit—beeping out the "Song of Kim Il Sung." Weeks later the U.S. intelligence community concluded that it was indeed a fireworks display, probably done for the fiftieth anniversary, but that the satellite had failed to reach orbit.[60]

In spite of a phalanx of noisy opposition in Washington and the high-level media din about the North Korean threat (one report even said that P'yŏngyang might unleash the smallpox virus on its enemies),[61] midlevel State Department officials patiently negotiated one agreement after another with North Korea, in a long series of talks on various problems. They also began a six-month-long review of Korea policy in the fall of 1998, which markedly changed the direction of U.S. policy and culminated in William Perry's mission to P'yŏngyang in June 1999. Dr. Perry finally issued a public version of his report (and this policy review) in October 1999, the essence of which was a policy of engagement predicated on the coexistence of two Koreas for another considerable period of time, a progressive lifting of the fifty-year-old American embargo

59. Selig Harrison interviewed a North Korean general who told him that whereas the North may call publicly for the withdrawal of American troops, in reality the troops should stay—to help deal with a strong Japan, among other things. See Harrison, "Promoting a Soft Landing in Korea," *Foreign Policy*, no. 106 (Spring 1997).

60. Tracing the missile's path and the number of stages required poring over radar tapes, which took several weeks; the announcement that it was, indeed, a satellite throw was buried in the American media.

61. *New York Times*, April 22, 1999.

against the North, a deepening of diplomatic relations between the two sides, and a substantial aid package for the North. The North, for its part, agreed to continue to observe the 1994 agreement, to suspend missile testing, and to continue talks with the United States about ending its missile program, including sales of missiles to the Middle East. This helped set the stage for the June summit in P'yŏngyang.

Kim Dae Jung also came rightly to believe that North Korea does *not* oppose a continuing U.S. troop presence in Korea if Washington were to pursue engagement with P'yŏngyang rather than confrontation (U.S. troops would continue to be useful in policing the border, that is, the DMZ, in assuring that the South's superior armed forces do not swallow the North, and in keeping Japan and China at bay); at the summit Kim Jong Il confirmed this view, telling Kim Dae Jung directly that he did not necessarily oppose the continuing stationing of U.S. troops in Korea. In this sense, President Kim's proposals constituted the first serious attempt in fifty years to achieve North-South reconciliation *within* the existing, American-shaped Northeast Asian security structure.

This summit, and the State Department's major review of policy, prepared the ground for a deal on North Korea's missiles that was deeply in the Korean, American, and world interest. North Korea was willing to forgo construction, deployment, and international sales of all missiles with a range of more than 300 miles. If President Clinton had been willing to do Kim Jong Il the favor of a visit to P'yŏngyang, American negotiators were convinced, Kim would also have agreed to enter the Missile Technology Control Regime (MTCR), which would limit all North Korean missiles to an upper range of 180 miles (and thus remove a threat felt deeply in nearby Japan). In return the United States would have provided $1 billion in food aid to the regime.[62] In other words, getting North Korea into the MTCR would cost $1 billion and a summit meeting between the American president and Kim Jong Il; national missile defense—said subsequently by spokesmen of the Bush administration to be directed particularly at North Korea—had already cost $60 billion.

President Clinton wanted to go to P'yŏngyang—indeed, his negotiators on Korea had their bags packed for weeks in November 2000—but as Clinton's national security adviser Sandy Berger later put it, it wasn't a good idea for the president to leave the country in November when they didn't know "whether there could be a major constitutional crisis."[63] After the Supreme Court stepped in to give the 2000 presidential election to George W. Bush, it was too late.

62. See Michael R. Gordon's investigative report, "How Politics Sank Accord on Missiles with North Korea," *New York Times*, March 6, 2001.
63. Quoted ibid.

The new administration was quickly at loggerheads over whether there had been any real progress in Korea or not, and within two years nearly all the gains of the 1990s had been lost. Trouble first became apparent when Kim Dae Jung visited Washington shortly after Bush's inauguration and was caught up short by the president's own hard line. Kim, fresh from winning the 2000 Nobel Peace Prize, was expecting to welcome the North Korean leader to Seoul in April or May of 2001, with this meeting being the follow-on to the previous summit. He returned home with his advisers publicly calling the meeting embarrassing and privately cursing President Bush—who proceeded to poison the well by calling Kim Jong Il a "pygmy" and telling the reporter Bob Woodward that he "loathed" Kim and wanted to "topple" his regime. It was really a pity, because with his persistent and patient policies President Kim did more to change policy toward the North than any other South Korean or American president going back to the end of the Korean War. But the backtracking on Korea since Bush assumed office is also an unfortunate example of the degree to which Washington still dominates the diplomacy of the Korean peninsula.

The Bush administration waited eighteen months before agreeing to a high-level meeting with the North Koreans in October 2002. Bush's emissary, James Kelly, used the meeting to accuse the North of having a second nuclear program, involving highly enriched uranium. Coming months after Bush had put the North into his "axis of evil" and a few weeks after his National Security Council had tabled a new doctrine of preemptive attack and preventive war, it was predictable that the North Koreans would respond badly: soon they again renounced the nonproliferation treaty, kicked out UN inspectors who had been at their nuclear facility for eight years, restarted their plutonium reactor, and most ominously, regained control of the eight thousand fuel rods that had touched off the 1994 crisis. From then on, the North Koreans claimed to have "a physical deterrent," one of the many ambiguous euphemisms they deployed to suggest that they had an atomic bomb, without testing a weapon or coming out openly as a nuclear state. Bush's subsequent invasion of Iraq only deepened the North's bluster—and its fears. In early 2005 the North finally asserted that it had nuclear weapons, but some observers—notably Defense Secretary Donald Rumsfeld—remained skeptical, short of an actual test.

The confrontation between Washington and P'yŏngyang in late 2002 created a stalemate and nearly erased the gains of the 1990s (construction of the light-water reactors went into suspension, but they were not dismantled; some experts still thought the North's nuclear facilities could be put back into a deep freeze). American foreign policy became overwhelmed by the violent occupation of Iraq, and North Korea returned to its tried-and-true strategy from the Cold War: stubborn intransigence. The war in Iraq, the North said with some reason, proved that if a country disarms under UN inspection auspices, it can still be invaded by the United States. In 2003 China put its prestige on the line by sponsoring first three-way and then six-party talks in Beijing (China, the two Koreas, the United States, Japan, and Russia), but by the end of the first Bush administration the talks had not accomplished anything. Stalemate is likely for the next several years, too, because the North will not give up its trump card (its nuclear programs) without a bundle of aid and normal diplomatic relations with the United States, and the Bush administration appears unable to agree to that, because it is split between those who want to make a deal with the North (mainly in the State Department) and those who want to pursue "regime change" (mainly civilian officials in the Defense Department).

The beginning of wisdom is to recognize that the United States continues to bear the greatest responsibility for peace on the Korean peninsula and, in many ways, for failing to resolve the Korean conflict fifty years after it began. Nowhere else in the world has the United States backed one side of a conflict so exclusively, with such minimal contact with the other side. Nowhere else does it directly command the military forces of another sovereign nation, as it continues to do in Korea. Therefore it was appropriate for the Clinton administration to take the initiative in expanding talks and trade with the North while continuing to support the South, and seeking through diplomacy to relieve tensions on the peninsula. The October 1994 framework agreement represented the first time since the Korean War that diplomacy has resolved any important problem in Korea.

KOREAN REUNIFICATION?

Historians are people who have enough difficulty explaining the past, without trying to predict a future that can only be imagined; furthermore, the past tells us nothing about how Korea might be reunified, since its national division has come but once in a millennium and today shows few serious signs of resolution. But events elsewhere after the Cold War ended have encouraged most Koreans to think that reunion might be around the corner: so what can be said about this critical issue, central to Korea's destiny as a nation?

Both Korean governments define themselves as the only legitimate sovereign entity on the peninsula, thus placing the other polity in a renegade status. From the 1940s onward the South has defined North Korea as an illegitimate anti-ROK organized entity (i.e., not a state but an anti-state organization), has maintained a shadow government for the northern provinces, and by law has a unification formula predicated on proportional representation according to population, rather than on the fifty-fifty geographic split that occurred in 1945. Political unification would thus be simple: hold elections in North Korea to fill one-third of the seats in the national legislature. Seoul has also predicated any reunification upon maintenance of Seoul's security ties with the United States, something that guaranteed no serious North-South relations if hostility between P'yŏngyang and Washington continued. As long as the global bipolar conflict endured, the ROK's enmeshment in the American security system was far more important to it than the questionable gains it might have obtained by dealing seriously with the North.

The South Korean official policy for many years was not to push for reunification but to assume the existence of two Koreas for the foreseeable future, and to try to melt the glacier the way Germany did: by small, low-level exchanges of visits (especially by members of divided families) and incremental increases of trade and other exchanges, over decades of time. Seoul thus emphasized modest improvements in North-South relations and confidence-building measures. Nordpolitik became possible only when the international environment changed to Seoul's advantage in the late 1980s, and as a way of responding to growing demands from the younger generation that something serious be done about reunification.

When the Western socialist states disappeared, the official line in Seoul was that it should prepare for a North Korean collapse on the German model, followed by its absorption into the Republic of Korea. Oceans of ink were spilled in the 1990s on the "German model" of Korean reunification. Study teams went off to Germany to examine its unification after the Honecker regime fell, and came back with worrisome stories about how much the process had cost and therefore how expensive it would be to bring northern Korea up to the level of the rest of the country. Meanwhile, the Seoul government relaxed restrictions on business with the North, leading to visits (and sometimes deals) by all the major business firms in South Korea. Seoul keeps a tight rein on citizen visits and continues to threaten any persons, no matter how prominent, with a jail term should they travel to the North without government permission. The late Reverend Mun Ik-hwan, for example, spent several years in jail after his 1989 visit to P'yŏngyang, and in 1995 his widow was jailed after she visited Kim Il Sung's grave on the first anniversary of his death.[64]

These core policies left the unification issue mostly in P'yŏngyang's

64. *Korea Herald*, July 10, 1995.

court, which fully exploited the propaganda worth of being the loud champion of the dearest value held by most Koreans. From the spring of 1948, when it sponsored a "unity conference" that succeeded in attracting moderates like Kim Kyu-sik and right-wing nationalists like Kim Ku, North Korea has identified itself as the innocent victim of "splittists" in the South, puppets acting at the behest of American imperialism. It took the ultimate step in 1950 of making war to unify the country, and that experience leads just about every external observer to discount P'yŏngyang's endlessly reiterated formula of "peaceful reunification." (In the spring of 1995 Ch'oe Kwang, head of the Korean People's Army, gave a speech where he said that Korea should be reunified in the 1990s, "even at the point of a gun.")

In 1960, after the war and internal reconstruction had been completed, Kim Il Sung tabled a scheme for a confederated republic that would maintain two systems under one nation, one state, and one flag; he revived the idea in the late 1970s and harped on it until his death. This would be the "Confederal Republic of Koryŏ," thus solving the problem of whether to call the country Han'guk or Chosŏn. (The North has always privileged the Koryŏ lineage as opposed to Silla, of course, viewing Koryŏ as the first truly unified "Korea.") The confederation plan always had a catch to make sure that it could not be implemented: no foreign troops or nuclear weapons would be allowed, for example, thus challenging the core of Seoul's unification formula. During the Cold War, confederated Koryŏ was to have been independent, neutral, and nonaligned, but these days I think the North would be willing to have its confederation aligned with the United States, should it ever come to fruition. Indeed, a unified Korea's diplomacy for the post–Cold War world might well recapitulate Huang Tsun-hsien's 1880 recommendation that it have "intimate relations with China, association with Japan, and alliance with America."

For decades North Korea has sponsored meetings at home and around the world on the unification question, yielding interminable conference transcripts and hundreds if not thousands of books, but there has never been a serious possibility that the South would accept the North's confederal idea. Instead, P'yŏngyang found the proposal useful in fortifying its bona fides as the party of unification and in playing upon traditional and nationalist ideas about what Korea ought really to look like—unbesmirched by things foreign, pure and virtuous (the Confederal Republic would, of course, follow the Juche idea), and, above all, whole once again. Even foreign allies of P'yŏngyang and its supporters in the South can be taken aback by the other continuous drumbeat that accompanied all the talk about confederation, to the point that all the southern people were yearning to be in the bosom of the Fatherly Leader, or that (in common and endlessly repeated P'yŏngyang parlance) "a certain Pak, living in Mokp'o, was heard to say that Kim Jong Il is, indeed, the iron-willed, ever victorious Commander who is the great disciple of Kim Il Sung and now the rightful father of the country."

Foreigners have had their own ideas about how Korea might be reunified, one of the best also having been tabled in 1960: after the overthrow of Syngman Rhee, Mike Mansfield, Democratic senator from Montana and onetime professor of East Asian history, proposed that Korea be neutralized under a great-power agreement, accompanied by the withdrawal of all foreign troops and an abrogation of security treaties with the great-power guarantors of the North and the South. Based on the successful and peaceful unification of Austria in 1955, this was an idea whose time in the Korean context had come in 1945. It could not work after the civil war and with the bipolar conflict at its height. Henry Kissinger, as we have seen, proposed a six-party conference to find a way out of the Korean dilemma, composed of the two Koreas and four powers connected to Korea (the United States, the Soviet Union, China, and Japan). Also known as a "four plus two" scenario, it was always denounced by the North Koreans because, they said, it left Korea at the mercy of the great powers and insinuated Japanese power back into the Korean situation. The real reason was that, by Kissinger's time, P'yŏngyang could not count on full and simultaneous backing from both Beijing and Moscow.

A unified Korea would be a strong economic competitor on the world scene, and a political force in East Asia. No doubt the combined economies of North and South, married to such a talented and well-educated people, would quickly rival Japan. That is one reason why Japanese leaders (at least those who held power through the LDP) have taken a dim view of Korean reunification, and in the past actively thwarted it by lining up almost exclusively with Seoul, whereas China recognizes both Koreas and tries to maintain a relative balance among them. The majority of Japanese citizens probably view Korea the way the French viewed divided Germany: "I like Germans so much that I'm happy there are two of them." The United States, on the other hand, might find it beneficial to have a friendly and unified Korea on its side, as rivalries between Washington and Tokyo, or Washington and Beijing, grow in the future. It was this possibility, combined with the evidence that North Korea was not going to go away anytime soon, that underlay the Clinton administration's willingness to pursue an extended and difficult diplomacy with P'yŏngyang.

Perhaps what foreign observers find most pertinent to Korea is the German model of unification. Unfortunately it is the wrong model. Korea differs from Germany mainly in that it suffered a terrible civil war, which killed millions, in recent memory. It is very hard to believe that People's

Army commanders who fought the South in such a bloody fratricidal war would allow the ROK to overwhelm the DPRK, by whatever means. The German Democratic Republic had 360,000 Soviet troops on its territory in 1989, whereas the DPRK has had none since 1948. East Germany collapsed because Gorbachev chose to do what none of his predecessors would ever have done, namely, keep those troops in their barracks rather than mobilize them to save the Honecker regime. Although Gorbachev sought similarly to pull levers against North Korea, he had none but the relatively small amounts of aid that Moscow had provided and that he eventually cut off. South Korea also flatters itself by comparing its status to West Germany's: many East Germans could see in West Germany some approximation to their socialist ideals, in its democratic politics, its social safety net, its widespread unionization (about 40 percent compared with 15 percent in the United States and a similar figure in the ROK), its early and favorable retirement benefits, and its good public order and strong civil society. By contrast, North Korean citizens can look forward to little or none of this in union with the South, but instead to the longest hours of labor in the industrial world on terms that South Korean firms would set.

By the mid-1990s a certain wisdom had come to Seoul's leaders about the reunification issue, as hopes (and fears) about the North's collapse faded and as Seoul came to understand that time was on its side—in part because North Korea had done so much to reform its own views and policies on interaction with the world economy, meaning that Seoul could expect that the dominant tendency in East Asia in the past twenty years—economic exchange sweeping political barriers away—would continue to erode obstacles in the path of North-South reconciliation. If the DPRK's socialist system were to collapse under the intense international pressures of the post–Cold War world, that does not necessarily mean its political system would decompress or disappear: probably the party and government apparatchiks will declare themselves to have been nationalists all along (with some measure of truth) and try to keep their hold on power anyway; the North's huge army will be the key element, should such a course unfold. It is an army that may well go down, but it will go down fighting.

There is still very little evidence that the political elite in either Korea is willing to sacrifice any important interest for the broader goal of reunification. The "division system" about which Paik Nak-chung has written so eloquently,[65] is ultimately and residually founded in zero-sum politi-

65. Paik, one of Korea's leading intellectuals and editor of Seoul's major intellectual journal, *Ch'angjak kwa Pi'p'yŏng*, is prolific in Korean. For some of his views in English, see "South Korea: Unification and the Democratic Challenge," *New Left Review*, no. 197 (Jan.–Feb. 1993): 67–84.

cal struggle, in which both sides expect that giving up power would mean trials and executions for political crimes, and a thorough rewriting of history to blot out the other side's achievements and highlight its transgressions. Over sixty years have passed since the national division, yielding half a century and several generations' worth of political solidification. Given that this is Korea, that means family solidification. In a country where family lineage is everything, to imagine bequeathing defeat to one's progeny is to imagine ultimate death as a member of the Korean nation.

The North Korean elite was originally formed around the Manchurian guerrillas, a group that takes visual and substantial form in the hundreds of bronze busts that populate the official cemetery atop T'aesŏng Mountain, near P'yŏngyang. By now the onetime guerrillas are all either in their graves or grandfatherly, but they have struck deep roots in the body politic through their children, their relatives, and, above all, their total control of the system. The favored generation now is Kim Jong Il's, a huge echelon of officials and elites in their forties and fifties, heir to every privilege that the system can bestow on those actively supporting the "Dear Leader's" succession over the past quarter century. Many, many sons and daughters of the founding guerrillas are among them; they constitute the power elite of North Korea, just as Yi Sŏng-gye's allies and merit subjects constituted the instant aristocracy of the Chosŏn dynasty in the fifteenth century. Like the Ming loyalists after 1644 and the Hongian elites of the late nineteenth century, P'yŏngyang's power elite assumes that fidelity to the old principles and the true way—in this case a socialism few believe in anywhere else, but then that was true of Ming loyalists, too—will allow their country to weather the adverse winds of the past two decades. In that judgment they are probably as wrong as were their predecessors, and therefore likely to meet a similar fate.

In South Korea the analogues would be the former landed elite, now ensconced in new forms of material wealth and very influential in cultural and educational realms; the favored military generations from the coup in 1961 onward, particularly the "T-K" (Taegu-Kyŏngsang) group, which came from the southeastern provinces and poured every manner of investment also in that direction; and a growing and broadening middle class (the analogue of the Kim Jong Il generation but much larger), freed from memories of a fratricidal war that came before they were born, but also unlikely to find its interests accommodated in anything remotely resembling the current regime in P'yŏngyang. It is much more in their interest to wait for their counterpart class to grow in North Korea, to the point that it would be willing to risk bursting the bonds of a regime still operating in the name of a now obsolescing proletariat.

Probably the most recalcitrant separatists will be the core families of the Manchurian guerrillas in the North and the core elements of the T-K militarists in the South. For either to give up the struggle would be to risk annihilation by the other side. The attack that Kim Young Sam launched against the top leaders of the T-K group in the fall of 1995 may come to signify the full political victory of the southern middle class and the solidification of South Korea's still-uncertain democratic commitments.

Kim Young Sam was the first civilian president since 1960 and will have his indelible place in history for his courage in bringing the former militarists Chun Doo Hwan and Roh Tae Woo to trial on sedition and corruption charges (Chun was sentenced to die and Roh to a long prison term; both were magnanimously pardoned by Kim Dae Jung in early 1998, after spending a long period in jail). Unlike any other former military dictatorship in the world up to that time, South Korea did not allow bygones to be bygones: the two former presidents ended up in jail, convicted of monumental bribery and treason against the state. Otherwise, however, Kim Young Sam was in every way a conservative and a product of the postwar South Korean system, as he demonstrated in his last year in office.

The falling out among the ruling groups and the trials of Chun and Roh, as well as the full glare of publicity on the slush fund scandals (big business groups had given more than $1.5 billion to Chun and Roh in the 1980s), bathed the state and the *chaebŏl* groups in a highly critical light and definitively put an end to the military's role in politics. This was a fine moment for Korean democracy. But it was an elite moment, making it important to remember that Korean democracy has come from the bottom up, fertilized by the sacrifices of millions of people. If they have not yet built a perfect democratic system, they have constructed a remarkable civil society that gives the lie to common stereotypes about Asian culture and values. The elections of Kim Dae Jung and Roh Moo Hyun have consolidated Korea's democracy, thus vindicating the masses of Koreans who had fought for democratic rule over the preceding fifty years. Today there is nothing to suggest that North Korean leaders have any intention of democratizing their system, however, and until they do, we can have little, if any, idea of what role the masses of North Koreans will play in the future.

It seems to me that for all these reasons, and short of a catastrophic war, no reunified Korea will emerge before a prolonged period of regional sovereignty, perhaps under one national name and one flag, perhaps for years to come. Let the elites hold on to power in Seoul and P'yŏngyang, and meanwhile let people-to-people exchanges, trade, tourism, and the sharing of a common ethnic heritage come well ahead of politics, which should be and (I think) will be the last phase of Korean reunification.

The Old Testament prophets, like the leaders of South and North Korea, knew the value of bringing fire and brimstone down upon the enemy, an eye taken for an eye, a tooth for a tooth. But they also learned the value of forgiveness, of reconciliation after ruin—that there is a time to die and a time to live. The time for reconciliation and reunion is now, so that Korea's ruptured and fragmented history can be knit together and made whole and so that the twentieth century can occupy its proper place as merely one of the past forty centuries—a calamitous century, but one that is now over and done with.

CONCLUSION

In the first years of the new century, Koreans can look back with a certain equanimity on decades of colonization, upheaval, war, political strife, ideological division, social turmoil, and pell-mell economic growth: through the cunning of history they ended a century of continuous crisis far better off than virtually any nineteenth-century foreigner would have predicted, save the unusually observant ones like Percival Lowell or Angus Hamilton. They have regained a world status that internal decline and foreign predation snatched from them, but on a different basis: no longer the country of the way, distinguishing itself through Confucian virtue and statecraft, but the avatar of rapid industrial growth, hell-bent-for-leather modernization, and world-class human talent.

We know what the Hongian purists would say, if they could speak (and many still do): what profits a Korean to gain the world and lose his soul? But that judgment is too harsh, since Koreans are merely doing what everyone else is trying to do in our time, including their Middle Kingdom communist neighbor across the Yellow Sea, namely, to get rich—and doing it better than just about anyone else. Still, we cannot say that South Korea's world-beating growth is enough to carry this nation forward to its true place in the sun. Korea remains divided, which means it deploys much less weight in the world, is far weaker and more vulnerable, than it would be if it were unitary. The North-South conflict still puts Korea at loggerheads with itself and with the ultimate telos of its modern history. Fifty years after the Korean War ended, huge armies remain poised to fight at a moment's notice. If South Korea has evolved in the direction of the "borderless world" that its leaders now speak of, North Korea is still peculiar in the Hongian style: having borrowed Western socialism the way old Korea borrowed Chinese Confucianism, it now finds itself in the Ming loyalist position after even the Mings give way, or in Ch'oe Ik-hyŏn's position on the doorstep of Korea's loss of nationhood: a "single topknot remaining atop the head, becoming the sole target for all of the arrows in all-under-heaven."

Korea is not a well-known country, and the rest of the world is only now discovering the talents of its people. The Spanish philosopher Ortega y Gasset wrote that "what makes a nation great is not primarily its great men, but the stature of its innumerable mediocre ones." Koreans in all walks of life, in both halves of Korea, are a spirited, hardworking, moral people with a great love of family and a wonderful belief in the virtues of education. This people deserves better from its own leaders, and it deserves better than it has gotten from a United States that has been deeply involved in the lives of Koreans for half a century, but knows them not.

Perhaps a century of conflict and turmoil, with millions of lives lost, will still have been worth it if a unified Korea has liberty as Koreans define it (*chayu*): liberty as a nation and liberty for its people to be what they want to be. Americans have forgotten how their liberty was born in war and revolution and sealed in a disastrous civil war. Tocqueville, however, saw the relation between liberty and conflict: "Liberty is generally established in the midst of storms; it is perfected by civil discord; and its benefits cannot be appreciated until it is already old." It is time to imagine a unified, dignified, and modern Korea, with a liberty "perfected by civil discord."

Bibliography

Ablemann, Nancy, and John Lie. *Blue Dreams: Korean Americans and the Los Angeles Riots.* Cambridge: Harvard University Press, 1995.

Aguilar-San Juan, Karin, ed. *The State of Asian America.* Boston: South End Press, 1994.

Amsden, Alice. *Asia's Next Giant: South Korea and Late Industrialization.* New York: Oxford University Press, 1989.

Appleman, Roy. *South to the Naktong, North to the Yalu.* Washington, D.C.: Office of the Chief of Military History, 1961.

Armstrong, Charles. "The Origins of the North Korean State." Ph.D. diss., University of Chicago, 1994.

Barclay, George W. *Colonial Development and Population in Taiwan.* Princeton: Princeton University Press, 1954.

Bishop, Isabella Bird. *Korea and Her Neighbors.* New York: Fleming H. Revell, 1897.

Blair, Clay. *The Forgotten War: America in Korea, 1950–1953.* New York: Times Books, 1987.

Blaut, J. M. *The Colonizer's Model of the World.* New York: Guilford Press, 1993.

Boettcher, Robert, with Gordon L. Freedman. *Gifts of Deceit: Sun Myung Moon, Tongsun Park, and the Korean Scandal.* New York: Holt, Rinehart and Winston, 1980.

Braudel, Fernand. *A History of Civilizations.* Translated by Richard Mayne. New York: Viking Penguin, 1994.

Buswell, Robert E. *The Zen Monastic Experience.* Princeton: Princeton University Press, 1992.

Ch'oe Yong-ho. *The Civil Examinations and the Social Structure in Early Yi Dynasty Korea: 1392–1600.* Seoul: Korean Research Center, 1987.

Choi, Jang Jip. *Labor and the Authoritarian State: Labor Unions in South Korean Manufacturing Industries.* Honolulu: University of Hawaii Press, 1990.

Choy, Bong-youn. *Koreans in America.* Chicago: Nelson-Hall, 1979.

Clark, Donald N., ed. *The Kwangju Uprising: Shadows Over the Regime in South Korea.* Boulder, Colo.: Westview Press, 1988.

Cohen, Jerome B. *Japan's Economy in War and Reconstruction.* Minneapolis: University of Minnesota Press, 1949.

Conroy, Hilary. *The Japanese Seizure of Korea, 1868–1910.* Philadelphia: University of Pennsylvania Press, 1960.

Cotterell, Arthur. *East Asia: From Chinese Predominance to the Rise of the Pacific Rim.* New York: Oxford University Press, 1993.

Cumings, Bruce. "Archaeology, Descent, Emergence: Japan in British-American Hegemony, 1900–1950." In *Japan in the World,* ed. H. D. Harootunian and Masao Miyoshi. Durham, N.C.: Duke University Press, 1994.

——, ed. *Child of Conflict: The Korean-American Relationship, 1943–1953.* Seattle: University of Washington Press, 1983.

——. "Corporatism in North Korea." *Journal of Korean Studies,* no. 4 (1983): 1–34.

——. "Kim's Korean Communism." *Problems of Communism* 23, no. 2 (March–April 1974): 27–41.

——. "The Origins and Development of the Northeast Asian Political Economy." *International Organization* 38 (Winter 1984): 1–40.

——. *The Origins of the Korean War: Liberation and the Emergence of Separate Regimes, 1945–1947.* Princeton: Princeton University Press, 1981.

——. *Origins of the Korean War.* Vol. 2, *The Roaring of the Cataract, 1947–1950.* Princeton: Princeton University Press, 1990.

——. *War and Television.* New York: Verso, 1992.

de Bary, W. Theodore, and JaHyun Kim Haboush, eds. *The Rise of Neo-Confucianism in Korea.* New York: Columbia University Press, 1985.

Dennette, Tyler. *Americans in Eastern Asia.* New York: Macmillan, 1922.

de Silva, Peer. *Sub Rosa: The CIA and the Uses of Intelligence.* New York: Times Books, 1978.

Deuchler, Martina. *Confucian Gentlemen and Barbarian Envoys: The Opening of Korea, 1875–1885.* Seattle: University of Washington Press, 1977.

——. *The Confucian Transformation of Korea: A Study of Society and Ideology.* Cambridge: Council on East Asian Studies, Harvard University Press, 1992.

Drake, Frederick C. *The Empire of the Seas: A Biography of Rear Admiral Robert Wilson Shufeldt, USN.* Honolulu: University of Hawaii Press, 1984.

Dumont, Louis. *Homo Hierarchicus: The Caste System and Its Implications.* Translated by Mark Sainsbury, Louis Dumont, and Basia Gulati. Chicago: University of Chicago Press, 1980.

Duus, Peter. *The Abacus and the Sword: The Japanese Penetration of Korea, 1895–1910.* Berkeley: University of California Press, 1995.

Eckert, Carter J. *Offspring of Empire: The Koch'ang Kims and the Origins of Korean Capitalism.* Seattle: University of Washington Press, 1991.

Eckert, Carter J., Ki-baik Lee, Young Ick Lew, Michael Robinson, and Edward W. Wagner. *Korea Old and New: A History.* Cambridge: Korea Institute, Harvard University, 1990.

Farris, William Wayne. "Ancient Japan's Korea Connection." *Working Papers in Asian / Pacific Studies.* Duke University, Asian / Pacific Studies Institute, 1994.

Foote, Rosemary. *The Wrong War: American Policy and the Dimensions of the Korean Conflict, 1950–1953.* Ithaca: Cornell University Press, 1986.

Franck, Harry A. *Glimpses of Japan and Formosa.* New York: Century, 1924.

Gale, James Scarth. *History of the Korean People.* Annotated and introduced by Richard Rutt. Seoul: Royal Asiatic Society, 1972. (First published serially in the mid-1920s.)

Goncharov, Sergei N., John W. Lewis, and Xue Litai. *Uncertain Partners: Stalin, Mao and the Korean War.* Stanford: Stanford University Press, 1993.

Gragert, Edwin H. *Landownership under Colonial Rule: Korea's Japanese Experience, 1900–1935.* Honolulu: University of Hawaii Press, 1994.

Griffis, William Elliot. *Corea: The Hermit Nation.* 3d ed. New York: Charles Scribner's Sons, 1889.

Gutzlaff, Charles. *Journal of Three Voyages along the Coast of China in 1831, 1832, & 1833, with notices of Siam, Corea, & the Loo-Choo Islands.* London: Thomas Ward, n.d.

Haboush, JaHyun Kim. *A Heritage of Kings: One Man's Monarchy in the Confucian World.* New York: Columbia University Press, 1988.

——. *The Memoirs of Lady Hyegyŏng.* Berkeley: University of California Press, 1996.

Halliday, Jon, and Bruce Cumings. *Korea: The Unknown War.* New York: Pantheon Books, 1988.

Hamilton, Angus. *Korea.* New York: Charles Scribner's Sons, 1904.

Han, Woo-keun. *The History of Korea.* Translated by Kyung-shik Lee. Edited by Grafton W. Mintz. Honolulu: University of Hawaii Press paperback, 1974.

Harrington, Fred Harvey. *God, Mammon, and the Japanese: Dr. Horace N. Allen and Korean-American Relations, 1884–1905.* Madison: University of Wisconsin Press, 1944.

Harrison, Selig, ed. *Dialogue with North Korea.* Washington: Carnegie Endowment, 1991.

Hart-Landsberg, Martin. *The Rush to Development: Economic Change and Political Struggle in South Korea.* New York: Monthly Review Press, 1993.

Hatada, Takashi. *A History of Korea.* Translated by Warren W. Smith, Jr., and Benjamin H. Hazard. Santa Barbara: ANC-Clio Press, 1969.

Hayes, Peter. *Pacific Powderkeg: American Nuclear Dilemmas in Korea.* Lexington, Mass.: Lexington Books, 1991.

Henderson, Gregory. *Korea: The Politics of the Vortex.* Cambridge: Harvard University Press, 1968.

Hicks, George. *The Comfort Women: Japan's Brutal Regime of Enforced Prostitution in the Second World War.* New York: W. W. Norton, 1995.

Hong Kong Daily Press. *The Directory & Chronicle.* Hong Kong, 1940.

Hong (Lady). *Memoirs of a Korean Queen.* Translated and edited by Choe-wall Yang-hi. London: KPI, 1985.

Hong, Wontack. *Relationship between Korea and Japan in Early Period: Paekche and Yamato Wa.* Seoul: Ilsimsa, 1988.

Hwang, Eui-Gak. *The Korean Economies.* Oxford: Clarendon Press, 1993.

Ienaga, Saburō. *The Pacific War: World War II and the Japanese, 1931–1945.* Translated by Frank Baldwin. New York: Pantheon Books, 1978.

Imperial Japanese Government Railways, *An Official Guide to Eastern Asia.* Vol. 1, *Manchuria and Chōsen.* Tokyo, 1913.

Illyŏn. *Samguk yusa* (Legends and history of the Three Kingdoms of ancient Korea). Translated by Tae-Hung Ha and Grafton K. Mintz. Seoul: Yonsei University Press, 1972.

Janelli, Roger L., and Dawnhee Yim Janelli. *Ancestor Worship in Korean Society.* Stanford: Stanford University Press, 1982.

Jeon, Sang-woon. *Science and Technology in Korea: Traditional Instruments and Techniques.* Cambridge: MIT Press, 1974.

Johnson, Chalmers. *MITI and the Japanese Miracle.* Berkeley: University of California Press, 1982.

Jones, Leroy P., and Il Sakong, *Government, Business and Entrepreneurship in Economic Development: The Korean Case.* Cambridge: Harvard East Asian Monographs, 1980.

Kalton, Michael C., et al. *The Four-Seven Debate: An Annotated Translation of the Most Famous Controversy in Korean Neo-Confucian Thought.* Albany: State University of New York Press, 1994.

Kang, Younghill. *East Goes West: The Making of an Oriental Yankee.* New York: Charles Scribner's Sons, 1937.

Kim, Choong Soon. *The Culture of Korean Industry: An Ethnography of Poongsan Corporation.* Tuscon, Arizona: University of Arizona Press, 1992.

Kim, Han-Kyo, ed. *Studies on Korea: A Scholar's Guide.* Honolulu: University of Hawaii Press, 1980. (This is an excellent guide to further reading on Korea.)

Kim, Key-Hiuk. *The Last Phase of the East Asian World Order.* Berkeley: University of California Press, 1980.

Kim, Nyung. "The Politics of Religion in South Korea, 1974–87: The Catholic Church's Political Opposition to the Authoritarian State." Ph.D. diss., University of Washington: 1993.

Kim Ronyoung, *Clay Walls.* Sag Harbor, N.Y.: Permanent Press, 1984.

Kim, San, with Nym Wales. *Song of Ariran: A Korean Communist in the Chinese Revolution.* San Francisco: Ramparts Press, 1973.

Kim, Se-jin. *The Politics of Military Revolution in Korea.* Chapel Hill: University of North Carolina Press, 1971.

Kim, Se-jin, and Cho Chang-hyun, eds. *Government and Politics of Korea.* Silver Spring, Md.: Research Institute on Korean Affairs, 1976.

Lautensach, Hermann. *Korea: A Geography Based on the Author's Travels and Literature.* Translated by Katherine and Eckart Dege. 1945; reprint, Berlin: Springer-Verlag, 1988.

Ledyard, Gari. *The Dutch Come to Korea.* Seoul: Royal Asiatic Society, 1971.

Lee, Hoon K. *Land Utilization and Rural Economy in Korea.* Shanghai: Kelly & Walsh, 1936.

Lee, Ki-baik. *A New History of Korea,* Translated by Edward W. Wagner with Edward J. Shultz. Cambridge: Harvard University Press, 1984.

Lee, Mun Woong. *Rural North Korea under Communism: A Study of Sociocultural Change.* Houston: Rice University Studies, 1976.

Lee, Peter H., ed. *Modern Korean Literature.* Honolulu: University of Hawaii Press, 1990.

Lee, Peter H., ed., with Donald Baker, Yongho Ch'oe, Hugh H. W. Kang, and Han-Kyo Kim. *Sourcebook of Korean Civilization.* Vol. 1. New York: Columbia University Press, 1993.

Lee, Warren. *A Dream for South Central: The Autobiography of an Afro-Americanized Korean Christian Minister.* San Francisco: Warren Lee, 1993.

Lee, Yur-bok. *West Goes East: Paul Georg von Möllendorff and Great Power Imperialism in Late Yi Korea.* Honolulu: University of Hawaii Press, 1988.

Lensen, George Alexander. *Balance of Intrigue: International Rivalry in Korea & Manchuria, 1884–1899.* 2 vols. Tallahassee: Florida State University Press, 1982.

Lew, Young-ick. "The Kabo Reform Movement: Korean and Japanese Reform Efforts in Korea, 1894." Ph.D. diss., Harvard University, 1972.

Lost Victory: An Overview of the Korean People's Struggle for Democracy in 1987. Edited by Christian Institute for the Study of Justice and Development. Seoul: Minjungsa, 1988.

Lowe, Peter. *The Origins of the Korean War.* New York: Longman, 1986.

Lowell, Percival. *Chosŏn: The Land of the Morning Calm.* Boston: Ticknor, 1888.

———. *The Soul of the Far East.* New York: Houghton, Mifflin, 1888.

Macdonald, Donald Stone. *U.S.-Korean Relations from Liberation to Self-Reliance: The Twenty-Year Record: An Interpretive Summary of the Archives of the U.S. Department of State for the Period 1945 to 1965.* Boulder, Colo.: Westview Press, 1992.

McCune, Evelyn. *The Arts of Korea: An Illustrated History.* Rutland, Vt.: Tuttle, 1962.

Mitchell, Tim. *Colonising Egypt.* Cambridge: Cambridge University Press, 1988.

Modin, Yuri. *My Five Cambridge Friends.* New York: Farrar Straus Giroux, 1994.

Myers, Ramon H., and Mark R. Peattie, eds. *The Japanese Colonial Empire, 1895–1945.* Princeton: Princeton University Press, 1984.

Nelson, Frederick M. *Korea and the Old Orders in East Asia.* Baton Rouge: Louisiana State University Press, 1945.

Ogle, George E. *South Korea: Dissent within the Economic Miracle.* Atlantic Highlands, N.J.: Zed Books, 1990.

Oppert, Ernest. *A Forbidden Land: Voyages to the Corea.* London: Sampson Low, Marston, Searle and Rivington. 1880.

Palais, James B. *Politics and Policy in Traditional Korea.* Cambridge: Harvard University Press, 1975.

———. *Confucian Statecraft and Korean Institutions: Yu Hyŏngwŏn and the Late Chosŏn Dynasty.* Seattle: University of Washington Press, 1996.

Park, Chi-Young. *Political Opposition in Korea, 1945–1960.* Seoul: Seoul National University Press, 1980.

Park, Kie-duck. "Fading Reformism in New Democracies: A Comparative Study of Regime Consolidation in Korea and the Philippines." Ph.D. diss., University of Chicago, 1993.

Park, Won-soon. *The National Security Law.* Los Angeles: Korea NGO Network for the UN World Conference on Human Rights, 1993.

Patterson, Wayne. *The Korean Frontier in America: Immigration to Hawaii, 1896–1910.* Honolulu: University of Hawaii Press, 1988.

Polanyi, Karl. *The Great Transformation: The Political and Economic Origins of Our Time.* 1944; reprint, Boston: Beacon Press, 1957.

Rhodes, Richard. *Dark Sun: The Making of the Hydrogen Bomb.* New York: Simon and Schuster, 1995.

Robinson, Michael. *Cultural Nationalism in Colonial Korea, 1920–25.* Seattle: University of Washington Press, 1988.

Savage-Landor, A. Henry. *Corea, or Chosen: The Land of the Morning Calm.* London: William Heinemann, 1895.

Shapiro, Michael. *The Shadow in the Sun: A Korean Year of Love and Sorrow.* Introduction by Susan Shira. New York: Atlantic Monthly Press, 1990.

Shin, Gi-wook. *The Politics of Popular Protest: The Roots and Legacy of Peasant Activism in Twentieth Century Korea.* Seattle: University of Washington Press, 1996.

Suh, Dae-sook. *Kim Il Sung: A Biography.* Honolulu: University of Hawaii Press, 1989.

——. *The Korean Communist Movement, 1918–48.* Princeton: Princeton University Press, 1967.

Suh, Dae-sook, and Edward J. Shultz, eds. *Koreans in China.* Honolulu: Center for Korean Studies, University of Hawaii, 1990.

Tillyard, E. M. W. *The Elizabethan World Picture.* New York: Vintage Books, 1942.

Toby, Ronald P. *State and Diplomacy in Early Modern Japan.* Princeton: Princeton University Press, 1984.

Tocqueville, Alexis de. *Democracy in America.* Translated by Phillips Bradley. Vol. 2. New York: Vintage Books, 1945.

Totman, Conrad. *The Collapse of the Tokugawa Bakufu, 1862–1868.* Honolulu: University of Hawaii Press, 1980.

Wade, James. *One Man's Korea.* Seoul: Hollym, 1967.

Wells, Kenneth M., ed. *South Korea's Minjung Movement: The Culture and Politics of Dissidence.* Honolulu: University of Hawaii Press, 1995.

Woo, Jung-en. *Race to the Swift: State and Finance in the Industrialization of Korea.* New York: Columbia University Press, 1991.

Wright, Mary C. *The Last Stand of Chinese Conservatism: The T'ung-Chih Restoration, 1862–1874.* New York: Atheneum, 1966.

——. "The Adaptability of Ch'ing Diplomacy: The Case of Korea." *Journal of Asian Studies* 17 (May 1958): 363–81.

Yi Sun-shin. *Nanjung Ilgi: War Diary of Admiral Yi Sun-shin.* Translated by Ha Tae-hung. Edited by Sohn Pow-key. Seoul: Yonsei University Press, 1977.

Zhang, Shu Guang. *Mao's Military Romanticism: China and the Korean War, 1950–1953.* Lawrence: University Press of Kansas, 1995.

Index